to Nancy, Judith, and Elizabeth

The Treatment of Emotional Disorders

The Treatment of Emotional Disorders

Seymour L. Halleck, M.D.

Jason Aronson
New York

Copyright © 1978 by Jason Aronson, Inc.

All rights reserved. Printed in the United States of America. No part of this book may be used or reproduced in any manner whatsoever without written permission from Jason Aronson, Inc. except in the case of brief quotations in reviews for inclusion in a magazine, newspaper, or broadcast.

Library of Congress Cataloging in Publication Data

Halleck, Seymour L
    The treatment of emotional disorders.

    Bibliography: 14pp.
    Includes index.
    1. Psychotherapy.   I. Title.

RC480.H275   616.8'914   77-18374
ISBN 0-87668-263-8

Manufactured in the United States of America

Acknowledgments

It is difficult for a person of my abilities to write a book while continuing to meet all of his personal and professional obligations. What usually happens is that I put work first and end up being less available to family and friends than I ought to be. During the four years I worked on this book my wife, my children, and my friends once again showed great tolerance for my narcissistic choices. Of course, I am grateful for their indulgence; but simply to state my gratitude in a perfunctory manner seems inadequate. I also want them to know how lucky I consider myself to be involved with them, and that I have missed a great deal these last four years by not maximizing that involvement.

While I borrowed liberally from the writings of hundreds of colleagues, the primarily integrative focus of this book did not require much direct consultation. I did need encouragement, however, and I am grateful for the continuous support of my publisher, Dr. Jason Aronson, of my esteemed former teacher and friend, Dr. Karl A. Menninger, and of my friends and colleagues, William Friedman and Gregory Johnson. Finally, I am grateful to my secretary, Mary Lou Allison, who interpreted my almost illegible handwriting, typed several drafts of this manuscript, and tended to dozens of organizational tasks involved in putting this material together.

Contents

Introduction   xv

Part I

CONCEPTUALIZING TREATMENT

Chapter 1   The Need For a Treatment Model   3

What Works with Whom? The Research Evidence   7
Good News and Bad News   20
Resistance to Integrative Models   22

Chapter 2   Relating Diagnosis to Treatment   29

Diagnosis   32
Individual-Environment Interaction   39
Biological Hypotheses   42
Learning Hypotheses   45
Informational Hypotheses   47
Environmental Hypotheses   50
Relating Hypotheses to Modes of Therapeutic Intervention   53
How Current Therapies Work   61
Values and Choice of Treatment   63

Chapter 3   Clinical Evaluation of the Patient
            and the Environment   69

   Evaluating Indications for Biologial Interventions   70
   Evaluating Indications for Learning Interventions   75
   Evaluation of Indications for Information Expanding
      Interventions   77
   Evaluation of the Environment   85
   [THE PRESYMPTOMATIC ENVIRONMENT • ACCIDENTAL VS. PATIENT
   CREATED ENVIRONMENTS • DEVELOPMENTAL CHANGE AND ENVIRON-
   MENTAL RESPONSE • EVALUATING THE POSTSYMPTOMATIC ENVIRON-
   MENT]
   A Summary of Clinical Evaluations Which Increase the Efficiency
      of Intervention   114

Chapter 4   Practical and Ethical Issues   119

   Practical Issues in Concurrent Use of Interventions   120
   [SEVERELY DISTURBED PATIENTS • MODERATELY DISTURBED PATIENTS •
   SYNERGISTIC INTERVENTIONS • THE CLINICIAN'S ATTITUDE • TIMING OF
   MULTIPLE INTERVENTIONS]
   Ethical Considerations   136
   [THE POLITICS OF THERAPY • MOTIVATION AND AUTONOMY • A NOTE ON
   TREATMENT CHOICE AND DEGREE OF SEVERITY • A LAST STATEMENT
   ABOUT ETHICS]

Part II

TREATMENT

Introduction   163

Chapter 5   Biological Interventions   165

   Territorial Issues   169
   General Diagnostic Issues   171
   Specific Diagnostic Issues   180
   The Use of Antipsychotic Drugs   193
   [SIDE EFFECTS OF NEUROLEPTICS • EXTRAPYRAMIDAL SIDE EFFECTS]

Contents   xi

Antidepressant Drugs   210
Lithium Treatment   217
Antianxiety Drugs   221
Electroconvulsive Therapy   224
Psychosurgery   228
Relaxation Training   229
The Ethical Use of Biological Treatments   232

Chapter 6 The Behavior Therapies   241

General Issues   241
The Uses of Behavior Therapy   245
Basic Learning Concepts   248
[CLASSICAL CONDITIONING • OPERANT CONDITIONING • OBSERVATIONAL OR INSTRUCTIONAL LEARNING]
Some Principles   251
[INCREASING A BEHAVIOR • DIMINISHING A BEHAVIOR]
Self-Control Techniques in Behavior Modification   258
Treatment of Fear Responses   261
Treatment of Appetitive Disorders   267
[TREATMENT OF SEXUAL VARIATIONS • TREATMENT OF SEXUAL INADEQUACY • BEHAVIORAL TREATMENT OF ALCOHOLISM • BEHAVIORAL TREATMENT OF EATING DISORDERS]
Behavior Modification Techniques and General Clinical
  Problems   279
Biofeedback   283
"Soft" Behavior Modification   284
Further Ethical Considerations   296

Chapter 7 Individual Psychotherapy   303

Psychotherapy and Responsibility   306
Territorial Issues   311
Diagnostic Issues: Who Should Receive Psychotherapy?   314
Theory and Technique   321
General Structure   322
Helpful Factors   326
[HOPE AND BELIEF IN THE POWER OF A SOCIALLY SANCTIONED HEALER • IDENTIFICATION WITH THE THERAPIST • CARING AND LOVINGNESS • TENSION REDUCTION • LEARNING IN PSYCHOTHERAPY • INFORMATION • EXPLANATION]

Some Personal Methods	363
Termination	368
Psychotherapy in Hospital Settings	371
Individual Psychotherapy and Other Interventions	375
Co-Therapists in Individual Psychotherapy	377
Ethical Issues	378

Chapter 8   Group Psychotherapy 387

Goals	389
Guides to the Prescription of Group Therapy	391
The Basic Format	395
Helpful Factors	397

[FAITH AND BELIEF IN THE POWERS OF THE HEALER • IDENTIFICATION • CARING AND LOVINGNESS • TENSION REDUCTION • LEARNING • INFORMATION • EXPLANATION]

A Brief Note On Encounter Groups	408
Additional Differences Between Group and Individual Psychotherapy	409
Further Technical Problems	411
Some Theoretical Concerns About Group Interventions	412
Ethical Problems	414

Chapter 9   Family Therapy 421

Who is the Patient in Family Therapy?	422
One-Dimensionality	425
Territoriality	427
Responsibility	427
Growth	429
Power	430
Varieties of Family Stress	432
Family Stress and Family Therapy	444
Indications For Family Therapy	452
Family Therapy and Other Interventions	456
A Basic Format of Family Evaluation and Therapy	457
Experiential vs. Structural Approaches	465
Co-Therapists in Family Therapy	466
Helpful Factors	467

[FAITH AND BELIEF IN THE POWERS OF THE HEALER • IDENTIFICATION • CARING AND LOVINGNESS • TENSION REDUCTION • LEARNING • INFORMATION • EXPLANATION]

Beyond the Family	481
Further Ethical Problems	483

Chapter 10	Back to Reality: Training and Service Delivery	487

References	503
Index	517

Introduction

These times are both difficult and exciting for professional healers of the emotionally disordered. The complexity of our society exerts a powerful influence upon the nature of the demands our patients make upon us. New scientific discoveries, a changing social consciousness, and new laws require the healer to seek a constantly expanding expertise in treating patients, in providing services for the community, and even in maintaining an acceptable professional identity.

Consider some of the more obvious questions with which the conscientious clinician must deal: What role does diagnosis play in rational treatment of the patient? What biological treatments can I use most effectively? What role do past environmental experiences play in initiating emotional disorders? What role do more recent experiences play? Should I focus upon psychoanalytic theories of personality and psychoanalytic methods, or should I invest my energy in mastering less complex and more empirical interventions based on learning theory? Of what value are group and family therapies? How can I use brief and supportive therapies? What relevance does the medical model have to my treatment endeavors? Do my interventions help to liberate patients or merely help them adjust to an oppressive society? Is my job simply to give patients what they are asking for or to try to return them to some state which fits in with an acceptable concept of normalcy? Is my task to help people realize their fullest potential, or is it simply to make them feel better? To what extent must I acknowledge the rights of my patient to be an informed and voluntary participant in his own treatment? When do I have the right to treat patients against their will? What are my responsibilities to the community? Do I have a right to restrict my services to only a few patient's, or must I seek to provide the greatest benefit for the greatest number? How can I decide between my allegiances to the patient and to the community when the needs of the two may not be compatible? How can I protect my patients' privacy? How can I most effectively participate in training those who will soon be my colleagues? What should my proper relationship be to members of other professions also committed to treating the emotionally disordered?

Although no clinician should avoid any of these questions, the search for answers is a staggering burden which can be successfully assumed only by those who have the energy, the commitment, and the intellectual capacity to deal with complexity.

There are several ways in which we can defend ourselves against the burden of complexity. One direction we can take is to specialize, allowing members of our various professions to develop high levels of proficiency in selected treatment and administrative skills and low levels of proficiency in others. To a certain extent we are already doing this. I believe that in taking this course we are failing to meet the needs of our patients. Specialization in the healing arts makes sense only when the indications for specific interventions are crisply defined and only when there is a relatively large cadre of generalists who know these indications and can serve as sources of referral.

Another way in which we can defend ourselves against complexity is through seeking superficial mastery of the issues. We can learn a little about all the treatment modalities, all the social problems, and all the administrative tasks which confront us; and we can be constantly alert to changing our ways when future developments call for it. This type of adaptive superficiality fails because it does not provide guidelines for real competence in the present and because it allows us to forgo a scrupulous intellectual inquiry into our problems that might prepare us for the future. If we practice as dilettantes mindlessly awaiting new scientific discoveries or drastic social changes to solve our problems, we are abdicating the responsibilities of health service professionals.

A third way of dealing with complexity is to simply deny its existence. There are still a few healers of emotional disorders who insist that things are never as complicated as they seem, that sticking to one theory, one orthodoxy, one model for dealing with

Introduction

patients and society is sufficient and safe. While the belief in simplicity is alluring, it can be achieved these days only by those with considerable capacity for denying reality. For a behavioral scientist trying to help people in the 1970s, simplicity is an illusion.

There can be only one approach to complexity. That is to face it head on and to try to develop models for integrating our understanding, our approaches, and our actions. Such models must be based upon a holistic view of man and society, must deal with the interrelatedness of the issues confronting us, and must be flexible enough to allow the integration of new scientific discoveries and social change. The integrated approach to behavior disorders must be multidimensional. It calls for a clinician with a protean view and demands a constant willingness to ask basic questions and to seek out those solutions which closely meet the needs of the patient and society.

This book is an effort to help students and practicing clinicians conceptualize and integrate their work by providing basic treatment models. There will be no new theories or discoveries presented here; I will merely seek to integrate what we already know. Throughout the text I will frequently refer to the healer as a *clinician*. I use this word in a special and revered sense. The clinician to my mind is a person who takes a multidimensional or systems approach to the treatment of patients. The clinician, while asking basic questions neither rejects complexity nor any idea or intervention that promises to help the patient. Obviously, this definition will not embrace all who practice psychiatry or psychotherapy.

I have tried to steer as far away as possible from territorial issues among the various mental health professions. These will at times be noted, but in a manner I hope is noninflammatory. One semantic compromise I have made to this end is to use the word *patient* to describe those who seek or need help, but to avoid using the word *illness* whenever possible and to substitute the term *emotional disorder*. I use the term *emotional disorder* to refer to any actions, thoughts, or feelings which cause a person sufficient mental anguish to seek professional help or which so interfere with his social functioning as to lead others to view him as needing it. This very broad definition will enable me to avoid an endless and often fruitless discussion of what is, and what is not, a mental illness.

This book is aimed primarily at practitioners of psychiatry, psychology, social work, and nursing who treat patients or who are involved in working with social systems that influence patients. While the material presented will be complex, it should not require unusual expertise to understand the text. A rudimentary knowledge of psychopathology and psychological or psychiatric treatment should be sufficient. Because of my basic medical orientation, the material here may be of most interest to practicing psychiatrists, psychiatric residents, or medical students. Many if not most of the issues, however, are relevant to all practicing health professionals as well as to those in training.

The integrated models presented here are primitive. They do not resolve problems; they simply provide the clinician a way of thinking about problems. Given the primitive or embryonic nature of my attempts at integrating so many issues, I have allowed myself considerable license in interjecting a number of my own approaches and biases throughout the test. This is presumptuous, perhaps, but I hope forgivable if it stimulates or provokes other behavioral scientists to work on models more extensively validated by experimentation.

Part I

Conceptualizing Treatment

Chapter 1

The Need for a Treatment Model

There is an new enthusiasm among those responsible for treating the emotionally disturbed. The clinician now has many alternatives. Drugs which have a powerful influence upon emotions and behavior are now available. Therapies derived from learning theory have proved to be efficient means of changing behavior. The influence of the family and interpersonal systems upon emotional disorders is better understood, and family therapy, as well as group therapy, has become a powerful tool for helping disturbed people. New psychotherapeutic techniques have been developed for enabling people to achieve their full psychological potential. And, as we begin to appreciate the influence of the environment on disturbed behavior, the clinician is prepared to utilize a number of social change strategies for therapeutic intervention.

With so much innovation in the mental health field, it might be thought that emotionally disturbed people will soon benefit from levels of health care comparable to those offered the physically ill. Unfortunately, there is little evidence of such a trend. Even with the new variety of treatments available, the person seeking help for emotional distress has absolutely no assurance of being offered the kind of treatment most likely to help. He may receive treatment that works too slowly and is unjustifiably expensive. Or he may receive treatment which diminishes suffering but leaves him in a worse life situation than before. Sometimes treament is so ineffective that the patient's suffering does not diminish but intensifies.

Much of the inefficiency in providing proper treatment for patients is the result of shortages and maldistribution of professional services. Certain treatments are simply not available to all classes of citizens. But most of the inefficiency resides in the attitudes and practices of mental health professionals. Those responsible for the treament of emotional disorders have failed to develop a rational model for trying to determine which person should receive which treatment at which time. Instead, most professionals belong to a particular school of therapy and tend to treat the majority of their patients with a single method or, at best but less frequently, with two. In actual practice there is a distressing tendency to fit the patient to the treatment rather than the reverse. Parochialism in the mental health field is deeply rooted. It is not simply a product of ignorance or laziness. Many therapists, believing that only the techniques they have mastered are effective, are skeptical of the usefulness of other therapeutic systems and even contemptuous of those holding to rival ideologies.

One of the most powerful therapeutic schools is made up of professionals who hold medical degrees and who treat patients primarily with physical methods. These professionals may give the patient an opportunity to ventilate his feelings or may provide him some reassurance, but both doctor and patient usually put most of their faith in the prescribed somatic treatments. Doctors who rely primarily on physical methods tend to be skeptical of other approaches. They often believe that insight oriented psychotherapies are wasteful and that they may even make the patient worse. Relatively unconcerned with the influence of the patient's environment and accepting almost totally a reductionist medical model, they are not likely to work with the family in a manner which identifies its role in creating or perpetuating an illness. Nor are they likely to try to modify other stresses in the patient's environment.

The derision directed by somatically oriented therapists toward other therapists is not easily detected in psychiatric literature. Major textbooks of somatic treatment advise the therapist to be eclectic and to combine somatic treatments with other methods, but in practice these admonitions are frequently ignored. The somatic therapist, in his conviction that emotional disorders can be treated by one-dimensional biological treatments, is prone to ignore obvious and critical interpersonal and social determinants of disturbed behavior. As a result, many of his patients who would have responded to learning, interpersonal, or social therapies are deprived of the opportunity of getting better.

Somatic therapists are not the only healers of emotional disorders who are prone to take a one-dimensional approach. Many with a psychoanalytic orientation have been equally arrogant and authoritarian in ascribing to the ideology of a "pure treatment." As psychoanalytic psychotherapy has developed in America, it has taken on the quality of a cult. Rigorous initiation rites for analytic trainees were instituted to ensure excellence, but they have also created a conformity in treatment approaches and have discouraged therapeutic creativity. Dynamically oriented psychiatrists must take some responsibility for having insidiously promulgated a belief among many students of therapy that any treatment that is not based upon psychoanalytic principles is somehow second-rate. Students in training are too frequently led to believe that when they prescribe drugs, work with families, or use behavior modification techniques, they are diluting the value of their work and deviating from the tenets of a true faith.

Although psychoanalysts have recently made some efforts to define the limitations of psychoanalysis as an effective treatment method, psychoanalysis and long-term psychoanalytically oriented psychotherapy are still prescribed too frequently. This is partly because of a continuing, but certainly unsupported, belief in the superior efficacy of the psychoanalytic method. It is also likely that too many patients enter long-term psychotherapy because the analytically oriented therapist they consult, many of whom are very prestigious professionals, have not learned other skills. Out of either apathy or the conviction that psychoanalysis is all there is, many psychoanalysts have so constricted their therapeutic vision that they mistakenly try to fit too many patients into the psychoanalytic mold. As a result, many patients have spent years of their lives in psychoanalysis when they might have obtained relief with simpler and briefer methods.

A similar cultism prevails in other schools of individual therapy. The reality therapist, the existentialist, the client-centered therapist, the gestalt therapist, and the rational emotive therapist all have an unrealistic commitment to the universal effectiveness of their treatment methods. While there is a certain similarity in technique employed by all individual therapists and while some research suggests that the therapist's personality and actual practice are more important than his ideology in determining outcome, it is conceivable that some patients would be better with one approach than with another. Little effort is being made to determine which patient might respond best to which method of individual psychotherapy. The clinician who searches for guidelines in determining the kind of individual psychotherapy to prescribe finds many claims, but no data (Harper 1975).

Unfortunately, new therapeutic developments are not simply incorporated into the treatment repertoire of the average therapist. Instead they become the focus for the development of a new school of therapy.

As new therapeutic techniques based on behaviorism have been developed, they have not been accepted by the majority of mental health professionals. The minority who are committed to behavior therapy, however, are primarily concerned with symptom removal and measurable behavioral change. They are convinced that this is most effectively accomplished by methods based on classical and operant conditioning. Some behavior therapists will not use drugs, nor will they send the patient to another therapist who might use drugs. Many behaviorists view long-term psychoanalytically oriented psychotherapy as irrelevant and a waste of the patient's time.

Family therapists have shown similar signs of cultism. They correctly understand emotional problems as systems problems related to the interaction of a given individual with his social environment, but in their fascination with the intricacies of the system they are prone to ignore techniques that may allow them to directly influence the individual patient, who is certainly a component of that system, but who may also be in great psychological pain. Patients who might have benefited quickly from somatic or other therapeutic approaches spend hours learning about their behavior in social systems while remaining as unhappy as they were before they started treatment.

Similar considerations apply to group therapists and particularly to those using group interaction techniques designed primarily to increase human potentiality and sensitivity. Groups based on these techniques are designed not to treat the disturbed but to help improve the quality of life of the relatively normal. Yet many highly disturbed people find their way into these groups, some of them counseled into joining by therapists who believe sensitivity methods can help just about anyone.

Not all therapists, of course, are cultists; some have a broad knowledge of various therapeutic modalities and are committed to fitting treatment to the patient's needs. But these clinicians are exceptions. The literature of the mental health professions consists for the most part of claims for a variety of mutually exclusive treatment approaches. Descriptions of a case or project in which more than one therapeutic approach was used are rare. The picture one gets of clinical practice in general is of a variety of methods being used to treat similar conditions, and of similar methods being used to treat a variety of conditions. What this means is that the consumer of mental health services is in a very vulnerable position.

WHAT WORKS WITH WHOM?
THE RESEARCH EVIDENCE

The disorganization which pervades the field of treatment of behavior disorders is sustained by the limitations of our scientific knowledge. Ideally, treatment for the emotionally disturbed patient should be determined by knowledge obtained from the scientific study of different treatments applied to patients with similar conditions. If we are to continue to advance our knowledge, it is even more desirable that our studies be based upon theoretical constructs as to what is wrong with the patient and how a given treatment influences or corrects that impairment. To what extent have we achieved these scientific goals, and what does research in the behavioral sciences tell us about treatment?

There has been endless theorizing and much useful research as to the biological, psychological, and sociological causes of human suffering. But while we have learned a great deal about the factors contributing to emotional disorders, we have not been able to develop unified theories which might explain how these factors interact with one another to produce suffering in a given individual. Nor have most behavioral scientists been able to relate their theories of causality to specific intervention modalities. Many of our treatments are best described as empirical. Most discouraging, it has been extremely difficult to determine which interventions, whether based on established theory or on empiricism, are actually effective.

In order to appreciate fully the usefulness and limitations of current knowledge, the clinician must have some understanding of the complexity of the methodological problems involved in studying treatment of patients. The problems begin with deciding what is wrong with the patient. Because it is so difficult to describe accurately the nature of a patient's disordered behavior, it is no small task to collect a group of patients with similar disorders so that the influence of a given treatment on this group can be evaluated. The clinician can seek to define the nature of the patient's disorder only in terms of what the patient reports and the clinician observes. Each patient describes his suffering in unique subjective terms. Some patients are good reporters of their experiences; others are not. Some patients exaggerate their suffering; others minimize it. Clinicians who observe the same patient do not always see the same thing. Even trained observers dealing with severely, rather than mildly, disturbed individuals cannot always agree as to how that patient is behaving. In milder disorders, the quest for observer consistency is even more elusive. The problem of defining which class of patient disorder will be studied can be resolved only by sharpening our observational skills and by developing test instruments which guide the patient in communicating his own experiences and the clinician in describing the patient's behavior. A number of rating scales, some of which can be filled out by the patient and others by those who observe him, have been a considerable help in facilitating resolution of these problems. These test instruments can never capture the full range or the nuances of human behavior, but they do force both patient and observer to make descriptive choices which allow for a least crude categorization or definition of the patient's disorder. The reader will quickly recognize how much simpler it is to define the patient population in nonpsychiatric medicine. Patients can usually describe bodily sensations more precisely than emotions or thoughts. Through physical examinations and laboratory tests doctors can arrive at relatively precise descriptions and categorizations of a patient's somatic condition.

A second problem in evaluating the usefulness of clinical interventions is defining the exact nature of the intervention utilized. If we are to determine whether drugs, behavior modification, or individual, group, or family psychotherapy is most effective, strict attention must be paid to the problem of dosages, length of treatment, and experience of the therapist. Even the personality, attitudes, and values of the clinician using a particular intervention must be considered. When studying the relative effectiveness of two or more types of interventions on a given patient population, the experience of the therapist and the length of treatment are especially critical. Some types of interventions are more easily learned than others, and if relatively untrained therapists are part of the study group, there would be some weighting of favorable outcome in the direction of the intervention most easily mastered. Duration of treatment is critical insofar as some techniques, such as psychoanalytically oriented psychotherapy, take considerable time before they are effective. A time-limited research project is likely to be weighted against positive results for interventions which are time-consuming.

A third, and probably the most difficult, problem in treatment research is measuring outcome. By what criteria shall we determine if a patient is improved? Outcome measures can be either specific or vague. If we are concerned only with the measurement of frequency of maladaptive behaviors or variables such as capacity to hold a job or remain outside of a hospital, the problems of evaluation are not too difficult. When we get into other issues, however, such as the patient's ultimate happiness, his emotional growth, his degree of self-knowledge, the quality of his life, or his capacity to enjoy such values as intimacy, freedom, or power, the problem of measurement becomes insurmountable. Yet many clinicians assert with considerable justification that these more elusive outcome measures are as important as symptom removal. Some of the problems of defining outcome can be partially resolved by developing rating scales which assess various aspects of the patient's condition. These allow the patient, the therapist, unbiased experts, and friends and relatives of the patient to describe or rate the patient before, during, and after treatment in an effort to assess change. The usefulness of these instruments is obviously limited. Test instruments allow us to make crude evaluations of the patient's comfort and effectiveness only in certain aspects of his life. Again, the reader is reminded that the research problem with regard to outcome is somewhat simpler in nonpsychiatric medicine. For decades, medical researchers have used such relatively noncomplex variables as symptom removal and physiologic change as outcome measures.

The problems involved in defining patient populations, treatment modalities, and outcomes do not exhaust the list of potential obstacles facing the researcher. There is also the problem of finding adequate control groups. We cannot assess the effectiveness of a given treatment unless we have some idea of how similar patients would fare without it. Patients who need help are, of course, reluctant to control subjects, and therapists who feel that they can provide help are often unwilling to withhold it from patients who might constitute a control group. There is also no way of monitoring the nature of therapeutic experiences available to those used as controls. Many who are viewed as having no treatment are actually receiving counseling from nonprofessionals. To be certain that a specific aspect of an intervention rather than such nonspecific variables as the clinician's authority or the patient's expectations of help is the critical factor in eliciting change, it would also be helpful to use placebos. These are readily available in evaluating drug therapies but a psychotherapeutic placebo may well be impossible to develop.

The researcher is also frustrated by the barely disguised reluctance of many therapists to have their results examined. Some therapists assert, often correctly, that such examinations would interfere with the confidentiality of the patient-therapist relationship. Others resist cooperating in research with outcome measures they feel stack the deck against them. Still others may fear that research findings will threaten their commitment to a long-held ideology and might lead them to question the meaningfulness of their lifework. Finally, a society increasingly concerned with consumer's rights imposes a number of restrictions upon research enterprises. Treatment which is researched does carry some risk of allowing a larger number of people access to the patients' secrets. The tests and evaluations which must be made in a comprehensive research project are also time-consuming. As consumerism grows, as government agencies put more emphasis on service, as the number of charity patients rapidly diminishes, and as skepticism toward medicine and psychology continues to remain high, it becomes increasingly difficult to maintain the professional enthusiasm, the public and private funding, and the patient voluntarism that are necessary for effective research.

Faced with these formidable obstacles, clinicians have been understandably slow in turning to research for answers regarding choice of treatment. Until only two decades ago, it was difficult to find even uncontrolled follow-up studies of the results of many interventions. Prior to the 1950s the major guides the clinician had in determining treatment were his theories, his clinical experience, and the unsupported claims of other therapists as to the efficacy of various procedures. One of the earliest efforts to bring scientific methodology to the field was intitiated in the 1950s by Carl Rogers (1951). He insisted that it was useful, feasible, and ethical to study the outcome of psychotherapy, and he devised a number of instruments for measuring therapeutic change.

The Need for a Treatment Model

Roger's efforts eventually stimulated adherents of other schools to conduct similar research. Individual and group therapists of all orientations began to conduct follow-up studies of therapeutic outcome; a few of these studies were controlled. Concurrently in the 1950s, major psychotropic drugs came into use, and since it was possible to regulate dosages and control for placebo effects, relatively sophisticated research on pharmacotherapeutic intervention became available (Elkes 1966). Behavior therapists, who traditionally have prided themselves on their scientific approach, began controlled studies of their techniques at about the same time (Franks 1969). We now have thousands of follow-up studies, some controlled and some uncontrolled, for every major intervention, and it is possible to cite some evidence for the usefulness of each.

In the last fifteen years research emphasis has moved beyond simple follow-up studies and simple comparisons of treatment groups with control groups to studies of the effects of different interventions or combined interventions on relatively similar conditions. These studies have become increasingly sophisticated, and while few are without methodological flaws, they are beginning to provide us information directly relevant to clinical work.

One way to illustrate th magnitude of the problem of comparing the effectiveness of various interventions and to appreciate the degree of care being exercised in current studies is to review briefly some of the methodological features of a recent and important study. Sloan et al. (1975), in attempting to evaluate the relative effectiveness of behavior therapy and psychoanalytically oriented psychotherapy in patients with neuroses and character disorders, insisted upon the following features in their study:

1. The use of experienced practitioners of behavior therapy and psychoanalytically oriented therapy
2. A wait list or control group for whom only minimal treatment was provided
3. Random assignment of patients to psychoanalytically oriented therapy, behavior, therapy, or wait list
4. The use of an independent assessment team who tried to make their follow-up assessment as nearly blind as possible and who resisted the temptation to analyze data until the last patient had been interviewed

5. The use of typical patients who attended a university psychiatric outpatient clinic rather than student volunteers
6. An independent team to analyze data during and after the study
7. Information from relatives and friends of the patient
8. Multiple outcome measures: target symptoms and measures of overall functions derived from therapist, patient, assessor, relatives, and psychological tests
9. Standardized procedures, definition of target symptoms, structured and scaled interviews to assess maladjustment for work and social maladjustment
10. A check on in-therapy procedures to show both qualitative and quantitative differences among treatments, therapist, patients, and therapist-patient interaction
11. A follow-up at one year and two years from original assessment

Some of the results of this and other studies will be noted shortly. For our purposes now, the methodology of the study is outlined, primarily to impress the reader with the degree of preparation, hard work, money, and therapist and patient cooperation which must go into any meaningful attempt to evaluate treatment.

If the clinician examines follow-up studies in which a specific intervention is utilized but in which no control group or comparison with other therapy is available, it is possible to find literature to support any intervention modality. There is no dearth of uncontrolled studies demonstrating the usefulness of pharmacotherapy, psychotherapy, behavior modification, group therapy, or family therapy in the treatment of disturbed individuals. These studies are, of course, encouraging and useful insofar as they set the stage for more sophisticated research, but of themselves they prove nothing. Without the use of a control group, there is no way of determining if it is the specific intervention that accounts for the patient's improvement or if other factors are involved. Uncontrolled research provides no firm guidelines for the clinician but rather allows him to strengthen his belief in the efficacy of the particular system of intervention to which he is most committed. Controlled research, which can demonstrate the superiority of a given treatment to no treatment, is much more useful in reassuring the clinician that a particular intervention may be helpful. Controlled research on single

The Need for a Treatment Model

treatments, however, does not provide guidelines in choosing treatment. It merely shows that a given intervention is superior to no intervention. The research most likely to assist the clinician in choice of treatment is that comparing the effectiveness of different interventions or combinations of interventions upon patients with similar conditions. The strengths and limitations of the research enterprises currently available, and their yield to the clinician in terms of treatment guidelines can be summarized as follows:

1. In dealing with neurotic and personality disorders, there is evidence that such interventions as behavior modification, psychotherapy, individual psychotherapy, and group psychotherapy are superior to no intervention at all (Eysenck 1959, Meltzoff 1970, and Baehr 1954). This statement could not have been made with much certainty until quite recently. Studies of patients applying for treatment but kept on waiting lists reveal that as many as one-third to two-thirds of this goup show improvement (Rachman 1971). The variations in percentage of those improved are dependent upon outcome criteria. It cannot be stated with certainty that these patients received no treatment at all, since they did receive therapeutic evaluation and were not followed extensively enough to determine what kind of therapeutically effective professional and nonprofessional intervention they may subsequently have experienced. Nevertheless, the burden of proof for the efficacy of professional intervention in minor disorders has always been on the practitioners of behavior modification and psychotherapy. Recent studies are beginning to relieve this burden. Depending on outcome measures utilized, in some studies almost twice as many treated patients have improved as compared to control groups (Sloane 1975). While the new research is encouraging and does justify the use of behavior therapies or traditional psychotherapies in the treatment of neuroses and personality disorders, the mental health professions must still be humbled by the realization that many patients get better with no treatment at all. Future studies of factors that might account for this high rate of improvement would be highly desirable. If it were possible to isolate factors which account for improvement of minimally treated patients, the efforts of professionals could be diverted more expeditiously to those definitely needing intensive treatment.

2. There are a few studies suggesting the usefulness of minor tranquilizers in combination with psychotherapy in the treatment

brief depression may respond to MAO inhibitors, but there are no controlled studies proving such treatment superior to psychotherapy (Shader 1975). Studies of combined antidepressant therapy and psychotherapy with severely depressed patients suggest that there is some advantage to combined treatment, particularly if outcome criteria are not restricted to symptom removal and include changes in social functioning (Klerman 1975). In most clinical practice today some form of psychotherapy, however perfunctory, is usually added to the pharmacotherapy regime.

6. Electroconvulsive treatment is clearly superior to no treatment or to psychotherapy in relieving the symptoms of severe depression (Detre and Jarecki 1971). It is also effective in reducing symptomatology of some schizophrenic and manic psychoses. Some studies indicate that ECT may be superior to pharmacotherapy in treating the most severe depressions (Davis 1975). For a variety of clinical and social reasons, however, ECT is not regularly used in treating depressions unless pharmacotherapy has failed. There is no evidence that ECT is superior to pharmacotherapy in the treatment of schizophrenic and manic psychoses, although some of these disorders do respond to ECT when pharmacotherapy has failed.

7. There is considerable evidence that techniques of behavior modification based on desensitization or operant conditioning are superior to the traditional psychotherapies in treating such circumscribed neurotic symptoms as phobias or habit disturbances (for example, smoking or bed wetting) (Gelder, Marks, and Wolff 1967, Wolpe 1969). In dealing with more general neurotic or personality disorders, however, there is surprising similarity of outcome whether behavior therapy or psychotherapy is utilized (Luborsky, Singer, and Luborsky 1975). Some studies suggest a slightly greater effectiveness for behavior therapy but the differences are usually not significant. It is interesting to note that available research indicates that it makes little difference what type of psychotherapy is used in treating neuroses or personality disorders. Group psychotherapy seems as effective as individual psychotherapy, brief psychotherapy as effective as long-term, and client-centered psychotherapy as effective as more traditional psychoanalytically oriented therapy.

8. There is very strong evidence that when psychotherapy is added to the medical regimen in the treatment of such psychosomatic conditions as ulcer, colitis, or asthma, the combination of treatments is superior to traditional medical treatments alone (Luborsky, Singer, and Luborsky 1975).

The Need for a Treatment Model

9. It is extremely difficult to find controlled studies which attempt to measure the impact of family therapy upon the family member perhaps arbitrarily defined as the patient. Most family therapists view pathology as residing not in the individual but within the family system. They are more concerned with measuring changes within the system than with measuring changes in the patient. Some would even hold that the systems approach is so important that it makes no sense to compare the effectiveness of family therapy with therapies focusing on only one element of the family system. There has, been controlled research in which people in marital or family therapy have been matched with couples or families who did not receive therapy, and based on such outcome criteria as improved communication, relief of sexual incompatibilities, and greater marital and family tranquility, the treated family groups have clearly done better (Beck 1975). There have also been studies of families in which one member presented a specific symptom, such as delinquency. These families were treated and, compared to control families receiving no treatment, showed considerable improvement (Alexander and Parsons 1975). What is not found in the literature are (1) studies which compare the effectiveness of family therapy for the patient with other therapies and (2) studies which examine the potential additive effect of family therapy when combined with other therapies. This lack is both regrettable and understandable. As compared to other treatments thus far discussed, family therapy is relatively new. The field is still largely dominated by ideology, and research enterprises have only lately gotten under way.

10. The effectiveness of hospitalization in treating acute emotional disorders is undocumented. In fact, most studies of day care and home care programs suggest that even severely disturbed patients do better if not hospitalized (Wilder, Levin, and Zwerling 1966, Langsley, Stephenson, and McDonald 1964). The question of hospital or custodial care for chronically ill patients is also controversial. Such patients can be maintained out of hospitals or domiciliary institutions, but it is questionable if this improves the quality of their lives.

11. Given the complexities involved in treatment of emotional disorders, it is probable that variables other than technique of intervention or the patient's symptomatology are significant. Characteristics of the treater, such as age, sex, social class, belief in the efficacy of treatment, values, and personality characteristics, may be significantly related to outcome. Similarly, characteristics of the patient, such as age, sex, social class, values, expectations of

treatment, and views or attributions as to the causes of their disturbance, may also have an effect on outcome. The literature in this area is vast and focuses primarily upon the matching of patient and treater in individual psychotherapy. There is good reason to pursue these studies. Therapists with similar training utilizing similar techniques with similar patients often have widely varying outcomes. Patients with similar symptomatology receiving similar treatments from therapists with similar training also have varying outcomes. In spite of the voluminous literature in this field, the firm conclusions that can be drawn from the research barely exceed common sense. Our current knowledge and its very real limitations can be summarized as follows:

a. Even with regard to pharmacotherapy, the attitude and personality of the clinician may be important. It has not been possible to directly relate given personality traits of the clinician to successful outcome, but the clinician's enthusiasm and commitment to pharmacological intervention seem related to successful outcome (Uhlenhuth 1966).

b. When therapist and patient are similar with regard to such variables as sex, socioeconomic class, value systems, and expectations regarding treatment, there is some indication that similarities between therapist and patient may be associated with successful outcome or at least associated with keeping the patient in therapy during the early phases of treatment (Landfield 1971).

c. Attempts to match patients and therapists with regard to personality characteristics measured by psychological tests have produced no clear sense of direction with regard to optimal matching of patients and therapists.

d. Over two decades ago, Betz and Whitehorn (1956) noted that some psychiatric residents performed well with schizophrenic patients while others did not. Those who did better were referred to as type A therapists. The poorer performers were called type B therapists. In attempting to find some characteristics which might distinguish the two groups, it was discovered that they had markedly different scores on the Strong Vocational Interest Blank. Type A therapists had Strong Vocational Interests scores similar to those of lawyers and accountants; type B therapists had scores similar to those of printers and science teachers. It was later discovered that type B therapists were somewhat more effective with neurotic patients than were type A therapists. These discoveries have stimulated a rash of laboratory research, generally testing the effect of A and B therapists on student volunteers in simulated therapy situations rather than on real patients. There is general agreement among researchers in this area that there is probably some powerful factor involved in the A/B differential, but there is not enough adequate outcome research to know how to use these findings (Razin 1971, Chartier 1971).

e. There is some evidence that experienced therapists have somewhat better results than inexperienced therapists (Cartwright and Vogel 1958).

f. There is general agreement throughout the literature, but no firm research evidence, that therapists with such highly desirable "healthy" personality characteristics as warmth, empathy, stability, tolerance, permissiveness, intelligence and acceptingness are more likely to be successful (Truax and Carkhuff 1967). In one research study, the quality of therapists' capacity for acceptance was positively correlated with success with highly anxious patients (Berzins, In press). This research indicates that therapists with high acceptance scores will be successful with patients who are highly anxious or moderately anxious, while therapists with low acceptance scores will be successful only with the latter group.

g. There is considerable evidence that patients of the opposite sex who are young, attractive, verbal, intelligent, and successful (the so-called YAVIS syndrome) are more likely to be accepted for psychotherapy by therapists regardless of ability to pay (Schofield 1964). Whether these patients have more successful outcomes or not is uncertain, but since they are more likely to receive treatment, it is more likely they will improve.

h. There is no conclusive findings relating personality variables in patients to success in treatment. There does remain among clinicians and researchers a strong conviction that patients who are highly motivated for therapy and who have an attitudinal set in which they anticipate relief of symptoms will do better in psychotherapy.

i. Recently there has been some tentative but intriguing research dealing with the manner in which patients explain their disability to themselves. It is assumed that patients who believe that important reinforcements are attributable to their own efforts, as compared to patients who attribute important reinforcements to chance, luck, and other external events, should require different therapeutic approaches or should respond differentially to a particular treatment modality. A few studies have indicated that patients who attribute their difficulties to external events and conditions are more likely to respond to directive approaches or approaches involving environmental manipulation, whereas patients who attribute their difficulties to internal processes may be more responsive to nondirective therapies (Valins and Nisbett 1971).

GOOD NEWS AND BAD NEWS

This synopsis of research which might guide the clinician in selecting treatment holds both good news and bad news. The good news is that in a few instances we have relatively convincing evidence that some treatments may be more suitable for some patients than for others. We have a little bit of data supporting the efficacy of combined treatments. We now know that most interventions help. We can also be somewhat reassured by the increasing volume and sophistication of research currently being undertaken. In this regard, it is well to remind ourselves that research as to the effectiveness of treatment is almost an infant science. While we have still not reached the point of investigating specific treatments or specific combinations of treatments for specific types of patients in any major way, the methodology for doing this is now available. If there is enough commitment on the part of researchers, enough funding, and enough freedom to do research, we can anticipate continued progress in matching the proper treatment and proper therapist to the proper patient.

The bad news is that, as of this moment, our research has yielded little in guiding the clinician in prescription of specific treatments for specific patients. With few exceptions a clinician can, in approaching a given patient, argue with impunity that his favored treatment, whether pharmacotherapy, behavior therapy, or group, individual, or family psychotherapy, is the treatment of choice for the patient; there is no data that anyone can invoke to fully disprove his contention. It is this lack of data which prolongs the ideological warfare and lack of precision characterizing current treatment of emotional disorders.

Given the lack of scientific guidelines in determining treatment, what is the clinician to do? Many mental health professionals have, as I have noted, responded to the complexity of the problem by eschewing science in favor of ideology. Others have resorted to a rigid empiricism and are disdainful of theory. The best clinicians have continued to practice, utilizing those techniques with which

The Need for a Treatment Model

they are most familiar and which are most compatible with their theoretical convictions, while at the same time supporting research enterprises and awaiting the time when research will provide them proper direction. This approach can also be combined with various degrees of empiricism. An experienced clinician may be highly committed to one or two interventions, but also be willing to try whatever seems to work, demonstrated either by his own clinical experience or by the experience and research of others. While this kind of pluralistic approach may seem the best we can currently do, I believe it inadequate. Pluralism is not sufficiently thorough; it merely directs the clinician's attention to all treatment modalities while providing no guidelines as to how to use them. It fails to alert the clinician to a vast amount of theory, research, and clinical experience which can serve to provide at least rudimentary guidelines to treatment specificity until more sophisticated research is available. The pluralistic approach also leads to complacency. It may increase the reluctance of clinicians to develop treatment models which might eventually lead to an integrated treatment of emotional disorders. Finally, it provides no help to consumers or regulatory agencies in making decisions as to which are the most useful treatments for given patients in given situations.

There is an urgent need for clinicians to move beyond pluralism to an integrative approach. Such an approach requires more than just theoretical eclecticism buttressed by clinical empiricism; it requires as well the development of a conceptual framework or model for prescribing treatment based on current knowledge. Such a model should be viewed not as a substitute for research but as a useful instrument for generating testable hypotheses. A model which would provide the clinician some guidance in treatment selection should have the following characteristics:

1. It should provide direction for defining a patient's problems and for dealing with those problems directly and efficiently. Stated in more conventional medical terms, it should allow the practitioner to understand how diagnosis can be related to a specific treatment or treatments.

2. It should provide the therapist a basis for understanding why a given treatment works and should, in a general way, help define the usefulness and limitations of every treatment that seems to work. No reasonable therapeutic intervention should be excluded from the model.

3. It should offer the therapist a basis for understanding not only how a given treatment affects the patient's immediate problem, but also how it affects the patient's long-term adjustment and quality of life. This means that the model should direct the clinician to consider successful outcome in terms of variables other than symptom removal.

4. It should be simple enough and sufficiently devoid of mysticism to be explained to consumers. The disturbed person should be able to understand what treatment alternatives are open to him and how they might be expected to work.

RESISTANCE TO INTEGRATIVE MODELS

While the task of developing this kind of model is formidable (some might call it grandiose), you would think that all therapists would welcome an integrated approach to treatment and would be willing to contribute to its development. This is not the case. Many of my colleagues defend the therapeutic status quo. They raise a series of objections to even trying to develop an integrative model, and their objections deserve serious consideration.

1. Some argue that the current laissez-faire approach to treatment is not as unscientific as it might at first seem. They insist that the current status of intervention in the mental health professions is not too different from the status of intervention in medicine. After all, surgeons and internists often prescribe quite different treatments for similar conditions. The thrust of this argument is that disagreements over treatment of the mentally ill are of the same order as those over treatment of nonpsychiatric illnesses.

There are several fallacies in this argument. Most nonpsychiatric illnesses can be diagnosed with some precision and an accurate diagnosis of the problem provides rather crisp treatment guidelines. In nonpsychiatric medicine, the results of treatment are much easier to measure than in psychiatry. Medical research can in most instances help us decide what is the best treatment. There is reason for the doctor to exercise clinical judgment in timing the duration and dosages of his therapies, but generally most doctors would treat pneumonia, pernicious anemia, and diabetes in roughly the same manner. There are some nonpsychiatric diseases which can be treated in a variety of ways and for which research findings do not provide unequivocal guidance as to

The Need for a Treatment Model 23

the best treatment. But even in dealing with these disturbances, the physician relies on knowledge as well as judgment and faith in coming to his treatment decision. Every surgeon who recommends surgery for a duodenal ulcer is at least aware of the rationale for more conservative treatments. The internist is equally aware of the arguments for surgery. Reliance on judgment and faith does not come until the usefulness of scientific knowledge is exhausted. This is not always true in decisions as to the proper intervention for emotional disorders. The healer of emotional disorders may never consider alternative treatments. He may even be unaware of them. The current process of selecting treatment for emotional disorders would be comparable with the state of affairs in nonpsychiatric medicine only if we had nineteenth century medicine in mind. The differences between various schools of treatment for emotional disorders are comparable not to differences between modern surgeons and internists but to the current differences between faith healers, naturopaths, and chiropractors.

2. It can be argued that the current situation is not really so bad, since hundreds of thousands of people are helped by whatever treatment they receive. Many people do get better whether they are drugged, psychoanalyzed, or have their social consciousness expanded. This argument implies that there are elements common to all aspects of mental healing (perhaps the concern, love, or authority of the healer), and that it doesn't really make too much difference which techniques the therapist uses. Those who cite this argument are lending support to the proposition that there may not be a real need for professional healers. If love, concern, or power were all that was important in treatment and if skill were unimportant, there would be little need for mental health professionals to develop complex skills in using various interventions. While I recognize that trained nonprofessionals can, at times, do a superb job in using certain interventions, and while I am aware of the critical role of the therapist's personality in treatment outcomes, I believe that there is a body of knowledge and skills which helps make a better therapist. Even the lay psychotherapist has to undergo some training before treating clients.

It must also be noted that there is considerable evidence that many patients are receiving treatments that are not helping them. Some patients are actually made worse by therapy (Malan 1973). In the last few years I have had the opportunity to personally observe some of the shortcomings of therapy. After many years of enjoying the splendid isolation of office psychotherapy, I returned to working on an inpatient unit. Treating inpatients gives the therapist the unique opportunity to learn something about what some of his colleagues are doing. The great majority of patients hospitalized on the two university services where I have worked were not new patients, but had been treated before hospitalization. Because their conditions failed to improve or worsened, these patients could be considered therapeutic failures. One of the striking characteristics of the prehospital treatment of this group was its one-dimensionality. With rare exceptions, these patients were treated only with drugs, only with individual psychotherapy, or only with group therapy. Most commonly, they had received only drug therapy (sometimes for years). In working with these patients, it was often possible to identify problems which proved amenable to new kinds of therapeutic intervention. These experiences helped confirm my belief that the current system of therapy is failing to meet the needs of many patients.

3. It can be argued that consumers of mental health services now have free choice to elect the kind of therapy they feel is most likely to fit their needs. Conceivably, any movement toward developing a system for determining treatment might be an unnecessary infringement upon the patient's freedom. This argument implies that treatment rationally prescribed on the basis of a conceptual model is ritualized or oppressive treatment. That is not the kind of treatment I am recommending. The clinician who is guided by a system for recommending therapy can still allow the patient choice.

I would note also that even with the current laissez-faire approach to treatment, many people have very little choice of therapist and therefore very little choice of treatment. The average person who cannot afford private therapy and who seeks help at a community clinic has little opportunity to ask his therapist for a specific kind of treatment. He is almost powerless in choosing a therapist or a therapeutic method and must accept whatever recommendations the community clinic proposes. Furthermore, even affluent and sophisticated people don't actually know very much about psychological treatment. Although they may be well read in popular psychology, their information is usually spotty and superficial. As a result, they are likely to be attracted to the popular or "in" therapy of the moment. Or they may rely on the advice of a friend and seek treatment with

The Need for a Treatment Model

the existentialist, the behaviorist, or the family therapist who they believe has helped others. The bitter disputes among mental health experts as to which is the "best" therapy also serve to confuse the consumer. As long as the consumer is bombarded with so much conflicting information, he is not likely to make a careful judgment as to what treatment he needs but is more likely, in desperation, to bow to the authority and the recommendations of the first therapist he consults.

Consider the now famous case of Senator Thomas Eagleton, whose treatment with electroconvulsive therapy became a subject of national concern. Senator Eagleton initially consulted doctors who were affiliated with Washington University Medical School in St. Louis. Psychiatrists at that institution are known to favor somatic treatments. (So are the doctors at the Mayo Clinic, where Senator Eagleton later was treated, but the choice of treatment in this case may have been influenced by the doctors' knowledge of the patient's earlier treatment.) I do not wish to be critical of the choice of treatment in this case, particularly since Senator Eagleton did get better. But, it seems likely that Senator Eagleton with all of his sophistication and power did not shop around in choosing his therapy. If he had, he might have found plenty of psychiatrists who would have treated him with antidepressant drugs instead of shock therapy. Others might have recommended long-term psychotherapy, behavior therapy, family therapy, or even group therapy. Given the limited public information about his case, it is not too far-fetched to speculate that the choice of treatment was in large part an accident of geography.

4. It can be argued that many of the best therapists who hold to a particular school are not really as rigidly one-dimensional as I have described them. Even the most doctrinaire therapist often uses a relatively eclectic approach in actual practice. Psychoanalytic treatment can be viewed as a rather prolonged variety of behavior modification. The drug-oriented therapist may provide brief individual or family psychotherapy. The behaviorist may encourage his patient to be more assertive. And behavioral principles can certainly be applied to family therapy.

I have little doubt that there are many therapists who try to fit treatment to the patient. But the conscientiousness and good intentions of these therapists do not negate the need for a conceptual framework for all therapists which would provide a rational basis for choosing treatment. Many of the therapists currently offering a plurality of treatments are operating out of intuition only; when they utilize a conceptual framework, it is usually poorly conceived. They might be far more effective if they had a basis for understanding why they choose certain treatments. Finally, it must be noted that the efforts of therapists to use techniques which go beyond their basic ideological systems are often perfunctory. It is a rare drug therapist who is willing to delve carefully into the dynamics of the family; it is a rare psychoanalyst who is willing to experiment with more precise behavioral techniques.

5. It has been argued that it would be a grandiose task to train therapists in all treatment modalities. There is simply too much to learn. It is easiest for me to respond to this question from the standpoint of psychiatry, the mental health profession I know best. I am convinced that psychiatric training programs do not expect enough of their trainees. The resident may experience considerable emotional stress during training, but his intellectual abilities are not sorely taxed. Most psychiatrists do not begin to master the intellectual aspects of psychiatry until they study for board examinations. In most residency programs now, the third year of training is almost entirely elective and many residents begin to set up unsupervised private practices long before the third year is completed. There is actually plenty of opportunity in three years of psychiatric training (and soon there will be four years of training) to acquaint students with all modalities of treatment.

Part of the problem is that training programs are not set up to teach an integrative or comprehensive approach. Many programs focus primarily upon teaching one particular system of treatment and teach other systems in a perfunctory manner. In most training programs the student rotates through a variety of clinics, in which he is given instruction in the theory and practice of the major forms of therapy, but these experiences are disjointed. The student is likely to be influenced by his most devoted and charismatic teachers, who are usually adherents of particular schools. All of this could be changed, without putting an undue burden upon the student, by providing an integrated curriculum in which the theoretical foundations and practical uses of each variety of intervention (as well as the indications for their use) could be taught.

The expectation that therapists already out of training will be able to broaden their knowledge so as to adopt a less parochial approach may well be unrealistic. Somewhere near the end of training or shortly after the mental health professional starts practicing, he tends to adopt a particular therapeutic style and philosophy. Most therapists currently practicing have become comfortable with an approach and are frightened or reluctant to learn others. Conceivably, they might be unwilling to take the time to broaden their treatment capabilities.

It might also be argued that if practitioners spent their time learning all varieties of intervention they would end up being jacks of all trades, masters of none. This is a real danger. After all, real skill requires learning certain areas in depth and scholarly research requires careful focusing of attention on specific issues. I am not advocating that all therapists be expert at every therapy, nor am I arguing against the idea that many therapists should devote most of their time to learning a particular type of therapy. I am insisting only that all therapists have some conceptual framework for determining which therapies are helpful in which situations and that they use this model in prescribing treatment. It is not necessary that every therapist be expert in a particular form of therapy, so long as he can rationally prescribe that treatment and see that the person who needs it gets it.

6. Perhaps the most serious criticism of an integrative conceptual framework is that it is unscientific. There is real danger that an integrative model could represent nothing more than an ecumenical statement that there is something good about all forms of therapy, thus impeding the scientific determination of which therapies are superior for which type of patient. It is certainly not my intention to argue that all therapies are equally useful. Undoubtedly, continued research will eventually show us that some therapies are far more efficient than others, and some currently popular therapies may not be taken at all seriously ten years from now. I am convinced, however, that all the treatment modalities considered in these pages are effective in certain situations, and that one of the tasks of the mental health professional is to know how to use these therapies in the proper situation.

It is certainly true that if more therapists learned to use more than one therapy concurrently, their work would be harder to evaluate than it is now. It is much easier to study the effects of a drug on behavior change when nothing else is done to the patient than when he receives individual psychotherapy or family therapy concurrently. On the other hand, a broader approach to treatment can certainly be evaluated if we are willing to increase the number of variables to be studied in outcome research.

Intervention into a disturbed person's life will have maximum effect if the therapist can intervene at all levels of the patient's dysfunction: biological, psychological, and social. The model I propose here will of necessity lead to an eclectic approach. Unfortunately, *eclectic* has become a dirty word. The eclectic approach has been ridiculed as comparable to putting the eight or nine elements of a gourmet dinner in a blender and insisting that the resulting puree is better than the sum of its parts. It has been viewed as a "shotgun" approach, used primarily by those not intelligent enough to master a theoretical framework and by those not courageous enough to commit themselves to a school of therapy.

Eclecticism can indeed become a watered-down approach, and it can become a refuge for the ignorant or the timid. But this is eclecticism which is not based on a conceptual framework or model. When the clinician has a model for making rational decisions as to which of many interventions are to be used, eclecticism is no longer a shotgun approach, but is the only scientific approach to the treatment of emotional disorder. Because the term *eclectic* has taken on so many pejorative connotations, I will frequently substitute the less controversial term *multidimensional*.

The first part of this book is an effort to describe a model for determining choice of treatment. The rationale for single or combined use of each of the major treatments will be reviewed. Case illustrations will be offered to clarify various arguments. In other works, I have discussed the social and political impact of therapy (Halleck 1971); in this book, I will also try to show how social and political variables must be considered in choice of treatment.

Chapter 2

Relating Diagnosis to Treatment

During the past four decades a number of clinicians have attempted to integrate approaches to the treatment of emotional disorders. In the 1930s Adolf Meyer developed a system of diagnosis and psychotherapy, called psychobiology, which provided direction for studying patients from both biological and psychosocial perspectives (Muncie 1959). Emotional disorders were viewed not as diseases but as reactions to multiple stresses in the patient's past and current life. Although Meyer's writings were not particularly influential, he did have considerable personal influence on many prominent American psychiatrists in the 1930s and 1940s. Meyer's common-sense approach to patients directed the therapist to investigate the whole person and to utilize a wide variety of therapeutic interventions. The psychobiologist was comfortable treating the same patient with drugs, psychotherapy, or environmental intervention and had at least a rudimentary framework to guide his eclecticism.

Unfortunately Meyer's influence waned during the latter part of the 1940s and the 1950s. These were years of intense commitment to psychoanalytic theory and of boundless if unfounded optimism as to its efficacy. It was also a time when psychologists such as Carl Rogers were developing highly popular and relatively easily mastered techniques for conducting individual psychotherapy. The rapid development of depth psychology and client-centered therapy served to polarize clinicians. Those in the majority committed themselves to individual psychotherapy based on one of several psychoanalytic or client-centered approaches, while a smaller number of primarily medical psychologists relied on somatic treatments. The few pioneers who experimented with behavior modification or family therapy were largely ignored. Students in psychiatric and clinical psychology training programs had little opportunity to learn more than one or two approaches to the patient. (My own training in the mid-1950s at the Menninger School of Psychiatry was more eclectic than most. There the residents learned both somatic treatments and psychoanalytically oriented psychotherapeutic techniques. A few of the faculty "bootlegged" some teaching of existential approaches in unscheduled evening meetings. There was no teaching of behavior or family therapy.)

The decline of Meyer's common-sense system of treatment was particularly unfortunate since it occurred at a time when new techniques of individual therapy were being developed and knowledge of behavioral, family, and social psychology was expanding. When new interventions became available to the mental health profession, there was no integrative *zeitgeist* which allowed for adequate evaluation of the role of the new therapy in dealing with the whole person. Instead each new innovation became the subject of heated debate, sometimes leading to the professional isolation of the innovator. One of the most shameful examples of this process was the treatment of behaviorists in the 1950s. Although at that time behaviorists such as Joseph Wolpe were producing impressive evidence of the value of their approach, they were unable to exert meaningful influence in psychiatric training. In fact, they were dismissed by the largely psychoanalytic establishment as misguided zealots or charlatans. It was only as data supporting the efficacy of behavior therapy accumulated and as increasing disillusionment with psychoanalytic technique developed that behavior therapy began to gain some legitimacy in clinical training.

While post-Meyerian treatment moved away from eclecticism, it must be noted that during the 1960s a number of prominent psychoanalysts did make serious efforts to integrate biological and psychological conceptions of behavior. Clinical investigations by psychoanalysts such as Masserman (1958), Grinker (1956), and Menninger (1963) led to the development of integrative theories of emotional disorder and to new views of diagnostic processes. Menninger's book "The Vital Balance" was an especially detailed study of the interdependent roles of biological, psychological, and social factors in producing emotional disorders. His restructuring of diagnostic categories implied multicausality and versatility in treatment techniques. Unfortunately the integrative efforts of Menninger and other psychoanalysts were highly theoretical. They did not have immediate implications for treatment and were not followed by development of conceptual models of multidimensional therapy. For the most part even the theoretical aspect of their integrative work generated little enthusiasm among psychotherapists.

Other integrative and nonpsychoanalytic studies of therapeutic techniques were published in the late 1950s and early 1960s. Jerome Frank (1961) argued that all therapies derived their usefulness from the authority of the socially sanctioned healer. Jay Haley (1963) presented a fascinating approach to all therapies based on communication theory and the struggle for authority and power between therapist and patient. As was the case with psychoanalytic writing, however, these publications were mostly theoretical and did not provide the student with a rationale for multidimensional therapy.

More recently Leston Havens (1972) has described four approaches to psychotherapy: the descriptive, the dynamic-analytical, the existential, and the interpersonal. Eloquently describing disagreements among the schools, Havens makes an effort to elaborate the usefulness of each approach; he does not, however, provide specific guidelines for the use of different techniques in different cases. He rests his hopes for progress in the behavioral sciences on what he calls "psychiatric pluralism"—the efforts of the various schools to refine their technologies and coexist separately. Throughout his writings is the implication that it would be impossible and unwise to seek an integrated system of therapy at this time.

Another psychiatrist, Aaron Lazare (1973) has commented upon four different conceptual models currently used in treating patients: the medical, the psychological, the behavioral, and the sociological. He notes that therapists are rarely precise in defining the model upon which their therapy is based and that this accounts for frequent misunderstanding of psychiatric treatment by other health providers and patients. Lazare calls for greater integration among the four approaches, but he is rather sanguine in believing that the current diversity of therapies reflects a healthy state of the science of mental healing. While Havens and Lazare have made interesting theoretical contributions to the science of behavior disorders, they have not undertaken the task of providing the clinician a method for determining which treatment to use and when.

The most comprehensive and integrated approach to treatment to date has been suggested by Arnold Lazarus (1971, 1973); he calls for a thorough evaluation of all aspects of the patient's dysfunction and for intervention based upon that evaluation. While Lazarus does not describe his multidimensional approach in depth, his conceptual basis for determining treatment is clear, and he uses a variety of interventions. Lazarus's work, if expanded, would provide an intriguing and useful model for all clinicians. While my approach differs from Lazarus's in theoretical orientation, we are pursuing the same basic goal.

With the exception of the work of Lazarus, I have been unable to find integrated approaches in the mental health literature. The reluctance of my colleagues to develop such an approach is understandable. At this point our knowledge of behavioral science is so primitive that it is impossible to develop any system that offers precise guidelines for the treatment of each patient. Still, I am convinced that there is a way of conceptualizing disturbed behavior which will at least suggest directions for intervention. Such a conceptualization must begin with an examination of the concept of diagnosis.

DIAGNOSIS

Diagnosis in both medicine and the behavioral sciences is based upon accurate observation of behavior. It will be helpful at this point to define how the term *behavior* will be used throughout this discussion. I will be using a broad definition, viewing as behavior any activity of the human organism. Obviously some organismic activities are easier to describe and measure than others. Motor activities, such as crying, fighting, verbal complaints of discomfort, tics, and flight responses, can be observed directly, and the sophisticated clinician can measure their frequency. Medical diagnostic techniques can be used to measure less observable organismic activities such as temperature, pulse rate, and respiration rate. The objectivity of description of behavior is drastically diminished when we enter the area of feelings, motivations, or attitudes. It is always difficult, and often impossible, to know what another is experiencing. Descriptions of such behavior must, in large part, be based on the patient's capacity to report subjective experiences and on the clinician's intuition. Nevertheless, the patient's phenomenological world is not a total mystery to the clinician. Empathic skills often enable the clinician to describe the patient's emotional state with some precision. Psychologists have also developed a number of tests that can provide the clinician a reasonable approximation of how an individual feels about himself and his world (Smith 1969). We may never be able to completely identify with the consciousness of another, but we can, and for purposes of treatment often must, gain an approximate understanding.

One common approach to diagnosis and treatment of emotional disorders is to try to link the current existence of a cluster of behaviors with predictable maladaptive behavior in the future. If among individuals who are delusional, who show disorganized thinking and inappropriate affect, and who do not show other behaviors such as confusion, depression or elation, a high percentage regularly experience a certain type of dysfunctional behavior at some future time, we can refer to this cluster of behaviors as a disorder, disease, or syndrome and give it a name such as schizophrenia. (Other variables such as the patient's age or his family history can also be used in defining the disorder.) If we observe that patients who show a slightly different cluster of behaviors have a different future, we can label this cluster differently and perhaps call it mania or psychotic depression. This kind of classification makes it easier for clinicians to communicate with one another about their patients. It also makes it possible to study the impact of various interventions on favorable alteration of the anticipated future, or prognosis, of those individuals who are viewed as having a particular kind of disorder. This diagnostic approach requires careful observation and classification of dysfunctional behavior. It brings some order to the mental health field and facilitates the compiling of experimental data as to which interventions are likely to influence the patient favorably.

A second approach to diagnosis and treatment may begin with observation, description, and classification of the patient's disorder, but it is characterized also by efforts to hypothesize the causes of the patient's dysfunctional behavior. Here, the clinician uses his previous experience and knowledge to hypothesize etiologic processes.

If it is possible to understand the processes which cause a behavior, the clinician has a theoretical as well as an empirical system for utilizing interventions. In making diagnoses based on etiological hypotheses, the clinician also seeks to relate similar behaviors to common processes. If there is reason to believe that a certain type of process is frequently present in patients who demonstrate a given set of behaviors, the clinician who encounters such a patient can formulate etiological hypotheses and relate them to treatment. In nonpsychiatric medicine, both observational and etiological diagnostic approaches are used, but the greatest progress in medical science has been brought about by emphasizing etiology. Even the labels the physician uses to classify a disease are more than just a description of the patient's behaviors; they denote certain processes that may be causing it. When the physician sees a person who complains of pain in the chest, several hypotheses as to what is causing the pain immediately flash through his mind. These are based upon his general knowledge and past experience. Further questioning of the patient, further observation, and various examinations or tests are then utilized to either confirm or refute these hypotheses. When the initial hypothesis is supported—or the process that is a major factor in causing the pain, such as myocardial infarction, pulmonary embolism, or pneumonia, is confirmed—there are usually rational directions for treatment. To the extent that we understand the processes involved in causation, we have an increased opportunity to modify them.

In the behavioral sciences, unfortunately, we currently lack sufficient knowledge to confirm most of our hypotheses. As a rule, the diagnostic statements we make represent only descriptions of observable behavior patterns. They do not represent descriptions of more complex mechanisms or processes, and they tell us very little about the cause of the disorder. Such diagnostic terms as *schizophrenia* or *manic-depressive psychosis* are, given our current state of knowledge, little more than careful descriptions of the observable behavior of the patient over a period of time. Unlike such diagnostic terms as *myocardial infarction* or *pneumococcal pneumonia*, they do not symbolize a definite process which may be causing the disorder.

In recent years we have become somewhat more sophisticated in relating certain kinds of depression to specific processes. We now believe that some forms of depression have biological determinants. There remains considerable disagreement, however, as to how severe a depression must be to consider it biologically determined and there still is no proven theory as to what biochemical changes have occurred. The various terms currently used to describe depressive disorders do not refer to etiologic processes. Some of the terms used to describe neurotic behaviors, such as *conversion reaction* or *obsessive-compulsive reaction*, do imply to most clinicians that the patient is experiencing some type of psychological conflict. But those diagnostic terms do not in themselves symbolize what type of conflict is involved or by what mechanism the conflict elicits the behavior. Even if one accepts a psychodynamic explanation of the above disorders (and not all clinicians do), there is a large variety of unspecified conflict situations that can have etiological relevance.

The diagnostic categories in the behavioral sciences most analogous to those in nonpsychiatric medicine are acute and chronic brain syndromes. In these categories not only is the patient's confusion and disorganization described by the term *brain syndrome*, but also the observation of the existence of a brain syndrome is a mandate for the clinician to search for its causes. If the clinician confirms that tumor, trauma, infection, metabolic disorder, or circulatory disorder is influencing the brain, then he has actually discovered a process that partially explains the patient's behavior, just as processes such as myocardial infarction or pulmonary embolism partially explain chest pain.

In actual practice mental health professionals use traditional psychiatric diagnoses as guides to treatment only some of the time. If there is no firm data indicating how a cluster of behaviors is best treated, the practitioner may simply label these behaviors and then base his intervention upon hypotheses he formulates as to what processes he believes are influencing the patient. In effect the clinician must utilize both an observational or classificatory approach and an etiologic approach to diagnosis and treatment. The observational or classificatory approach is essential when experience or data tell us that certain precisely defined behaviors respond better to certain treatments than to others. Here the clinician must be prepared to use whatever intervention has been observed to be effective, whether or not there is a good theory to explain its mechanism of effectiveness. But observation or classification alone provides an inadequate guide to treatment. There are relatively few instances in which we can say with certainty that classifying a given patient's behavior provides us a clear idea of how to treat him; the clinician must also try to hypothesize the processes which cause it, and each such hypothesis should logically suggest a specific type of intervention.

The obvious problem with the etiologic approach is that we have so many unproven hypotheses. Does it make sense to impose treatment upon patients which is based on theories rather than on facts? It is important here to reemphasize that some type of hypothesis, however tacit, governs the choice of intervention in most clinical situations. Choice of treatment is in large part determined by the clinician's belief in a theory that the prescribed intervention will remedy some dysfunctional process influencing his patient. I feel that we should continue to use such an approach as long as we acknowledge the hypothetical nature of our methods and as long as we are committed to being extremely thorough and comprehensive in considering every hypothesis that might be relevant in a given case.

The key to effective use of the combined classificatory and etiological approach is systematization and thoroughness. Each patient's disorder should be carefully observed and described. If there is good evidence that the particular disorder can be influenced by a particular intervention, that intervention must be given first consideration. But whether or not such evidence is available, the clinician must also begin to consider the causes of the patient's disorder. He must consider all of the biological, psychobiological, and social processes that may be influencing the patient's behavior and must develop a system for judging which processes are most critical.

The hypotheses themselves can be viewed as crude analogues to more sophisticated etiological diagnoses in nonpsychiatric medicine. When clinicians in the mental health field talk about the patient having certain conflicts, utilizing certain defense mechanisms, being scapegoated by a dysfunctional family system, or having a defect in certain neurotransmitter systems, they are hypothesizing the existence of processes which explain dysfunction and are making diagnostic statements which suggest specific treatments.

Two groups of mental health professionals might disagree with this approach. Some psychiatrists, primarily of biological orientation, support the need for diagnosis based on observation and classification but are skeptical of efforts to develop systems of diagnosis or intervention based on theory. They argue that we know practically nothing about etiology and that we should base most of our interventions on data provided by research. When these practitioners do invoke etiology, they try to restrict their hypothesis of causality to biological processes (Woodruff 1974). Certain behaviorists would be even more emphatic in rejecting my approach. They argue that there is no need for any diagnostic system and that one does not have to understand the causes of

Relating Diagnosis to Treatment

behavior or even know its natural history in order to change it (Skinner 1971). Both groups emphasize the argument that we possess techniques for changing behavior even if we are not sure why they work. They point out that behavioral scientists have developed a more scientific system for changing emotional disorders than they have for explaining what causes them. Many treatments, including relationship therapy, free association, electroshock therapy, and drug therapy, were believed useful (and in some instances were so validated) long before there were theories explaining how they worked. Similarly, behavior modification techniques derived from learning theory can be used quite effectively by clinicians understanding nothing of how the maladaptive behavior was learned.

While I am impressed with the commitment to scientific purity which characterizes those who reject the etiological approach to diagnosis, I am also concerned that failure to consider causality carries certain risks for the patient. First of all, the clinician who does not seek to determine the many possible causes of a given behavior may forfeit the opportunity of discovering a variety of different and sometimes lifesaving modes of intervention. Treatment which is not based on causality is usually one-dimensional. Second, whenever behavior is treated without regard to its causes, neither patient nor therapist will likely have the opportunity to learn how to prevent recurrences. Finally, there is a very real danger that the patient so treated may find his behavior changed in a way that makes his total life situation worse than before treatment.

These concerns are especially critical when the issue of diagnosis is totally ignored. Consider what might happen if a behavior therapist who rejects the value of diagnosis is asked to treat a common dysfunctional behavior such as a pronounced tendency to withdraw from interpersonal relationships. Let us assume that some therapeutic intervention has been developed which increases the patient's sociability and his capacity to relate to others. The use of such a technique without concern for the issue of how or why the patient has become withdrawn might be harmful to the patient for a variety of reasons. The patient's withdrawal might be based on confusion resulting from organic brain disease. Or it might be related to a schizophrenic process in which the patient's disordered perception has seriously compromised his capacity to relate to others. In these instances, simply treating the behavior without searching for its causes might limit therapeutic intervention and deprive the patient of either lifesaving or palliative treatment. Or what if the patient's withdrawal is actually related to being in an environment which is hostile or dangerous to him? There are times when withdrawal is adaptive. Treating such withdrawal without doing something about the environment might seriously compromise the patient's psychological and political status. A behavioral technique might be the most appropriate intervention when the patient's withdrawal can be considered a simple manifestation of shyness. But the clinician could not know that the problem is simply shyness until he did a diagnostic evaluation which included consideration of all possible determinants of the patient's behavior.

Biologically oriented psychiatrists who are skeptical of the etiological approach to diagnosis would probably not treat the specific symptom of withdrawal unless it was associated with other symptoms and could be considered the manifestation of a disease or syndrome. They would certainly be concerned with etiology insofar as they would carefully consider and try to rule out the presence of an acute or chronic brain syndrome. If they totally ignored the issue of causation by nonbiological factors, however, they might conclude that the patient's withdrawn behavior is not part of a disease picture and that it therefore should not be treated. The patient might then be deprived of a behavioral intervention that could alleviate his symptom. Conversely, they might conclude that the patient's withdrawal is part of such a picture and might treat the syndrome pharmacologically while failing to note that the patient's withdrawal is also related to such modifiable environmental factors as being scapegoated by a family system. Exclusive reliance on the observational or classificatory approach, just like exclusive reliance on a nondiagnostic approach, cannot provide the clinician with safe and rational guidelines to effective treatment.

For the sake of completeness, it should be noted that a few practitioners accept an etiological approach but reject the value of diagnosis based on observation and classification. Their inadequacies have already been noted. An even more deviant group of practitioners have argued the uniqueness of causal sequences, finding each relevant to a single individual on a single occasion (May, Angel, and Ellenberger 1958). They have insisted that individuals are so different that common processes in the development of a similar disorder in two different individuals will never be discovered. In effect, they call for each patient to have his own unique diagnosis. This highly individualistic and seemingly humanistic approach to the problem of treatment may appeal to the unsophisticated clinician but is entirely impractical and intellectually unsound. Obviously no two people are alike, but if we view each patient as being influenced by unique processes, we must ignore a great deal of clinical data which suggest that there are common processes with causal significance in eliciting similar behaviors. Furthermore, such a nihilistic approach is inconsistent with the realities of clinical practice. Whenever the clinician makes a decision to intervene on the basis of causal hypotheses, he is heavily influenced by his previous experiences with other people. Delving into a patient's past, dealing with the patient's present life, or seeking to understand and empathize with the patient is always based on some hypothesis of human behavior which the clinician assumes is relevant to the patient, because the clinician's experience or knowledge has taught him that such an hypothesis has been relevant to patients or other people he has known. Thus it is impossible to discard the notion of common causality in diagnosis, and literal acceptance of the idea of each individual having his own unique diagnosis must be based on romantic rather than scientific values.

The basic arguments of this section are worth repeating. Diagnosis is essential to rational treatment and the clinician needs a system of diagnosis that provides direction for treatment. Diagnosis based solely on observation and classification provides only limited guides to intervention. We need an approach to diagnosis which is based on causation. This approach requires the formulation and testing of multiple hypotheses as to the processes which cause various types of dysfunctional behavior. Given the infant state of our science, it is critical that no hypothesis or set of hypotheses should be so revered as to make us less open to other hypotheses. Being open to a variety of hypotheses will not in itself provide the clinician a precise guide for knowing which treatment to use, and when. A willingness to consider all classes of hypothesis is essential, however, if there is to be a comprehensive and systematic approach to the patient.

INDIVIDUAL-ENVIRONMENT INTERACTION

Any human behavior is determined by who a person is (genetic makeup, physical strengths and weaknesses, past learning experiences) and by where he is (the nature of all the interpersonal and social forces in his environment). All behavior is determined by an individual's interaction with his environment. Still another way of putting this is that behavior may be considered in terms of how an individual responds to environmental stimuli. We have to consider how the individual's biological makeup and previous learning experiences define and sometimes limit that individual's capacity to respond to environmental stimuli.

When behavior is examined from this perspective, it is necessary to invoke field or process models of explanation. No single factor can be viewed as causing a behavior, nor, for that matter, can the listing of several factors associated with a behavior be viewed as explanatory. Rather, each of many causative factors exerts influence within a complex system, and the power of any factor to change behavior is dependent upon several other factors. Given the enormous variation in people's genetic makeup, in their past learning experiences, and in their present environments, it is rarely possible to predict that the coexistence of any group of factors will produce a given behavior disorder. At best we are dealing with probability. We can only say that certain biological deficits, certain learning experiences, and certain environments increase the probability of a certain behavior's developing.

The multidetermined nature of human behavior is confirmed by the clinical data of the behavioral sciences. We know that there is an important genetic factor in some behavior disorders such as mania or schizophrenia. But we also know that some people suspected of having a high genetic propensity toward such a disorder behave quite normally throughout their lives. Hereditary factors do not totally determine psychotic behavior. We also know that people acquire neurobiological disabilities. But suspicion or knowledge of the existence of organic impairment is never a sufficient explanation of a behavior disorder. People with quite similar brain pathology often behave differently. Variables related to the individual's heredity, past learning, and present environment must be considered in accounting for these differences.

It is also apparent that an individual's past learning experience cannot totally explain his present behavior. If it were theoretically possible to raise two people in identical environments, they would not learn similar patterns of behavior because they would have different genetic makeups. Even if it were possible to find two people with identical genetic makeups who were raised in an identical environment, their behavior would differ once each was exposed to a different environment. Finally, changes in the recent or present environment can never fully account for an individual's behavior. People exposed to the most oppressive environments react differently. Because of differing genetic and acquired traits, some tolerate oppression well, others fight it, and others succumb to it by developing highly maladaptive behavior patterns.

Any well-trained clinician is aware of the multidetermined nature of human behavior and knows that only models based on the interrelationship of many causal factors can explain human behavior scientifically. Unfortunately, it is difficult to use such models as guides to treatment. Systems approaches provide a broad picture of what is happening to the patient, but they do not provide clear directions for intervention unless certain parts of the system are examined, at least temporarily, in isolation from others. Research in the behavioral sciences is also simplified if the researcher studies the effect of one or two variables, rather than attempting to study all the ramifications of systems change. For practical purposes the clinician must learn to examine components of a system, at the same time keeping the total system in mind.

There are serious drawbacks to such an approach. As the clinician compartmentalizes his thinking, he is tempted to mistake the part he is focusing on for the whole, or for a more important causative factor in the patient's disturbance than in fact it is. Too much of the literature of psychiatry and psychology reflects the clinician's need to focus upon specific components of behavioral systems and to ignore other components. The debates over the etiology of schizophrenia are representative. Those who favor developmental theories focus upon past environments created by schizophrenic parents who have either failed to allow the child to develop a sense of identity or have communicated with the child so inconsistently that the child begins to behave in a psychotic manner (Jackson 1959). Organicists, on the other hand, argue that when the parents of the schizophrenic child behave so perversely, it is because they are forced to raise a biologically impaired child who cannot respond normally (Kety 1974). More socially oriented therapists have politicized or romanticized schizophrenic behavior as an adaptive response to a corrupt or "sick" society (Laing 1967).

In spite of the risk of developing a constricted view of the patient, the clinician must, in my opinion, temporarily compartmentalize his thinking so that he can formulate hypotheses as to how classes of determinants, such as the patient's biological condition, the patient's past learning experience, or the patient's present environment, are related to the patient's current behavior. Only after the clinician has considered the relevance of all categories of behavioral determinants can he begin to integrate them. With such an approach, thoroughness is the clinician's major protection against developing a one-dimensional or constricted view of the patient. It is therapeutically productive to focus intensively on one group of etiologic factors only if the clinician is committed to eventually considering all etiologic factors.

When behavior is viewed as a product of the individual's interaction with the environment, four groups of possible etiologic factors or hypotheses can be distinguished: biological hypotheses, learning or educational hypotheses, informational hypotheses, and hypotheses relating to the nature of the present environment. In reviewing these categories, it will be necessary periodically to remind ourselves how they interrelate to one another in causing a given behavior.

BIOLOGICAL HYPOTHESES

Because of the historical perspectives of the behavioral sciences and because biological dysfunctions often require urgent interventions, the clinician usually begins the process of diagnosis by asking himself: Is there some inherited or acquired biological dysfunction that is contributing to this patient's behavior? When the patient is confused, disoriented, or delirious, the clinician is always accurate in postulating some biological dysfunction and with careful evaluation can often determine its cause. When severe alterations of mood or schizophrenic behavior are observed, the clinician can fall back upon a certain amount of genetic, laboratory, and clinical evidence and assume some biochemical dysfunction. There is, of course, always some biological change in the organism accompanying any observable behavioral change. The clinician does not ordinarily invoke biological hypotheses unless the behavioral change is severe. Behavior that is not associated with intense suffering or that does not deviate greatly from the patient's past behavior or from the norms of the patient's subculture is not usually assumed to be heavily influenced by biological determinants. Obviously, the judgment of whether or not a behavior is dysfunctional enough to be viewed as having important biological causes must often be somewhat arbitrary.

When biological causes of such behaviors as mania, schizophrenia or depression are hypothesized, it is always difficult to determine the relative influence of predisposing genetic as opposed to environmental factors in creating the biologic dysfunction. Inherited biologic deficits are undoubtedly important factors in creating susceptibility or predisposition to grossly disturbed behavior, but a patient may also become predisposed to developing a biological disorder by virtue of experiencing certain physical, psychological, and social stresses engendered by the environment. (The nature-nurture problem here is exceedingly complex. Genetic predispositions may lead to behaviors that elicit stressful responses from the environment. The congenitally hyperactive infant, for example, may elicit reactions of overprotectiveness, withdrawal, or rejection from his distressed mother. These maternal responses will put stress on the child and contribute to the later development of a personality disorder.) Environmental stress may of itself elicit biological changes irrespective of the issue of predisposition. For example, some behavioral scientists have hypothesized that depression may begin as an adaptive response to stressful life events (Akiskal 1975). If these events are prolonged and severe enough, the biochemical changes which accompany the depression may increase or remain constant even when the patient's life situation has improved. The patient can remain depressed when the environmental causes of depression have disappeared. Perhaps those who remain depressed have some predisposition to developing this state. But it is also conceivable that sufficient stress can elicit the prolonged biological dysfunction associated with depression in almost any person.

In the early stages of evaluation the clinician should focus upon detecting or inferring the simple presence of severe biological dysfunction. We cannot, as yet, describe the mechanics of the processes associated with dysfunction, but if we believe such processes are operating, we can use a number of therapeutic agents (usually drugs) to ameliorate or partially reverse them. Even when the clinician hypothesizes the simple presence of severe biological dysfunction, he can usually say very little as to how such dysfunction directly influences the patient. If we could unquestionably demonstrate a biological abnormality in schizophrenia, we would still not have a clear idea of how that abnormality could lead to a complex behavior such as a delusion. Most current theories assume that biological impairments influence behavior by interfering with highly complex perceptual systems. The impaired individual cannot accurately evaluate his environment and responds to environmental stimuli in an aberrant manner. Such responses are in turn influenced by learning and environmental variables. When we speak of biological "causes" of behavior, we are never describing a linear relationship between a biological change and a symptom. It is nevertheless clear that biological dysfunctions are frequently associated with behavior disorders. Hypotheses which infer that such dysfunctions are present usually direct the clinician to consider the use of biological interventions. This aspect of diagnosis and treatment is illustrated by the following case.

A twenty-two-year-old man, who had recently graduated from college, began to feel anxious and depressed shortly after he started his first job, as assistant athletic director at a high school. He gradually began to withdraw from people. His co-workers noted that there were times when he did not respond to ordinary social communication and seemed to be staring off in space. After three months on his new job he was fired. He did not take a new position but stayed home with his parents and was relatively uncommunicative and inactive. He slept poorly, and his parents noted that he frequently wandered about the house during the late hours of the night and seemed to be talking to himself. They persuaded him to see a doctor, who recommended psychiatric evaluation. The patient complained to the psychiatrist that he felt that his body was deteriorating and that he was losing his strength. He felt that this was perhaps some type of test that God was putting him through and that he might emerge from his suffering as a special kind of being. He wondered if perhaps he really were Christ and finally confided that he was hearing voices which were tempting him to do bad things. The examining psychiatrist noted inappropriate affect, some blocking in the patient's flow of speech and some tendency on the patient's part to speak in an irrelevant or illogical manner. The diagnosis of acute schizophrenic reaction was made and the patient was hospitalized. Tests were conducted to rule out other neurological and metabolic diseases and these were negative. It was hypothesized that the patient was experiencing a schizophrenic reaction characterized by some form of biological dysfunction which would respond to neuroleptic medications. The patient was started on Thorazine and after a week of treatment there was considerable diminution of his more severe pathological behavior.

LEARNING HYPOTHESES

After seeking to determine whether severe biological dysfunctions are present, the clinician proceeds to examine the nature of the patient's past learning experiences and tries to determine how these experiences influence the patient's present behavior. Again, it must be emphasized that we are always dealing with interrelated factors. The nature of the learning experience in any environment will be influenced by the individual's biological state, including his level of biological maturity and the learning he has experienced in earlier environments. A new learning experience will also influence an individual's biological state (Pelletier 1976). In formulating learning hypotheses the clinician usually relies on his knowledge of learning theory, which explains how behavior is shaped in the various environments the patient encounters through life. The clinician can also broaden learning hypotheses and use psychoanalytic theory to help him understand how the patient has learned to repress certain emotions and has learned to solve conflict situations in ways that are maladaptive. It will not be necessary here to try to explain psychoanalytic theory in learning terms. This task has been undertaken with considerable success by others (Dollard and Miller 1950). There is general agreement among behavioral scientists that psychoanalytic explanations can be viewed as complex, sometimes esoteric hypotheses as to how the patient has learned his current maladaptive behavior. The methodologies of treatment in psychoanalysis and behaviorism may differ, but the efforts of both schools to deal with causality are rooted in similar theories.

The clinician's attempt to formulate hypotheses of disordered behavior on the basis of the patient's previous learning experiences will require some evaluation of the individual's past. There is considerable disagreement among clinicians as to how extensive this evaluation should be. Behaviorists are not deeply concerned with the patient's past. They assume that if symptoms are present maladaptive learning has taken place, and they focus upon factors in the present that reinforce symptoms. Psychoanalysts are much more concerned with the details of the patient's past life. They believe that new and better learning can take place only through a careful evaluation of past learning. My own position, which will be developed throughout subsequent chapters, is that the clinician must evaluate past learning experience and that the learning-oriented hypotheses the clinician develops while formulating a diagnosis should be detailed, but not as detailed as those routinely made by adherents to a strict psychoanalytic approach.

The influence of past learning on current dysfunction is illustrated by the following two cases:

A thirty-one-year-old married woman consulted a psychiatrist complaining that for the past six months she had been practically unable to drive her automobile. Whenever she tried to drive in traffic, she would experience an overwhelming sense of panic, would feel like she was going to faint, and would begin to tremble. She related her symptoms to having observed a severe traffic accident in which several people were hurt. She did not have any trouble driving away from the accident but the next day experienced her first panic attack while driving. A review of the patient's life situation revealed that at the time the symptoms developed she was having considerable difficulty with her husband. She felt that he was away from home too much, was not helping sufficiently in raising the children, and was generally less interested in her than he had been in the early years of marriage. A review of the patient's past history indicated that she had always been a relatively passive individual who tried to accommodate herself to the needs of others. She had been raised in a strict fundamentalist home and had been taught that the expression of any kind of anger and assertiveness was inappropriate and undesirable. She could recall having frequently felt intense anger toward people she cared about, but felt incapable of expressing it. In this instance, it was hypothesized that the patient's phobic behavior was a learned response which seemed to have been elicited by her observance of the capacity of an automobile to do great physical damage to others. It was further hypothesized that the precipitating event may have had special significance for her because she was trying to solve serious conflicts in her marriage and that all of her previous learning had taught her to fear and deny angry feelings. Another tentative hypothesis which relied on unconscious determinants of behavior was that her inability to drive was based on a fear that she might inadvertently express her repressed aggression and hurt someone while driving.

A sixteen-year-old boy was referred for psychiatric evaluation by his probation officer. He had been involved in a number of delinquent activities, including stealing, truancy, and use of illegal drugs. In addition, his foster parents, his teachers, and legal authorities were troubled by his surly, aggressive attitude and his inability to place any trust in adults.

Relating Diagnosis to Treatment

The patient did not reveal very much about himself to the examiner but did say that most of his friends were involved in similar illegal activities and that he was part of a gang which included a number of young men more skilled in criminal behavior. History obtained from the probation officer and foster parents revealed that the patient had been abandoned by his real parents and had been raised in a succession of foster homes. During his early years he had received very little affection from adults, at times had been subjected to physical abuse, and had never enjoyed the material advantages available to most of his schoolmates. It was hypothesized that the patient's delinquent behaviors were in part learned from association with other young boys and men who had engaged in similar activities. It was further hypothesized that the patient's susceptibility to such learning and his general distrust of adult figures were related to a long series of past learning experiences which had caused him to fear and distrust authority figures.

INFORMATIONAL HYPOTHESES

One of the critical factors in determining maladaptive behavior is the patient's lack of information about himself or his environment. We usually think of these deficits of information in terms of awareness or insight. Psychotherapists are most concerned with the effects of the patient's lack of self-awareness. There is considerable clinical evidence that people are not always fully aware of how they respond to environmental stimuli and that disturbed individuals are especially prone to lack awareness of the emotions and thoughts such stimuli elicit. We learn to block certain feelings and thoughts from awareness in order to preserve our psychological equilibrium. Sometimes such repression serves us well, but sometimes it does not. A person who is not aware of aggressive or sexual feelings engendered by certain stimuli is likely to respond inappropriately. A person who is unaware of the emotional needs he is seeking to gratify in interactions with others or who is not fully aware of his motivations may also behave inappropriately. Causal hypotheses related to lack of information as to one's own emotions and motivations can be considered a subtype of hypothesis related to maladaptive past learning. The person who lacks an adaptive level of awareness can be viewed as a person who has been subjected to learning experiences in which awareness of certain thoughts or feelings has come to be negatively conditioned or extinguished through association with great anxiety. In effect, such a person learns to repress his awareness of certain aspects of his past learning experiences. While lack of self-awareness can be understood in terms of learning theory, the therapeutic interventions derived from hypotheses related to an individual's lack of awareness of his own thoughts and feelings are different from the interventions derived from hypotheses related to other aspects of defective learning. Hypotheses of defective learning—other than those related to informational deficits—suggest a variety of ways of structuring the environment so as to provide new learning. Such learning can be achieved without expansion of awareness of information. Hypotheses of learning focused upon defective information suggest a specific need to structure a type of learning environment in which the patient will have the opportunity to gain new information.

Informational deficits can also be examined in terms of the patient's lack of awareness as to how he influences others. An individual who is not aware of the impact of his behavior upon his environment may repetitively behave in a manner that is disadvantageous to himself. When a patient behaves in a manner that irritates, bores, offends, or enrages others without being aware of his own role in eliciting such unwelcome responses, he may experience the unpleasant reactions of others as gratuitous and will find little motivation for changing. If, on the other hand, the patient can develop awareness of how he is influencing others, he can begin to visualize how, by changing his own behavior, he can exert greater control over the environment.

Behavior can also be adversely influenced by lack of adequate awareness or information as to the nature of the present environment. A person who does not receive clear communications as to the way others are trying to influence him will behave inappropriately. An individual is more likely to have gratifying relations with others if he knows what they expect of him. Accurate information as to the nature of one's immediate environment, and particularly as to expectations in the interpersonal environment, enables a person to make rational self-serving choices. To the extent that a person lacks such awareness or information, his actions will appear less rational and will be less adaptive. One of the clinician's tasks, therefore, is to formulate hypotheses of emotional disorders which are based on the extent to which the individual lacks general information about his environment and lacks awareness of the expectations of his environment. It will be apparent that such formulation requires evaluation of the environment and that informational hypotheses, in addition to being sub-types of learning hypotheses, are likely to overlap with environmental hypotheses. The following four cases illustrate various ways in which informational deficits can contribute to the causation of emotional disorders:

Returning to the case of the thirty-one-year-old housewife who had developed a driving phobia, we can view the issue of her repressed anger as an informational hypothesis. She was aware of being angry in certain situations, but both she and others described her usual behavior as so ingratiating, so docile, and so passive that it was assumed that many of her aggressive feelings were outside of her awareness. When asked how she might respond in situations which would normally call for anger, the patient repeatedly insisted that she would not show aggressive responses because it was wrong and unchristian to behave in such a manner.

The clinician hypothesized that the patient lacked awareness as to how certain environmental stimuli led to her experiencing aggressive feelings. It was further hypothesized that the patient lacked awareness of the nature and extent of her aggressive feelings.

A twenty-three-year-old medical student was placed in a sensitivity group as a part of his first year psychiatry experience. During the course of the group meetings, he complained bitterly about his isolation from other medical students. He felt they did not like him and resisted his overtures of friendship. Although he was doing well in school, he felt that his poor relationships with classmates were affecting his sense of well-being and making him anxious. In the course of several sessions, his classmates reported to him that they had tried to be friendly toward him but had felt put off by his extraordinary competitiveness and competency. They saw him as somebody who had everything under control, who was interested only in academic performance, and who seemed to have little need of frienship. Some of them reported that they were even afraid of him because he seemed so self-assured. This student was generally surprised to hear these revelations. He had not seen himself as coming across in this manner, and it was easy to hypothesize that some of his difficulties were related to inadequate information as to how he influenced others.

A twenty-five-year-old married woman consulted a psychiatrist with the fear that she was becoming paranoid. She said that although her marriage had been good for the first three years, she had in the past six months noted an increasing estrangement on her husband's part. He seemed so cold, distant, and preoccupied that she began to suspect he was seeing another woman. Frequently he would come home late, claiming to have been doing extra work at the office. She wanted to check up on him at these times but felt such suspicion unwarranted. When she asked her husband what was wrong, he insisted that he loved her as much as ever and that whatever distancing he was doing was related to problems he was experiencing at work. She began to see herself as a nagging, suspicious person and wondered why she could not just simply accept her husband's explanation of the situation. During the first conjoint interview with the husband, he revealed that he had fallen deeply in love with another woman and had not up until that point been able to bring himself to tell his wife. Much of his physical and emotional distancing had been obviously related to his being interested in another person. In this instance the hypothesis that the patient did not have adequate information as to certain happenings in her environment seemed quite justified in explaining her feeling that she was becoming paranoid.

A twenty-seven-year-old resident in psychiatry came to see the director of the training program complaining of anxiety and mild depression. At the time, the resident was working in an outpatient setting which primarily treated chronic schizophrenics, and he was discouraged over his inability to influence his patients. His fellow residents seemed more successful with their patients. When the resident asked his supervisors how he was doing, he received only perfunctory feedback that his performance was satisfactory. As he brooded about his situation, the resident contemplated leaving the field of psychiatry. It was hypothesized that the resident's distress was partly generated by lack of information as to the realities of being a psychiatric resident and lack of feedback as to his own performance. The problem was handled by reassuring the resident that most trainees experienced similar difficulties and that his fellow residents might not be having as sanguine an adjustment as he thought. He was urged to communicate with them. In addition his supervisors were urged to give him more specific and more frequent feedback as to his strengths and weaknesses.

ENVIRONMENTAL HYPOTHESES

In considering hypotheses relevant to the patient's immediate environment, the clinician must be aware of the wide variety of

Relating Diagnosis to Treatment

environmental stimuli which influence behavior. People change as the environment changes. Hardly any patient is disturbed for twenty-four hours a day, and there are times in the waking day of even highly disturbed individuals when they feel reasonably good. A person can be anxious at work and relaxed at home or anxious with some people and at ease with others.

One of the most remarkable aspects of human behavior is that it can be drastically modified by changing the environment. A sudden change in attitudes of family, friends, or employers can bring about a startling change in mood. A change in finances or an upheaval in the local political situation may have a similar result. The most disorganized individual diagnosed as a schizophrenic or as a manic-depressive can often be taught to behave in a socially acceptable manner by placing him in a carefully controlled environment. There are, of course, variations among patients as to the degree to which they can be influenced by environmental change. Serious disorders such as psychotic depressions, mania, or catatonia are less influenced by environmental change than are less severe neuroses or psychoses. (But even here there can be dramatic exceptions. Many years ago, while I was working on a ward which cared for regressed schizophrenics, our hospital was warned of an approaching tornado. In the ensuing safety drill, all of my patients behaved impeccably in going through a number of complex actions which increased the probability of their survival. When the tornado alert was over, the patients immediately returned to their regressed postures.)

The protean influence of environmental variables can be further illustrated by considering a common behavior such as depression. Sometimes depression is precipitated by object loss. It may be precipitated by loss of positive reinforcement related to economic failure, aging, moving to a new location, or the effects of poverty or racism; it may follow a sudden success with a change in self-image and the assumption of new responsibilities; or it may appear suddenly without any apparent environmental change. It may be sustained only in highly stressful environments, it may appear in quite benign environments, or it may be manifest only when the patient is exposed to certain highly specific environmental reinforcements. Understanding a depression occurring in each of the environments listed above requires a different causal hypothesis as to how a given individual has been influenced by each environment. To the extent that the clinician seeks to diagnose without such hypotheses, he can obtain only a limited picture of the patient's disorder. To put this somewhat more forcefully, diagnosis which ignores the influence of environmental variables is both incomplete and inadequate.

Two major categories of environmental hypotheses can be invoked in explaining disturbed behavior. First, the environment can be examined in terms of the manner in which it reinforces or rewards certain behaviors which the patient or others may find undesirable. Quite often a careful examination of the disturbed individual's environment will reveal that certain individuals or institutions in the individual's life are overtly or subtly encouraging maladaptive behavior. Second, the environment can be examined in terms of the amount of stress it imposes upon the individual. We know that excessive stress is a key factor in eliciting disturbed behavior. Stress emanating from interpersonal or social forces is usually a precursor of the suffering that drives a patient to seek help. The relevances of environmental hypotheses can be illustrated by returning to the case of the thirty-one-year-old phobic housewife:

Further evaluation of the patient's environment revealed that she felt herself under unusual stress. She and her husband had recently moved to a new town. The husband's new job kept him more busy and preoccupied than either of them would have wished. The patient found herself burdened with the responsibilities of raising children and running a home with little help from her husband and the other supporting figures available to her previously. In addition the husband was not as available as he had been previously. When she complained to him he became angry, and the couple fought. The stressfulness of this situation seemed clearly related to the patient's symptomatology. It was also noted that when the patient's phobic symptoms began, her husband became much more attentive and warm. Whenever she experienced a phobic attack, he would become more attentive and concerned. His supportive responses to her phobic behavior served as reinforcements for her symptomatology.

Having recommended that the clinician systematically consider four classes of hypotheses—biological, learning, informational, and environmental—in evaluating the patient, it is necessary to reemphasize that in going through the steps of formulating hypotheses, the clinician should not simply list factors and assume they exert influence in an additive manner. The clinician must consider the interaction of all factors. Whatever troublesome behavior is eventually defined as the patient's symptom will always be the product of complex individual-environment interaction over a period of time. Compartmentalizing one's thinking by putting hypotheses into categories has heuristic value only insofar as it directs the clinician to think through the various means that are available for changing the patient's behavior.

RELATING HYPOTHESES TO MODES OF THERAPEUTIC INTERVENTION

The hypotheses that can be invoked to explain an individual's behavior will, in a general way, suggest strategies for therapeutic intervention. One obvious way of changing behavior is to change something about the individual's biological state so that the individual part of the individual-environment interaction is altered. Biological treatments are based upon hypotheses that behavior is either caused or sustained by some biochemical or neurological change. It is possible to significantly modify an individual's brain chemistry or physiology through the use of drugs, psychosurgery, or electroconvulsive therapy. The patient's biological state can also be less drastically modified by physical therapies such as yoga, relaxation, exercise, massage, or electrosleep. Biological interventions will have a direct effect upon the individual and will also influence his interactions with the environment. Even slight changes in an individual's biological state are likely to significantly change his response to environmental stimuli. The person who is anxious in a given environment will be less anxious in the same environment if he is tranquilized. A person who is depressed will respond to his day-to-day environment in a more appropriate manner if given a drug that diminishes his depression. A biologically induced change in the patient's behavior will also elicit changes in the patient's environment. People react differently to a person who behaves in an anxious or depressed manner than to one who does not.

Patients can also change by having experiences that teach them new ways of responding to their environments or by having experiences that teach them that old ways of responding are undesirable. Interventions which focus upon learning are logically related to hypotheses that disordered behavior is at least partially caused by maladaptive learning. In designing a reeducative treatment, it again becomes apparent that individual and environment cannot logically be separated. The new learning experiences that help the patient change can be made available only by changing some aspect of the patient's environment. Even the learning that takes place in nondirective or psychoanalytic psychotherapy is primarily shaped by the environment that the therapist tries to create in his interaction with the patient. The emphasis in almost all schools of individual psychotherapy is upon an intimate patient-therapist relationship. Under the benevolent guidance of the therapist the patient may learn to face and overcome fears previously experienced as overwhelming. The patient will be encouraged to experiment with new behavior with the therapist and will be praised for doing so. Or the patient may learn that some of his behaviors are undesirable or unnecessary. If the therapist, whose approval the patient learns to seek, disapproves of certain actions, ignores them, or considers them trivial, the patient will be less likely to repeat them. It is always hoped that the favorable learning experiences that take place within the context of the intimate therapeutic relationship will be repeated in less benign environments or that they will be generalized to situations outside the psychotherapy session.

All of these learning experiences can be explained in terms of classical and operant conditioning. Fears diminish in psychotherapy partly because the patient is actually desensitized. That is, he learns to deal with previously feared situations while under the benevolent, relaxation-inducing care of his therapist. The patient learns also to experiment with new behaviors through a form of operant conditioning in which the therapist reinforces the patient whenever the patient behaves in a "healthy" manner. Finally, the patient may learn to abandon certain undesirable behaviors if the therapist fails to reinforce the patient or punishes him (by expressing disapproval) whenever these behaviors appear. When the therapist indicates disapproval of a certain action, he is initiating a process of aversive conditioning. When he ignores a certain behavior, he may help extinguish it by failing to provide reinforcement.

While individual psychotherapy is an effective intervention, there are formidable limits to the clinician's power to change behavior by relying on the environment of patient-therapist intimacy. The learning process in such therapy is usually slow. The patient can spend only a small fraction of his time with the

Relating Diagnosis to Treatment

therapist. There are also limits to what the therapist can do to control the rate at which the patient will interact with the therapist in ways that provide for new learning. Furthermore, if the favorable learning arising out of the therapy experience is not reinforced by other experiences in the patient's environment (or is not *generalized*) the patient may not change very much. He may develop a comfortable relationship with the therapist, but may continue to suffer in his relationship with the rest of the world.

Clinicians have understandably sought and have succeeded in developing modes of intervention not totally dependent upon the therapist-patient relationship as the environment for new learning. When the patient comes to the clinician for help, the patient places a great deal of trust in the authority of the clinician. In effect, the patient has added a new factor to his environment, a source of authority or direction. The clinician can use his authority to persuade the patient to experiment with new behaviors and to enter into or create other new environments.

One of the most common interventions based on the authority of the clinician is hospitalization. In the hospital it is possible to create a therapeutic milieu in which the patient is constantly exposed to learning experiences which shape his behavior in a manner that he or others find desirable. Because hospitalization makes it possible for the clinician to control most aspects of the patient's environment, it can be used to create experiences which meet the learning needs of the patient with a high level of precision. Where less control of the environment is desired, the patient can be treated in day hospitals or partial care clinics. Here the environment is orchestrated for only a limited number of hours each day.

The clinician can also use his authority to urge the patient to seek out environments which will provide new experiences. The patient may be asked to join recreation, task-oriented, or church groups. Encouragment to initiate relations with people the patient has previously avoided can also be provided. The therapist has still other options in the use of authority. Patients can be directed to change their behavior in order to create new responses from others. A husband can be persuaded to be more attentive toward his spouse, or a parent can be encouraged to be more permissive with his children. A patient can also be urged to respond to other people's behavior in a new manner. Directives such as "The next time you wife wants to talk to you, why don't you listen" or "When you boss tells you to do something you don't like, why don't you let him know how you feel about it" will hopefully create new responses from others (a changed environment) which will in turn facilitate salutary learning experiences. Or the patient may be persuaded to change his own responses to his own behavior and thereby create a new set of circumstances. The therapist may say, "The next time you can't sleep, why don't you get up and work rather than lie around and worry about your inability to sleep" or "When you fear you are going to be impotent, why don't you concentrate on enjoying foreplay with you wife and avoid having intercourse." Such directives, if obeyed, will temporarily change the patient's behavior and will also change the consequences or environmental responses which follow the behavior. The therapist hopes that such alteration of the postsymptomatic environment will provide new and favorable learning experiences.

It is not entirely naive to ask why all symptomatic behavior does not respond to the authority of the clinician. Why, after all, cannot the therapist change even highly disordered behavior by persuading or ordering the patient to change? Some clinicians have argued that most behavioral change can be related to a desire to conform to the authority of the therapist (Frank 1961). The patient learns to behave in a way that pleases the therapist or minimizes his displeasure. While this kind of mechanism may operate in may successful therapeutic encounters, most clinicians have discovered its practical limitations.

Anyone with considerable authority over another, including the power to restrain him, will be able to shape much of his behavior. But even such unusual power is limited. Even the warden of a prison or the director of a mental hospital cannot exert complete control over the environment of his clients for a twenty-four hour period and, therefore, cannot totally control his inmates' behavior. In clinical practice we deal with voluntary clients and here our authority tends to be transmitted through persuasion. The clinician is viewed by most people as a trusted authority and most rational people will be expected to follow his advice. But patients do not always behave rationally. Some will be unwilling and some unable to follow the clinician's directions. Even if the patient follows the clinician's advice to experiment with a new behavior, it is unlikely that the new behavior will be sustained unless it meets the needs of the patient and is environmentally reinforced. A therapist can urge a patient to deal with angry feelings toward a nagging wife by talking and listening to her, rather than by beating her. If the wife then changes her own

Relating Diagnosis to Treatment

behavior, the therapist's initial directives could lead to permanent changes in the patient's behavior. If the wife continues to nag, however, the therapist's directives will eventually lose their power. (The situation might be different if the patient had decided on his own that he wanted to stop beating his wife. If the patient's behavior had changed because of some type of new learning which changed his perception of his wife, her continued nagging might have less influence in extinguishing his new behavior.) The power of persuasion or authority to change behavior is inherently limited by the clinician's inability to totally control the environment's response to the patient. The most the therapist can do is to use directives to try to create situations in which there is an increased probability that the patient will be optimally reinforced.

Behavior can also be changed by helping the patient discover new information that allows him to entertain alternative courses of action and make more effective choices. Gaining information about how and why the patient behaves in a certain way can be viewed as a major purpose of most forms of psychoanalytically oriented individual psychotherapy. Some of this kind of information may also be obtained through group or family therapy. There is much controversy as to the degree to which new information or insight facilitates behavioral change. Psychoanalysts believe that it is a powerful factor in eliciting change, while behaviorists consider it relatively unimportant (Freud 1955, Wolpe 1964). While I would agree with most behaviorists that insight is neither necessary nor sufficient for behavior change, I am convinced there are times when it can be a powerful factor. Some of the ways in which expanding information may facilitate behavioral change will be briefly reviewed.

We are all regularly influenced by environmental stimuli, but we are not always aware of how we are influenced. If we knew how certain situations adversely affect us, we might avoid them or prepare to cope with them. In addition to being helped by accurate knowledge of environmental influences on us, we benefit also by reexamining the manner in which we perceive environmental stimuli. Sometimes emotional states we are unaware of can distort our perceptions of stimuli. Awareness of these emotions may enable us to respond more adaptively to our environment. A patient who has always viewed women as seductive temptresses may treat them in a cold, distant manner. If the patient gains awareness that he actually has great fears of closeness to women, he may appreciate that his fear has led him to perceive them incorrectly. Once he begins to perceive women more appropriately, he may be able to consider other ways of dealing with them.

The causes of an individual's misperceptions of current stimuli can be discovered by investigating his past learning. While such investigation is possible in group or family therapy, awareness of past learning is most effectively expanded in psychoanalytically oriented individual psychotherapy. Insight or awareness of past maladaptive learning provides both clinician and patient guidelines as to what new types of learning the patient will find helpful. Such insight enables them to use direct learning interventions based on classical and operant conditioning to shape new and more desirable behaviors. Techniques for shaping or extinguishing behavior can be used most efficiently only when patient and therapist have the maximum amount of precise information as to how past learning is influencing present behavior. Such information provides a more exact definition of what behavior should be changed. (This is an appropriate place to note that there is no inherent incompatibility between insight-oriented psychotherapy and behavior therapy. Insight or awareness merely increases the efficiency with which behavioral or learning interventions can be used.)

Expansion of the patient's awareness of his motivations can also be critical in changing his behavior. In the example above, the patient's distant mode of relating to women could have been sustained by repression or by lack of awareness of his need for intimacy. If the patient could appreciate the depth of this need, he would also become more aware of his need to find a new way of relating and could be expected to be more willing to experiment. Finally, awareness of how and why he has behaved maladaptively in the past provides the patient a cognitive map or a sense of direction for avoiding maladaptive behavior in the future. Once our patient understands how women influence him and why they influence him in just that way, he can try to structure his social life so that he encounters the least threatening women in the least threatening situations.

Information as to how one's own behavior influences others also enables the patient to consider alternative behaviors. If a person believes he is behaving in a manner pleasing to others but discovers that his actions really irritate them, he has some idea of what he can do to change the way others relate to him. All of the conventional psychotherapies—individual, group, and family— are at least partly directed toward helping the patient achieve greater awareness of how others perceive his behavior. Group and family therapies are especially effective in expanding the patient's knowledge of his impact upon others.

Finally, accurate information as to the nature and expectations of the environment can help the patient to cope. It enables him to make rational decisions as to what he needs to do and how he must interact. It helps him decide what can be done to satisfy and please others and at the same time defines the limits of self-serving behavior. A clear understanding of the environment enables one to separate friends from enemies. Finally, it allows the individual to make the most economical use of his resources.

A person stressed by forces that cannot be recognized is likely to respond with inappropriate or ineffective behavior. The wife whose husband is having an affair but does not know about it may react to her husband's coolness toward her by blaming herself or becoming more irritable toward others. Once she discovers that her husband has an important role in causing this stress, she can deal with her environment more realistically. The child whose parents constantly tell him that they seek nothing but his own happiness and yet put enormous pressure on him to succeed would be in a better position to cope with these conflicting messages if he could appreciate the reality of this parental pressure. Even new information about the political environment can change behavior. Oppressed groups such as blacks and women, who so often blame themselves for their low status and who so often have lashed out at inappropriate targets, have in recent years, by appreciating the intensity of the social forces aligned against them, made impressive changes in behavior.

Several forms of conventional therapy help expand awareness of the external environment. In individual psychotherapy the patient examines not only himself but also his relationship to the environment. The therapist can try to help the patient understand how interpersonal and social factors are influencing the patient's life. Group therapies provide similar learning experiences. In family therapy the patient has an opportunity to learn new information about significant figures in his life by communicating with them directly and by observing their behavior "in vivo."

While the importance of environmental variables in shaping behavior has long been recognized by clinicians, interventions based on altering the natural environment have, until recently, been largely ignored. Most of the predominant schools of psychotherapy, such as psychoanalysis, initially placed greatest emphasis on the learning and insight that takes place in the artificial environment created by an intimate therapist-patient relationship. They have taken considerable pride in avoiding efforts to change the natural environment on the grounds that such efforts represent manipulations which interfere with the patient's control of his own destiny. The authority of the psychoanalyst has been primarily directed at helping the patient learn from the therapeutic relationship and to generalize that learning to life situations which the therapist does not try to influence. Environmental manipulation outside the relationship has traditionally been viewed as appropriate only for the psychotically ill or for the child.

The clinician today is free to use many more methods in trying to change the patient's environment. He is not restricted to structuring such artificial environments as the hospital, which may provide temporary solace for his patient; he can also strive to influence those who interact with the patient to behave differently and thereby create a new and more therapeutic natural environment. The opportunity to actually change the patient's natural environment substantially increases the modern clinician's power to change behavior. Currently, intervention dealing with the natural environment is most effectively initiated through the technique of family therapy. The definition of family therapy I will employ throughout this text is not restricted to work with the nuclear or even the extended family. I consider family therapy quite broadly, as conjoint therapy with any significant figure in the patient's life: spouse, lover, parent, child, friend, employer, or co-worker. The term *significant figure* includes any individual who is involved in an affectional or power relationship with the patient.

In family therapy the therapist can use a variety of techniques to influence those who are involved with the patient to change their responses to the patient's behavior. A parent can be persuaded to be more or less firm in dealing with a child. A husband can be urged to listen more or less attentively to his wife's complaints. An employer can be persuaded to be more or less tolerant of his employee's work performance. Each of these interventions will change the patient's natural environment by changing the nature of environmental reinforcement. The patient's natural environment can also be changed by diminishing the stress that significant figures impose upon the patient. By persuading family members or other significant figures to change the manner in which they communicate and relate to one another, the therapist can restructure small social systems so that they are less stressful to the patient.

The intervention of stress alleviation can also be applied to social systems larger than the family. In a democratic society the clinician has an opportunity to attenuate the negative impact of social stress. Social agencies may be called upon to provide services which alleviate some of the stresses of poverty. The therapist may also work to alleviate stress generated by social institutions by helping schools, churches, and other institutions understand how their practices may oppress certain individuals. Finally, the therapist might try to change some aspect of the larger social order. There are limits, of course, as to what the therapist can do to change society. He can always remind himself, however, that anything that can be done to improve the patient's sense of political or economic power is likely to be helpful. In this regard, I try to teach students who are dealing with poor and powerless patients to always try to imagine how their patients' symptoms would be altered if the patient could suddenly receive a large sum of money. This usually helps the student appreciate the role that stress in the total environment plays in the disorder and may also help the student to appreciate the need to do whatever is reasonable to help the patient improve his economic and social status.

HOW CURRENT THERAPIES WORK

It will be useful at this point to briefly review how each of the major therapies can work to alleviate a hypothesized dysfunctional process. Drug therapies and other somatic therapies are based on hypotheses of biological dysfunction and work directly upon the individual by changing aspects of his biological responsiveness. Individual psychotherapies are based upon hypotheses that the patient's learning has been inadequate or defective and that new learning is desirable. Such learning is facilitated by restructuring part of the patient's environment through the creation of an intimate patient-therapist relationship. The relationship itself becomes an environment in which new learning takes place and can also provide leverage for directing or persuading the patient to change various aspects of his behavior. Individual psychotherapy may be offered with or without concurrent efforts to expand the patient's awareness of self and environment. The kinds of information that can be provided through individual psychotherapy include knowledge of how the patient influences and is influenced by others, knowledge of how past learning influences the patient's present behavior, and knowledge of what the environment expects of the patient. Those individual therapies which are directed toward expanding the patient's awareness tend to be lengthier than those that are not, but they provide both patient and therapist a more precise idea of how the patient's behavior should be modified.

Group therapy helps by creating an artificial environment in which the patient can be influenced by other patients as well as by the therapist. Its direction of influence upon the patient is determined by the manner in which the therapist tries to orchestrate the group response. Within the group environment the patient can gain new information, particularly as to how he influences and is influenced by others. The group environment can also be used to shape new adaptive behaviors and to extinguish the maladaptive.

The family therapies, as I have defined them, elicit change in a variety of ways. In addition to providing an environment in which new learning can take place, family therapy provides an excellent means of changing the patient's natural environment either by changing the manner in which others reinforce the patient's behavior or by diminishing the amount of stress others put upon the patient. Family therapy can also provide the patient with new information about the manner in which he influences and is influenced by others. It is especially helpful in expanding the patient's knowledge of others' expectations of him. This multivectored aspect of family therapy may account for its often powerful impact in producing rapid behavioral change.

Thus far, I have not discussed behavior therapy as a specific intervention. Behavior therapy is best viewed as a series of techniques which provide the patient with new learning by creating precise changes in the patient's environment which help to reinforce, shape, or extinguish specific behaviors. Principles of behavior modification are involved in any form of psychotherapy, but they are not usually labeled as such unless the therapist acknowledges the deliberate and precise nature of his efforts to change the environment. Behavioral techniques can also be used as specific or exclusive interventions in situations in which the clinician does not seek to establish a close relationship with the patient. The behaviorist may merely try to direct the patient or

Relating Diagnosis to Treatment

those involved with the patient to create situations or events in which adaptive behaviors are reinforced and maladaptive behaviors are extinguished. Throughout this text I will use the words *new learning* and *reeducative* to refer to that element of helpfulness, whether in individual, group, or family therapy, that is based on principles of classical and operant conditioning. When techniques based on these principles are used with no concurrent effort to expand the patient's information or to focus on the therapist-patient relationship, I will refer to such interventions as *direct behavior modification* or *direct behavior therapy*.

Brief mention should be made of behavior modification techniques which involve efforts to create new learning by altering the patient's biological status or which alter the patient's biological status by changing environmental reinforcement. In one technique called systematic desensitization, biological change (through drug-induced or self-induced methods of muscular relaxation) is paired with environmental change or fantasied environmental change. The patient is taught to relax, thus changing his biological state, and while relaxed is asked to imagine being in a variety of feared environments. Eventually, the patient learns to confront the feared stimulus and to be comfortable in environments which had previously elicited maladaptive responses. Here the clinician is combining biological and learning interventions. In a different type of technique, based on principles of biofeedback, the patient is placed in environments in which autonomic responses are changed by providing new kinds of reinforcements. Here, biological responses are changed through environmental manipulation.

VALUES AND CHOICE OF TREATMENT

It is usually possible to formulate some biological, some educational, some informational and some environmental hypotheses as to the causation of every patient's disturbance, and each of these hypotheses logically suggests a direction for intervention. The most powerful behavioral changes should, in theory, be brought about by intervening in as many areas as possible. If an individual shows signs of severe depression and is living in a highly oppressive environment, we could anticipate that maximum behavioral change would be brought about by giving him a drug that would alleviate his depression (biological treatment) and by at the same time doing something to alleviate the stressfulness of his environment (family therapy). If that same person's life experiences had led to his having developed unsatisfying and maladaptive interpersonal relationships, he could also benefit from interventions which would provide him with new learning experiences and with new information (individual, family, or group psychotherapy). There is a simple logic here. Attempting to modify as many of the factors that have caused a disturbance as possible should have the maximum effect in alleviating the disturbance.

The use of multiple interventions can also have more than a simple additive impact upon the patient's behavior. Any single intervention will have reverberations throughout the total system of individual-environment interaction. A salutory change in an individual's biological state should make him more amenable to learning better means of adaptation by eliciting more benevolent responses from those around him. Similarly, changes in the environment will provide the patient new learning experiences and will ultimately influence his biological state. When the therapist deliberately sets out to intervene in more than one area at a time, different interventions often potentiate one another with a resulting escalation of behavioral change.

Using the same type of reasoning one can see the limitations of one-dimensional intervention. A favorable change in the individual may elicit more gratifying responses from the environment, but it may not. If the environment does not reinforce the patient's new behavior, the stability of the patient's new learning or new comfort may be jeopardized. At the same time favorable changes in the patient's environment may not be helpful unless the patient is capable of perceiving them. A severely depressed or psychotically disorganized patient may gain more benefit from individual or family psychotherapy if his capacity to interact with others is enhanced through pharmacologic intervention.

Theoretically, the patient should benefit most when the clinician can use every therapy called for by his diagnostic hypotheses. Justification for such a multidimensional approach to treatment is slowly gaining experimental as well as theoretical support. A few articles are beginning to appear in the literature which provide evidence for greater efficacy of treatment with combined pharmacological and psychotherapeutic approaches (Grinspoon and Shader 1975, Klerman, DiMascio, and Weissman 1974, Hogarty, Goldberg, and Schooler 1975). I anticipate that we will someday have evidence of the advantages of using even larger combinations of treatments.

Relating Diagnosis to Treatment

With all of the theoretical advantages of a multidimensional approach to treatment, there will always be limits as to how comprehensive the clinician can be in utilizing interventions. These limits are generally defined by the clinician's values. The value which influences the clinician most powerfully is efficiency. It is rarely necessary to change the biology, the educational experiences, the social environment, and the informational input of a patient, even if the clinician can formulate hypotheses which justify each intervention. Often the patient's needs, both long- and short-term, can be met by simply reassuring him. Some patients need no help other than being told they do not need help. The long- and short-term needs of other patients may be met by calming them temporarily with medication, teaching them something new, or slightly modifying the environment. In the interest of efficiency it would be absurd to do more than one of these things, if one were sufficient.

Implied in the value of efficiency is the value of economy. (Throughout this book I will use the term *efficiency* to include both effectiveness and economy. When I use the term *effectiveness* to describe an intervention, I am referring to the adequacy of its capacity to accomplish a certain result. When I use the term *efficiency* to describe an intervention, I am referring to the adequacy of its capacity to accomplish a certain result with the least expenditure of time and effort.) Even if it would be most desirable, in terms of optimum results, to treat every patient with all forms of intervention, it would be impractical to do so. There are too few trained clinicians and too many people seeking help. The clinician usually seeks maximum therapeutic change with minimum therapeutic intervention. Issues of triage are important here. The clinician may wish to reserve the most expensive and time-consuming interventions for the most disturbed patients. Whether working in private practice or for a government agency, the clinician may also be concerned with cost-benefit ratios or whether the cost of a treatment to the patient or to society could outweigh the benefits to either.

Values such as efficiency provide obvious guidelines for determining treatment, but other less obvious values must also be considered. One of these is that the patient should not be physically or psychologically harmed by treatment. Direct and immediate harm is obviously undesirable. But it is also important that therapeutic change be accomplished without sacrificing the patient's future potentialities. This value puts limits on the use of many interventions. The need for such limits can be conceptualized by speculating upon the effects of excessive interventions. Most patients with obsessive-compulsive behavior could probably be "cured" quickly by a prefrontal lobotomy. The ensuing limitation of the patient's potentialities might, however, be so severe as to have made the treatment worse than the illness. Moving to a less provocative hypothetical situation, it can be noted that many minor forms of behavioral distress can be temporarily alleviated by drug therapy. The unpleasant physiological side effects of psychotropic drugs, however, might be so unpleasant as to leave the patient worse off than before. It is also, in theory, possible to reeducate a patient so massively that he will learn to behave in ways that may be too conforming, or alternatively, too abrasive to allow him to live in a way that maximizes his potentialities. Or it is possible to so overload a patient with information about himself and his environment that the patient is unable to enjoy the kind of ease that comes with lack of self-consciousness or the temporary peace of mind that is needed, at least some of the time, if one is to survive in a world plagued by chaos and oppression.

A corollary to the value that treatment should not compromise the patient's future potentialities is the value that treatment should not totally disrupt the patient's future environment. This value also limits the extent of some therapeutic interventions. One can speculate that stress-free environments which would provide positive reinforcement for socially adaptive behavior could be created for almost any patient in a manner that would temporarily leave the patient symptom free. The problem here is that such restructuring of the patient's environment might also result in destruction of human ecological systems. Whenever a patient is hospitalized or otherwise removed from the stresses of everyday life by being put into a sheltered situation for a long period of time, the community as well as the patient may lose a great deal. The community loses the contribution of the patient. Even at the family, as opposed to the community, level the clinician must observe some limits as to the extent of change imposed upon the environment created by other family members. The clinician, who has the capacity to influence how family members interact with the patient, must exercise sufficient caution that his interventions do not elicit serious disturbances in other members of the patient's family or totally disrupt the family system.

There are, of course, times when both the patient and others may benefit from drastic changes in the environment. I have argued elsewhere that in seeking to treat the patient the clinician has as much right to try to change the patient's environment as he does to change the patient (Halleck 1971). The major point here is that there must be limits (defined by an ethical system) as to how far the clinician is willing to go in changing either. Potential risks to the environment must be compared to potential benefits for the patient.

Another value which may dictate the clinician's choice of treatment is compassion. The clinician's major commitment is always to alleviate the patient's suffering. When the patient is experiencing great distress, the clinician will often seek rapid alleviation of symptoms by using biological interventions. There are times, however, when the value of compassion may conflict with the value of not diminishing the patient's future potentialities. This value conflict must be resolved by weighing long-term needs against short-term. An intervention such as psychotherapy may, in some circumstances, be preferable to a biological intervention, even if psychotherapy does little or nothing to alleviate the patient's immediate suffering. This is because there are situations in which psychotherapy carries less risk of compromising the patient's future and will eventually produce more salutary long-term change. There is much controversy among clinicians as to whether the value of compassion is too often compromised in an effort to avoid poorly defined social dangers or to achieve esoterical long-term goals. Such a value controversy is highly desirable. Theoretical commitments to a particular school of therapy may obscure the clinician's commitment to the value of compassion. I firmly believe that clinicians who would withhold interventions which might alleviate immediate suffering should assume the burden of proof that their slower therapies actually avoid danger to the patient and serve his long-term needs.

A final value which helps define the nature of intervention is respect for the patient's autonomy. It is usually desirable for the patient to play as great a role as possible in determining his own treatment and in working toward achieving his desired behavioral change. This value is most relevant to a democratic society in which individuality and self-determination or self-governance are considered desirable.

The values of efficiency, economy, protection of the patient and his environment, compassion, and autonomy provide important guidelines to treatment, guidelines which can be developed by considering the following propositions:

1. Some interventions are more likely to change a given behavior or class of behaviors than are others. The clinician must utilize theory, clinical experience, and whatever experimental data are available to evaluate the patient, so that he can determine which variety of intervention will be most effective and least expensive for a particular patient. One aspect of the value of efficiency is that some therapies cannot be used concurrently. The use of one intervention may mitigate the effectiveness of another. The clinician must have some awareness of how various interventions may conflict with one another and must have some idea as to the proper timing of each intervention.

2. Efficiency is not a sufficient guide to treatment. Some interventions physically damage the patient. Many interventions change the patient and the environment in a manner that makes it unlikely that the patient can assume the same sociopsychological status he occupied before he became disturbed. After treatment neither the patient nor those around him are likely to be the same. This raises powerful questions as to the ethical basis of any therapy. The value of protecting the patient must be considered not only in biological but also in social and political terms.

3. The patient should play at least some role in deciding what kind of intervention will be utilized. Every patient comes for help with certain motivations, a certain degree of sophistication, and certain ideologies. All of these qualities should have some influence in determining the kind of therapy he receives. The clinician must develop a system for respecting the patient's wishes with regard to treatment, while at the same time seeing that the patient receives the most helpful treatment.

4. The severity of the patient's disturbance will have some relationship to the type and number of interventions which can or should be used. Where there is severe disturbance, the values of compassion and efficiency may supersede all other values in dictating the use of specific treatments. Where disturbance is minimal, the clinician can be much more tentative in recommending specific interventions.

Chapter 3

**Clinical Evaluation of the Patient
and the Environment**

This chapter deals with the proposition that some interventions are more efficient than others in changing a given behavior or class of behaviors. I have already alluded to some aspects of treatment effectiveness, but neither my previous remarks nor the material presented here will exhaust my discussion of the value of efficiency. Some of the indications for, and limitations of, a particular intervention are better understood when the student is familiar with the technical problems of actually using an intervention. It is not possible, for example, to fully understand the limits of group therapy or behavior modification unless one knows something about group or behavioral techniques. Therefore, in the second part of the book, when I discuss how various treatments work, I will make additional references to the issue of efficiency. There will necessarily be some repetition in this approach, but my hope is that viewing the same issue from varying perspectives will help the reader to develop a more comprehensive approach to choosing the most efficient interventions.

The primary emphasis in this chapter is on accurate evaluation and how it enables the clinician to select the most effective treatment. Accurate evaluation is dependent upon the clinician's skills in history taking, in observation, in establishing rapport with the patient, and in understanding the patient's phenomenological world, as well as upon the practitioner's clinical and scientific knowledge. The clinician's first task is to describe the patient's current and past behaviors as precisely as possible. These observations are evaluated in the light of the clinician's theoretical knowledge, past clinical experience, and awareness of experimental data. The clinician can then use the model developed in the previous chapter to make systematic decisions as to which interventions will be most efficient in treating specific types of dysfunctional behavior.

In developing guidelines for evaluating the indications for various interventions, the clinician may have to temporarily put aside his concern with other values, such as the patient's long-term needs and the patient's autonomy. Much of the discussion in this section will reflect a mechanistic approach to the patient; modifications of the approach will be considered in later sections.

Throughout this discussion, I will be assuming that the reader is at least in the process of developing skills in history taking, in establishing rapport with the patient, and in observation of behavior. I will assume also that the clinician has a rudimentary knowledge of the varieties of emotional disorder and of the major hypotheses as to their causes.

EVALUATING INDICATIONS FOR BIOLOGICAL INTERVENTIONS

As noted in chapter 2, biological hypotheses and biological interventions are not usually invoked unless the patient's behavior disturbance is severe. The clinician must, in the initial examination of any patient, evaluate the severity of the patient's suffering and incapacitation, and must seek concurrently to describe the exact nature of his distress. The clinician is especially concerned with the manner in which the patient experiences his symptoms. Efforts are made to have the patient describe his thoughts and feelings in as explicit a manner as possible. The clinician also observes how the patient responds to the clinician's inquiries, and is particularly concerned with the patient's responses to questions designed to assess the patient's intellectual functioning. These activities are part of a routine mental status examination designed to expand the clinician's knowledge of the patient's perception, cognition, and emotionality. They help the clinician formulate an opinion as to the need for biological intervention and as to the type of biological intervention likely to be most useful.

There are six types of highly disturbed behaviors, each of which, given our present state of knowledge, is best treated with a somewhat different somatic intervention. Detailed descriptions of

Clinical Evaluation of the Patient and the Environment

these behaviors can be found in any textbook of psychiatry or psychology. For our purposes here, these behaviors will simply be listed as follows:

1. Confused behavior in which the patient, usually as a result of brain dysfunction, may be disoriented, delirious, forgetful, highly agitated, emotionally labile, and unable to think clearly or to adequately evaluate the environment.

2. Schizophrenic behavior in which the patient may show emotional blunting, speak incoherently, be unwilling or unable to think logically, be detached from reality, experience delusions and hallucinations, and, if untreated, show gradual social deterioration. Such behavior is usually not accompanied by the type of confusion associated with demonstrable brain dysfunction.

3. Manic behavior in which the patient may show agitation, hyperemotionality, irritability, extreme egocentricity, increased verbal and motor activity, impaired judgment, and be able to behave in a relatively normal manner between periods of disturbance.

4. Depressed behavior in which the patient shows inappropriate sadness and impoverishment of affect, poor appetite and weight loss, psychomotor retardation or agitation, insomnia, suicidal preoccupation, and intense feelings of hopelessness and worthlessness.

5. A combination of manic and depressed behavior in which the patient over a period of time may experience cyclic or asymmetric episodes of both mania and depression. Occasionally mania and depression may follow one another in cyclic form but more often the patient experiences a preponderance of one or the other behavior.

6. Anxious behavior in which the patient experiences frightening thoughts and a sense of helplessness as well as a variety of uncomfortable psychophysiological changes.

(The reader who is upset with my cavalier approach to psychiatric nomenclature is urged to bear with me for a while. In the second part of this book I will have more to say about traditional nomenclature and classification.)

The above sets of behavior do not usually appear in isolation from one another. Patients who are confused can become depressed, anxious, and hyperactive. Schizophrenic behavior is often associated with considerable depression or anxiety. It is often difficult to say if a patient's behavior is more suggestive of schizophrenia or of mania, and there has been much recent controversy as to whether many psychotic behaviors which were once thought of as forms of schizophrenia can be more appropriately viewed and treated as variations of mania (Lipkin, Dyrud, and Meyer 1970). With all of these uncertainties the clinician must still try to determine how the patient's behavior might fit into one of the above categories, because some categories have, on an experimental basis, been shown to respond to specific treatments, and because other categories can be explained by hypotheses which logically lead to a use of specific treatments.

Confused behavior suggests hypotheses of serious brain dysfunction and directs the clinician to thoroughly examine the patient to discover the presence of infection, tumor, toxicity, trauma, or circulatory, metabolic, or degenerative disorders. If the cause of the patient's confusion can be ascertained, appropriate medical treatments can be initiated. Schizophrenic behavior is currently believed to be associated with a defect in biogenic amine metabolism and its most distressing manifestations can be attenuated by treatment with such antipsychotic or neuroleptic drugs as phenothiazines, butyrophenones, or thioxanthenes. Manic behavior will respond to neuroleptic drugs and is also likely to remit after treatment with lithium carbonate. The precise mechanism of action of any of these drugs in alleviating schizophrenia or manic behavior is unknown. Severe depression is believed to be associated with changes in catecholamine or indoleamine metabolism and can be partially alleviated by treatment with tricyclics or monoamine-oxidase inhibitors. Depressed behavior occurring in a person who has at some time in his life experienced manic behavior, as well as some types of recurrent depressed behavior, may respond to either lithium or antidepressant medications.

There is one nonpharmacological intervention that alleviates many of the more distressing symptoms of schizophrenic, manic, and depressed behavior. Electroconvulsive therapy can produce remarkable alleviation of extreme emotional distress. While the thought of using an induced convulsion to change behavior often terrifies the patient (and sometimes the clinician), there are times when this treatment is essential to the preservation of life. Severely agitated psychotic or depressed patients who do not respond to drugs are often spared excruciating and life-threatening suffering by the proper use of electrically induced convulsions.

Where extreme anxiety exists without concomitant confused, schizophrenic, manic, or depressive behavior, such anxiety is

Clinical Evaluation of the Patient and the Environment

generally assumed to be primarily determined by recent stress or by previous maladaptive learning experiences which have created psychological conflicts. Severe anxiety, however, is also accompanied by alterations of function of the vegetative system and may be associated with alterations of brain metabolism. While the clinician will usually elect to treat even severe anxiety (if unaccompanied by other manifestations of highly disturbed behavior) with psychotherapeutic techniques, it is clear that this behavior can be rapidly, if temporarily, modified by the so-called major or minor tranquilizers. For the sake of completeness, it is also worth noting that paralyzing and unremitting anxiety associated with obsessional thoughts and dysphoric affect can sometimes be relieved by psychosurgery.

There are other less powerful somatic interventions which when combined with learning, informational, or environmental interventions are valuable adjuncts to the treatment of milder forms of anxiety. These include electrosleep or electrosome treatment, deep muscular relaxation, hypnosis, massage, or yoga. All of these treatments can be used to produce a state of increased calmness and lowered metabolic activity which is called the relaxation response (Benson, Beary, and Carol 1974). There is much disagreement in the behavioral sciences as to whether the more powerful somatic treatments such as neuroleptic drugs or electric shock should ever be used in treating anxiety which is not accompanied by more disorganized behavioral changes. Usually, because of concern with not harming the patient or not restricting the patient's future potentialities, the majority of clinicians restrict their somatic treatments of anxiety to minor tranquilizers or to interventions which induce the relaxation response.

The patient's history provides additional clues to the choice of biological intervention. Some patients have family members who have experienced schizophrenic, manic, or depressive disorders, and knowledge of this history may help the clinician to categorize the nature of the patient's disturbed behavior when symptoms alone are not definitive. History of the patient's previous responses to pharmacological agents may be helpful in determining what treatments are likely to be effective. A history of previous physical illness, of previous trauma, or exposure to toxic substances or of patterns of drug abuse may alert the clinician to the possibility of organic brain disease. Knowledge as to the onset and course of a disturbance also helps in categorization. Some severe disorders such as schizophrenia are likely to become manifest at an early age. Manic and depressive disorders are likely to begin at a later age. Schizophrenic disorders tend to have a course characterized by steady deterioration. Manic and depressive disorders tend to have a course characterized by remissions followed by recurrences.

As I will detail later, evaluation of the circumstances critical in precipitating a disorder provides many clues for efficient presription of a variety of environmental interventions. Knowledge of precipitating circumstances can also help the clinician use biological treatments more efficiently. When stresses preceding the disorder have been severe and are modifiable, the patient's prognosis may be better and the clinician may wish to limit the extent and duration of biological interventions (Eitlinger, Laane, and Langfeldt 1958). When premorbid stress is minimal and the disturbance is nevertheless severe, the clinician must be more willing to use biological treatments and more cautious in discontinuing them.

While somatic or biologic treatments may be sufficient conditions of temporary behavior change, they do not "cure" the patient. Unlike antibiotics, neuroleptic or antianxiety drugs do not act directly to abort specific pathologic processes. Nor can they be viewed as replacement therapies, as can insulin. Each of the current somatic therapies influences many biological functions other than those that may be directly related to the patient's disturbance, and each can have effects which the patient experiences as unpleasant or unwelcome. If used for brief periods, somatic therapies do not protect the patient from recurrence of symptoms. Even over longer periods, they have limited usefulness in sustaining desirable behavior change. The problem of long-term use of somatic therapies will be discussed in greater detail in the chapter on biological treatment. For our purposes now, it is important to note that somatic therapies are most efficient in bringing about short-term change.

There are still some practitioners who insist that severe depression, acute schizophrenias, and mania can be successfully treated without somatic intervention. While some of these therapies do, at times, have spectacular success with long-term psychotherapy or family therapy alone, the preponderance of evidence leans toward the use of somatic treatment during the acute phase of sever disturbances (Klerman 1975b, Klein and Davis 1969, Shader 1975). Given what we know now, efforts to treat severe emotional disturbances without drugs or other somatic interventions are primarily useful as research enterprises. Too often they are based on the therapist's relentless commitment to the value of autonomy, a commitment leading to an irrational distrust of doing too much to the patient.

EVALUATING INDICATIONS FOR LEARNING INTERVENTIONS

One general evaluation that must be made prior to recommending learning intervention is that of the patient's overall capacity to learn. Such capacity may be limited by relatively fixed intellectual deficits. It is difficult to teach complex interpersonal skills to the mentally retarded. Learning capacities may also be limited by the presence of severe psychological dysfunction based on biological abnormalities. The kinds of new learning proposed for a patient suffering from a disorder which leads to progressive intellectual impairment (such as pre-senile dementia) will of necessity be limited. Generally patients suffering from severe forms of schizophrenia, mania, or depression benefit most from learning quite basic responses such as trust, self-acceptance, temporary accommodation to limited potentialities, and good hygiene. Learning of more complex interpersonal skills may have to be delayed until the patient's general level of functioning has improved. Even mild anxiety can impair some types of learning, and until the patient has achieved a certain level of tranquility, the clinician's learning interventions may have to be quite modest.

Decisions as to what the patient must learn in the present are to a large extent based upon evaluation of what the patient has learned in the past. Here the clinician relies upon history taking and his assessment of the patient's current needs. Two general types of question are asked: First, What behaviors has the patient learned in the past that are causing him trouble in the present? and, second, Are there behavioral responses which may help the patient solve problems in the present which are not available to the patient because he has failed to learn them in the past? Examples of maladaptive past learning would include avoidance of closeness, excessive dependency, overcontrollingness in relationships, or unrelaistic fears of relatively commonplace environmental stimuli. Examples of failure in learning would be deficits in abilities to form interpersonal relationships, inadequate coping devices, inability to regress when circumstances require regression, or inability to be assertive. Often when we speak of maladaptive learning or deficient learning, we are talking about different ways of viewing a similar phenomenon. The person who fears closeness to others will usually have deficient interpersonal skills. The person who is overcontrolling will usually have difficulty in regressing. There may be times, however, when deficits in learning may not be directly equated with maladaptive learning. A patient may, for example, have failed to learn responses appropriate to establishing intimacy with members of the opposite sex because he or she has had insufficient opportunities to develop such responses. Such a patient may need to learn new interpersonal skills but does not have to unlearn anything.

It is likely that every person has experienced some learning that would impair his capacity to cope with stressful situations, and certainly none of us has learned all of the social skills we might wish to have. In adhering to the value of efficiency, the clinician cannot always take the time to evaluate the full extent of each patient's behavioral maladaptations and deficits. Instead the clinician focuses initially upon the patient's current symptomatology. It is always useful for the clinician to try to evaluate whether all or some symptoms are circumscribed behaviors which can be objectively measured. Circumscribed and measurable behaviors, sometimes called target behaviors, can be diminished or increased through use of techniques of direct behavior therapy. Some examples of target behaviors are phobias, compulsions, obsessional thoughts, tics, overeating, drug abuse, and sexual inadequacy. Whenever the clinician observes one of these, particularly if it is chronic, he should consider the use of direct behavior modification.

Other symptoms cannot be circumscribed and are difficult to measure. Vague complaints of anxiety and depression, feelings of meaninglessness, hopelessness, alienation, or existential despair are common symptoms in clinical practice. They can, in a broad sense, be viewed as learned responses, but since they are so difficult to measure, they are difficult to treat with direct behavioral techniques. They are also unlikely to be markedly influenced by biological interventions. Usually they must be treated with some type of individual, group, or family therapy. (Informational and environmental factors as well as learning factors must be carefully evaluated in dealing with vague and poorly circumscribed complaints. Evaluation of informational deficits and of the environment will be discussed shortly.)

Once the patient's symptomatic behaviors have been considered, evaluation of learning should focus on the kind of repetitive interpersonal response patterns or personality traits the patient has developed which seem to repeatedly put him into stressful situations or which make him vulnerable to them. Here the clinician must examine the patient's past interpersonal history and try to determine which learned personality traits, such as abrasiveness, passivity, or demandingness, have gotten him into trouble, and which insufficiently developed traits, such as honesty, assertiveness, patience, or independence, might have increased his coping abilities. As will be elaborated later, the presence of persistent response patterns which serve the patient poorly should lead the clinician to favor the use of individual or group therapy.

EVALUATION OF INDICATIONS FOR INFORMATION-EXPANDING INTERVENTIONS

The evaluation of indications for information-expanding interventions requires the clinician to make judgments based on inference as well as on observation. Here the quality of evaluation is determined by such variables as the clinician's level of experience and his inferential skills. The nature of the problems involved in making subjective evaluations can be illustrated by beginning with the problem of evaluating the extent to which the patient accurately perceives his own impact on the environment. There are inherent difficulties is assessing the extent to which an individual is unaware that he behaves in a certain manner. An individual may see himself as behaving in a certain way and will have a private view of the impact of such behavior. Others may share that view, but sometimes not. When there is disagreement between the patient and others, it is important to ask whether the picture others have of the patient's behavior is more accurate than the patient's own perceptions. Those who evaluate the patient's behavior, including the clinician, can easily make subjective and erroneous interpretations of its impact.

The clinician's problem is to find as objective a means as possible of determining how the patient's behavior affects others. Sometimes the clinicians can be relatively objective in making such evaluations if the patient is hospitalized and several members of the treatment team can report how they respond to the patient. Or family members and friends may be available to provide history as to what impact the patient's behavior has had upon them.

Sometimes the clinician can determine from the patient's own revelation of his history that those around the patient have seen the patient's behavior quite differently than the patient has. When family interviewing (described in chapter 9) is added to the evaluation process, the clinician may be able to observe directly how the patient influences certain important figures in his life. But the chief tool the clinician has in evaluating the patient's impact upon others is the evaluation of the patient's impact upon the clinician. Evaluation here is subjective. Whatever objectivity is involved is provided by the clinician's determination to avoid letting his own biases influence his evaluation of how the patient comes across to him. Every clinician must eventually develop skill in assessing the manner in which the patient relates to him. The use of this skill can be demonstrated by the following case vignettes:

A twenty-five-year old woman who became depressed after termination of a love affair complained that men were taking advantage of her. She wondered why they saw her only as a sex object and did not wish to relate to her as a person. As the interview progressed, the interviewer noted that everything about the patient's dress and mannerisms was sexually seductive. The patient's verbalizations centered around sexuality, and the clinician found himself becoming moderately aroused by her.

It is possible in this instance to hypothesize that the patient was not fully aware, or was unable to acknowledge to herself, how she was coming across to the clinician and others. To satisfy her wish to form a stable relationship on an intimate, rather than on a purely sexual basis, she would have to find a better way of demonstrating her needs and would have to stop frustrating her own wishes by behaving seductively. It is unlikely she could do this, however, unless she gained more awareness of the impact of her seductive behavior upon others.

A thirty-year-old man complained of depression and loneliness. He insisted that although he tried to be nice to everybody, people did not seem interested in being his friend. He could not understand this, since he was convinced that he was a warm person who wanted to give and share with others. In the course of the interview, the clinician noted that the patient was subtly demeaning toward the clinician. The patient made small insults relating to the clinician's sincerity and abilities. As the

Clinical Evaluation of the Patient and the Environment

interview continued, the clinician felt himself getting angry and feeling distant from the patient.

It is reasonable to hypothesize in this situation that the patient did not have full awareness of his impact upon the clinician and perhaps upon others. The patient saw himself as kind and friendly but came across quite differently. It seemed likely that he would continue to have difficulty in making friends until he became more aware of how he was offending others.

In these examples, the clinician developed responses to his patient's behavior, evaluated his responses, and assumed they were similar to responses others had. There are obvious pitfalls to this approach. The clinician may err in relating his own feelings to the patient's behavior. Conceivably, the clinician may be responding to internal or unconscious cues which have more to do with his own problems than with the patient's. The clinician may also err in judging his responses to the patient as being similar to those of others. Even if the clinician's response to the patient is similar to that of some significant figures in the patient's life, it may differ from the responses of other significant figures. The clinician and some significant figures may share certain qualities which lead them to evaluate the patient's impact idiosyncratically.

One straightforward way of facilitating the evaluation of the patient's awareness of his impact on others would be to tell the patient how he is influencing the clinician and to observe how the patient reacts to this communication. The clinician could, for example, tell a patient that his is coming across as seductive or aggressive. The patient's responses to such a communication might provide clues as to the accuracy of the clinician's hypothesis. Unfortunately, there is considerable risk in using this technique. Patients can be deeply upset by statements which imply that they do not know how they are coming across. Such statements can be viewed as powerful interpretations which attribute responsibility for his difficulties directly to the patient and which demand behavioral change. They are best offered only after the clinician and patient have developed a trusting relationship.

Even granting the subjectivity involved in such evaluations, if the clinician feels relatively certain that the patient needs to know more about how he influences others, the clinician should recommend some form of psychotherapy (individual, group, or family) which provides this kind of feedback. Lengthy therapy may not be required and the patient can sometimes learn a little about how he influences others even during the course of the evaluation interview. There are some patients, however, who have exceptional difficulty in appreciating their impact. Friends and relatives may have told the patient about how he influences them, but the patient may never have accepted such feedback. The clinician might, on the basis of his own response to the patient, believe that the patient's friends and relatives are accurate in their assessment of the patient's impact on them and yet sense that it would be difficult to convince the patient of their accuracy. If the clinician elected to try to provide feedback in the context of individual psychotherapy, he might have to take an exhortative approach which would probably not be helpful. Here group therapy may be of use. The group can provide continuous feedback verified by several individuals. In the process of group therapy many situations will occur in which the patient's behavior and its impact can be examined more or less "in vivo." These situations will develop gradually in a benign environment and the patient will not be deeply threatened. The patient will have the opportunity to become convinced that his behavior is having an undesired effect.

The clinician will also encounter patients who seem to have a fairly good idea of how they are influencing others, but who feel powerless to do anything about it. These individuals can often describe some aspects of their interpersonal response patterns or personality traits quite accurately. They may express a desire to change but complain they do not know how to. Here the clinician has the choice of prescribing some type of psychotherapy which will teach the patient how to relate to others differently or of deciding that the patient can make more effective changes by seeking information as to why he is behaving so maladaptively. The former prescription calls for a psychotherapy in which the individual can directly learn new response patterns through reinforcement, shaping, and extinction. The latter prescription calls for a psychotherapy which, in addition to being reeducative, facilitates the reorganization or reinterpretation of old information or helps the patient to discover new information as to his perceptions, emotions, and motivations.

Many factors are involved in the choice between reeducative and information-expanding therapies. As noted, a major advantage of information expansion is that it increases the precision with which learning problems can be defined. It may also be chosen for a variety of ethical reasons to be discussed later. Economy is important as well, since information-expanding therapies are as a rule more lengthy than those with the more modest goal of training the patient to behave differently. Another major factor requiring early evaluation is the patient's capacity to deal with the stress inducing techniques often involved in insight-oriented psychotherapy. Still another factor is the patient's degree of "psychological mindedness," or interest in and capacity to assimilate new information. Patients have varying degrees of psychological mindedness. Some people are intrigued with the possibility of gaining new information about their emotions and motivations, while others find the prospect tedious or even frightening. Some have the capacity to develop and accept new emotional experiences and new explanations of their emotionality; others have a great deal of difficulty being introspective. In general the clinician tends to recommend information-expanding psychotherapy primarily for those patients he evaluates as having a relatively high capacity to deal with stress and a high degree of psychological mindedness.

A second major evaluation the clinician must make in deciding upon the use of information-expanding interventions is the extent of the patient's awareness of how he is influenced by the environment. The clinician asks himself: How much does the patient know as to how his thoughts, feelings, and actions are related to the influence of other people and external events? Here evaluation of how the patient responds to the clinician has only limited usefulness. The clinician can observe how the patient responds to stimuli the clinician emits and may ask the patient how aware he is of these responses. But since there is not an intimate therapist-patient relationship at this point, the patient's responses are quite likely related to the anxieties engendered by being evaluated by an authority figure. The clinician can learn something about how the patient responds to anxiety and to authority figures—as well as how aware the patient is of these responses—but this knowledge may not be very relevant to the patient's everyday behavior. When family interviewing is added to the evaluation process, more information can be obtained. In the family interview the clinician can observe how the patient responds to significant individuals and can ask the patient how aware he is of these responses. Generally, however, the clinician's assessment of how the patient is influenced by others is based on two operations. First the clinician, by delving into the patient's past history, tries to develop a picture of how the patient has been influenced by various environmental stimuli. The clinician looks for repetitive responses to similar situations. In developing a picture or map of the patient's response pattern, the clinician will make many inferences based on his knowledge of human behavior. Second, after the clinician has some idea as to how the patient responds to the environment, he can ask the patient directly what he knows about such influence. Generally, patients are not threatened by such questions and are eager to know how they are influenced by others.

Patients usually have varying degrees of awareness as to what kinds of interpersonal and environmental stimuli make them fearful, angry, sad, or withdrawn. In evaluating the patient's complaints, the clinician can ask the patient to try to define the stimuli that preceded them. A large number of questions can be asked which are directed toward relating symptomatic behaviors to external events. Some patients turn out to have very little knowledge of how they respond to the environment. They may not, for example, be able to relate feelings of anger or depression to situations in which they felt rejected. They may fail to note they become anxious only in certain situations or with certain people at certain times. The clinician can help these patients by encouraging them to carefully examine all of the situations which seem related to their symptoms. At the very least the new knowledge gained through this examination will help them avoid aversive stimuli; at best it will encourage them to find new ways of coping. Some of this kind of information expansion can be accomplished in the process of evaluation, but brief individual, group, or family psychotherapy will often be needed.

Other patients will turn out to have fairly good knowledge as to how they are influenced by the environment, will be unhappy with the nature of these responses or personality traits, but will feel powerless to change them. Here (as in the case of dealing with the patient who cannot seem to change the way he influences others) the clinician has two choices: reeducative or insight-oriented therapy. The latter approach will focus heavily upon helping the patient understand why he has come to perceive stimuli in a certain way and how these perceptions can be changed through gaining new information as to past learning experiences. Again the clinician's decision to elect an information-expanding approach will be dependent upon many factors, including his assessment of the patient's capacity to deal with the stresses of therapy and his patient's psychological mindedness.

There is still one more factor, rather complex, which can influence the clinician in favor of reeducative or information-expanding therapy. It is sometimes useful for the clinician to evaluate the extent to which the patient already possesses such awareness. This assessment is best made by inquiring as to the patient's past history and by focusing upon situations or events that might have led to maladaptive learning. The patient can then be asked to describe how he believes these experiences have affected him, and his assessment can then be compared with the clinician's. To the extent that their assessments are similar, the patient may be assumed to possess insight. While such evaluation relies heavily on inference, it is nevertheless useful. A patient with little awareness of the influence of past experience might gain more from long-term intensive psychotherapy than one with considerable awareness. The latter might well be more responsive to direct learning interventions.

It is also useful to evaluate the quality of the patient's understanding. Often the clinician must deal with a patient who has already learned something of himself in previous psychotherapy. Such a patient may understand the causes of his behavior in an intellectual manner and still fail to experience the emotions that are part of a broader understanding. The patient may logically conclude that he is angry in certain situations and yet be unable to perceive that anger. One way in which the clinician can try to distinguish between intellectual and emotional understanding is by focusing upon the patient's emotions as he discusses his behavior. If the patient describes a situation in which he was angry at his boss but does this in a stilted, dispassionate manner, the clinician can raise questions as to the quality of the patient's emotional awareness. The clinician can also observe the patient's emotionality in interactions with him and can thereby make rough estimates of the extent to which the patient actually experiences the feeling he reports. Where the clinician estimates a considerable lack of awareness of the feeling states or emotions associated with explanations of behavior, or where the patient still seems distant from his expressed feelings, there can be some assumption that the patient still lacks useful information as to why he behaves as he does. There are good reasons for trying to formulate the extent to which the patient's understanding is either intellectual or emotional. It is often useful to continue information-expanding therapy with a patient who, though psychological minded, possesses only intellectual insight. On the other hand, the patient who has emotional as well as intellectual understanding of his problems and who still cannot change his behavior, may be more effectively treated with more direct learning techniques.

Finally, the clinician must evaluate the extent of the patient's knowledge as to what others might be doing that influences him and his knowledge of what others expect of him. There are two major reasons for ignorance in these areas. First, the patient's knowledge may be defective because the environment is not sending out signals in a fashion clear enough to let him determine what others are doing to him or might need or expect of him. Second, it is possible that the signals are clear but that the individual is not interpreting them correctly. If signals are not being transmitted clearly, if they are ambiguous or covert, the patient could be helped by the clinician's urging significant figures in the environment to communicate more directly. Or if this is not possible, the individual can receive some type of training in deciphering ambiguous or covert messages. If the individual is interpreting the environment incorrectly, however, the most logical intervention must be directed at changing something about that individual. Most but certainly not all behavioral scientists tend to assume that deficits in information about the environment are best explained by focusing on individual dysfunction. There is a tendency, except in schools relying heavily on family therapy or communication theory, for clinicians to look first, and sometimes only, at the individual. This, I am convinced is an inadequate approach to assessment.

The clinician must, of course, be concerned with the patient's capacity to detect signals from the environment. Biological changes that may impair perceptions must be evaluated. Sometimes the patient's knowledge of the environment is so minimal that it can be assumed that he has, for a variety of possible reasons, deliberately avoided learning about it. Or the patient's perceptions may be so bizarre that the clinicians can suspect that the patient is distorting the messages he is receiving. More commonly the patient's history may reveal that he has a pattern of reading environmental signals incorrectly. Still, all of these observations

Clinical Evaluation of the Patient and the Environment

can never leave the clinician convinced that the patient is receiving enough direct information to function effectively. The only way in which the clinician can assess the quality of communication the patient is receiving is to actually evaluate the manner in which others are communicating. This means that the clinician must interview significant figures in the patient's life, preferably together with the patient.

There are many good reasons for routinely doing a family interview as part of the diagnostic process, but one of the most important is to assess the nature and quality of information the patient is receiving. In the family interview the clinician looks for patterns of ambiguous communication. He tries to determine if information is being withheld, either deliberately or out of lack of appreciation of its importance. He also wants to know if communication is distorted or blatantly dishonest. If he believes that any of these communications problems exist, he must help the patient gain new information, sometimes through individual or group therapy, but more often through family therapy.

EVALUATION OF THE ENVIRONMENT

This section deals with evaluation of the environment preceding and following the appearance of symptomatic behavior. Evaluation of the presymptomatic environment is especially complex but can provide indications as to the use of biological, learning, and informational interventions as well as for the use of interventions which change the natural environment. Evaluation of the postsymptomatic environment is less complicated, but the clues it provides are largely restricted to the use of interventions which change the natural environment. In trying to adhere to the model presented in the previous chapter, I have left for last the issue of evaluation of the environment. The reader should appreciate, however, that in actual practice evaluation of the environment, particularly of the presymptomatic environment, is usually undertaken very early in the diagnostic process. It may also be useful to remind the reader that the environment cannot be evaluated without considering how it both influences and is influenced by the individual. Some of the evaluations already discussed could not have been made without considering the environment.

A certain amount of arbitrary judgment is involved in calling a given environment a part of the patient's remote past, recent past, or present. Environments change from day to day and from second to second and should be viewed as representing a continuous flow of interconnected conditions and events. For the purposes of this discussion, the presymptomatic environment will be considered that which confronted the patient in the space of the days, weeks, or (more rarely) months preceding the appearance of symptoms. Usually, but not always, some major alterations of the patient's environment have preceded the onset of his disturbance. The clinician's evaluations would be simpler if there were some certainty that conditions and events in the patient's environment had changed in some circumscribed time period such as a week or day before the disturbance. But there is never certainty as to when exactly critical environmental changes became manifest, and the clinician's definition of the presymptomatic environment or recent past must be quite broad. The postsymptomatic environment is more easily defined as that which immediately follows the disturbance up until the time the patient consults the clinician. This environment includes all the conditions and events, including treatments by other practitioners, which influence the patient once he has been identified by himself or by others as behaving in a disturbed manner.

There will be times when the clinician will be concerned with much narrower time frames. In assessing ways of treating circumscribed target behaviors such as phobias or tics, the behaviorist will often want to know what stimuli preceded the symptom by minutes or even seconds and how the environment responded minutes or seconds afterward. Assessment of the immediate antecedents and consequences of a given behavior is essential if direct behavior therapy is to be used, and should always be made if the clinician can identify a target behavior. This, however, is only one relatively circumscribed way of evaluating the environment and in the remainder of this chapter, I will consider pre- and postsymptomatic environment in terms of much broader time frames.

Investigation of the patient's interaction with the environment both preceding and following the development of a disturbance provides clues that can lead to the richest opportunities for therapeutic intervention. Learning that has taken place in the remote past is difficult to modify. Usually it can be changed only by creating totally new environments. The old environments in which maladaptive learning took place cannot easily be resurrected. The recent past and present, on the other hand, are characterized by environmental conditions and events that are more easily changeable. If the patient can be favorably influenced by these conditions and events, he will undergo a fresh process of learning.

The Presymptomatic Environment

When the patient's recent history is carefully reviewed, preferably with family as well as individual interviews, it is usually possible to determine that the precipitating environment was characterized by changes which the patient experienced as stressful. Disturbances can, of course, develop with very little apparent change in the environment. Some people seem to become disturbed "out of the blue," and neither the patient nor his family are able to relate the disturbance to any environmental change. But such presentations should be viewed with suspicion by clinicians. There are good reasons for patients and families to avoid acknowledging recent environmental changes. To the extent that such events have adversely affected the patient or continue to trouble him, the patient may wish to avoid the unpleasantness of examining them. Some of the changes which may have taken place are likely to have involved conflict within the family, and family members are not always eager to have the family system examined. For many patients and families the first response to the patient's disturbed behavior is to view it as a "happening," an event mysteriously unrelated to environmental change. Unless the clinician vigorously searches for evidence of recent change, neither he nor the patient will ever learn about it. Too many patients who are considered to have developed a disturbance on a purely biological basis are viewed this way because the clinician has not made an adequate effort to explore the patient's environment.

It must also be acknowledged, however, that even with diligent examination, there will be times when no obvious changes in the disturbed patient's recent environment can be detected. Where the patient is severely incapacitated and where there is little evidence of recent environmental change, the clinician should be suspicious of the presence of organic brain disease and most of his diagnostic focus should be on searching for evidence of confused behavior and signs and symptoms of physical illness. (This does not mean that organic brain disease is necessarily absent when there are discernible changes in the precipitating environment, but simply that the absence of such changes should make the clinician more suspicious of an organic disorder.) If organic deficits are found they can be treated with biological interventions. The following case represents the diagnosis and treatment of a patient whose disturbances developed in an apparently unchanged and benevolent environment.

A forty-one-year-old man came to the doctor at the urging of his family. A successful executive, he had never demonstrated emotional instability until a few weeks earlier, when he began to show signs of forgetfulness, irritability, and confusion. A previously gentle husband and father, he had begun to criticize other family members for actions he once shrugged off. His co-workers also noticed that he was becoming less efficient at his job. On talking to both the patient and his wife, it was apparent to the clinician that there had been no unusual changes in the patient's recent environment. The behavior disorder seemed almost to have been "inflicted" upon him. When he was hospitalized and given a thorough neurological work-up, a space-occupying lesion in the right frontal area, which later proved to be a meningioma, was discovered and surgically removed. Shortly after recovery from the effects of the surgery, the patient began to behave like his former self.

There is some controversy as to whether disorders other than brain syndromes ever develop in the absence of some major environmental change or stress. Certainly the clinician sees many schizophrenic and major affective disorders which seem to develop in apparently benign and constant environments. There is an old clinical dictum that disorders which develop under conditions of minimal stress are difficult to treat and have a poorer prognosis than disorders which are more easily related to stress (Langfeldt 1956). While the data on this issue are inconclusive, my own clinical experience supports this dictum.

Some practitioners argue that there is always a significant environmental change preceding any disturbance, but that the change may be too subtle to be detected by ordinary means. They insist that minor shifts in the patient's relationship with family members or others can be detected if one is diligent enough. It should be apparent that there is no way of proving or disproving this contention. Minor changes in family and social systems occur constantly. The diligent observer can always find some shift in the system which preceded the disorder and consider that shift etiological. These considerations pose a serious problem for clinicians. Environmental change or stresses are undoubtedly an etiologic factor in many disorders. But while it is necessary to be as thorough as possible in evaluating the environment, the clinician cannot view just any change as etiological. He must have some criteria for determining what kind of stress is likely to elicit dysfunctional behavior and then evaluate whether such stress was present in the presymptomatic environment. Here again we are hampered by lack of data. The best we can do is to devise criteria based on theory and clinical experience. I have found it useful to evaluate environmental stress as a significant etiological factor when any of the following three conditions exist in the presymptomatic environment:

1. The environment puts new demands upon the patient
2. The environment does not respond to the developmental needs of the patient
3. The environment begins to provide a diminished level of positive reinforcement for the patient

(Throughout this section, *positive reinforcement* is not used in the strict behavioral sense as any event which immediately follows a behavior and increases the probability of its being repeated but in a more general sense as approval, praise, concern, attention, love, or appreciation.)

Each of these kinds of stresses can be studied in terms of the patient's interactions with smaller social systems such as the family and with larger social systems such as the community as a whole. New demands can develop within the family when the patient is asked to behave differently toward another family member. Because of changes in their own perceptions of their needs, other family members may demand more or less interest or time of the patient, or require him to assume more or less responsibility within the family system. The latter demand is often related to the patient's age or state of development. As individuals pass through pubescence, adolescence, middle age, old age, and senescence, they are assigned different levels of responsibility within the family as well as within other social systems. New demands can also develop within the patient's work environment. An employer may insist that the patient increase his productivity or may ask the patient to take on new responsibilities. Finally, changes in the society as a whole create new demands for every individual. We all have some difficulty in adjusting to the rapid rate of change which characterizes technological society. Changes in values concerning such issues as women's liberation can place individuals of both sexes in new roles which are demanding and stressful. A woman may feel forced to seek a career beyond that of homemaker. A man who has previously devoted most of his energies toward developing his own career may feel more obligated to help with housekeeping.

Developmental changes within the individual not only elicit new environmental demands but also tend to create a new set of needs. An adolescent, for example, needs different kinds of responses from his parents than does a prepubescent child. Some families seem to maintain a satisfactory equilibrium and meet one another's needs adequately until one of the family members begins a new phase of development. The community as a whole may not have the flexibility to meet the developmental needs of some of its members. Currently two age groups in our society are particularly stressed—adolescents and the elderly. Technological society has experienced increasing difficulty in developing appropriate and meaningful roles for both these groups.

Reinforcement within small social systems such as the family can diminish when various members because of their own needs become more involved with their careers or other people and less involved with the patient. Or the patient may interact with family members in a manner that leads to estrangement and loss of reinforcement. Sometimes developmental factors such as aging put the patient in a role of diminished responsibility. If he was previously reinforced for assuming responsibility, he will now have to accustom himself to receiving less reinforcement. Aging also leads to greater isolation with fewer opportunities for reinforcement. Diminution of reinforcement in work situations can occur when, either through his own inadequacy or for reasons more or less accidental (shifts in the economy, increases in work requirements), the patient performs poorly or is fired from his job. In a rapidly changing society even an individual who has worked hard to develop skills and personality traits which may receive high reinforcement is in a precarious position. Many of the skills and attributes that help an individual achieve a certain distinctiveness within the family or the society can today suddenly become irrelevant.

It should be apparent that the three categories of stress I have delineated are interrelated. New environmental demands put people into situations where they risk losing reinforcement. Developmental changes put people into situations where more or less is expected of them and where more or less reinforcement is available. The failure of family or community systems to meet the age-appropriate needs of individuals can also be described in terms of the environment's failure to provide sufficient positive reinforcement.

As a rule the clinician will find at least one of these categories of stress to be operative in the presymptomatic environments of anyone developing an emotional disorder. The mere observation and elucidation of the effects of these stresses, however, does not provide direct clues to intervention. We cannot "cure" patients merely by changing stressful factors in the presymptomatic environment. Some of these are beyond our influence, but even if we could influence the environment to meet precisely the patient's needs, it would still be necessary to have more precise knowledge of the conditions under which presymptomatic stresses develop. Three issues must be evaluated:

1. The extent to which the individual because of biological, learning, or informational deficits interacted with the environment in a manner that made the environment more stressful
2. The extent to which accidental events which the individual could not influence created a stressful environment
3. The extent to which new developmental needs upon the part of the individual led to the environment's becoming more stressful

Accidental versus Patient-Created Environments

In trying to determine the extent to which an individual actually participates in the creation of a stressful environment, it is important to recall that the individual not only is influenced by his environment but also has varying degrees of influence upon it. The patient is not merely an object that responds to a stimulus. He is himself a stimulus, and his interactions with others elicit new environmental responses. When the patient behaves in a disturbed or unusual manner, there is an especially high probability that the environment will respond adversely and will withdraw reinforcement. Sometimes the patient's role in creating a stressful environment is minimal; sometimes it is critical. This varying role may be illustrated by considering the cases of four individuals who became depressed:

Case 1. A forty-three-year-old aeronautics engineer lost his job following cutbacks in the aerospace industry. Because of his age and lack of skill in other areas, he had great difficulty in finding new employment. This resulted in a marked change in his life style. In addition to having to reduce his standard of living, the patient felt deprived of status and began to spend more and more time at home. His wife found both her diminished social role and her husband's new behavior irritating. Both partners were frightened, and they quarreled frequently. The patient began drinking heavily and finally was arrested for drunken driving. When he went to court, he was confronted with a judge who, for various reasons apparently having little to do with the patient, was in an irritable mood. The judge repeatedly demeaned and insulted him, and eventually the patient was provoked into saying something disrespectful. As a result, instead of receiving only the temporary driver's license suspension usual in such cases, the patient was given a thirty-day jail sentence. The patient appealed the sentence and continued to live at home, but his quarrels with his wife became more violent. At one point, following a particularly bitter fight, his wife threatened to leave him. The patient reacted by becoming fearful and despondent. For the next three days he stopped arguing but began to dwell on the hopelessness of his plight. On the third night he took an overdose of sleeping pills. His wife happened to wake during the night, noted that the patient could not be roused, and called for an ambulance. The patient survived after treatment with gastric lavage and intensive medical care.

Case 2. A twenty-two-year-old woman, married two years, was experiencing difficulty with her husband. They could not seem to communicate, and she perceived him as quite insensitive to her needs. She was especially troubled by his unwillingness to help with the care of their nine-month-old child. The patient had a much warmer relationship with her in-laws and spent many hours with them. She felt like they were a new set of parents. Six months before the onset of her depression her mother-in-law died. The patient mourned this loss appropriately and then proceeded to develop a very close relationship with her father-in-

Clinical Evaluation of the Patient and the Environment   93

law, who was a minister. This relationship became even closer when the patient hired a housekeeper and went to work for her father-in-law. At this time, in addition to providing emotional support for the patient, the father-in-law was also providing a considerable amount of financial support and promising to provide even more money in the future. One month before the patient's disturbance the father-in-law announced that he was going to remarry. The patient was totally surprised and angered by this revelation and immediately began to show signs of mood disturbance. She became somber, apathetic, and uninterested in her work. She stopped working but was unable to take care of her household or her child. When she tried to talk to her husband about her feelings he could say little more than that it was all right for his father to remarry and that they could get along without him. The patient's symptoms intensified to the point of serious depression requiring hospitalization.

Case 3. A thirty-five-year-old business executive had throughout his adult life taken on heavy work responsibility in an effort to achieve power and financial security. His ambition led him to work many evenings. The patient's first wife had left him because she could not tolerate his lack of attention to her and his commitment to work rather than to family. Eventually his second wife also began to complain, and their marital relationship deteriorated. At this point the patient, as in his first relationship, began to have extramarital affairs. As time passed, he became exclusively involved with one of his paramours, toward whom he began to develop deep feelings of affection. While she initially did not make demands upon him, she eventually began to ask him to divorce his wife and marry her. The patient did not want to get a divorce and, in fact, remained quite attached to his wife. Faced with this conflict and continued stresses in his work, the patient began drinking heavily. His work performance deteriorated. Shortly after receiving a harsh but deserved reprimand from his employer, he began having symptoms of anxiety, insomnia, and overwhelming sadness. After a particularly anxiety-ridden day and sleepless night, he decided to seek help.

Case 4. A twenty-two-year-old male student became depressed shortly after enrolling in the same university for the third time. He had had an outstanding record of academic achievement in high school and was considered a young man of great intellectual promise. Yet he had dropped out of school on two previous occasions because he had not been able to bring himself to do the necessary assignments. These dropouts occurred at a time when student activism was at its peak. The patient, like many others during that period, had found more gratification in political activism or drugs than in studying. His parents reacted to his nonconventional behavior with considerable tolerance but were also explicit in communicating their concern that he was wasting his life. By the time the patient entered school for the third time, student activism had cooled, and the patient had begun to believe that it would be necessary for him to have a more conventional career. His parents encouraged his new attitude, but having almost given up on the hope of their son leading a conventional life, were prepared for his failing again and were resolved not to interfere with his activities. He reentered school with great determination and high hopes. For the first few weeks of the semester he worked hard, attended all classes, and did well. After about two months, however, he started to neglect his assignments and began skipping classes. As his concern over not being prepared increased, he responded by becoming even more delinquent in his responsibilities as a student. He handled his guilt and anxiety by increasing his use of marijuana and minor tranquilizers. When the deterioration of his work became evident to university officials, he was called into the dean's office and told he was failing. At this point the patient became sad, tearful, and anxious. He was referred to the student counseling service by the dean. By this time he was having fantasies of suicide and was grateful for the opportunity to seek help. This young man was advised to once again drop out of school. He did this but remained depressed. He constantly berated himself for his past failures, feared for the future, and could not motivate himself to take a job or seek a career that did not require academic success.

The above cases illustrate a number of concepts. To begin with, they demonstrate that a behavior such as depression can have different environmental determinants. They also illustrate the manner in which individual and environment interact so as to eventually produce a behavior the patient or someone else defines as an emotional disorder. A third and therapeutically critical principle can be inferred from these cases. In each of the first two cases the conditions and events leading to the disturbance originated with environmental changes beyond the patient's control. The patient's response to these changes, of course, played a role in the eventual development of the depression, but it is reasonable to assume that depression might not have developed at the time it did had certain *chance* or *accidental events* not occurred. In the second two cases, the elements of chance was much less

Clinical Evaluation of the Patient and the Environment   95

significant. In a sense, the latter two patients created the conditions and events that defined their precipitating environment, or they created it to a far greater extent than did the first two.

The capacity to influence one's environment becomes greater with age. The infant is helpless. He cannot choose his parents. Even if the parents' reactions to the child are determined, in part, by the child's inherited levels of activity or need for intimacy, the child can do little about his parent's own needs and personalities. As a person matures and develops personality traits, or more or less fixed ways of relating to people, those traits begin to exert greater influence upon the manner in which others respond to him. The older one gets and the more fixed his personality traits, the more likely he is to create significant events and conditions in his environment. But no person can ever exert a great deal of control over his environment. Changes in the society as a whole can rarely be influenced by a single person. People close to the patient may, for reasons of their own, change their behavior toward the patient in very drastic ways. A rejection by a loved one, the death of a loved one, a casual insult, an employer going out of business and having to fire the patient, a change in values in the society which diminishes the patient's sense of belonging, an accident, or the sudden development of a physical illness are stressful events beyond the patient's influence.

Most of us find some satisfactory way of adapting to chance or accidental stress. There would be some reason to suspect that if time passed without either the engineer's or the housewife's disturbance escalating (as it did in the case of the engineer when, because of a series of partially self-created and partially chance circumstances, he found himself facing a jail sentence), the natural course of events would have led to abatement of the disturbance. Eventually the engineer would have found a job. The housewife would have found new people to whom she could relate in a dependent manner. Such salutary events would not, of course, have diminished either patient's vulnerability to certain kinds of future chance occurrences, but they would nevertheless have allowed the patients to return to their premorbid patterns of behavior.

In the natural course of events there would be little probability of the environment changing in a way that would alleviate stress upon the executive or the student. The executive's immediate problem might have been alleviated if his mistress or his wife had abandoned him. But such events of themselves would undoubtedly have created new stresses. And there would be little reason to doubt that he might once again have sought a new mistress. It is hard to envision any change in the environment that would have helped the student without an accompanying change in his capacity to cope with school or a major change in his attitude toward achievement.

Another difference between cases 1 and 2 and cases 3 and 4 is that the first two sustained direct losses (job and loved ones) while the second two were primarily threatened by a fear of not achieving and a fear of eventual loss of loved ones or of self-esteem. It must be pointed out, however, that object loss is not the critical issue here. Direct losses can also be experienced by patients who play a significant role in bringing about such losses. If the engineer (case 1) had become depressed after suffering his fourth job loss in a row, it could then be assumed that he played a major role in creating the precipitating environment. His situation would then be similar to that of the student's (case 4). An important factor in distinguishing the extent of the patient's involvement in creating his environment is repetitiveness of behavior. There is usually critical difference in the genesis of depression in a woman who becomes depressed after being rejected by her first lover and the woman who becomes depressed after being rejected by her sixth. The element of chance is likely to have played a greater role with the first woman and it can be assumed that the second woman is doing something to create a climate in which she is rejected.

It is, of course, unusual for people to become disturbed solely as a result of chance events or solely because of preexisting personality traits which lead them to create certain environments. The engineer reacted to his loss of employment by excessive drinking and by becoming more aggressive, behaviors probably influenced by his genetic makeup or previous learning experiences. He played a role in creating at least some of the conditions and events which eventually elicited his depression. The housewife reacted to her loss so severely and failed to find the support she needed from her husband partly because of certain traits of her own. In this case her passivity and dependency played a role in shaping conditions and events which increased her depression. Conversely, cases 3 and 4 can, to a certain extent, be viewed as having encountered poor luck. The executive might have avoided paralyzing conflict for a longer period of time had he encountered a more nurturant mistress or had pressures at his job not been so intense at that time. The student might have done better had he encountered superb teachers who understood his problem. He was also unfortunate in having made the decision to return to school at a time when academic standards and student competitiveness were high.

Though sharp discrimination of the degree to which the patient creates a stressful presymptomatic environment cannot always be made, efforts at even broad discrimination may help the clinician choose an intervention. Many patients whose disturbances are related to events they cannot influence are helped by understanding that their disorders may be the result of a unique and highly unlikely series of events, actually a combination of circumstances that may never occur in the same manner again. When the patient is taught to view his disorder in such a nonmystical and natural manner, he receives several benefits. It becomes clear to the patient that there was nothing preordained about his disorder. He can be reassured that if he learns to deal with the unanticipated events which have changed his life, his condition will improve. If the manner in which these chance events contribute to his disturbance can be explained to the patient, there is a greater likelihood that the patient will develop an appreciation of the complex forces which determine his behavior, and he wll be less likely to blame himself or others for his distress. In cases 1 and 2, this kind of information could have been an important part of treatment. For patients 3 and 4 it would have had far less relevance. Though they may have developed their personality traits as a result of chance events in their remote past, a naturalistic explanation of how this happened would take considerable time and exploration to develop and would have little influence in alleviating the patient's current state of distress.

In cases 1 and 2 it is also apparent that certain changes in the natural environment could have rapidly diminished the patients' suffering. The unemployed engineer, for example, could have been helped by finding something that increased his self-esteem. A therapist could not have found a job for the patient, but could have tried to structure a series of activities for the patient that would have kept him busy and preserved his self-esteem. The depressed young housewife could have been helped, at least temporarily, by finding other sources for gratification of her dependency needs. The therapist could have encouraged the patient to seek out new relationships, could have involved her with new groups, could have hospitalized her, or could himself have served as a new source of dependency gratification.

There are also some relatively unspectacular, stress-reducing interventions directed at making small changes in the family system that could have been utilized in the first two cases. The engineer and his wife could have undergone marital therapy to prepare both of them to cope with a difficult situation. The wife might have learned how to react differently to a man who had previously been financially successful but was now unemployed. The housewife who sustained two major losses in a brief period of time could have been helped if her husband had been taught to be more responsive to her needs. Again, family therapy could have created an environment that might have enabled her to cope with a crisis.

With both the executive and the student, the possible effectiveness of immediate stress reduction through family therapy would be limited. One could not know whether it would be desirable to work with the executive's wife, his mistress, or both. If either the wife or mistress became more tolerant of the patient's behavior, the patient would still be faced with a dilemma. In patients with problems similar to those of the student, it is often true that parents exert pressure to achieve goals beyond those the student seeks for himself. Brief family therapy is then quite useful in changing the environment by encouraging the parents to diminish this pressure. But in this case, the parents had long since abandoned great hopes as to their son's performance. Pressures which initially were probably created by earlier experience with the parents were by this point solidly internalized as part of the patient's personality and, to a considerable extent, existed independently of their present expectations. Family therapy could have shown how these pressures were learned, but it would have had little immediate value in diminishing stress upon the patient.

Many family therapists would not accept this analysis, arguing that both the executive's and the student's maladaptive responses could be directly related to their continuing involvement in dysfunctional family processes. This is not an appropriate place to consider the validity of what often is esoteric family theory. In a later chapter I will spend more time discussing this issue. I will note simply that I am speaking here of brief family therapy, and

Clinical Evaluation of the Patient and the Environment

doubt that even the most enthusiastic family therapist would be very optimistic about helping the executive or student in just a few family sessions.

In general there are only two ways in which either the executive or the student could have resolved his problem. They would either have had to become more successful at the tasks they undertook (achieving power and a conflict-free capacity to relate to multiple partners in the case of the executive; achieving academic success in the case of the student), or they would have had to have changed their attitudes or ways of relating to other people. The focus of therapy would in either instance be on changing the individual.

The above analysis suggests that interventions directed at changing the environment will be useful to the extent that environmental changes are accidental or out of the patient's control. It is possible, for example, to try to create an artificial environment that will restore lost reinforcements. Thus a highly reinforcing form of individual psychotherapy is indicated, as well as other interventions that increase reinforcement in the natural environment. The clinician can actively work with the family and help strengthen the patient's emotional support system. He can work with the community and help the patient find a new job or financial assistance. To the extent that the patient creates his own precipitating environment, he is more likely to need treatment directed at changing something about himself. Coping skills may be increased through providing the patient new learning experiences based on direct behavior modification techniques. Or the patient through some combination of reeducative and information-expanding psychotherapy, can come to appreciate that his behavior is self-defeating and can proceed to learn new behaviors based on changes in his attitudes. Environmental interventions, including family therapy, might be useful for this group of patients, but would generally not be as effective as in situations in which accidental or chance occurrences are etiologically critical.

While I have tried to present a system for distinguishing between two ways in which stressful environments develop, the reader should be reminded that such either/or distinctions can rarely be made in actual practice. Patients whose disorders can be viewed as significantly related to events outside of their influence can also benefit from therapies directed at providing new learning. Certainly the engineer could have learned a great deal about the determinants of his impulsivity, and the housewife could have benefited from a clarification of the determinants of her excessive dependency needs. Such learning might have increased their capacity to cope with accidental stressful events. The point to be made here is that there are modes of therapy, other than those directed at bringing about major changes in the individual, which may be sufficient treatments for patients whose disorders are related largely to accidental circumstances. Where the patient creates his own unfavorable environment, brief intervention is not likely to be effective and there is a greater likelihood of recurrences of disturbed behavior if the patient does not learn new patterns of adaptation.

One way of summarizing this section is to suggest that when the clinician encounters a patient whose disturbance is related largely to accidental events, the clinician must ask, What can I change about either the patient or the environment that will enable him to survive this ordeal? Intervention here can be brief. Where it appears the patient plays a major role in creating the presymptomatic environment, the clinician must ask, How can I teach the patient to stop creating unfavorable environments? or How can I help him increase his coping skills so as to allow him to withstand unusual stress of his own making? Here the task of treatment is more formidable and is likely to require the use of lengthy learning and information-expanding therapies.

Developmental Change and Environmental Response

In evaluating environmental influences in creating an emotional disorder, the clinician must also consider the extent to which the environment is influenced by the patient's developmental needs. Human development can be viewed as a process in which biological changes associated with maturation or aging lead to important shifts in individual-environment interaction. As an individual matures or ages, the environment will have new expectations of him. At the same time the maturing or aging individual will have new needs of his environment. The new social expectations related to development are usually obvious. On reaching adolescence a child is expected to assume greater responsibility and to begin to prepare for marriage and a career. During the years of childrearing the individual must assume new obligations to care for others. On the other hand, less is expected of the elderly. The new individual needs created by development are less apparent. The adolescent, in contrast to the latency age child, needs more opportunity to take a role in decisions as to how he will structure his daily activities. He needs less nurturance and more opportunity to experiment with independent activities. There are other times in the life cycle when people need less independence and a larger degree of nurturance and support. During the course of pregnancy, childbirth, and child rearing, a woman may need a great deal of support from her husband or others. As people get older and are deprived of reinforcement they once received from work activities or from now deceased loved ones, they need an increased level of nurturant support.

Sometimes the process of development is especially stressful because the patient is burdened with biological or learning impairments. Certain biological defects may not appear until an individual reaches a certain state of development. Defective or inadequate past learning will also compromise an individual's capacity to deal with developmental change. An overprotected child will have trouble leaving home in late adolescence. An immature man or woman will have difficulty assuming the burdens of parenthood. Individuals with biological or learning impairments will have difficulties meeting new social expectations and will need especially propitious responses from the environment when they reach a point in life when they are expected to assume responsible roles. In evaluating dysfunctional behavior which occurs as an individual moves into a new developmental phase, the clinician must consider the inadequacies of the individual as well as the expectations and responses of the environment. Evaluation of biological, learning, and informational deficits have already been considered and these must be kept in mind as the clinician observes the manner in which developmental change elicits dysfunction. The primary emphasis in this section, however, is on the evaluation of the extent to which the presymptomatic environment has imposed unusual expectations upon the patient and has failed to meet the patient's age-appropriate needs. The presence of these environmental conditions will direct the clinician to considering the use of interventions which change the natural environment. Consider the following case:

A nineteen-year-old male was admitted to a hospital complaining of fears that he was going to be homosexually assaulted and of an inability to think clearly. Shortly after hospitalization he admitted that he had been hearing voices which accused him of being "queer." He showed frequent evidence of *blocking*, or inability to stick to a particular train of thought. Several aspects of the patient's recent history were especially important. He reported his symptoms as having begun three weeks before admission and to have gradually become more severe. A month prior to the appearance of his symptomatology he had engaged in homosexual activity with an older male. Two months prior to the onset of his symptomatology he had dropped out of his first year of college and had returned home to live with his parents. His experiences in college had been marked by lack of success and loneliness. He found college work extremely difficult even though he studied almost constantly. He had made no close friends at school and did not date. When his loneliness approached unbearable proportions and when he realized he was going to fail in school, he returned home. He took a menial job as caretaker in a pool hall. It was in this setting that his homosexual experience occurred. The patient condemned himself severely for his failures in school. He repeatedly said that he had disgraced his parents and particularly his mother. Even during the early stages of his disorganization he insisted that he wanted to get back to school as quickly as possible and do something his mother could be proud of.

The patient responded well to neuroleptic medication and on the tenth day of hospitalization he and his parents were seen together in a family interview. Here it was noted that both parents viewed him as a highly intelligent and gifted youth from whom they anticipated exceptional performance. (Actually, the patient had low-normal intelligence.) While they expected him to perform exceptionally, they had provided him few opportunities to develop the skills he had. They had always been overprotective of him, never allowing him to work while in high school and discouraging him from dating. They had insisted that he attend a college located only a few miles from home, and even while he was away at school he was required to call his mother at least three times a week. It was also apparent that the mother was inconsistent in her communication to the patient. Although she repeatedly insisted that she only wanted her son to do exactly what he wanted, she made it abundantly clear that she would be disappointed if he did not live up to her expectations.

It was reasonable to hypothesize in this case that maladaptive learning experiences and some type of biological deficiency had impaired the patient's capacity to deal with the pressures of achieving manhood. But it also seemed reasonable to hypothesize that certain factors in his presymptomatic environment were directly impeding his adjustment. He was being put under pressure to perform beyond his ability and at the same time was not given the opportunity to find ways of separating from the family or of developing age-appropriate social skills. In this case biological intervention in the form of neuroleptic medication was essential in relieving his psychotic symptomatology. Learning and informational-expanding interventions were indicated as a means of increasing his capacity to cope with the stresses of maturation. It was also felt that treatment would be incomplete unless some effort were made to treat the family system and to diminish the stresses the family was putting upon him.

With some patients who become disturbed as a result of developmental changes, the indications for changing the natural environment are even more powerful:

A thirty-year-old woman became extremely anxious and moderately depressed following the birth of her third child. Her older children were under five years of age. From the moment she had come home from the hospital with her infant, she had been plagued with fears that she would be unable to take care of three preschool children. She ruminated about her potential inadequacies and began to worry that she would fail to perform some task which might result in harm to one of her children. She began to have difficulty in sleeping and complained to her husband that she could not go on taking care of the children. At this point the couple agreed to hire a part-time housekeeper who would also help with the children. This was done, but the patient's symptoms did not abate.

During the family interview it was noted that the third child was born at a time when the husband was highly committed to success in his job and was working up to seventy hours a week. He was concerned about the burden that had been put upon his wife but expected that she would work as hard with the children as he was working on his career. He made some effort to help his wife with household tasks, but since he was away from home so frequently and was so fatigued when he was at home, these efforts did little to relieve her burden. The patient needed little prompting to reveal how deeply she resented her husband's absence from the home and his expectations that she be the sole provider of care for the children. She had harbored career aspirations of her own and resented the fact that he enjoyed his work so much, while she was stuck with the children.

While hypotheses of a postpartum metabolic abnormality or of maladaptive learning leading to rigid obsessional traits were considered, the major aspect of treatment in this case was directed toward helping the couple renegotiate their family responsibilities. The husband agreed to stop his evening work and to accept at least a temporary curtailment of his drive for success. He stayed home more frequently and became actively involved in raising the children. After several weeks the patient's symptoms abated. She decided to ask her housekeeper to work longer hours and began to consider returning to school on a part-time basis.

A fifty-year-old woman became depressed two months after the marriage of her youngest child. Her depression was manifested by insomnia, weight loss, and abuse of alcohol. At the same time the patient was experiencing menopausal symptoms and was preoccupied with a fear of growing old. She complained that with the departure of her youngest child and the loss of her youth there was nothing worth living for. She had no occupational skills and throughout the twenty-seven years of her marriage had been content to be a homemaker. Her husband was a successful executive who found many gratifications in his work and in weekend fishing and hunting trips with male friends. The couple had stopped having sexual relations five years before this patient became depressed. She anticipated a future in which she would have to deal with the problems of aging without the support of a close relationship with her husband. During the family interview it was noted that the husband too had many concerns about his future. He wanted more involvement with his wife and was troubled by their inability to enjoy each another's company. In spite of all their difficulties this couple insisted that they wanted to try to improve their relationship and to remain together for the rest of their lives. The husband seemed especially willing to renegotiate the conditions of the marital relationship. While the patient could well have been treated with antidepressant medication, she responded so well to the first marital interview that it was decided to use couple therapy as the primary intervention. As the couple dealt with the issue of separating from their children and learning to provide more gratifications for each other, her symptoms of depression diminished.

In the above cases the family system complicated each patient's developmental task by imposing unrealistic expectations upon the patients, by failing to provide a climate in which age-appropriate skills could be learned, or by failing to provide sufficient emotional support. The environment can also make certain developmental processes, such as aging, more stressful, by failing to lower its demands on a patient whose physical capacities are diminishing. In such instances the presymptomatic environment, if superficially examined, may seem to have undergone no change at all, and it is possible to conclude that the patient's symptoms developed "out of the blue." Careful evaluation of small social systems might, however, reveal that the environment has actually been stressful by failing to accommodate itself to the patient's new limitations. Sometimes interventions directed at changing the natural environment can alleviate this situation:

A fifty-year-old black male sought help for symptoms of anxiety and depression. He had lived at a poverty level for most of his life, was uneducated, and supported himself and his family through manual labor. In recent months he had noticed this his physical strength was ebbing. In the initial interview it was relatively easy to ascertain that the patient's symptoms were related to his fears that he would soon be unable to earn a living. Neither the patient nor his family could determine anything about the patient's environment that had recently changed. It seemed in this case that the patient's symptoms were related to a normal aging process which made it difficult for him to continue to survive in a capitalist society. In this case the patient was fortunate to have an unusually flexible employer. The patient and his employer were seen together, and the employer was persuaded to give the patient a job which required less physical strength. When this decision was made, the patient's emotional distress was appreciably relieved.

While I have tried to categorize three factors—accidental events, the patient's influence on the interpersonal environment, and the environmental response to the patient's developmental needs—which can increase environmental stress, it is important to emphasize the interrelationship of these factors. In actual practice the clinician commonly sees patients in whom both the elements of chance and the patient's own personality have played major roles in creating the presymptomatic environment. Patients with dysfunctional responses to developmental changes may also have individual characteristics (biological deficits or learned personality traits) which elicit undesired environmental responses. Accidental events will often compromise the individual's capacity to deal with developmental tasks.

Even given complex interrelationships, it is still useful for the clinician to try to define a class of patients who have certain characteristic modes of interpersonal interaction which seem to elicit stressful responses from the environment. These people are usually labeled personality or character disorders. Their problems tend to be chronic and their maladaptive behavior patterns are characterized by a constant level of vague dissatisfaction, punctuated during times of stress by moderate to severe anxiety or depression. Their symptoms tend to be poorly circumscribed and difficult to measure. Much of their stress-creating behavior can be explained in terms of hypotheses of maladaptive learning or informational deficits. Since the major problem here is attempting to modify relatively fixed and chronic modes of interaction and not just dealing with periodic exacerbations of anxiety or depression, the task of intervention is likely to be prolonged and difficult. These individuals will usually need long-term individual or group psychotherapy (which will, of course, make use of principles of behavior modification). They may also, at times, be helped by long-term family therapy.

Dysfunctional responses to accidental stressful events or to stress associated with developmental change are sometimes referred to as *crisis reactions* (Langley and Kaplan 1968, Caplan 1964). This term is most likely to be used when the individual was felt to be functioning in an adequate manner before the new stresses developed. To the extent that the clinician can determine that the patient's presymptomatic personality traits were not a major factor in creating the crisis, the goals of treatment here are to restore the patient's earlier level of functioning and to help him use the crisis experience to learn new coping skills. Long-term individual or group psychotherapy are not usually indicated. Biological treatment will be needed if the response to the crisis is severe. Brief individual psychotherapy based on reeducation and information expansion will be useful. Interventions such as family therapy, which are directed at changing the natural environment, will be especially useful.

Evaluating the Postsymptomatic Environment

While easier to define than the presymptomatic, the postsymptomatic environment must nevertheless be defined somewhat arbitrarily. We are dealing with a continuum of conditions and events over time and it is extremely difficult to say at what point behaviors should be called symptoms and at what point they should be considered part of a process leading to the development of symptoms. In the case of the aeronautical engineer who lost his job, events following the patient's drinking rather than events following his suicide attempt might have been viewed as the critical part of the postsymptomatic environment.

With this reminder, consider the question Why do symptoms persist? The environment in which symptoms develop can change quickly. Certainly where chance events contribute to the stressfulness of the environments, there is a high possibility of stress alleviation after only a brief period. Even stressful environments created by the patient are likely to become less stressful over time, and until the patient re-creates them, he may find himself in a relatively benign environment. It is true also that many people under stress will have sufficient psychological strength to change their coping patterns and master a difficult environment without seeking help. Actually, many symptoms do go away without any therapeutic intervention at all (Eysenck 1952).

Still, there are many patients who remain disturbed or who become more disturbed after they identity themselves as being troubled. This may happen even when they or their environment have changed salutarily. How can this be explained? Different schools of behavioral science put forth different hypotheses. Those of biological orientation believe that when some symptoms develop there may be concurrent changes in the individual's biological processes which tend to perpetuate symptoms even if the environment becomes more benign (Pincus 1974). Psychoanalysts believe that a symptom is only a partial solution of a conflict and never fully gratifies the patient's needs. As long as the patient's needs or wishes remain unsatisfied or unrecognized, the symptom may linger (Alexander and Ross 1952). Social psychologists argue that there are certain social responses to deviant behavior or illness which increase the level of stress imposed upon the patient (Scheff 1966). In the most extreme form of this argument it is sometimes asserted that much of the patient's maladaptive postsymptomatic behavior is determined by the label others put upon him. Behaviorists view symptom maintenance as related primarily to environmental reinforcement (Storrow 1967). They argue that, even if the environment seems to have become more benign, either those around the patient continue to reinforce disordered behavior or the patient through some as yet poorly understood mechanism learns to provide internal reinforcements of his own behavior. There are times when each of these explanations of symptom maintenance seems appropriate, and sometimes all may have a certain relevance to understanding and treating a given patient. Certainly when biochemical changes are suspected, somatic treatments should be strongly considered. Psychoanalytic hypotheses suggest reeducative and informational approaches which, though time-consuming, may be helpful. But the most useful clues to intervention can be formulated by focusing upon how the postsymptomatic environment changes so as to increase the level of stress imposed upon the patient (sociopsychological hypotheses) or to reinforce disturbed behavior (behavioral hypotheses).

A variety of new stresses can develop once a person begins to behave differently, and these may sustain or even escalate maladaptation. Sometimes, when those in the patient's environment become angry, the threatened loss or reinforcement may make the disturbance worse:

A thirty-five-year-old man began to experience severe anxiety attacks both at home and at work. He was barely able to function at his job, and at home curtailed many of his activities. As soon as he was home from work, he would insist he was too tired to do anything but rest. Much of his time at home was spent watching television or sleeping. He began to lose interest in sex. The patient's symptoms elicited an angry response from both his employer and his wife. He was reprimanded at work for not being as productive as he used to be. His wife, who was deeply annoyed because of restrictions put on the couple's social life and the patient's lack of interest in sex, began to chide and eventually berate the patient. These critical responses to his behavior made the patient angry, guilty, and fearful. His condition deteriorated rapidly.

Sometimes those around the patient react to the patient's symptoms by withdrawing from him. This increases the patient's stress level by depriving him of intimacy which had previously helped sustain him.

A thirty-year-old married woman developed symptoms of abdominal pain and nausea. After several thorough physical examinations which revealed no organic pathology, the patient was told her symptoms were related to emotional stress and she was treated with minor tranquilizers. The patient, however, continued to complain bitterly. Much of her conversation with her husband focused entirely on her symptoms. The husband did not become openly angry, but after a while he stopped listening. He worked longer hours at the office and began to invest more emotional energy in his children, friends, and co-workers. The patient reacted to her husband's withdrawal by feeling even more insecure, and this made her symptoms worse.

Sometimes those around the patient react to the patient's symptoms by becoming frightened or even awestruck. This can result in withdrawal of support by those upon whom the patient relies. It also increases the patient's fear that something terrible is happening to him.

A twenty-five-year-old married man was arrested for exhibiting his genitals to a small girl. There was a good deal of publicity about the case, so the patient's family and most of his friends learned of his behavior. Although the patient had viewed himself as having had a normal marital adjustment prior to this time, and although the patient had no motivations to physically harm anyone, he found that his friends began to treat him like a pariah. They would not bring their children to his house, and they tried to avoid him in social situations. Even his wife seemed somewhat frightened of him and found it difficult to enjoy sexual relationships with him as much as she had previously. All of this contributed to the patient's anxiety. He began to respond to this new tension by indulging in fantasies of exhibiting himself and eventually he again succumbed to this temptation.

Sometimes the person who develops symptoms is labeled as sick and is not considered responsible for his actions. When this happens, the patient loses power. His feelings, thoughts, and acts do not receive the same degree of consideration they used to, and as his influence wanes, so does his self-esteem.

An eighteen-year-old youth was hospitalized and treated for a psychotic reaction following the use of LSD. During the hospitalization, there was some uncertainty on the doctor's part as to whether the patient was experiencing a schizophrenic reaction or whether the psychosis was primarily drug-induced. This uncertainty was communicated to the patient's parents. They had for at least a year been seriously troubled by the patient's drug use, his values regarding sex and society, and his rebelliousness. Once the patient returned home, they tried to be kind to him, but whenever he disagreed with them in any way, they reminded him that he was sick and that those of his behaviors and ideas which they did not like were products of his illness. Instead of recovering from his illness quickly, as doctors had predicted, the patient continued to function at a regressed level for many months.

One step the clinician can take in evaluating the stressfulness of the postsymptomatic environment is to ask the patient how he perceives others' reactions to his symptoms. Some patients may be unaware of stressful environmental responses to their behavior, while others may exaggerate the severity of such responses. But frequently patients can quite rationally explain how they have been troubled by how others respond to their disturbance. The clinician can also detect stress in the postsymptomatic environment by doing a family interview. Here he can listen to more than one version of the events that followed the patient's symptomatology. He can also corroborate or disprove the patient's perception as to what has happened by actually observing how various significant figures are dealing with the patient's disturbance.

The most obvious way to diminish the negative impact of stressful postsymptomatic environments is to alleviate the patient's symptoms as quickly as possible. In actual practice, of course, symptoms often remit slowly, and once the patient has been labeled deviant or ill, even total remission of symptoms may not diminish the stressfulness of the postsymptomatic environment. A more practical approach is to make direct efforts at changing a stressful postsymptomatic environment once it has been observed. Significant figures in the patient's life can be urged to curb their tendencies to withdraw reinforcement. They can be encouraged to relate to the patient as an autonomous, responsible person and can be instructed as to the unfortunate long-term consequences of using psychiatric labels to explain the patient's behavior. Sometimes it is useful to work with significant figures who respond in a stressful manner without the patient's being present. As a rule, however, modification of the harmful effects of the postsymptomatic environment is best accomplished in the context of conjoint family therapy.

Often environmental responses to the patient's symptoms may seem supportive rather than stress-inducing. Those involved with the patient may treat him more considerately, and even indulgently after symptoms develop. But these apparently benign responses may actually sustain the patient's symptoms. Viewed in terms of operant conditioning, they are reinforcers. The manner in which symptoms are reinforced by supportive or indulgent responses can be illustrated by the following case vignettes:

A thirty-year-old married woman developed a fear of leaving her house alone. Her phobia quickly escalated so that she was soon unwilling

Clinical Evaluation of the Patient and the Environment

to perform such routine tasks as shopping. She began to curtail her social life. Prior to the onset of her symptoms, her husband had been rather exploitive of her. He paid little attention to her emotional needs but demanded that she keep house and be an adequate partner in bed. With the onset of her symptoms, her husband was required to be more solicitous. He felt compelled to regularly express concern for her. He began driving her about on her errands and spent much more time in her company. Whenever her husband would attempt to withdraw his interest in the patient, her symptoms would return.

A fifty-five-year-old married woman developed Raynaud's disease. In the process of diagnosing this disorder, the patient underwent many tests and was hospitalized several times. Eventually she was told she had a very mild form of the disease and that it should not in any way interfere with her leading a normal life. By this time, however, the patient was plagued with severe headaches, frequent insomnia, and feelings of hopelessness. Her husband, who was an Army officer, retired early so that he could help her more around the house. The family moved to the vicinity of a military hospital that could provide them readily available service. Their whole life style for the next several years was focused around her symptoms and well-being, an environment heavily reinforcing her illness. Eventually she became severely depressed and had to be hospitalized.

Indulgence is not the only environmental response that reinforces symptoms. Sometimes even annoyed or angry responses by significant figures (these might also be viewed as stressful-producing responses) seem to reinforce the patient's behavior. While the mechanism of such reinforcement is not clearly understood, its manifestations are often apparent and are especially evident in work with children. Such symptoms in young people as bed wetting, temper tantrums, or tics sometimes elicit angry responses from parents. Too often the anger does not seem to serve as an aversive stimulus but may actually encourage the repetition of the child's behavior. The key issue here may be attention, and conceivably any kind of attention will be a reinforcer. But whatever mechanism is involved, the clinician must be prepared to consider the possibility that efforts of those around the patient which seem directed toward getting rid of a symptom may actually serve to perpetuate it.

Evaluation of reinforcment in the postsymptomatic environment requires that the clinician interview not only the patient but those interacting with the patient. Conjoint family interviewing helps the clinician develop a history of reinforcements experienced by the patient since symptoms become manifest. The clinician can ask how family members respond to the patient's disturbed behavior and what effect this has on the symptoms. The family interview also allows the clinician to observe how others reinforce the patient's symptoms. Here the clinician should pay particular attention to how others react when the patient talks about or demonstrates symptoms. It is not uncommon to discover that patients receive attention only when they behave symptomatically.

The easiest way to change patterns which reinforce symptomatic behavior is to instruct family members to change their responses and to reinforce more adaptive behaviors. This instruction may be provided in a setting where family members are seen without the patient, but it is likely to have more impact in the conjoint family therapy setting.

One other symptom-sustaining aspect of the postsymptomatic environment remains to be evaluated. Unfortunately the treatment efforts of professionals are not always successful; they may in fact make the patient's situation static or even worse. Any therapy incorrectly or injudiciously applied can increase the patient's level of stress. Unnecessary or imprecisely prescribed drugs can worsen his condition. Demands that he learn new behaviors he may be unwilling or unable to learn are highly stressful. New information may be imposed upon him before he is ready to deal with it. Unnecessary hospitalization may terrify him. The clinician can also reinforce symptoms by prematurely labeling them as a disease, by being overindulgent or solicitous, or by fostering excessive dependency upon the professional relationship. A patient who comes to view his behavior as a disease totally out of his own control will, in addition to being stressed, experience diminished motivation to change his behavior. A patient may come to so value the attention of his therapist that he is consciously or unconsciously unwilling to abandon his symptoms for fear of losing the relationship. He may remain in the sick role because the therapist has inadvertantly taught him he is sick or because he has learned to use the sick role to sustain the therapist's attention. All of these things can happen even when the practitioner is skilled and his motivations are altruistic. It is impossible to practice psychiatry, psychology, social work, or psychiatric nursing without making mistakes.

Clinical Evaluation of the Patient and the Environment 113

There are, of course, highly skilled mental health professionals and poorly trained mental health professionals. There are honorable, responsible professionals and greedy, insensitive professionals. While skilled and honorable professionals outnumber the poorly trained or dishonorable, I have practiced psychiatry long enough to be always sensitive to the possibility that the patient has been financially or sexually exploited by a previous therapist.

In evaluating the postsymptomatic environment, the clinician must always take a careful history as to the patient's past treatment. This information will be of direct value in determining current treatment. It will give the clinician some idea of what has worked or not worked in the past, what treatment should be avoided and what may be useful. The clinician must also be alert to adverse effects of previous treatment. Knowledge of those effects may direct the clinician to prescribe a new learning experience for the patient. When the patient and his family have been told that the patient has a certain type of disorder and the current evidence indicates that this information is incorrect, family members, as well as the patient, must learn that the patient has been inappropriately labeled. The patient who has become excessively dependent upon therapy must learn other means of gratification. The patient who has learned to seek insight as a means of remaining dependent upon his therapist rather than as a means of changing his behavior must be acquainted with other forms of therapy. The patient who has been financially or sexually exploited must learn that other, more benevolent professional relationships are available.

Clinicians, probably out of a wish to protect their colleagues, are often too superficial in investigating or remedying adverse effects of previous therapy. Such superficiality is unfortunate if earlier interventions have unduly stressed the patient or reinforced his symptoms. If this has happened, the clinician has a moral obligation to discover ways of diminishing these effects. When the patient's previous therapist have behaved ethically, these issues can be considered openly with the patient without disparaging one's colleagues. In fact many enlightened clinicians will welcome the opportunity to try to ameliorate adverse results of their earlier treatments and will often be eager to consult with the new clinician. The previous therapist may even be willing to become a participant in a kind of family therapy in which examination of the initial therapist-patient relationship helps the patient resolve his conflicts about the previous therapist or helps reestablish the relationship with him.

If the clinician suspects that the patient's previous therapists have behaved stupidly or unethically, the clinician's problem is far more difficult. On the one hand, it is neither safe nor enjoyable to disparage one's colleagues. On the other hand, the patient has the right to know how he was mistreated, since such information will make it easier for him to understand and perhaps to change his current maladaptive behavior. The clinician should move cautiously in making negative comments about previous treatment or previous therapist. There is always the possibility that the patient's perception of his interactions with previous therapists is inaccurate or distorted. Before the patient is given even a hint that his previous treatment was harmful, the clinician must review old records and contact the previous therapist in order to hear his version of what happened. Through evaluating information from both participants, the clinician can make a realistic assessment of how previous treatment may have affected the patient. Fortunately such assessment usually reveals that the undesirable effects of previous treatment were the result neither of incompetence nor exploitation, and it is then possible to discuss the unsuccessful treatment openly with the patient without disparaging one's colleagues. If the clinician, after thoroughly evaluating the situation, is convinced that previous treatment damaged the patient because of the practitioner's incompetence or exploitiveness, and if the clinician believes the patient will benefit by knowing he has been adversely influenced, the clinician should provide him that knowledge. In so doing the clinician risks both litigation and unpopularity within his professional group. If he is truly committed to his patient, however, he has no other choice.

A SUMMARY OF CLINICAL EVALUATIONS WHICH INCREASE THE EFFICIENCY OF INTERVENTION

The material presented in this chapter has been complicated and has been organized in a manner perhaps unfamiliar to many clinicians. It will be useful, then, to review the problem of evaluation in terms of the format the clinician ordinarily uses in making a diagnostic evaluation. I will list the traditional steps the clinician takes in making an evaluation and show how each step relates to the task of diagnosis and treatment.

Clinical Evaluation of the Patient and the Environment

One: The clinician begins by evaluating the patient's complaints. He notes their severity and duration. He makes some effort to classify them in terms of any dysfunction he detects in the patient's perception, cognition, or emotionality. Efforts are made to determine whether the complaints suggest confused, schizophrenic, manic, or severely depressed behavior. These, unlike less severe depression or moderate forms of anxiety, usually require biological interventions. The clinician tries also to determine if any of the patient's complaints can be viewed as target behaviors, or as behaviors that can be observed and measured in terms of frequency. Target behaviors can be treated with direct behavior modification techniques.

Two: The clinician moves from evaluation of the nature of the patient's complaints to evaluation of the environment which preceded them. In dealing with target behaviors he is sometimes concerned with antecedent events that may have preceded behavior by minutes or seconds. Usually, however, he is concerned with broader aspects of the presymptomatic environment and tries to develop a picture of how individual and environment have interacted over a period of weeks or months so as to have brought the individual to his current plight. The clinician tries to evaluate the stressfulness of the presymptomatic environment. Where the disorder is severe and presymptomatic stress was minimal, the clinician is especially sensitive to the need for first ruling out a biological disorder. If stressfulness is more evident and the clinician can determine that the patient's personality traits were significantly involved, then individual or group therapy is likely to be indicated. If on the other hand the clinician determines that he is dealing with a crisis reaction related to accidental events or developmental needs, then brief individual and family psychotherapy are more useful. If the response to crisis is severe, biological interventions will also be needed.

Three: The clinician then turns to evaluation of the postsymptomatic environment. His first concern here is with the type of treatment the patient has received between the appearance of symptoms and the patient's first visit with the clinician. Knowledge of previous treatment will give some indication of which interventions are likely to work and which are not. It may also give clues as to how previous treatment might have imposed additional stress upon the patient or reinforced his symptoms. Asking the patient about events that have occurred between him and significant figures in his life since the development of symptoms will also give some clues as to what stresses and reinforcements in the natural environments have helped sustain his symptomatology. When the postsymptomatic environment is sustaining symptoms, it can be modified directly by teaching significant figures to change their responses to the patient's disorder. Usually this is done in the context of conjoint family therapy.

Four: The clinician then thoroughly reviews the patient's past history and tries to learn whatever he can about the patient's family, early development, and educational, occupational, sexual, and marital experiences. Here the clinician is looking for evidence of emotional disorders in other family members. Such information may help substantiate a diagnosis of a schizophrenic or affective disorder. In reviewing other aspects of his patient's history, the clinician is primarily concerned with the kind of learning the patient has experienced throughout his life. It is important to determine if the individual encountered past situations which led to his developing ineffective or maladaptive methods of coping. It is necessary also to determine if the patient has had learning experiences sufficient to prepare him to deal with his current needs. These evaluations give the clinician some idea as to what the patient must learn or unlearn in individual, group, or family psychotherapy.

As various aspects of the patient's past life are discussed, the clinician can inquire as to the patient's awareness of how in each situation he either influenced or was influenced by the environment. Such an inquiry will reveal something about the patient's psychological mindedness and will also provide clues as to the indications for psychotherapeutic interventions directed at expanding information about past learning.

Five: During all of the above evaluations, the clinician is continuously trying to assess how he and the patient are interacting. He tries to determine how aware the patient is of how he is coming across to the clinician and how he is influenced by the clinician. He tries to make some inferences as to how aware the patient is of his own feelings. When the clinician hypothesizes deficits in any of these types of awareness, he gives more serious consideration to the use of psychotherapeutic interventions emphasizing expansion of information.

Six: The clinician expands his evaluation of the patient's complaints by doing a formal mental status examination. This involves asking questions which test the patient's perception and

Clinical Evaluation of the Patient and the Environment   117

cognition. At this point a thorough physical examination is also essential. When the clinician is a physician he can do this himself. If he is not, he must make sure the patient's condition is thoroughly evaluated.

Seven: Most of the time the clinician does the family interview after the patient has been interviewed alone. There can be variations on this format, however, depending upon the clinician's orientation and the patient's needs. Some patients may be too disturbed to provide useful historical information; in such cases, the family interview may provide this information. The family interview is especially useful in elucidating the influences of various events in the pre- and postsymptomatic environment. Often during the interview, patterns of family interaction can be observed which are clearly stressful to the patient or which reinforce symptomatology. The presence of such patterns indicates direct family intervention. Family interaction can be observed to evaluate how the patient influences and is influenced by one major aspect of his environment. The clinician can then compare his own with the patient's perception of the patient's interactions with significant figures. This procedure sharpens the clinician's evaluation of informational deficits. Finally, the family interview allows the clinician to assess the quality of communication the patient is receiving from significant figures and to formulate strategies for expanding the patient's knowledge of his environment.

In my experience it takes from two to five one-and-a-half-hour sessions to make these evaluations. At least one of these sessions must be a family interview. The experienced clinician can sometimes do an adequate job in two sessions, one with the patient alone and one with the family. It should be apparent that the process of evaluation, particularly if it goes on beyond an hour or two, is itself an intervention which includes many of the helpful elements of individual or family psychotherapy.

I have tried to show how both observational or classificatory and etiological approaches to diagnosis can be used to evaluate indications for various treatments. Efforts to continue to refine indications for treatments will be made in the second part of this book when specific treatments are discussed. But before getting to that it is necessary to discuss certain practical and ethical issues which may also influence the nature of intervention.

Chapter 4

Practical and Ethical Issues

Suppose a fifty-year-old woman who has always had difficulties getting along at work and at home, but who has never felt disturbed enough to seek psychiatric help, becomes severely anxious and depressed following the death of her son in a driving accident. Suppose further that the patient has always been mildly phobic about driving but is now too frightened to even enter a car and is unable to work. As she stays home and mourns, she loses weight, has difficulty sleeping, and begins to contemplate suicide. Here we have a patient who might need a biological intervention (for her depression), a behavioral intervention (for her target phobic behaviors), a learning-informational intervention (individual or group psychotherapy for her long-standing personality disorders), and an intervention that deals with the natural environment (family therapy to help her through a crisis situation). Should this patient, or patients like her, receive all of the above treatments?

Up to now, my answer to this type of question has, with certain qualifications, been yes. As long as each of several interventions which might be used are believed to be effective on the basis of plausible hypotheses, the clinician should not put restrictions on the use of multiple interventions unless such multidimensional treatment is economically unjustified. With the exception of long-term psychotherapy, most interventions are brief and inexpensive enough so that they unduly stress neither the patient's financial resources nor the therapist's time and energy. On the basis of efficiency alone, the clinician can usually be comfortable utilizing pharmacotherapies, behavior therapies, and all varieties of brief psychotherapies with the same patient. But it would be naive not to assume that the use of multiple interventions might have some adverse effects when superimposed upon a complex system of patient-environment interaction. There are clinical realities which impose limits on the use of certain combinations of therapies, particularly when these treatments are used concurrently. Though these limits are not formidable, they are important enough to be considered in some detail.

PRACTICAL ISSUES IN CONCURRENT USE OF INTERVENTIONS

Severely Disturbed Patients

Sometimes different interventions do not complement but interfere with one another. Indiscriminately used, the resulting whole of multidimensional therapy, in terms of outcome, can turn out to be less, rather than more, than the sum of its parts. While clinicians tend to exaggerate the extent to which interventions may antagonize one another, the issue is nevertheless real. In planning the treatment of some seriously disturbed patients, it becomes obvious that certain interventions obviate the use of others. A patient being given electroconvulsive treatment is unlikely to be benefited by concurrent information-expanding psychotherapy. Similar arguments would apply to insight-oriented therapy with a patient who has been lobotomized. Even the patient who is being treated with major tranquilizers is a less than optimal candidate for some forms of information-expanding psychotherapy. The problem here is that many somatic interventions cloud the sensorium and make complex learning difficult. A patient whose perceptual functions have been altered by some biological intervention finds it especially hard to process new information, whether knowledge of one's own behavior or of the environment. However, learning is still possible even when the sensorium is impaired. Emotional support can be provided through most forms of psychotherapy, and more simple types of learning based on operant conditioning models can certainly take place in a patient receiving somatic treatments.

The problem of providing concurrent emotional support while the patient may be dealing with serious symptoms of disorganization—and is perhaps receiving biological treatments—needs some elaboration. If the patient is hospitalized, much emotional support can come from a structured milieu. But in outpatient and sometimes hospital settings, it can also be provided through one-to-one or group relationships. Such relationships can be considered a supportive form of individual or group psychotherapy. (Family therapy can also be considered supportive. Unlike individual or group psychotherapy, however, it may not provide a great deal of support to the patient during the actual treatment session, but is most useful in activating support systems in the natural environment.) The use of psychotherapy as a means of providing emotional support to a patient is a poorly conceptualized intervention in clinical practice. In a general sense, all psychotherapy is, or should be, supportive. The patient must, for a while, gain sustenance from the therapist, and even if psychotherapy may at times impose stress upon the patient, that stress should be viewed as something helpful in the long run. Nevertheless, most therapists agree that there are patients who, either for brief or for extended periods of time, cannot tolerate stresses created by insight-oriented or information-expanding psychotherapy. These patients may need the intimacy and the positive reinforcement of psychotherapy, but they do not need its more stressful aspects. Yet it is often difficult to know which of the therapist's actions are stressful and which are not. Psychoanalytic therapists view supportive therapy as an intervention which strengthens rather than attacks defenses (Kubie 1950). This can be a useful criterion of support, but there are, nevertheless, times when even the most disturbed patient can be comforted by receiving information that one or more of his behaviors (which can be viewed in psychoanalytic terms as defense mechanisms) is serving him poorly.

I consider supportive psychotherapy to be a form of therapy in which the patient is provided with a caring, loving, interpersonal environment in which he has the opportunity to learn new and gratifying behaviors without being unduly stressed. Supportive therapy should emphasize positive reinforcement (in the sense of praise, approval, or appreciation) of the patient. It should provide an environment in which the patient's positive attributes rather than his weaknesses are emphasized. The therapist must clearly demonstrate his acceptance of and concern for the patient. At the same time that the patient is reinforced, the supportive therapist avoids overloading the patient with information about either self or environment. The supportive therapists helps the patient to learn to deal with day-to-day problems. Even when the patient asks to learn new and difficult skills such as assertiveness, the supportive therapist will move slowly and try to convince the patient that the patient will be accepted by the therapist whether or not the patient changes his behavior. In supportive psychotherapy, the therapist does not make comments or interpretations which threaten the patient's self-concept, which demand behavioral change, or which free up anxiety-laden memories. Nor does the therapist use techniques such as confrontations, silence, or impersonality which are likely to confuse the patient. The supportive therapist should reveal himself as a concerned human being who is willing to explain things to the patient, to answer questions, and to provide clear verbal messages as to what kind of behavior on the patient's part would be useful and what kind not useful. The use of supportive psychotherapy requires flexibility on the part of the clinician. Supportive psychotherapy can be brief or prolonged. It can gradually merge into other forms of psychotherapy which are more stressful and which demand greater behavioral change on the part of the patient.

Most important for our purposes here, supportive therapy can be a useful intervention with the patient who is confused or disorganized. A disorganized patient who is receiving large amounts of neuroleptic drugs may benefit greatly by a relationship in which the patient has an opportunity to explore what is happening to him together with an empathic, concerned human being who strives to teach the patient what kind of behavior is most desirable under the circumstances. The trust engendered by such a relationship will be a critical factor in encouraging the patient's continued cooperativeness in taking medication. When the patient has improved, his trust will make it easier for him to accept a more stressful kind of psychotherapy in which he can develop new learning and new awareness.

The following case illustrates the concurrent use of pharmacotherapy and supportive psychotherapy:

A twenty-one-year-old male student was hospitalized for symptoms of depression, difficulty in concentrating, and inability to get along with fellow students. His fellow students had noted that he was behaving bizarrely, sometimes talking to himself and sometimes failing to understand their efforts to be helpful. When interviewed, the patient admitted to serious difficulties in thinking and to experiencing auditory hallucinations. He was also plagued with fears of impending bodily harm. The patient was viewed as experiencing an acute psychosis, most typical

Practical and Ethical Issues 123

of schizophrenic behaviors and was started on treatment with one of the phenothiazines. He was also told that he would see one of the staff doctors regularly, three times a week for a half hour. The patient was informed that these interviews would be designed to help support him through a difficult time. He was also told he could use the session to talk about whatever he wanted to, but that the therapist might try to help focus the discussion. In the sessions, the therapist made some effort to control the flow of material by selectively reinforcing certain kinds of responses through the use of words and gestures. Once the patient had described his own perception of what was happening to him, little emphasis was placed on discussing the patient's psychotic behavior. Instead the patient was praised when he discussed day-to-day problems and his efforts to deal with them. A good deal of time between therapist and patient was spent in asking about the patient's past history. This was never done in a probing manner; rather, the therapist tried to convey his interest in wanting to learn about the patient and to know him better. The therapist was not adverse to discussing issues seemingly unrelated to the patient's disorder, such as sports and recreation. Sometimes the whole session was devoted to reminiscences of activities such as fishing. Through the therapist's warmth, enthusiasm, and use of positive reinforcement, the patient was regularly reminded that he was liked. Aside from efforts to urge the patient not to express certain aspects of his psychotic behavior which might get him into trouble (such as paranoid feelings about other patients), no pressure was put on him. Whenever he asked for more activities, more responsibilities, or more privileges, he would be reminded that he had been through a great deal of stress and would be urged to be sure that he was ready to take on new tasks. This was done primarily to reassure the patient that he would be liked and accepted by the therapist whether or not he began to behave more conventionally.

There is usually little problem in adding interventions based on behavior modification to the treatment regime of the patient already receiving biological treatment. Often patients who are highly disorganized and who need somatic treatment are hospitalized or placed in environments where they can receive extensive care and observation. The primary purpose of these environments is to protect the patient and those around him, but these are also environments in which new learning can take place. There is much that the patient can learn while experiencing a severe emotional disturbance. Some of this learning is not always helpful, but some of it may be beneficial. The patient can experience the existence of unanticipated benevolence on the part of others. He can learn to deal with feelings he did not previously own to be part of himself. He can develop greater appreciation of his strengths and limitations. And he can also learn new ways of relating to others. The kind of learning the patient experiences is in large part based upon the environment or milieu created for him. While benevolence and lovingness must be included, much of the structure of the therapeutic milieu is based on principles of operant conditioning. In a "good" milieu the patient is reinforced by praise or privileges (or in some highly sophisticated behavioral modification units, by tokens which "buy" him privileges) for being sociable, rational, and concerned with learning more adaptive behavior. At the same time, if the patient behaves irrationally or uses symptoms to gain attention, he is either ignored or punished by being given mild reprimands. The level of sophistication and precision with which this process of reinforcement and extinction is carried out varies from unit to unit. But some form of behavior modification based on operant conditioning is always being used with any patient who is placed in a closely supervised environment, whether or not that patient is receiving concurrent somatic treatment.

Modified forms of group therapy which focus upon providing emotional support can also be utilized with disorganized patients who are concurrently receiving pharmacotherapy. Supportive group therapy is based on principles similar to those involved in supportive individual psychotherapy, but also provides patients the opportunity to learn that their problems are not unique and that they can help one another. The use of concurrent family therapy and pharmacotherapy with highly disturbed patients is more controversial. Disturbed patients who are receiving large dosages of medications which influence their sensorium may have difficulty assimilating the new information usually generated in family interviews. On the other hand, these patients also benefit from the changes in patterns of communication and the stress reduction which can result from even brief family therapy. Not uncommonly, a psychotic patient will look much more sane during and after a productive family interview. My own practice in dealing with severely disturbed patients receiving concurrent somatic treatments is to postpone the initial family interview until the patient has shown some capability of understanding the communications he receives from me, and until I believe he can sit in a room with his family for an hour and a half without becoming panicky or combative. If the patient tolerates the initial family evaluation session well and if there are good indications for family therapy, I will use concurrent family and pharmacological interventions.

Moderately Disturbed Patients

Most clinicians appreciate the advantages of utilizing multiple interventions in treating confused and disorganized patients. There is more controversy over the issue of using multiple interventions with the less disturbed. Much of this controversy is related to the concerns of those highly committed to individual psychotherapy. Conceivably, individual psychotherapy based on provision of new learning and new information may be less effective when combined with other types of intervention. Psychoanalytically oriented psychotherapists, in particular, have striven to keep their interventions pure (Freud 1952, Harper 1961). Some become concerned if their patients use even minor tranquilizers. Others feel that the environmental interventions involved in the behavioral therapies interfere with the psychotherapeutic process. Still others are concerned that the learning and information provided in group and family therapies, and particularly the changes in the natural environment engendered by family therapy, may be disruptive to the process of individual psychotherapy. Their concerns can be specified as follows:

1. The patient in intensive psychoanalytically oriented psychotherapy needs to experience a certain amount of anxiety in order to have optimum motivation to explore his unconscious processes. The use of even minor tranquilizers may diminish the patient's anxiety at crucial moments in psychotherapy so that motivation for new learning is diminished and repression of information about himself is reinforced.

2. The use of behavioral techniques to extinguish symptomatic behavior may in a similar manner diminish the patient's motivation to gain new information about himself.

3. A small number of individual psychotherapists fear that concurrent group therapy might diminish the power of the transference relationship between therapist and patient and might therefore interfere with the course of psychoanalytically oriented individual psychotherapy.

4. Some analytically oriented psychotherapists fear that interventions into the patient's natural environment will either

dilute the intensity of the individual therapy learning situation or diminish the patient's motivations to work at individual psychotherapy. There is the additional concern that, when family therapies are grafted onto individual psychotherapy, the patient may be encouraged to look outward and to view his problems as "caused" by external forces. This may distract the patient from focusing upon his internal psychodynamics.

5. There is also a thread of concern running through almost all schools of individual psychotherapy, whether psychoanalytic, client-centered, or reality oriented, that the patient receiving concurrent drug, behavioral modification, or family therapy (in this case group therapy would not cause as much concern) may experience some erosion of his sense of autonomy. It is feared that if the patient cannot feel that he is accomplishing change largely upon his own, without the assistance of drugs or environmental manipulations, the patient may lose pride, self-respect, and a feeling of responsibility for self (Ford and Urban 1965, London 1964).

Combining individual psychotherapy with pharmacologic, behavior, and group or family therapies could in some instances diminish the patient's motivation to work at individual psychotherapy or attenuate the power and meaningfulness of the individual psychotherapeutic relationship. But I do not believe, nor do I suspect the majority of enlightened psychotherapists believe, that there is a great likelihood that such combination of therapies will have these effects. The small amount of data we do have suggests that pharmacotherapy may often facilitate psychotherapy (Group for the Advancement of Psychiatry 1975). While symptom alleviation may at times decrease motivation to explore feelings, it may at others provide the patient the strength to undertake such exploration. Similar considerations are relevant to the issue of combining behavior modification with psychoanalytically oriented psychotherapy. There are no data to suggest such combinations are deleterious, and it is reasonable to speculate that patients who are relieved of symptoms of paralyzing anxiety might be more self-assured or more motivated to work on long-standing personality problems.

More justified, perhaps, are fears that the power of the therapist to provide effective individual psychotherapy might be diluted if the patient is concurrently receiving group or family therapy. Since the patient will have more than one source of support, such combined therapy might conceivably diminish the patient's dependence on the therapist providing individual therapy. (This would obviously be less of a problem if the same therapist were conducting group or family as well as individual psychotherapy.) If the patient is less dependent, the therapist's power to influence the patient through suggestion, reinforcement, or interpretation could be diminished. There is no way of knowing if this actually happens, but in my opinion there are many factors other than the patient's dependency which provide the therapist with power. Much of the therapist's power, as I shall elaborate later, derives from his skills and his role as a socially sanctioned healer. Some psychoanalysts may also fear that providing the patient with two or more varieties of psychotherapy concurrently will drastically limit the patient's transference responses in individual psychotherapy. It has been my experience that transference responses do not diminish where the patient is having other therapeutic experiences. Sometimes transference responses to individual psychotherapy may be even richer or more intense as a result of concurrent experiences in group or family therapy.

Psychoanalysts could be right when they worry about family therapy distracting the patient's attention from internal psychological processes, but I would not consider such distraction a therapeutic disaster. Often the patient's major problems reside in his interactions with the environment, and it may be therapeutic for him to deal with these problems directly. I also believe that patients who are sophisticated enough to benefit from psychoanalytically oriented individual psychotherapy are capable of focusing upon internal dynamics and current environmental interactions at the same time.

There still remains a question as to whether the patient in individual psychotherapy will lose autonomy if he is concurrently provided biological, behavioral, and family therapies. Here it is important to realize that there are some behaviors and some life situations that an individual cannot simply change through willpower or self-awareness. An individual's autonomy is not diminished if he is helped to deal with situations he can hardly control. When the patient's suffering is extreme and is not responding rapidly enough to individual psychotherapy, the value of autonomy must be tempered by the value of compassion. There is nothing inherently dehumanizing about temporarily allowing others to guide one's destiny. Even the individual psychotherapy relationship fosters a certain amount of dependency and by no means ensures that the patient will obtain greater autonomy. The sense of personal responsibility and autonomy with which the patient leaves therapy will ultimately depend upon the attitudes with which any form of therapy, whether behavioral, family, or somatic, is actually conducted.

Synergistic Interventions

All clinicians should remind themselves that the overall goal of treatment is simply to help the patient and that the goal is more important than the process. If several concurrent therapies are more efficient than one particular therapy, then neglecting one intervention in order to increase the effectiveness of another reflects more of an ideological than a therapeutic purpose. Most patients can, after the acute phase of their disturbance, benefit from the use of medications—including antidepressants, lithium, and major tranquilizers—and intensive psychotherapy at the same time. Behavior therapies can be used concurrently with awareness-expanding therapies. These treatments are likely to enhance one another's effectiveness and can be called *synergistic*. Behavior therapy may make it easier for the patient to work on personality problems, and information generated in intensive psychotherapy will allow the clinician and patient to discover new areas of maladaptive learning which can be changed by behavioral techniques. A similar synergism may exist between group or family psychotherapy and individual psychotherapy. The learning that takes place in the family or group situation can often be examined, expanded upon, and reinforced in the individual psychotherapy situation. At the same time, the learning that takes place in individual psychotherapy can be put to use and perhaps reinforced in the group or family situation.

The following cases illustrate how combined therapies can be used effectively and, at times, synergistically:

A twenty-four-year-old unemployed man requested continuing psychotherapy following the sudden death of a therapist he had been seeing for approximately four years. Five years earlier the patient had been attending college and doing quite well until he began using psychedelic drugs. Following the ingestion of LSD, he experienced an acute psychotic reaction characterized by confusion, great fear of being with people, withdrawal, and obsessional ruminations as to whether he had any special purpose in being put on this earth. He did not hallucinate but often felt that his body was changing, that he might be shrinking, or that his sex might be changing. The patient's illness was severe enough that he had to be hospitalized for several months, and upon release from the hospital, he entered long-term intensive psychotherapy. During four years of therapy, the patient showed only slight improvement. Although able to live outside the hospital, he continued to have distressing symptoms. He became preoccupied with cannibalistic fantasies and also became quite fearful of any inadvertent contact with feces. He constantly feared that he would accidently step on animal droppings and structured much of his life around this fear. For example, on one occasion a friend who had unexpectedly stepped on some dog feces got a small amount of feces on the patient's car. After this the patient refused to drive or go near the car. While the patient's intellectual functions were intact and while he could clearly appreciate the absurdity of his fears (and even make rather clever jokes about them), these fears nevertheless dominated his life. He did not return to school. He did not work and became very dependent on his parents. They catered to his fears and tried to protect him from stress-inducing situations. By the time the patient was seen by his second therapist, he was feeling reasonably comfortable but was in effect leading a sedentary and protected life, was largely withdrawn from social contacts, and had given up all vocational aspirations. The new therapist took a multidimensional approach. The patient was seen in twice-weekly psychotherapy which focused largely upon development of a trusting relationship between him and the therapist. Much time was spent in discussing existential issues and in trying to devise strategies which would facilitate the patient's making small steps toward returning to a less protected existence. At the same time, in spite of the diffuseness of his fears, a program was instituted to try to desensitize him to some of his phobias and obsessions. This work was conducted by another therapist. At the same time a number of sessions were held with the patient and his parents: there was open and frank discussion of the manner in which the parents were reinforcing the patient's sedentary existence. They had for a long time wanted to be less coddling of the patient but were afraid to be more firm lest it result in his relapsing and needing hospitalization. With this combination of individual psychotherapy, behavior modification, and family therapy, the patient gradually began to make changes. As he began to understand both the primary and secondary gains related to his symptoms, he felt strong enough to leave his parents' home and rent his own apartment. He began working part-time. Eventually he moved away from his parents' town and went back to college. He began to date girls occasionally. None of this came easily, and the patient continued to have recurrences of his fear reaction as well as periods of moderate depression. A great deal of the depression, however, was related to his sense of having wasted so many critical years of his life. While the patient still remains somewhat incapacitated in terms of his earlier potentialities, he currently functions fairly well. In this instance the use of behavior modification and family therapy in no way compromised the intensity of the patient's relationship to the individual psychotherapist. In fact these treatments helped provide him the confidence, the focus, and the determination to work more effectively on his existential problems.

A thirty-two-year-old married woman artist sought therapy because of recurrent depression. At the time she was seen, she had just come out of a hospital where she had received a course of electroconvulsive treatments. Her history revealed that she had been hospitalized at least three different times; in each case, severe and massive depression had been preceded by a period of mild elation and great hyperactivity. The patient was a highly energetic, often histrionic, and creative person who related her problems to intense competitiveness with her siblings, a wish to get closer to her father—whom she idolized but who seemed remote—and an inability to establish a relationship with her mother in which she could be treated as an independent adult. In addition, the patient felt there was a great deal wrong with her marriage. She professed to love her husband, but there were times when she could not feel he was providing her enough attention or dependency gratification. At these times she had been prone to seek out extramarital sexual relations, which were unsatisfying and left her feeling guilty. The patient's psychotherapy began just prior to the general acceptance of lithium as a treatment for bipolar affective disorders. She was treated solely with psychotherapy for about a year. During this time she seemed to be making slight progress. Near the end of the year her husband became involved with another woman and began to withdraw from the patient, who began to show symptoms of both hyperactivity and depression. By this time lithium therapy was available and was instituted. The patient's more distressing symptoms were quickly alleviated. As she felt better and more confident about the capacity of newer treatments to abort future attacks of mania or depression, she was able to relate much more honestly to the therapist and to do some working through of her serious problems with her parents and husband. As with many manic patients, she was so narcissistic, so self-satisfied, and so resistant to psychological exploration when feeling well that progress came slowly. It is unlikely that she would have made much progress in psychotherapy, however, without concurrent lithium therapy.

Practical and Ethical Issues

A thirty-year-old single male professor sought intensive psychotherapy for symptoms of disturbing obsessional thoughts and moderate feelings of anxiety in most of his interpersonal contacts. He was quite successful in his work but had few friends. He felt that his sexual involvements were casual and uninteresting. During the first six months of intensive analytically oriented psychotherapy, the patient was highly cooperative and talkative but relied heavily on intellectualization. Feelings were discussed but not expressed. Transference responses were minimal. On the advice of an acquaintance, the patient decided to attend a weekend marathon which was being held in the same town by a Gestalt therapist of some repute. The patient asked the therapist's permission to participate, and the therapist, with some trepidation, gave it. At the marathon session the patient was rather heavily worked over for his aloofness, his intellectualization, and his conveying of a sense of superiority. The patient found himself desperately wanting to be accepted by group members and yet constantly coming across to them as uninterested, cold, and distant. He returned to psychotherapy somewhat shaken. In the next few weeks, however, he began to talk about noting deep feelings of dependency toward the therapist which he found both enjoyable and frightening. He was able to relate many of these feelings to earlier childhood experience and in the next few months was able to free up a great deal of repressed emotionality and experienced considerable symptomatic relief. While sensitivity groups which focus on attacking the participants' defenses can be harmful to some patients, in this instance the group experience served to catalyze the patient's responsiveness to individual psychotherapy. The patient had received a powerful message as to how he was influencing others. This shattered his composure and greatly increased his motivation to discover the reasons for his behavior.

A twenty-year-old male student entered psychotherapy somewhat reluctantly after several brushes with the law involving the sale of illegal drugs and sexual relations with a sixteen-year-old girl. He had been put on probation and one of the conditions of probation was that he start psychotherapy. His parents had also put a great deal of pressure on him to seek help. Although an intellectually gifted person, the patient was functioning marginally in school, just doing enough work to get by, and spending most of his time "partying," seducing women, and experimenting with a wide variety of drugs. One aspect of this patient's personality problem, which was immediately apparent in psychotherapy, was his ambivalence toward authority figures. He seemed to want the therapist to like him and also seemed to like the therapist but had almost conditioned responses of disdain, distrust, and abrasiveness in his therapeutic interactions. His behavior to professors and other authority figures was quite similar. After two months of therapy the patient's parents were asked to come in for conjoint therapy, and several sessions were held with the family unit. During these sessions the parents together with the patient were able to clearly delineate certain patterns of interaction. The patient seemed to desperately want to be closer to his father, but somehow or other he always reacted with hostility when such closeness seemed obtainable. At the same time the patient felt too dependent upon his mother, whom he considered a "soft touch" who could be manipulated to indulge his whims. Following these family sessions the patient's individual therapy continued and there was a marked shift in the patient's perception of the therapist. The patient was able to allow himself to be somewhat more dependent and began to talk more desperately about his wish to respect his father. He revealed how disappointed he had been during early adolescence when he first became aware of his father's limitations. As the patient discussed these issues, he was able to become more acceptant of his father. Some of his authority problems became less pronounced, and his school work dramatically improved. He also became more aware of the extent of his dependency upon his mother and of how he was generalizing his resentment of her to other women. As he worked on these issues, his relationships with women became less exploitative and slightly more loving. In this instance family therapy (while not exactly concurrent with individual therapy) served to clarify the problem, to increase the patient's transference responses, and to increase his motivation to work on intrapsychic conflicts. In a sense, family therapy served for this young man as an "in vivo" opportunity to receive direct information as to the reasons for his current behavior. The patient had previously possessed a fairly good understanding of how he was behaving, but family therapy, by facilitating his understanding of his motivations, led to a striking change in his willingness to explore new patterns of behavior.

A nineteen-year-old woman student complained of chronic feelings of anxiety with regard to her school work. Although she was performing quite well, she constantly felt that she was not doing as well as she should be and was haunted by vague fears that something was wrong with her. Her social life seemed quite satisfactory although it was at times compromised by her obsessive concern with school performance. Her friends would tease her about being so preoccupied with schoolwork that

Practical and Ethical Issues   133

she avoided real involvement with them. The patient did not know the roots of her uneasiness. She insisted that she could not have learned such behavior from her parents, who had always told her that they had no expectations of her other than wanting her to be happy and to enjoy life. After several individual psychotherapy sessions the patient's parents as well as her older brother and sister were seen in a conjoint interview. While the parents continued to espouse their reluctance to put pressure on the patient and while they repeatedly stated they were concerned only with her happiness, her siblings revealed that they had always felt under great, if subtle, pressure from their parents to be vocationally and academically superior. The older sister was an A student who had already been accepted to medical school. When confronted with the communication of the older siblings, the parents conceded that they both had extremely powerful wishes for their children to be highly successful. Both parents felt that they had not accomplished up to their potentials in life, and they nourished not-too-secret wishes that their children's performance would compensate their own deficiencies. At the same time they felt it wrong to push their children and had tried to convince themselves that they could avoid putting undue pressure on them. As the patient heard all this, she began to appreciate that much of her anxiety was related to inconsistent communication as to the expectations of her parents. She used this new information well and in subsequent individual therapy hours worked hard on trying to determine what part of her motivation was internalized and unrealistic and what part was a response to continuing but covert family pressures. As she worked on this problem, her anxiety significantly diminished and her interpersonal relationships improved. In this instance family therapy helped the patient to understand the impact that a significant part of the environment was having upon her, and she was able to use this information to clarify the extent to which intrapsychic and environmental factors were influencing her. In the process of such clarification she was able to come to a realistic acceptance of her own motivations and limitations and was also able to deal more directly with covert but powerful messages from her environment.

The Clinician's Attitude

The attitude of the clinician may be the most important factor in the successful use of concurrent multiple therapies. Many patients have simplistic views of causality. If they receive multiple therapies and their condition improves, they will often attribute their change to only one of the therapies and may lose some of their inclination to participate enthusiastically in the others. Since somatic therapies bring on powerful and rapid behavioral changes and require little active participation on the part of the patient, they are likely to be viewed as the sole initiators of change. When this happens, there is some danger that the patient will be less motivated to work in other therapies and will develop a passive outlook toward therapy in general. The clinician can mitigate this tendency by carefully explaining to the patient how each therapy works and that each intervention is only part of the treatment process. If the clinician communicates to the patient his feeling that one modality of therapy is far more powerful than another, the patient is likely to relate his improvement to that modality. But if the clinician carefully explains the role of each intervention, the patient will have a rational basis for understanding how both his own efforts and the treatments have contributed to his improvement.

The following case illustrates how the clinician's failure to provide sufficient explanation of treatment effects can be harmful to the patient:

A couple sought family counseling after the wife became depressed upon learning of her husband's long history of and recent involvement in homoerotic acts. The husband had received considerable individual psychotherapy and was convinced that while he could do nothing about changing his homosexual feelings, he could control his homosexual behavior and have a happy marriage. The wife claimed to be hurt by her husband's recent sexual behavior, but could feel no anger toward him. She did feel distant and estranged from him. After a few weeks of family therapy, the wife's depression deepened. She asked for antidepressant medication, which I was reluctant to prescribe. Finally, after a session in which she seemed to be experiencing great psychic pain, I prescribed a moderate dosage of Elavil. That same night the couple had a stormy fight in which she for the first time expressed the anger she felt toward her husband. She took her first Elavil tablet, went to bed, and awoke the next morning feeling relieved of all symptoms. Her improvement was sustained, but she was reluctant both to give up her medication and to continue marital therapy. While her depression did not return, it took me several months to persuade her to discontinue drug therapy because she was convinced the drug was essential to her cure.

In this case it would seem unlikely that medication could have done anything more than ensure the patient a good night's sleep.

Practical and Ethical Issues

Her improvement was probably more directly related to the enhanced communication between her and her husband, her awareness of her anger, and her ability to express it. Continued marital therapy might have helped both partners learn more about their interactions and might have helped to prevent future depressions. But the patient was no longer interested in such therapy and instead for several months took a drug she probably did not need. In retrospect, I feel that my attitude in prescribing the antidepressant drug influenced the patient's attitude toward her "cure." My reluctance to prescribe the drug may have convinced her I was withholding a potent agent of change, and my failure to explain its effects and overall place in the treatment plan may also have helped her to see it as the sole "curative" agent.

Timing of Multiple Interventions

I have argued that, with the exception of combining powerful somatic therapies with stress-inducing psychotherapies, there is little justification for rejecting the use of concurrent therapies. This does not mean that the patient must be exposed to a variety of concurrent interventions from the first day of treatment. In practice the patient's first experienced intervention is diagnostic evaluation by the clinician. This evaluation, which is usually supportive and exploratory at the same time, embodies many of the attributes of individual psychotherapy. For a brief time, such "evaluation therapy" may be the only intervention the patient receives. Somatic interventions are not immediately initiated unless the patient's disturbance is severe. Behavior modification should not be utilized for clinical and ethical reasons until the patient's learning problem is rigorously defined. The indications for group therapy may not immediately be apparent. And key family members may not be available to help in the diagnostic or therapeutic process. Thus most intervention begins with a brief dyadic psychotherapeutic approach. The clinician obviously has much flexibility in determining when a new intervention is to be added. Ordinarily, the clinician can follow guidelines offered in the previous chapters in deciding when to add a new intervention.

Just as interventions may be introduced at different times, they may also be terminated at different times. The multidimensional approach does not demand that the clinician use all modalities of intervention indiscriminately and indefinitely. A given intervention should be used only so long as there is a diagnostic hypothesis that justifies its use. Many patients receiving antidepressant therapy can discontinue their medication after being asymptomatic for several months. At the same time it may be necessary to continue these patients in some kind of psychotherapy. There is some argument as to when patients who behave in a schizophrenic manner should have their antipsychotic medication discontinued, but my own experience is that after several months of remission the biological processes which sustain psychotic behavior have changed and that many of these patients function as well with psychotherapeutic approaches alone. Behavior therapies can be discontinued once target behaviors have changed. Family therapies can be dropped once environment-related problems have been dealt with, and then the patient, if motivated, may continue to learn more about his personality difficulties in individual or group psychotherapy. Conversely, individual or group psychotherapy can be discontinued and family therapy continued when it becomes clear that the patient's current problems are related primarily to environmental factors.

ETHICAL CONSIDERATIONS

Thus far my focus has been largely upon the value of efficiency. Passing references have been made to ethical issues, but the overall approach has been rather cold-blooded and has not focused on the influence of treatment upon social systems, the patient's wishes, or the patient's rights. It is now time to turn to ethical considerations which may be critical in determining choice of treatment. My discussion here will focus upon general problems related to the values of autonomy, preserving the patient's potentials, and compassion. I will delay extended discussion of the risks and ethical problems involved in the use of specific therapies until the second part of the book.

The Politics of Therapy

Clinical interventions have powerful social and political consequences for patients and those involved with them. It is not possible to change people's behavior without altering the nature of their interaction with interpersonal and social environments. Behavioral intervention, whether heroic or tentative, always leaves the individual in a social position somewhat different from that enjoyed or suffered before intervention. Sometimes the social results of intervention are obvious. A person who is lobotomized may behave in a more socially acceptable manner but will at the same time be deprived of the opportunity to fully enjoy many gratifying human experiences. The social consequences of most other interventions are less obvious. But whenever we do things to patients that change the way they relate to others or the way others see them, we have modified their social position. And, of course, when we treat patients' family systems or other natural parts of the environment we are again changing their social position. Most of the time we assume or hope that our interventions not only will make our patients feel better but will also favorably affect their relationship to a future environment. This is not always true. The least benign appearing intervention can alter individual-environmental interaction so as to effectively diminish the patient's potential.

The dictum that interventions should not greatly compromise an individual's potential imposes an additional complexity upon clinical practice. People exist as elements of social systems, within which they have a certain degree of status and power. Used insensitively, most forms of psychological intervention can subtly strip the patient of both of these. Many practitioners have an orientation toward emotional disorders which encourages them to ignore environmental variables as etiological factors and to focus almost entirely on the individual. If the problem is seen as residing within the individual and if significant figures in the patient's environment are viewed as blameless, there is a subtle shift in power relationships between the patient and those around him. To the extent that the patient is viewed as diseased, "mad," irrational, and in need of help, and the environment is viewed as neutral or normal, the patient loses power, and those that may have played a role in creating his illness gain power. This process is much more intense when the patient is given some type of psychiatric label and is viewed as not being responsible for his behavior. The oppressive potentiality of psychiatric labeling is well documented (Szasz 1965, Lemert 1972). Once labeled as sick, an individual's judgments, actions, and opinions may not be taken seriously, and much of the capacity to influence others is lost.

An approach to diagnosis and treatment which ignores the influence of environmental variables not only fails to meet the patient's needs, but also is unscientific. Behaviors which we view as psychological symptoms always have some important relationship to the patient's environment. Up to now I have focused upon the way symptoms may be created or influenced by stressful environments and have noted that symptoms can have an influence on the environment which lead to their being reinforced. Here it will be useful to expand upon the nature of reinforcement and upon the manner in which symptoms have a communicative purpose. Symptoms provide the patient certain social benefits. They can sometimes be viewed as purposeful efforts to deal with an oppressive environment by creating conditions which require the environment to change in a manner that provides the patient certain gratifications. A husband who feels that his wife has been ignoring him can regain her attention by communcating to her that he is depressed or anxious. A wife who feels oppressed by a dominating husband who takes great pride in his sexual prowess may diminish his influence by becoming sexually unresponsive. Symptoms can also have purposes which neither patients nor those around them are fully aware of. The anxious and depressed husband, for example, could also be trying to tell his wife to treat him like a child or to feel guilty for having contributed to his misery. The sexually unresponsive wife could be trying to let her husband know that she feels unloved and is angry with him.

The use of symptoms, on a largely unconscious basis, to change a social system is illustrated in the following sense:

A twenty-four-year-old married woman entered the hospital with an initial complaint of a compulsive need to clean her house. This symptom had been present for eight months, and since such compulsive behavior is not usually incapacitating, it was intitially unclear to the hospital staff why she had voluntarily sought hospitalization. An examination of her social situation, however, revealed serious conflicts. The patient had married while in high school. Her husband had been an athletic hero who, upon graduation from high school, lost much of his status in the community and worked at a menial job. The patient saw herself as being much more intelligent, sensitive, and sophisticated than her husband. Yet he insisted on dominating the relationship. He would not let her visit with certain friends, insisted upon having his meals on time, and in general, behaved like a stereotyped male chauvinist Shortly before the onset of her symptoms the patient had a brief love affair with a traveling salesman who, she stated, treated her tenderly and convinced her she was a "beautiful person." During this time the patient lost interest in sexual relations with her husband. Nevertheless he insisted on having sexual relations and, with vigorous and sustained efforts, would usually succeed in getting her aroused even when she did not wish to be. During this period the compulsive housecleaning began.

The patient obviously felt great ambivalence about remaining in the marriage, but also seemed genuinely unaware of her wish to get out of it. In her first interview she reported two dreams, one in which her legs had been cut off and the other in which her wedding ring had been suddenly swept off her finger and flushed down the drain. It appeared that while there may have been many intrapsychic or previously learned determinants to her compulsive symptomatology, including massive guilt, one of the purposes of her symptoms was to avoid involvement, particularly sexual involvement, with her husband. One of her purposes in seeking hospitalization was to try either to do something about a totally unbearable equilibrium in the marriage or to get out of it. Her coming to the hospital did succeed in arousing the husband's concern about their relationship sufficiently that he agreed to participate in family therapy. She returned home and, while the marriage remained stormy, her husband did make several concessions and her symptoms totally disappeared. It should be clear in this instance that if the compulsive behavior had been treated without recognition of the social circumstances engendering it (this could easily have been done using some form of behavior modification), there would have been serious questions as to the ethical propriety of such intervention.

Even behavior that is defined as symptomatic or unreasonable by those associated with the patient can be viewed as having an influence-seeking purpose. For example, a person who is aggressive toward others or who regularly breaks the law is usually trying to change something in his environment. He may not actually know what it is he is trying to change; he may feel that he is just doing what he must do in order to survive in a hostile world. But his actions may in part be determined by an unconscious wish to change the nature of relationships or the distribution of power within his family. They might also be viewed as efforts to modify his perceived status as an oppressed person within the community. While the net result of aggressiveness or delinquency is unpredictable, the patient's aggressive actions will always change some aspect of his relationship to the family or the community system.

I have argued that symptoms can be viewed as indirect or symbolic attempts to communicate. Because those around the patient have difficulty deciphering the messages communicated by symptoms, their responses to symptoms are likely to be less predictable than if the patient had communicated more directly. The wife who is attempting to make her husband more attentive may accomplish this through frigidity, but her symptoms could also anger the husband and make him even more withdrawn. The delinquent child who is trying to alter an oppressive environment may find that his aggressive actions change relationships within his family system or within the community, but might also find that his aggressiveness leads his family or the community to retaliate by committing him to an even more oppressive environment, such as a training school. Communication through symptoms is risky. Many variables outside the patient's control determine whether such communication diminishes or increases the patient's power. But when those involved with the patient care about him, symptoms may represent the only influence the patient has over his family or other significant figures.

All of this means that the practitioner who simply focuses upon problems within the individual and treats the patient's symptoms without helping the patient deal with other aspects of the environment is taking an incomplete and unscientific approach to treatment and risks compromising the patient's future potentials. Practitioners who focus primarily upon changing the individual often use biological interventions or forms of behavior therapy primarily directed at relieving symptoms. These therapies are not usually designed to change or help patients deal with oppressive environments. The short-run gain of symptom relief in such cases may not be worth the long-term perpetuation of oppressive conditions which could have been changed by dealing with the environment as well as the individual. If a woman develops symptoms of severe anxiety in response to her husband's lack of interest or cruelty, treating her anxiety with a drug or with some form of behavior modification would still leave her facing a highly oppressive marital situation. If an economically and emotionally deprived child behaves in an aggressive manner and is treated for his aggression with some type of drug or behavior modification technique, he would not only still be trapped in the same environment but also would lose some of his ability to sustain any kind of socially useful aggressiveness which might enable him to escape that environment.

A general rule can be derived from these considerations. Unless the patient is experiencing great distress, treatments focusing on symptom relief (usually biological treatments and behavior modification) should not be used as the sole form of intervention without first thoroughly evaluating the patient's environment, and then only if the therapist has a firm belief that simple relief of symptoms will not compromise the patient's future potentials. In most instances the clinician will discover that environmental factors play a significant role in the patient's disturbance and will wish to use at least some type of information-providing or environmental-stress-reducing intervention in addition to symptom therapy. At the very least the patient is entitled, either through his talks with the therapist or through some type of family therapy, to gain a clear picture of just what those in the environment expect of him and are doing to him. It is even more desirable for the patient to learn the extent to which his symptoms are related to environmental stress and how his symptoms influence the environment. Ideally, the patient should also be assisted by interventions that help change his environment. Sometimes the additional interventions must be intensive, but often the patient can be helped to learn about or deal with his environment in a few sessions or even during the process of evaluation.

While it should be almost a mandate for the clinician to always be prepared to combine symptomatic treatment with some sort of intervention designed to help the patient deal with the environment, there are some exceptions. I have already alluded to the issue of the severity of symptoms. If a patient is in great distress, his symptoms should be treated immediately and the environment investigated later. There are other situations in which symptomatic treatments alone may be adequate. Once a particular behavior pattern has proved useful to the patient in dealing with his environment, the patient may continue that behavior even after the disturbing situation has changed. His symptoms can then be viewed as either bad habits or physiological sysfunctions which linger on to plague him long after their causes have disappeared. If a woman with a brutal and insensitive husband learns to be frigid in trying to gain some control over the marital relationship, she may remain frigid even though her husband becomes more solicitous. If she finds a new husband who treats her considerately, she may still be frigid. Similarly, an aggressive youth may continue to act the same way even if he is placed in a truly benevolent environment. It is always possible that these patients are now having their deviant behavior reinforced by a benevolent environment. Sometimes, however, the presence of such reinforcement is not ascertainable and the clinician may assume that the process of symptom perpetuation has, on some type of biological or learning basis, become internalized.

Symptoms no longer related to environmental determinants can be thought of as autonomous symptoms. In terms of the patient's current needs, they are purposeless. Although every symptom has a certain communicative value, there may be some justification for trying to treat autonomous symptoms directly without trying to help the individual cope with or change the environment. If the environment has already become more benevolent, the patient could, in theory, benefit by ridding himself of symptoms through the use of somatic therapies or some form of behavior therapy.

This statement should be qualified by a reminder that the clinician must make a strenuous effort to ascertain that a benevolent environment is not reinforcing the autonomous symptom. A frigid woman may find that her sexual unresponsiveness even with benevolent partners elicits certain responses from them which are gratifying insofar as they allow her to retain power in the conjugal relationship. An aggressive youth may continue to be aggressive in a benign environment at least partly because people treat him solicitously when he is belligerent. If a benevolent environment is reinforcing symptoms that appear to be autonomous, the clinician may not be doing harm to the patient by using only symptomatic treatment and avoiding dealing with the environment, but the clinician's task will certainly be facilitated if he combines symptomatic treatment with family therapy designed to diminish reinforcement of symptomatic behavior. The issue here seems more practical than ethical, but the ethical implications should not be ignored. In the case of the frigid woman or the aggressive youth, symptom relief will still be accompnied by loss of power, and in each case the patient as well as the clinician should be aware of this possiblity. Conceivably a patient who is fully aware of the social implications of symptom removal, even in a benign environment, might elect to keep his symptoms.

Another type of ethical problem can arise when the clinician is too vigorous in exposing and changing stressful family systems. Patients who suddenly gain awareness of how other family members have been influencing them can become quite aggressive

Practical and Ethical Issues

in interacting with people toward whom they had previously behaved passively. Sometimes in the course of treatment a family member who had been persuaded to enter treatment in order to help the patient may become so disturbed by the patient's change in manner of relating that he too will become symptomatic. This happens often in family therapy, but fortunately such disturbances are usually transitory and as a rule a more satisfactory mode of relating can be worked out for all participants. Nevertheless the clinician can never be assured of a happy outcome and has the ethical responsibility to protect people who may never have sought treatment in the first place from being harmed by his interventions.

So far I have considered the ethical problems of intervention primarily as they relate to small social systems such as the family. But the community or society as a whole may also be stressful. (It may even reinforce maladaptive behavior by providing selected individuals with greater monetary rewards for being sick than for being well.) Interventions can be used to encourage adjustment to the social system or to encourage rebelliousness. There is always some risk that our interventions will make some patients adjust to a "bad" environment and make some patients too rebellious to adjust to a "good" environment. Our interventions can certainly strengthen the political status quo and more rarely they can help to change it. In *The Politics of Therapy* I discussed this problem in great detail and tried to emphasize how the clinician might help the patient in dealing with a "bad" environment (1971). I concluded that the clinician had a right to try to change social institutions he judged oppressive and had an obligation to increase his patient's awareness of how social oppression might contribute to their disorders. My opinions have not changed. I still believe that many social conditions in our society, including poverty, racism, and sexism, are important factors in causing many emotional disorders. Patients are benefited by becoming more aware of these conditions. Such awareness may allow the patient to adopt an explanation of his disturbance which is not self-punitive and will provide him a sense of direction as to how social conditions might be changed to improve his plight. There can be no guarantee that awareness of social oppression will lead to the patient's doing anything about it, but the patient with that awareness does at least have the choice of accepting or trying to change the status quo.

While I remain convinced that the clinician should help the patient find new ways to change an oppressive environment, I have no new guidelines to offer the clinician in accomplishing this task. I have some hope, however, that the system of diagnosis and treatment I have presented will minimize the oppressive use of therapeutic interventions. If the multidimensional approach does nothing else, it at least directs the clinician and patient to look at the total social environment as well as the individual. Neither the clinician nor the patient may know how to change the most pernicious stresses within that environment, but a willingness to consider the impact of the environment at least diminishes the possibility that the clinician will utilize a one-dimensional intervention that will do nothing but encourage the patient to make a desperate adjustment to oppressive conditions. In my more optimistic moments I can even convince myself that scrupulous adherence to a multidimensional model not only increases the efficiency of treatment but also increases the probability that the clinician's approach will be liberating and humanistic.

Motivation and Autonomy

Another factor thus far neglected in developing a model for selecting treatment has been the wishes of the patient. In a society which values individual autonomy, the patient's wishes should be a major factor in determining treatment. For a variety of reasons it is a much less powerful factor than mental health practitioners usually assume. Many practitioners exaggerate the patient's role in choosing treatment because they are unduly influenced by their experiences in treating an elitist group of patients who are highly informed as to the varieties of behavioral intervention, who are usually well-off financially, and whose troubles are not likely to be incapacitating. There are patients, for example, who are eager to undergo psychoanalysis and who, for reasons of professional improvement, prestige, or ideological commitment, would be unlikely to consent to any treatment other than psychoanalysis. There are other patients who have similar feelings about Gestalt therapy, transactional analysis, or reality therapy. The clinician who sees mainly sophisticated patients who approach treatment without urgency and without too much concern as to the costs can easily convince himself that most patients exercise free choice in selecting treatment. But in clinical practice sophisticated patients are the exception rather than the rule. The great majority of

Practical and Ethical Issues

patients who seek help know very little about therapeutic interventions and do not voice preference as to how they should be treated. Generally they request only that they be treated as quickly and as inexpensively as possible.

There is another group of patients (but still a minority) who may not have a clear idea of what kind of treatment they want but who have definite opinions about what kind they do not want. Some will be vigorously opposed to involving their families in any aspect of their treatment. Some will resist behavior therapy on the grounds it is dehumanizing. Other patients will be unwilling to participate in group therapy, while still others will vigorously oppose any form of biological intervention. Unless the clinician can dissuade these patients, their wishes must be honored. Treatment cannot be imposed upon unwilling patients unless they have been civilly committed and found incompetent.

With the exception of highly sophisticated patients or those with some unusual preference or distaste for a particular treatment, the mass of patients exercise little choice in determining their treatment. Most people come to the clinician because they are suffering. In their desperation they will cooperate with their therapist whether they are told to explore their unconscious, to get in touch with their feelings, to understand their "child," to be more responsible for their actions, or to take medicines which will make them feel better. The majority of patients treated in America, whether by medical or nonmedical therapists, are swayed by the authority of the healer. They follow the advice of the therapist, and are likely to be treated in a manner their therapist believes best for them.

When the patient's motivations occasionally influence the clinician's choice of treatment, such influence is likely to lead to exclusion of certain treatment. The clinician may note that some patients are seeking goals not likely to be met by certain treatment modalities. A patient not interested in more gratifying relationships with family members might not be a good candidate for family therapy. A patient who is not introspective and who has no wish to expand his self-awareness might not be a good candidate for psychoanalysis. A patient who does not want to change his manner of relating to others might not be a good candidate for group psychotherapy or intensive individual psychotherapy. Sensitive clinicians will consider these issues in determining treatment and will not be too vigorous in recommending interventions that seem incongruent with the patient's expressed motivations.

Most patients, however, are flexible and do not come to treatment with powerful motivations that would preclude the use of most therapies. These patients may have some idea of what kind of treatment they need but, easily influenced by the therapist's perceptions of their needs, they often in the course of evaluation come to redefine their goals accordingly. The patient may be convinced that he has been seeking too much or too little. He may be persuaded that independence from the family cannot come about until he has made peace with his family. He may be persuaded that his need to focus on the present cannot be gratified until he has come to terms with his past. Or he may be persuaded that his wish to dwell on the past is really a resistance to making changes in the present. In the process of negotiation of goals and values between therapist and patient, it is the therapist who wields the greater power. Even the nondirective therapist provides powerful messages that the pursuit of certain goals is essential to the patient's cure. The psychoanalyst may spend years subtly trying to help the patient learn to accept either more modest or more ambitious goals, while the existential or growth-oriented therapist may directly or indirectly influence the patient toward greater ambition.

The pure behaviorist probably comes as close as any therapist to trying to give patients exactly what they want. If the patient is able to define a target behavior that he wants removed or developed, the behaviorist tries to comply directly with the patient's wishes by creating an environment providing appropriate extinction or reinforcement. But even the behaviorist cannot always accede to the patient's wishes. Patients may request behavioral changes that the therapist may view as unethical or illegal. To use an extreme example, it is unlikely that a behaviorist would try to use systematic desensitization in treating a "second-story man" who has developed a fear of heights. It is also true that behavior therapists have become increasingly concerned with the patient's need to develop new behaviors, such as assertiveness, which they feel will influence the patient's overall adjustment as well as his symptoms. Greater assertiveness is rarely a conscious goal of patients who seek behavior therapy. When assertiveness training becomes a standard part of the treatment program, it is the behavior therapist and not the patient who is exercising the greater influence in determining goals.

Practical and Ethical Issues   147

   Although I have argued that the patient has little influence in determining the choice of treatment, neither I nor most other clinicians are content with this situation. The patient's autonomy is severely compromised when he is too passive a participant in treatment decisions. Most clinicians would prefer to deal with patients on a more egalitarian basis and to allow the patient to have considerable influence in selecting treatment. How this can be done when the clinician is also committed to providing the patient the most effective treatment is a problem best dealt with by trying to expand the patient's knowledge of what is wrong with him and how his disorder might be treated. The degree of self-serving choice available to the patient is directly proportional to his degree of knowledge.
   I believe the clinician has the responsibility to inform the patient at each stage of the diagnostic evaluation just what the clinician thinks is causing the disturbance. The clinician also has the responsibility to inform the patient as to which treatments might help him and to describe the potential benefits and disadvantages of each. In effect the clinician should list a series of possible treatments or combination of treatments, should describe their probable effectiveness as determined by weighing possible benefits against possible costs and risks, should indicate his own treatment preferences, and should then be willing to ask the patient to participate in the selection of his own treatment. Patients who are not severely disorganized will then become relatively informed participants in a dialogue that determines choice of treatment. Most fully informed patients will still accede to the clinician's preferences, but they will at least have a greater opportunity to insist on a different treatment, and some will. Through this kind of sharing of knowledge the clinician both expands the autonomy of the patient and increases the probability that the patient's consent to receive a given treatment meets the legal criteria for informed consent.
   Let me try to anticipate some of the urgent and troubling questions my discussion may have raised.
   Question: Are you actually urging the clinician to tell a patient his diagnosis? Would you tell a patient he is schizophrenic?
   Answer: My preference is to avoid putting diagnostic labels on patients whenever possible since our current labels lack the precision of labels in other fields of medicine. Most often I find it useful to describe to the patient as accurately as I can how he has been behaving and then to present hypotheses I have formulated

which might explain that behavior. Some patients insist on a label or have a tendency to impose a label upon themselves, either by imagining the worst or by consulting textbooks of psychiatry. When I anticipate this, I try, if I can truthfully, to tell the patient he does not have the "disease" he fears. Sometimes, however, it makes sense to tell people who are sophisticated and worried about themselves exactly how they might be labeled under current nomenclature. It need not be devastating to tell someone that he has evidenced a cluster of behaviors we have come to define as schizophrenic as long as we are clear in presenting the uncertainty and multiplicity of hypotheses of schizophrenic behavior, can point out the possibilities of a hopeful prognosis, and can point to treatment modalities that will change the undesirable behavior.

Questions: Are you urging the clinician to spell out to the patient those psychodynamics he can detect in the patient before treatment starts? Won't the patient use this knowledge as a resistance in subsequent treatment? Won't such knowledge upset the patient?

Answers: It is hard to determine at what point the clinician should decide to share with the patient those hypothetical musings still embryonic in the clinician's mind. I do feel, however, that if the clinician has firm convictions as to the dynamic process going on within the patient or within the field of the patient's interaction with others, and if these convictions have some relationship to the choice of treatment, they should be shared. I am not urging clinicians to provide patients elaborate conceptualizations of their psychodynamics. Most of these speculations are irrelevant to the immediate question of choice of treatment. I am urging that the patient be provided simple explanations of his problem and how it indicates certain treatments. In general, information related to how the patient is behaving is most relevant in the early stages of evaluation or treatment. Causal information, particularly as it relates to the influence of an individual's past learning or present behavior, is more difficult to formulate and must be presented more gradually.

It is always possible that premature explanations of his behavior will be rejected by the patient. But there is no reason why this should discourage him from seeking further treatment. If the patient should elect to undergo long-term psychotherapy, he might conceivably use intellectual insights gained from the therapist's early explanations as a resistance to further self-exploration. But this possible deleterious effect of sharing information with the patient may well be counterbalanced by such positive effects as the promotion of psychological mindedness. Intellectual insights are not always used as resistances. They can also prepare the patient to accept a more meaningful, emotional awareness.

There is a more ominous possibility, that the clinician's formulation of the problem may be destructive of the patient's self-esteem. I believe we generally underestimate the patient's ability to face hard truth, but the clinician must of course exercise some caution to avoid overwhelming the patient with unwelcome information. Any of the clinician's hypotheses which might be devastating to the patient can be withheld until the clinician feels the patient is able to hear them without being overly stressed.

Question: Can patients actually understand explanations of what is wrong with them and how various interventions can help them?

Answer: The clinician should always assess his patient's cognitive abilities and not overwhelm the patient with complicated explanations. It is critical that the clinician's explanations be free of jargon. Actually, if the clinician truly comprehends his hypotheses with regard to the patient's disorder he should be able to explain them in jargon-free language to a rational patient of average or near-average intelligence. I have always felt that the ability to explain diagnostic and treatment issues to the patient without using jargon is one of the best indices of professional competence. Obviously, if a patient is disoriented or irrational, the clinician's sharing of information will be postponed.

Question: Do you recommend that the clinician inform patients of the role their family and society have played in determining their behavior, even when this role may be somewhat malevolent?

Answer: Yes. The patient has as much right to know about the environment's impact upon him as he does about his own impact upon the environment or his own intrapsychic process. In those instances where the clinician may have interviewed family members without the patient present, there is sometimes a temptation on the part of family members to reveal information they ask not to be shared with the patient. If the clinician does see a family member without the patient present, it should be made clear that no secrets will be kept from the patient. The patient has a right to know whatever the clinician knows.

The clinician will certainly wish to be careful that he does not overemphasize environmental determinants to the extent that the patient is encouraged to resist looking at his own role in creating his disorder. Nor should family or other social factors ever be viewed as factors which can be invested with complete blame or responsibility for what the patient does. Rather the clinician should as matter-of-factly as possible explain the manner in which he feels the patient's environment has influenced the patient's disorder. Some clinicians fear the patient's early discovery of malevolence on the part of those close to him may be detrimental. This has rarely, in my experience, been the case. Such revelation may lead to a profound emotional reaction on the part of the patient, but generally these experiences are followed by considerable relief and a sense of well-being.

The clinician's social and political sophistication of course determines the extent to which he can interpret how the patient has been affected by society. Here, of course, there will be much disagreement among clinicians as to what type of information should be offered. Some clinicians are more likely than others to see the current status quo as desirable. Others will be much more aware of the manner in which social conditions create or sustain emotional dysfunction. In my own experience, there are social causes of certain behavior disorders which are obvious; these should be made explicit to the patient. If a man's depression is related to an early retirement with an inadequate pension, the clinician would be remiss in not reminding the patient that social circumstances have a great deal to do with his illness. Some might argue that simply reminding the patient of harsh environmental realities is little more effective than rubbing salt in a wound. I believe, however, that to whatever extent the patient can identify the sources of his oppression he is more capable of rationally dealing with them. To put it somewhat pithily, a person who knows he is "being screwed" by others can retain more equanimity in the face of adversity than a person who feels he has in some mysterious way injured himself. Again there is a question of balance here. The clinician must invoke all possible hypotheses and not fall into the trap of allowing the patient to blame external sources for his difficulty when the patient is still very capable of doing something about his situation. A man who loses his job because of social changes he cannot control, might, for example, find useful alternatives for dealing with his loss if he could overcome some of his intrapsychic problems.

It is well, in this regard, to recall that although most schools of psychotherapy tend to hold the individual totally responsible for

Practical and Ethical Issues 151

his behavior, there are always some things in life an individual can do little about. One cannot, for example, be responsible for his genes or for a defective state of his brain function. The individual can be held responsible for the manner in which he deals with biological defects, but the individual is not responsible for having them. There are also sociological limitations upon behavior. People cannot choose to do just anything. Their choices are limited by social and political conditions. The black child raised in a ghetto who is deprived of proper nutrition and schooling and who grows up to be illiterate and unsuccessful cannot be told that he is responsible for having shaped such a destiny. There are things he can do about his situation, but there are also stringent social limits upon his choices. It helps the patient to be aware of such limits, since he will then be less inclined to flagellate himself for having fallen into oppressive conditions of life he cannot change.

Question: In recommending a list of possible treatments, should I, as a clinician, list treatments I do not believe will work?

Answer: I am not recommending that the clinician go through an intellectual exercise in which every possible treatment is listed just for the sake of thoroughness. If the clinician were to be meticulously academic, for example, it might make sense to list lobotomy as a possible treatment for every obsessive or anxious person. This would be absurd. The clinician should recommend only treatments he sees as potentially useful. At the same time, the clinician should seek to purge himself of biases which lead him to dismiss certain treatments too cavalierly. The clinician who believes most strongly in psychoanalytic techniques should be willing to recommend behavior therapies when these are indicated. The clinician who holds most avidly to a biological approach should be willing to recommend psychoanalysis.

Question: What if the clinician cannot provide the treatment or treatments that are indicated?

Answer: When the clinician does not have the skills to perform the most desirable treatment he is obliged to find another clinician or practitioner who will. In most parts of the United States there is usually some person available who has the technical skills to provide the particular form of intervention the clinician recommends. It is also possible for the conscientious clinician located in a relatively understaffed area to teach himself a new technique. Except for psychoanalysis, the skills involved in most interventions do not require an enormous amount of training. A well-trained clinician should be able to learn to provide behavior, family, or group therapy without inordinate difficulty. If he has medical training, psychopharmacology can be self-taught. I am assuming that any person coming out of a training program in psychiatry, psychology, or social work would also have at least some skills in individual psychotherapy.

Question: You are recommending that I tell my patients about the possible adverse effects of each treatment I recommend. Won't this lead some patients who are suggestible to actually develop these effects on an hysterical basis? Wouldn't it cause other more obsessive people to develop anxiety worrying about the possible side effects of treatment?

Answer: There are certainly risks involved in the approach I am recommending. It is conceivable that people will respond to treatments with adverse effects if they know of their possibility. It is also conceivable that people will worry about things they might not have worried about if they were ignorant of them. Again, however, I believe that the overall general benefits of an open approach outweigh these risks. There are considerable therapeutic advantages reaped when the patient is informed about negative effects. Patients can watch for these effects and be more alert to discovering means of aborting them should they develop. Patients will also be somewhat less terrified if forewarned of the possibility of what they find happening to them. Finally, it must be noted that even when patients are told little about possible negative side effects, people we think of as having hysterical personality traits do find out about these effects from reading, from friends, or from observing other patients. Such people are better off informed by the clinician than allowed to glean inaccurate information on their own. It is also true that patients we think of as obsessive worry about undesirable side effects of treatment whether informed of them or not. Sometimes a clear understanding of what is likely to happen may take some of the mystery and fear out of the obsessive patient's rumination.

Question: Once I have revealed my knowledge of the patient's case and my treatment biases so openly, can I still work with the patient in some kind of long-term psychotherapeutic relationship if that is the treatment of choice? Will my having revealed so much about my own prejudices influence the course of treatment?

Answer: There may still be some psychoanalytic purists who would feel that the amount of communication which the clinician provides the patient in the method I am recommending would give the patient so much knowledge about what kind of person the

Practical and Ethical Issues

clinician is that it would impede transference. My own experience and my reason tells me that this is silly. Simply being a straightforward, relatively scientific type of human being does not put the clinician in such a light as to make it impossible for the patient to develop transference responses toward him. I have noted elsewhere (1971) that transferences can develop and be worked with effectively even when the clinician is quite open about his own feelings and values. Undoubtedly, when the clinician talks openly with the patient, the clinician loses some of the magical power the patient invests in him. A desperate patient seeking help from a distant and silent therapist is likely to be easily influenced by that therapist. The therapist's silence, if not carried to the point of absurdity, gives him power. But such power is not essential for helping patients, and if is too great, it will necessarily diminish the patient's autonomy.

Question: There has always been considerable belief that successful healing resides in the authority and charisma of the healer. If I give up my techniques of mystification and openly discuss diagnosis and treatment with patients, won't I lose the power to heal by virtue of my authority and charisma?

Answer: To begin with, we do not precisely know how the authority of the clinician contributes to healing. Some authority is undoubtedly necessary, but too much authority infantilizes the patient. In treating emotionally disturbed patients we assume they are responsible for some of their behaviors but not for others. We use our authority to help them change things they seem unable to change by themselves, but we also urge them to take as much responsibility for their own actions and treatment as possible. In the latter role the clinician uses authority only to help the patient achieve autonomy and freedom from authority. If the clinician is viewed as overly powerful, the patient may develop feelings of powerlessness and dependency rather than feelings of autonomy.

Even if we assume that the clinician's authority is a crucial factor in most treatment, it cannot be assumed that demystification of the clinician-patient relationship will automatically diminish that authority. It is hard to see how the patient could fail to respect the clinician who provides an explicit picture of the patient's disorder and its possible treatments. In the process of presenting this information, the clinician will demonstrate skills the patient cannot help but appreciate. There is also a certain type of power that is obtained by openness. The clinician who is open is more likely to gain a kind of trust from the patient that will ultimately give the clinician considerable influence. It is also important to distinguish between charisma and authority. Charisma implies authority based on divine power or special gifts. The charismatic healer is a magical healer. I am very skeptical as to the value of behavioral change brought about through the charisma of the healer. Such changes are, in my experience, likely to be temporary. Furthermore, the charisma of the healer always carries as much potentiality for hurting the patient as for helping him. "Magic" can be used for evil as well as for good.

The practice of telling patients what is wrong with them and discussing the advantages and disadvantages of various treatments will strike some of my colleagues as obviously useful and rational. Others will view it as a cumbersome waste of time. Still others will view it as a revolutionary and dangerous approach to clinical practice. Although convinced such an approach is entirely sensible and necessary, I expect its initiation to meet such massive resistance that its justification must be considered in greater detail. What is accomplished by sharing with the patient what we know as to what is wrong with him, or by speculating with him as to the disadvantages or advantages of various treatments? I have just argued that one major advantage is that it gives the patient some true choice in what will happen to him, far more than is now granted patients treated in a more mystical manner. A second advantage is that such open practice will meet consumers' rapidly expanding demands for unbiased information. Increasingly, consumers of medical services are unwilling to accept passively whatever the professional imposes on them. Increasingly, our courts are supporting the malpractice suits of patients who have unfavorable responses to treatment after consenting to various medical procedures without full information about potential risks. The doctrine of informed consent is gaining ascendancy in the relationship of consumer groups to medicine (Ayd 1974). If we as clinicians do not adopt the kind of open clinical practice I am recommending, it will eventually be forced upon us.

A third reason for fully informing the patient is that demystification facilitates treatment. Even if the patient is provided a highly speculative explanation of his disorder, such an explanation is at least something the patient can consider in naturalistic terms without having to deal with the aura of shame, fear, and mystery that has come to be associated with mental illness. Naturalistic explanations of the patient's difficulty are particularly reassuring when external or accidental events have played a major role in the development of the disorder. The clinician can then point out how the disorder was the product of a certain combination of circumstances occurring at a certain point in time. This provides reassurance to the patient that such circumstances are unlikely to occur together in exactly the same way in the future and that there is no inexorable tendency toward further illness. Unless the patient has a history of having repeatedly created environments that turn out troublesome, the clinician can avoid such mystical and frightening interpretations as *repetition compulsion* or *life script* which imply that the patient is afflicted with a drive toward self-destruction. Great harm is done patients when we, with little evidence, sagely imply to them that they are ordained to a lifetime of self-injury. Explanations of the effectiveness and disadvantages of treatment modalities also helps take them out of the realm of the mysterious. The clinician can be completely frank in acknowledging that he does not know why some interventions work. In this case the clinician and patient can share a sense of mystery rather than having the patient bear the burden of mystery alone.

A fourth benefit closely allied to demystification is that, when the clinician discusses alternative modes of treatment and lists his preferences, patient and clinician are likely to engage in some dialogue as to each other's values. In *The Politics of Therapy* (1971) I argued that it is almost impossible for the clinician to avoid imposing some of his values upon the patient, but that this process could be attenuated by the patient's having greater knowledge of the clinician's values. As the clinician discusses his picture of what is wrong with the patient and as he tries to convince the patient that one intervention is better than another, some dialogue will take place as to the clinician's view of such values as intimacy, power, freedom, and responsibility. This dialogue will reveal the clinician as a real person and may protect the patient from the subtle but powerful inculcation of the therapist's values which occurs in many forms of psychotherapy.

Finally, any effort the clinician makes to explain diagnosis and alternative treatments to the patient requires the clinician to do some hard thinking about his patient. It is one thing to look at a person, to observe that he is depressed, and to prescribe antidepressants. This process does not demand unusual skill or effort on the part of the clinician. Nor is it very difficult to spend an hour or two interviewing a neurotic patient, to observe and formulate one or two psychodynamic conflicts, and to recommend psychoanalysis. It is something else again to collate all of the data the patient and the family have presented and to try to put it into a jargon-free explanation of what is happening. It takes great concentration and commitment on the clinician's part to go through the exercise of formulating various hypotheses as to causality and trying to see how these hypotheses relate to specific interventions in a given individual. Such efforts cannot help but increase the clinician's efficiency.

A Note on Treatment Choice and Degree of Severity

When the patient is severely disturbed, the value of compassion and frequently the value of efficiency dictate the immediate use of somatic interventions. Evaluation of the severity of the disorder may also influence choice of intervention after the most acute phase of the disturbance has passed. The patient who has experienced severe disorganization or depression will have good reason to be troubled about what has happened to him even after he seems to be feeling better. He will have experienced serious assaults on his confidence, his self-esteem, and his status with regard to his family and community. He may be asked to continue to take medications which affect his body image and which curtail previously enjoyed social activities such as sex or drinking. Most important, he will feel vulnerable and fear a recurrence of his disability—a not unrealistic fear since such behaviors as schizophrenia, mania, and depression do recur.

I have come to automatically view almost every severely disturbed patient as requiring multidimensional intervention. A severely depressed patient who is hospitalized, for example, should receive antidepressant medication or electroconvulsive treatment, supportive or information-expanding therapy, group or individual therapy, and family therapy. The ward environment should be structured so as not to reinforce depressed behavior and to provide reinforcement for any behavior likely to enhance the patient's self-esteem. In an outpatient setting it is advisable to rely upon medication, individual or group psychotherapy, and family therapy. When the patient is not hospitalized, behavior modification techniques can be taught to family members so that they, rather than the hospital staff, can learn to reinforce behaviors which are to the patient's advantage.

Indications for the use of multiple interventions are somewhat less clear in patients who have threatened or attempted suicide. Some of these patients will show concurrent signs of schizophrenia, mania, or depression. The elderly suicidal patient, for example, is almost always depressed. But younger suicidal patients may not be severely depressed or may be so only transitorily. They may show no signs of schizophrenic or manic behavior. Many younger suicidal patients have learned persistent patterns of maladaptive behavior which impair their capacity to find intimate relationships or to function effectively in occupational roles. Their suffering is severe during the period preceding the suicidal act. At other times they may feel reasonably well and make marginal or satisfactory adaptations.

Treatment of the younger suicidal patient does not usually require antidepressant medication or electroconvulsive treatment. Brief hospitalization may be indicated while the patient is actively suicidal, but the patient usually is most in need of new learning experiences, better understanding of his environment, and perhaps a change of behavior on the part of significant others. Such change is most likely to be brought about by individual or group therapies accompanied by family therapy. Behavior therapies may also be used with specific symptoms or behavioral patterns. Shy individuals, for example, whose suicidal preoccupations may be related to fears of permanent loneliness, can be taught to overcome some of their shyness through modeling, behavior rehearsal, and proper timing of positive reinforcement. (I am, for the purpose of this discussion, omitting the question of involuntary treatment of suicidal patients and am assuming that all of the treatments mentioned would be accepted voluntarily once the patient has full knowledge of their effects.)

Severely anxious patients benefit from early treatment of symptoms. When severe anxiety can be related to specific situational events, as is usually the case with phobias and compulsions, behavior modification is most helpful. Anxiety states which seem independent of antecedent events (sometimes called free floating anxiety) can be treated with antianxiety agents or sometimes with tricyclics. As with depressed or psychotic patients, the debilitating or demoralizing aspects of these symptoms are usually severe enough to warrant psychotherapeutic interventions even when personality disorders, crises, or noxious postsymptomatic environments cannot be defined. The clinician should also bear in mind that a small number of individuals with severe anxiety benefit little from behavior therapy or drug therapy but may benefit considerably from family therapy or long-term individual psychotherapy.

As severity of the disturbance diminishes, so does its usefulness as a guideline to treatment. Many patients who seek help are not incapacitated with depression, anxiety, or psychosis, are not suicidal, but are plagued with chronic feelings of inadequacy and occasional experiences of moderate anxiety or depression. Biological determinants are rarely manifest in this group and there has in recent years been considerable debate among behavioral scientists as to whether they should be considered proper subjects for treatment, particularly by medical specialists (Schwartz 1974). In spite of this debate, when these people ask for help they are usually treated by medical or nonmedical professionals with a large variety of interventions.

The extent and type of intervention in these patients should, in my opinion, be partially determined by the value of compassion. While these patients may not be incapacitated, when they do become anxious or depressed they are entitled to whatever relief the clinician can bring them. Antianxiety drugs and relaxation inducing techniques can be used to help them through periods of intense suffering. Brief individual, group, and family psychotherapy may have a salutary influence on symptoms of anxiety or depression and can also help such patients learn something about avoiding situations which elicit symptoms. Indications for long-term individual psychotherapy for patients with personality disorders who are also experiencing considerable distress should be determined by the failure of other techniques to provide relief and by the clinician's assessment of the patient's role in creating a pathogenic environment. In my own practice, I recommend long-term individual or group psychotherapy for moderately anxious or depressed patients who seem to have repetitively played a substantial role in creating their own pathogenic environments and who have failed to respond to other interventions.

Some patients complain only of feelings of meaninglessness and chronic unhappiness. They are neither terribly anxious nor depressed, just chronically troubled. One can argue that these people would do just as well to go through life without help or that they might seek the help of friends or nonprofessionals. On the other hand, it can also be argued that when these people ask for help, the clinician must consider that those who have experienced chronic unhappiness are high risks to develop more serious physical or mental disturbances. With so much ambiguity and with the clinician possessing little capacity to discern when justifiable human unhappiness should be considered an emotional disorder, there can be few clear guidelines to treatment. Patients with personality disorders manifested almost entirely in existential problems are easily exploited and are susceptible to fads in psychotherapy. Too often, they are urged to spend large segments of their lives and large proportions of their wealth in futile therapeutic ventures. While some of these patients can greatly improve the quality of their lives by undergoing long-term individual psychotherapy, they should be fully informed that there is little guarantee that the benefit of treatment will be worth the cost. If a patient who is neither anxious nor depressed and who is not living in an oppressive environment requests individual psychotherapy for existential problems, I try to help him but will promise him as little as possible. He is advised that his struggles are not too different from the struggles of most people, that life in general is difficult, that behavioral change is not easily accomplished, and that only great motivation on the patient's part is likely to lead to a favorable outcome.

A Last Statement about Ethics

A final comment is in order concerning the disturbing tendency among many practitioners to consider ethical issues apart from treatment issues. Sometimes it is even argued that a preoccupation with ethics will diminish the clinician's effectiveness. I have tried to show that, if the clinician makes an effort to define a set of values that will fully protect the patient and then tries to use these in prescribing treatment, the issue of ethics then becomes an integral factor in treatment choice. Ethics simply means doing what is right or what is good for the patient. Determination of what is right or good is made by comparing therapeutic outcomes with previously stated values. Viewed in this light, treatment cannot be good unless it is ethical, and cannot be ethical unless it is good.

Part II

Treatment

Introduction

The conceptual model presented in Part I provides a crude but more or less comprehensive guide for selecting appropriate treatment or treatments for a given patient. The emphasis in that section was on offering the clinician guidelines in deciding what treatment to use. In the second part of the book there will be further elaboration of diagnostic issues, but the emphasis will be upon the question how can the available treatments be used most effectively?

There is no dearth of "how to do it" books dealing with each of the major therapies. My purpose here is not to duplicate the work of others but to present a concise review of how each of the current therapies can be used in an integrated or multidimensional framework. Each class of treatment will be considered in terms of the value systems I have outlined and considerable attention will be paid to the ethical issues involved in the use of each intervention.

As in Part I, it will be assumed that the reader has some knowledge of basic psychopathology and interviewing techniques. An effort has been made to present the material in language as jargon-free as possible so that it can easily be followed by third-year medical students or advanced social work, nursing, or psychology students. While nonmedical or nonnursing professionals may be unfamiliar with a few of the terms and concepts used in the discussion of biological interventions, I would urge them to review this material and to employ extra effort in trying to comprehend the role of biological treatments in the behavioral sciences. Because psychologists and social workers are usually excluded from active participation in the use of these treatments, they often fail to appreciate their value and do not learn how they may appropriately be used with other treatments.

Such disorders as tumor, trauma, metabolic disorder, circulatory disorder, infection, or toxicity, which cause acute and chronic brain syndromes, usually require complex medical and surgical interventions. These interventions I will not discuss. In dealing with brain syndromes, the task of the healer of emotional disorders is generally limited to diagnosis and treatment of symptoms. Some psychiatrists may be exceptionally skilled in treating the disease processes underlying brain syndromes, but most are less skilled than their medical and surgical colleagues; once these underlying disorders are diagnosed, the psychiatrist will rarely carry out specific treatments without consultation. Nonpsychiatric clinicians must, of course, always seek consultation in treating the causes of organic disorder once a diagnosis has been made.

With the exception of a few comments in the section on family therapy, there will be no material presented regarding treatment of children. It would have been highly desirable to have discussed the use of an integrated approach with children, but such a presentation would require knowledge and experience I do not have.

Chapter 5

Biological Interventions

In terms of capacity to effect rapid changes in behavior, biological treatments are the most powerful interventions currently available. Effective and inexpensive, they quickly alleviate profound suffering and on the basis of compassion alone are often necessary. Their effectiveness and cost are relatively easy to measure, and government, hospital, and peer review committees can evaluate their efficiency with much more precision than is usually possible in evaluating other therapies. With all these advantages, the use of biological interventions has greatly expanded over the past two decades, but not without controversy. There is growing concern over the abuse of biological therapy.

Ethical problems in using biological treatments arise when the values of efficiency and compassion are weighed against the values of not diminishing the patient's autonomy and future potential. Biological treatments may seriously compromise both. The kind of value conflicts which plague the clinician can be dramatically illustrated by presenting some experiences I had in treating a patient and in attempting to respond to various colleagues' assessments of that treatment.

In the course of writing this book I was invited to speak at a symposium examining the ethical and social impact of psychiatric

Recommended dosages in this chapter are based on my experience and the recommendations of two or more sources in addition to PDR; they should not be accepted unreservedly. Dosages must be considered carefully in each case, and the clinician, when prescribing medication with which he is unfamiliar, should consult more than one source.

intervention. From the nature of the publicity surrounding the meeting, it was clear that its theme was to be critical of conventional psychiatric practice. In the days preceding the meeting, I was deeply concerned about one of my patients. She was a twenty-three-year-old woman who, four weeks after the birth of her first child, had been hospitalized with symptoms of confusion, inability to communicate or think clearly, feelings that people were trying to kill her, doubt that the child was actually hers, and fears of being near her husband. Although she did not admit to hallucinating, she frequently stared into space and was noted to be mumbling to herself. During the first few days of hospitalization, she was coherent at times and was able to provide some history. Her condition soon deteriorated, however, and she was started on treatment with chlorpromazine (Thorazine). She showed slight improvement but quickly developed a severe allergic reaction, and the drug had to be discontinued. She was then started on thiothixene (Navane). Again she developed a severe allergic reaction, and the drug was discontinued. Rather than immediately begin a course with a third group of antipsychotic drugs, such as the butyrophenones, I decided to allow her to be drug free for a few days. My decision was motivated partially by concern (which may not have been realistic) that she would be allergic to butyrophenones as well, but was based primarily on certain historical data and observations made by myself and the treatment team. The patient had not wanted her baby. Shortly before she became pregnant, she had for the first time in her life found an interesting job and was experiencing herself as a mature person. She was also becoming disillusioned with her husband, whom she increasingly viewed as an uninteresting, unsympathetic person who could not meet her intellectual or emotional needs. A family conference held shortly after admission revealed that the couple had been having serious marital difficulties and that the patient had been considering divorce in the weeks just prior to her illness.

While convinced that the patient had a severe biological disorder, I hypothesized as another factor in her psychosis the wish to change or get out of an oppressive marital situation. The patient came from a fundamentalist religious background, and my experience with such people when they become psychotic and recover is that they tend to seal over and deny problems that may have been quite apparent to both themselves and others before or during the psychosis. I wanted the patient to achieve some new learning about her situation and, since she was allergic to perhaps

Biological Interventions 167

all the major antipsychotics, I hoped she would turn out to be one of those patients who could, while psychotic, be successfully treated with psychotherapy and milieu therapy.

My optimism was unjustified. The patient quickly deteriorated, and twenty-four hours after thiothixene was discontinued she became mute, periodically stuporous or excited, and unwilling to take fluids or eat. In the succeeding twenty-four-hour period, she began to rip her clothes off and became incontinent of urine and feces. At this point, I viewed the patient as critically ill and, unwilling to risk her being allergic to other antipsychotic drugs and fearful of waiting until they took effect, I recommended emergency electroconvulsive therapy. The first treatment was given on the morning of the day I was to leave for my meeting. By the time I left for the airport that afternoon, I was gratified to note that the patient was taking fluids and was far less agitated. Although in the care of competent colleagues, she was very much on my mind as I traveled to the meeting.

The first day of the meeting left me angry and depressed. I had been invited to speak because of critical positions I had taken on some aspects of psychiatric practice, but the depth of my fellow speakers' distrust of and contempt for any biological aspect of therapy was so great that I felt I was among hostile strangers. None of the speakers and, judging from their response to the speakers, none of the audience seemed to have the least respect for clinicians who use biological therapies. In listening to their diatribes, I couldn't avoid thinking about how most of my medical colleagues would respond to them. Most psychiatrists would have considered the antibiological statements made to be misguided at best and malicious or dangerous at worst.

When my turn came to speak, I decided to try to persuade the audience to consider a more balanced view of biological treatment by presenting the details (in disguised fashion) of the case which had been preoccupying me all week. I presented all of my doubts about the ethical issues involved in using drug treatment and ECT in this case and at the same time offered no apologies for my decisions. My hope was that consideration of the case might help the audience question their certainty and appreciate the ethical dilemmas involved in treating highly disturbed people.

I didn't come close to achieving my goals. Most of the audience were openly hostile. I was accused of insensitivity and brutality. Several persons asked why I hadn't tried to keep the patient alive with intravenous feeding. Many were critical that I had merely "shocked" the patient into what would be a life of conformity, had failed to help her learn from her illness, and had contributed to strengthening an oppressive status quo.

Subsequent events proved that the concerns of my audience were not wholly inappropriate. When I returned home, the patient was much improved. She showed some post-ECT confusion but was otherwise rational, in reasonably good spirits, and fully ambulatory. She was given a total of seven electroconvulsive treatments and, as her post-ECT confusion cleared, efforts were made to involve her in individual and marital psychotherapy. The patient, however, was stubbornly resistant to any type of continued treatment. She claimed that she had simply experienced a metabolic illness related to pregnancy, denied she had not wanted the baby, denied she was dissatisfied with her marriage, and insisted upon leaving the hospital as soon as possible. She was unwilling to take any medication. Her husband and his family were delighted with her progress and attitude and took her home. Both the patient and her husband refused any follow-up treatment. I was able to contact the patient several months later. She was working part time and was having some success in taking care of the baby. Except for a few mildly paranoid feelings regarding her treatment, she seemed quite rational but sad. She was unwilling to talk about her interpersonal relationships or to consider further treatment.

It is hard to know how to evaluate the usefulness of this patient's treatment. Most probably she did have some type of postpartum metabolic disturbance that was an etiological factor in her psychosis. It is likely, however, that her symptoms were also precipitated by powerful interpersonal stresses, and insofar as she did not acknowledge or deal with them, she did not learn anything from her illness. I did not know her before she became ill, but I suspect she was a happier, more "together" person than she is now. Perhaps I could have kept her alive with tube or intravenous feeding and then treated her with psychotherapy, but there is really no way to know whether she would have sealed over any less defensively with such treatment. Perhaps a nonbiological psychotherapeutic approach might have prevented further remissions, but it is also possible that this was a psychosis that will never recur anyway. Some of my colleagues would consider my treatment of this case competent, thoughtful, and successful. Others would consider it an atrocity. My own view is ambivalent.

I began this chapter on biological treatment with a case that poignantly illustrates the ethical dilemmas involved in such treatment to remind the clinician of the need to avoid becoming prematurely decisive in the use of biological interventions. Ideally, every clinician should carefully weigh the values of efficiency and compassion against the values of not compromising the patient's autonomy and future potentials before making any decision to use biological treatment. Deliberation regarding value issues may be burdensome to the clinician but does not preclude decision making.

TERRITORIAL ISSUES

Another important issue in considering biological treatments relates to territorial conflicts among the various mental health professions. To use biological interventions effectively one must have medical skills. But while these may be necessary for actually providing biological treatment, they are not essential in most aspects of the diagnostic process. There is no reason why the nonmedical clinician who works together with a family physician or internist cannot develop sufficient skills to formulate biological hypotheses or diagnoses of most emotional disorders. The traditional medical evaluation rarely provides information to substantiate the diagnosis of an emotional disorder but simply helps the clinician to rule out the presence of measurable physical disorders. With the exception of the brain syndromes, there are at present no physical or laboratory findings which substantiate or differentiate emotional disorders. Rather, the positive aspect of diagnosis, or the capacity to observe and describe behaviors that are characteristic of an emotional disorder, is based on skills in observation, in interviewing, and in psychological testing. These skills have been mastered by many who are not physicians.

Once a hypothesis of biological disorder is made, and once biological interventions are recommended, we have a totally new situation. We then must thoroughly evaluate the patient's physical condition to detect any physical disorders which may be aggravated by the use of the biological agent. We must also be prepared to deal with the physical changes which biological agents impose upon the patient. Every time a patient is given a major biological treatment, his physiological and biochemical processes are drastically altered. The patient is not simply brought back to where he was before he became disturbed; his physiology and biochemistry are altered in a way that requires continued monitoring and treatment. Another way of putting this is that once a major biological intervention is used, it creates serious side effects which can be considered biological disorders. It should be apparent that medical skills are required in the actual treatment process but not in diagnosis—a nonpsychiatric clinician should be able to diagnose biological disorders and recommend biological treatments as long as a physician is available to initiate them.

This issue can be clarified and perhaps defused if we imagine that a new drug has been developed which has a salutary effect on all types of learning disabilities but which also has many serious effects upon bodily functions. There are, of course, some forms of learning difficulties which are related to specific physiological and anatomical disorders. But diagnosing the existence and causes of most of these disabilities does not require skills in physical medicine. It requires instead skills in using interviewing techniques and psychological testing to assess intellectual functioning. Psychologists are more likely to have mastered these than are psychiatrists. If our hypothetical new drug has become widely used, physicians would be responsible for actually prescribing it and would also have to treat the side effects or biological dysfunctions its use occasions. It would still, however, be desirable to ask nonmedical experts to play major and responsible roles in the diagnostic process.

The practice of having biological treatment administered solely by physicians and ancillary medical personnel is based upon rational needs. Unfortunately, the necessity of such restrictions has subtle but powerful influences upon the manner in which the various mental health professions view biological interventions. Psychiatrists tend to be highly committed to biological interventions not only because they are effective, but also because such treatments allow them to use their medical skills and solidify their identification with other medical practitioners. Nonpsychiatric clinicians tend to be somewhat reluctant to formulate hypotheses that call for biological treatment. They know that they cannot independently provide this treatment and fear that once it is invoked they will be excluded from the treatment process. Economic factors may also be important. Biological treatments are more likely to be reimbursed by third-party payment than are nonbiological treatments. The psychiatrist is rewarded for recommending biological treatment; the nonpsychiatrist is not.

While this is not the place to dwell upon the nonaltruistic motivations in the various mental health professions, it would be a mistake to ignore the manner in which territorial considerations have colored professional views of biological interventions. Too many psychiatrists have committed themselves to a one-dimensional biological approach to practice. Too many nopsychiatric professionals have deprecated the use of biological interventions and have failed to learn the indications for their use. As a result, both groups risk developing styles of practice which may deprive the patient of essential treatment.

GENERAL DIAGNOSTIC ISSUES

Some of the less powerful biological interventions, such as muscular relaxation or drugs of the benzodiazepine class are often used as nonspecific treatments of general anxiety without making efforts to relate treatment to precise diagnosis. This nonspecific approach is tolerated in clinical practice because the hazards of such therapy are minimal or at least not immediately apparent. The situation with more powerful psychoactive drugs and ECT is different. Because of their very powerful physical, psychological, and social effects, their use is difficult to justify in the absence of a firm observational or classificatory diagnosis. Errors in diagnosing biological disorders can be quite harmful to the patient. Patients who are misdiagnosed may be given potentially harmful biological treatments when they don't need them, may be deprived of biological treatments when they do need them, or may be given the wrong biological treatment.

Most clinicians, particularly psychiatrists, are trained to search for pathology and to assume that the troubled patient has some type of serious pathology until it is proved otherwise. This attitude, essential when the presence of life-threatening but treatable disorders is suspected, leads to a certain amount of overdiagnosis but is justified by the need to preserve life. Many emotional disorders, however, are not life-threatening. A false positive diagnosis may be detrimental to the patient's social position and may lead to the use of unnecessary and potentially harmful treatments. While overdiagnosis and overtreatment in these cases is not as dangerous as underdiagnosis and inadequate treatment of life-threatening conditions, it is still bad for the patient. Throughout most of the following discussion, I will focus on the pitfalls of overdiagnosis. This does not mean I am complacent about misdiagnosis or underdiagnosis. It is simply that I believe the latter errors are sufficiently discussed during the clinician's training and are heavily emphasized in textbooks of psychiatry and psychology. On the other hand, overdiagnosis is usually neglected in clinical training, and many clinicians are not sufficiently aware of its dangers.

The discovery of empirical biological treatments of major emotional disorders has had both negative and positive effects upon treatment practices. The positive effects are obvious. In addition to alleviating the suffering of patients, the new pharmacotherapy has improved our science by directing us to make efforts to categorize behaviors that will respond differentially to drugs. It has encouraged much useful research as to heredity patterns and changes in brain chemistry which are associated with such behaviors. We now have fairly good criteria for categorizing certain clusters of behavior and sufficient evidence to hypothesize different biological mechanisms that may be associated with these clusters. An unfortunate negative byproduct of the new pharmacotherapy, however, may be an increased tendency to try to fit too many patients into the diagnostic categories for which we now believe there are treatments. The discovery of lithium treatment for manic behavior has led to a more frequent use of the diagnosis of bipolar affective disorder. Some of the "new manics" probably come from a population previously called schizophrenic, but there are also some whose behavior might previously have been labeled neurotic. The discovery of useful antipsychotic medication has also, in my opinion, led to an overdiagnosis of schizophrenia. Similarly, the discovery of antidepressant medication has encouraged too many practitioners to consider mild depression, normal grief, or mourning reaction as diseases which must be treated.

It is easy to understand why the existence of a new and effective treatment leads to its increased use and to a lack of "crispness" in diagnosing the conditions it will influence. There are some analogies in nonpsychiatric medicine. When antibiotics were first discovered, they were used initially to treat a wide variety of conditions which they could not possibly have influenced. Excessive use of antibiotics has harmed patients. The consequences of unnecessary or careless use of psychotropic drugs in treating the emotionally disordered are much more serious. These drugs act on the brain and influence every aspect of the patient's psychological and social life. To put this issue as forcefully as possible, it is well to remind the reader that most biological interventions change the patient's chemistry and physiology in ways that distress the patient as well as help him. It is not too farfetched to argue that each biological intervention creates an illness as well as treats one. However one defines illness, there is as much justification for considering such extrapyramidal symptoms as tardive dyskinesia as illnesses as for so considering schizophrenia.

Effective rather than excessive use of biological treatment is dependent upon two factors: the clinician's ability to make accurate diagnoses, and the relative specificity of the biological agents used. In current clinical practice diagnoses are not optimally accurate, nor are the effects of pharmacological agents optimally specific. There is little that the practicing clinician can do about the latter situation except to patiently await the day when research provides us agents with greater therapeutic specificity. There is much, however, that the clinician can do to improve his diagnostic skills. It will be useful at this point to briefly review how failure to develop these skills leads to inaccurate diagnosis.

Behaviors which are part of the symptomatology of severe emotional disorders are primarily defined by what the clinician observes and the patient reports. Rating scales and psychological tests may help support our assessments, but when we say a patient is confused, delusional, hallucinating, disorganized in his thinking, euphoric, or depressed we are simply making a judgment as to what we believe is happening to the patient. We can be more assured of our judgments when there is consensus with other colleagues or with our past experience. But consensus does not assure accuracy in describing symptoms. Such accuracy is dependent upon the technician's observational skills and experience and upon three additional factors: first, the clinician's ability to achieve sufficient rapport to enable the patient to be precise and honest in reporting experiences; second, the clinician's commitment to be as thorough as possible in investigating all aspects of the patient's symptomatology; third, the clinician's awareness of situational, socioeconomic, and cultural variables which may influence the patient's behavior, particularly in the evaluative situation.

The clinician can fail to make accurate observations because he has not attained sufficient rapport with the patient. A patient who does not wish to confide in the clinician will offer little data that cannot be conveyed through monosyllables. The clinician needs to know much more than whether the patient reports hallucinations, looks depressed, or shows evidence of blocking. Sufficient rapport, by putting the patient at ease and encouraging him to communicate, enables the clinician to obtain this additional information. Once good rapport is achieved, the clinician must ask questions whose answers will allow him to define precisely the nature of the patient's disturbing experience, the environments in which it occurred, what preceded it, how the patient responded to it, how others responded to it, and how the patient interprets it. This information substantiates the pathological nature of the patient's behavior and allows the clinician to judge whether such behavior is part of a clinical syndrome.

Failure to seek rapport with the patient and failure to be thorough in investigating patients leads to innacurate diagnosis and overdiagnosis. In the well-publicized study "Being Sane in Insane Places," Rosenhan (1973) arranged for bogus patients to be admitted to a mental hospital and for each to complain of only one quite unusual hallucinatory experience. The bogus patients acted normal in every way. Nevertheless, these patients were uniformly diagnosed as schizophrenic, and efforts were made to treat them with neuroleptics. The authors cite the diagnosis and treatment of these "patients" as evidence of the unreliability of the concept of mental illness. I view it as unforgivable sloppiness on the part of examining physicians. There can never be any justification for putting the label of schizophrenia on a patient on the basis of that patient's reporting only one symptom, however bizarre.

Errors can also be made in evaluating the meaning of the patient's behavior when the clinician does not have enough understanding of the human condition or enough sociological perspective to appreciate what might be normal behavior and what might not be. Too many clinicians are pathology oriented and probe for symptoms in the manner of inquisitors. Psychiatrists especially, having been trained in a medical setting where signs and symptoms of disease are viewed as "positive" findings and signs of health as "negative," learn as students to anticipate praise for discovering pathology. This orientation leads to too many false positive diagnoses of emotional disorders. The clinician must be as willing to consider the possibility that the patient's troubling behaviors are a normal variant of the human condition as to discover in them evidence of severe pathology.

Some behaviors are more easily observed and viewed as pathological. Confusion, for example, can usually be noted when the patient appears perplexed, says he is confused, and cannot respond appropriately to simple tests of orientation and memory. Even with such data, however, the clinician must ascertain that the patient is not exaggerating or misreporting experiences. The clinician must also assess the extent to which the patient's confusion may be related to the stress of being interviewed or to the patient's intellectual limitations. I have seen patients in hospital settings who were neither psychotic nor brain damaged, but who were too anxious to respond appropriately to simple tests of orientation and memory. Before judging the patient's confusion as symptomatic of a disorder, the clinician either must be assured that the patient is not responding to overwhelming anxiety or must have additional evidence of confused recent behavior in other environments.

Evaluations of such intellectual functions as ability to think abstractly or to do simple calculations are more difficult. The clinician infers deficits in such functions on the basis of his assessments of the patient's verbal responses during the interview and of the patient's capacity to handle certain simple tests. Again, the patient's ability to communicate, his intellectual limitations, his motivation, and his expectations of the evaluator may influence his responses. The inexperienced clinician often expects far too much of the patient in asking the patient to respond to verbal tests of memory, of abstraction, or of arithmetical ability and tends to overdiagnose cognitive deficits.

There is never any way the clinician can be absolutely certain that a patient is hallucinating. A patient may say he is hearing voices, but there is no way of knowing if the patient is lying, is simply having thoughts which he chooses to believe he can hear, or is misinterpreting hypnogagic phenomena as hallucinations. The patient who appears to be hallucinating may also be a member of a subculture in which the experiencing of visions may be acceptable or even desirable. There is greater probability that a patient is hallucinating if he actually responds to hallucinations in a direct manner. Sometimes patients suffering from organic psychoses such as delirium tremens respond vigorously to, and appear terrified of, visual objects which others cannot see. But less bizarre responses to the environment are not sufficient evidence. There is no certainty that patients who stare off into space or mumble to themselves are responding to hallucinations. Lots of people who don't hallucinate talk to themselves and stare into space.

It is also difficult to be certain when a patient is delusional. A delusion can be defined as a false belief engendered without appropriate external stimulation and maintained in spite of what, to other people, seems incontrovertible evidence to the contrary. By this definition, blatant delusions are not too difficult to detect. But many beliefs of undue influence or fear of harm from others, often considered evidence of delusional thinking, should not be so labeled if the clinician sticks to the above definition. Often we assume that evidence contrary to the patient's beliefs is incontrovertible without taking the time to examine its validity. Only several years ago people who talked of assassination conspiracies and government persecutions would have been viewed as delusional. Today, because we have much more data, we examine their statements more carefully before jumping to conclusions. I do not mean to be flippant in discussing this issue, but simply wish to emphasize that the clinician should train himself to give the patient the benefit of the doubt and not automatically consider the expression of a bizarre or idiosyncratic viewpoint as prima facie evidence of delusion. It is useful to assume that the patient is not delusional until there is sufficient contradictory information from other sources which when presented to the patient does not moderate the tenacity with which he clings to his beliefs.

Unless they are blatant, disorders of the process of thinking are also difficult to describe with certainty. Even the most psychologically intact people are at times illogical. All of us experience blocking in thinking and we are particularly likely to do so under the stress of an interview. Similarly, we are all at times circumstantial, tangential, irrelevant, or overinclusive (in the sense of feeling driven to report all we are experiencing without regard to conceptual boundaries). When there are no obvious delusions or hallucinations and no gross disturbance in thinking, the clinician who diagnoses the presence of a thought disorder is actually weighing the rationality of the patient's thinking against his own and, in doing so, must be constantly aware of the patient's intellectual capabilities, personality traits, cultural and socioeconomic background, and reponse to the interview situation.

Assessment of the patient's mood is also a complex art. Some patients exaggerate sadness; others hide it. Some patients have an innately sad view of the world and their chronic moroseness is more a fixed personality trait than a symptom. A patient's morbid perception of himself and the world around him, which is usually considered a primary symptom of depression, may reflect an accurate assessment of reality rather than a symptom. Many elderly people who are sad over having lost certain capabilities or over the oppressive treatment they receive from others are quite correct in feeling pessimistic. Those who look at the world situation and find it depressing may be insightful rather than disturbed. During the latter part of the 1960s when student unrest was at its height, I would often give speeches in which I explained student behavior on the basis of their reacting to the dismal future of our planet. Many in the audience who did not want to hear this message argued that I must be depressed. Today, when the majority of American people expect things to get worse rather than better, my pessimism is interpreted as good reality testing rather than depression.

Manic behavior in extreme forms is easily documented. But the patient who is moderately hyperactive, euphoric, or irritable may merely be acting quite appropriately to a variety of life situations. Quite often young people who feel they have solved some major identity problem experience a sudden burst of energy and euphoria which is likely to be accompanied by contempt for authority and moderate antisocial behavior. There is a disturbing tendency these days to diagnose such adaptive but troubling behavior as mania.

Even such relatively concrete symptoms as insomnia and weight loss must be viewed in terms of the patient's total situation. Many patients exaggerate their reports of these symptoms. The clinician must ascertain the circumstances involved in the timing of weight loss. Sometimes it is related to dieting or to concurrent physical illness. Insomnia is a ubiquitous symptom in our society; millions of Americans who have minimal sleep disturbance are preoccupied with the nature and quality of their sleep. Questioning them about sleep patterns can lead to many false impressions unless the clinician is quite precise. Too often, changes in sleep patterns which are related to a change in working hours for the patient or the patient's spouse, to the rearing of children, to changes of noise levels in the environment, or to changes in levels of physical or mental activity may be interpreted as a serious form of insomnia. Or a sleep disturbance that has been present for years and is really a learned behavior (primary insomnia) may be viewed as a definitive symptom of depression when it is not.

It should not be necessary to include most of this material on diagnosis in a book of this type. Every clinician should be fully aware of the dangerousness of arbitrary descriptions of symptomatology and should almost reflexively be committted to thoroughness and precision. I felt obligated to include these reminders, largely because I have observed an increasing mechanistic stance toward diagnosis and treatment in the last ten years, primarily among psychiatrists, who are the main providers of biological treatments. In observing the work of my students and in examining candidates for certification by the American Board of Psychiatry and Neurology, I have noted a disturbing tendency, particularly on the part of my younger colleagues, to ask suggestive questions regarding symptomatology and to accept the patient's affirmative response as evidence that the symptom is present. I have seen too few psychiatrists who are sufficiently concerned with establishing good rapport with the patient. I have also noted a disturbing lack of appreciation of human variation or any understanding of the broad ranges of normality. Many young psychiatrists are too eager to consider minor behavioral variations as major symptoms. While I fear that my nonmedical colleagues may be underdiagnosing psychoses and other disorders that would respond to biological treatments, I have seen too much evidence of overdiagnosis among psychiatrists to be sanguine concerning the practices of my own profession.

Most of the abuses of pharmacotherapy related to overdiagnosis probably involve the use of antidepressant medication. It is not uncommon in an inpatient setting, however, to encounter blatant overdiagnosis of psychosis and subsequent misuse of other types of medication. Consider the following case:

A twenty-three-year-old man sought help for complaints of anxiety which he related to a fear that his parents might hospitalize him involuntarily. He had just left a hospital where he had been voluntarily treated with a course of lithium. As near as he could tell, the lithium treatment had no effect upon him. His evaluation of this treatment was later validated by his parents. The patient's initial hospitalization and treatment had come about because of concern on the part of his parents and co-workers regarding his behavior. For several weeks preceding his lithium treatment, the patient had been irritable around his parents. They noted that he seemed excited and overly energetic. The patient worked for his father, who owned a large and successful business. The father had decreed that if the patient wanted to come into the business, the patient would have to start out at the bottom. The patient initially acceded to this condition without complaint. In the weeks preceding his lithium treatment, the patient began to upset his father and other executives in the firm by making many suggestions for changes in the

Biological Interventions

operation of the business. There was a general feeling in the firm that the patient did not have the authority or experience to be making suggestions and some concern that his suggestions were impractical and grandiose.

The patient had for most of his life viewed himself as a placid, frightened, and obsequious person. He had always done exactly what his father had said and had many doubts as to his self-worth and masculinity. About six months prior to the onset of his behavior change, he had become intimately involved with a woman. This relationship helped him to feel more self-assured. She encouraged him to be more aggressive in dealing with his co-workers and his parents, and the patient soon began to chafe at his lowly position in the firm. He described himself as experiencing a combination of feelings of confidence and frustration and he became determined to prove to himself and to his parents that he was capable of holding an executive position in the family business. He viewed these changes as accounting for his new behavior at work and at home. Upon reflection he was able to see that many of the things he did to prove himself could have troubled and offended his parents and others. When his parents threatened him with commitment if he did not seek psychiatric assistance, he reverted to his more passive behavioral patterns and did not resist. Anger toward his parents, however, emerged in a more blatant and powerful manner after his brief hospitalization and lithium treatment had failed to influence him.

A series of family conferences with the parents and the girlfriend revealed that the patient's ideas for changing the business were hardly irrational but merely reflected inexperience. His ideas were rejected more because of the overenthusiastic and somewhat obnoxious manner in which he presented them than because of their irrelevance. It was also clear from the family interviews that the parents were used to seeing their son as a placid, obedient person and would have interpreted any assertiveness on his part as evidence of a major behavior change. In many ways the father came across in the family interviews as a highly energetic, irritable, and sometimes volatile person whose ordinary behavior was not too much different from that ascribed to the patient during his alleged illness. Continued family therapy with this patient resulted in the father's willingness to allow the patient to advance more rapidly in the business and to the patient's becoming more appropriately assertive. While there were limits to the success of treatment (the patient remained in a highly dependent relationship with his parents and girlfriend), the patient has been followed for over a year and there have been no recurrences of excited behavior.

In this case the possibility that the patient's behavior represented a mild or borderline form of bipolar affective disorder must still be considered. Certainly if the behavior recurred in more exaggerated form, the diagnosis might have to be changed. But even the suspected presence of mania in this case did not justify biological intervention. Thorough diagnostic efforts might have spared the patient an unnescessary and potentially harmful treatment.

None of this means that biological diagnoses should not be made or that biological treatments should not be provided. The clinician will find many patients who, if examined carefully enough, will demonstrate behaviors which justify biological interventions. It should be apparent, however, that a diagnostic hypothesis which requires biological treatment should, except in emergency situations, be made slowly. Outpatients should not be started on biological treatments unless the diagnostic criteria for their use are relatively clear. If suffering is moderate and there is diagnostic uncertainty, the evaluative process in an outpatient setting should continue for several days. If the patient is experiencing great suffering and the diagnostic picture is uncertain, the patient should be hospitalized and at least several days spent evaluating the patient and developing a firm basis for a biological hypothesis before any biological intervention is utilized.

SPECIFIC DIAGNOSTIC ISSUES

Forewarned as to the ease with which he can overdiagnose, the clinician must always be aware of the possible existence of behavior patterns that are likely to have biological determinants and are responsive to biological intervention. In this aspect of clinical practice classification is essential. It is especially important for the clinician to have some criteria which allow him to distinguish brain syndromes, schizophrenic disorders, and affective disorders. To make it easier to emphasize certain theoretical and practical aspects of treatment, these criteria will be briefly reviewed. More detailed discussions of descriptive diagnosis may be found in several of the sources referred to throughout this chapter.

The patient afflicted with a brain syndrome may show disturbances in perception, in memory, in verbal, spatial, and

Biological Interventions

numerical ability, and in level of consciousness. The presence and severity of any of these symptoms depend upon the stage and the seriousness of the disorder. Disturbances of level of consciousness in the form of delirium are not seen unless there is a major insult to the brain. Sometimes in the early stages of a brain syndrome, there are only minor signs of memory or intellectual loss. Changes in personality are also characteristic of brain syndromes. Irritability, poor judgment, and restlessness may be present in varying degrees. When the problem is more severe, illogical thinking and severe alterations of mood may also be present. Delusions and hallucinations may be present as in both schizophrenic and affective disorders. Visual hallucinations, however, are more characteristic of organicity and are rarely seen in schizophrenia or affective disorders.

A person experiencing some impairment of brain function is likely to be anxious. There are few experiences as frightening as the awareness that mental functions once accomplished automatically seem now to be failing. Anybody who has ever parked a car in a crowded parking lot and forgotten where he left it can empathize with what the organically impaired patient must experience regularly. It is natural that the patient will seek to deny both to himself and others, the reality of his loss of mental functioning. The clinician must be aware that patients experiencing organic deficits will try to minimize them through confabulation, denial, or evasiveness. Such defensiveness is highly protective to the patient. The clinician cannot permit himself to be too aggressive in exposing these deficits to the patient or others for fear of arousing even greater anxiety in the patient. All mental-status and psychological testing with patients suspected of organicity must be conducted in a gentle manner which allows the patient to save face when his performance is poor. This can be done while, simultaneously, the clinician remains committed to extreme thoroughness in examining the patient's intellectual functions.

If the clinician is ever to be guilty of overdiagnosis, it should be in the area of organicity. Proposing an hypothesis or organic dysfunction does not mandate immediate treatment but rather directs the clinician to make an immediate and thorough search for specific biological disturbances. Once the processes which underlie the disorder are discovered, they can be treated by specific medical and surgical intervention. There are also some relatively nonspecific biological treatments available to the clinician when the organically impaired patient is highly agitated, uncooperative, severely depressed, or assaultive. When these behaviors are present, small dosages of antipsychotic or antidepressive medication can be useful. These drugs do not influence the process that intitiated the brain syndrome, but they do control highly disturbing behaviors associated with it.

The diagnosis of a schizophrenic disorder is usually made on the basis of the presence of a thought disorder manifested by hallucinations and delusions or some other form of conceptual disorganization. The patient may occasionally show deficits in memory, in orientation, and in other intellectual functions similar to those of the organically impaired patient, but these deficits are likely to be transitory. The schizophrenic patient usually has sufficient intellectual intactness to perform adequately when he is motivated or when his anxiety is diminished. Schizophrenic disorders, unlike organic disorders, cannot be identified by detecting biological changes in the organism. Negative physical and laboratory examinations in a psychotic patient are, at this point in the state of our knowledge, one of the criteria used in diagnosing schizophrenic disorders.

Schizophrenic behavior tends to run in families. In contrast to organicity, which can appear at any age and is most characteristic of the elderly, schizophrenic behavior characteristically appears for the first time during early adulthood. Once the patient develops the behavioral picture of schizophrenia, the eventual outcome with or without treatment is for a high probability of recurrence and for considerable deterioration in social functioning. Yet there is never any certainty that the patient who shows schizophrenic behavior for the first time will have recurrences or will fail to regain his premorbid level of social functioning. There has been much debate in psychiatry over whether a good or bad prognosis for schizophrenic behavior can be made on the basis of initial symptomatology. Some clinicians believe that a healthy premorbid personality, acute onset, and a certain degree of organiclike confusion during the initial pyschosis support a good prognosis and that poor premorbid adjustment, insidious onset, and an absence of confusional behavior support a poor prognosis (Schofield et al. 1954, Kant 1940, Vaillant 1962). The issue is far from resolved, but most clinicians, myself included, are more hopeful of a favorable outcome when a good premorbid adjustment and an acute onset can be documented.

The issue of distinguishing schizophrenic from manic behavior has in the last decade become highly controversial. It has always been assumed that schizophrenic behavior is associated with some affective disturbance, in the form of either blunted or inappropriate affect. Patients with thought disorders who demonstrate a great deal of emotionality, in the form of depression, excitement, or euphoria, have traditionally been diagnosed as schizoaffective disorders, a subtype of schizophrenic disorder. Today, primarily because we have discovered that many of these patients will respond to lithium therapy, the boundaries of the diagnostic categories of schizophrenia seem less clear. Many clinicians question whether some of the behaviors traditionally considered schizophrenic should not really be considered affective disorders (Lipkin, Dyrud, and Meyer 1970). This uncertainty makes for difficulty in devising criteria for the biological treatment of psychotic disorders. In general, when the psychosis is manifested in a thought disorder, when it begins early in life, when it has no major affective components, when it is not accompanied by detectable organic deficits, and when similar behaviors have been noted in close family members, the currently available neuroleptic or antipsychotic drugs are the preferred biological treatment. When the patient shows these characteristics but also has pronounced affective components to his disturbance, lithium treatment may be indicated.

Manic behavior is diagnosed by the presence of euphoria, irritability, hyperactivity, social intrusiveness, and speech characterized by rapid digression form one idea to another. Sometimes the apparent euphoria may be quickly supplemented by hostility when the patient is frustrated or by sadness when the patient is discussing a troubling life situation. In mild form, manic behavior is not necessarily maladaptive. Many creative and successful people may be abrasively or charmingly hyperactive and are sometimes considered to have a mild form of mania called hypomania. In more severe forms, manic behavior can be of psychotic proportions and be manifested by delusions, hallucinations, irrational thinking, and poor judgment. The disordered thinking in manic behavior is often distinguished from that in schizophrenic behavior by a certain congruence of affect and idea. The manic patient is easier to empathize with and to understand, even when quite disorganized, and is often amusing.

Manic behavior can be cyclical and may also be associated with depressed behavior. The patient may be intact during periods when mania or depression are not apparent and does not, as a rule, experience the severe social deterioration experienced by the schizophrenic. There is considerable evidence that manic behavior runs in families. When manic behavior is present in severe or psychotic proportion and particularly where there is a family history of affective disturbances, treatment with antipsychotic drugs or lithium is indicated. The indications for lithium treatment and lithium prophylaxis increase if the behavior is cyclical, is associated with or alternates with depression, and is characterized by reasonably good functioning during intervals. Lithium treatment as noted earlier may also be considered in some conditions which psychiatrists used to classify as schizoaffective disorders.

Depression is one of the easiest disorders to detect. It is characterized by inappropriate sadness, psychomotor retardation or agitation, insomnia, anorexia, weight loss, suicidal preoccupations and intense feelings of worthlessness and hopelessness. While these symptoms are not difficult to observe, it is extremely difficult to know when their presence should direct the clinician to consider biological hypotheses and treatment. This is because there are so many degrees of severity of depression and so much variation in the environment in which depression occurs. The complexity of the problem is demonstrated by the confused state of our nosology. Depression has been classified as reactive (precipitating events can be ascertained) or endogenous (precipitating events are not evident); as agitated (accompanied by a great deal of anxiety and agitation); or retarded (accompanied by withdrawal and psychomotor retardation); as neurotic (the patient is in good contact with reality); as primary (no other medical or psychiatric conditions preexist or seem related to the onset of depression) or as secondary (other medical or psychiatric conditions precede, and may precipitate, the depression). Primary depressive disorders are also divided into unipolar affective disorders (where there are recurrent episodes of severe depression) or bipolar affective disorders (where there are recurrences of both depression and mania or recurrences of mania). The latter pair of categories may have the most clinical usefulness, since recurrent depression does run in families and recurring cycles of mania and depression or recurring periods of mania also run in families. Involutional melancholia is another diagnostic category which refers to severe depression, often of psychotic proportion,

Biological Interventions

which is seen for the first time in persons entering late middle life. For the sake of completeness, some mention should be made of the transient but often severe depressions which tend to recur in people who have long-standing personality disorders, usually of the hysterical type.

Classifications of depressions are of some usefulness in prescribing treatment, but they do not supply the clinician with consistent guidelines for determining when and what type of biological treatment should be used. The distinction between reactive and endogenous depressions has some relevance to treatment, but ascertaining the presence and meaning of precipitating circumstances requires considerable time and skill. Often a depression is judged endogenous simply because the clinician has not been vigorous enough in searching for precipitating events. Conversely, it is possible that a depression may have little to do with recent events but is judged reactive because the patient in his depressed condition desperately seeks to attribute his behavior to recent events. Sometimes depressions which seem to have clear and powerful environmental determinants are simply not responsive to environmental change but will respond to biological treatment. The most that can be said here in terms of guidelines is that a high level of stress preceding the disorder should alert the clinician to go slow in invoking biological treatments. Patients who have recently sustained severe object or narcissistic losses may respond well to therapies that bring about small environmental changes. On the other hand, they may not respond to antidepressant medications. One special class of patients show many of the symptoms of depressed behavior but rarely need biological treatments. Those who have recently lost loved ones experience after the death a sadness quite similar to that of the depressed patient; it is usually helpful, however, for the patient to live with and feel that grief for as long as several months. Efforts to prematurely obliterate the patient's grief with drugs should not be too heroic.

A forty-four-year-old married woman was hospitalized for the second time in a space of two months for treatment of sadness, tearfulness, and anxiety. She expressed fears of growing old and being useless. Although she had, with the exception of time spent in hospitals, continued to be gainfully employed as a school teacher, she stated that she simply was not enjoying life. There had been some insomnia, both difficulty in getting to sleep and early awakening, but no weight loss. During the previous hospitalization she had been treated with tricyclic drugs, but this treatment had not led to any substantial improvement. In the hospital setting, the patient's depression did not seem severe. She was able to relate well to other patients and staff and participated effectively, if not joyfully, in all ward activities.

The history revealed that the patient had been subject to an unusual amount of stress in the year preceding her first hospitalization. Her husband had taken on a new job which required a move to a new location. She had experienced her loss of friends and loss of status in the old community as a severe blow. One of her children had left to go off to college that year and another had left home to go to work. Most important her mother had died that year after a long illness. The patient's husband, preoccupied with his own sense of loss and the need to succeed at a new job, had not been able to give the patient much support.

It was decided that the patient was experiencing a grief or mourning reaction and that the biological causes or concomitants of her depression were not critical. Accordingly, antidepressant medication was stopped, and the patient was given individual psychotherapy to help her ventilate her feelings of grief regarding her losses and family therapy to help both her and her husband assist one another during a difficult period. The patient was discharged from the hospital and urged to return to work. On this regimen the patient improved slowly and after six months was feeling very much her old self.

Grief reactions are usually distinguished from depressive disorders on the basis of a history of recent loss of a loved one. The diagnostic discriminations, however, are rarely easy to make. A grieving person may appear very disturbed. Sometimes the loss of a loved one can precipitate a depression which will neither remit nor respond to psychotherapy, but which will respond to biological treatment. Some clinicians believe that clues to the differentiation of grief and depression can be found in the nature of the patient's behavior. The grieving patient complains more of the emptiness of the environment; the depressed patient complains more of emptiness withing himself. The depressed patient is also more likely to show a symptom called anhedonia, the loss of ability to experience pleasure in ordinary activities that are usually gratifying.

The distinction between psychotic and neurotic depressions has some clinical usefulness. Depressions associated with psychotic

Biological Interventions

behavior require more drastic intervention, sometimes calling for the use of neuroleptic or antipsychotic as well as antidepressant medication. Distinctions between retarded and agitated depressions have slightly greater clinical usefulness. Retarded depressions often respond well to tricyclics. Agitated depressions respond less well to both tricyclics and MAO inhibitors, and patients who are both agitated and depressed may require antipsychotic drugs as well as antidepressants in the early stages of treatment.

The distinction between primary and secondary depression is useful insofar as many depressions which seem related to the demoralizing effect of other disturbances, such as phobias, organic impairment, or schizophrenia, will be more effectively treated if the underlying disorder has been evaluated and treated. Depression associated with organic brain disease or a schizophrenic disorder can be treated with antidepressants but usually requires other biological treatments as well. Depression related to the lengthy incapacitation or ineffectiveness often associated with severe anxiety can often be relieved by merely treating that anxiety.

A thirty-six-year-old man came to the hospital for treatment of excessive drinking and depression. Both symptoms had been present for approximately four years. He had been treated by a number of different doctors, who had used both tricyclics and MAO inhibitors without success. The patient's depression was characterized by chronic feelings of hopelessness and dread, difficulty in falling asleep, sadness over his future, and feelings of self-depreciation. His drinking patterns were characterized by daily use of between two and ten ounces of alcohol. If he drank more than a few ounces, he would feel more depressed and hung over the next day, but he often felt he needed large doses of alcohol to get him through the day. Both Librium and Valium had been substituted for alcohol with no success.

Extensive history taking revealed that the patient's symptoms began with a panic attack during lunch with a business associate. The patient, a salesman, began to fear that these attacks would recur whenever he contacted a customer. He would get panicky in such situations and soon began to experience anxiety even in social situations that did not involve business dealings. Eventually he was anxious even with close friends. While alcohol was effective in relieving his anxiety, it left him feeling ashamed, guilty, and fearful as to how long he could continue to function as a successful businessman.

It was decided to stop all medication and treat the patient with systematic desensitization. According to the method developed by Wolpe, hierarchies of fear responses associated with dealing with people were developed, and these were paired with muscular relaxation until the patient could in fantasy feel relaxed in each threatening situation. The patient was then encouraged to try making social and business contacts without the use of alcohol and was highly praised when successful. After several months of supportive therapy, the patient felt in control of his drinking, and both his anxiety and his depression were markedly improved.

Unipolar and bipolar depressions are repetitive, tend to run in families, and are appropriately viewed as having biological determinants. Though they are usually treated with antidepressants, neuroleptics, lithium, and ECT are also used. Even here, however, the clinician must not be too mechanistic in prescribing biological treatments. Sometimes depressive behavior recurring for the third, fourth, or fifth time may no longer respond to medication that has previously helped and may prove quite responsive to environmental interventions.

Involutional melancholia is best treated with electroconvulsive therapy, although neuroleptic and antidepressant drugs in combination may be effective. Recurrent depressions in patients with hysterical personality traits are not responsive to tricyclic antidepressants, but there have been some recent claims that they do respond to monoamine oxidase inhibitors and that these drugs may be useful in preventing recurrences (Shader 1975b).

While efforts to classify categories of depression provide some treatment guidelines, the clinician must still make highly subjective judgments in making decisions as to whether to treat depression with biological interventions. These judgments are as difficult as any that are made in clinical practice. One criterion that influences the clinician's judgment is the severity of symptoms, that is, the degree of sadness, of self-criticism, of feelings of hopelessness, of suicidal rumination, of anhedonism, and of such vegetative symptoms as insomnia or weight loss. Severity also influences the type of biological treatment chosen. When the patient is extremely disturbed and when symptoms threaten life either because of suicidal motivation or because the patient is severely restless and in poor health, ECT is often used in preference to drug treatment because it works so much faster.

Biological Interventions

Before treating depression with biological interventions, the clinician must also ask himself whether environmental interventions could, if powerful enough, relieve the symptoms relatively quickly. There is, of course, no way of answering this question without experimenting with some nonbiological treatment, putting the clinician in a very difficult position. If he experiments with a nonbiological intervention and it does not work, effective biological treatment will have been delayed. If he fails to so experiment, he risks prescribing a biological treatment which may be unecessary, may have harmful side affects, and may not be helpful. The clinician is forced to speculate whether he is dealing with a depression that is responsive only to biological interventions, only to environmental interventions, or to both. In this speculation, the clinician can use some of the guidelines above. I have also found the following assessment useful:

1. The patient should always be asked what changes in his life might make him feel better. Often the patient will respond with a request for a relatively unspectacular environmental change, such as more attention from loved ones, which can be initiated. The patient who says that nothing can help is a more likely candidate for biological treatment.

2. The clinician should try to imagine (and sometimes ask the patient) whether highly favorable economic changes in the patient's life might help. This is a highly subjective evaluation, but when the clinician senses that spectacular changes might help, it is worthwhile considering the possibility that minor environmental changes might also help.

3. The extent of the depressed patient's involvement with other people should be evaluated. Some show little affect in relating to friends, family, and clinical personnel. Others show a great deal. With the latter there is some justification for delaying biological treatment.

4. The possibility of recent losses should be carefully investigated. In these days of high divorce rates and rapid shifting from one sexual partner to another, many depressions are precipitated by dissolution of relationships. Usually the partner who wants to sustain the relationship is the one who gets depressed. That partner, although capable of suicidal depression, is very much preoccupied with the lost love object, is experiencing a type of grieving, and may respond to individual or family psychotherapy.

5. The clinician should try to ascertain if there are certain environments, such as situations which distract the patient or put

him into contact with friends or family which dramatically relieve the symptoms of depression even temporarily. When the patient is hospitalized, he can be observed in a variety of environments. Family interviewing creates another environment in which dramatic changes can be observed. Patients whose depressions seem to temporarily remit in certain environments may be good candidates for nonbiological treatment.

In my own practice I always attempt such speculations and if I feel that some form of psychotherapy may work and that the patient's suffering or suicidal potential is not great, I will experiment with individual or family therapy before using biological treatments. If psychotherapeutic interventions fail, a diagnosis of biological depression is, of course, supported. Both clinician and patient lose valuable time when nonbiological interventions fail. For this reason, I will not extend my experimentation beyond two or three weeks. If the patient shows no signs of getting better and if his suffering is even moderate, I will add a biological intervention to the treatment regimen. Using this method I am able to avoid using biological treatment in as many as half of my moderately depressed patients without exposing them to unnecessary suffering.

A cautious diagnostic approach as opposed to a reflexive pharmacotherapeutic approach to treating depression can sometimes spare the patient unnecessary and potentially harmful treatment. Psychiatrists trained in the last ten years have become inured to treating depression biologically. They rarely have the opportunity to see depression treated in other ways and fail to appreciate how often this disorder can be reversed, sometimes quickly, without biological treatment. Older clinicians have some obligation to remind their younger colleagues that even severe depressions do not always have to be treated with drugs or ECT. Some of my own clinical experiences may help make this point:

Fourteen years ago a twenty-two-year-old woman medical student was sent to me by one of her professors after she had complained to him of profound depression. She had been experiencing sadness for several months. She cried frequently, felt that her future was hopeless, and was seriously contemplating suicide. Her appetite had deteriorated, and in the preceding months she had lost ten pounds. She was also complaining of difficulty in falling and staying asleep. While her reality testing was good, this patient had all of the symptoms of the kind of severe

Biological Interventions 191

depression which today would be almost automatically treated with medication.

During our interview she expressed her sadness in a very powerful manner, but was able to relate it to her dislike of medical school. She was a third-year student and was pursuing a medical career largely to please her parents. An exceptionally creative person, she did not find medical work overwhelming but did find it rather uninteresting. She felt it deprived her of time she wanted to spend pursuing other interests. As a woman medical student in an era when medical students were almost exclusively male, she also felt estranged from and oppressed by her classmates. She yearned to get out of medical school and yet was afraid of her parents' reactions if she quit.

In two long sessions over a period of two days the patient ventilated most of her ambivalence about her situation. I took no stand but indicated that I would try to provide emotional support for her whether or not she decided to remain in school. In the course of the second hour the patient made a firm decision to drop out of medical school. As she did this, I could almost visualize the lifting of her depression. She left the hour looking like a different person. She proceeded to drop out, went home to explain her decision to her parents, took a brief vacation, and then enrolled in graduate school in the humanities. A year later she dropped by to thank me. Quite pleased with her own decision, she had not experienced any major depressive symptoms from the moment she had made it. (This case still makes me wonder as to the potential rapid reversibility of biological changes associated with depression particularly in the early phase. The patient was not in the least histrionic and yet moved from a state of moderately severe depression to one of normal mood within the space of a few minutes.)

An eighty-two-year-old woman was hospitalized for the seventh time for the treatment of depression which had been recurrent since her early sixties. She had all of the classical symptoms of sleeplessness, sadness, weight loss, feelings of hopelessness. She had received electroconvulsive therapy in all of her previous hospitalizations. I was somewhat reluctant to repeat this treatment because at that time our techniques for minimizing risks with ECT were not that good, and she had a worsening cardiac condition. In the course of making up my mind whether to use ECT, I had the time to take a more extensive history and discovered that in the two years following her last hospitalization the patient had been cared for by a charismatic physician who often prescribed small amounts of alcohol. The patient had acquired the habit of taking two glasses of beer daily, one in the morning and one before bedtime. She seemed to do fairly well on this regimen until her doctor died. Just two months before her current hospitalization, she went to see a new doctor who told her to stop drinking beer. The patient was able to date the onset of her most recent depression to this deprivation. Armed with this information, I advised the patient that the new doctor's opinion was not necessarily right and I advised her to return to drinking beer. The patient was grateful for my advice and her spirits very quickly perked up. Within two weeks she said she was feeling her old self. I was not able to follow this patient but was impressed that a patient who today would be diagnosed a unipolar affective disorder and would immediately be treated with a biological intervention was quickly relieved by what at first glance appears a minor or trivial intervention. (Some might not view my intervention as all that trivial. I doubt if the beer had much direct phamacologic effect, but I did give the patient permission to return to the use of a heavy positive reinforcement, and I did rekindle her faith in the powers of her deceased doctor.)

A sixty-two-year-old widow was referred to me with complaints of severe insomnia (zero to three hours of sleep per night for several weeks), agitation, a feeling of hopelessness, and powerful suicidal preoccupation. Given the severity of these symptoms, her reality testing was remarkably intact. The patient stated that she had mourned her husband's death several years ago but had not been really depressed until a few months prior to seeing me, when a widowed aunt had asked to move in with her. The patient had always liked this aunt and, since she too was widowed, could see no reason for refusing the aunt's request. The decision to have the aunt move in turned out to be unfortunate. The patient found herself resenting her lack of privacy. Her aunt had changed over the years and was now perceived by the patient as demanding, obnoxious, and critical. Yet the patient could not bring herself to ask the aunt to leave. As she brooded over the situation, her condition deteriorated.

I was sufficiently concerned by the depth of the patient's depression and her suicidal preoccupation to have her hospitalized. In those days, one of the treatments often provided for depressed patients was ordering them to do menial tasks. This was done in an effort to structure their time and to diminish their preoccupation with depressive thinking as well as to provide them an environment in which they might, hopefully, experience and express anger. One of my residents was assigned the task of seeing to it that this elegant and highly educated woman scrub several floors daily. He went about his task in a rather overenthusiastic manner which the patient perceived as sadistic. One day while he was complaining about the poor quality of her work, she exploded. She screamed at him as she had never screamed at anyone before. She threatened him with violence and soon afterward felt as if years of pent-up anger had somehow or other been released. In discussing this episode with me the next day, the patient stated that she felt somewhat different; that she was still depressed, but that she thought perhaps she could confront her aunt and work out a fair and humane way of removing her from the home. The patient proceeded to do this and also continued to receive psychotherapy outside the hospital. Just two months after I first saw her, she was totally relieved of symptoms. Treatment was terminated. Several years later I came to know this woman much better when we became neighbors. She led a very active and interesting life with absolutely no sign of depression until she died at the age of eighty.

THE USE OF ANTYPSYCHOTIC DRUGS

There are several classes of drugs currently available which influence psychotic behavior, and which are particularly useful in the treatment of schizophrenia. These drugs are sometimes referred to as *major tranquilizers*, but the term is misleading since tranquilization is not an accurate description of their complex effects, and the terms *neuroleptic* or *antipsychotic* have come to be preferred. Of the several classes of neuroleptic drugs available for use in this country, the three most commonly used are classified as phenothiazines, butyrophenones, or thioxanthenes. Each of these classes is characterized (a) by some effectiveness in diminishing psychotic behavior at dosages below what would produce major sedative or hypnotic effects and (b) by additional effects they have upon the autonomic and extrapyramidal nervous systems.

The apparent effectiveness of neuroleptic agents in attenuating psychotic behavior has stimulated an enormous amount of laboratory and clinical research on the biology of psychosis. We do not know exactly how neuroleptic drugs work, but do know they influence the way a substance called dopamine is metabolized in the brain (Snyder 1976). (Dopamine is one of several chemical agents involved in transmission of nerve cell impulses.) We know also that these drugs are the most active and effective agents for rapidly removing such observable symptoms of psychosis as delusions, hallucinations, agitation, aggressive behavior, paranoid ideation, social withdrawal, and catatonia. As such they are remarkably useful in controlling behaviors that are highly offensive to others, and there is good reason to believe that they at least temporarily alleviate the patient's suffering. We have also learned a great deal about the side effects of these agents, effects so important that it will be necessary to consider them in some detail as the use of each type of drug is described.

The phenothiazines are the most widely used neuroleptics. There are three clinically useful subclasses of phenothiazines, which differ in molecular structure, and there are several clinically useful compounds in each subclass. Depending upon molecular structure, phenothiazines are divided into aliphatic, piperidine, and piperazine subclasses, and compounds in each subclass have certain characteristic effects.

At this point it is well to warn the reader that there is a disturbing lack of consistency in using brand or generic names in describing various psychotropic drugs. Brand names are frequently used in clinical work or in informal communication, while generic names are regularly used in scientific writing. Wherever appropriate in this discussion, I will provide both generic and brand names to avoid confusion. The aliphatic phenothiazines, of which chlorpromazine (Thorazine) is the most commonly used, have more sedative effect than the others. In terms of undesirable side effects, the aliphatics are more likely than the other phenothiazines to produce transitory lowering of blood pressure (usually when the patient assumes a standing position), allergic skin reactions, and convulsions. They are less likely than the piperazines to produce extrapyramidal side effects. The piperazines produce a high incidence of extrapyramidal effects but less sedation and hypotension than the aliphatics. The piperidines can cause damage to the retina as well as ejaculatory disturbances, but have fewer extrapyramidal side effects than the other phenothiazines. They are similar to the aliphatics in their effect upon blood pressure.

Phenothiazines vary in milligram per milligram potency. The aliphatic subclass has the lowest potency and the piperazine the highest. The approximate dosage equivalence of some of the more common phenothiazines is illustrated in Table 1 (Klerman 1975, Appleton 1976).

TABLE 1

Phenothiazine Subclass	Ratio (to Thorazine)	Compound Generic Name	Brand Name	Dosage (Equaling 100 mg. Thorazine)
ALIPHATIC	1:1	Chlorpromazine	Thorazine	100 mg.
	1:4	Triflupromazine	Vesprin	25 mg.
PIPERIDINE	1:3	Mesoridazine	Serentil	35 mg.
	1:10	Piperacetazine	Quide	10 mg.
	1:1	Thioridazine	Mellaril	100 mg.
PIPERAZINE	1:70	Fluphenazine	Prolixin	1–2 mg.
	1:10	Perphenazine	Trilafon	10 mg.
	1:6	Prochloperazine	Compazine	16 mg.
	1:10–20	Trifluoperazine	Stelazine	5–10 mg.

The butyrophenones are a class of neuroleptics chemically unrelated to the phenothiazines. Several drugs of this class are now available, but the discussion here will be restricted to the one butyrophenone which is most commonly used in this country, haloperidol (Haldol). This is a potent neuroleptic agent (1 mg. of Haldol equals 50 mg. of chlorpromazine) which has few side effects upon the autonomic nervous system but has moderate extrapyramidal side effects.

The thioxanthenes, the third class of neuroleptics to be considered here, are chemically similar to the phenothiazines and are quite similar to them in range of therapeutic effects and side effects. The two most important are chlorprothixene (Taractan), which has a milligram to milligram dose equivalent to Thorazine, and thiothixene (Navane), which has high potency in low dosages (1 mg. of Navane equals 20 mg. of chlorpromazine).

Recently a new class of neuroleptic compounds (the dibenzoxazepines) have been approved for marketing in this country. Experience with these drugs is at present minimal and they will only be mentioned here. One of them, however, clozapine, is of special interest insofar as it allegedly has little or no extrapyramidal effects. One of the first classes of antipsychotics used in this country, the rauwolfia alkaloids, has proved relatively ineffective compared to other neuroleptics and is rarely used today. Most of the following discussion will be restricted to one aliphatic phenothiazine (Thorazine), one piperidine phenothiazine (Mellaril), two piperazine phenothiazines—fluphenazine (Prolixin) and trifluoperazine (Stelazine)—one butyrophenone (Haldol), and one thioxanthene (Navane). These are the agents with which clinicians now have most experience. Psychiatrists should know how to use these drugs and other clinicians should have some familiarity with the principles underlying their use.

Psychiatrists have labored arduously over the past decade trying to determine if some neuroleptic drugs are better than other neuroleptic drugs for patients who exhibit psychotic symptoms. As of this moment the rewards of their labor have been negligible. There are no clear rules for determining which neuroleptics will be most effective in which type of schizophrenia or with which type of nonschizophrenic psychotic behavior. While each of the six most popular drugs can be effective in treating psychotic behaviors there are patients with similar conditions who respond to one neuroleptic drug but not to another. This phenomenon may be related to differences in the way the drugs are absorbed into the blood stream and metabolized. Some patients will also have side effects with one drug which will not appear with another. All of this means that it is difficult to develop clear guidelines to neuroleptic therapy. The clinician must be willing to experiment, trying a different drug when one appears not to be working, and constantly seeking to titrate the dosage so that the patient is receiving the minimum amount of drug for control of symptoms. In practice the choice of drug is most often related to such clinical considerations as the patient's age, health, degree of agitation, degree of cooperativeness, the potential threat to his well-being or health, the various side effects of the drug and to historical considerations such as the patient's past responsiveness to different neuroleptics and even to the responsiveness of his blood relatives to different neuroleptics. It is important also to note that the simultaneous use of two or more neuroleptics offers no advantage over the use of a single drug. The use of multiple neuroleptics with the same patient is not only uneconomical and inefficient, but may increase the probability of undesirable side effects (Hollister 1975).

Biological Interventions

Chlorpromazine (Thorazine) is the most widely used neuroleptic, partly because it is the agent with which psychiatrists have the most familiarity and partly because it is highly effective in sedating the patient and controlling aggression and hyperactivity. Often it is the first drug considered in treating an agitated, psychotic patient, providing the patient does not have serious cardiac problems. Physical and laboratory examinations of the patient are essential before use. Particular attention must be paid to the patient's cardiac status, blood count, and liver functioning. Chlorpromazine, like other neuroleptics, can in rare instances produce liver dysfunction or interfere with the manufacture of white blood cells. Compared to some other neuroleptics, in the early stage of its use it has a more powerful effect in lowering blood pressure, particularly when the patient moves from a recumbent to a standing position. Other neuroleptics such as trifluoperazine (Stelazine) and particularly haloperidol (Haldol) may be preferable for patients with serious cardiac problems.

With highly agitated and uncooperative patients, chlorpromazine (Thorazine) can be administered *parenterally* in an initial dose of 25 mg. This term refers to injection of a drug into soft tissue, muscle, or veins. With neuroleptics only intramuscular injections are used. An additional 25 to 50 mg. injection can be given an hour later if the patient is still not responsive, and subsequent doses of 50 mg. can be given every four to six hours for the next few days. High dosages of intramuscular chlorpromazine are usually unnecessary, since after 24 to 48 hours of parenteral treatment the patient is likely to be willing to take oral medication. With cooperative patients oral medication is begun at a dosage of 100 mg. the first day and is then gradually raised over several days to the 400 to 800 mg. range, not to exceed 600 mg. in the first twenty-four hours. There are no clear-cut rules to follow in reaching an optimum dosage, and different patients will react differently to the same dosage. Some will respond well to low dosages of chlorpromazine (Thorazine), while some will not show improvement until they are receiving as much as 1000 mg. daily. Dosages should rarely exceed 1500 mg., and high dosages should be restricted to nonchronic patients. Some clinicians suggest that in using any neuroleptic, but particularly with Thorazine, it is wise to give a small test dose (25 mg. I.M. or 50 mg. orally) and observe the patient for signs of hypotension or other idiosyncratic effects for two hours. If side effects are manageable, the dosage is gradually decreased (Shader 1975b). In using any neuroleptic it is usually economical, effective, and safe to give single large dosages in a twenty-four-hour period rather than multiple small dosages. This is especially important in using chlorpromazine (Thorazine), where a single bedtime dose will help the patient sleep and will spare him some of its unpleasant side effects. Because neuroleptics are relatively long-acting the patient will still be receiving the therapeutic influences of the drug during his waking hours.

The clinician must observe the patient's behavior daily and be prepared to adjust dosages according to the patient's needs. If all goes well with chlorpromazine (Thorazine) therapy, the patient becomes more cooperative and less hyperactive within five days, becoming more sociable but continuing to show signs of thought disorder for the next several weeks. Eventually the patient behaves in a manner not grossly psychotic. As the patient improves, dosages can be lowered to between one-third and one-fifth the peak dose, drug holidays can be instituted (skipping Sundays, weekends, or every other day), and depending on issues to be considered later, the drug may be discontinued.

Thioridazine (Mellaril) has slightly less effect on the autonomic and extrapyramidal nervous system than chlorpromazine (Thorazine) and is particularly useful in calming elderly patients and outpatients. It does not come in injectable form. Oral dosage can be initiated in a manner similar to that used with chlorpromazine (Thorazine). Dosages should not exceed 600 to 800 mg. daily because of the danger of damage to the retina. Thioridazine (Mellaril) has a slightly higher tendency than other neuroleptics to create sexual dysfunctions in the form of ejaculatory disturbances, and should be used cautiously with young men who are especially concerned with sexual potency. Recently there has been some concern as to the cardiotoxic effects of thioridazine (Mellaril), and it may be wise not to use this drug with patients with cardiac problems (Sugerman 1975).

Fluphenazine (Prolixin) comes in oral and injectable forms. There are three injectable compounds. Two of them, fluphenazine enanthate and fluphenazine decanoate, have an extended duration of effect and are referred to as depot fluphenazines. Because of their prolonged effects, the enanthate and the decanoate forms are primarily used in treating chronic patients unwilling or unable to take regular oral medication. Oral dosages of fluphenazines range initially from 2.5 to 10 mg. and, as with other neuroleptics, the dosage can be raised to control symptoms. Maximum oral dosages of the drug should not exceed 20 mg. (There is also a relatively short-acting injectable fluphenazine, the hydrochloride form, which can be used in approximately one-half to one-third the amount used for the oral preparation.) When the depot fluphenazines are used, the patient's responsiveness to fluphenazine can first be evaluated with a trial of oral fluphenazine; alternatively, treatment can begin with the depot fluphenazines. When using the decanoate form, a dosage of 12.5 to 25 mg. (0.5 to 1.0 milliliters) may be given initially. The patient usually responds in 48 to 96 hours, and the effects of a single dosage may last as long as six weeks. Further dosages are determined by the patient's clinical condition. In using the enanthate form, a dosage of 25 mg. every two weeks is usually adequate.

Trifluoperazine (Stelazine) is a frequently used phenothiazine which has relatively minor sedating effects and is useful as a maintenance drug with outpatients. It used to be thought that this drug was of value in energizing highly withdrawn patients, but it now appears that its energizing effects are the result of an extrapyramidal side effect called akathisia, which is characterized by intensely uncomfortable motor restlessness (Hollister 1975). Generally trifluoperazine (Stelazine), like all the piperazines (including fluphenazine), produces a high incidence of extrapyramidal symptoms. Trifluoperazine (Stelazine) is usually initiated in dosages of 2 to 5 mg. twice daily, although dosages as high as 40 mg. are not unusual. Intramuscular trifluoperazine is available but is rarely used since highly agitated, restless patients seem to respond more effectively to intramuscular chlorpromazine (Thorazine), haloperidol (Haldol), or thiothixene (Navane).

Haloperidol (Haldol) is allegedly more effective than the phenothiazines in treating highly agitated patients with a maniclike component to their psychosis. It has relatively fewer automatic side effects and less sedating properties than chlorpromazine and is often useful in treating elderly patients. In low dosages it is especially useful in controlling the psychiatric behavior of elderly patients suffering from brain syndromes. Used parenterally, haloperidol (Haldol) should be started in dosages of 2 to 5 mg. This dosage or dosages up to 10 mg. can be given hourly until the patient's behavior is controlled and oral medication instituted. When it is used orally, there is a great variation in range of the dosage, depending upon the patient's age and severity of symptoms. Dosages of 3 to 5 mg. daily are common, although dosages of up to 100 mg. daily are not unusual. Extrapyramidal reactions are common.

Thiothixene (Navane) is alleged to have greater sedative and mood-altering effects than the other neuroleptics, but this is unproven. It does have autonomic and extrapyramidal effects similar to those of the aliphatic phenothiazines. An initial oral dose of 10 mg. daily in severely disturbed patients may be gradually raised to 60 mg. daily. For highly disturbed patients injectable Navane may be used in dosages of 4 mg. and administered 2 to 4 times daily. The maximum recommended intramuscular dosage is 30 mg. daily, and most patients are controlled and able to switch to oral medication at dosages of 20 mg. per day.

A brief mechanistic description of the common neuroleptics cannot convey the extent to which art and skill (clinical judgment) and tenacity are involved in searching for the proper drug and titrating its proper dosage. The clinician must always seek the minimum effective dosage, and there is danger in erring by under- or overdosing. As a rule, daily observation of the patient is essential in the early stages of neuroleptic treatment and this goal is most often achieved by hospitalization.

The reader will note the frequent use of the word *control* in the preceding discussion. Neuroleptic drugs do allow the providers of treatment to gain considerable control over the behavior of the recipients. Because neuroleptics are available in parenteral form, they can be easily administered to an unwilling patient. When a patient acquiesces and agrees to take oral medication after several hours or days of parenteral medication, we tend to assume that the patient is getting better and is more rational. But perhaps he is merely getting tired of being stuck with a needle or has learned to cooperate because of an appreciation of his powerlessness. The entire issue of the use of neuroleptics with involuntary patients is complicated by the ethical problems to be considered later in this chapter.

Side Effects of Neuroleptics

Passing references have already been made to the autonomic and extrapyramidal effects of the major neuroleptics. These effects, as well as others, are highly varied and range in seriousness from mildly irritating to potentially fatal. Obviously, it is important that psychiatric clinicians know how to manage these side effects; it is perhaps equally important for all clinicians to assess the psychological impact of these side effects upon the patient when decisions are made whether to use these drugs. The decision to use a neuroleptic should be made not only on the basis of diagnosis but on the basis of value considerations. One such consideration is weighing the obvious benefit of treatment against the obvious danger of side effects as well as the often subtle psychological consequences of these side effects.

Among the milder autonomic side effects of neuroleptics are symptoms such as dry mouth and throat, blurred vision, dry skin, and nasal congestion. These symptoms tend to lessen after the first few weeks of treatment, but they may be quite irritating to the patient. In the case of people who gain pleasure or earn their living from reading, blurring of vision during early treatment can be extremely distressing. Because of their slight anticholinergic effects (or tendency to diminish the activity of an important transmitter substance called acetyl choline), neuroleptics can cause urinary retention, particularly in men who have prostatic hypertrophy. There is a slight risk of precipitating painful attacks of glaucoma, a disorder of the eye which can lead to eventual blindness. There may also be some slowing of bowel function manifested by constipation. All of these risks are slight but increase significantly if neuroleptics are combined with other anticholinergic drugs such as antiparkinson drugs or tricyclic antidepressants.

Previous references have been made to effects on blood pressure. In the early stages of treatment, patients on neuroleptics (particularly the aliphatic and piperidine phenothiazines) may experience sudden lowering of blood pressure on moving from a recumbent to a standing position. Such postural or orthostatic hypotension rarely results in circulatory collapse and can usually be treated by teaching the patient to stand up slowly. In instances of circulatory collapse which may occur after parenteral medication, it is useful to raise the foot of the patient's bed. If the blood pressure remains low, norepinephrine (but never epinephrine) may be utilized.

There is no conclusive evidence of major cardiac complications with neuroleptic therapy. Thioridazine (Mellaril), which is often used with older patients, does sometimes produce electrocardiographic changes and cardiac irregularities, but these symptoms are reversible. Some clinicians prefer to use haloperidol (Haldol) or a piperazine phenothiazine in elderly patients or in patients whose cardiac situation is compromised.

Skin reactions are relatively common. Allergic reactions to neuroleptics can vary from mild to severe and are sometimes severe enough to require switching to another drug. Patients receiving chlorpromazine (Thorazine) may be particularly sensitive to light and should avoid exposure to direct sun. Prolonged use of phenothiazines (and perhaps other drugs which have simply not been available for as long as phenothiazines) can cause pigmentary changes in the skin and eyes. Typically blue-gray or slate-gray metallic discoloration is seen in areas of skin exposed to sunlight. Patients showing skin pigmentation will generally show eye pigmentation as well, beginning in the lens but also appearing later in the cornea and retina. Thioridazine (Mellaril) in high dosages may produce pigmentary retinopathy without lens or corneal changes. Visual acuity may be impaired but usually returns when the drug is discontinued.

Disturbances of white blood cell production (agranulocytosis) is a rare side effect of neuroleptic treatment. The effect often appears early in treatment and is likely to be manifested in symptoms of local infection. It is controlled by stopping the drug and treating the concurrent infection with antibiotics. Jaundice is a rare complication of phenothiazine treatment. Most cases appear in the first few weeks of treatment, often paralleled by symptoms of malaise, joint pains, fever, and nausea. An unexpected fever during phenothiazine treatment should always suggest jaundice or agranulocytosis. Phenothiazine induced jaundice is usually effectively treated by discontinuing the drugs. Butyrophenones or thiaxanthenes can then be used safely.

Neuroleptics may also influence endocrine functioning. Phenothiazines raise blood sugar. Although they do not cause thyroid disorders, they do have some influence on heat regulatory systems of the organism and should be used with care in cases of hypo- or hyperthyroidism. Lactation, breast engorgement (in males as well as females), ejaculatory disturbances, and diminished libido have been reported with neuroleptic treatment. While these symptoms are no threat to life, they can be extremely disturbing psychologically. Many patients will also gain weight on neuroleptic medication. It is important that these patients not be given antiappetite drugs of the amphetamine class since these drugs may exacerbate the psychotic process.

Currently there is no evidence that neuroleptics increase the risk of birth abnormalities when given to pregnant women. When used during labor or lactation, however, these drugs may be passed on to the fetus.

Biological Interventions

It should be apparent that in addition to thorough physical and laboratory examinations preceding use the patient taking a neuroleptic should be checked regularly for symptoms of urinary or bowel dysfunction, changes in sexual function, and unexplained fever. The patient's eyes should be checked regularly for pigmentary changes and intraocular pressure should be measured, particularly if the patient is also using other anticholinergic drugs. Some authorities recommend weekly blood counts during the first three months of treatment. The physician should also be aware of adverse interactions when other drugs are administered concurrently with neuroleptics. Epinephrine should never be used for neuroleptic induced hypotension. Phenothiazines decrease the effect of MAO inhibitors and potentiate the effects of antihistamines, antihypertensives, central nervous system depressants, and reserpine.

Extrapyramidal Side Effects

All the neuroleptics (with the possible exception of experimental drugs such as clozapine) produce extrapyramidal symptoms or disorders of movement related to dysfunctions of specific regions of the brain. The most common of these dysfunctions is the parkinsonian syndrome, indistinguishable from postencephalitic parkinsonism and characterized by akinesia (loss of mobility) and muscular rigidity. The syndrome places severe restrictions not only upon the patient's mobility but also on psychological behavior, interpersonal relationships, and mental processes. The patient moves slowly and stiffly, speech is monotonous in tone, with difficulty in raising its volume. In severe forms there is major loss of arm movement, a stooped shuffling gait, "pill-rolling" movements of the hands, and excessive salivation. These complications usually appear after several weeks of treatment. Severe parkinsonism is obviously incapacitating to patients who require control over fine movements in their work. Treatment consists of reduction of dosage of the neuroleptic drug, the addition of antiparkinson medication, or both. Antiparkinson drugs are synthetic anticholinergic agents. The two most commonly used are benztropine mesylate (Cogentin) and trihexyphenidyl (Artane). Cogentin can be used both parenterally and orally, usually in dosages of 1 to 4 mg. once or twice daily. Artane should be started in low dosages of 1 to 2 mg. one to three times a day and increased gradually not to exceed a maximum of 15 mg. daily. These drugs are not without their own side effects. They have anticholinergic effects and can occasionally produce toxic psychoses.

In dealing with extrapyramidal symptoms, antiparkinsonian drugs should not be used prophylactically but only when extrapyramidal symptoms have appeared. Prolonged maintenance with antiparkinson medication is often unnecessary and it is useful to discontinue it after one to three months to see if extrapyramidal side effects are still present. When a patient has been taking both neuroleptics and antiparkinson drugs for a while and the neuroleptic is discontinued, it is usually wise to continue the antiparkinson drug for a week afterward, since neuroleptics are eliminated from the body more slowly than antiparkinson drugs.

Another important extrapyramidal complication seen early in treatment (usually 24 to 48 hours after the outset of treatment) is acute dystonia or acute and bizarre-appearing muscle spasms which predominantly effect the head, neck, and facial muscles. The extraocular muscles can also be effected, resulting in the patient having a fixed upward gaze (oculogyric crisis). These reactions are more common in younger men. Because of their sudden and bizarre nature, they can be misdiagnosed as hysterical in origin. The acute dystonias are treated with intramuscular injections of antiparkinson agents (Cogentin 2 mg.), intramuscular antihistaminics, or intravenous Valium. These drugs produce a dramatic remission and neuroleptic treatment can then be continued.

Akathisia is a third variety of extrapyramidal complication. It is characterized by an internal feeling of restlessness and by an inability to sit still. The patient appears agitated, walks up and down, and may be unable to sleep. Too often, this restlessness is not recognized as being drug related, and the patient is given even larger dosages of neuroleptics; this, of course, only aggravates the symptom. The akathisias, when present, are understandably powerful factors in the patient's unwillingness to take neuroleptics. Akathisia, when it is seen within a few days of the onset of neuroleptic treatment, is relatively easily treated with antiparkinson drugs.

Akathisia occurring after weeks, months, or years of neuroleptic treatment is more difficult to treat without reducing or discontinuing the neuroleptics, and may be associated with tardive dyskinesia, undoubtedly the most severe extrapyramidal side effect of neuroleptic treatment. Characterized by chronic, bizarre, and involuntary movements of the face, mouth, and tongue, it is most commonly seen after prolonged use of high dosages. Though more common in the elderly, particularly in women, it can occur also in young patients and in males after only brief periods of treatment at low dosages. Tardive dyskinesia begins with exaggerated chewing movements or licking of the lips. Abnormal movements of the tongue can be observed on examination. As the condition progresses, there is a constant mouthing, chewing, and licking of the lips as well as protrusion of the tongue. Although these movements are quite bizarre (almost grotesque), schizophrenic patients rarely complain about them. The condition may also involve writhing movements of the arms, trunk, and pelvis. Some researchers estimate that as many as 40 percent of elderly patients and 20 percent of young chronically institutionalized patients develop tardive dyskinesia (Crane 1973).

Unfortunately there is no treatment for tardive dyskinesia currently available. The symptoms can be suppressed temporarily by increasing the dosages of neuroleptic medication, but since it is the drug which causes the disorder, this may lead to an escalation of symptomatology. Concomitant use of antiparkinson drugs with neuroleptics can exacerbate or precipitate the condition. The most effective treatment available now is gradual withdrawal of neuroleptics. Realizing the frequency and dangerousness of tardive dyskinesia, pharmacotherapists have in the past few years called for increasing caution in neuroleptic treatment, recommending the use of minimal dosages and drug holidays. Increasingly, pharmacotherapists are insisting as well upon precise diagnosis of schizophrenic psychosis before neuroleptics are prescribed for a patient.

A few more neurological and psychological complications should be considered. Neuroleptics lower the seizure threshold and may provoke seizures in those susceptible to epilepsy. Delirious states can be induced by the combined anticholinergic effects of antiparkinson and neuroleptic drugs. Finally, a sizable number of patients show increased or sustained psychotic symptomatology or major symptoms of depression in the second to fourth month of treatment. It is difficult to know whether such symptoms are a result of inadequate treatment, are directly related to the effect of neuroleptics on the central nervous system, or are a response to certain side effects of the drug. Postpsychotic depression, or symptoms of depression which appear as psychotic symptoms remit, may be a natural response to the experience of psychosis but appears more frequently following neuroleptic treatment.

All the neuroleptics have varying degrees of influence upon the patient's body image. When questioned closely, most patients on neuroleptics report that they feel the drugs alter their body in some way and may report that this alteration makes them feel strange. Alterations of body image and feelings of strangeness are often part of the schizophrenic picture to begin with, and it is difficult to know the extent to which these changes in schizophrenic patients may be drug related. It is reasonable to conjecture, however, that patients with schizophrenic symptomatology may be especially distressed by medication that has a wide variety of autonomic and neuromuscular effects. Subtle distortions of body image produced by neuroleptics can either sustain psychotic symptoms or be factors in eliciting depressive responses.

This summary of the major complications of neuroleptic treatment should impress all clinicians with the formidable impact their use can have upon patients. Researchers in neuropsychiatry have been scrupulous in describing adverse reaction to these drugs and have shown the customary conscientiousness of the medical profession in warning doctors as to their dangers. Yet most psychiatric articles describing the side effects of neuroleptic treatment usually conclude with the argument that these effects are minimal when compared to the advantages of such treatment. It is sometimes pointed out that in terms of danger to life the neuroleptics may be safer than such commonly used drugs as aspirin (Shader 1975a). While this may be true, such a view does not recognize the enormous deleterious impact neuroleptics can have upon the quality of the patient's life. Consider, for example, what the life of a patient on neuroleptics might be like. Some patients must avoid sunlight. Most should monitor their alcohol intake carefully. Chronic feelings of drowsiness, nasal stuffiness, stiffness, and lethargy may be present. The patient risks obesity. Most important, the patient is constantly suscesptible to disorders of movement which are not only profoundly uncomfortable but which may also preclude work in many professions. It is a rare patient who takes his drugs cheerfully. Not too many take them willingly and as many as 40 percent will stop taking them if given the opportunity (Blackwell 1973). All of this should make any clinician humble and cautious in prescribing neuroleptics, and indeed some clinicians have recently questioned whether treatment with neuroleptics may be worse than the disease (Gardos and Cole 1976).

When patients are severely disturbed and a decision is made to use neuroleptics with or without the patient's consent, there is a limited but still substantial value in explaining the potential advantages or side effects of the drugs. The use of these agents can be explained quite simply to disturbed patients as something that is being done to calm them and to help their thinking. Some warning as to the occurrence of drowsiness, of autonomic nervous system effects such as hypotension and dry mouth, and of changes in the patient's perceptions of muscular and motor activity should be provided in a direct and simple manner. Warnings as to the rarer autonomic and extrapyramidal symptoms which must be watched for are probably best delayed until the patient's more blatant psychotic activity has diminished. When these warnings are eventually given, the clinician must exercise great skill not to frighten the patient yet must at the same time be scrupulously honest. The patient can be forewarned of the necessity to be alert to the appearance of side effects and still be assured that most side effects are usually nonlethal and treatable.

It is especially important that the acutely disturbed patient, in addition to being informed that the drug will make him feel better and think more clearly, should be informed that the drug may effect his body image. Unless specifically forewarned that neuroleptics can do these things, a psychotic patient may not attribute anticholinergic or extrapyramidal effects to their use. The psychotic patient who attributes unpleasant changes in body image to something about himself or something about the external world other than the fact of his taking a new medication may become quite frightened and even more disturbed.

Once the patient's more acute psychotic symptoms have subsided, the patient's freedom to reject the use of neuroleptics is markedly increased. There are few instances in which a competent patient can or should be forced to submit to a treatment. Patients who are hospitalized may be subjected to considerable verbal coercion to continue taking medication, but they also realize that if they behave appropriately and are released from the hospital, they will be free to stop taking the medicine. I have found it useful at this stage in treatment to give up much of my authoritarian stance with the patient and to try to enlist the patient's cooperation as a relatively autonomous participant in the decision to continue taking medication. This tactic requires scrupulous honesty in terms of explaining the benefits and risks of continued treatment as well as the risks of discontinuing it. It is important to be frank in admitting uncertainties and ignorance about the patient's disorder and its current treatment. Some of the more pessimistic messages the patient may receive can be tempered by a justifiable optimism as to the possible development of newer and more effective interventions.

Unfortunately in their passionate commitment to biological treatment modalities, many psychiatrists present a mystical picture of pharmacotherapy to their patients. The patient is told that he must take his medicine if he is going to get better and that failure to continue medication for a lengthy period will result in recurrence of symptoms. Neither of these statements is absolutely true and, as I will note shortly, the latter statement may have as much as a 50 percent chance of being inaccurate. It can be argued that white lies to the patient are justified if they help him cooperate in necessary treatment. But the facts are that an authoritarian approach to drug therapy still does not prevent many patients from resisting this intervention. It has been estimated that as many as 25 to 50 percent of outpatients fail to take prescribed neuroleptic medication, and as many as 20 percent of inpatients somehow avoid ingesting their medication (Ayd 1975). This failure cannot be interpreted as perversity on the part of these patients or as a manifestation of their illness, but is in my opinion an understandable, if sometimes ill-advised, decision to try to escape the unpleasant influence of these drugs. Treating the patient as a responsible person increases the probability that he will continue to use medication he might need. Another benefit of this approach is that when the prescription of drugs is based upon an appeal to the patient's more rational self, the clinician immediately sets up an expectation in the patient that he will be treated as a fully respected human being and will be expected to seek and achieve more rational behavior in all aspects of his life.

Duration of treatment with neuroleptics should be as brief as possible. In the past many people diagnosed as schizophrenic have been told they must remain on neuroleptics indefinitely. Yet most studies show that only 45 percent of chronic schizophrenics relapse if their medication is withdrawn (Troshinsky, Aaronson, and Stone 1962, Hirsch et al. 1973). In assessing research on discontinuing medication in chronic schizophrenics, Gardos and Cole (1976) concluded that as many as 50 percent of chronic schizophrenics receiving maintenance neuroleptic therapy could be safely withdrawn. In view of the substantial risks of tardive dyskinesia, they concluded that every schizophrenic outpatient maintained on antipsychotic medication should have the benefit of an adequate trial without drugs. (The withdrawal of neuroleptic medication after many months or years of usage is not without hazards. Tardive dyskinesia can begin once treatment is withdrawn.)

In treating patients who have experienced acute psychotic episodes, the general practice has been to retain them on medication at least six months and often indefinitely. Where other modalities of treatment such as psychotherapy are available to the patient, my own practice has been to experiment with gradual drug withdrawal very early in treatment (after six to eight weeks) if the patient has been relatively symptom free for as long as two weeks and to make at least one effort to withdraw the patient before six months of therapy has elapsed. Often the patient's psychosis seems to run its course over a period of several weeks and neuroleptic treatment may be either superfluous or a factor in symptom maintenance. My own experience and that of some other clinicians is that a surprising number of psychotic patients do well following withdrawal of drug treatment early in the course of their disturbance—providing other modalities of treatment are available (Carpenter, McGlashan, and Strauss 1977). Of course a sizable number of patients will relapse after early treatment withdrawal. Their drug treatment can be immediately reinstituted. Just as the clinician is concerned with risk-benefit evaluations when initiating therapy, he must be concerned with risk-benefit evaluations in terminating it. Here again the ethical problems are thorny. Does a reasonable probability that the patient will do as well or better without drugs justify the risk of the patient's psychotic symptomatology returning? My own answer to this question is usually yes, since the adverse consequence of prolonged drug use may be more serious than any relapse.

While there has been little documentation of the usefulness of combining neuroleptic medication with psychotherapy, most clinicians believe that combined therapy is desirable. Currently the extent of psychotherapy provided varies from perfunctory to extensive. Even in hospital settings, the extent of interpersonal contact within the milieu which may have a psychotherapeutic purpose varies greatly. In outpatient settings, the patient's symptoms may be merely checked out during regular visits to his doctor, just as his blood pressure or intraocular pressure are checked out, and the patient may be encouraged to continue medication. Such contacts with a helping person may be supportive to the patient and might in a general sense be called psychotherapeutic. Thorough clinicians are likely to spend more time inquiring as to the patient's feelings and the nature of the patient's involvement with other people. The patient may be seen every few months, monthly, weekly, or several times a week. Obviously, clinicians who are most committed to change through psychotherapy see their patients most often.

While I am aware that most studies fail to show any marked advantage to combining psychotherapy and neuroleptic therapy (given the outcome measure of symptom change and capacity to avoid hospitalization), I am convinced that treating psychotic patients with some perfunctory form of individual, group, or family therapy is inadequate. The patient recovering from a psychosis needs help in dealing with the devastating psychological effects of having lost his sanity. He needs the support of a trusting relationship. He needs an individual or individuals whom he can repeatedly use as models to improve his capacity to deal with reality. And perhaps most of all he needs help in coping with the stressful events and conflicts he will encounter in his efforts to lead a fulfilled life. While I realize that drug therapy without psychotherapy is certainly the most economical way to treat schizophrenic patients, I am confident that research will eventually show that combined therapy, as compared to drug therapy alone, is more efficient (in terms of enhancing the patient's capacity for intimacy and for work), diminishes the probability of compromising the patient's future potentials, and eventually increases the patient's sense of autonomy.

ANTIDEPRESSANT DRUGS

There are three classes of antidepressant drugs, the tricyclics, the monoamine-oxidase (MAO) inhibitors and the stimulants. Since stimulants, such as amphetamines, have no proven role in the treatment of adult emotional disorders, they will not be considered here. The tricyclics are the most commonly used antidepressants. Their generic and brand names and approximate dosages are listed in Table 2.

Except for some recent research suggesting that people who excrete low levels of 3-methoxy-4 hydroxyphenylglycol (MHPG) may be more reactive to imipramime (Tofranil) and that those who excrete normal or high levels of MHPG may be more reactive to amitriptyline (Elavil), there are no clear guidelines in the choice of a particular tricyclic (Appleton 1976). Nor is combined use of tricyclics ever desirable. In current practice the patient put on tricyclics is most likely to receive imipramine (Tofranil), amitriptyline (Elavil), or doxepin (Sinequan). Serious depressions which are not complicated by major sleep disturbances are usually treated with imipramine. Amitriptyline has a mild sedative or hypnotic effect and is frequently used when the patient is troubled with sleeplessness. Doxepin is alleged to have fewer anticholinergic side effects than imipramine or amitriptyline and is often used with elderly patients. Like amitriptyline, it has some sedative effect. Imipramine and amitriptyline are usually started in dosages of 50 mg. twice daily and the ensuing dosages are increased according to the patient's symptomatology on a gradual, fixed schedule up to

TABLE 2

Compound Generic Name	Brand Name	Approximate Dose Range
Imipramine	Tofranil	75–300 mg.
Desipramine	Pertofrane Norpramin	75–200 mg.
Amitriptyline	Elavil	75–300 mg.
Nortriptyline	Aventyl	50–150 mg.
Protriptyline	Vivactil	10–60 mg.
Doxepin	Sinequan	75–300 mg.

300 mg. daily. (Lower dosages are often adequate and certainly safer in elderly people.) Doxepin is usually started at dosages of 25 mg. three times daily with gradual increase of dosage up to 300 mg. daily.

All of the tricyclics are characterized by a lag period of five days to three weeks before positive effects are seen. Often the patient will be observed to be less depressed and behaving more normally for several days before he actually experiences himself as feeling better. Because of the time lag in drug effectiveness and because so many depressed patients are treated in settings where tricyclic medication is combined with one or more other treatment modalities, it is often difficult to know if the patient's improvement is related to the drugs or to other interventions. There are controlled studies, however, which demonstrate that tricyclics are superior to psychotherapy or placebo in the alleviation of severe depressive behaviors (Klerman et al. 1974).

In general the tricyclics are most useful in treating depressions commonly described as retarded, endogenous, involutional, psychotic, or unipolar. There is considerable agreement throughout the literature that depressed behavior which seems to be reactive or associated with either long-standing characterological problems or bereavement does not respond as well to tricyclics (Shader 1975b). There is some evidence that tricyclics and MAO inhibitors may be of value in treating phobic reactions, but as of this writing they are not commonly used for this purpose (Tyrer, Candy, and Kelly 1973). Sometimes tricyclics are used in treating the depression which commonly follows recovery from psychotic behavior. The usefulness of this practice is poorly documented and, because of the combined anticholinergic effects of tricyclics and neuroleptics, the clinician must be alert to problems created by using them concurrently. Patients with a history of manic episodes are occasionally given tricyclics during periods of depression. This practice is risky because there is considerable danger that the tricyclics may induce a manic episode. The use of tricyclics in severely suicidal patients must always be carefully monitored, as there is not a wide difference between therapeutic and lethal dosages of these agents.

Tricyclics are anticholinergic drugs which produce a wide variety of troubling side effects through their influence upon the autonomic nervous system. Such symptoms as dryness of the mouth and skin, tremor, blurred vision, and palpitations are usually annoying, but are transitory. More persistent symptoms, such as weight gain or difficulty in thinking and concentrating, may be more troubling. In elderly patients using tricyclics constipation and urinary retention are common; because of the latter, the drugs must be used carefully in males with enlarged prostates. Tricyclics must also be used cautiously in patients with certain types of glaucoma, and, since these drugs tend to reach high concentrations in heart muscle, their use must be carefully monitored in patients with cardiac difficulties. They should never be used in patients who have recently experienced myocardial infarctions (heart attacks). Other side effects, such as agranulocytosis, allergic reactions, endocrine dysfunctions, and such neurological symptoms as difficulty in motion and balance, are rare. Delusions and confused states occur more commonly in elderly patients, particularly those receiving tricyclics concurrently with other drugs having anticholinergic effects.

As potent anticholinergics, the tricyclics have certain adverse effects when combined with other drugs. They may diminish the effectiveness of antihypertensive drugs and they potentiate the effects of alcohol. Their concurrent use with MAO inhibitors is controversial since these drugs in combination potentiate the anticholinergic effects of each other and can produce tremors, hyperpyrexia (sustained high body temperatures), convulsions, delirium, and sometimes death.

In certain instances tricyclics may be judiciously combined with other psychotropic drugs. Depressed patients who are moderately anxious and are having sleep disturbances, even while taking such tricyclics as amitriptyline or doxepin, may receive symptomatic relief of anxiety from concurrent use of minor tranquilizers of the benzodiazepine class such as diazepam (Valium), chloradiazepoxide (Librium) or flurazepam (Dalmane). When the depressed patient is highly agitated or psychotic, combined use of neuroleptics and tricyclics may be helpful. Here it is usually wise to use the neuroleptic drug while the patient is being brought under control and then to discontinue it while continuing the tricyclics. One combined preparation useful in treating agitated psychotic depressions is Triavil, which contains perphenazine (Trilafon) and amitriptyline (Elavil).

Depression, particularly when cyclical, has a time limited quality; once the symptoms remit they may not reappear for a long time. In comparison to the neuroleptics, there has been much less tendency for clinicians to maintain patients indefinitely on antidepressant medication as a prophylaxis. Generally the patient is advised to continue on a maintenance dosage of the drug for six months after symptoms have improved. Perhaps because of their awareness that the period of drug use has a definite end point and perhaps because of the extremely distressing nature of depressive symptomatology, depressed patients are usually cooperative in taking their medication even when the side effects make them uncomfortable. Although amitriptyline (Elavil) and imipramine (Tofranil) are available in parenteral form, there is little occasion to use parenteral antidepressants since the biological treatment of depression is characterized by far more doctor-patient cooperation than is seen in the treatment of schizophrenic behavior.

Finally, it should be noted that a substantial number of patients treated with tricyclics (as many as a third) do not improve. If biological treatment is still felt to be indicated, the clinician is advised to try MAO inhibitors or ECT.

While it is believed that both tricyclics and MAO inhibitors combat depressive behavior by increasing the amount of norepinephrine at the neuron receptor site, the mechanism by which the two classes of drugs accomplish this effect is different. The tricyclics are alleged to block uptake of norepinephrine at nerve endings, while the MAO inhibitors are believed to increase the concentration of monoamines in the brain by slowing their rate of destruction. Because MAO inhibitors have not shown a superior efficacy over the tricyclics and because they have more serious side effects, they are used infrequently in this country, usually when tricyclics have failed. There are two classes of MAO inhibitors, the hydrazides and the nonhydrazides. The hydrazides available in this country are isocarboxazid (Marplan) and phenelzine (Nardil). The only available nonhydrazide is tranylcypromine (Parnate).

MAO inhibitors may begin to have a positive effect within a few days, although sometimes three weeks is required before changes are noted. These drugs are usually started at fairly high dosages and the dosage is not increased appreciably. In using isocarboxazid (Marplan), 15 mg. may be used twice daily and, once improvement is noted, the dosage is cut back to from 10 to 20 mg. daily because the drugs tends to have a cumulative effect. Phenelzine (Nardil) is begun at dosages of 15 mg. three times daily, and the maximum recommended dosage is 60 mg. daily. Tranylcypromine (Parnate) is started at 10 mg. twice daily; daily dosages should never exceed 30 mg.

The MAO inhibitors produce most of the anticholinergic side effects seen with the tricyclics but in somewhat milder degree.

They have other characteristics, however, that make them highly potent agents which can be used to commit suicide. Insofar as these agents inhibit the action of an important enzyme, monoamine oxidase, throughout the body, they have a number of troubling side effects. Tranylcypromine (Parnate) and, to some extent, phenelzine (Nardil) may have a stimulant effect similar to that of the amphetamines. The patient may experience central nervous system and cardiac stimulation leading to insomnia, agitation, restlessness, hypertension, cardiac palpitations, and headaches. Damage to the liver is more common with the MAO inhibitors than with the tricyclics. The MAO inhibitors may also have an effect in reducing blood sugar levels, and they must be used cautiously with diabetics taking insulin because they potentiate and prolong the insulin-induced reduction in blood sugar.

The most serious side effect of MAO inhibitor usage is the so-called hypertensive crisis which occurs when certain food or other drugs are combined with MAO inhibitors. Usually this complication is heralded by extreme headaches, but the patient may also experience palpitations, nausea, vomiting, flushing of the face, photophobia, and sometimes cardiac and pulmonary complications. Blood pressure can suddenly rise to very high levels followed by stroke or death. These drugs are obviously contraindicated in patients with liver or cardiovascular disease, but even the physically healthy person must be observed carefully. Restrictions must be put on the ingestion of foods with a high content of tyramine—cheese, red wine, beer, pickled herring, yeast extracts, chicken livers, chocolate, fava beans, meat extracts, and game. Not every patient on MAO inhibitors who enjoys such food experiences a hypertensive crisis, but the risk is considerable. Certain commonly used drugs which have even a slight effect on blood flow and blood pressure, and which are available in common cold remedies and nasal decongestants, must also be avoided. There is still much controversy in the United States regarding the usefulness of MAO inhibitors, particularly regarding the advantages and disadvantages of using them concurrently with tricyclics. The dangers of hyperpyrexia and severe neurological side effects are always present with combined medication, but some authorities have claimed that the efficiency of combined treatment is sometimes worth the risk (Schukit, Robins, and Feighner 1971). When used concurrently, either both drugs are started at the same time or the tricyclic is started first and the MAO inhibitor later.

There are excellent reasons for providing the depressed patient extensive information as to what effects antidepressant drugs will have upon him, and there rarely are any reasons for withholding it. The anticholinergic symptoms of the tricyclics should be fully explained, and the patient should be warned that certain changes in bodily sensations may occur. The depressed patient, like the schizophrenic, can easily misinterpret bodily changes which are caused by drugs as having other origins and can become quite upset if not forewarned. Asking the patient to be aware of changes, particularly those relating to functioning of the eyes, bladder, and colon, is also of obvious value in helping the physician discover adverse effects. It is also important to inform the depressed patient of the probable lag in time between initiation of treatment and perception of positive results. Many patients expect drugs to work immediately, and when a drug that has been prescribed as a possible cure has no apparent effect, the patient may experience his situation as hopeless. Actually, once the patient is fully informed of the side effects of antidepressant medication and the rate at which the drugs work, the clinician can justifiably communicate a strong sense of optimism to the patient.

There is a greater tendency to use combined treatment modalities with depressed patients than with schizophrenics. The research in this area does not suggest that antidepressant medication interferes with psychotherapy, and does indicate that patients who receive psychotherapy along with pharmacotherapy do somewhat better on such outcome measures as sociability and adjustment (Weissman et al. 1974). Some pharmacotherapists have feared that providing psychotherapy to severely depressed patients could be harmful insofar as it would put demands for change upon them they could not meet. This concern might be realistic if psychotherapy were used with severely depressed individuals without combined pharmacotherapy but, when the two are used together, there is no indication of any harmful psychotherapeutic effect.

Most depressed patients in this country are treated with some combination of pharmacotherapy and psychotherapy, with varying degrees of emphasis on the intensity of the psychotherapy. Patients may be seen only briefly to check medications and symptoms and to provide reassurance, or they may be seen frequently and their intrapsychic processes and interpersonal relationships may be intensively explored. Family therapy is increasingly being used with depressed patients, and in my own experience a combination of family therapy and pharmacotherapy is highly effective in treating severe depression. There is as yet no good experimental data to substantiate my impressions.

LITHIUM TREATMENT

In the last decade lithium carbonate has been used extensively in the treatment of recurrent manic or recurrent manic and depressed behavior. The mechanism of action of this drug is unknown, but it is believed to alter sodium transport in nerve and muscle cells and to both block the release of norepinephrine and stimulate its re-uptake. While the drug is most effective in the treatment of manic episodes, it may also, when used prophylactically, reduce the intensity of recurrent manic episodes; in bipolar patients who also experience depression, it may attenuate the severity of depressive attacks. The use of lithium in unipolar depression is more controversial, but some studies suggest it may be as effective as the tricyclics (Fieve et al. 1975). Lithium has also been suggested as a possible treatment for a wide variety of character disorders, but its efficacy in these conditions is unproven (Rifkin et al. 1972).

Lithium carbonate is marketed under the brand names Eskalith, Lithane, and Lithonate. These products are similar in potency and effect. In the treatment of acute mania, the patient is started on 600 mg. three times daily and the dosage may be raised to 2500 mg. daily until a proper blood level and symptom remission is achieved. Because four to ten days of lithium treatment are usually required to achieve remission of manic symptomatology, highly disturbed patients are frequently started on neuroleptics to control their behavior until lithium is effective. One crucial issue in lithium treatment is that there is only a small difference between therapeutic and toxic dosages. Fortunately, lithium blood levels are easily measured. The patient who is started on lithium therapy should be hospitalized so that lithium blood levels can be monitored and overdosage avoided. Once the drug is started, blood levels should be checked every two days, preferably (because lithium is rapidly absorbed and eliminated) six to eight hours after the most recent dose. A good time for checking blood levels is in the morning, before the patient takes the first dose of the day. When lithium levels are brought up to 1.5 to 2.0 milliequivalents per liter, manic behavior usually remits. At this point the dosage should be lowered to as little as one half the acute treatment dosage. This is because the remission from manic symptoms is associated with decreased tolerance to lithium, and toxicity may occur if the patient is maintained on the initial dosages. Once symptoms remit, the patient can usually be managed on 600 to 1800 mg. of lithium daily. Lithium blood levels at this point should be kept at 0.5 to 1.0 milliequivalents per liter. When symptoms remit, blood levels should be checked every week until the patient is stable. Once the patient is stable, his lithium levels should be monitored every one to two months.

Lithium is excreted primarily by the kidneys. Any condition which compromises kidney functioning, such as renal or cardiovascular disease, severe debilitation, or excessive sweating and diarrhea may contraindicate the use of lithium. Caution must be used in instituting lithium treatment for patients needing low salt diets or diuretics. Lithium can also exacerbate latent hypothyroidism and produce a nontoxic swelling of the thyroid. This effect can be controlled by reducing lithium dosage or by administering drugs which compensate for disturbed thyroid function.

When the drug reaches its peak levels of absorption (at one to three hours), the patient may experience symptoms of nausea, vomiting, dizziness, muscular weakness, and a dazed feeling. These symptoms may not be serious and can be controlled by spreading out the intervals of dosage. At the same time the clinician should be aware that vomiting and sleepiness may be signs of toxicity. When these symptoms appear for the first time, an immediate check of blood levels is desirable. More persistent side effects of lithium therapy are fine tremor of the hands, thirst, and polyuria (frequent urination). These symptoms are difficult to treat but represent no major threat to the patient's life. A few patients may gain weight during lithium therapy. Skin rashes, changes in the blood count, and episodes of confusion have also been reported.

Lithium poisoning is heralded by symptoms of slurred speech, drowsiness, coarse tremors, muscular twitching, nausea, vomiting, and diarrhea. If the drug is not stopped, the patient may experience severe neurological dysfunction including coma, increased deep tendon reflexes, fasciculations, and attacks of hyperextension of the arms and legs. Death may follow. The patient's condition can be helped by any measures which rid the body of the lithium ion, including dialysis.

The evidence for the prophylactic value of lithium maintenance is relatively good although there is some question as to whether lithium maintenance merely attenuates, rather than aborts, future attacks (Coppen, Peet, and Bailey 1973). Since the drug has few side effects if administered in proper dosage, patients with a documented history of recurring manic behavior can be maintained on the drug indefinitely. Older patients and those who tend to have rapid cycles of mania or mania and depression will not do as well as other patients on prophylaxis. One might imagine that, with the relative paucity of side effects and with the dramatic reversal of mania with lithium treatment, manic patients would be glad to stay on lithium. This is not always the case. Many patients resist taking lithium not because of unpleasant side effects but because they do not feel like themselves on the drug, fear that it will stifle their creativity, and perhaps yearn for the euphoria that is sometimes associated with the manic state. Beyond persuasion and reason, there is little the clinician can do to ensure that patients continue to take lithium. Manic patients, except in the acute phases of their disorder, are rarely dangerous, either to themselves or to others. They cannot be forced to take a drug they do not want, even if their resistance puts them at risk of further dysfunction and embarrassment.

Manic patients, who may be extremely disorganized at times, cannot always comprehend and use accurate information regarding treatment. The patient, however, should be told as much as possible, as soon as possible. This is especially important in lithium treatment, since the patient can be a valuable partner in distinguishing transient or long-term side effects which do not herald toxicity from those which may indicate overdosage. As in the case of depression, there are good reasons for the clinician to prescribe lithium medication with a strong sense of optimism. The natural history of manic-depressive disturbances is not as grim as that of schizophrenia, with or without treatment. The manic patient can, in most instances, be assured that he will not experience remissions and that his life in general is likely to be more productive and happier if he continues lithium therapy.

Still, the clinician will see exceptional cases of mania which lead him to question the ethics of lithium intervention. An occasional manic patient may look upon his manic begavior as relatively appropriate and desirable, even after he has experienced remission. Often he will wonder if he is better off as a result of his treatment. Occasionally the clinician will have similar doubts.

A sixty-six-year-old man was brought to the hospital by his children primarily because he was behaving inappropriately. He would keep an unloaded shotgun with the barrel open in his place of business, and sometimes he would carry his gun with him during visits to local restaurants and to the bank. Because the gun was visibly not loaded and not in a position to be fired, he was breaking no law, but his actions, for obvious reasons, were disturbing to others. The patient stated that he needed the gun for protection because there were so many robberies in the community. The patient was also showing symptoms of hyperactivity and grandiosity. He had experienced manic attacks before and readily admitted to symptoms of restlessness, insomnia, and feeling "high," which he viewed as characteristic of his manic attacks.

While the patient was showing demonstrable manic behavior and had a history of such behavior in the past, he was not terribly uncomfortable and, in fact, the attention he was getting because of his behavior and his grandiose fantasies may have been helping to sustain him at a very difficult time in life. As a retired schoolteacher, separated from his wife and living alone, he was a very isolated person who in his nonmanic periods was desperately lonely. He had come to the hospital as a volunteer patient only because of great pressure from his family and the community. He reluctantly agreed to resume lithium therapy, which in the past he had always stopped once he had recovered from the acute phase of his disturbance.

The patient's manic symptoms abated once therapeutic levels of lithium were reached, but the hospital staff were discouraged to note how much more sad the patient became as his hyperactivity and grandiosity diminished. With lithium treatment he was not actually depressed but he was certainly far unhappier. The patient had argued from the beginning that the appropriateness of his behavior should be tested in a court of law and that he should not be hospitalized or treated. After results of our treatment were apparent, some of our staff were inclined to agree with him. He was discharged on a maintenance dose of lithium after efforts had been made to work with the family and community to define acceptable terms of behavior on his part.

This is the kind of case that Dr. Thomas Szasz and his advocates would view as a classic example of the use of psychiatric treatment to obfuscate legal issues and to diminish the patient's autonomy (Szasz 1970). Our staff justified treatment in this case because the patient accepted it and because we feared that his inappropriate behavior and the community's intolerance might have led to harm to himself or others, or to his eventual placement in a long-term hospital or nursing home. We were not especially gratified by the patient's response to treatment, and realized that we had made powerful social judgments as to what was best for him. Our concern as to the ethics of our intervention was mitigated only by the knowledge that our control was temporary and that the patient would ultimately have greater freedom to choose to continue or discontinue lithium therapy.

Psychotherapy should be added to the long-term treatment regimen of manic patients. My own experience in doing psychotherapy with these patients has not been encouraging. I find their egocentricity and narcissism so pervasive as to make it difficult for me to develop the kind of therapeutic relationship in which they can learn and process new information. Other clinicians have had more encouraging experiences and feel that concurrent psychotherapy should be an essential part of the treatment process (Benson 1975).

ANTIANXIETY DRUGS

There are a wide variety of preparations available which diminish anxiety. Some, such as the barbiturates, have a powerful hypnotic or sedative effects and have little current value in the treatment of emotional disorders other than as sleep-inducing agents. (Barbiturates, of course, have important medical uses in the treatment of epilepsy, in anesthesiology, and in the detoxification of patients addicted to hypnotics.) Even in dealing with sleep disturbances, however, barbiturates and other purely sedative or hypnotic drugs such as chloral hydrate, paraldehyde, gluthethimide (Doriden), ethclorvynol (Placidyl) and menthyprylon (Noludar) need rarely to be used because other less addictive drugs with fewer side effects are now available.

In the last two decades a new variety of drugs frequently referred to as minor tranquilizers have practically replaced the barbiturates and other sedative agents in the pharmacotherapy of anxiety disorders and sleep disturbances. These drugs have moderate sedative effects but do not produce as much drowsiness as the barbiturates. They are less addicting than the barbiturates and are far safer since there is a considerable range between therapeutic and toxic dosages. These agents act upon the brain to reduce anxiety in a manner not currently understood. Their antianxiety effects may also be enhanced by their capacity to relax the neuromuscular system. In contrast to neuroleptic or antidepressant drugs, they have no central nervous system side effects and no autonomic side effects.

The two classes of antianxiety drugs or minor tranquilizers most frequently used are the glycerol derivates and the benzodi-

TABLE 3

Compound

Generic Name	Brand Name	Dosage
Diazepam	Valium	5-20 mg. daily
Chlordiazepoxide	Librium	15-100 mg. daily
Oxazepam	Serax	30-120 mg. daily
Clorazepate dipotassium	Tranxene	15-60 mg. daily
Flurazepam hydrochloride	Dalmane	15-30 mg. daily

azepines. Meprobamate (Equanil, Miltown) in dosages of 800 to 3200 mg. daily is the most commonly used glycerol derivative, but tybamate (Tybatran) in dosages of 600 to 1200 mg. daily is occasionally used and is alleged to rarely lead to withdrawal symptoms if abused. Table 3 lists the commonly used benzodiazepines.

Those prescribed most often are Valium (diazepam), Librium (chlordiazepoxide), and Dalmane (flurazepam). Their use is so widespread that Valium and Librium have become the number one and number two most frequently prescribed drugs of any type in the United States. Valium and Librium are absorbed and metabolized rather slowly; Dalmane is a better choice for sleep disturbances since it is metabolized rapidly and does not interfere with dreaming (or REM) sleep. Used intravenously or orally, both Valium and Librium have important medical value in withdrawing patients from alcohol. Intravenous Valium is also effective in relieving intractable, repetitive seizures.

Since all antianxiety drugs have sedative effects, they potentiate the effect of alcohol and other psychotropic drugs and patients must be warned against their combined use. The major problem in using antianxiety drugs, including the glycerol derivates and benzodiazepines, is that they are habituating. In contrast to neuroleptics, antidepressants, or lithium, these drugs make people feel good and patients are not only willing but eager to take them. Addiction can be an especially serious problem with meprobamate;

withdrawal from this agent can produce some of the same complications, such as seizure disorders, that are seen with barbituate withdrawal. In spite of the awareness of the medical profession and much of the public of the potential abuse of these agents, habituation to them is rising at an alarming rate. Much of the blame for this must be assumed by physicians, who frequently, in my opinion, use these drugs inappropriately.

The patient who is acutely anxious is clearly experiencing some disturbance in his biological functioning. We don't have any idea what alterations in brain functions accompany the subjective experience of anxiety, but there are usually measurable autonomic nervous system changes in the anxious patient. Whatever biological changes are present, however, are probably transient because, while anxiety attacks may be recurrent, they are also likely to be easily reversible by environmental change. Thus only two kinds of biological hypotheses of anxiety disorders can be formulated. One is that the patient has some type of disorder which renders him more susceptible to transient episodes of anxiety. The other is that the patient experiences anxiety because of certain environmental events and only during the brief and transient period of anxiety can we think of him as being biologically disordered. While some clinicians believe that there is a genetic basis for susceptibility to anxiety, we currently have no evidence to support this. More important, there is no evidence whatsoever that any of the minor tranquilizers are useful in influencing the patient's susceptibility to anxiety. (It is possible that some of the tricyclics may actually exert a susceptibility reducing effect in the treatment of phobias, but this is unproven.) The only rational use of anitanxiety drugs is as agents for temporary relief of the actual symptoms of a transient but recurring disorder. Since most clinicians continue to believe that anxiety attacks can best be understood and modified by examining the patient's past learning experiences and current environmental interactions, the only rational indication for using antianxiety drugs would be for temporary relief of symptoms. They should be prescribed with the same therapeutic rationale used when aspirin is prescribed for a headache or a cold. (I am not suggesting that antianxiety drugs should be prescribed in as cavalier a manner as aspirin is currently prescribed, but am merely noting an identical rationale for their use.)

Unfortunately, many physicians prescribe antianxiety drugs on a regular basis. Patients are told to take two to four doses a day and are allowed to continue this for weeks or months. This is a clinically unsound and dangerous practice. It is rare for any patient to be continuously anxious for more than a few hours. When minor tranquilizers are prescribed on a regular basis, they are being used as though the patient has a chronic biological condition which is influenced by the drug when there is absolutely no evidence either that the patient has such a condition or that the condition is drug responsive. Given their physician's sanction to continue using a drug which has a pleasant and sometimes euphoric effect, many patients will become dependent on and eventually habituated to the antianxiety drug.

My own preference is to tell patients that these drugs are highly habituating and that they should be responsible for using them judiciously. Sometimes I will prescribe daily dosages for as long as three or four days if the patient is highly demoralized by his anxiety. In treating milder forms of recurrent anxiety, I will provide the patient with a certain amount of the drug and tell him to use his own judgment in using it only when anxiety seems too burdensome to cope with otherwise. My experience in using this system is that patients are able to gain the beneficial effects of the antianxiety drugs and are less likely to abuse them. The approach also makes the patient a more autonomous partner in the treatment enterprise and reinforces a sense of responsibility. In at one research study in a hospital unit, a similar approach was tried and patients were allowed to use Valium on demand (Winstead et al. 1974). It was noted that when patients were given this responsibility, they tended to use smaller amounts.

The habituating properties of the antianxiety drugs put clinicians in the often difficult position of having to persuade patients not to use them. This is in sharp contrast to the situation with other psychopharmacologic agents: there the clinician is often attempting to persuade patients to use medicine they do not wish to take. The irony of this situation is apparent. More often than not, the clinician is in an adversary relationship with his patient, telling the patient to take things the patient doesn't want to take and telling him not to take things he does not want to take. Some practitioners tire of this adversary stance and easily succumb to the patient's demands.

ELECTROCONVULSIVE THERAPY

For almost four decades, electroconvulsive therapy has been an effective intervention in treating patients presumed to have emotional disorders based on severe biological dysfunction. Its use should be limited to manic behavior, highly excited or catatonic schizophrenic behavior and severe depression, particularly depression in older people which is accompanied by features of agitation and psychosis. Until the last two decades the treatment was experienced by patients as quite unpleasant. Patients feared the convulsion resulting from the passage of an electrical current through the brain. One realistic aspect of their fears was that the convulsive movements associated with the electrically induced seizure sometimes produced fractures of the spine. These days ECT is usually preceded by intravenous administration of a general anesthetic such as a fast-acting barbiturate (Brevital). The patient is taken, before breakfast, to a treatment room where the barbituate is injected and the patient becomes unconsicous. The patient is then given a muscle relaxant (Anectine) and the electroshock treatment is administered. The patient wakes up several minutes later and is given breakfast. The muscle relaxant limits the convulsions to minor shaking of the toes. The major body movements usually seen in grand mal convulsions are absent.

The process by which ECT modifies disturbed behavior is unknown. It is difficult to hypothesize what combination of circumstances would lead to a single intervention modifying such widely differing behaviors as mania, depression, and catatonia. We do know that ECT treatment produces an acute brain syndrome characterized by a certain degree of confusion and a drastic loss of recent memory. It may be that temporarily freeing the patient of the troubling thoughts and feelings which accompany his disorder may be critical in the effectiveness of ECT, or it may be that more complex biological mechanisms are involved.

In this age of pharmacotherapy it is not generally appreciated that ECT has, in most controlled studies, been proven superior to pharmacotherapy in the treatment of severe depression (Avery and Winokur 1976). There are still some clinicians who use ECT regularly in treating severely depressed behavior, but most clinicians prefer using antidepressant medication. In one state, California, efforts have been made to bar physicians from using ECT until all other therapeutic modalities have been tried. The reluctance of some clinicians to utilize ECT is difficult to understand when it is appreciated that, as currently used, there are few dangers to the patient's life with ECT and, indeed, a patient with cardiac difficulties may be more at risk using tricyclics or MAO inhibitors than reciving ECT. Even older patients with a variety of chronic illnesses can safely be given ECT. The only major general contraindication is increased intracranial pressure, and this condition can be ruled out by neurological examination and laboratory tests.

It is reasonable to ask why so many clinicians are loathe to use a treatment demonstrably superior to pharmacotherapy. There are several answers. One is that the public, and perhaps clinicians too, have come to view ECT as a drastic and perhaps cruel tampering with the patient's mind and body. Lack of knowledge as to the mechanism by which ECT works continues to be perplexing and makes many clinicians feel frustrated by the magical aura and sense of powerful control over the patient which may be involved in use of ECT. Too many patients and physicians still think of ECT as "shock therapy" and associate it with the potentially dangerous and often grotesque convulsions usual before the use of anesthetics and muscle relaxants.

A more rational reason for not using ECT more frequently is that the brain syndrome it produces can be quite incapacitating. Post-ECT confusion can be attenuated by applying the electrical leads to only one side of the brain, rather than two sides, but some confusion may still occur. Furthermore, there is always concern that the patient will experience permanent brain impairment. A small percentage of patients do report difficulty with memory for months and sometimes for years after receiving ECT.

A third reason for using ECT sparingly is that it diminishes motivation for psychotherapy. Immediately after treatment the patient feels very good, cannot recall many of the conflicts which were bothering him, and has little motivation to explore his past learning experiences or current environment. Once the patient has received ECT, it is difficult for him to view his disturbance as anything but an affliction unrelated to his own behavior or that of others, or to view his cure as anything but the magic imposition of a powerful doctor. After receiving ECT, patients, in my opinion, lose some of their sense of autonomy and much of their motivation to cope with psychological and social problems.

Finally, the relapse rate following ECT is high. Once symptoms are relieved, it is often necessary to intitiate prophylactic tricyclic or lithium therapy; some practitioners prefer to utilize periodic maintenance ECT. Such treatment appears to cut down on relapses, but it involves continuous use of potentially dangerous biological interventions in patients who for the most part become resistant to other less dangerous interventions such as psychotherapy. My own practice (with the exception of an occasional catatonic or manic patient, elderly psychotically depressed patients, or depressed patients with cardiac disabilities) is to use ECT only for major disturbances and only after other interventions have failed. My hope is always to try to produce a remission which does not leave the patient refractory to the benefits of other interventions. Over the years, however, I have become increasingly more willing to use ECT when other interventions are clearly not working, particularly when there is a threat to the patient's life or if the patient's suffering is great.

Although ECT is probably used too infrequently by most clinicians, it is used far too frequently by a few. There are still "shock mills" in this country where patients with minor symptoms of anxiety or depression will almost automatically receive ECT. Some clinicians sincerely believe ECT to be the treatment of choice for even minor disorders. Yet in some instances it may be that overuse of ECT is in part determined by economic incentives. ECT treatment is profitable for the psychiatrist. It requires little time and the fees are substantial. The public and the medical profession have reason to be concerned that ECT may be prescribed too often, just as there is concern that some surgical procedures (such as hysterectomy) are prescribed too often.

Recently one of my colleagues wrote a letter to a psychiatric news bulletin in which he made a simple but ingenious suggestion for diminishing much of the abuse of ECT. He noted that these days the major skills involved in providing ECT are administration of anesthesia and prevention of side effects related to premedication or to the seizure. In most settings, an anesthesiologist is present and responsible for dealing with adverse reactions. The main function of the psychiatrist these days is simply to set the proper current, place the electrodes on the patient's head, and press the button. Whatever benefits might accrue to the psychiatrist-patient relationship by virtue of the psychiatrist's presence at the time of treatment are questionable since the patient is already unconscious, and in some settings it may actually be a rotating psychiatric resident who provides treatment. My colleague argued that anesthesiologists might assume the entire burden of administering ECT. Psychiatrists might then prescribe ECT, but they would not actually perform the procedure or get paid for it. Under such a system, direct financial incentives would never be involved in its prescription. More important, the patient would be assured of having the person who is most skilled in dealing with dangerous side effects present at the time of treatment. Predictably, my colleague's suggestion was not greeted with enthusiasm. Many letters critical of his position were sent to the news bulletin. They warned of the dangers of separating psychiatry too far from medicine and of depriving the patient of the psychiatrist's presence during the actual treatment. In our current political and economic climate, psychiatrists justifiably resent efforts of government or other regulatory agencies to dictate the conditions of practice. But making the anesthesiologist responsible primarily for the actual provision of ECT seems nevertheless a rational and progressive move.

PSYCHOSURGERY

Brief mention should be made of the most controversial biological intervention: that involving direct efforts to alter an individual's neuroanatomy by cutting brain tracts or destroying other brain tissue. These procedures are usually referred to as psychosurgery. The most common of these procedures is the prefrontal lobotomy, a procedure designed to cut or ablate brain tissue in the prefrontal cortex. Prefrontal lobotomy was introduced as a treatment for abnormal behavior four decades ago and until the emergence of neuroleptic drugs was a relatively common treatment for schizophrenic behavior. Lobotomized patients demonstrated a diminished emotional reaction to their delusions and hallucinations. They were more placid and more easily manageable in hospital settings. These changes, however, were accompanied by other highly undesirable side effects. The patients experienced marked blunting of personality, impairment of cognitive functions, and occasional convulsions. In effect, the psychosurgical procedure produced a chronic brain syndrome.

In the past decade much more sophisticated techniques of prefrontal lobotomy have been developed which produce a disconnection of relatively discrete functioning areas of the orbital and medial frontal cortex from intermediate limbic circuits. These techniques destroy a relatively small amount of brain tissue and are not accompanied by the massive, highly undesirable side effects seen in the earlier procedures. There has also been a shift away from using lobotomy as a treatment for chronic schizophrenics and toward using it to treat intractable affective illness and severe obsessional or anxiety neuroses. Some neurosurgeons and psychiatrists have reported excellent remission of depressive, obsessive, and anxiety states with minimal adverse personality changes in patients previously incapacitated by their symptoms (Livingston 1969, Kelly 1973).

Another form of psychosurgery, perhaps even more controversial, is based on the theory that some people become violent because of abnormal discharges from a part of the brain called the amygdala. The violent behavior, sometimes referred to as episodic dyscontrol, is considered a form of seizure. In these cases, efforts have been made to perform amygdalotomies. The early researchers in this area reported some success, but there is much controversy as to the effectiveness of the procedure and as to the potential hazards it presents to the patient (Mark and Ervin 1970, Shevitz 1976).

Currently most psychiatrists agree that psychosurgery is never a treatment of choice but may sometimes be a treatment of last resort. If a patient is suffering from a severe affective, obsessional, or anxiety disorder, if he is completely incapacitated, is he has been treated with every other rational mode of treatment available, and his symptoms have still not responded, then psychosurgery may be seriously considered. In my own practice of psychiatry, which spans almost twenty-five years and has included work with highly disturbed patients in prisons, prison hospitals, veterans' hospitals, and state hospitals, I have never had occasion to recommend psychosurgery. Since I do not reject the intervention out of hand, this might suggest how rare are the circumstances in which its use might seriously be contemplated.

The ethical issues involved in psychosurgery are so apparent they need not be elaborated. When the clinician uses psychopharmacological agents, he alters only the chemistry of the brain and can hope that such alterations are reversible. In electroconvulsive treatment some slight brain damage may occur, but there is little danger that the patient will be permanently incapacitated. With psychosurgery, however, brain function is permanently altered. Whatever intellectual or emotional losses a patient suffers as a result of this procedure can never be regained.

RELAXATION TRAINING

The treatment of emotional disorders would be more efficient and far less ethically complicated if we could find some means of altering an individual's biological state without using drugs, electroconvulsive therapy, or psychosurgery. It would be even more desirable if these alterations could be under the control of the individual himself. We are a long way from developing such interventions but have been recently rediscovering what some Eastern cultures have known for decades, that an individual can teach himself to induce a physiological state which may be quite effective in reducing anxiety. There are now a variety of methods, some of which are highly popular, for helping people to induce what is called a relaxation response or a generalized decrease in activity of the sympathetic nervous system and perhaps a generalized increase in activity of the parasympathetic nervous system. The relaxation response is often accompanied by demonstrable physiological changes which include muscle relaxation, a decrease in heart and respiratory rate, and a decrease in oxygen consumption and carbon dioxide elimination. Subjectively the individual also experiences diminished anxiety and tension.

The most important technique for the clinician to master and to teach the patient is progressive relaxation. This technique, easily learned by both clinician and patient, takes relatively little practice and does not interfere with the patient's life style. Most patients who conscientiously practice progressive relaxation experience considerable diminution in anxiety and report an improvement in their sleep. Patients who use antianxiety drugs or alcohol to deal with anxiety report that the practice of progressive relaxation enables them to diminish their reliance on these agents.

Tape recordings of instructions in progressive relaxation are available and can be provided the patient, who can listen to them and begin training on his own. In my experience, however, it is usually desirable for the clinician to teach this technique to the patient directly. One highly useful description of how this is done has been presented by John Paul Brady (1972):

In this procedure the patient learns to relax one gross-muscle group at a time by first tensing the muscles of that group and then releasing their tension. Relaxation is carried out with the patient in a comfortable reclining chair or couch; it is essential that he not have to exert any effort to maintain posture. The room is quiet, the lights are dimmed, and he is asked to close his eyes. Typical instructions during the first session follow. I begin with relaxing the right upper extremity.

1. "I am going to teach you to relax very deeply. To do this I will ask you to concentrate on and relax one group of muscles at a time. We will

Biological Interventions

start with your right hand, forearm, i.e., your right upper extremity. Now you will find it easier to relax these muscles completely if you first tense them. To do this, make a tight fist, flex your hand and forearm and tense all the muscles of the limb as much as you can." (If the patient is not clear what to do, I passively move the limb into the correct position or demonstrate the position to him.) "Now tense the muscles until you can feel the limb tremble. When I say 'Relax,' in a few seconds, simply release all the tension, let the muscles go and relax completely."

After about 5 seconds of tension I tell the patient: "Relax. Release all the tension in the muscles. Feel the tension drain out of your limb. Keep on letting go until the limb is completely limp." After about 25 seconds of relaxation this tension-release exercise is repeated once or twice more or until the limb is indeed deeply relaxed. This is ascertained by questioning the patient and by direct examination of the limb (passively moving and palpating the limb). I then proceed to have the patient relax each of several other gross-muscle groups in an analogous manner, using similar verbalizations, and having the patient repeat each tension-release cycle once or twice as needed. These other groups are as follows:

2. Left upper extremity.
3. Upper portion of face. Here I have the patient strenuously frown, which tenses the muscles of the scalp, forehead, and around the eyes.
4. Lower portion of the face. The patient is instructed to draw back the corners of his mouth in a wide grin, which tenses the lower facial muscles and some muscles of the jaw and neck.
5. Upper portion of trunk. The patient takes a very deep breath and slowly exhales.
6. Lower portion of trunk. Tightening the abdominal muscles as though anticipating a blow is used here.
7. Right lower extremity. I have the patient extend the leg and dorsiflex the foot to tense the muscles.
8. Left lower extremity.

When the preceding is completed, I give some general relaxation instructions and some suggestions in a monotonous tone that is similar to those used in hypnotic induction. However, actual hypnosis is rarely inadvertently induced in this procedure. Typically, I will say to the patient: "Now relax all the muscles of your body—let them all go limp. Let the last vestiges of tension drain out of your body. A pleasant heavy feeling may come over your body, and you may seem to be sinking deeper into the reclining chair. You may notice a pleasant, warm sensation in your abdomen as you relax more and more completely." And so on. It is important at this point to ask the patient if in fact he feels completely relaxed. If he reports some residual tension in some part of his body, additional tension-release exercises or suggestions of relaxation should be directed at the problem area. It is also useful at times to have the patient vividly imagine a scene or situation he finds especially relaxing, such as watching clouds drifting by overhead, floating in a pool of warm water, or lying on the warm sand at the shore.

Usually a portion of the first three or four treatment sessions is devoted to relaxation training. In addition the patient is instructed to practice progressive relaxation at home at least 20 minutes daily between sessions. The time required for the patient to attain a deeply relaxed state should become shorter with practice. The preliminary tensing of muscles before relaxing them can usually be omitted after the first few weeks of training.

There are several other methods for inducing the relaxation responses and I will describe them briefly:

1. Hypnosis: This technique is largely based on efforts to suggest relaxation and drowsiness. Physiological states can vary in different directions depending upon the nature of the suggestion.

2. Autogenic Training: This technique involves exercises which focus on feelings of heaviness and a sensation of warmth in the limbs, on cardiac regulation, on passive concentration on breathing, on cultivating a sense of warmth in the abdomen, and on cultivating a feeling of coolness in the forehead (Luthe 1969).

3. Yoga: This is a combination of meditation and exercises. Appropriate posutre and control of respiration are essential elements.

4. Transcendental Meditation: In this method an individual is taught a systematic method of repeating a word or sound (the mantra) without attempting to concentrate on it specifically. It is easily learned, is not time consuming, and is becoming very popular (Glueck and Stroebel 1975).

5. A technique used by existential therapists consists of learning control of breathing and posture and concentrating on *koans*, illogical problems such as "What is the sound of one hand clapping? (Benson, Beary, and Carol 1974)"

THE ETHICAL USE OF BIOLOGICAL TREATMENTS

Perhaps the most critical ethical issue in biological treatment is that of forcing such treatment upon a patient who does not want it. This complex ethical and legal problem is intertwined with the

Biological Interventions

whole problem of civil commitment to hospitals and would require almost a separate chapter or volume to deal with comprehensively. Here I will only highlight some of the medical and ethical issues the clinician should consider in reaching decisions as to when to attempt treatment of a noncooperative patient.

The clinician's dilemma in dealing with a patient who is suffering from an incapacitating disorder but does not want to have it treated is excruciating. On the one hand, the clinician feels a mandate to alleviate misery and suffering whenever possible. If a biological agent is available which will do this, he will want to use it. On the other hand the patient's autonomy must be honored. We live in a society which tolerates, or at least purports to tolerate, a great deal of variation, and no clinician has a legal or moral right to arbitrarily impose treatment upon a person just because that person is acting strangely or seems to be experiencing psychic pain. The dilemma is compounded by the clinician's realization that the patient may have a disorder of brain function which actually impairs the patient's competence to make a rational decision with regard to receiving treatment.

The clinician can most effectively deal with this dilemma by considering his responses to three questions. First, is there an imminent probability that the patient will hurt himself or others? Second, is there a considerable probability that the treatment the clinician wishes to use will help the patient? Third, is there a high probability that the individual's disorder is actually impairing his ability to make a rational decision with regard to treatment? If all three of these conditions exist or if the answer to all three questions is yes, the clinician should feel free to either begin treatment when the law allows him to do so, or to petition the courts to set up legal machinery that would allow for involuntary treatment. If the clinician can respond affirmatively to only one or two of these three questions, the clinician is best advised to seek some type of consultation before involuntary treatment is instituted, even if the law is relatively permissive about allowing the clinician to proceed independently. Of course many patients who resist treatment are already involuntarily committed to the hospital. In some jurisdictions the fact of involuntary commitment allows the clinician to proceed with most forms of involuntary treatment. This usually simplifies the ethical as well as the legal problem for the clinician because in many states involuntary commitment does not take place unless there is some evidence of dangerousness to self or others, some evidence of incompetence, and some hope of treatability.

Without digressing too far into forensic issues, I believe physicians should become much more comfortable with letting judicial agencies make final determination with regard to treating involuntary patients. Most jurisdictions allow the physician considerable leeway in the emergency treatment of acutely psychotic individuals who are violent, suicidal, or whose lives are in danger because of malnutrition or hyperactivity. Here involuntary commitment can be instituted immediately and, as a rule, treatment can be provided once such commitment has been initiated. It is imperative that clinicians have the freedom to act relatively independently in emergency situations. In all other situations the clinician should accept a more passive role. He should see himself primarily as an expert who recommends a given treatment on the basis of a good diagnosis and humanistic motivations and should allow the final decision with regard to the actual institution of the treatment to be made by the courts. Our society has wisely decided that the imposing of treatment upon a person who does not want treatment is sometimes too important an issue to be decided solely by physicians (Brooks 1974). The need to constantly go through legal jurisdictions is a source of constant annoyance and frustration to physicians. It uses up our time, compromises our authority, and sometimes makes it impossible to treat people who are not dangerous to themselves or others, but who are ruining their own lives and the lives of those around them. Nevertheless we must appreciate that some values, such as freedom, may at times supersede values such as health and that in the long run increased protection of patient's civil rights may help more patients than it hurts.

Other ethical problems with regard to the use of biological interventions have been alluded to frequently throughout this chapter. In the main, problems arise either because of inaccurate or inadequate diagnosis. When a patient is incorrectly diagnosed as suffering primarily from a biological disorder, he is likely to be labeled as diseased and to receive a treatment that will help convince him he is diseased. That patient may unnecessarily lose status and power within social systems. If other individuals within his social network have had some role in creating the disorder, they may be totally absolved of responsibility. There is likely to be considerable compromising of the patient's future capacity to deal with aspects of his social network which may be oppressive. If inaccurate diagnosis is accompanied by a one-dimensional

Biological Interventions 235

approach in which nonbiological treatment modalities are neglected, the patient's future may be compromised even further.

In using the term *inadequate diagnosis*, I am referring to the tendency of many practitioners to fail to examine all aspects of causality and to consider all forms of intervention. Neglect of environmental variables is crucial here. An individual can have a biological dysfunction and yet his symptoms can still be, in part initiated or sustained by an oppressive environment. Failure to deal with that environment may make the patient's future situation worse, even if the biological treatment is successful in relieving some of his symptoms.

There is, finally, one subtle issue which is both ethical and practical and which is especially important in using biological interventions. It relates to how the patient and those around him explain the patient's disorder in terms of responsibility or blame. To put this issue in oversimplified terms, we can assume that there are only three ways in which a patient can invoke blame or responsibility for his disorder. First, he can blame himself and believe that he is suffering as a result of his own action or inaction. He is then likely to view his treatment in terms of future changes in behavior which he must initiate. Second, he can blame others. He may then believe that relief from suffering will be dependent upon the willingness of others to change or upon his own capacity to change their behavior. Third, he can view his suffering as an affliction or as an act of nature or of God, in which case he must rely on the ministrations of some external healing force for his cure. Most patients probably invoke some element of all three of the above explanations in understanding their own disorders. In a general sense, it is probably true that the healing process can usually be expedited by actions one takes on one's own behalf, by changes others may make, or by treatments imposed by those with the authority to treat afflictions. It is also true, however, that most patients (and some practitioners) have a great deal of difficulty in grasping concepts which involve multiple explanations. Many patients are likely to cling to one of the above three explanations as most relevant to their disorder and will have little incentive to seek or accept modalities of treatment which may philosophically be based on the others.

When a patient is treated with a biological intervention other than antianxiety medication or relaxation techniques, he is given a powerful message that he has an affliction or disease. That message can be either reassuring or fightening. On the one hand, it absolves the patient of a certain amount of responsibility for his behavior and enables him to avoid blaming himself needlessly. It will also absolve others in his social network of responsibility and diminish the patient's tendency to blame others. On the other hand, acceptance of the disease concept puts the patient in a position where he feels diminished control of his own destiny and feels diminished capability of changing his own behavior. People react differently to the message that their disorder is an affliction, but many will react to the message by accepting their condition passively and by diminishing their efforts to change themselves or those in their environment. While this response may spare the patient needless anguish and activity, it may also have undesirable effects. The patient may have less motivation to participate in such interventions as individual and family psychotherapy. His diminished motivation to examine psychological and social problems may deprive him of therapeutic gains and increase the probability that he will remain disturbed. In this sense, labeling the patient as diseased, together with the provision of powerful biological treatment, may have something of the quality of a self-fulfilling prophecy.

While I have previously referred to research which indicates that pharmacological therapy does not compromise the value of concurrent psychotherapy, this research cannot tell us how many patients who are treated with biological intervention avoid psychotherapy altogether because they totally explain their disorder to themselves as an affliction. My own suspicion is that many psychotic and depressed individuals may resist exploration of self and environment partly because they have developed an affliction model of their disorder which has been reinforced by biological treatment. It is common, in my experience, to see patients and families with modifiable nonbiological problems grasp on to the affliction model of disorder and tenaciously resist all efforts at individual or family system exploration.

While the clinician cannot avoid reinforcing affliction models of explanation in patients and their families every time he prescribes a biological intervention, there are some steps he can take to diminish the probabilities of compromising the patient's capacity to benefit from other interventions. The clinician can be scrupulous in considering all levels of explanation and can relate to the patient with an attitude that implies that attribution of responsibility for the patient's disorder can be seen in various ways. To put this differently, the main message which the clinician must get across to the patient and his family is that the presence of a biological disorder should never be used as a rationalization for avoiding self-examination or examination of family interactions. At the same time neither the patient nor the family should be psychologically flagellated for events or conditions they cannot control. The clinician merely asks the patient and family to explore the possibility that they had some role in creating the disorder. He avoids imputing blame and never imputes total blame to individuals. The clinical attitudes I consider most useful in dealing with this problem can be illustrated by a case example.

A twenty-year-old man was admitted to my hospital unit with classical symptoms of mania. His behavior was so disturbing to himself and to others that lithium treatment was instituted after only a few days of hospitalization, and it was almost immediately effective. The doctor who worked with the patient told him that there was a good probability that the disturbance was the first episode of a bipolar affective disorder and that the patient should think of himself as having experienced an illness. The patient readily accepted this explanation and felt relieved that he did not have to feel wholly responsible for some of the abrasive and embarrassing acts he had performed while disturbed. At the same time, however, the patient was told that it was likely that other emotional problems, both intrapsychic and related to his family, may have played some role in eliciting his disturbance. The patient was an intelligent, introspective young man and was able to accept this multiple explanation. He said that he had been troubled about himself and his relationship with his family for many years and had seriously thought of seeking psychotherapy in the past.

At this point the patient's doctor asked me to conduct a family diagnostic interview, and I saw the patient together with his father, his mother, and his four younger brothers for approximately two hours. I began the conference by pointing out that the patient had just experienced a disorder which we could think of as being an illness, that I would be glad to answer questions about what psychiatrists have learned about manic disorders, but that I also wanted to investigate as fully as possible any psychological or social factors, particularly those relevant to the family, that might help us understand the disturbance. For the first forty-five minutes I was besieged with questions, primarily from the patient's brothers, as to the causes and treatment of manic-depressive illness. Questions relating to genetics, to the effects of lithium, and to the likely prognosis were repeatedly asked. On one occasion the mother reported her own hypomanic tendencies, and the depressive illness of her own mother, and wondered if she was the "carrier" of the manic disorder. I answered each question as thoroughly and as patiently as I could. Eventually the family seemed to run out of questions.

I then asked what ideas the various family members might have as to how they would have tried to explain his behavior if we did not have so much evidence of its biological origin. Being an intelligent and psychologically open family, they quickly began to identify problem areas. It soon became apparent that both parents, and particularly the father, had put extraordinary pressure upon all of the boys to succeed. The brothers were very competitive with one another, yet very close. All of them perceived the father as a powerful and sometimes frightening person, and frequently they would band together to oppose him. It also became clear that the patient was not accepting of his father's values and wanted to pursue a career in music rather than in one of the academic professions. Just prior to the manic episode, the patient had experienced an important failure in his musical aspirations, and this had elicited an "I told you so" response from the father. Much information relevant to the patient's own behavior was also obtained. The brothers reported that they felt that he had sometimes been treated specially by the parents, that long before he became ill he seemed to have an angry quality about him that frightened them, and that they had always seen him as a somewhat unhappy individual. All of the family members ventilated previously unexpressed feelings toward one another and left the meeting feeling that a great deal had been accomplished. The patient was highly motivated to begin individual psychotherapy, and the family was willing to continue family therapy.

I do not know whether any therapeutic work was accomplished during this interview. I do not know the extent to which this delightful, apparently well-adjusted family could have played a role in eliciting the patient's illness. Nor do I know to what extent the patient's earlier learning had generated intrapsychic conflicts which might have played a role in his illness. I believe, however, that the efforts of my staff and myself to present an open minded position with regard to causality and blame to both the patient and his family will make subsequent treatment easier and success more likely.

The reader will probably note that it is rarely so easy to get a patient who has just experienced a psychosis, or his family, to look at psychological issues once a diagnosis of a severe disorder has been invoked. Admittedly, the family I have described was sensitive, intelligent, and remarkably free of defensiveness. Most of the time the clinician has to work much harder in urging the patient and the patient's family to look beyond the affliction model.

Chapter 6

The Behavior Therapies

In the last two decades a number of techniques for treating emotional disorders have been developed based on principles of learning. These behavior therapies are derived from an approach in which a behavior is viewed as determined by environmental circumstances rather than by drives, forces, or traits residing within the individual. Maladaptive behaviors are viewed as having been learned in past and recent environments, but they are actually treated by creating new environmental circumstances in which an individual can be trained to stop behaving in a certain way or to develop new behaviors. Because the behaviorist believes that behavior is determined by the environmental events that precede or follow it, he seeks to modify behavior by changing these antecedent or consequent events.

GENERAL ISSUES

Behaviorism focuses primarily upon motoric and verbal behaviors which are relatively easy to measure and upon the environments in which these behaviors occur. Little emphasis is placed on thoughts, feelings, or other nonobservable activities of the organism. It takes a considerable shift in perspective for the clinician trained in medical or depth psychology to accept this approach. The clinician who wishes to use behavioral approaches will also discover that he will be urged to abandon medical models of explanation which are based on hypotheses of defective biological or psychological processes. Behavior therapy is based on the assumption that all behavior, whether we call it deviant, disordered, sick, or normal, is developed and maintained in accordance with universally relevant principles of learning. A behavior may be labeled deviant because it does not serve the individual or society well, but it is assumed that it was learned in accordance with the same principles involved in learning a behavior considered highly adaptive. According to social learning theory, a person who experiences sexual gratification only by exhibiting his genitals to young girls learned this behavior under the governance of the same principles by which another person learned to gratify sexual needs through heterosexual intercourse. The only difference between the two individuals is that they have been subjected to different learning experiences. In theory, each can undergo new learning experiences so as to be trained to behave like the other.

The traditional clinician who wishes to utilize behavior therapy is also urged to accept an unfamiliar focus in viewing causality. Behaviorists believe that a large variety of phobic, compulsive, antisocial, and even psychotic behaviors are probably learned many months or years before the patient seeks help. They have little interest, however, in trying to elaborate the exact nature of this learning process; even when they have tried, they have had little success in developing hypotheses which adequately explain how the undesirable behaviors may have been learned. Explanations of past maladaptive learning are of some theoretical interest to behaviorists, but they have practically no relevance in planning treatment. Instead, behaviorists focus upon causal learning factors that exert influence in the very recent past and in the present. These factors are the events that immediately precede and follow the troubling behavior.

Diagnostic processes in behavioral approaches differ radically from other approaches. The behaviorist considers the labeling of behaviors as illness to be unscientific and sometimes socially destructive. Attempts to study the natural history of clusters of maladaptive behaviors or their possible genetic linkages are usually viewed as unnecessary. Biological processes are viewed as important only insofar as they set limits upon the individual's capacity for learning. The role of informational deficits in creating disorders is seen as critical only by certain schools of behaviorism. While environmental hypotheses are paramount, environmental diagnosis is limited to objective assessment of the manner in which certain stimuli and certain reinforcements shape a specific behavior. No effort is made to interpret the social and interpersonal meanings of events which impinge upon the patient. The concept that environmental stress can be a stimulus or series of stimuli which the patient may perceive as oppressive or which may actually be harmful to the patient is rarely considered.

Behavioral diagnosis (behaviorists prefer the term *assessment*) is almost entirely dependent upon observation of motoric and verbal behaviors. There is little emphasis on efforts to discover what the patient is experiencing. The skills which are prized in behaviorism are skills in distinguishing specific behaviors which trouble the patient or others and skills in determining what events precede or follow these behaviors. Skills in establishing rapport with the patient or in establishing an intimate therapist-patient relationship are viewed as desirable, not insofar as they expand information but primarily insofar as they enlist the patient's cooperation in planning a treatment program.

Finally, behavior therapy may be strange to traditional clinicians because it is so frankly based on the authority of the therapist. Successful behavior therapy requires either total control over the patient's environment or total cooperation from the patient. It is assumed that the clinician "knows best" and that the clinician's license to structure environments in which learning will occur should not be jeopardized. Such therapeutic authority is familir to clinicians who primarily use biological interventions, but is somewhat alien to individual, group, or family psychotherapists. In varying degrees, each of the traditional psychotherapies can be characterized by a certain amount of nondirectiveness, that is, by few efforts to provide advice and by lack of insistence that advice will be followed. (A certain amount of resistance to the therapist's wishes may even be viewed as helpful to the treatment process.) While traditional therapists undoubtedly exert considerable control over their patients, many are reluctant to advise specific remedies. Behaviorists have no such qualms.

Partly because the approach of behaviorism is so alien to traditional psychotherapists, particularly psychiatrists, it has had a surprisingly modest impact on clinical practice. Much of the work of behavior modification currently takes place in nonclinical settings such as educational or training institutions. When behavioral techniques are used with patients, they are usually initiated by psychologists. The practices of psychiatrists, social workers, and nurses have, with some notable exceptions, been relatively uninfluenced by behavioral techniques. As is true for biological interventions, there may be some professional rivalries operating here. Psychologists, who are usually well versed in learning theory, have been the major innovators in the field of behavior therapy. Their critiques of nonbehavioral approaches have, at times, been strident. Nonpsychologist clinicians may be reluctant to master the principles of an approach which threatens their belief systems. Psychiatrists in particular may be troubled by the tendency of behaviorists to reject medical models. Furthermore, the physician's medical training does not provide him any advantage in mastering behavioral techniques. If he is to use behavior therapy, he must accept the role of student and realize that whatever expertise he develops will be available to members of many other professions. Such egalitarianism does not come easily to those trained in medicine.

My own efforts to generate enthusiasm for the use of behavioral approaches among psychiatric colleagues and trainees have left me frustrated. Colleagues often maintain defensively that they use a common sense type of behavior modification anyway. They also raise poorly conceptualized ethical objections to behaviorism. Psychiatric residents often resent being taught a technique of therapy by psychologists. They also complain that the actual process of behavior modification requires activities on the part of the therapist that are tedious and boring. There may be some substance to the latter complaint. Compared to the excitement involved in watching patients respond to drugs or develop new insights, the precise bookkeeping and repetition of activities involved in some behavioral techniques are often very tedious indeed.

The reluctance of nonpsychologist clinicians to develop skills in behavior therapy is unfortunate. Unlike the situation with biological interventions, where years of medical training may be required before one can judiciously and safely use them, skills in behavior therapy may be mastered relatively quickly, and profound knowledge of learning theory is not a prerequisite for their use. Any clinician willing to do some reading and to practice behavior modification techniques under the supervision of colleagues can gain some degree of proficiency. At the very least, any clinician can familiarize himself sufficiently with behavioral techniques to be able to determine when and how they should be used, to cooperate with other clinicians in implementing behavioral programs, and to appreciate their limitations.

In terms of models developed in the first part of this book, behavior therapy is best viewed as a series of techniques which deal with changing the patient's environment. Sometimes artificial environments have to be created, but often the patient or those around him can be persuaded to change aspects of the natural environment. Viewed in this manner, behavior therapy has many elements in common with other interventions. One characteristic which distinguishes it, however, is its precise and exclusive focus on readily measurable events. Behaviorists bring exacting scientific methodology to their work, but the cost of this is a limited attention to such important therapeutic variables as thoughts and feelings, which are difficult to measure.

To the extent that behaviorism is a system which rejects multidimensional diagnosis and phenomenology, it can never be a complete system for treating the wide variety of emotional disorders. On the other hand, it provides a useful set of methods for treating certain troubling behaviors with considerable efficiency. Sometimes behavioral techniques relieve extreme suffering quickly and are justified by the value of compassion alone. While behavior therapy, like biological therapy, carries risks to autonomy and future potential, the techniques of behavior modification are so useful that it is no longer possible to be an effective clinician without having some knowledge of their application.

THE USES OF BEHAVIOR THERAPY

One key to the success of behavior therapy is the capacity of the patient and the clinician to define precise behaviors which can be changed. Behavioral techniques are not applicable to such general complaints as alienation, despair, malaise, confusion, hopelessness, and poor self-concept. They cannot help the patient who is looking for emotional growth or self-actualization. Their use is limited to situations in which troubling behaviors can be precisely defined as *target* behaviors, or where the patient is unable to perform some specific, or target, behavior. When symptoms, such as fear responses, can be related to specific events, when the patient is troubled by some observable and measurable behavior, such as exhibitionism, or when the patient is unable to perform certain behaviors, such as those required for pleasurable sexual intercourse, behavior therapy is likely to be either the treatment of choice or a very valuable treatment adjunct.

Given the territorial aspirations of all schools of therapy, it is not surprising that behaviorists have worked to expand the scope of their involvement by diligently seeking to translate vague complaints of human suffering into precise behavioral components. The extent of behaviorism's contribution to the treatment of patients is directly related to its capacity to reduce the complexity of human experience to easily measurable and observable acts. There is always considerable danger that in being committed to such reductionism (reminiscent of that seen in one-dimensional biological approaches), behaviorists will oversimplify problems and overdiagnose the presence of target behaviors that they have some skill in changing. I believe this happens with distressing frequency. Just as the availability of new biological therapies may lead to overdiagnosis of mania and schizophrenia, the availability of new behavior modification techniques may lead to an overdiagnosis of such disorders as phobias. In over twenty years of practice I have seen less than a dozen patients whom I would have assessed as suffering from phobic disorders. Many of my colleagues who are not behaviorists report similar experiences. Yet behaviorists report treatment of thousands of phobic individuals. One gets the impression from the behavioral literature that the majority of patients who seek help suffer from some form of anxiety reaction or behavior which can be easily related to immediate environmental events. I often wonder where these patients are coming from. Conceivably, phobic patients may be avoiding me and other psychiatrists and bringing their complaints directly to the behaviorists; but, since I am a general psychiatrist who practiced long before behavior therapy became popular, this seems unlikely. The best explanations are either that my colleagues and I are underdiagnosing phobic disorders or that the behaviorists are overdiagnosing. My bias toward the latter explanation gains some indirect support from the observations of Isaac Marks (1976), a prominent medical behaviorist, who believes that behavioral techniques are relevant to the treatment of no more than 10 percent of the population ordinarily seen by psychiatrists.

There is an assumption regarding causality in behaviorism to the effect that most human misery is determined by how an individual acts or by his observable behavior. To the extent that an individual can behave in an appropriate self-serving way, he will, according to the behaviorist, be rewarded by his environment and will be well adjusted. Behaviorists insist that favorable changes in observable behavior usually precede the patient's reports of favorable changes in thoughts and feelings. In most other schools of therapy there is an assumption that favorable changes in thoughts and feeling are necessary antecedents to favorable changes in observable behavior. Unfortunately there is no evidence that either view is totally correct. In my own experience I have at various times noted both sequences. Focusing upon the patient's observable behavior is most useful when it is the motoric behavior itself which is generating the patient's misery. But there are many instances in which the treated observable behavior has little relevance to the patient's suffering and in which failure to deal with thoughts and feelings prolongs the patient's suffering.

In fairness, I am probably characterizing an extremist position within behaviorism. Some behaviorists such as Lazarus (1971, 1974) take a more eclectic position and argue that the patient's thoughts, feelings, and interpersonal relationships must be thoroughly examined before a behavioral program is instituted. Indeed, Lazarus makes a strong argument, similar to mine in earlier chapters, to the effect that proper evaluation or diagnosis must precede the institution of behavioral treatment. Lazarus fears, probably correctly, that many of his colleagues are functioning as psychotechnicians and are making only perfunctory efforts to evaluate the patient's difficulties.

The type of clinical error likely to be made when thoughts and feelings are ignored can be illustrated by considering the case of a woman who came to me complaining of frigidity. She had never been orgasmic with her husband and had never had sex with other partners. She said she did not particularly mind her lack of pleasure in sex, but that she very much wanted to become an adequate sexual partner because this would please her husband. An investigation of her marital situation and her entire life pattern revealed her to be a highly intelligent and competent but self-demeaning person who always submerged her needs to those of others. Her husband had obtained considerable success in a job which he enjoyed immensely and led an interesting life with few obligations at home. She felt obligated to take care of all problems related to home and family. Occasionally she felt resentful over her oppressed marital status, but she did not feel she had the right to communicate her dissatisfactions to her husband.

In this type of case (which is, incidentally, quite common in clinical practice) it would have been futile and probably unethical to try to treat this woman's frigidity without examining her life style and her attitudes and feelings regarding her marital relationship. Even if by some extraordinary effort I could have cured her frigidity, it is unlikely that this would have helped her general sense of despondency related to her marriage. Lazarus (1971) reports a similar case of sexual dysfunction, in this instance impotence in a male, which was totally refractory to behavioral techniques but which proved easily treatable once the patient's feelings toward women were elaborated and clarified.

In practice behavioral techniques are most effective in dealing with three types of problems:

1. Anxiety or fear reactions characterized by avoidance of situations which do not objectively threaten the patient but which are responded to as though they did. Included are phobic reactions and some compulsive reactions in which certain maladaptive rituals enable the patient to avoid a feared event such as contact with dirt.

2. Disorders or variations of appetitive functions such as eating, ingestion of alcohol, and sexuality. Behavioral techniques have been used to alter excesses or insufficiencies relating to eating, to diminish excessive use of alcohol, to increase heterosexual competence, and to diminish variant sexual behaviors which trouble the patient or others.

3. General clinical problems in which the frequency of a behavior may be disturbing to the patient or to others. Both low and high frequencies, depending on the behavior, may impair adaptation to social systems. A wide variety of behaviors, including ability to converse with members of the opposite sex, assertiveness, defective study habits, or withdrawal from social contact, can be developed or altered by using techniques based on operant conditioning. In an outpatient setting such techniques can be used to improve adjustment within families. More rarely, individuals may request help in becoming more proficient at a certain behavior, such as dating or studying. Perhaps the most widespread use of operant techniques is in hospital or institutional settings where they can be employed to influence patients to react in ways that society (and sometimes the patient) deems appropriate.

BASIC LEARNING CONCEPTS

There are a number of basic concepts which underlie the use of behavioral modification techniques. To comprehend the manner

The Behavior Therapies

in which behavior therapy works, the clinician must have at least a rudimentary notion of the principles involved in learning and how these principles have been utilized to develop techniques of behavioral change. Behaviorists are concerned with three types of learning: classical or respondent conditioning, operant or instrumental conditioning, and observational or instructional learning.

Classical Conditioning

There are stimuli in our environment which automatically elicit reflex responses in human objects. Food will elicit salivation. Noise or shock may elicit the perception of pain or muscular movement. Stimuli which automatically elicit reflex responses are called unconditioned stimuli. The reflex responses they elicit are called unconditioned responses. Any unconditioned response to an unconditioned stimulus is an innate property of the human organism. It is not learned. The behavior produced by unconditioned stimuli is frequently referred to as respondent behavior.

Respondent or reflex behavior can also occur in response to stimuli which do not automatically elicit the unconditioned response. Neutral stimuli may, through chance or through intention, be paired or presented at the same time as the unconditioned stimuli. When food (an unconditioned stimulus) is placed in the mouth it elicits salivation (an unconditioned response). If a neutral stimulus such as the sound of a buzzer is presented at the same time, it will after a number of pairings elicit the response of salivation when presented alone. At this point classical conditioning has occurred. The neutral situation (in this case, the sound of the buzzer) is called a conditioned stimulus, and the response it elicits (salivation) is called a conditioned response.

Classical conditioning is derived from the seminal work of Pavlov and has been used to produce a variety of behavioral changes in both animal and human subjects (Watson and Rayner 1960, Jones 1924). By pairing neutral stimuli with unconditioned stimuli, the behaviorist can teach animals to perform autonomic responses such as salivation at the sound of a buzzer or tone. Similarly, human subjects can be taught to fear previously neutral stimuli by pairing these stimuli with unpleasant or aversive unconditioned stimuli. The principles derived from classical or respondent conditioning are employed in some forms of aversive therapy and in systematic desensitization.

Operant Conditioning

There are limits to the extent to which behavior is developed or modified through classical conditioning. Most human behavior is not elicited by stimuli and is not involuntary but is rather emitted spontaneously. These behaviors are controlled primarily by their consequences and have some influence on the environment. They can be said to operate upon the environment insofar as they generate environmental consequences, and they are referred to as operant behaviors. Most human responses, such as talking, walking, playing, or smiling, are freely emitted and are examples of operants. Many of the behaviors which trouble patients are controlled by, and can be altered by changing, their consequences. Many of the behaviors which patients wish they could perform more frequently but cannot can be increased in frequency by creating new consequences to their appearance. If a consequence is to alter behavior, it must be made dependent upon or contingent upon the occurrence of that behavior. For a consequence to be called contingent, it must be delivered or appear only after the target behavior is performed and not otherwise. Behaviorists frequently use the term *contingency* to refer to the relationship between the behavior and the events which follow it.

The principles of operant or instrumental conditioning were largely developed by B. F. Skinner (1953, 1971, 1974). They have had enormous influence in educational and training settings and have been used clinically to diminish fear reactions, to change appetitive behaviors, and to diminish or increase behaviors which the patient or others may want developed or changed.

There is considerable controversy within behaviorism as to whether operant or classical conditioning is involved in many types of learning. Some behavioral interventions cannot be categorized precisely in terms of their derivations from operant or classical conditioning. It should also be noted that in both classical and operant conditioning the influence of stimuli occurring before the behavior is produced is important. In classical conditioning, learned or conditioned stimuli develop the power to elicit certain behaviors. In operant conditioning stimuli may also control behavior by increasing the probability that a behavior may be emitted. Much of our behavior, such as eating, sleeping, working, studying, or lovemaking, is influenced or controlled by a large number of stimuli or cues which precede the act. We cannot make a simple dichotomy and say that respondent behavior is controlled by altering antecedent events or stimuli and operant behavior is controlled by altering consequences. Operant behavior is primarily controlled by consequences, but it may also be controlled by altering antecedents. The process by which behavior is determined by antecedent stimuli is referred to as stimulus control.

Observational or Instructional Learning

While seeking to avoid consideration of what they consider the private and unobservable area of thoughts and feelings, behaviorists recognize that a certain amount of learning is acquired through cognitive processes. People learn when they are told how to perform a task or when they are shown by someone else how a task might be performed. Being told how to do something is an example of learning through observation or modeling. Modeling is learning by watching another person perform an act. In this type of learning a response capability may be created or learned without being actually performed.

Techniques involving modeling are frequently used in behavior therapy. It is ofen useful to show a patient how to perform some desirable behavior so that the patient will have an increased likelihood of performing it. The desired behavior can then be reinforced. Modeling procedures have been used to alter fear responses. The concept of modeling is also involved in role playing and assertiveness training. Finally, behaviorists argue that much of the benefit of classical individual psychotherapy is actually derived from the kind of learning that is related to imitation or modeling. The patient observes the therapist's responses to various situations or stimuli and learns to follow the therapist's example.

SOME PRINCIPLES

One relatively simple way of conceptualizing the varieties of behavioral techniques is in terms of their capacities to increase or decrease a behavior. A deficiency of this type of classification is that it is difficult to apply to fear responses. In treating phobias and compulsions, similar techniques are often utilized either to increase a behavior (such as going into a feared situation) or to decrease a behavior (such as diminishing constant hand-washing related to fear of dirt). The whole area of fear reactions is difficult to conceptualize in pure behavioral terms. When we assume that a patient who reports anxiety upon approaching certain stimuli is in fact anxious, we are probably considering thoughts and feelings as well as observable behavior. In treating fear reactions, we are trying to diminish one subjective experience which can be called a behavior (fear) and either increase or decrease an observable behavior (such as performing a previously feared behavior or stopping a ritualistic behavior).

Setting aside the problem of treatment of fear reactions, it is useful to consider how various behavioral interventions either increase or decrease the frequency of a behavior. Behaviors can be developed or increased by positive reinforcement, by negative reinforcement, and by regulating the events that precede the behavior (stimulus control). Behaviors can be diminished or removed by a process of intervention referred to as *extinction*. Stimuli can also be regulated so as to diminish a behavior. Another important principle in behavior therapy is that an undesirable behavior can be diminished by developing a different behavior which may be (a) more socially adaptive than the undesired behavior or (b) incompatible with it. A patient who seeks sex with children but is trained to deal with sexual arousal by engaging in sexual relations with mature partners will be less likely to molest children. A patient who learns to clench his fists when tempted to suck his thumb is thereby prevented from doing it.

Increasing a Behavior

A positive reinforcer is defined as any event that quickly follows a response and increases the probability or rate of that response's recurrence. While a common sense approach would indicate that gratifying or rewarding events would be most reinforcing, it is often difficult to predict which events will be reinforcing for a given individual at a given time. Positive reinforcers need not be rewards. Events which outside observers might interpret as nonrewarding to the patient may actually increase a given behavior in a given patient. When a patient behaves in an abrasive manner and other people respond to that behavior with expressions of anger, even the anger may be a positive reinforcer. Conceivably, the attention provided by the angry response may be specifically reinforcing to that patient.

The issue of positive reinforcement is critical in understanding how certain highly maladaptive "sick role" behaviors develop. Clinicians, especially those who are physicians, often pay a great deal of attention to the unusual behavior or complaints of their patients. This is absolutely necessary if the physician is to be

The Behavior Therapies

thorough, but it may also result in the positive reinforcement of illness behavior.

Many events positively reinforce human behaviors. Food, water, sexual activity, and warmth are sometimes called unconditioned reinforcers since they do not depend on special training to acquire their reinforcing value. Social attention, praise, grades, and money are examples of reinforcers which have been conditioned or learned. Some reinforcers, such as tokens or money, are frequently associated with other events which are also reinforcing since money and tokens can be used to bring on other reinforcing events. They are referred to as generalized conditioned reinforcers. Participation in a desirable activity can be used as a reinforcer. Allowing a person to watch television, stay in his room, or visit with a friend or therapist can be a reinforcer which may be made contingent upon the performance of other behaviors.

Depending upon the type of behavior to be developed, behaviorists pay considerable attention not only to the timing, quantity, and type of reinforcement but also to the regularity with which it is delivered. Continuous reinforcement is often quite effective in the early stages of training a behavior, but intermittent reinforcement may be more useful in sustaining the behavior over a period of time. Positive reinforcement is more effective when the patient is presented with feedback, or information as to how he is doing. Positive reinforcement is also facilitated by efforts to help the patient initiate the desired response so that reinforcement can take place. To do this, environmental prompts or cues are utilized. Frequently one can initiate a desired behavior by demonstrating it to the patient. The clinician or someone else can model the desired behavior. These efforts to initiate a behavior (called response priming) set the stage for the delivery of positive reinforcement.

One important technique based on positive reinforcement is called shaping. In this technique a behavior is gradually developed or built up by providing selective positive reinforcement. The therapist either waits for or prompts some response, such as a mute patient speaking or a phobic patient entering a feared situation, and immediately follows this initial response with positive reinforcement. This increases the probability that the response will be repeated. By gradually increasing the criterion for reinforcement, the desired behavior is eventually built up or shaped. A mute patient, for example, might initially be reinforced for merely moving his lips. As speaking behavior is shaped, however, reinforcement will be made contingent on speaking words and eventually on speaking sentences.

Negative reinforcers increase a behavior in a different manner. They are usually aversive or unpleasant events which, when removed, result in an increase in the probability of the occurrence of a certain behavior. Some examples of negative reinforcement are putting on a coat in cold weather or taking medicine to relieve pain. Putting on a coat removes the sensation of coldness (a negative reinforcer), and taking medicine relieves pain (a negative reinforcer). The wearing of warm clothing or the taking of medication are reinforced by removing the aversive event or negative reinforcer. Some events, such as pain or loud noise, are unconditioned negative reinforcers. Through training, such events as the abrasive behavior of other people may become conditioned negative reinforcers.

Behaviorists distinguish between situations in which a negative reinforcer is terminated by a response and situations in which it is prevented by a response. If an event such as a father's angry look or scowl is terminated by a child's beginning to cry, this is spoken of as an escape response or escape learning. If the child has learned, however, that crying will, in certain situations, diminish the probability that the father will become angry or scowl, the child may begin to cry before the parent actually does anything aversive, and in this situation behaviorists speak of the crying as an avoidance response or as an example of avoidance learning. The reader should be aware that concepts of negative reinforcement and avoidance learning are complex and sometimes nebulous, since both classical and operant conditioning seem operative. Notwithstanding this conceptual problem, behaviorists believe that many of the phobic and compulsive reactions encountered in clinical practice are best understood as avoidance responses.

While the concept of negative reinforcement may sometimes be invoked to explain the learning of fear response, there are few practical uses of negative reinforcement in clinical work. It is possible to use aversive stimuli to get people to perform behavior that would terminate those stimuli, and such practices have occasionally been employed in order to make withdrawn children develop affectionate responses or to direct patients to initiate certain kinds of sexual activity. In general, however, behaviorists have tried to avoid using painful stimuli to develop new behaviors because it is usually easier to develop new behaviors through positive reinforcement. As a corollary of this approach, behaviorists try to persuade family members to restrict their use of such negative reinforcers as crying or shouting in trying to shape behavior of other members. This principle has been borrowed by all schools of family therapy.

Behaviors can also be increased by altering antecedent conditions and by training people to perceive what cues or stimuli in their environment may subsequently be followed by positive reinforcement (altering the conditions of stimulus control). People act differently in the presence of different stimulus situations. They act differently in an expensive restaurant than in a tavern. They act differently toward a warm, affectionate person than toward a surly, rejecting person. The probabilities of eliciting a desired behavior can be increased by placing the patient in stimulus situations which favor that behavior. People can also learn what situations or stimuli lead to positive reinforcement. Some cues in the environment suggest the impending appearance of positive reinforcement. Some do not. By creating proper conditions for positive reinforcement through instruction, modeling, and prompting, the efficiency with which a behavior is developed can be increased.

Diminishing a Behavior

The term *extinction* is used to describe a series of processes which decreases the future probability or rate of a given response. The least complicated process of extinction involves withholding reinforcements from a previously reinforced response. There are many effective uses of this simple process in clinical practice. The clinician, those who work with the patient, or those who live with him can determine which of their responses have been reinforcing the patient's behavior and can stop making these responses. There can be some undesirable side effects to this process. The cessation of reinforcement may cause the patient to develop emotional responses such as agitation, frustration, feelings of failure, or rage. Behaviorists usually advise that when this form of extinction is used, efforts should also be made to develop a behavior to replace the response that is eliminated.

The question of extinguishing negatively reinforced responses is much more complicated. Recall that in a negative reinforcement a response develops as a means of escaping or avoiding an aversive stimulus. Many of the fear reactions seen in clinical practice can be viewed as avoidance reactions. These are extremely hard to extinguish because the individual is often unwilling to place himself in situations in which the aversive stimulus might appear, even after the dangers of the aversive stimulus being present are minimal. An analogy to laboratory experiments might be helpful in understanding this phenomenon. An animal which learns to avoid an aversive event, such as electric shock, by jumping into a different part of a cage will learn to perform the response of jumping when a previously neutral stimulus, such as a tone, is paired with the shock. Eventually the animal will jump to a different part of the cage when it hears the tone, even if no shock is presented. The animal continues to perform this maladaptive response because it has no opportunity to learn that the conditions which originally elicited the avoidance response are no longer present. If the animal is forced to remain in the cage where it initially experienced shock (response prevention), however, it will eventually learn that the sound of the tone is no longer followed by an aversive stimulus and the response of avoiding the tone will be extinguished. In human subjects it has been discovered that the most effective way to extinguish avoidance responses is to expose the patient to the feared situation. Usually by the time the clinician sees the patient, whatever aversive conditions that may have produced the avoidance reaction are no longer present, and exposure to the feared situation is likely to result in the extinction of the fear response.

Behaviors can also be diminished through classical conditioning by pairing the undesired behavior with an aversive stimulus. In the treatment of alcoholism, the sight or smell of alcohol has sometimes been paired with chemical substances which induce nausea. Classical fear conditioning has also been used in treating homosexuality. The homosexual stimulus, usually a picture or slide, is presented to the patient simultaneously with an aversive stimulus, such as a brief electric shock. After repeated pairings of the two stimuli the patient will develop a response to the homosexual image similar to that he experiences with the shock.

In a more sophisticated form of aversive therapy known as covert sensitization vivid descriptions of extremely unpleasant scenes such as vomiting and nausea are actually described to the patient in conjunction with descriptions and fantasies of the undesirable behavior. With some homosexual patients, for example, efforts have been made to describe a homosexual liason to the patient accompanied by vivid descriptions of disgusting experiences that might be associated with such activity. Since

The Behavior Therapies

covert sensitization is a technique which employs only fantasy and does not require the presentation of painful events, it has some ethical advantages over other forms of aversive therapy.

A more frequently utilized form of extinction is punishment. In punishment, events which are usually experienced as aversive are presented *after* the occurrence of a clearly defined behavior. There are two operations involved in the technical process of punishment. After a response, aversive events may be presented or positive events removed. Typical aversive events are mild electric shock, chemicals producing unpleasant reactions, and threats. When positive events are removed, patients are deprived of previously anticipated positive reinforcement. Patients can also be put into situations where they are removed from all positive reinforcers for a certain period of time. Psychiatrists have traditionally referred to such procedures as *seclusion* but behaviorists have given it the more benign label of *time out* or *time out from reinforcement*.

The use of punishment, whether in the form of an aversive event or of deprivation of positive reinforcement, obviously requires a situation in which there is a great deal of control over the patient. Behaviorists are justifiably sensitive to the ethical appropriateness of punishment and other aversive techniques as treatments and also have concerns about their effectiveness. Suppressing an undesirable behavior does not guarantee that a desirable behavior will take its place. Punishment trains an individual in what not to do rather than in what to do. It may lead to undesirable emotional reactions, such as crying or anger, which interfere with new learning. It can also lead to the learning of new avoidance reactions for escaping punished behavior or can elicit aggression toward the punishing agent and others. In general, when punishment is used as a technique for diminishing behaviors, behaviorists believe it imperative that positive reinforcement also be utilized to model new and more desirable behaviors.

Varying the conditions of stimulus control can diminish a behavior. Many appetitive behaviors such as eating, smoking, or sex are cued by environmental stimuli that may have little to do with actual bodily need or pleasure seeking. Obese people, for example, may learn to eat under certain conditions of social interaction, boredom, or frustration. Deviant sexual patterns such as exhibitionism or child molestation may be cued by such situational variables as being in places where the victims can be approached. By controlling these stimuli, it is possible to diminish the frequency of the behavior.

SELF-CONTROL TECHNIQUES IN BEHAVIOR MODIFICATION

In the last decade behaviorists have become more eclectic—less rigid in their commitment to strict Skinnerian and Pavlovian approaches. Increasingly they are concerned with thoughts and sometimes with feelings, which they have traditionally referred to as private and unknowable events. Some behaviorists now believe that these events or activities are influenced by operant conditioning. They describe images and fantasies as covert responses or coverants (Kazdin 1975). Since behaviorists believe that only the individual has access to coverant responses, it is the individual who is in the best position to deal with them. But they now believe that the therapist can play an important role in teaching the patient how to influence his own responses. Obviously if patients can learn to control coverant behavior through the help of a therapist, the range of applicability of behavioral techniques can be appreciably expanded.

These considerations have led to the development of a new school or series of techniques of behavior modification, which is referred to as self-control (Mahoney and Thoresen 1974, Kanfer 1971). When an individual deliberately performs behaviors to achieve outcomes he selects himself, he is engaging in self-control behavior. Some behaviorists believe that self-control can be developed without external reinforcers or contingencies arranged by other people and are convinced that self-control methods free the behaviorist of concern with many troubling ethical issues. Self-control techniques have even been referred to as humanistic behaviorism (Thoresen and Mahoney 1974). It must be noted, however, that it is the therapist who must teach the patient these methods. In the process of such teaching, the therapist retains control over many contingencies, and it is unlikely that self-control can be totally independent of external reinforcement.

Self-control methods usually require that the individual learn to sacrifice short-term positive reinforcement for long-term positive reinforcement. A student may study rather than go to a movie; in so doing, he elects to sacrifice immediate reinforcement for later reinforcement. Similar considerations apply when an individual elects to diet and substitutes long-term gratifications of health and

The Behavior Therapies

attractiveness for the short-term gratification of eating. Behaviorists have noted that self-control behavior is a part of the maturation process of any individual. We must all learn to make compromises in order to achieve ultimate gain. Psychoanalysts would describe the same process as one in which an individual learns to behave in accordance with the reality principle rather than with the pleasure principle.

In examining the manner in which self-control behavior is learned, behaviorists seem to have rediscovered other psychoanalytic concepts. They note that through early training, an individual models himself after significant figures in his life and develops certain standards and patterns of self-reinforcement and self-punishment. This statement would hardly be disputed by psychoanalysts. As behaviorists have ventured into considerations of human development, their explanations of emotional disorders begin to be more congruent with traditional explanations. Indeed even the techniques involved in promoting self-control of behavior, while couched in a totally different jargon, are not unfamiliar to psychoanalytically oriented psychotherapists.

The major self-control techniques utilized by behaviorists are:

1. Stimulus control, in which individuals are taught how to structure or avoid stimuli so as to produce a desired behavior. People who want to develop better study habits are taught to study in certain situations. People who want to lose weight are taught to recognize and avoid situations in which eating behavior takes place for reasons other than relief of hunger. Psychoanalysts might view this process as that of gaining insight into the nature of one's responses to various environmental situations or stresses. In a general way, the concept of insight, in the psychoanalyst's jargon, includes the concept of discrimination training (learning which stimuli precede reinforcement) in the behaviorist's jargon.

2. Self-observation, in which individuals are instructed to carefully observe, and usually to record, their behavior. It is probable that individuals reinforce themselves when they behave in a manner they perceive as favorable, and do not reinforce themselves when they behave in a manner they perceive as unfavorable. At any rate it has been clearly demonstrated that the process of self-observation or feedback can result in change in behavior. Psychoanalysts would probably describe this process as one of gaining accurate information or insight as to how one is behaving. Self-observation surely answers the psychoanalytic dictum "Know thyself."

3. Self-reinforcement and self-punishment, or efforts on the part of the individuals to reward themselves when they are behaving favorably and to punish themselves when they are not. Patients may be instructed or may learn to reinforce themselves with activity such as play or with self-praise when they have behaved appropriately. They may learn to punish themselves by applying a painful stimulus or by being self-denying or self-critical when they behave inappropriately. Psychoanalysts would view this process as a series of efforts to influence and change the superego or the individual's conscience and ego ideal.

4. Self-instruction involves learning to control the messages or language used in determining and evaluating one's behavior. Behaviorists believe (as do psychoanalysts) that children develop a self-directed verbal repertoire which derives from interactions with parents and other significant figures. As people develop, they in effect learn to think out loud, and their thoughts influence their action. By learning to think more positive or rational thoughts, patients can change their behavior. Patients are also trained to recognize when they are presenting themselves with self-defeating verbalizations and to try to control them. These techniques have much in common with Albert Ellis's Rational Emotive Therapy (1962, 1973). They would probably be viewed by psychoanalysts as efforts to change the nature of the superego by modifying the introjects or internalized representatives of parental figures or parental injunctions which guide individual behavior.

5. Alternative response training, in which the individuals learn to develop responses which interfere with or replace responses they wish to control or eliminate. Individuals can be trained to relax and to think pleasant thoughts in order to control tension in difficult situations. They can also learn to perform more adaptive motoric responses which replace maladaptive responses. A patient who constantly scratches himself, for example, can be instructed to stroke himself in a pleasant manner every time he feels like scratching. A patient who feels compelled to engage in some ticlike movement can learn to perform a muscular movement which is incompatible with the tic whenever he feels that the ticlike behavior is impending. It may be stretching a point, but psychoanalysts would probably see some aspects of alternate response training as emotional growth or as expansion of information which enables the individual to experience alternatives to neurosis.

These five self-control methods are currently utilized in many therapeutic enterprises, and have been most successful in the treatment of appetitive disorders, particularly sexual disorders and obesity. While I have emphasized the similarity between self-control and traditional psychotherapeutic techniques, there are two important differences. First, self-control techniques require direct instruction to the patient and, therefore, direct intervention into the patient's life. In keeping with other behavioral techniques, there is little room for nondirectiveness or permissiveness. Second, the use of self-control methods by behaviorists has not been accompanied by any lessening of their commitment to seek precision in defining symptoms, technique, and outcome. Measurement and a willingness to have procedures and results rigidly scrutinized still characterize the behavioral movement and still distinguish it sharply from all other schools of psychotherapy. It is to be hoped that as behaviorists continue to explore areas that were previously left to psychoanalysts and other traditional psychotherapists, their commitment to retain a scientific, experimental approach will have a contagious effect upon all clinicians.

TREATMENT OF FEAR RESPONSES

Although clinicians disagree as to their prevalence, there are undoubtedly a certain number of emotional disorders which are characterized by fear of specific situations or events. Individuals may fear heights, open spaces, closed spaces, social intercourse, public speaking, or many forms of travel. They may show a profound unwillingness to enter into stimulus situations in which such fear might be experienced. People may also fear contamination with dirt, germs, or excrement. They may develop rituals, such as compulsive cleanliness or hand-washing, which are designed to diminish the anxieties associated with possible contamination. In both types of behavior, we assume that a major causal factor is previous learning (although the responsiveness of some phobic behaviors to antidepressant drugs also raises questions as to the relevance to biological factors). Behaviorists most commonly view fear reactions as engendered by avoidance learning, although they concede that it is usually difficult or impossible to demonstrate the precise manner in which those behaviors were initially learned.

Fear reactions can be trivial or incapacitating. Many people have fears of animals such as snakes or spiders. Many more people are quite frightened of public speaking. Often these minor phobias do not interfere with the individual's leading a satisfying life. People who experience minor phobic disorders may never seek help. They can lead satisfying lives by simply avoiding the stimuli they fear. On the other hand, phobic and compulsive behavior can totally incapacitate an individual. Some phobic individuals reach a point where they are unable to leave their houses or meet with other people. Some compulsive individuals structure their lives so that they are almost constantly performing rituals which isolate them from others, and which are a source of great humiliation and psychic pain.

There are also obvious variations in the degree of reality associated with a fear reaction. Sometimes one wonders if those who fear flying are simply more realistic and careful than the rest of us. Fears of snakes and spiders may be adaptive, particularly in regions where poisonous snakes and spiders are plentiful and when one does not have the expertise to make quick discriminations between poisonous and nonpoisonous animals. (When I lived in Wisconsin, where there were many rabid bats but no poisonous snakes, I developed a fear reaction toward all bats and felt quite comfortable when I encountered a snake. Since I have moved to North Carolina, where there are few rabid bats but many poisonous snakes, I no longer fear bats but have learned to be extra alert when walking through the woods and have developed a fear response to the sight of a snake.) There are usually good reasons for most of us to fear public performances. We may have little to say, and there is always the danger we will say something to alienate the audience or that we will make fools of ourselves. In our larger cities walking in the streets at night or even in the daytime is accompanied by realistic dangers. It doesn't do a patient much good to overcome his agoraphobia only to be mugged in the street.

If services are to be provided efficiently, the clinician must make some judgments as to how disabling a fear response is to the patient before undertaking its treatment. The clinician should treat only those fear reactions which the patient defines as inappropriate and which are seriously compromising the patient's enjoyment of life. Fears of walking on a pleasant country road, fears of indulging in conversation with friendly people, fears of public speaking when one has a great deal to communicate, fears of

The Behavior Therapies

flying when one is a successful professional entertainer or athlete, and fears of dirt when reasonable hygienic conditions are present are highly maladaptive responses. They may trouble the patient greatly and successful treatment may vastly improve the quality of the patient's life.

For many years behaviorists have claimed that behavior therapy is superior to traditional psychotherapy in treating fear responses. Much of the original research using behavior modification techniques to treat fear responses was done with nonpatient volunteers and was not controlled. Many clinicians remained unconvinced of the superiority of behavior therapy in this area. More recent research with behavior therapy has, however, been done with actual patients (rather than student volunteers), has used control groups, and has been compared with traditional therapy. All of this research indicates that behavior therapy is the more effective treatment for fear reactions (Marks 1972). My own limited experience leads me to suggest the qualification that behavior modification is most useful in treating *chronic* fear responses. When a fear response has recently developed and when the symptom is being influenced by immediate conflict situations and is not functionally autonomous, almost any kind of psychotherapy may be effective, and classical individual and family psychotherapy may have ethical advantages.

Behavioral techniques for treating fear responses are based on the principle that the patient must be exposed to the feared situation. Exposure in itself seems to extinguish the response. Behaviorists are far from certain as to how the technique of exposure exerts therapeutic influence. Analysis of avoidance learning in animals provides clues as to what might be happening, but these clues are not really explanatory. It is probable that after a period of time, feared situations lose their aversive properties. As the patient ceases to avoid the feared behavior, it is possible for him to learn that its aversive properties have decreased.

There are a variety of well-studied techniques which employ different methods for bringing the patient into contact with the feared stimulus. The first of these to be used in an organized therapeutic manner is the method of systematic desensitization developed by Joseph Wolpe (1961). In working with cats Wolpe noted that animals trained to fear certain situations could overcome this fear if they were very gradually placed in the feared situation and were at the same time presented with the pleasurable unconditioned stimulus of food. Wolpe reasoned that the presence of a fear response might be incompatible with the presence of a pleasurable response and viewed this form of desensitization of cats to phobic situations in terms of classical conditioning. The pairing of the feared stimulus with the gratifying unconditioned stimulus was called *counterconditioning*. From this Wolpe made a speculative leap and reasoned that human subjects who fantasized feared situations while they simultaneously experienced a pleasurable bodily state might also be counterconditioned to their phobias.

Using the technique developed by Edmund Jacobson (Brady 1972), Wolpe trained his patients in deep muscular relaxation (described in chapter five). He also asked his patients to describe a number of situations related to the feared event and to rank them in order of their fearfulness. A person who had a snake phobia, for example, might rank looking at a picture of a snake low on a hierarchy of fearful events, while he might rank touching a snake quite high. When a series of possible situations associated with a feared event could be described in hierarchial order, Wolpe asked the patient to fantasize the least feared situation while the patient was put into a state of deep muscular relaxation. As soon as the patient reported feeling comfortable with the fantasy of this stimulus, the patient was asked to fantasize the next most feared stimulus in his hierarchy, again while in a state of relaxation. Eventually patients were able to tolerate imagination of the most fearful aspect of their phobia while in a relaxed state.

Wolpe's patients showed high rates of improvement, actually overcoming their phobias. The theory he elaborated to explain this improvement was based on the belief that a fear response would be difficult to maintain in a condition of total relaxation. In effect the patient was eased into an exposure situation in a fantasy while experiencing minimal or no anxiety and was in the process desensitized to the phobia. For many years systematic desensitization was considered the major technique for dealing with phobic responses. A number of different methods for inducing relaxation, such as hypnosis or injection with Brevital (a rapidly acting barbituate), were developed, but the principles of the technique remained unchanged.

While systematic desensitization is not a particularly arduous treatment for the patient, it is unfortunately, a very uninteresting task for the therapist to perform. There are few interventions in the behavioral sciences as boring to the therapist as sitting with a patient while he learns to relax and then encouraging the patient

The Behavior Therapies

to fantasize various steps of his hierarchy. Most behaviorists have probably welcomed the newer research which indicates that the only critical feature to Wolpe's method is exposure to the feared stimulus in fantasy. Recent research indicates that exposure in fantasy alone will yield results similar to systematic desensitization (Marks, Boulougouris, and Marset 1971, Marks 1976). Relaxation training can be totally omitted from the procedure. It has also been shown that muscular relaxation without exposure in fantasy is of little value. Experiments have even been done in which hierarchies have been turned around so that the patient was exposed to the most fearful situation at the beginning rather than at the end of the treatment, and satisfactory results were still obtained.

In recent years a new series of techniques or procedures for treating fear responses has been developed. They share the common element of omitting relaxation and attempting to relieve fear by directly confronting the patient with the fear-provoking situation. All these techniques may be described under the rubric of *flooding* (Wilson 1967). Treatment by flooding can occur in a variety of ways. The exposure or confrontation may take place in imagination or reality. If fantasy is used, the patient may simply be asked to imagine various aspects of his feared stimuli. This can be done in a way which elicits either minimal or considerable anxiety. In one technique called *implosion therapy*, efforts are made to have the patient experience maximal anxiety by vividly imagining his worst fears. Although great claims have been made for implosion therapy, the levels of anxiety experienced through exposure by flooding do not seem relevant to treatment outcome (Marks 1976). Flooding in fantasy with minimal anxiety is also effective.

Flooding "in vivo," or actually persuading the patient to enter the feared situation, seems even more effective. Here a number of techniques based on instrumental and observational learning can be used. The patient's behavior can be shaped so as to encourage him to face the feared situation by rewarding a behavior that is a small step in the direction of facing the feared situation. Future reinforcement can then be made contingent upon higher levels of performance. This procedure is sometimes called *reinforced practice*. Modeling can also be used to help the patient intitiate the desired response. The therapist may accompany the patient into a feared stimulus situation and actually confront that stimulus while observed by the patient. Then the patient will be asked to confront the stimulus.

Certain general statements can be made as to the effectiveness of flooding techniques. Outcome seems unrelated to the level of anxiety the patient experiences during the treatment process. The duration of exposure to the feared stimulus, on the other hand, seems much more critical. It is more useful for the patient to face the feared stimulus for a long period of time, such as two hours, rather than to face it during smaller increments of time on several different occasions. It is believed that certain accommodation mechanisms come into operation with prolongation of exposure to the feared situation. Finally, there is evidence that flooding "in vivo" is more effective than flooding techniques employing fantasy.

Behaviorists have also noted that a number of techniques which are based on quite a different therapeutic rationale may actually function to alleviate phobic distress through the principle of exposure. The most important of these is Victor Frankl's technique of paradoxical intention (1960), which involves asking the patients to cease fleeing or fighting their symptoms and instead to try deliberately to bring them on or exaggerate them. This technique was originally developed out of an existential approach and was based on cognitive theories that such efforts might dramatize to patients the absurdity of their symptoms. Other therapists such as Jay Haley have postulated that the technique works because it takes control of the patient's symptomatology away from the patient and puts control in the hands of the therapist (Haley 1963). To the extent that the patient uses symptomatology to control the environment, this technique undercuts the power of the symptom. Behaviorists reason that paradoxical intention may be effective simply because it exposes the patient to the feared situation in fantasy. (The technique of paradoxical intention is mentioned specifically here because I found it useful in helping to alleviate a number of distressing situations not usually dealt with by behavior therapists; these will be discussed later in this chapter.)

It has probably occurred to the reader that a treatment which is alleged to cure a symptom by exposing patients to situations which elicit the symptom may not be welcomed by patients. It is often difficult to persuade patients to enter "in vivo" situations. Some will even resist facing their fear in fantasy. The process of persuading the patient to face his fear may require extensive negotiation between therapist and patient, and will be influenced by the therapist's authority, persistence, and capacity to gain the patient's trust. At some point ethical questions arise as to how much authority can be invoked in pushing a patient to do something that is frightening. With some patients exposure "in vivo" will be so resisted as to preclude any but coercive use, and the clinician will have to use techniques which involve exposure in fantasy.

TREATMENT OF APPETITIVE DISORDERS

Sex, eating, and, to a lesser extent, drinking intoxicating beverages are among the more pleasurable activities known to humankind. For most people, each of these activities is conducted with a certain social appropriateness or moderation which produces pleasure. Often, however, there are excesses, deficiencies, or variations in these behaviors which may cause great distress for the person who experiences them or may lead to irritation or great concern upon the part of others. Excessive intake of alcohol is of obvious concern, both to those who overindulge and to those around them. Excessive eating, as well as inadequate eating, can be a severe and life-threatening problem and can certainly be a major source of concern for the families of patients. Variations in preferred style for obtaining sexual gratification may be of little concern to those who enjoy them, but may be quite troubling to other people in our society who demand a standardization of such activity. When the variation in sexual activity takes the form of exhibitionism, child molestation, or rape, it may be a source of great irritation or real danger to others. Deficiencies in sexual funtion or sexual inadequacy are of obvious concern to those who experience them.

Neither biological interventions nor traditional psychotherapeutic approaches have been of much value in treating appetitive disorders. On the other hand, techniques derived from behavioral modification have shown a little more promise. It is essential that the clinician have some knowledge as to how these techniques can be implemented.

Treatment of Sexual Variations

The behavioral treatment of sexual variation is fraught with ethical complications. Some of the disorders which behaviorists have chosen to emphasize in their treatment paradigms do not trouble the patient and represent no actual threat to society. Homosexuality between consenting adults, for example, is rarely viewed as a problem by those who practice it and does not pose a realistic threat for those who don't. Too often behaviorists have been overly vigorous and insensitive in applying behavior modification techniques to homosexuals whose motivation to change is questionable, vague, or determined entirely by social pressure. This questionably ethical use of behavior therapy has not gone unnoticed by other behaviorists. Some have even wondered if by offering to treat homosexuality, therapists are not actually promulgating a notion that homosexuality is a disease or a "bad" behavior that must be treated, and in the process of doing this, they may actually be worsening the homosexual's plight (Davidson 1976, Halleck 1976a).

In dealing with homosexuality, the behavioral approach usually involves some effort to extinguish the offending behavior and to replace it with socially acceptable heterosexual behavior. Aversive techniques, including classical conditioning, punishment, and avoidance learning, are used in these efforts. Homosexuality has been treated by applying a mild electrical shock to the patient while he views a slide of an attractive homosexual object. Covert sensitization has also been utilized, a process in which the patient may imagine a homosexual scene while the therapist tries to pair this fantasy with new images intended to elicit profound disgust and revulsion. This technique requires the therapist to paint a picture in which the normally pleasurable activities involved in homosexual contact are presented as frightening, unappetizing, or disgusting.

In a more sophisticated aversive treatment of homosexuality a type of avoidance learning is utilized in which the patient learns to turn off a picture or slide of a homosexual object in order to avoid receiving an electrical shock. The patient may be shown a slide and then be given an electrical shock which is terminated when the patient presses a button turning off the slide. Eventually the patient can learn to avoid shock entirely by turning off the slide shortly after it appears. Often the removal of the homosexual slide is followed by a picture of a heterosexual object, and it is hoped that the aversion relief involved in this change will come to be associated with reinforcement of heterosexuality.

Other efforts to treat homosexuality are directed toward increasing the heterosexual response. Systematic desensitization of fears related to heterosexuality is frequently employed. Responses to masturbation may be influenced by instructing the patient to begin to masturbate with a homosexual fantasy or by looking at a homosexual slide and then instructing him to replace either the fantasy or the slide with a heterosexual stimulus. When a heterosexual object is available, "in vivo" attempts to shape more adequate heterosexual functioning can be employed using the same techniques involved in treating sexual inadequacies. (This will be discussed shortly.)

Finally, self-control measures are occasionally used. The patient may be taught to avoid stimulus situations in which homosexual encounters are likely, or to provide himself an aversive stimulus, such as snapping an elastic band on the wrist in a painful manner whenever a homosexual impulse emerges.

In treating exhibitionism, behavioral techniques are focused almost entirely upon aversive measures. The technique of covert sensitization has been elaborated by pairing fantasies associated with exhibitionism not only with images of revulsion but also with nausea induced by the presence of foul-smelling chemical substances. Self-control measures, including stimulus control in the form of learning to avoid situations in which exhibitionistic impulses are likely, are also used. The shaping of adequate heterosexual responses is not a large part of the behavioral treatment of exhibitionism since many exhibitionists are already able to perform adequately with heterosexual partners.

Treatment of transvestism and fetishism (which are hardly serious disorders in terms of suffering to the individual or others) is again most readily accomplished through aversive techniques. Here it is relatively easy to practice punishment procedures "in vivo." The patient can receive a mild electrical shock while cross-dressing or while fondling the fetishistic object.

Recently a highly innovative and socially useful behavior modification technique has been utilized in the treatment of homosexual child molesters. Efforts have been made to strengthen the patient's capacity to enjoy homosexual relationships with adult partners using "in vivo" sexual training with volunteer partners (Kohlenburg 1974). This technique (using volunteer adult female partners) would also seem to be promising with heterosexual child molesters. To the extent that any child molester seeks immature objects because of inadequacies or fears related to performance with mature objects, techniques designed to enhance functioning with mature sexual object would seem to have a logical and useful function. They may be limited in application, however, because many of our citizens find them socially objectionable. The few efforts that have benn made to treat major sexual dysfunctions by using "in vivo" training with mature partners have been confined to outpatient settings. Our society is not yet ready to allow this treatment in the cases of convicted sex offenders.

I firmly believe that the eventual usefulness of behavior therapy techniques in the treatment of sexual variations will be dependent upon the extent to which they are applied to serious variations which are highly troubling to the patient and which represent threats to others in the community. The use of behavior therapy or any other therapy for treatment of less serious sexual disorders is always open to justified ethical question and should never be instituted lightly. A careful examination of the individual's total environment, including the forces allegedly motivating him to seek treatment, is essential. Judgments must always be made as to the oppressiveness of the forces which may shape the patient's motivation. In order to illustrate the ethical problems involved in treating sexual variations, I have whimsically created a case example of a woman who sought treatment to change her sexual orientation from heterosexual to homosexual. The case, of course, is fictitious, but I am not sanguine as to the possibilities that sooner or later some "liberated" therapist may not use such techniques.

A twenty-one-year-old woman sought help, asking that she be relieved of her impulses to have sex with men and learn to overcome her revulsion toward having sex with women. She had had a number of relationships with males in the past, and although she found herself attracted to her partners and physically gratified by them, she always felt they were exploiting her. She could not develop a feeling of real intimacy toward her partners and felt that her sexual needs left her vulnerable to developing relationships in which she was objectified and used. Shortly before seeking therapy, she had become involved in the feminist movement and had made several close relationships with other women who shared her views. Some of these women were lesbians who suggested to her that she might overcome her vulnerabilities to men and find real sexual gratification by experimenting with homosexual behavior. She tried to have homosexual relationships with one of her friends but was not sexually aroused during the preliminary phases of lovemaking, and as the act continued, she experienced feelings of revulsion. It was at this point that she decided that treatment was essential.

Treatment was begun with a type of avoidance learning. The patient was exposed to slides showing pictures of the kinds of males she found attractive; she learned to avoid electric shock by turning off the slides and having them replaced by pictures of attractive females. Covert sensitization techniques were also used to try to institute a certain amount of disgust associated with the heterosexual act. When the patient began to report some diminution in her interest in males and could visualize the possibility of fantasizing sex with females without being disgusted, efforts were made to have her masturbate, first using her old heterosexual fantasies. When she began to be comfortable masturbating with homosexual fantasies, "in vivo" training was instituted with a voluntary female partner. Using techniques of gradual erotic stimulation, combined with efforts to relieve performance anxiety (a technique that will be described more fully in the next section), the patient eventually learned to overcome her revulsions and to experience orgasm through mutual masturbation and cunnilingus with female partners. She now reports she is no longer tempted by men and is quite happy with her sexual life as a homosexual.

Treatment of Sexual Inadequacy

There are probably millions of Americans who are dissatisfied with their sex lives. Many new sex therapies and sex clinics have been developed, and the conglomerate efforts of therapists to treat sexual dysfunction have become a multimillion-dollar industry. Much of the emphasis of the new sex therapies is on mechanical skills. It is possible that too much emphasis on mechanical skills can degrade sexuality by encouraging patients to ignore the humanistic aspects of lovemaking. Elaborate techniques have been developed, for example, to treat premature ejaculation. But this "disorder" is hardly a major problem when two lovers are intimate, understanding of each other's needs, and willing to be responsive to them. At its worst, sex therapy can improve two lovers' sexual performance while they continue to hate and hurt each other.

An exaggerated emphasis on sexual techniques and sexual performance may also have unfortunate long-range social consequences. It may be that our preoccupation with sexuality is part of a defensive maneuver which allows us to avoid consideration of more realistic and more grim existential or social issues. The rapid proliferation of a variety of sex therapies may simply contribute to this process of distraction. While our society's current rejection of puritanical attitudes toward sex and its new openness in discussing sexual issues is highly desirable, our preoccupation with sexuality has reached "overkill" proportions. This trend is reflected in both professional and nonprofessional media. Books on improving one's sexual abilities abound. Several journals devoted entirely to human sexual function have become popular. Many of our professional journals and books repetitively emphasize the importance of mechanical techniques for obtaining sexual happiness and pay only lip service to interpersonal and humanistic approaches to sexuality.

Still, there can be no doubt that sex therapies are helpful. In many instances sexual therapists are simply trying to enhance the quality of people's erotic experience. While the use of large numbers of trained clinicians to merely improve peoples' sex lives may not represent the wisest investment of our mental health resources, those who can be taught to have better sex lives will usually be happier people, and there are certainly many people who suffer from sexual dysfunction. Symptoms of impotence and frigidity are not only distressing in themselves but lead to impairment of self-concept and interpersonal relationships.

There are a number of structural and metabolic abnormalities which may lead to frigidity or impotence. No form of psychotherapy or behavior modification should be instituted until the possibility of organic etiologies of sexual distress have been identified and, if possible, eliminated. Once organic disorders have been ruled out, a good deal of the treatment of sexual dysfunction is based on techniques derived from learning theory.

While it is easy to use behavioral techniques for treating sexual dysfunction in a very mechanistic fashion and while I suspect that many sex therapists are doing just that, some of the acknowledged experts in the field of sex therapy (including Masters and Johnson) are forthright in emphasizing that behavioral methods are only a part of the total treatment of sexual dysfunction (Masters and Johnson 1970, 1972, Kaplan 1974). They appreciate that lack of information, poor communication, and disturbed interpersonal relationships are usually an essential factor in creating and sustaining sexual disorders. They emphasize that treatment of sexual disorders must involve much more than a mere mechanistic use of behavioral techniques, but must also be based on efforts to thoroughly assess and deal with problems of misinformation and lack of communication. If one or both parties to an erotic relationship are experiencing sexual difficulties, the focus of treatment must include not only the actual behavior of the persons experiencing difficulty but also an examination of the total relationship.

In effect the best sex therapists begin their treatment with a form of couple or marital therapy. During the course of this therapy it is important that the therapist correct any misconceptions either partner has about normal male or female sexuality. Often such misconceptions are a major factor in sustaining dysfunction. Men must learn that sexual potency can be compromised by anxiety, that it is not a capacity available to them in every sexual liason, and that there are many ways of satisfying a woman without performing the act of coitus. Woman must learn that there are many ways of achieving orgasm and that they cannot be expected to achieve orgasm unless they are aroused, usually through enjoyable foreplay. It is also essential that lovers like each other. Animosities which develop in any intimate relationship often follow the couple into the bedroom and make enjoyment of sexual intercourse impossible. My own experience is that couple or marital therapy which focuses upon poor communication and animosities in the relationship often results in relief of the sexual dysfunction even before any specific advice based on behavioral principles is provided. In this regard it is worth noting that the bedroom often becomes a battlefield in which one or another partner may satisfy needs for power by failing to perform in a manner that gratifies the other. Sometimes symptoms such as impotence or frigidity simply represent a fear of being controlled or a means of demonstrating to the other partner that their enjoyment of sexuality cannot be used to obscure other conflicts or feelings which are more powerful. Another way of putting this is that, at least in the early stages of their development, many symptoms of sexual inadequacy are purposeful and have interpersonal meaning.

Several years ago I was treating a young woman who had many complaints, one of which was inability to achieve orgasm in sexual relationships with her boyfriend. Whenever she talked about this difficulty, she seemed only slightly distressed and sometimes even pleased. I was treating this woman with a modified psychoanalytic approach, and toward the end of one of our hours she was quite silent. I asked her what she was thinking about, and she said that she desperately craved a cigarette but didn't have any money to buy them when she left the office. I offered to loan her money, and she responded to my offer by stating that she would never borrow anything from me because she never wanted to be indebted to me. At this point I made what I thought was an incisive interpretation and remarked that it was no wonder that she could not accept an orgasm from her boyfriend if she could not even accept the price of a pack of cigarettes from me. The patient quickly deflated my therapeutic narcissism by breaking into laughter and saying, "Dr. Halleck, your problem is that you think sex is more important than power." In subsequent therapy the patient overcame her fears of men and her need to handle these fears by retaining an inordinate degree of power in such relationships. As these problems resolved, she had no further sexual problems. I should also add that she helped me learn that power sometimes is more important than sex.

Behavioral techniques are best utilized only after the clinician has made a concerted effort to determine that the interpersonal problems that may have nurtured the sexual dysfunction have been resolved or are in the process of resolution. Having made this assessment, the clinician will still find people who remain impotent or frigid even when their nonsexual relationship has been reasonably good, or has been plagued by difficulties which have subsequently been resolved.

One of the oldest behavioral techniques for treating sexual dysfunction, both impotence and frigidity, is the use of desensitization procedures. The patient is asked to fantasize a graded series of sexual situations which may be associated with anxiety and is taught to pair these fantasies with muscular relaxation. Desensitization principles have been carried over into a wide variety of "in vivo" techniques in which the patient is taught to shape sexual performance by gradually performing sexual acts which do not arouse anxiety. The purpose here is always to try to keep the patient's sexual arousal in ascendency over the patient's anxiety and to eliminate pressures on the patient to perform. Patients are taught to concentrate on their sexual feelings and enjoyment of their feelings in the hopes that this will eliminate a morbid self-consciousness or self-grading which leads to self-defeating expectations of performance and subsequent anxieties.

"In vivo" treatment of sexual dysfunction of course requires the availability of a cooperative partner. The couple is usually instructed to perform certain erotically pleasing acts which do not generate anxiety in either partner, and they are specifically told not to go beyond those acts and seek more sexual fulfillment until they have experienced total relaxation at each step. At the beginning the couple may be instructed to practice touching one another in nongenital areas of the body and simply to focus upon the pleasurable aspects of this behavior. Once the couple is perfectly relaxed in doing this, they may move on to some exploratory touching of the genital area. They may then experiment with simultaneous genital manipulation to the point of orgasm. Finally, when there is no indication of performance anxiety, the couple is permitted to have intercourse. Throughout the entire procedure there is also a focus upon the needs of individual partners, and both partners are urged to communicate exactly what they would like the other partner to do to please them. The basic element in these techniques, again, is an elimination of anxiety by focusing upon sexual pleasure and diminishing self-consciousness and feelings of pressure to perform.

A number of other techniques which may be considered under the rubric of behavior therapy involve gradual shaping of sexual gratification from masturbatory activities to coitus. Many women who report inability to experience orgasm during intercourse are able to experience orgasm through masturbation. Techniques have been developed in which the patient is taught to transfer the capacity for orgasm by allowing the partner to gradually take over clitoral stimulation until the partner is able to bring her to orgasm manually. Clitoral stimulation may then be paired with intromission, usually from a posterior position, until the woman is able to experience orgasm with intromission alone.

Premature ejaculation may be treated by temporary withdrawal of the penis, and by having the patient focus on nonerotic thoughts and images while engaging in sexual intercourse. Masters and Johnson have also developed the squeeze technique. When the man is about to ejaculate, the woman is instructed to squeeze the partner's penis for about three seconds. Rather strong pressure is applied under and behind the glans. One drawback to the squeeze technique is that it may sometimes produce temporary impotence.

There are a variety of formats used in treating sexual dysfunctions. Some therapists may combine sex therapy with individual as well as marital therapy, particularly if one partner has specific sexual disturbances. Masters and Johnson insist on a brief but intensive marital approach using two therapists, one female and one male. The couple is isolated from the usual responsibilities involving their family or work during the course of treatment. While there are too many sex therapists who focus primarily upon the mechanical aspects of sex, the best sexual therapies do represent good examples of a multidimensional approach in which individual, family, and behavior therapies are skillfully combined to produce effective treatment.

Behavioral Treatment of Alcoholism.

Many behaviorists view alcoholism as a learned response. They have tried to diminish alcohol abuse both through respondent conditioning in which an aversive stimulus is paired with alcohol intake and by operant methods involving stimulus control and altering the consequences of drinking. While the success of behavioral methods in the treatment of alcohol abuse has been limited (as has been the success of all other treatments), there have been sufficient case reports of successful outcome to warrant consideration of behavioral techniques in this area. Any tentativeness here is related to the lack of controlled studies convincingly demonstrating the superiority of behavioral methods.

One intriguing aspect of the behavioral approach to treatment of alcoholism is that it is characterized by rejection of the disease model. Many behaviorists believe that the concept of alcoholism promulgated by Alcoholics Anonymous and most physicians, which is predicated on the belief that alcoholics are biologically incapable of controlling drinking behavior, may be erroneous (Franks and Wilson 1975). If the behaviorists are right, their techniques may ultimately turn out to be quite promising because they could be used to teach alcoholics to control their drinking rather than to seek total abstinence. This might make treatment acceptable to many more alcoholics. (While it is not my purpose here to elaborate current controversies regarding the etiology of alcoholism, it is worth mentioning that the current behavioral literature does not take note of recent research which suggests a genetic basis to alcoholism and probable biological determinants in at least some alcoholics; (see Goodwin et al. 1973.)

The earliest approaches to behavioral treatment of alcoholism involved asking alcoholics to drink at the same time that nausea and vomiting reactions were produced by the ingestion of such drugs as emetine or apomophine. The pairing of these two events was accompanied by verbal instructions to the patient that after treatment he must never taste or experiment with liquor. The patient was encouraged to smell, taste, and swirl the liquor around in his mouth before swallowing it. These instructions were given just before nausea and vomiting occurred. Remarkably good results after only several treatment sessions have been reported using this method. Unfortunately these data are not adequately controlled. Other early approaches using classical conditioning involved pairing drinking with mild electric shock. There is now general agreement among behaviorists that aversive treatment in which the unconditioned stimulus is electrical shock is of little value in the treatment of alcoholism.

Principles of operant conditioning have also been used in treating alcoholism. Negative reinforcements such as *time out* have been made contingent on alcohol intake. The patient can avoid the negative reinforcer by diminishing alcohol intake. A number of avoidance learning techniques have proven quite successful in at least temporarily diminishing the amount of alcohol the patient ingests. The long-term usefulness of these techniques has, however, not been documented. Much of the more recent impetus in behavioral treatment of alcoholism focuses upon stimulus control. Patients are taught to recognize situations in which they are likely to ingest alcohol and learn either to avoid these situations or to develop responses alternative to drinking when these situations are encountered.

Behavioral Treatment of Eating Disorders

The problem of obesity seems almost endemic in the United States. Many Americans are overweight, and the pernicious effect of this condition upon an individual's psychological and physical health is well documented. Obesity is highly refractory to almost any kind of intervention. Traditional psychotherapy and self-help groups, such as TOPS (Take Off Pounds Sensibly) and Weight Watchers are sometimes effective, but the overall results of these interventions are disappointing. In the last several years there has been an increasing effort to use behavioral modification principles in the treatment of obesity. The results, at least in terms of bringing about short-term weight loss, seem promising. There is, however, no firm evidence at present supporting the effectiveness of behavioral techniques in maintaining weight loss over a lengthy period (Mahoney 1974, Harris and Bruner 1973).

There are usually five basic elements involved in the behavioral approach to obesity:

1. The patient is instructed to change his eating behavior. This may involve directions to eat at a much slower pace and to chew each morsel of food thoroughly. The patient is instructed always to leave some food on his plate at the end of the meal.

2. Techniques involving stimulus control are important. The

patient must learn to eat at specific times and only in certain places. Emphasis is placed upon eating only at the dinner table and avoiding eating while standing, conversing, or engaging in such activities as watching television. The patient is also instructed to remove excess food from the environment.

3. Patients on weight loss programs are encouraged to diligently plan meals and caloric intake in advance. Careful counting of the amount of calories ingested at each meal is encouraged.

4. The patient is taught to develop alternative responses to boredom. Many patients claim they eat when they are bored. The patient may be instructed to practice alternative behavior, such as exercise, working, or visiting with friends, when boredom appears.

5. The patient is rewarded for changes in eating habits and for weight loss.

For reasons which are not clear, feedback both as to caloric intake and changes in weight seems an important ingredient in any behavioral weight loss program. It also appears useful to put as much control of reinforcement in the hands of the patients as is possible. One type of reinforcement which has proven quite useful in developing self-control techniques is money. The patient may at the beginning of treatment put a certain amount of money aside or deposit it with the therapist. Regaining this money is then made contingent upon weight loss. This technique is suitable for external reinforcement procedures where the therapist controls the money, or for self-control techniques where the patient determines his own rewards.

Behavioral methods also have been used for the much more rare, and dangerous, condition of deficient eating. Physicians have long experienced considerable difficulty in treating patients, usually young females, who seem to deliberately avoid eating almost to the point of starvation. When this behavior pattern is severe enough to produce symptoms of malnutrition, severe weight loss, and endocrine changes, it is called anorexia nervosa. This disorder is extremely difficult to treat and can be viewed as lift-threatening.

Behavior modification of anorexia nervosa requires total control of the patient's environment and must be conducted in a hospital setting. Once in the hospital, the patient is deprived of most of the privileges or positive reinforcements available in everyday life, and efforts are made to discover which behaviors may be positively reinforcing. Behaviors such as watching television, attending recreational events, having time to spend talking with certain ward personnel, or access to total privacy may be made contingent upon weight gain. The patient is at regular times given meals which are usually substantially greater than ordinarily ingested. Sometimes the amount of food provided is gradually increased as the patient gains weight. The patient is instructed to carefully monitor food intake, and is weighted regularly. One of the critical factors in this procedure is the provision of feedback to the patient regarding both caloric intake and weight.

This cursory description of the behavior modification program for anorexia nervosa cannot begin to capture the intricate planning, careful bookkeeping, and commitment and "togetherness" of the ward team which are necessary to implement such a program. Some of these issues will be considered in the next section.

BEHAVIOR MODIFICATION TECHNIQUES AND GENERAL CLINICAL PROBLEMS

Techniques of behavior modification have been used in a wide variety of situations where a given behavior or behavioral deficit interferes with an individual's capacity to adapt to various social systems. Sometimes it is the individual who requests a change in his behavior repertoire in order to adapt more adequately to a social system. Sometimes family members or community agents of control request that the patient's behavior be changed.

Institutions which treat involuntary patients have made extensive use of behavior modification techniques. Insofar as patients in these settings may not initially present high levels of cooperation and may not be motivated to change their behaviors, the effectiveness of behavior modification programs is dependent on maximum control of the environment. Hospitals which treat voluntary patients also use some type of behavior modification in trying to shape the behavior of their patients. In any psychiatric ward some effort is usually made either to positively reinforce patients when they behave in a manner defined as healthy or to ignore them or apply punishment when they behave in a manner judged unhealthy. In most psychiatric hospitals, however, it is very difficult to apply reinforcement contingently. The natural reaction of hospital personnel is to pay attention to illness behavior. Most hospital workers will show a high degree of tenderness, warmth, and concern (responses which are likely to be positive reinforcers) when people appear to be suffering. This is, of course, laudable and essential in a humanistic milieu. But it also makes for great difficulty in providing reinforcement contingent upon healthy behavior.

The discrepancies in attitude between the medical and behavioral approach has led to an unfortunate all or none situation with regard to the use of behavior modification with inpatients. Some hospital units have been specifically structured for the utilization of behavioral principles. Staffs are extensively trained to deliver reinforcement contingent on desirable behaviors. Psychiatric hospital units not highly committed to a behavioral approach have difficulty in shifting to such an approach with occasional patients who need it. When they use behavior modification techniques, they often use them sloppily; and when they don't work quickly, the staff tends to question their worth. Many staffs in traditional hospitals are also fearful that the use of behavior modification techniques will put unwanted restraints on their wishes to be loving and caring in their interaction with patients. My own experience has been that rigorous behavior modification techniques can be used on an ordinary psychiatric unit only if special efforts are made to explain the rationale of the treatment to staff members and to ensure high levels of communication among them. Treating an anorectic patient in an ordinary psychiatric milieu, for example, requires almost daily team meetings in which various staff members have to be reinforced for exerting control over the expression of certain feelings, such as tenderness, disgust, or anger. In particular, hospital staff members must learn to avoid expressing sympathy when the patient complains about restricted privileges. They must also learn not to lecture, reprimand, or exhort the patient when eating patterns are highly deviant.

Behaviorists have found their greatest acceptance in settings where patients have previously received minimal levels of medical and nursing care. Chronic psychotic patients in back wards of state hospitals are not likely to be showered with attention or tenderness. Understaffed state hospitals have paid little attention to these patients and have sometimes welcomed the efforts of behaviorists to work with them. Some of the most effective behavior modification units have been set up on chronic wards of

The Behavior Therapies

these hospitals. Here the behaviorists find a small and untrained staff that may be open to learning new approaches. There is also considerable freedom to experiment with new techniques. In such a setting both shaping and punishment have been used to help highly deviant people develop more socially appropriate behaviors.

One of the more interesting forms of behavior modification used in institutional settings has been the so-called token economy (Wexler 1973). Patients are instructed that certain privileges, such as watching television or taking walks, will not be available to them unless they can be purchased with tokens. Obtaining tokens, however, is contingent upon appropriate behavior. Good grooming, proper eating habits, and rational social behavior are reinforced by the presentation of tokens. The patient then uses these tokens to purchase other reinforcements. In this sense, tokens are operating as general reinforcements. The use of a token economy approach requires almost total control of the hospital environment. Obviously, difficult ethical issues are involved in such an approach. One baffling issue is whether the reinforcements, which are initially denied patients and then made contingent on certain behaviors, are really privileges or actually rights. Many would argue that access to a certain amount of recreation is a right of all patients, whether they behave appropriately or not. Elimination of such a right would appear justified only when the patient's life or the safety of others is threatened.

The use of behavior modification techniques to develop more adaptive behaviors in voluntary patients is much less controversial. One of the most interesting and currently popular approaches involves training people to be more assertive. Many patients complain of shyness, inability to stand up for their rights, or to express either positive or negative feelings. The treatment of such symptoms is not, of course, the exclusive province of the behaviorist, but the behavioral school has placed considerable emphasis on assertiveness training and has developed a number of methods for implementing it. Their techniques consist of a mixture of role playing, modeling, and social reinforcement aimed at teaching appropriate or adaptive interpersonal responses. Usually the therapist tries to structure situations in which the patient has previously failed to demonstrate the desired assertive behavior. These situations are rehearsed with the therapist, who gives feedback as to the appropriateness of both verbal and nonverbal behavior for that situation. Sometimes the therapist will demonstrate a model of the desired behavior, and the patient will rehearse it. Assertiveness training can take place in groups. The group setting is especially useful for employing adjuncts such as videotape replay, in which the patient can receive direct feedback as to how he is coming across to others (Stoller 1969).

One interesting aspect of assertiveness training is that its use implies that some of the stimuli determining the patient's behavior have social meaning. When the behaviorist trains a person to stand up for his rights, the therapist is making an assumption that the events influencing the patient's behavior may well be oppressive. Assertiveness training is another area in which behaviorists are moving away from more rigid Skinnerian models and are considering the impact of the relationship between the patient and the social systems in which the patient operates.

Another class of behaviors that are favorably influenced by behavioral techniques are nervous habits, for example, nail biting, thumbsucking, or tics, such as head jerking or eyelid blinking. These are easily measurable target behaviors. They have been successfully eliminated by a combination of techniques in which the patient learns to anticipate the internal stimuli which precede the habitual response and then is taught to engage in a muscular movement the reverse of the normal habit each time he is tempted to perform, or has actually performed, the habit. Patients habituated to thumsucking, for example, can be asked to place their hands by their sides and clinch their fists powerfully whenever they feel tempted to suck their thumb or have just done so. Positive reinforcement is provided the patient when he is cooperative and indicates that he is motivated to change his behavior (Azrin and Nunn 1973).

As behaviorism becomes more concerned with social systems, it has also made important contributions to the treatment of family systems. Family members, in addition to developing problems in communication and problems in dealing with the stresses they may impose upon one another, often fail to provide one another adequate positive reinforcement. The term *positive reinforcement* is used imprecisely here to refer to responses which have a high probability of being reinforcing, such as praise, appreciation, or tenderness. In any interdependent relationship people usually want more positive reinforcement from others than they are getting. One way of dealing with this situation is to have all parties involved communicate to one another the manner and type of changes they would like to see the others make and at the same time define the types of reinforcement they are willing to offer one another in return for these changes. In any type of family therapy that is successful, there is usually some shifting of reinforcements between various parties. Behaviorists try to accomplish this in a precise manner by having the parties in a relationship contract to behave in specific ways and to provide reinforcements for one another when they perform these new behaviors. Behaviorists refer to this technique as contingency contracting. The contracts usually specify the relationship between behaviors and their consequences. The technique of contingency contracting is an important contribution to family therapy based on behavioral approaches, and will be discussed further in the chapter on family therapy.

BIOFEEDBACK

Throughout most of its history behaviorism has been dominated by the belief that automatic responses can be altered only through classical conditioning and cannot be brought under the control of operant conditioning. Even Skinner (1953) concluded that such autonomic behaviors as blushing, salivating, or crying could not generate the kinds of consequences that could be reinforced. Unfortunately there is only a limited amount of control that can be brought over bodily functions and emotions through classical conditioning. To the extent that it is possible to control emotions and bodily functions through altering environmental contingencies, it would theoretically be possible to bring about massive changes in the total behavior of the organism by directly controlling feelings.

In the past fifteen years there has been a gradual accumulation of evidence that some autonomic responses can be modified through negative or positive reinforcement (Kimmel 1974, Miller 1974). The most interesting aspect of these investigations has been the use of modern instrumentation to provide a person moment-to-moment information about a specific physiological process which is under the control of the nervous system but which ordinarily is not clearly or accurately perceived. In effect, sophisticated electronic instrumentation is utilized to provide a person with feedback as to his own biological processes. Such biofeedback helps the person increase his perception of internal stimuli. This process can be adequately explained in terms of operant conditioning. Electronic information that a desired biological response is taking place will cause the patient to positively reinforce himself; information that a desired response is decreasing may lead to self-punishment.

In terms of models discussed earlier in this book, biofeedback training changes people by simultaneously altering their biology and by teaching them how to bring on and sustain such alterations. Biofeedback holds out the theoretical promise of enabling clinicians to alter highly maladaptive, and sometimes physically incapacitating, responses. The new interest in autonomic conditioning has generated much research and enthusiasm. Efforts to alter heart rate and blood pressure have helped some patients with cardiac arrhythmias or hypertension (Barber 1974). Considerable success has been claimed in treating migraine headaches through biofeedback training which involves raising the temperature of the hands relative to the temperature of the forehead and helping the patient relieve muscular tension through electromyography (Mitchell and Mitchell 1971). With all of the enthusiasm for biofeedback techniques, however, it must be noted that there is little evidence at present that biofeedback techniques are useful in the treatment of emotional disorders (Blanchard and Young 1974). Efforts to induce relaxation and sleep through biofeedback methods involving electromyography have had some success. (Since these efforts are directed at changing the responses of striated muscles, they do not actually involve autonomic responses. They are, however, generally referred to under the rubric of biofeedback.) Beyond this, none of the claims for the efficacy of biofeedback training in modifying emotional disorders can, at this moment, be documented.

"SOFT" BEHAVIOR MODIFICATION

If there is any distinguishing feature to the behavioral approach, it is the commitment to rely on scientific methodology and careful observation of treatment and outcome variables. Given this consistency there is still a wide variation in therapeutic outlook among behaviorists. Behavior therapy can be visualized as an all-encompassing approach to the treatment of emotional disorders, or it can be viewed as a series of helpful techniques complementary to other approaches. My own prejudice, which is surely clear to the reader by this point, is that the behavior therapies are best viewed as a series of techniques which are occasionally sufficient treatments in themselves but more often serve as highly useful complements to other treatments. There are rarely any contraindications to combining behavior modification with other forms of treatment, and, indeed, behaviorists have argued (correctly, in my opinion) that much of the change that takes place in other psychotherapies is based on principles of behavior modification anyway.

Techniques of behavior modification can be utilized at the same time that one is exploring the unconscious, examining characterologic defects, or focusing upon the way an individual interacts in social systems. The authority which the clinician must invoke in behavior modification may at times interfere with the kind of nondirectiveness some therapists feel necessary for the development of complete expression of feelings and transference. When this conflict arises, it can be handled relatively easily by splitting therapeutic functions between two clinicians. I have on a few occasions been treating patients in individual psychoanalytically oriented psychotherapy when it became apparent that some fear response or appetitive disorder was making the patient miserable and would not quickly respond to my nondirective approach. On such occasions I have simply asked a colleague more skilled in behavior therapy than myself to treat the specific symptom and have comfortably continued to work with the patient on murkier areas such as self-concept, identity, existential commitment, or unconscious motivation.

In combining specific forms of behavior therapy with most forms of individual, group, and family psychotherapy, a splitting of therapeutic functions is not usually necessary. As long as the patient understands what the therapist is doing and agrees to the behavioral procedures, it is usually relatively easy to stop exploratory processes for a while, to be directive, and to set up a program aimed at modifying specific responses. In family therapy, for example, I have often found that where family members have been hurting one another for years and can produce nothing but negative responses toward one another, it is sometimes useful to employ the technique of contingency contracting, just to provide enough temporary peacefulness so the family can continue their other psychotherapeutic work.

In spite of being far more impressed with the specific than the general uses of behavior therapy, I must admit that the behavioral approach has, in more recent years, also had a subtle impact on many aspects of my overall therapeutic behavior. When performing any kind of psychotherapy, I am much more aware of how I use positive reinforcement and punishment. I am a little more insistent than I used to be that patients be precise in defining their problems. And I am a little more curious as to the therapeutic outcome and more willing to have such outcomes measured. I believe my attempts to study behavior modification have given me some insights into dealing with patients, and have led me to use periodically a "soft" or relatively imprecise behavioral approach to many clinical problems. Some clinicians might see this approach as merely reflecting good common sense, but I believe that better understanding of behavior modification may expedite a common-sense approach to the patient.

One area in which behaviorism can expand the clinician's vistas involves the deleterious effects of labeling and overdiagnosis. Sociologists have for decades been accusing psychiatrists of perpetuating illness by labeling and treating people who are merely behaving differently than others as though they were ill (Rosenhan 1973, Matza 1969). These critiques are difficult to appreciate unless one considers in behavioral terms the impact of medical diagnosis upon the patient. Physicians and all those who work under the traditional medical model must be concerned with the discovery and elucidation of pathology. Anything that the patient says or does that is suggestive of a disorder must be totally investigated. There is really no choice. If the physician fails to be hyperalert to the possible existence of pathology, there is a real risk that an important treatment will be ignored and that a partially curable illness will not be treated and will incapacitate or destroy the patient. In effect, the physician is locked into an interaction with the patient in which the physician must pay scrupulous attention to the patient's illness behavior and, at the same time, will have far less commitment to pay attention to the patient's healthy behavior. By virtue of his training and social rule, the physician will engage in activities which tend to reinforce sick behavior and to extinguish healthy behavior. The dangers that traditional medical practice will lead to reinforcement of illness behaviors are present from the moment the diagnostic process begins.

Many lay persons in our society have learned a great deal about psychiatric disorders. They know which symptoms are likely to be viewed as signs of illness and they know which behaviors are likely to arouse the attention of medical practitioners. In effect many patients learn to mimic illness behaviors. There are many reasons for this. Sometimes the patient is unaware of the potential gains of illness behavior but may resort to it to resolve an unconscious conflict. More often the patient appreciates that illness behavior provides him certain new reinforcements but is unaware of the extent to which his illness behavior is motivated by a wish to receive those reinforcements. Sometimes the patient is quite aware of the advantages of illness behavior and knows that he is consciously mimicking it in order to achieve those advantages. The degree of awareness of the gains created by illness behavior and the degree of awareness of motivations that might create illness behavior will vary from patient to patient and often will vary in the same patient from moment to moment. It is always difficult to know how much of such behavior is based on malingering or deliberate creation of symptoms and how much on motivations of which the patient is totally unaware. For purposes of discussion, it is convenient to ignore such questions as How deliberate is this behavior? and Can the patient control it? I will refer to as *mimicry* all forms of behavior which resembly physical and mental illness but which are actually created by the patient to gain attention and to resolve problems in living. The term includes conversion reactions, exaggeration of psychophysiological responses, and a cluster of behaviors that have been described as hysterical personality disorders.

Mimicry of neurological and other medical disorders has been well known to clinicians for over a century. Mimicry of psychotic and depressive behavior has, in my experience, become much more prevalent in the last two decades. The increase seems to parallel growing public sophistication and interest in psychological issues. In conducting a diagnostic interview with the patient who may be exaggerating symptoms of depression or who may be exaggerating minor difficulties in cognition or perception so that they begin to sound like symptoms of psychosis, the physician is faced with an incredibly difficult task. These patients are usually quite miserable. They would not be seeing a doctor if they did not want help. However, if the physician shows excessive interest in the symptom, he will reinforce a behavior that would be better extinguished. Here the clinician's task is far broader than simply discovering and treating severe pathology. He must also help the patient deal with conflicts or problems in living that have led to the use of mimicry in the first place, a task rendered far more difficult when the physician reinforces presenting symptoms.

There is ample evidence that clinicians reinforce certain kinds of complaints from their patients and in so doing may reinforce the illness behavior of their patients (Halleck 1967). Experienced or not, clinicians can reinforce illness behavior by becoming more interested when the patient discusses symptoms, by looking more troubled when illness is discussed, by remaining silent and noncommittal when the patient inquires as to the significance of symptoms, or by failing to even inquire as to aspects of the patient's more healthy behavior. In my experience the most powerful reinforcer of illness behavior is mystification. Patients who use mimicry are usually worried about the seriousness of their condition. Clinicians who refuse to answer reasonable questions, relentlessly use silence to put pressure on patients, and use gestures, intonation, or remarks to indicate knowledge of something ominous which will not be shared become potent reinforcers of illness behavior.

To avoid this, clinicians must try to relate to patients in a manner which allows for thorough assessment of behavior but which minimizes reinforcement of symptoms while maximizing reinforcement of desirable behavior. Sometimes such a relationship seems unattainable. There are a few suggestions, however, that may be helpful. In trying to avoid reinforcement of symptoms, I have learned to be extremely matter-of-fact, but thorough, in investigating any behavior that can be considered a symptom. Such an approach does not preclude the expression of empathy, concern, and even tenderness at appropriate times. I am committed to answering any reasonable questions the patient might ask and to explain thoroughly the reasons for any consultations or laboratory examinations I order. At the same time I inquire thoroughly as to the patient's ability to deal with symptomatic behavior and other aspects of life. My effort to focus on the patient's strengths is intended to reinforce adaptive behaviors. A case illustration of this approach may be useful:

A twenty-two-year-old woman was hospitalized for evaluation of symptoms of depression and depersonalization. Until six weeks prior to admission, she had functioned adequately as a college student. Although her academic work had been marginal, she had had many friends and had been elected president of her sorority. Her difficulties began after she was told of her younger sister's plans to get married. The patient felt pleased on hearing this news but soon began to ruminate about her own situation. While she had many friends, men did not usually regard her as a desirable sexual partner. She began to ask herself if all the things she was doing to please her parents, other members of her family, and her sorority sisters were worth the effort. Three days after she received the news of her sister's impending marriage, she experienced a sense of panic while taking an examination. She left the examination uncompleted, went back to the sorority house, and tried to talk to her friends: this did not alleviate her anxiety. A few hours later she began to experience a feeling that she was unable to concentrate and that her body seemed detached from her mind so that she constantly seemed to be observing herself. At this point she called her parents and returned home. A psychiatrist was consulted. He talked to her briefly and started her on 5 mg. of Stelazine. The medication did not influence her anxiety or depression but did leave her quite drowsy. She consulted another psychiatrist, who advised hospitalization. She then entered my hospital unit.

Since symptoms of depersonalization and depression in a young person often herald a schizophrenic process, I was obligated to take her symptoms very seriously. I spent a great deal of time trying to document the nature of her feelings of sadness and trying to get her to describe as precisely as possible her feeling of being outside of herself. Other aspects of her perception, thought processes, and emotionality were thoroughly investigated. All this was done in a matter-of-fact way. I tried to communicate to the patient, both verbally and nonverbally, that I understood she was miserable, but that my primary interest was in diagnosing her misery and treating her.

In the second interview I asked her if she thought she was going crazy. She replied affirmatively. I responded by pointing out that we did not yet know how ominous her symptomatology might be, but I also pointed out how rationally she was able to relate to myself and others, how capable she was of describing her symptoms, how she managed to retain a good sense of humor even while feeling miserable, and that there were many times during the day when she felt relatively comfortable and did not seem depressed. She was told that certain tests would be ordered to rule out organic dysfunctions and to test her overall psychological strength. When these tests failed to show any evidence of gross pathology but did indicate that she was a person with an immature personality structure who had excessive dependency wishes and feelings of inadequacy, the patient was fully informed of our findings. At this point I told her that while I was very impressed and concerned with the degree of her suffering, I felt that her symptoms would be most expeditiously relieved if she focused upon efforts to understand herself and her relationship to her family. The hospital staff were encouraged to treat her as an unhappy but highly responsible young woman who should receive no special solicitousness on their part. The patient was initially quite resistant to our plans and insisted that we were not taking her seriously enough and that we had simply failed to detect some serious illness. After six stormy weeks of using this approach, however, the patient became completely asymptomatic and left the hospital with a determination to find a more gratifying life style.

I believe my determination to take care of this patient's medical and psychological needs while not reinforcing her symptoms was an important part of her successful treatment. I also believe that I could not have stuck to my approach if I had not already developed some appreciation of the ease with which symptoms can be reinforced in medical settings.

"Soft" behavior modification can also be quite helpful in treating depressed patients in hospital settings. Hospital staff can be instructed to limit their empathic responses to repetitive complaints of symptoms such as insomnia, constipation, worthlessness, and hopelessness. As the patients improve, they can be assigned graded tasks such as spending a certain amount of time in the day room or making coffee, and these behaviors can be positively reinforced. Such interventions probably have little influence in reversing a depressive process when the depression has powerful biological determinants. They do, however, help make life much more comfortable for both the patient and the staff while the patient is getting better. It is imperative that this behavioral approach not be used in a cold or cruel manner. Psychiatric hospital personnel, who are usually trained to deliver reinforcement noncontingently, have a great deal of difficulty in learning that the delivery of contingent reinforcement still allows them to express tender and loving feelings toward the patient. They must simply learn to redirect their loving responses to situations in which the patient is behaving appropriately.

In treating outpatients who use mimicry, particularly those who might be considered to have hysterical personality disorders, I have learned to respond to illness behaviors (once they have been thoroughly evaluated and I am relatively certain they are not indicators of more ominous pathology) by empathizing with the patient's suffering but refusing to spend much time discussing it. I tell the patient, "Look I am very much aware of your symptoms, and I certainly know how deeply you are suffering. There is really no point in your repeatedly telling me about it. Your task in therapy is not to tell me about your suffering, which I am already aware of and sympathize with, but rather to try to solve problems that may be causing your suffering." This tactic to a certain extent cuts off free association and may seem a cruel denial of the kind of permissiveness that is so characterisitc of nondirective therapies. Used with gentleness, however, it is quite helpful to the patient.

Sometimes refusing reinforcement to a chronically ill patient with a conversion or hysterical personality disorder seems unusually cruel. Yet I have almost reluctantly come to appreciate that such deprivation or even the threat of it may turn out to be the kindest treatment of all.

A forty-one-year-old woman came to the hospital with complaints of chronic jerking movements of the trunk and extremities which had disabled her over the past four years. Her muscle spasms even influenced her speech and she was at times dysarthric. The patient's symptoms had begun almost immediately after the birth of an unwanted child. When the symptoms appeared, she took to her bed, and the tasks of housekeeping and child rearing were left to her husband and older children. She had been hospitalized many times for treatment of this condition and had been thoroughly examined by neurologists. Every examiner was convinced that there was no organic basis for her disorder. Neither hospitalization nor outpatient treatment had helped her.

Because the patient's illness behavior closely resembled a number of serious and potentially lethal neurological disorders, our staff repeated the neurological evaluation. Again, we could find no evidence of organic dysfunction. At this point we told the patient that we could not determine what was wrong with her but that we were firmly convinced that she had the capacity to function more adequately in her role as housewife and mother. We insisted that she perform certain simple tasks such as taking care of her hygienic needs and clothing and spending time in the day room. Gradually demands were put on her to do her own ironing, washing, and some volunteer work in another part of the hospital. Such activities were, of course, positively reinforced. While this shaping procedure was going on, several family interviews were held in which efforts were made to determine what stressful or reinforcing conditions in her home environment were contributing to her condition. We found that the husband had behaved oppressively during the early part of the marriage, but that once her disturbance seemed to have stabilized, he had become a model of self-sacrifice. He and his children treated the patient kindly, and because they were so concerned and troubled by the patient's illness behavior, tended to indulge her. A form of individual psychotherapy was also utilized. The patient was told that she could talk with her doctor about any of her problems in life, but that she could not talk about her symptoms for more than five minutes a day.

Under this "soft" behavioral regime the patient showed considerable improvement. She soon was working in the hospital for most of the day and was socializing with other patients. Improvement in her social functioning seemed to be correlated with considerable improvement in her symptoms. After four weeks of this gradual improvement, however, we discovered that the patient was pregnant. She asked for an abortion and this procedure was done in the hospital. Following the abortion her symptoms recurred in as severe a form as ever. Efforts were made to try to relate her feelings about the abortion to her earlier unwanted pregnancy and to her life problems and symptoms in general. She seemed uninterested in discussing these issues. In our family work it soon became apparent that her husband and children were becoming more desperate. They talked of giving up on the patient and sending her to a nursing home or a mental hospital. The patient responded to such threats by crying and by dramatically proclaiming her helplessness. Eventually the patient's pathetic pleas had an effect on one of her older daughters. During a family conference the daughter volunteered to give up her last year of college to return home and take care of her mother. As the daughter talked about her plans, it also became clear that such a move might also lead to her having to leave her fiancé and give up plans for marriage.

I was deeply moved by the extent of the daughter's intended sacrifice and by its futility. At this point I said to the husband and daughter with considerable passion, "Look, we may have reached a point when nothing can be done for your wife and mother, and our real concern should be with the survivors." I then proceeded to tell the daughter that her efforts to abandon important life gratifications in order to take care of her mother would probably be futile, and I very strongly told her that she should feel no guilt if she refused to do so. At this point the husband, who had also become deeply moved by the interaction, said that he had made up his mind that he would not take his wife home and would have her sent to a nursing home or a state hospital. After much discussion the rest of the family members concurred in this decision. While all this was being discussed, the patient was in tears and was warning her family that they were destroying her. I left the hour distressed as to the patient's plight, and worrying as to whether I had acted ethically in failing to support her immediate goals.

Amazingly, two days later the patient's symptoms dramatically improved and she asked to go home with her husband. The family was delighted and took her home; several weeks later they reported to me that her symptoms were almost entirely gone and that she was functioning with apparent contentment as a housewife and mother.

This spectacular cure seemed to be based on the patient's receiving the very solid message that there was no way in which she would continue to be reinforced for her symptoms. My role in helping to bring this change about might be perceived by some as cruel or even unethical. Nevertheless, this case has increased my belief that a real commitment on the clinician's part to work to diminish reinforcement of illness behavior can ultimately be advantageous not only to patients but to those around them as well. Our entire ward staff was so impressed with this patient's change that we all began considering ways of being less reinforcing of symptoms of mimicry. While I have no way of documenting this, I am convinced that our treatment team is "curing" conversion reactions much faster than it used to. We do this not by the aid of hypnosis, amytal interviews, or even powerful suggestion but simply by being kind to the patient while offering reinforcement which is primarily contingent on adaptive behavior.

The case above raises a tangential issues related to behavior modification. Sometimes, a patient who has suffered for many years, usually with a phobia or compulsion but occasionally with an hysterical disorder, will experience a dramatic cure through some type of behavior therapy. Such patients usually have a need to somehow or other justify or rationalize to themselves the existential issue of having wasted many years of their lives in unnecessary inactivity and suffering. The patient I have described here seemed relatively untroubled by the need to save face or to explain her four years of inactivity, but I have seen other patients suddenly "cured" by behavioral techniques who became moderately depressed when they began to consider the opportunities that had been wasted during years of incapacitation. I have begun to wonder if some patients fail to respond to behavioral or other treatments because removal of symptoms might result in great loss of face and self-esteem. (Perhaps this is why faith healers sometimes do much better than clinicians in treating conversion symptoms. If God heals the patient, there is little need to explain either the origins of behavior or its cure.) One face-saving technique which I have found useful and which does not require the therapist to be supernatural or to have magical powers involves giving patients total reassurance that there is nothing physically wrong with them and providing them the explanation that their symptomatology may have been prolonged by their uncertainty as to their physical condition. Once they begin to improve, they can be told with considerable truthfulness that their anxiety over the possible presence of organic disease could very well have accounted for the prolonged duration of their symptoms.

A forty-eight-year-old male patient suffered periods of intermittent dizziness for three years. Symptoms began on his job as a meat-packing house foreman, where he was required to work around machinery. While at work one day he suddenly felt weak and dizzy and fell to the floor. He was given a brief physical examination and told to take a few days off. He then returned to work, but his symptoms recurred, first, at work, with a frequency of several times a week, and then, at home, with a similar frequency. At this point the patient was hospitalized and extensive neurological tests were done. The electroencephalogram showed a mild and diffuse abnormality, but all other procedures, including skull films, a brain scan, and a pneumoencephalogram revealed no abnormalities. All other aspects of the physical and laboratory examination, including assessment of the patient's metabolic status, revealed that he was in excellent health. The patient's experience of weakness and fainting spells was not characteristic of any known seizure disorder. Although he seemed unconscious after he fell to the ground, he could be immediately revived with ammonia.

The patient left the hospital but felt incapable of working and applied for retirement and disability. This turned out to be a long and tedious process in which both his and his family's life were seriously disrupted. Shortly before his second admission to my service the patient was awarded full disability compensation. By this time, however, his relationship to his wife and children was seriously strained. They were angry over his inactivity and helplessness, which they viewed as in part contrived, but they could not say this to the patient. Even with the disability award, the patient's symptoms persisted and he had also begun to have symptoms of depression.

The Behavior Therapies

We began our second evaluation by repeating the neurological evaluation. We also made use of a relatively new instrument for evaluating brain damage called computerized axial tomography, or the EMI (Electric Music Industry) scan. The patient was told that this expensive and highly complicated procedure would give us the most definitive answer yet available as to whether he suffered from any brain disease. When the EMI scan was reported as negative, the patient was told that we were as sure as we ever could be that he did not have a serious disease. We further told him that there must have been good reasons why he fainted on the job originally, but that there was probably no way we would ever be able to really understand what had happened. We speculated with him that the perpetuation of symptoms could have been related to issues of disability compensation, but that they were probably also related to his anxiety and fear that he may have had a potentially fatal illness. This same explanation was given to members of the family, and in a conjoint interview they were give the opportunity to express their resentment as to how the patient's condition had affected their lives. They seemed willing not to press their resentment, and the patient seemed eager to accept our presentation of the situation and get on with the process of living. In a few weeks he reported that his depression had lifted, that he had experienced no more dizzy spells, and that he was planning a new career.

Our treatment of this patient can certainly not be characterized in terms of pure behavior modification. What we did was cut off, as firmly as possible, any physician-based reinforcements of illness behavior. More important, we presented him with a face-saving device and helped him to reestablish more open communication with his family.

A final comment will be made on the technique of paradoxical intention, which is sometimes classified as a behavior modification technique and which I sometimes use in treating disorders that are not defined as fear responses. People who ruminate over troubling thoughts suffer greatly and more or less continuously. It is sometimes useful to ask these patients to deliberately bring on these thoughts in as disturbing a manner as possible for a limited period of time, perhaps twenty minutes a day. Many patients will refuse to cooperate with a technique which threatens to escalate their suffering. Others will try to cooperate and find that they cannot seem to follow my directions. Often, however, the mere attempt to perform this task leads to slight improvement in symptomatology. Patients who are able to perform the task may experience even more relief. I have no idea whether behavioral principles of exposure, principles related to power struggles, or existential principles are involved in the process. I do know this technique can be a useful adjunct to treatment of patients who are painfully obsessive and who are not responding to other treatments. The technique should not be invoked in a cavalier manner. A good relationship with the patient and a willingness to share speculations as to why the technique may be helpful are essential factors in its effective use.

FURTHER ETHICAL CONSIDERATIONS

Behavior therapies, like biological therapies, carry a high risk of compromising the patient's autonomy and future potentials. Many if not most of the techniques of behavior modification require that the patient submit completely to the clinician's authority. When behavior is controlled by altering contingencies, the patient, who had not fully participated in the decisions to alter these contingencies, must learn to accept a certain degree of powerlessness. To the extent, of course, that any treatment is imposed upon a patient without fully informed consent, the patient's autonomy will be eroded. The danger of compromising future potentials is greatest when behavioral techniques are employed without due regard to the possibly oppressive nature of the environment. New training which is focused only upon the relief of symptoms can leave the patient more vulnerable to the ravages of an oppressive relationship or other oppressive environment. The long-term usefulness of such behavioral change is questionable when symptoms are still in a stage of development and can be clearly related to interpersonal and social conflict.

As is true for biological treatments, the dangers of providing ethically questionable behavioral treatment are diminished to the extent that the clinician is committed to thorough diagnosis of the environment as well as the individual. Such diagnosis should include assessment not only of the immediate antecedents and consequences of behavior but also of the potential oppressiveness of environmental stimuli. Even with a thorough diagnostic evaluation, ethical problems persist. But treatment decisions can then, at least, be made in terms of data which allow for consideration of potential risks, costs, and benefits. There are times when a painstaking, thorough, and unhurried assessment of the patient dissuades the clinician from trying to initiate a behavioral change which the patient initially professes to desire but may not actually want. A more leisurely assessment may also call attention to long-standing characterological and family problems which call for more emphasis upon traditional psychotherapeutic approaches.

In the course of writing this chapter, I was responsible for the treatment of a twenty-seven-year-old woman who came to my service with a diagnosis of anorexia nervosa. Her weight had dropped from 130 to 85 pounds over a period of eight months. She deliberately rejected most foods and had developed habits of eating only certain low calorie foods such as vegetables and fruits. She had no organic disease which would account for her behavior. When she came to the inpatient unit, she had not menstruated in several months and was beginning to show signs of malnutrition. She said that she was distressed about her condition and wanted to gain weight. She offered to cooperate in whatever treatment was recommended. When I reviewed the patient's case, I immediately asked the staff to begin preparing for a behavioral approach to her treatment, in which we would try to determine what responses or events would serve as positive reinforcers for her and to prepare to restrict her privileges so that we could make these reinforcements contingent upon her eating more food and gaining weight. The staff seemed to groan collectively as I made these recommendations. (I have already noted how deeply nurses and doctors who are not fully committed to behavioral approaches dislike having to implement them.) One of my residents reminded me of my own teaching and said that I was premature in recommending a behavioral approach. He argued that in the first two days of hospitalization the patient had already begun eating enough to take her out of immediate physical danger. He strongly suspected that the patient had serious marital problems and was ready to work on them. Most of the staff agreed with the resident in recommending a combined individual and family psychotherapy approach. I relutantly agreed to their plan, warning them that if the patient's weight fell below 80 pounds, I would invoke my authority and insist upon a behavioral approach.

The patient was seen daily in individual psychotherapy and twice weekly for marital therapy. She was given no special diet but was allowed off-ward privileges so she could supplement her eating any way she desired. No attention was paid to caloric intake. She was weighed once weekly, primarily at my insistence. It quickly became apparent that the patient was a highly controlling person with a poor self-concept and limited aspirations and was locked into a marriage in which she felt extremely dependent upon a man who seemed to have lost interest in her. Her husband complained bitterly that she was dull and nonspontaneous. These behavioral traits irritated him far more than her anorexia. He admitted that he had in the previous year withdrawn much of his emotional involvement from her and paid as little attention to her as possible. He made it clear to her that only her unusual eating habits and her weight loss were able to sustain his attention. She desperately wanted to continue the relationship and felt that perhaps it was her weight loss and pitiful condition that kept her husband from leaving her completely. He conceded that her observation was probably accurate.

Our focus in marital counseling was to help the couple either to find a way of experiencing a more gratifying marriage or to get divorced. We took a strong stand against the maintenance of the status quo, which we viewed as highly reinforcing to her illness behavior. In individual psychotherapy, the focus was upon increasing her self-esteem, searching for psychodynamic explanations of her deviant eating behavior, and trying to increase her assertiveness. The patient left the hospital after eight weeks with her problems far from resolved. She and her husband agreed to separate, but they continued to see each other on an almost daily basis and would not talk seriously of divorce. The patient became somewhat more assertive, believed she had a greater understanding of herself, and liked herself a little better. She also had gained 13 pounds by the time she was discharged.

The patient is continuing in treatment, and it is far too early to determine how things are going to turn out. It is clear, however, that she is quite ambivalent about regaining her normal weight. She is willing to keep her weight at a level where her health is not endangered. But she now talks of consciously wanting to hold on to her symptom and clings to the belief that her disorder may help her salvage her marriage.

Many speculations can be made about this case. Perhaps, if we had forced the patient to gain even more weight than she did, the husband would have been encouraged to be more attentive to her since she would have been a more attractive sexual partner. There is no way of knowing if her weight gain in the hospital was related to some resolution of her psychological conflicts and to her feeling better about herself or if it was related to a fear of authoritarian

The Behavior Therapies

treatments which she knew might eventually be utilized. It is also difficult to know if a strict behavioral approach to her problems might have compromised her future potential. We eventually discovered that the patient, contrary to her initial statements, was ambivalent about gaining weight and felt that weight gain might have compromised her possibilities of staying married. On the other hand, there is good reason to question whether maintenance of the marriage would have served her long-term interests. The only thing that is clear from this case is that my staff's commitment to thorough diagnosis prevented us from intitiating a treatment which would not have been lifesaving and which the patient did not actually want. If we had gone ahead and implemented the highly coercive control that is involved in a behavior modification program for anorexia nervosa, we might also have created a climate in which the kind of permissiveness and trust necessary for family and invididual psychotherapy would never have been available.

This case highlights the whole issue of motivation as it relates to the ethics of behavior modification. Behaviorists are quite willing to concede that the coercive use of behavior modification if often unworkable and unethical. They are especially aware of the ethical problems involved in using aversive stimuli and are usually fastidious in demanding that extinction techniques be accompanied by efforts to shape new behaviors. They are also aware that individuals, particularly those who are institutionalized, may consent to treatment because of societal pressure. Like all other clinicians, they try to initiate treatment only when the patient can freely provide informed consent. But behaviorists are prone to dodge many ethical issues by arguing that ethical questions do not exist when patients are motivated to have their behavior modified. They argue that they are merely providing patients what they ask for. I have partially dealt with this issue in chapter 4, where I argued that efforts to satisfy the motivations which the patients verbalize may be incompatible with therapists' ethical constructs and that initial verbalizations of the desired behavioral changes may turn out to be different from their real wishes or antagonistic to their needs. The latter issue is especially critical.

When approaching the issue of motivation, behaviorists seem to forget their own theories. They seem almost to assume that the patient's statement of motivation is a manifestation of self-determination or free will. What they forget is that the patient's verbalization of specific motivations is itself an operant response. It is shaped by negative reinforcement when the patient learns to seek help in order to avoid aversive interpersonal stimuli, and by positive reinforcement when the patient anticipates that others will approve of the desire to seek change. It is risky to assume that the intentions of those who provide the negative and positive reinforcements which shape the patient's motivation will be benevolent. It is conceivable, and often probable, that the environment has trained the patient to seek goals that are not in the patient's ultimate interest.

Several years ago a young girl came to me for treatment, asking me to help rid her of feelings of possessiveness and jealousy. When asked why these feelings were bothering her, she revealed that she had several months previously fallen in love with a young man who believed in communal living and who asked her to join his commune. She left school in order to live with him and several other young people. This action seriously strained her relationship with her conservative and religiously fundamentalist family. For a few months her lover paid exclusive attention to her, and she was happy. Then he began to insist on his right to have sex with other women, and she felt rejected and hurt. She began to plead with him to abandon his sexual involvement with other women. He told her that she was free to have sex with other men in the commune. She found this suggestion unacceptable. At this point her lover, as well as the communal group, attacked her verbally. They accused her of being controlling and pathologically possessive. They urged her to seek psychiatric help. While this patient was highly motivated and while I would probably have devised some behavioral method for trying to treat her, I really was much more concerned with her lack of capacity to deal with oppression than her inability to handle her feelings of possessiveness. Undoubtedly some therapist would have tried to comply with her requests, but I was deeply troubled with what such treatment would do to her future potentials. Her motivation had been shaped by her experiences in a recent and oppressive environment. Her situation was not too different from many other patients, particularly homosexuals, whose request for help is often shaped by negative reinforcers in the environment.

In theory it may be impossible to ever determine the patient's true motivations. All motivation is shaped by early as well as more recent learning. All learning is, therefore, influenced by the environment. Eventually the clinician must make value judgments and decide that some goals or motivations are more likely than others to promote the patient's happiness if fulfilled. I believe that patients are most likely to seek goals that are of optimum value to them if they take the time to consider the type of learning they have experienced in both recent and remote environments and if they share with the clinician their assessment of what goal should be sought and compare the clinician's assessment of what change is needed with their own. As noted several times previously, all of these considerations may be subservient to the value of compassion. When the patient's suffering is severe, the clinician's concern with ethical issues need not be so tortured. But behaviorists treat many symptoms which do not cause unbearable suffering to the patient. Even when the patient verbalizes motivation for specific behavioral changes, the behavior therapist cannot dodge consideration of those thorny ethical and political issues which are associated with any clinical intervention.

Chapter 7

Individual Psychotherapy

Individual psychotherapy is a treatment in which a trained person deliberately establishes a professional relationship with an emotionally troubled person and, through a process of mostly verbal interaction, helps the troubled person find a more comfortable and effective adaptation. There are elements in this definition which need elaboration.

First, the helping person is defined as someone who is trained and who deliberately establishes a professional relationship with the patient. The training and professionalism of the therapist is one factor which differentiates psychotherapy from friendship. As a professional, the psychotherapist will try to keep feelings toward the patient from influencing the manner in which the patient is treated. Friends can certainly help one another, but if their relationship is sustained, the person in the helping role will eventually have certain needs of the other. These needs will compromise the therapeutic effectiveness of the helper. Psychotherapists, on the other hand, ask nothing from the patient other than the patient's cooperation and professional gratification in the form both of monetary compensation and of the knowledge that their craftsmanship has been adequate. Another way of putting this is that a helping friend risks becoming entangled in the problems of the individual who is counseled. A professional can retain a certain degree of detachment and can respond to the patient's maladaptive behaviors in a nonreinforcing manner.

The second element in my definition of psychotherapy is that it involves a relationship between two people in which there is mostly verbal interaction. Certainly the patient and the therapist often communicate with one another through gestures, facial expressions, and even through silence; but the primary interactive process in psychotherapy involves two people talking to each other. The emphasis on verbal interaction excludes all biological interventions from being defined as forms of psychotherapy, with the possible exception of biofeedback or relaxation training. It also excludes those forms of behavior therapy in which there is little verbal communication with the patient. Most forms of behavior therapy require verbal interaction with the patient and can legitimately be called psychotherapy. While it will be convenient in much of the subsequent discussion to distinguish individual psychotherapy from most behavior therapy techniques, the reader should keep in mind that such distinctions are somewhat arbitrary.

The third element in the above definition is that psychotherapy helps a troubled person find a more comfortable and effective adaptation. Psychotherapy is not defined as a process which simply changes or relieves troubling behaviors or symptoms but as a process that influences an individual's total adaptation. With somatic interventions, the clinician is primarily concerned with relieving symptoms. With behavioral techniques, he is primarily concerned with increasing or diminishing the frequency of a given behavior. However, with psychotherapy, the clinician purports to do much more. The goal of psychotherapy is not only to alleviate symptoms (comfort), but it is also to help people lead better lives (effectiveness). Psychotherapy is a far more ambitious treatment than any that have thus far been considered. It is often alleged that the patient who is successful in completing psychotherapy is not only relieved of his suffering but emerges as a better and happier person than he was before his suffering became apparent (Rogers 1961). Psychotherapy has become such a familiar enterprise in Western culture that we tend to take its expansive goals for granted. But if clinicians fail to be impressed by the awesome task demanded by psychotherapy, it is not because the founders of the various schools of psychotherapy have been deceptive or unduly modest in defining its goals. All psychotherapists, whether traditional psychoanalysts or proponents of newer self-actualizing treatments, share a common concern with improving the total life of the patient. Throughout the literature, all schools of psychotherapy proclaim that the successfully treated patient will develop better coping mechanisms for dealing with the stresses of life, will develop better attitudes toward himself and others, will emerge from treatment with a new and more agreeable picture of himself, and will be in an improved position to achieve his full potential. All of these changes can be subsumed under the term *emotional growth* (Fagen and Shepherd 1970, Berne 1966, Boss 1963). Even when psychotherapy is primarily supportive or nonstressful, the therapist is still hopeful that the intervention will have a salutary effect upon many aspects of the patient's life other than his symptoms.

Removal of symptoms is a relatively straightforward goal. Helping patients achieve emotional growth, however, is a grander task, which immediately involves the clinician in issues that go far beyond the realm of traditional medicine, psychology, or any other science. If the patient is to lead a better life, there must be standards for deciding what that better life shall be. Decisions must be made as to what coping mechanisms, what attitudes, what kind of relationships, and what levels of understanding are best for a given individual. Ultimately such decisions must be based on the values which the therapist and the patient bring to the treatment situation. To the extent that the psychotherapist is concerned with helping the patient find a good or better life, the therapist must assume some of the functions of guidance which are usually relegated to spiritual leaders.

Many in our society have questioned whether it is appropriate for those in the mental health professions to assume such lofty functions (Akiskal and McKinney 1973, Busse 1972). Their questions are especially poignant when directed at psychiatrists who are physicians and who frequently practice psychotherapy. Physicians as a rule tend to avoid detailed consideration of the quality of the patient's life. The patient comes to the doctor with certain symptoms, the physician offers certain treatments, and if the symptoms are relieved, the patient is dismissed. The goal of emotional growth requires an expanded view of the process of healing in which the clinician concerns himself not only with altering a temporary biological imbalance but with altering the patient's total experience of his existence. In spite of the apparent grandiosity of such a goal, I believe it is entirely appropriate that psychiatrists, as well as other clinicians, seek it. The quality of a life is directly related to happiness, and there is a point at which unhappiness becomes a major factor in eliciting both physical and emotional dysfunction. Many patients will not be relieved of symptoms until they have changed significant aspects of their attitudes, their world view, or their life style. Furthermore we now have some evidence that psychotherapy which is designed to help the patient achieve emotional growth also relieves symptoms (Sloane et al. 1975).

PSYCHOTHERAPY AND RESPONSIBILITY

Although different schools of psychotherapy place different emphasis on what changes should be called emotional growth, all schools emphasize that such growth is related to the capacity of the patient to take responsibility for his own behavior. Responsibility can be defined as the capacity of an individual to hold himself fully accountable for what he does, thinks, or feels. The responsible individual accepts his behavior as his own. He accepts blame for what he does poorly and praise for what he does well. He also believes that he has choice in determining his behavior, can control his own actions, and can exercise a certain amount of will. The patient who successfully completes therapy should be able to say to himself, "When I act, think, or feel in certain ways, it is I who am doing it. All of my activities represent an effort to realize my own needs and wishes. Although there will be times when my behavior does not further my best interests or the best interests of others, I am always choosing to do what I want to do." This kind of responsibility is intimately associated with values such as freedom and autonomy. The capacity to make choices expands one's freedom, and being free necessitates making more choices. A person cannot feel independent and in control of his own behavior unless he feels that it is he who determines how he will behave.

Psychotherapists view the assumption of responsibility not only as a goal of successful treatment, but also as an essential element in sustaining the treatment process. Freud (1961) insisted that in the practice of psychoanalysis the patient must be held responsible for all thoughts and feelings, conscious or unconscious. Rogerians and existentialists teach that people are not moved by gargantuan or mysterious forces but hold power within themselves to choose and to govern their own actions (Rogers 1970, May 1969). In one school of therapy, known as reality therapy, the patient is regularly instructed to learn to take total responsibility for every aspect of his behavior (Glasser 1965). Rational emotive therapists repeatedly tell their patients that they are giving themselves unrealistic messages which they have the power to change (Ellis 1962).

Individual Psychotherapy

The concept of responsibility is also invoked by psychotherapists in their efforts to explain the origin of symptoms. In most schools of psychotherapy, the patient is viewed as having to some extent played a willful role in creating his own disturbance. In the first part of this book I noted that some patients seem to play an obvious role in creating environments which are ultimately oppressive. Other patients, thrust into oppressive environments by accident or by developmental changes, might be viewed as having been too vulnerable to such environments because of their commitment to unrealistic gratifications or their failure to have prepared themselves for developmental change. Most psychotherapists never allow the patient to plead total helplessness. The patient is discouraged from viewing his symptoms as an affliction or something caused by others and is encouraged to view symptoms as behaviors he himself has helped to develop and which he has the power to change. Finally, psychotherapists are impressed with the patient's capacity to resist change and to cling to symptoms. Whether such resistance is viewed as conscious or unconscious, the patient is held accountable for not trying hard enough to get well.

(On the basis of superficial observation, it might seem that many forms of psychotherapy may actually absolve the patient of responsibility rather than teach him to be more responsible. Psychoanalytic psychotherapy, for example, has sometimes been viewed as a treatment in which the patient learns to blame his plight on his parents, his society, or his unconscious. Some of the more extreme critics of psychoanalysis have even argued that by absolving the patient of blame, psychoanalytic psychotherapy encourages a form of permissiveness that borders on lawlessness. While it is certainly true that some patients in psychoanalytically oriented psychotherapy do at times seem to blame their disturbance totally on others, their reactions should be viewed as undesirable by-products or failures of treatment rather than as desired products of treatment. The psychoanalyst, like all other psychotherapists, does not want the patient to settle on a view of his disturbance which impugns outside sources.)

In practice the psychotherapist's insistence on the patient's assuming responsibility is neither stern nor condemning. Psychotherapists are gentle in assigning responsibility to the patient and try to divorce the issue of responsibility from the issue of punishability. This mode of assigning responsibility distinguishes psychotherapists from judges or theologians. In law the imposition of responsibility upon a person for a given act usually results in blame or punishment. In religion thoughts and feelings as well as acts may be considered blameworthy. In psychotherapy, however, the emphasis tends to be primarily upon the patient's merely accepting thoughts, feelings, actions as his own. Psychotherapists rarely punish the patients by making remarks that would make them feel ashamed or guilty.

Providing the patient the message that he is responsible for his behavior creates expectations within the patient that he will be able to initiate self-change. It diminishes the capacity of the patient to develop externalized explanations of his behavior, and to view it as something over which he has no control. By constantly providing the message You can do better, the therapist deprives the patient of reinforcement for ineffective behavior. He also subtly promises reinforcement for effective behavior. Finally, by an insistence that the patient be totally responsible for everything about himself, the therapist directs the patient to focus upon those less lovable or unacceptable aspects of himself which he would ordinarily be reluctant to examine. When all of this is done in a climate in which little blame and no punishment is invoked, the patient experiences a willingness to continue the painful process of viewing himself as responsible for his behavior.

Unfortunately psychotherapists rarely bother to conceptualize why they invoke this technique. Some psychotherapists seem to actually believe that people are always responsible for all of their behavior. Others believe that the effort to lead a responsible life is an essential condition of human existence. And there are probably a few therapists who would view responsibility as merely a necessary fiction created by society in an effort to train individuals to behave in accordance with prevailing mores. Psychotherapists also tend to avoid confronting the dilemmas created when they ask the patient to assume total responsibility for behavior. Little effort has been made, for example, to define those situations in which the patient's responsibility, will, or capacity to choose might be compromised. Forensic psychiatrists and psychologist have, of necessity, done considerable thinking as to how certain psychological impairments may mitigate responsibility (Waelder 1952). But their theoretical discourses and debates are not generally related to clinical practice.

My own belief is that efforts to define the limits of responsibility are as important in clinical as in forensic work. Certain structural and physiological dysfunctions clearly impair an individual's

Individual Psychotherapy

capacity to choose. A person with a broken leg cannot choose to run in a race. A mentally retarded person cannot choose to do mathematical equations. A person in a manic phase of a bipolar depression cannot choose to be contemplative. Rarely is the person diagnosed as physically ill asked to review his own role in creating his illness. To put this absurdly, we do not ask a patient with cancer how he could have chosen not to have the disease, nor do we ask how he intends to behave in the future so as to prevent the disease's recurrence. It is a reality of clinical practice that it is futile and even destructive to exhort certain types of emotionally disturbed patients to do better or to examine the manner in which they may have created their own suffering. The severely depressed patient has had many admonitions from friends and relatives that he is capable of snapping out of it and doing better. The message that he is capable of curing himself through his own efforts can be a cruel one. The severely depressed patient tends to equate responsibility with blame. To the extent that he feels he has created his own illness and to the extent that his efforts to be responsible and to work at changing his behavior do not result in amelioration of symptoms, he blames himself even more for failing to accomplish something he is not really capable of doing.

The clinician who combines psychotherapy with other treatment modalities or who does psychotherapy with patients whose capacities for choice have been compromised needs a model for conceptualizing how he will approach the issue of responsiblity with each patient. He must learn when to demand that the patient assume an attitude of responsibility and when to modify such a demand in accordance with the patient's capabilities. In my own work I have gradually developed such a model, which for the sake of convenience I will present in terms of how I might instruct a hypothetical patient, beginning psychotherapy, as to the limits of his responsibility.

"You will progress more comfortably and effectively in psychotherapy and in life in general, to the extent that you assume responsibility for your behavior. I will always be trying to inculcate this attitude into your thinking. At the same time I will try never to blame or punish you for your shortcomings. I don't want you to punish or blame yourself, but I do expect you to hold yourself accountable for everything you think, feel, or do. There are some conditions or circumstances which can limit your capacity to choose, and I will constantly try to be aware of those. Obviously, you cannot be held responsible for failing to behave in an adaptive manner when others in your environment, or circumstances in your environment, prevent your doing so. If you have been oppressed throughout your life, have been poor, uneducated, and discriminated against, it would be absurd to hold you fully responsible for not having developed effective work habits. Physical disabilities will also impair your capacity to choose. If your thinking and emotions are impaired because of some biological process, these conditions will also impose limits upon your capacity to choose. If you are biologically depressed, for example, you may not be able to work and may have to live for a brief time in a hospital. Within that hospital setting some choices will be available to you and others will not. You may choose, however, whether to spend your time lying in bed or going for a walk. Another factor which may compromise your capacity to be held accountable for your actions is your lack of access to information as to what the environment expects of you. If you are hospitalized, I cannot hold you responsible for behaving inappropriately in the hospital setting until you have been fully informed as to what is expected of you in the environment. There may be other factors which, in perhaps less powerful ways, compromise your capacity to choose. Your failure to be aware of needs or motivations which are important to you may lead you to seek gratifications which are not in your best interests. You may, because of your experience in early childhood, have learned to distort your perceptions of certain environmental situations. I will try to help you become aware of your motivations and perceptual distortions, and such awareness may enhance your capacities or circumstances which impose limits upon your behavioral repertoire. I cannot hold you responsible for these limitations; I can only try to ameliorate or diminish them. I can, however, ask you to take responsibility for how you deal with these limitations and I will."

This is one mode of explanation that may be too complicated to be presented verbatim to the patient. What is most important here is that the clinician has a model for dealing with the issue of responsibility firmly fixed in his mind before approaching the patient. The clinician's task is to urge the patient to try to change things he is capable of changing, but it is the clinician who must assume responsiblity for trying to change things the patient cannot. Thus the clinician must operate in two spheres of influence at the same time. He must sometimes behave authoritatively and do things for the patient, such as provide medication or set up selective reinforcement schedules. At other times he must

Individual Psychotherapy

encourage the patient to do things for himself. The clinician must guard against both asking too much of the patient and asking too little. This is one of the most difficult conceptual and practical problems the clinician will ever face. I believe that however tortuous or convoluted my own model for dealing with this issue may be, its use in clinical practice is preferable to using systems of treatment which are based entirely on the assumption either that the patient is helpless or that the patient is responsible for healing himself. It is also preferable to a laissez-faire approach in which the clinician indiscriminately, and without bothering to conceptualize the reasons for doing so, switches from a mode of interaction which views the patient as totally helpless to one which views the patient as fully responsible.

TERRITORIAL ISSUES

Emotional disorders have since the beginning of civilization been treated by techniques involving verbal and emotional interaction with another concerned person. Priests, shamans, and witch doctors performed psychotherapy long before the mental health professions existed. As psychotherapy has evolved in the modern era, it has been performed by a wide variety of professionals, including physicians, psychologists, social workers, nurses, educators, religious advisors, and, occasionally, by nonprofessionals as well. Professional educators and religious advisors often refer to their work with troubled people as counseling rather than psychotherapy. They usually try to avoid treating people who are highly disturbed, but sometimes they knowingly or unknowingly work with people with quite serious difficulties. Nonpsychiatric physicians frequently become involved in verbal interactions with a patient, directed toward solving the patient's problems, and these interactions would fit most definitions of brief psychotherapy. They tend to refer more difficult problems to their psychiatric colleagues but there are times when they will try to treat highly disturbed patients. Psychologist, social workers, and nurses will initiate psychotherapy with a wide variety of patients. They tend to avoid treating more highly disturbed patients, particularly those who may have a biological disorder, but occasionally they will treat even psychotic or severely depressed patients.

Psychiatrists have the broadest license to provide psychotherapy in the United States. Historical factors are important here. Sigmund Freud, working as a physician, developed the most influential theory and technique of psychotherapy, and his followers brought psychotherapy away from psychology and religion and toward medicine. While Freud did not view psychoanalysis as a treatment which should be practiced solely by the medical profession, many of his disciples who were physicians felt differently. In the United States there was an especially powerful thrust to restrict the practice of psychoanalysis and related psychotherapies to the medical profession. The psychiatrist, while often retaining skills in physical diagnosis and biological treatment, came to see his primary professional identification as that of a doctor who does psychotherapy. In recent decades, however, other professions have increasingly sought to define their identity in terms of their psychotherapeutic capabilities. They have developed techniques of psychotherapy which differ slightly or significantly from psychoanalysis and have insisted that proper use of these techniques does not require medical training. Nonpsychiatric therapists have laid claim to a major portion of what might be called the psychotherapy market. At the same time psychiatrists, while expanding their identification as doctors who utilize many interventions other than psychotherapy, have sought legal and social sanctions to strengthen their role as the most legitimate purveyors of psychotherapy.

In a society in which economic incentives are important to the psychotherapist, in which safety and efficiency are important to the patient or consumer, and in which there are no definitive data indicating which profession can perform psychotherapy most effectively, various professions struggle over control of the psychotherapy market. In this struggle psychiatrists are most powerful. They not only have access to skills which allow for complete diagnosis and treatment, but they have access to the most prestigious forms of training in psychotherapy. To the extent that emotional problems are defined as medical problems, the psychiatrist is also the professional who is likely to be compensated for doing psychotherapy by private and public insurance programs. Psychologists have staked out a certain territory for themselves by developing standards of licensure for psychological psychotherapeutic practice. Other professionals who practice psychotherapy are similarly seeking to legitimate their own psychotherapeutic interventions.

Individual Psychotherapy

The stakes in this territorial war are high. Psychotherapy, as practiced in this country, is a multibillion dollar industry. Unfortunately, the economic aspects of the current territorial controversy have not fostered a rational approach to the question of who should do psychotherapy. The medical profession's rigid hold on on psychoanalytic psychotherapy has probably been a significant factor in encouraging the development of many new systems of psychotherapy which can be practiced by nonpsychiatrists. As schools of psychotherapy develop and proliferate, they develop their own criteria for training and for assessing competency. Praising the virtues of a given school is determined not only by ideology but by the needs of the practitioner to stake out a territory which provides him assured access to the psychotherapy marketplace. Viewed in this light, the current pluralism in the field of psychotherapy can hardly be viewed as facilitative of a scientific approach to clinical theory or practice.

It would help if we had rational standards for determining who should do psychotherapy. My own position is that psychotherapy is not the exclusive domain of any of the currently active health professions. As long as psychiatrists are the only professionals dealing with emotional problems who have access to medical training, they should continue to have primary responsibility for carrying out the type of diagnostic process I have described in earlier chapters. There is no rational argument, however, behind psychiatrists' claims that they should be the sole or main purveyors of psychotherapy, which is only one of many interventions they might prescribe. Recent efforts of some psychiatrists to distinguish between medical and other forms of psychotherapy are, at best, based on a kind of sophism in which there is failure to distinguish between diagnostic and therapeutic roles. At worst they reflect a concern with economic rather than professional values. The skills required of the psychotherapist can be mastered by individuals who have had absolutely no medical training, and indeed many of our most prominent and creative psychotherapists are not physicians. There are no data proving that psychotherapy performed by psychiatrists is in any way superior to psychotherapy performed by other professionals. Our professions and our society need to devise standards for licensing psychotherapists, which are based on ensuring the competence of psycotherapists and protecting the public from those who are inadequate. These standards should not be influenced by the status or economic needs of the various professions.

DIAGNOSTIC ISSUES:
WHO SHOULD RECEIVE PSYCHOTHERAPY?

In chapter 2 I described psychotherapy as an intervention in which a new environment is created that allows the patient to experience new learning and to receive new information. Such an environment begins to be created during the process of diagnosis. In a very broad sense any person who is distressed enough to seek help receives a form of brief psychotherapy while he is being evaluated. It will be useful at this point to review and elaborate upon some of the previously developed guidelines as to which patients are most in need of a psychotherapeutic experience that extends beyond the diagnostic process.

There are three types of patients who are in special need of individual psychotherapy:

1. Patients who are experiencing acute but moderate symptoms of anxiety and depression related to recent changes in the environment brought about by accidental events or by changes in the patient's development. These symptoms can be viewed as responses to crises, and one effective form of crisis intervention is individual psychotherapy. This kind of psychotherapy can be brief. Family therapy might be equally useful for these patients, but I will not consider that intervention here.

2. Patients who have been disabled by severe emotional disturbances such as schizophrenia, mania, or depression. These patients need a long term psychotherapeutic experience which will help them adjust to their disabilities. Usually they do not get it.

3. Patients who periodically suffer from moderate feelings of anxiety and depression and who have chronic feelings of inadequacy and discontent. These patients do not usually have circumscribed symptoms such as phobias or compulsions but usually experience a more vague sense of unhappiness and disease. When their symptoms become exacerbated, it is often possible to determine that environmental changes have taken place which the patients have themselves helped to create. In clinical terms these individuals are currently described as having *personality* or *character disorders*, but they can also be considered in sociological terms as *alienated* individuals who have failed to develop adaptive means of dealing with the problems of existence. While these patients are often helped by group or family therapy, most require a rather prolonged period of therapy which is conveniently provided in the dyadic setting.

Individual Psychotherapy

The reasons for using individual psychotherapy in crisis situations characterized by moderate symptomatology are as follows:

1. Most of these patients do not need and are unlikely to be benefited by biological interventions other than brief use of antianxiety drugs or training in inducing the relaxation response. There are, of course, exceptions: patients who develop more disabling symptoms in response to a crisis may require major biological interventions

2. Behavior modification techniques may be extremely difficult to implement with these individuals because their symptoms are often vague and poorly circumscribed.

3. The symptoms experienced by the patient in crisis are directly influenced by a number of internal and external factors which can be examined and modified. Even if the patient's symptoms are relatively circumscribed and can be described as target behaviors, they are not yet autonomous, but are still "alive." In the process of psychotherapy, the patient is likely to learn something about himself and his environment. He may develop new attitudes, become aware of new feelings, and develop more appropriate coping mechanisms which will assist him in dealing with future crises. In short, the patient who seeks treatment for acute moderate symptomatology is in a position to experience emotional growth. If such a patient is treated only by manipulating environmental contingencies, there is a risk that his future potential will be compromised. The behavior therapies can of course be held in reserve to be used if brief psychotherapy does not work, and if the symptoms take on a chronic or autonomous quality.

4. Patients in crisis situations do not usually respond well to group therapy. The reasons for this will be explained in the next chapter. These patients may, however, do quite well with family therapy or combined individual and family therapy, particularly when family members are directly involved in the creation of the crisis situation.

It is possible, and certainly economically desirable, to keep treatment for this group of patients relatively brief. One way of doing this is to set a limit on the number of sessions. Efforts are then made to focus primarily on recent environmental changes which seemed to initiate the disturbance and on the patient's responses to these changes. Wherever possible, the patient is urged to try to define one problem or one symptom (whether circumscribed or not) and to try to focus upon this area during the entire course of therapy. Once the focus of therapy is determined, a variety of techniques can be used to bring about rapid change. (These techniques will be described more comprehensively in a later part of this chapter.) Some therapists will concentrate primarily on providing an empathic, tension-reducing environment and hope that this is sufficient for the patient to achieve control of the situation. Others will focus upon developing new learning experiences within the therapeutic relationship or will try to create some of the frustrations and anxieties characteristic of the psychoanalytic paradigm. Some therapists will be liberal in providing direction and advice to patients. Others will emphasize nondirectiveness. Some will try to influence environmental variables either in the community or in the family, while others will choose to restrict their involvements solely to working with the individual. All practitioners of brief therapy will try to provide their patients some explanation of how the disturbance developed.

Some of the more vigorous efforts to do brief psychotherapy have developed out of the psychoanalytic movement. Recently, psychoanalytically oriented psychotherapists have claimed considerable success in using modified techniques of anxiety induction and transference interpretation in treating acutely disturbed individuals (Mann 1974, Sifneos 1974). Their results, however, seem dependent upon the selection of patients who have demonstrated considerable psychological strength before their disturbance developed. Brief psychoanalytically oriented psychotherapy is most effective with those of above average intelligence, who have been able to develop meaningful relationships with others, are able even during the first interview to show some emotional relationship to the therapist, and are highly psychologically minded and motivated for behavioral change. The rigidity of selection criteria, particularly regarding the patient's motivation, would seem an extremely important factor in the success of brief psychoanalytic psychotherapy. Patients accepted for this form of treatment are expected to show:

1. An awareness that their symptoms are largely psychological in nature
2. A tendency to be introspective and honest
3. A willingness to be active in therapy
4. Curiosity and willingness to understand themselves

5. A willingness to try to change and to explore and experiment with new behaviors
6. Realistic expectations of possible outcomes of psychotherapy
7. A willingness to make reasonable sacrifices in order to achieve therapeutic benefit

In considering treatment for patients disabled by a severe emotional disorder, it would seem logical that, whether their disorders were brought on by learned or by biological determinants, they, more than others, would benefit from learning as much as possible as to the nature of their disturbances as well as learning how they and others respond to the disturbances. Many of these individuals had failed to develop adequate coping mechanisms even before their major disturbances developed. Their major disorders compromise their adaptive capacities even further. Patients who have been disabled by psychotic or depressive disorders need as much support, information, and coping skills as they can get. Yet, as noted previously, it is rare for such patients to receive long-term psychotherapy. This is especially perplexing because there are very good data that adding psychotherapy to the medical treatment of patients with certain disabling psychophysiological disorders, such as asthma or peptic ulcer, markedly improves their adjustments to life and to their illness (Luborsky, Singer, and Luborsky 1975). If psychotherapy is so effective in helping this group of patients deal with their biological disorder, why can't it help psychotic and depressed people (who probably also have a biological impairment) deal with theirs? We don't know the answer to this question because there have been few controlled studies in which experienced and highly motivated psychotherapists have worked with psychotic or severely depressed patients.

I have several times throughout this text lamented the reluctance of practitioners to offer psychotherapeutic services to those with severe physiological disabilities. Conceivably when the organ of the body that is impaired is the brain, talking about the disturbance or talking about problems related to the disturbance may be threatening to the patient's self-esteem and body image. Clinicians may simply feel that the psychotherapeutic process is too stressful for the highly disturbed patient. It is also true that many practitioners have not mastered the techniques of supportive psychotherapy. They have not learned how to help highly disturbed people examine their lives and maximize their potentials without imposing undue stress upon them. Psychotherapists are understandably confused as to the role of biological versus learning determinants in creating psychoses and depression, and most do not have a system for dealing with the issue of the disturbed patient's degree of responsibility. It is possible that they avoid individual psychotherapy with highly disturbed patients because they fear that in the course of therapy they may demand conditions of responsible behavior on the part of the patient which the patient cannot possibly meet. A better explanation of the reluctance to provide individual psychotherapy to disturbed patients is that work with these people is intellectually and economically unrewarding and requires a high degree of emotional involvement and staying power. If we accept this explanation, the most efficient way of providing psychotherapy for these people would be a health care delivery system providing clinicians greater rewards for working with more difficult patients. I will have more to say about this in the final chapter.

One important reason for recommending the highly expensive intervention of long-term psychotherapy for patients with personality and character disorders is that these individuals are usually unresponsive to any other treatment. Medication rarely helps, and behavior modification only ameliorates a few of the multitude of symptoms they periodically develop. By the time many of these people reach their thirties, they have already had one or more unsuccessful experiences with briefer psychotherapies. Family therapy is helpful to them during periods of crisis, when symptoms are exacerbated, but these patients may continue to have difficulty after major family system problems have been resolved.

Personality or character traits are learned over a long period of time. They are maintained by patterns of self-reinforcement and environmental reinforcement that are difficult to extinguish. The patient may never relate these traits to his experience of anxiety or depression. Even when his personality traits are experienced as sources of interpersonal difficulty, the patient may be unwilling to give them up. The patient can usually resist the therapist's efforts to order or persuade him to behave differently. It is only through a prolonged process of relating and learning that most of these people can find a better life.

It will be useful at this point to try to elaborate on the problem of diagnosing the presence of a personality or character disorder.

Individual Psychotherapy

Given their constitutional predispositions and the series of learning experiences encountered throughout childhood and adult life, all individuals eventually develop a variety of relatively consistent ways of dealing with life stress. These behaviors can be looked upon as personality or character traits. Some traits, such as lovingness toward others, assertiveness, willingness to assume personal responsibility, and a capacity to enjoy work and play, are adaptive in most environments. Other personality traits may interfere with people's capacity to function effectively in most of the environments they encounter in Western culture. These traits will influence the interpersonal environment and may elicit responses from others that the patient experiences as oppressive. When that environment becomes too oppressive, these patients experience anxiety or depression. Patients with maladaptive personality traits may also lack capacity to cope with oppressive events created by accident or by the demands of maturation. Again they are vulnerable to anxiety or depression. Their immediate experience of suffering can be resolved by changing environments, or through finding new jobs, new people to relate to, and new diversions, but if their response patterns remain unchanged, sooner or later they will experience new difficulties. The general life course of these individuals is unhappy. Their unhappiness should be distinguished from the unhappiness of those who are simply oppressed by poverty and discrimination. Maladaptive personality traits can certainly develop in response to social oppression, but here I am concerned with traits that seem to persist even when the social environment is not depriving the patient of material needs or restricting his freedom.

The personality traits which are most frequent and which are usually maladaptive in American society are:

1. An inability to be appropriately aggressive or assertive. Some individuals are regularly aggressive in a manner which offends others. Others are too passive and unable to assert their rights and needs. Still other people have difficulty in developing the right response for the right situation, and are aggressive when passivity would be most adaptive and passive when they should be aggressive.

2. A tendency to blame others for whatever dissatisfaction one has with one's status in life. This behavior serves as a justification for avoiding efforts to initiate behavioral changes, and preserves the patient's self-esteem at the price of creating unfriendly responses on the part of those who are blamed.

3. A tendency to lead a life in which one denies responsibility for past or present actions, and to either explain much of one's behavior as a form of illness, or to develop behavioral patterns which mimic illness. With the expansion of medical and psychiatric care in the country, this adaptation has become disturbingly commonplace.

4. A tendency to seek control of interpersonal situations so that one is not left vulnerable to the prospect of loss of interpersonal nurturance. This tendency can be manifested in a variety of ways, but most commonly it leads to seeking power over others, or to a structured approach to other people that is characterized by rigidity and lack of spontaneity.

5. A tendency to be exploitive of others in a manner which is not socially acceptable. While our society condones competitiveness, qualities such as greed and selfishness are not acceptable when they are expressed in manners which go beyond socially ordained rules. Many people never learn to gratify aggressive and sexual needs in a manner inoffensive to others.

6. A tendency to fear closeness to other people, which results in an inability to obtain the gratifications which are inherent in a loving relationship.

The current tendency in clinical practice is to give each of these behavior patterns a name. People who have difficulty in modulating aggressiveness are called passive-aggressive personalities; individuals who blame others for their own inadequacies are called paranoid personalities; individuals who lead a nonresponsive life and exploit the illness role are called hysterical personalities; individuals who seek power and orderliness are sometimes called obsessive-compulsive personalities (although there are usually other traits associated with this label); individuals who exploit others and who are not successful at it are called sociopathic personalities; and individuals who are too socially withdrawn are called schizoid personalities. My own position is that such labeling adds little to our understanding of these people or to their treatment. While it is often possible for the clinician to note that some people use one of these behavior patterns to excess, this does not mean that such traits dominate most aspects of these individual's lives. The unhappy patient is likely to use more than one of these response tendencies in his daily relationships. In describing a patient it would make much more sense to try to evaluate the extent to which he uses any or all of the above responses than to label him primarily on the basis of

Individual Psychotherapy

the existence of the predominant trait. (The reader should also be aware that I am only describing some of the most common patterns of maladaptive personality traits and that any individual has probably developed a rich pattern of interpersonal responses, many of which are maladaptive in certain situations.)

While I have described patients with personality or character disorders as individuals who are primarily experiencing problems in living, I do not mean to deemphasize their plight. At times they are profoundly miserable and many are at risk of becoming suicidal or developing depressions which must be treated with biological intervention. Others are at risk of developing psychophysiologic disorders. These considerations provide some justification for long-term psychotherapy with these individuals even though the evidence for the superiority of this method is not overpowering and even though it is an intervention which strains our economic and manpower resources.

Given the current realities of psychotherapeutic practice in the United States, there are conditions which limit the number of people with personality disorders who will seek and receive long-term psychotherapy. Patients are most likely to accept such treatment if they are highly motivated to change, are psychologically minded, and are capable of meeting the high expenses of prolonged treatment. Therapists who spend a significant portion of their working lives intimately involved with such people naturally try to select patients who will keep them interested and who fit the general criteria of the YAVIS (Young, Attractive, Verbal, Intelligent, Successful) patient. Another large group receiving long-term psychotherapy in America today are individuals who are either practicing psychotherapy or are in the process of becoming professional therapists. This is a unique and interesting situation insofar as one of the major indications for being a patient in long-term psychotherapy is a high motivation to become a psychotherapist.

THEORY AND TECHNIQUE

While clinical judgment or artfulness is a factor in efficacious use of biological interventions and behavior therapy, it is not too difficult to conceptualize and communicate the technical knowledge that is required for their use. Given the availability of accurate information about the patient, it is possible to make fairly good predictions about what the effects of a given pharmacological or behavioral intervention will be. Many of the skills of biological or behavioral intervention can be taught by verbal or written instruction. The situation with regard to psychotherapy is different. Psychotherapy involves a series of transactions between therapist and patient which have an unlimited range of content and form. There are dozens of ways in which the therapist can respond to the patient's communication of a thought or feeling and dozens of possible responses of the patient to the responses of the therapist. The most that can be taught is that some responses to the patient's presentation of problems are more useful at certain times than others, that some responses are generally safer when the therapist is uncertain as to what is happening, and that other responses may be quite harmful to the patient. Some aspects of psychotherapeutic intervention can be studied successfully, but in practice psychotherapy is a skill or art which must be mastered by repeated practice, observation, and supervision. Writing about psychotherapy is difficult. Most textbooks on how to do psychotherapy focus more on the theory of technique than on technique itself. The writers try to teach technique by explaining how common elements influence the process of psychotherapy, by illustrating how problems which frequently arise can be handled, and by reproducing case material which illustrates psychotherapeutic practices. No one has been able to develop a "cookbook" approach to psychotherapy.

My own approach will certainly suffer from lack of specificity. In this section, my efforts will be restricted to isolating those elements in the psychotherapeutic process which are essential and helpful and showing how these can be used to influence the patient. Before doing this, however, it will be useful to review some more specific but generally accepted rules which are used to structure individual psychotherapy,

GENERAL STRUCTURE

Psychotherapy should begin with a contract. The clinician offers to try to help the patient achieve some goal such as relief of symptoms, personal growth, or both. Some therapists are quite specific in defining the goals which they will try to help the patient achieve. Others are deliberately vague and are prepared to change goals as the patient reveals more information regarding his wishes

Individual Psychotherapy

and needs. In return for the clinician's commitment, the patient is expected to pay a fee, to be diligent in keeping appointments, and to be punctual. He is instructed as to how to cancel an appointment because of illness or emergency and is told under what circumstances he will be excused from paying for missed hours. If the patient is in long-term therapy, arrangements regarding the timing of both the therapist's and patient's vacations may also be made.

The extent of the therapist's commitment to the patient should be spelled out in terms of the number of hours the therapist will be available. Some therapists prefer to do time-limited therapy and will tell the patient that they will be available for a certain number of weekly or monthly visits for a certain number of weeks or months. Other therapists view their commitment as indeterminate and usually tell the patient that they will be available for as long as it takes for the patient to feel better. The frequency of therapy is determined by the therapist's goal and theoretical orientation. If information-expanding therapy based on psychoanalytical principles is offered, the patient is likely to be seen several times weekly. When supportive approaches are used, the patient is seen once a week or once every other week. As a rule, therapists do not present the patient with contingency plans as to what different approaches will be tried if the initial therapy does not go well. Such neglect may be justified by the need to create a climate of optimism for the patient. The clinician should, however, have a sufficient commitment to the patient to ascertain that other modes of intervention will be available if the patient does not get well or gets worse.

The patient should have some idea of what approach the clinician will take from the beginning of therapy. If therapy is to be conducted entirely at a verbal level this should be stated. If it is to include experience in achieving the relaxation response or in becoming aware of bodily sensations through prescribed exercises, this too should be stated. It is especially important for the clinician who is nondirective and who may often be silent to clarify the reason for his silence. Sophisticated patients may anticipate and understand the therapist's silence, but others will experience it as frightening or rude. My own practice, when doing psychoanalytically oriented psychotherapy, is to tell the patients in the first hour that I will often be silent and may not observe ordinary social amenities, because this is an important technique for helping them gain access to out-of-awareness information.

The therapist must try to create a climate in which the patient feels free to disclose his problems. This requires that the therapist seek to maximize the confidentiality of communication between himself and his patient and that the patient have complete knowledge as to the limits of confidentiality. The patient must be informed as to what kind of records will be kept and with whom the therapist may share information regarding the patient. The clinician and the patient must be aware that records can be subpoenaed. The patient must also know that if he uses medical insurance to pay for part of his treatment, and if he subsequently applies for a job or insurance and is asked whether he has had previous psychiatric treatment, he will have to answer affirmatively. The employer or insuror may then ask the patient for permission to see his treatment records. If the patient should fail to admit he has had previous psychotherapy, his omission can be detected through use of computerized data which have been recorded because of his previous use of medical insurance. All of this means that clinicians should be sensitive as to what kind of material is put in psychotherapy records. Clinicians who work in private practice have some freedom to keep unrevealing or perfunctory records. Those who work in public institutions do not. As a rule the clinician is wise to keep any material that might be used to limit the patient's future potentials out of the record. Material which if made public would be embarrassing to the patient should also be deleted. Many clinicians these days tape-record psychotherapeutic interviews. While this practice may be valuable for research and teaching purposes, it carries serious potential hazards for the patient. Patients may readily consent to having interviews tape-recorded, without appreciating the risks of the tapes becoming public record. I do not believe that the patient can be considered to have given informed consent to have psychotherapeutic interviews recorded until the patient has full information as to the potential future use of the recordings.

I strongly favor allowing the patient full access to his psychotherapy records. Such an arrangement makes the therapist-patient relationship more egalitarian. It diminishes the degree of power the therapist gains through mystification. It is also likely to make the therapist more conscientious in deciding what is to be included in the record.

Patients must also be informed as to whether the therapist will discuss their case with other clinicians. Even experienced therapists will desire consultation in dealing with difficult cases and beginning therapists will wish to share material with supervisors. The only rule to be observed here is that the patient know the extent to which the clinician will share information with his colleagues. The issue of sharing information with the patient's relatives or friends is more serious. As a general rule information about the patient should not be shared with any friend or relative of the patient without the patient's explicit permission. Sometimes the psychotherapist is unexpectedly called by a friend or relative of the patient who informs the therapist about certain of the patient's behaviors. The therapist may then be urged not to tell the patient that such information has been given. Confidentiality in such cases should not be honored. The therapist has no contract with the friend or relative and should tell him that the patient will be informed of the contents of the call.

There are three reasons why issues of confidentiality and record keeping are so important. First, many forms of psychotherapy are based on a kind of trust between patient and therapist that can only be obtained with total confidentiality. Second, the information obtained in psychotherapy is likely to be more detailed and embarrassing to the patient than that obtained in ordinary diagnostic interviews. Third, many patients who enter psychotherapy do so electively. They do not view themselves as sick, and may not know their problems will be catalogued in medical records, or that various agencies and institutions might eventually come to label them mentally ill. Confidentiality is, of course, a critical issue in any clinical intervention. It is especially important in psychotherapy.

A final issue which must be settled in the initial negotiations between patient and therapist is the extent of contact the patient will be allowed to have with the therapist outside of regularly scheduled interviews. Some therapists permit extra hours on the patient's demand and do not object to phone calls. Others are far more rigid and try to discourage any disruption of the planned schedule of appointment, or any contact outside of the treatment sessions. My own policy is to provide extra hours when the patient seems to be having difficulty and to ask the patient to call me if he is deeply troubled. I also tell the patient, however, that I will accept these deviations from structure only during crisis periods and that I do not expect crises to recur repeatedly. The patient knows he can see me more often or call me if he feels it is necessary, but he also receives a message that I will be unwilling to reinforce disturbed behavior indefinitely.

HELPFUL FACTORS

A number of prominent psychotherapists have recently tried to define those factors in the therapeutic process which are most influential in promoting desirable change. They have concluded that whatever the theoretical orientation of the therapist there are certain characteristic events and conditions in all therapeutic processes which are essential to successful therapy. I also believe that common helpful factors in psychotherapy exist and that it is easier to understand, study, and practice psychotherapy by focusing upon these factors than by focusing upon the theories and practices of the various schools. The factors I will consider are difficult to isolate. They tend to overlap, and the reader should be cautioned that they are classified primarily to promote clarification and communication. My own list of factors which are effective in psychotherapy differs only slightly from the lists of such writers as Jerome Frank (1971), Judd Marmor (1975), or Irvin Yalom (1975). It includes one factor that must be present before treatment begins and six factors which exert influence by virtue of the interactions which take place within the therapeutic process. The factor which operates most powerfully before therapy even begins is the patient's hope and belief in the power of the socially sanctioned healer to help him. The factors that are critical once the therapeutic process begins are:

1. Identification with the therapist
2. The climate of caring and lovingness created by the therapist
3. The opportunity to relieve tension by verbalizing and expressing uncomfortable thoughts and emotions
4. The process of learning new behaviors and unlearning old behaviors which is determined by the therapist's management of the contingencies of reinforcement and which can be explained in terms of operant conditioning
5. The attainment of new information on the part of the patient as to how he interacts with the environment as well as information as to how he is influenced by past experiences
6. The therapist's ability to explain the patient's behavior in a manner that allows the patient to tolerate and forgive himself for undesirable behaviors in the past and which serves as a guide for preventing such behaviors in the future

Hope and Belief
in the Power of a Socially Sanctioned Healer

Jerome Frank (1961) has been arguing for over two decades now that successful therapy is dependent upon the patient's faith in the powers of the therapist. Few experienced therapists would disagree with him. The patient who is experiencing emotional stress is demoralized, his attitudes toward life do not help him find gratification, and his explanations of what is happening to him are unsatisfactory. He seeks out a healer who can provide moral guidance, explanation, and a sense of certainty. If the healer is to provide such guidance, he must be sanctioned or invested with powers of healing either by the society as a whole or by the patient's subculture. For most people the licensed psychotherapist may be viewed as having the strongest healing powers, but for others it may be the priest, the shaman, the witch doctor, or the unlicensed but charismatic encounter-group leader. Through the patient's faith in the therapist and through the therapist's belief in his own system of healing the patient experiences hope, faith, a slight but significant change in his belief systems, and eventual improvement. A key element in this process is the patient's acceptance of the therapist's authority and power. This elicits the patient's innate wish to please the person who has this authority and power. The easiest way to please the therapist is to follow his instructions and get well.

Other writers have expanded on Frank's observations and have argued that psychotherapists have merely usurped a role that was formerly given to priests and witch doctors. They believe that with all of our scientific theories, the elements of belief and faith remain the most powerful curative factors in psychotherapy. An extreme view of this position is that the elements of faith and belief taken together produce a placebo effect which is the only important factor in psychotherapy (Fish 1973, Harper 1975). Proponents of this view have seriously suggested a form of placebo therapy in which the therapist deliberately seeks to provide the patient explanations and experiences which are compatible with the patient's world view and which the patient will accept as confirmation that a healing process is taking place. These writers view even the time, energy, and money which the patient invests in therapy as important elements in the process of healing, since the patient cannot justify such expenditures unless he can believe he is better.

In writing this section, I frequently reminisced over my own psychoanalysis, which I began at the age of thirty-one. At that time, I was a practicing psychiatrist, eclectically trained but firmly committed to belief in the theory and practice of psychoanalysis. When my analyst accepted me for psychoanalytic treatment after only one interview (in those days analytic patients were selected quite rigorously), I was elated. I felt as though a great burden had been lifted from me, and in a very real sense I believed (falsely, of course) that my salvation was assured. My enthusiasm, as well as my analyst's enthusiasm, kept me locked into the process of psychoanalysis four times a week for almost four years. During this time I learned to accept my limitations and the limitations of the analytic process. Although psychoanalysis did not "remake" me or assure my salvation, when I finished I felt that I had received more than my money's worth.

In my last hour of therapy my analyst did what in retrospect appears a strange thing. He presented me with my psychoanalytic lineage or genealogy back to Sigmund Freud, pointing out that his analyst had been analyzed by one of Freud's original disciples who, in turn, had been analyzed by Freud. This established me as a fourth generation analysand and assured all of my future patients of a fifth generation lineage to Freud. Both of us laughed as we discussed this, but in retrospect I think that, in addition to enjoying the humor of the situation, we were quite serious. I felt I had been anointed. It is difficult for me to know in retrospect to what extent the elements of faith and commitment to a historically significant world view accounted for my satisfactory response to psychoanalysis. My experiences as a patient have, however, reinforced my belief that therapy is most successful when the therapist is invested with authority in which the patient believes and when the therapist believes in his own authority. I doubt that such belief is a sufficient condition of therapeutic progress. I am not even sure if it is a necessary condition. But I have few doubts that the therapist is most likely to be successful if he sustains a healthy respect for his social role, believes to some extent in what he is doing, and accepts and uses the mantle or authority he has been granted.

Identification with the Therapist

In addition to being viewed as an authority, the therapist also is viewed as a person who has something to teach the patient. Some schools of psychotherapy are quite straightforward in referring to psychotherapeutic work as a didactic process. Even the more

Individual Psychotherapy

nondirective schools of psychotherapy refer to their work as reeducative. Didactic schools of psychotherapy rely heavily on training through instruction and imitation. The therapist or teacher may provide verbal descriptions of how the patient is to respond to certain situations, or the therapist may, through role modeling or through discussion as to how he would handle a situation, provide a demonstration of adaptive behavior. Observational learning will also take place in nondirective therapies. The patient will imitate the therapist even if the therapist does not deliberately instruct the patient and does not deliberately model desirable behaviors. In the course of therapy the patient observes a variety of cues which the therapist emits and uses these cues to develop a mental picture of the therapist. The patient tries to determine how the therapist thinks, feels, and acts and then tries to shape his own behavior so that it is similar. Whether the therapist deliberately seeks this response or not, the process by which it develops can be called identification.

As an authority, teacher, and healer, the therapist appears to the patient as a person of extraordinary interest, even fascination. The patient, of course, wonders what the therapist thinks and expects of him, and what kind of behaviors would please the therapist. He also begins to wonder about the personal qualities of the therapist. "What is he really like?" "How does he solve his problems?" "How does he live?" "How would he be handling my problems if he were in my shoes?" The image the patient builds of the therapist is not left entirely to fantasy. The therapist gives cues as to how he thinks, feels, and acts both in and out of the psychotherapeutic relationship. These cues can be very explicit when the therapist deliberately shares his thoughts and feelings. They can be implicit when the therapist acts in certain ways or asks questions and provides responses which give hints as to how he actually does think and feel about various issues. In either case the patient learns to identify with many of the therapist's attitudes and values.

The therapist also strengthens the process of identification by either willingly or unwillingly reinforcing the patient's efforts at imitation. Didactic or directive therapists may deliberately try to serve as models for their patients, with the intention of positively reinforcing them as soon as they can imitate the models presented them. Even the most nondirective therapists, however, find it hard to conceal their pleasure when their patients follow their example. Therapists as a rule show only their better traits during the therapeutic interaction. Being human, they are gratified when they observe the patient's eagerness to emulate these traits.

All schools of psychotherapy recognize the occurrence of the phenomenon of identification with the therapist during psychotherapy, but there are differing assessments of its value as a curative factor. Some therapists view it as of negligible importance, and try to keep identification minimal by revealing as little of themselves as possible. Other therapists view identification as a significant factor in healing and try to reinforce it whenever it occurs. My own view is that identification is an important factor in psychotherapy and it operates as an effective force whether or not the therapist seeks it. While the power and intensity of identification will vary directly with the frequency and length of therapy, some element of identification with the therapist probably operates in even the briefest therapies.

No matter how detached, no matter how unobtrusive, no matter how mechanical the therapist seeks to be, he will reveal a great deal about himself to the patient during the first interview. Even the physical details of the therapist's office will tell the patient something about the therapist. The spaciousness of the setting, the comfort and expensiveness of the furnishings, and the tastefulness of the color combinations will reveal something about how the therapist deals with closeness, about his taste, and about his financial situation. Diplomas, pictures of loved ones, and art objects reveal something about the therapist's status and outside interests. As therapists rise in status, they often furnish their offices in a tastefully elegant manner, conveying a subdued but expensive atmosphere. The patient usually gets a clear message that the therapist believes that the quest for comfort and even opulence is not a vice. This impression is likely to be reinforced by the therapist's clothing and grooming. Most therapists, as befits their upper-middle-class status, dress well and tend to conform to the latest styles. The patient quickly learns that he is in the presence of an individual who accepts many of the values of capitalist society. (Those colleagues who have watched me at work might be chuckling to themselves if they read this. I usually dress casually, and my office is always messy. I see patients in the same office in which I do my other work, and as a rule, papers, letters, and books are scattered in every conceivable location. A casual look at the office suggests that the occupant is disorganized, unconcerned with conventional values, or trying to impress others with his differentness—this last point may be valid. But the

Individual Psychotherapy

amount of manuscripts, letters, and reprints scattered about also tells the visitor that the occupant works hard. Sooner or later most of my patients make some comment about my office, hostile or humorous or both, but it is apparent from these comments that they correctly identify my commitment to productivity and hard work.)

From the moment the therapist begins to inquire about the patient's problems, he conveys a willingness to listen. As time passes and as the therapist listens empathically, the patient learns that the therapist values tolerance, patience, calmness, and rationality. The patient, in most forms of psychotherapy, receives a powerful message that a cognitive or contemplative approach to the problems of life is desirable. For the sake of completeness, it should be noted that some schools of therapy try to convey a different message. These are "body psychotherapies" which emphasize efforts to bring out people's emotionality and place more value on expressiveness and spontaneity than on cognition.

Once the therapist begins to discuss fees, he usually reveals himself as a rational, economically motivated individual who is unashamedly willing to take advantage of the high market value placed upon his services. Most therapists make fair and reasonable contracts with their patients in accordance with the principles of a free enterprise social system. There are, of course, exceptions. Therapist who work in community clinics are less concerned with fees, and will accept fees that are less than the marketplace value of their services. Some schools of psychotherapy, such as that established by Karen Horney, emphasize the availability of low fee services.

As the patient continues in therapy, it is hoped he will note that the therapist can be loving and concerned. The patient will be particularly impressed with the manner in which the therapist seeks to preserve the patient's dignity, even when the most sordid and humiliating subjects are being discussed. Honesty and an appropriate degree of humility are also modeled by the therapist. If the therapist makes an error or behaves inappropriately, he will usually acknowledge that he has done something wrong in as direct a manner as possible. Over a period of time the patient should also learn that the therapist is incorruptible. Efforts to seduce, placate, bribe, enrage, manipulate, or ridicule the therapist are usually not met with the responses one anticipates in ordinary social intercourse. The therapist does not respond to seduction, but rather tries to understand why the patient is seductive. The therapist does not respond to efforts to anger him, but tries to focus on why the patient is trying to make him angry. There are exceptions. Some therapists will, at times, deliberately be flirtatious, some will respond in a nonphysical manner to a seductive patient, and others will allow themselves to become angry with patients and will even argue with them. In general, however, most therapists hold strongly to the belief that they should not use the patient to satisfy their own needs, and they tend to be incorruptible in holding to this position. As a result, their patients receive a powerful statement as to the value of consistency and self-discipline.

I have noted that therapist differ in terms of the directness with which they reveal themselves to patients. Some therapists are subtle in influencing patients to identify with their values and may even profess not to have such influence. Other therapists are quite open in revealing their own values and may deliberately encourage patients to identify with them. The psychoanalyst is an example of a therapist who seeks to keep his opinions and values out of the therapeutic relationship. One reason for this is that psychoanalysts want the patient to project feelings, thoughts, and wishes onto the therapist which are similar to what the patient experienced toward important objects or persons in his past. This process is referred to as transference, and transference responses are essential if the clinician is to elicit information regarding unconscious motivations. Psychoanalysts believe that transference responses will be diminished if the therapist is self-disclosing, and they deliberately strive for a certain degree of secrecy or mystery in presenting themselves to patients. There is good reason to question whether the psychoanalyst's efforts to appear as a blank screen to the patient really prevents the patient from learning a great deal about the therapist. Any therapist must respond selectively to the patient's verbalizations. Some of the patient's behaviors will be responded to by the therapist in a manner that is reinforcing, while other responses will favor extinction of certain behaviors. The astute patient can surmise a great deal about this therapist's value system by observing these patterns of delivering reinforcement.

Therapists who are not as concerned with eliciting transference reactions or who feel that transference will take place whether the patient knows the therapist as a real person or not are much more open about themselves. Such openness facilitates the process of identification. In being willing to discuss his own responses to the patient's problems, the therapist is communicating the values of honesty and self-disclosure. The therapist's openness also provides the patient a very clear picture of an alternative way of dealing with problems which can either be rejected or partially incorporated into the patient's future repertoire of behaviors. My own prejudice is that the therapist's willingness to be open about his values does not force the patient to identify with these values but does give the patient an opportunity to weigh them objectively and to learn to identify with them if they are relevant to his own situation. I doubt that this therapeutic posture leads to identifications any more powerful than those which take place when the therapist is evasive or secretive about his own values and the patient must do the work of discovering them. Secret attitudes, once discovered, may seem weightier, more important, and more worthy of emulation than those which are freely revealed.

In my own work, I will not volunteer my views regarding value-laden issues to the patient unless he asks about them. Even if the patient inquires as to my views, I will often ask him to fantasize what he thinks my views may be, in order to clarify his relationship to me at that moment and to identify transference distortions. Once the patient has responded to this request, however, I will answer any questions the patient puts to me, as long as they are reasonable and do not infringe too deeply upon my privacy. I have no hesitation in discussing my views regarding child rearing, sexuality, marriage, divorce, religion, or politics with any patient, and I have not found that this kind of openness has any notable effect upon the formation of transference reactions. Transference behaviors are ubiquitous. They occur whether the therapist is an open book or a blank screen.

There are some other techniques I utilize which influence patients through the process of identification. Periodically I will acknowledge that I have thoughts and feelings similar to those which I assume the patient must have. If the patient is describing a situation in which I surmise that he has been experiencing intense aggressive feelings but is denying them I am likely to comment that, were I in his situation, I would have quite hostile feelings. I similarly confess to feelings of fear, dependency, and eroticism. In doing this I am trying to give the patient the following message: "If I have these kinds of feelings and seem to be comfortable with them and have even risen to a position of authority while struggling with them, you are not in such a helpless or unique position. While you may not like these feelings, you can certainly tolerate them as an evidence of an existential frailty that you, I, and all humans share." This technique of mentioning the unmentionable contains some elements of empathy and information expansion, but it is also a direct and provocative means of furthering a goal that is usually left implicit in most psychotherapies, that is, having the patient identify with the therapist's conscience or superego. It is usually safe to assume that in areas related to the patient's difficulties, the therapist's superego is likely to be less condemning than the patient's.

Another quality which I deliberately try to convey and which I hope the patient imitates is a certain degree of playfulness and an appreciation of the absurdity of the manner in which both of us behave during the therapeutic hour. I periodically chide either of us when we are too solemn or pompous. I do not mean that I take the patient or his symptoms lightly, but I do hope to teach the patient that therapy is not always a life and death matter, and that it can be fun. My efforts to accomplish this goal include joking and occasional teasing directed both at myself and the patient. I try to convey the message that I don't take myself too seriously, and I hope that the patient also learns not to take himself too seriously. Periodically I remind the patient that psychotherapy is only one of several methods human beings have developed to help deal with the issues of unhappiness, meaninglessness, and existence. The patient is told that psychotherapy will help with some of his problems but will still leave him vulnerable to a variety of miseries which plague all human beings. To the extent that the patient identifies with this view, he is better prepared to deal with the reality that successful therapy does not necessarily bring happiness and that the struggles of life continue even after one is "healed."

Caring and Lovingness

Without a considerable degree of intimacy, caring, respect, and mutual liking between therapist and patient, psychotherapy is unlikely to be helpful. The patient is more likely to identify with, learn from, and listen to the therapist if he has a high degree of positive emotional involvement with the therapist. Unless the patient feels understood and cared for by his therapist, he will be unlikely to experiment with new behaviors which can later be positively reinforced. Responsibility for creating a climate of care and lovingness falls upon the therapist. The patient's capacity to care about and love the therapist is directly related to the

Individual Psychotherapy

therapist's capacity to care about and love the patient. A therapist can, in theory, successfully treat a patient he doesn't love, but this is uncommon, and in actual practice clinicians usually select patients they find lovable. (The reader may object to the term *lovable* as used in this context and should feel free to substitute such terms as *likable* or *attractive*.) This should not be surprising because the criteria that make for a good psychotherapy candidate also make for a lovable person. An individual who is highly motivated to change, who is psychologically minded, who is relatively helpless, who presents no threat to the therapist, and who is respectful enough to tolerate or invest the energy and money involved in psychotherapy has an inherent lovability. Even patients who initially seem unlovable tend to change as therapy progresses. As such patients improve, they are likely to become more honest and more open and to develop increased control over character traits that are offensive to others. The therapist will be pleased with these changes and will find that, as therapy progresses, the initially unattractive patient becomes more and more attractive.

While it is difficult to describe such vague concepts as loving or caring, the behaviors of the therapist which create a climate of intimacy can more easily be described as those which provide empathy and positive reinforcement and those which communicate the therapist's commitment to be helpful. Empathy is most simply defined as the process by which one puts oneself into the psychological frame of reference of another person in an effort to understand and perhaps predict that person's thinking, feeling, and acting. There are other definitions of empathy which have an almost mystical or spiritual quality and focus upon a communion between therapist and patient which is alleged to transcend the ordinary sensory processes involved in communication. For our purpose here I will be using the simpler, more direct definition of empathy, but I will add to that definition by noting that empathy is most helpful in psychotherapy when it is complemented by the therapist's compassion. The therapist seeks not only to understand but also to understand compassionately.

There are three important questions with regard to empathy; How does the therapist get it? How does he demonstrate it? and, Why is it helpful?

It is difficult to teach people to be empathic. The capacity to understand what others are experiencing is largely related to depth and variety of experience. It is also related to the capacity to be open or sensitive to experience. The capacity to be empathic is developed by having lived, having suffered, having observed others suffering, and having been intensely aware of these experiences. It is likely that older and more experienced therapists are more capable of being accurately empathic simply because they have lived longer and spent more time cultivating their capacity to understand others. The easiest way for the therapist to become empathic is to see more patients. He is also in a better position to understand what the patient feels during the course of psychotherapy if he has been a patient himself. The beginner in psychotherapy is often overwhelmed by the realization that capacities for empathy do not develop quickly (and may, for some individuals, never develop adequately). The most the beginner can be taught is to listen to people, to read about people, and always, when with the patient, to be asking himself, "What is this person experiencing?"

There is also little that can be taught about how to communicate empathy. Attentive listening certainly helps, but if the therapist is really not in touch with what the patient is experiencing, this will soon become apparent to the patient. When the therapist truly understands what the patient is experiencing, empathy can be communicated by statements which describe the patient's feelings, such as "You must have been very angry" or "You must have wanted to please him and hurt him at the same time," or by expressing concern as well as understanding through such statements as "That must have been an awful experience" or "You really must have felt that intensely," or by asking such questions as "How do you feel about that?" in a way that implies that the patient must have had strong feelings about the situation and that the therapist senses what these might be.

Nonverbal cues play a significant role in the expression of empathy. My colleagues, who have watched me interview patients on a daily basis for a period of years, tell my that it is relatively easy to determine when I am feeling close to the patient and my empathic feelings are on target. They note that my voice, posture, and general sense of involvement with the patient seems to change and that the patient seems to become involved with me. I have noted similar nonverbal cues on the part of my collegues and students which seem to communicate varying degrees of empathy. These experiences have convinced me that, in teaching the communication of empathy, it is essential to focus upon the internal processes by which the therapist strives to understand

and feel with the patient. Here it is important that therapists become more aware of how their own emotional responses to various patients impair their capacity to be empathic. The therapist who has learned how he is influenced adversely as well as compassionately by various patient behaviors can separate these responses in his own mind and try to focus on the compassionate part of his responsiveness. If he is successful, empathy will probably be communicated nonverbally, and the technical correctness or incorrectness of actual verbal statements the therapist might make is not too critical.

Beginning therapists tend to feel pressured to communicate empathic responses. Often they will say to patients, "You seem angry" or "You seem depressed," when the patient may not be experiencing such an affect or, if he is experiencing it, does not wish to acknowledge it. In general it is wise to use verbal empathic responses somewhat sparingly and only when the therapist feels relatively certain of their accuracy. The process of continuing the exploration of the patient's problems and feelings by questioning, by clarifying, or even by interested silence will often be more reassuring and comforting to the patient than an inappropriate or ill-timed empathic response.

Most people probably feel safer when they are understood, but this is not always true. It is the addition of compassion to the process of understanding that determines the therapeutic value of empathy. Compassion implies warmth, concern, and acceptance. The kindliness, implied in the therapist's voice and actions, gives the patient the message that the therapist cares about the patient and does not condemn the patient for having certain thoughts or feelings. The process of being accepted as well as understood by a concerned and powerful individual is an inherently positive experience for most people. In successfully communicating understanding and compassion, the therapist is telling the patient that he either has had experiences similar to those troubling the patient, or has had significant interactions with others who have had similar experiences. In either case the patient can be assured that he is being treated by an experienced person. The communication of compassion and understanding also serves as a positive reinforcement for the patient to continue discussing problems and expressing feelings.

In addition to being empathic, the therapist can provide the patient other responses usually associated with positive reinforcement. Any of the therapist's responses which communicate to the patient that he is worthwhile or lovable will help create a caring therapeutic environment. Spontaneous or deliberate expression of enthusiasm, interest, and tenderness on the part of the therapist provides the patient *strokes*, or responses associated with positive interpersonal reinforcements. The presentation of such unsolicited concern allows successful therapists to subtly convince patients that it is a pleasure to be in their presence and that it is a privilege to treat them. As the patient basks in the tender concern of such an important person as the therapist, the patient is likely to experience a substantial increase in feelings of self-esteem. The kind of reinforcement I am discussing here is similar to what Carl Rogers (1961) describes as the successful therapist's capacity to provide unconditional positive regard. I would paraphrase this quality and call it the therapist's capacity to provide unsolicited and noncontingent positive reinforcement to the patient. The therapist tries to tell the patient that approval will be forthcoming not only if the patient behaves as the therapist wishes but also because the patient is inherently worthwhile and lovable.

The therapist's commitment to the patient is another factor in enhancing the patient's sense of worth. Such commitment usually does not become manifest until treatment has progressed for some time, and the therapist's loyalty, honesty, and incorruptibility have been tested. In the course of treatment many patients will experience periods of emotional turmoil and will make new demands on the therapist's energy and availability. The therapist's capacity to weather these demands amiably and fairly communicates his capacity for commitment. The therapist's willingness to increase his availability to patients in a time of crisis is an even more powerful indicator of commitment. As noted previously, psychotherapists differ in their willingness to make themselves more available. Many will stick to the original therapeutic contract and may not change the frequency of contact even when patients are deeply troubled. My own belief is that it is better for the therapist to be flexible. Patients who are having a difficult time often respond favorably to an increase in the number of visits. This may be due to the greater amount of therapeutic work that can be done during these visits, but I suspect the patient's improvement is, in large part, related to the therapist's demonstration of his commitment. Therapists also have opportunities to demonstrate their commitment to the patient by taking responsibility for finding other therapists for the patient when they cannot be available or when therapy is not going well and in fiercely

Individual Psychotherapy

protecting the paient from intrusions of privacy which may be initiated by the patient's friends, relatives, or employers.

Tension Reduction

There are techniques inherent in all forms of psychotherapy directed toward relieving the patient's tension. The simple act of discussing one's problems with a professionally trained person and sharing disagreeable or shameful information about oneself is helpful for a variety of reasons. When the patient reveals or confesses unpleasant thoughts, feelings, or actions, he is likely to receive a nonaversive response from the therapist. Confession followed not with condemnation or recrimination but with a response of understanding allows the patient to feel accepted and forgiven. There is a powerful learning experience taking place here. Fears of punishment, which the patient anticipated from others if he shared his thoughts and feelings, turn out to be unrealistic. Punishment the patient has inflicted upon himself is partially extinguished.

In discussing painful events in the remote and recent past or painful affects in the present, the patient also expresses powerful feelings. It is quite likely that the mere expression of such feeling in the presence of a concerned, helping person has inherent therapeutic qualities. There is probably some biologic mechanism by which expression of emotion relieves tension. In all cultures the expression of emotionality, either verbally or nonverbally is viewed as desirable in prescribed social situations. People feel good when they dance, sing, or engage in athletic competition. Following the death of a loved one, mourning characterized by weeping, singing, and other physical manifestations of lamentation may ease the bereavement process. Sexual intercourse is often more enjoyable if it follows an emotional experience such as an argument. Behaviorists have noted that even phobic behavior may be diminished after the patient powerfully expresses an emotion such as anger (Marks 1976). Some psychotherapeutic methods such as psychoanalysis put great emphasis on abreaction, or the bringing to consciousness of repressed emotions with an accompanying discharge of affect during the therapeutic hour. In the far more controversial primal therapy, efforts are made to help the patient relive and reexperience highly traumatic events of childhood (Janov 1970). Almost all schools of therapy emphasize the need for patients to be in touch with their emotions and encourage or permit patients to express emotionality during therapy hours. Usually efforts are made to confine emotionality to verbal interchange, but Gestalt therapists may encourage limited physical expressions of emotionality in order to teach patients how bodily awareness can relieve tension (Perls 1969).

The tension-relieving aspects of the therapeutic situation are enhanced by the quietness and pleasantness of the consultation room, by furnishings designed to maximize the patient's comfort, by the therapist's gentle verbal ministrations, or by the therapist's teaching of exercises which bring out the relaxation responses. The patient's willingness to express emotions attached to secrets or to unpleasant ideas is related to the extent to which the patient views the therapist as a person worthy of respect and trust. It is difficult to describe how the therapist earns these attributions, but one prerequisite is the therapist's commitment to providing the patient total confidentiality. Patients will not tell their innermost secrets and will not allow themselves to investigate or reexperience repressed emotionality unless they are assured that their self-revelations are held in confidence. Another important factor in gaining the patient's trust is the therapist's capacity to be as noncondemning of the patient's past behavior as possible. The therapist does not have to approve of everything the patient has thought, felt, or done, but he does have to help the patient feel like a lovable person whose status as a human being will not be diminished by whatever he reveals.

Learning in Psychotherapy

I have noted repeatedly that much of the effectiveness of psychotherapy is determined by processes that can be explained in terms of learning theory. The role of identification in producing behavioral change has already been considered. Techniques based on operant conditioning are also used to bring about behavioral change in psychotherapy. Positive and negative reinforcement, as well as extinction, can be used to shape the nature of the material the patient brings to therapy. Extinction and positive reinforcement can also be used to change the manner in which the patient behaves both in and out of the therapeutic hour.

The process of extinction operates from the moment the therapist begins to react to the patient's complaints. Therapists do not respond to complaints in the same manner as other concerned people. The presentation of complaints to friends and relatives ordinarily elicits a response of alarm and attention, and this response is usually focused upon the complaints themselves. The therapist, in contrast, will listen seriously to the patient's

Individual Psychotherapy

complaints, but will be interested in learning about other aspects of the patient's life. Once the therapist makes an assessment of the severity of the complaints and their impact upon the patient's functioning, the therapist's attention to complaints will rapidly diminish. As a rule the therapist's inclination to focus upon the patient's total life situation, rather than upon the patient's complaints, leads to extinction of verbal presentation of symptomatic behaviors and, perhaps, to some extinction of the symptoms themselves.

As efforts are made to focus upon the patient's total life situation, the patient will begin to bring behaviors into the therapeutic situation which were learned in previous interactions with other individuals. These behaviors may be judged maladaptive by the therapist. Their appearance in therapy can be explained in different ways. The patient may simply be viewed as repeating a learned behavior, or he may be viewed as transferring attitudes and feelings toward the therapist which were once directed toward significant others in his past. Whatever explanation is invoked, it is probable that these maladaptive behaviors the patient brings to the therapy hour are being repeated in some of the patient's interactions outside of therapy and that the patient will be better off if these behaviors are extinguished. Psychotherapists have developed a number of techniques for extinguishing maladaptive behavior patterns. All of them have certain elements in common. These techniques require that the therapist respond to the patient's behavior in a way different from the way others have responded to it in the past and in a way different from what the patient anticipates.

A sixteen-year-old boy who was being treated for delinquent behavior had a history of difficulty in cooperating with male authority figures. He usually began relationships with such individuals by being friendly but would quickly become derisive and contemptuous toward them. After the first few sessions with a male therapist, which were characterized by a great deal of enthusiasm and cooperation on the patient's part, he began to show signs of uneasiness during the hours. He questioned the therapist's motivations, honesty, and skills. He then began to attack the therapist more directly and was quite clever in making derisive comments concerning aspects of the therapist's appearance and mannerisms that he was sensitive about. When the patient had behaved this was toward adult males in the past, the eventual result was an angry and even violent response on the part of the person he was tormenting.

In this instance, however, the therapist merely pointed out that the patient was trying to elicit an angry response, just as the patient had tried with other adult males. The therapist acknowledged that the patient's behavior was annoying, but he did not respond in an annoyed manner. Instead he urged the patient to try to understand the meaning of his provocative behavior.

A twenty-two-year-old woman in therapy for problems of mild anxiety and depression became seductive toward her therapist. She talked openly about how she found him sexy. She began to dress in a very appealing manner and made clear that she would be quite willing to have a love affair with him. The patient had a long history of using her sexual attractiveness to gain control of situations in which she felt insecure. However, after she began a sexual relationship with a man, she would quickly become guilty and depressed. The therapist in this case acknowledged the patient's advances, said he felt complimented that she found him attractive, but also pointed out that, since both of them were involved in a professional relationship in which she was seeking help for emotional problems, it would be most fruitful to spend their time investigating the purpose or meaning of her seductive behavior.

A thirty-five-year-old woman entered therapy for symptoms of moderate depression. In the tenth hour of treatment she reported that she had had a fight with her husband the night before, which she admitted to having started because she felt that he was too detached from her and emotionally unavailable. They had fought a good part of the evening until he threatened to leave the house. At that point she implied that if he departed she would make a suicide attempt. Her husband stayed home and was quite attentive to her the rest of the evening. The patient told her therapist that she was still feeling very upset and that, for a number of reasons, her husband's reluctant attentiveness was not gratifying. As she discussed these issues during the hour, she became more depressed and began to have suicidal ruminations. She complained that the therapist could do more for her if he really wanted to. In this case the therapist did not respond by being more attentive. He did point out the similarities in the way the patient had related to her husband and to him, and asked the patient if there were some response she might develop to satisfy her needs other than becoming depressed and suicidal.

These three vignettes are typical of many of the important transactions that take place in psychotherapy. The patient behaves in a manner which has customarily elicited certain

Individual Psychotherapy

responses in others. These responses have become reinforcers. But the therapist does not behave as the patient anticipates and does not provide the expected reinforcements. Instead he directs the patient to look at the interpersonal meaning of his behavior and to behave more responsibly. The therapist's response, in addition to putting pressure on the patient to seek new information or develop new behaviors, is likely to diminish the frequency of the patient's previous maladaptive behavior, at least during the therapy hours. Over time such changes might generalize to situations outside of therapy. Some therapists would view such interactions as a process in which the patient has a corrective emotional experience (Alexander and Ross 1952). The most parsimonious explanation of the process, however, is that failure to provide anticipated reinforcement for a learned behavior leads to eventual extinction of that behavior.

Positive reinforcement and, to a lesser extent, negative reinforcement are used by the therapist to encourage people to examine themselves, to talk about significant issues, and to search constantly for new information. The use of negative reinforcement to shape the patient's verbalization during the hour will be discussed further in the section on information. Positive reinforcement is used to shape the patient's behavior during the hour, in a very direct manner. When the patient acts toward the therapist in a manner that the therapist views as healthy, the therapist will praise the patient. Phrases such as "I'm glad you were able to say that to me" or "It must feel good to be able to relate to me differently" are used as reinforcers. If the patient is able to behave more adaptively outside of the hour, the therapist can also use positive reinforcement to increase the probability that the adaptive behavior will be continued. Here he uses words and statements such as "good," "You're making progress," or "It sounds like that really helped you."

Perhaps the most difficult problem in any type of psychotherapy is to get the patient to perform a behavior which can then be reinforced. This can be accomplished within the therapeutic hour by relentlessly refusing to reinforce maladaptive behaviors, and either waiting for the patient to try a new behavior or persuading him to try it. Outside of the hour the task is more difficult. One tactic the therapist can use is persuasion. If the therapist has been successful in creating a therapeutic climate of care and lovingness and if the patient respects and trusts the therapist, he will often do what the therapist asks. Some therapists are direct in ordering or suggesting that the patient experiment with a new behavior. Others who think of themselves as nondirective use a more subtle form of persuasion. As the nondirective therapist begins to understand the patient's problems more fully, he provides the covert but powerful cues as to what behaviors the patient might initiate to solve them. The therapist guides the patient in discovering the best course of action and gives him permission to initiate the new behavior. Consider the following therapeutic interaction:

Patient: I'm feeling very nervous today, and I think I know what it's about. Yesterday my boss was giving me a hard time. I don't know what was bothering him, but he kept putting me down and treating me like a child. When I got home, I was so nervous I had three martinis.
Therapist: What were you feeling while this was happening?
Patient: I'm not sure, mostly hurt and intimidated but, well, maybe there was more feeling too. I don't have to put up with that kind of crap. I'm a valuable employee. I deserve respect. I guess I was just plain angry at him.
Therapist: In retrospect what do you think you wanted to do with your anger?
Patient: I guess now that I think about it, I was so mad I would have liked to have slugged him. But that doesn't make sense. You don't go around slugging bosses. Besides, I kind of like him, and ordinarily he's a pretty good guy. I guess I wish now that I simply told him to lay off me. I'm sure if I'd done that he would have understood and backed off.
Therapist: What stopped you from doing that?
Patient: I'm not sure. I always had trouble sticking up for my rights. I guess I'm kind of scared. You can never predict what will happen if you talk back to people. Maybe I'm just chicken.

While the above vignette may not be a classical example of a nondirective approach, it is fairly representative of an approach commonly used by nondirective therapists. The therapist leads the patient into considering his feelings and what he would have liked to have done about them. When the patient states that he was unable to behave as he wished, the therapist in effect asks, "Why couldn't you?" This is an invitation for the patient to explore his motivations and feelings more deeply. But there is also a clear message that the patient should have been more assertive and that the therapist would have approved of assertive behavior. Note that the therapist does not tell the patient to be more assertive.

Rather he helps the patient appreciate that assertiveness is one of the patient's goals and gives subtle encouragement and permission for the patient to seek that goal.

As therapy progresses, the patient will usually develop some ideas as to what changes in behavior might be approved by his therapist. As long as the patient is not ordered or urged to engage in a new behavior, the patient can select the time at which he will experiment with it, and he is likely to feel that he is the primary agent responsible for the therapeutic change. Once the patient experiments with the desired new behavior, the therapist's positive reinforcement is seen as a well-deserved reward for a self-motivated and responsible act. The patient retains a greater sense of autonomy or self-determination than if he were merely ordered to change.

Efforts are sometimes made to distinguish between indications for nondirective and directive therapy on the basis of the patient's degree of psychological mindedness or his social class. It is probably true that a person who is not sensitive to his own motivations or who is unskilled in detecting cues as to what others expect of him, will have difficulty responding to a nondirective approach and will be more responsive to overt suggestion and persuasion. The issue of social class is more complicated. Certainly poor people are likely to seek rapid and direct solutions to their difficulties. Some therapists have argued that these people will not tolerate the ambiguities and intricacies of a nondirective therapeutic approach (Mechanic 1969). My own experience is that it is difficult to make generalizations about the capacity of lower-class people to respond to nondirective therapy. There are so many economic pressures upon the therapist to achieve a rapid cure of poorer patients that the therapist may simply resort to a directive approach because it seems to work faster than a nondirective approach. In working with delinquents and criminals (who are certainly likely to be members of lower socioeconomic groups), I have often found them to be highly responsive to a nondirective approach. Other therapists have had similar experiences (Stürup 1968). The antisocial lower-class person may, however, be different than other lower class patients. Usually, he has had plenty of unsuccessful experiences with directive counseling before entering psychotherapy. He is likely to be seeking a high degree of autonomy, and his distrust of authority may be tempered by nondirectiveness.

Once the patient begins to experiment with new behaviors outside of therapy, the therapist's task of providing reinforcement is relatively straightforward. If the patient behaves adaptively, he can be assured of the therapist's praise and support. Eventually the patient may begin to provide himself the same kind of reinforcement (internal or self-reinforcement) that was initially provided by the therapist. One constant uncertainty in this process is whether other individuals in the patient's natural environment will reinforce his new behavior. Since the practitioner of individual psychotherapy has little control over contingencies in the natural environment, there are inherent limits to his capacity to provide the patient an experience of mastery or success outside of the therapeutic relationship.

Information

In earlier sections I noted how expanding the patient's awareness of self and environment can be helpful to him. Here the emphasis will be on describing how the therapist goes about developing and using such information to bring about behavioral change in a dyadic psychotherapeutic relationship.

There are obvious limits to the amount of information that can be generated in a two-person interaction. The only sources of data are the patient's descriptions of his own behavior outside of the therapeutic hour and the therapist's observations of the patient's behavior within the hour. This contrasts with group or family therapy, where there may be many sources of information and many interactions which can be studied directly. The interaction in a two-party relationship in which one person seeks maximum information about another is rather delicate. The therapist must strive to maintain a constant interaction between himself and the patient. There is no way that either can step out of the therapeutic field and be alone for even a brief period of time. All of these considerations place considerable demands on the therapist. Conflicts do not simply unfold in individual psychotherapy as they so often do in group or family therapy. The therapist is always at work. There are times when showing empathy will keep the patient committed to generating new information. At other times, it may be important to put pressure on the patient by frustrating wishes for support and reassurance or by remaining silent. Patients search for new information rather grudgingly. The therapist must step lightly, providing the proper mixture of support and frustration to keep the patient motivated to work. This is one of those areas in psychotherapy which requires a skill almost impossible to describe. A skilled therapist can examine a videotape or a transcription of a therapist-patient interaction and speculate as to what therapeutic interventions at what time might have led to more information-generating behavior on the part of the patient, but it is very difficult to generalize such technical knowledge from patient to patient.

The therapist, of course, must do much more than help the patient search for new information. It is necessary for the therapist to use information derived from the patient's self-revelations and behavior during the therapy hour to formulate hypotheses as to how the patient is interacting with the current environment and as to how this interaction is determined by past experiences. The therapist is always looking for new explanations of the relationships between the patient's behavior and the way in which the environment responds to it. These hypotheses, once communicated to the patient, provide either new information for the patient or new conceptualizations of old information. (For the sake of convenience, I will in the subsequent discussion consider the formulation of new conceptualizations of old information to be synonomous with the discovery of new information.) The capacity to formulate such hypotheses is a skill which can be taught only through direct supervision and which can be sharpened only through experience in understanding human relationships and in actually doing psychotherapy.

The therapist must also find a way either of communicating new information to the patient or using it in a manner that benefits the patient. It is essential that any new information presented to the patient have a reasonable chance of being heard and accepted. This means the therapist must have evidence to support his hypotheses and must time his presentations so that they reach the patient at a propitious moment. The therapist must also use new information about the patient to guide him in responding to the patient. New information will provide the therapist cues as to which of the patient's behaviors are best reinforced or extinguished and how the therapist can model behaviors the patient can identify with. Again, the process of obtaining and integrating this information requires skills that are best taught by direct supervision of psychotherapy.

Using the models developed in the first part of the book, it is convenient to begin examining techniques for providing new information by considering the patient's impact upon the environment. The therapist tries to help the patient learn how he comes across to others and how his self-presentation may create unwelcome responses. In individual therapy there are only two ways of gaining this information: listening to the patient's description of how he interacts with others, and observing the impact the patient is having upon the therapist. Here the individual psychotherapist is at a distinct disadvantage to the group or family psychotherapist. He must always attempt to assess the reliability of the patient's observations and has little or no data from outside sources to support his conclusions. The therapist's assessment of the impact the patient is having upon him is limited in accuracy by the extent of the therapist's sensitivity and by idiosyncratic aspects of the patient's responses. In practice the individual psychotherapist tries to help the patient describe situations in which the patient seems troubled or surprised by the responses of others and seems to be uncertain as to his own role in eliciting such responses. If the therapist begins to detect a tendency in himself to want to respond to the patient the same way the patient has complained of, then the therapist may be in a position to hypothesize something about the impact the patient has upon others. The manner in which the therapist can discover such behavioral patterns, relate them to the patient's difficulties, and communicate them to the patient is illustrated by the following case:

A twenty-three-year-old medical student sought counseling because he was anxious about his work. He had recently been told by one of his clinical teachers that his work was not up to par and that he was functioning below his capabilities. The therapist tried to create a climate in which the patient felt free to talk about his anxieties and his experiences in medical school. In the second hour the patient reported that he felt uncomfortable in most of his clinical rotations because his teachers seemed to be irritated with him and to treat him as though he were inept. The patient did not feel that his teachers' responses were justified. He viewed himself as a hard-working and conscientious student who was quite eager to please his instructors. The patient was asked if he could think of anything he might be doing to irritate others or create an impression of ineptitude, but he could think of nothing. In the subsequent three hours the patient began each session by asking the therapist what would be most useful to talk about that day. When the therapist would respond by noting that it was up to the patient to decide

Individual Psychotherapy

what to talk about. the patient would respond by pleading that he did not know what to say. He would then become quiet and sullen.

It occurred to the therapist that the patient was showing little initiative and, in an almost childish manner, was demanding that the therapist provide direction. The therapist found this behavior somewhat irritating but reacted to the patient's complaints by remaining silent. After a few minutes of silence the patient seemed to extract himself from his passive stance and began to talk about highly relevant thoughts and feelings. Under the prodding of the therapist's silence, he seemed quite capable of taking some initiative and responsibility for what happened during the hour and was able to be a "good patient" in the sense of being willing to examine and reveal himself. At this point the therapist hypothesized that the patient had not yet learned to trust his own abilities, was still seeking more dependency gratification and guidance than he actually needed, and was coming across both in therapy and in his clinical work as less competent than he actually was. When the patient began the fourth session in a row by demanding guidance from the therapist, the therapist felt it was time to make a point of how the patient was behaving and to remark that such behavior was sometimes irritating to the therapist since it was so obvious to both patient and therapist that the patient was capable of taking initiative on his own. The patient seemed quite troubled as he heard this and remained silent for over a minute. He then said, in a very tentative manner, that perhaps the same kind of thing was happening on his clinical rotations. He speculated that he might, because of feelings of insecurity, have been showing less initiative and competence than he actually possessed and that this might be why he was coming across to his teachers as uninterested or inept.

In this case the patient made his own connection and related his impact upon his therapist to his impact upon his teachers. This was highly advantageous to the patient insofar as it enhanced his sense of autonomy and diminished his sense of dependency. If the patient could not have seen the relationship between his maladaptive behavior in therapy and in school, however, it might have been appropriate for the therapist to have pointed it out.

Therapists should exercise restraint in making interpretations to patients as to how they are coming across to others. Such interpretations are messages to patients that they have failed to perceive rather obvious aspects of their behavior. Usually, such messages are unflattering and put pressure upon the patient to change. They imply that the patient is responsible for past behavior and can choose new behaviors. The patient uses the new information to reason that "if others treat me in ways I don't like because of things I now know I am doing, then it is now within my power to get them to treat me differently by changing my own behavior. I will have to do something about this." Interpretations as to how the patient influences others should be used sparingly in treating patients who are experiencing a great deal of anxiety or disorganization. These patients may view the new information as a demand for change which they are not capable of meeting.

In collecting, evaluating, and presenting information as to how the environment is influencing the patient, the individual psychotherapist is once again limited to data obtained in a two-party interaction. The patient can describe how various interpersonal events influence him, and the therapist can note how his own responses to the patient influence the patient. It is extremely difficult, however, to assess whether the patient is receiving accurate information from the environment, how direct others in the environment are in communicating to the patient, what others expect of him, or how they reinforce or punish him. The clinician can gain some knowledge as to what the environment is doing to the patient by listening to the patient talk, but this provides nowhere near the data base available in group or family therapy. Still, there is enough data generated in individual psychotherapy to help the patient learn some important aspects of his responsiveness to environmental stimuli. Part of this learning process may be somewhat cognitive and involves a direct effort to determine a relationship between antecedent events and a behavioral response. This kind of therapeutic work is similar to the efforts behaviorists make when they study stimulus control in order to increase the patient's self-control. As the patient repeatedly talks about environmental events and describes his responses to them, it is possible for both therapist and patient to make connections and to note that whenever a given event occurs the patient seems to respond with a given behavior. The patient can then either avoid the event, try to change it in some way, or try to change the way he responds. The development of information is less cognitive when the therapeutic focus is upon how the patient responds to the therapist. Often, powerful and inappropriate emotional responses to the therapist help the patient appreciate the existence of similar emotional responses to stimuli in the natural environment:

Individual Psychotherapy

A twenty-five-year-old man sought help because of fears of homosexual impulses. Although he had experienced satisfactory heterosexual relationships, he was occasionally plagued by fantasies or dreams in which he was being forced to submit to the sexual overtures of powerful males. These fantasies and dreams were sometimes accompanied by erotic pleasure, but the patient experienced them as distinctly frightening and unpleasant. He saw himself as wanting to maintain a heterosexual orientation and feared that his symptoms were an indication that he was not really masculine. In the course of exploring the patient's thoughts and feelings about these symptoms as well as the environment in which they seemed to occur, a definite stimulus-response pattern emerged. Usually the homosexual fantasy or dream occurred shortly after the patient had been in a situation in which he viewed his dignity or status as a respected male as having been compromised. If he was put down by male superiors, if he was in any way embarrassed or humiliated by a woman, or if he lost out in meaningful competition with peers, he would have some type of homosexual fantasy or dream the next day. The therapist initially took a direct and cognitive approach in trying to help the patient make the appropriate connection between certain stimuli and his pseudo-homosexual responses. The patient, however, was not convinced this was actually happening and continued to worry that his fantasies and dreams were generated by some mysterious defect in his personality.

During the course of therapy, the patient asked to change the time of his hour, feeling that an afternoon rather than a morning hour would be more compatible with his work schedule. The therapist was unable to comply with patient's wishes, and this made the patient somewhat irritated. A dialogue followed in which the therapist was adamant in refusing to change. The patient finally acquiesced. That night he dreamed he was being forced to perform fellatio upon a powerful male. In this case, the patient was able to make the connection that he had seen the therapist's refusal to change the time of the hour as evidence of the therapist's superiority and wish to put the patient down. He was able to see his experience with the therapist as one of many situations in which an event he viewed as humiliating elicited homosexual fantasies or dreams. He began to worry less about being homosexual and to focus upon his problems in dealing with authority figures and gaining power.

Patients often have considerable difficulty in directly experiencing or communicating many of their responses to the stimuli emitted by the therapist. Sometimes they are aware of powerful feelings but cannot define them. Sometimes the feelings are repressed and, as in the case of the pseudo-homosexual patient, are revealed through a dream. One of the therapist's tasks is to encourage the patient to talk freely about any thoughts or feelings he has toward the therapist. The therapist must then use his knowledge and sensitivity to try to determine when the patient is behaving inappropriately in response to some cue the therapist has emitted. Usually the patient will be responding inappropriately to similar cues in the actual environment and will have the opportunity to learn to avoid these cues or to deal with them more adaptively.

In trying to understand how the patient is responding to him, it is especially useful for the therapist to be sensitive to the patient's use of latent or metaphorical language. Patients will frequently talk about situations which seem unrelated to the therapeutic process but which may be a disguised and safe way of presenting thoughts and feelings very definitely related to the therapist. If the therapist comes late to a session and the patient begins to talk about how others in his life do not seem sufficiently concerned about him, the patient may be indirectly talking about whether the therapist is sufficiently concerned. If the patient talks about how a friend may have been taken advantage of by another psychotherapist, he may be communicating his fears about his own therapist. By being sensitive to the use of latent or metaphorical communication, the therapist can discover patterns of response which occur in the natural environment as well as in the therapeutic situation.

The tendency to use latent communication is inversely related to the patient's psychological strength, and the degree of safety he feels in the therapeutic relationship. While the therapist is usually tempted to interpret the patient's metaphoric responses in more direct language, it is not always wise to do so. Disturbed patients who do not feel safe with the therapist may not accept a direct interpretation or may find such interpretation stressful. Sometimes the therapist is well advised to simply use the latent communication as a piece of data which expands his knowledge of the patient's response tendencies. With highly disturbed patients the therapist may even wish to continue the pattern of indirect communication and stay in the metaphor. A patient who complains that another therapist has taken advantage of a friend may be reassured that most therapists don't do this or that the friend may have misinterpreted the therapist's response. Use of this technique may enhance the patient's feeling of safety within the therapeutic relationship.

Some mention must also be made of the issue of helping the patient learn how he responds to himself. (I did not consider this problem in the first part of the book, because it is more easily understood after the reader has some knowledge of the techniques of self-control discussed in the chapter on behavior therapy.) It is desirable that patients have some understanding of their own reactions to their behavior or knowledge of the manner in which they have learned to reinforce or punish themselves. This knowledge is acquired primarily through a direct examination of the kinds of messages the patient gives himself or the kinds of feelings he experiences when he behaves in certain ways. The patient is urged to study and become more aware of the thoughts and feelings which accompany his actions. Sometimes the therapist may use his observations of the patient during the therapeutic hour to help the patient become more aware of internal reinforcements and punishments. The therapist may note that the patient is inordinately pleased with himself while engaging in behavior that is not adaptive or may note that the patient's reactions of guilt or shame with regard to a given behavior are irrational or extreme. When these dysfunctional self-control mechanisms are pointed out to the patient, he is put under considerable pressure to change his behavior.

If the patient's thoughts or feelings reinforce undesirable behaviors or are aversive responses to innocuous behaviors, the patient can be urged to develop alternative responses, and the therapist can try to model more adaptive responses. The patient who becomes guilty and self-punitive whenever he is assertive can be told that he should congratulate rather than punish himself at such times; the therapist may also describe or demonstrate how he is able to be assertive without being guilty. If these techniques are not successful, the patient may be asked to delve into the origins of his maladaptive responses to his own behavior.

Up to now, information-providing techniques have been considered in terms of the patient's behavior in the present. Certainly much information can be generated by focusing upon the patient's interactions in the here and now, and some therapists believe that the major thrust of therapy should be directed toward elucidating the present. Others believe that therapy which focuses solely on the present is insufficient and that the patient should also learn how current patterns of behavior are influenced by past experience. The advantages of focusing on the past have been noted in the first part of this book, but it will be useful to repeat them here. Emphasis on the past expands the therapist's capacity to explain why the patient behaves as he does in the present. If the patient learns how he effects others, how others effect him, or how he responds to himself, he may still be unable to change his behavior unless he understands the cause of these responses. Such causes can be found in past learning experiences which influence the patient's motivations and perceptions in the present. The awareness of previously repressed motivations and distorted perceptions becomes a new factor in the patient's total experience of his plight, and such awareness expands his capacity to make choices. The patient's new understanding of the causes of his behavior will provide him an explanatory or cognitive map which may guide him in making more adaptive future decisions. Information related to the past will also help the therapist develop a clearer picture as to what types of maladaptive learning the patient has experienced, and will guide the therapist in trying to provide corrective learning experiences within the therapeutic interaction.

One of the simplest ways to learn how the patient's past experiences influence present behavior is to ask the patient to thoroughly review his life history. As the patient reviews his life experiences from childhood to adulthood, attention can be paid to how the patient's inherited characteristics and learning experiences through various phases of life have interacted to lead to his present troubling behavior. Such investigation may be quite comprehensive, even exhaustive. The richness of the understanding it offers the patient is dependent upon the therapist's capacity to keep the patient talking about himself and to help the patient develop an integrated picture of how his behavior has come to be influenced by the interaction of biological, psychological, and social factors. This type of therapy can be conducted without making efforts to bring unconscious material into awareness. There is a great deal of information about the past that can be used to explain the patient's behavior in the present if the patient is willing to try to recall it and reconstruct it. Using a commonsense, logical approach, the therapist can help the patient relate past events to present conditions or conceptualize old information in a new manner. The patient can make constructive use of his new understanding to avoid mistakes and misinterpretations which have produced troubling behavior in the past. This rather cognitive approach to psychotherapy was developed by Adolf Meyer and is called distributive analysis (Polatin 1966). At one time it was quite popular in this country and was viewed as a sufficient means of bringing about behavioral change.

Most therapists these days believe that there are limits to the extent to which understanding can be obtained by focusing solely upon conscious material. Much of the past, particularly past thoughts and feelings which have been troubling, is repressed and cannot be brought to consciousness through simple efforts at recall. Psychotherapists who are influenced by psychoanalytic theory seek a more thorough understanding of the patient's problems by gaining access to the unconscious. The effectiveness of psychoanalytic treatment is probably based on all of the factors which make other forms of psychotherapy effective, but psychoanalysis is distinctive in its emphasis on highly complicated techniques for making unconscious information available to the patient.

The reader should note that in developing information as to how the patient interacts in the present, the therapist is often dealing with unconscious processes and will use techniques designed to uncover out-of-awareness material. Some of these techniques, such as clarifying the response patterns between patient and therapist, have already been described. I will focus here primarily upon that aspect of psychoanalytic technique which is directed toward elucidation of how the past influences the present.

I will list only the major elements of psychoanalytic technique here. Therapy usually begins with a fairly rigid contract in which the patient is told how many hours he will be seen weekly. From the first hour the patient is encouraged to verbalize everything and anything that comes to mind without regard to its content, whether embarrassing or distasteful, critical of the therapist or affectionate. He is urged to omit nothing and to express everything regardless of whether or not he considers his verbalizations pertinent, relevant, or logical. This verbal behavior is called free association. Its purpose is to permit unconscious material to find expression by reducing the patient's tendency to deliberately censor it. Much of the material the patient brings up in free association will relate to the past, and the therapist may reinforce exploration by tactful questioning. A significant proportion of the material the patient brings up, however, will also relate to the present, and efforts are made to encourage the patient to focus upon that part of the present which constitutes the therapist-patient relationship.

One of the crucial aspects of the early stages of psychoanalytic treatment is that it puts considerable stress on the patient. The therapist seeks to be gentle and kind but provides the patient relatively little stroking or positive reinforcement. Instead, deliberate efforts are made to frustrate the patient by at times, withholding emotional support, by failing to respond to the patient's demands, or by remaining silent. Eventually, the patient experiences a regression, or series of responses to the therapy situation, reminiscent of the patient's behavior during childhood. The rationale for creating this type of stressful and frustrating environment (which is always accompanied by just enough concern and positive reinforcement on the part of the therapist to keep the patient motivated to continue therapy) is that it will make it easier for the patient to recover infantile memories through the formation of transference responses. As the patient regresses, he develops feelings toward the therapist similar to those he held toward significant individuals in his past. These transference responses, in effect, bring the patient's past into the here and now, where repressed feelings and ideas can be examined with a certain degree of objectivity. (In psychoanalytic theory the totality of the patient's transference responses is referred to as a transference neurosis.) The therapist, if not unduly influenced by his own unrealistic attitudes toward the patient based on his own childhood experiences (countertransference), can respond to these previously repressed thoughts and feelings in a rational, accepting, and nonthreatening manner.

The analyst is constantly seeking opportunities to explain how unconscious thoughts and feelings, developed in response to past events, influence present behavior. These integrative explanations or interpretations may focus at various times on clarification of past events, on understanding of the transference relationship, or on understanding of the patient's relationships with others. Psychoanalytic theory also postulates that patients tend to resist discovery of unconscious impulses and to resist behavioral change. Liberal interpretations are made as to the patient's use of such resistance. Considerable attention is also paid to the patient's dreams, which are felt to provide relatively direct information as to the patient's unconscious processes.

This synopsis cannot begin to capture the intricacies of psychoanalytic treatment. One of the most interesting and difficult tasks for the psychoanalytic therapist is that of trying to

Individual Psychotherapy

be helpful and supportive to the patient, while continuing to frustrate him. This complex task is facilitated by the therapist's use of attentive silence. The patient quickly learns that the analyst is always involved and concerned. He also learns, however, that the analyst will not respond to him in an explanatory or reassuring way unless the patient reveals information that is relevant. The patient must therefore continuously dig for unconscious material. In effect the therapist's silence is used as a negative reinforcer to make the patient talk about issues he might wish to avoid. The therapist's nonresponsiveness is most effectively terminated by the patient's verbalization of material that allows the therapist to make a comment or interpretation.

The therapist's skill in making connections between unconscious material and current behavior and in helping the patient understand such connections is also critical. In formulating these interpretations, the therapist must rely primarily upon his own experience and good sense. As in any other kind of intervention which provides the patient new information, the information must be presented when the patient is ready to hear it. This means that the therapist must have considerable evidence to support the interpretation and some sense that the patient is close to making the interpretation on his own. The same interpretation may have to be repeated several times and related to several different themes in the patient's life before it can influence him. The first time a patient hears a certain interpretation he may accept it only intellectually. After several similar interpretations he may experience a more powerful emotional response. As the patient moves from an intellectual to an emotional response to an interpretation, he seems to say, "Yes I know, I know, I know...by God, I really know."

I have noted how access to unconscious information may be helpful to the patient in itself, but that such information also gives the therapist a more specific idea as to which behaviors are best reinforced or extinguished. This issue is not usually given adequate consideration in discussion of psychoanalytic techniques. Yet it is probable that much of the usefulness of psychoanalytic therapy resides in its capacity to provide the therapist rich data as to which of the patient's behaviors need to be changed. Psychoanalytic therapy is especially useful in expanding the patient's information regarding his feelings. Psychoanalysts have developed a variety of techniques for helping the patient deal with awareness of new feelings. When the patient expresses guilt feelings previously repressed, the analyst will often try to diminish their influence by pointing out their irrationality or inappropriateness. The analyst directly or indirectly tells the patient, "I dont't blame you for what happened in the past, and it hardly makes sense for you to blame yourself." Both of these statements are designed to diminish the patient's use of self-punishment. Feelings of aggression or sexuality are handled somewhat differently. The analyst will usually reinforce verbal discussion of such feelings, as long as he feels that the patient is not using such talk as a form or resistance. If the patient wishes to act upon previously repressed sexual or aggressive feelings, however, the analyst tries to place limits upon such direct expression. Within the therapeutic relationship the analyst will insist that the patient confine himself to talking about sexual and angry feelings; physical manifestations of sexuality or aggressiveness are strongly discouraged.

The patient's expression of newly experienced sexual and aggressive feelings outside of the hour will be selectively reinforced depending upon the analyst's opinion as to whether such expression is adaptive. If the patient becomes more intimate, loving, and experimental in relations with relatives and friends, these behaviors will be reinforced. But if he becomes promiscuous, he is likely to have his behavior carefully examined and interpreted. If the patient becomes more assertive and hardworking in his natural environment, he will be reinforced. But if he becomes argumentative and abusive toward others, he will be asked to explore the meaning of his behavior.

The issue of regression deserves an additional comment because it has certain practical implications. Those analysts who have remained loyal to the idea that regression and development of a transference neurosis are essential elements of cure have become committed to progressively longer treatment. When psychoanalytic methods were first being developed, treatment of less than a year's duration was common. Currently, psychoanalytic treatment is likely to last from two to five years. Commitment to the goals of regression and development of a transference neurosis have also encouraged psychoanalysts to restrict their interaction with the patient and to reveal as little about themselves as possible. The analyst's efforts to remain a blank screen limit the kind of therapist-patient interactions in which the patient can experience how he comes across to the therapist and how he is influenced by him. In classical psychoanalytic treatment, there is

Individual Psychotherapy

much less person-to-person encounter than is available in therapies which are more present oriented. There is also less opportunity to use positive reinforcement as a supportive maneuver or as a technique for shaping the patient's behavior outside the hour.

In the last two decades psychoanalysts have placed greater emphasis upon developing briefer interventions, which are called psychoanalytically oriented psychotherapy (Offenkrantz and Tobin 1974). In these interventions the therapist investigates unconscious processes in the past and present and, while he interprets transference responses when they occur, he does not deliberately seek to create a regression and a transference neurosis. There is more therapist-patient interaction than in classical-psychoanalysis and more willingness on the part of the therapist to be positively reinforcing. There is also less use of interpretation or resistance and less interpretation of transference responses which seem based on resistance.

It is extremely difficult to evaluate the role of psychoanalytic technique in modern psychotherapy. Most schools of therapy, whether they have moved away from pure Freudian theory while still considering their method a form of psychoanalysis, or whether they have rejected Freudian doctrines and have adopted new theories and techniques, still borrow liberally from the Freudian method. Many of the differences between the predominant schools revolve around differing degrees of commitment to the belief that expanding information as to how previously learned unconscious thoughts and feelings influence present behavior is the primary factor in healing emotional disorders. My own commitment to that belief is rapidly diminishing. The acquisition of new information is only one of the helpful elements in psychotherapy, and the acquisition of information as to how past events of which one is unaware exert influence in the present is an even smaller element. Since the process of retrieving repressed past information is so long, tedious, and expensive, there are few indications in ordinary clinical practice for prescribing classical psychoanalytic psychotherapy.

Explanation

Most patients either desire or demand explanations as to how their disorders developed, and in most forms of therapy these explanations are provided. It is conceivable that there is something innately therapeutic about having one's difficulties explained. What is explainable is less mysterious and, therefore, less frightening. The explanation provided by the therapist will be less indicting or critical than the one the patient may have entertained before therapy. For many patients, explanation is viewed as forgiveness. The patient who understands the causes of a maladaptive behavior will also feel a sense of control or mastery over the behavior. Explanations also provide guidelines for future adaptive behavior. They help patients determine what they should do or not do if they are to avoid future difficulty. (It should be apparent that the helping factors of information expansion and explanation are intimately related. Explanations are frequently based on the information developed in the course of therapy, and the kind of information the therapist seeks to develop is often based on his explanatory system.)

In my experience, the accuracy or scientific verifiability of the explanation offered the patient may not be too important. What is important is that the patient believe the explanation. Many years ago I became involved in working with a group of incarcerated sex offenders who had received psychotherapy consisting primarily of the presentation of didactic explanations of their disorders, using pure Freudian terminology. These men had received indirect instruction that their release from prison would, in large part, be determined by their capacity to parrot back a Freudian explanation of their difficulties to the prison authorities. I was initially dismayed by the nature of this kind of psychotherapy and predicted to myself that these men would continue to have considerable trouble both in and out of prison. I was wrong. As a group, they were more comfortable than other sex offenders while in prison, and once released their rates of recidivism were no greater than those who had received less cognitive or more expressive psychotherapy. Apparently the largely mythological explanations those men received were helpful to them. In subsequent years I have often been amazed to observe an occasional patient, who may have had many years of unsuccessful previous treatment, suddenly respond to the explanatory message of a transactional analyst, Gestalt therapist, reality therapist, or rational emotive therapist by enthusiastically accepting it and experiencing symptom remission. These dramatic changes often take place in situations in which there has not been time for an intimate therapist-patient relationship to develop. The easiest way to comprehend the phenomena is to postulate that these individuals have finally found an explanation of their difficulties that makes sense to them and that their new understanding has relieved them of an enormous burden.

Many of the technical operations involved in individual psychotherapy are determined by the therapist's commitment to a particular explanatory system. The type of questions the therapist asks, his selective attentiveness, and the interpretations or integrating comments he offers are largely determined by the therapist's theoretical commitments. Whether or not the therapist is explicit in providing explanations, the patient, who is very much concerned with how the therapist views his disturbance, will pick up many cues as to the therapist's explanatory system. Even therapists who view themselves as nondirective do a good deal to facilitate the process of explanation. Patients may finish a nondirective therapy experience feeling that they have worked out the details as to the causality of their disturbance on their own. But it is likely that their conceptual framework for understanding causality is indirectly cued by the therapist and that the patient's explanation will in large part reflect the therapist's belief system.

If a large group of therapists of different orientations were to sit down and try to explain why they thought a particular patient was disturbed, there might be considerable overlapping in their explanations. Depending on theoretical commitments, however, it is also likely that each therapist would focus at least part of his explanation on a particular aspect of the patient's experience, either the recent and remote past or the patient's present experience. Freudian therapists tend to explain the patient's suffering in terms of repression of thoughts and feelings related to sexual or pleasure-seeking activities during early life. The patient's efforts to sustain the repression are alleged to lead to maladaptive responses which leave him ill prepared to deal with the stresses of the present (Menninger 1958, Wolberg 1967, Alexander 1956). Adlerian therapists make similar formulations but stress the patient's striving for power and recognition rather than the patient's sexuality (Adler 1924, 1931). Jungian therapists are more concerned with the patient's lack of awareness of the symbolic meaning of his behavior, both in terms of the patient's intrapsychic processes and in terms of the collective meanings of these symbols in the patient's culture (Jung 1929, 1953). Hornevian therapists are concerned with unconscious processes but also place considerable emphasis on the patient's inability to find security in a society which puts emphasis on the attainment of goals which are not congruent with the patient's real self (Horney

1937). Sullivanian analysts emphasize how earlier interpersonal experiences produce both distortions in the patient's view of others and diminished self-esteem, which then compromise the patient's capacity to find satisfactory interpersonal relations in the present (Sullivan 1953). Existential therapists emphasize the patient's unwillingness to experience and deal with the present, particularly the manner in which his entire being, including bodily functions, responds to the present (Maslow 1968). Reality therapist emphasize the patient's failure to take responsibility for past and current behavior (Glasser 1965). Rational emotive therapists focus upon the internalized messages or reinforcements and punishments the patient has been presenting to himself (Ellis 1962). Rogerian therapists emphasize the patient's past exposure to learning experiences which lead to his developing negative self-regard toward manifestations of his true self and which prevent him from self-actualizing, or realizing his potentials (Rogers 1954, Truax and Carkhuff 1967). Transactional analysts focus upon how the patient's difficulties in discerning his ego states of parent, child, and adult and how his tendency to follow irrational parental injunctions (based on early learning experiences) eventually lead to self-defeating behavior (Berne 1964).

Each of the above emphases is based on slightly different views of the patient's biological needs, the patient's capacity to take responsibility for his own behavior, the influence of the past, the influence of the present, and the importance of the social environment. There is, at this point, absolutely no evidence that any explanatory mode or any set of techniques based on that explanatory mode can be used to provide a psychotherapy experience that is superior to any of the others. All individual psychotherapies (with the exception of the use of behavior therapy for certain types of well-circumscribed disorders) seem to produce similar results. In making the above statement, I do not wish to imply that all forms of psychotherapy are equally effective for all types of patients. The aggregate data obtained by current research methodologies do not tell us what is happening to individual patients. It is probable that some explanatory modes and the techniques derived from them are better for certain patients than for others. Research on how the patient is likely to be influenced by differing modes of explanation and how the patient eventually explains his disturbance to himself may someday help us to match specific patients to specific psychotherapies. Nor do I

Individual Psychotherapy

wish to suggest that there are no skills which the therapist must master and use consistently in order to help patients. The therapeutic efficiency of proper use of authority, idenification, lovingness, tension reduction, new learning, and new information can be assessed even with current research methodologies. There are certain techniques for utilizing these helpful features that are more efficient than others, and these techniques are teachable.

The diversity of explanatory systems and the lack of evidence for their usefulness or validity force the therapist to make difficult choices in developing his own style of explanation. One alternative is to master a single system of explanation and to use it with all patients. This approach has the advantage of allowing the therapist to become quite proficient in using that system. The disadvantage is that it can close the therapist off from new ideas and can lead to a kind of religiosity which discourages the effective use of interventions other than a particular form of individual psychotherapy even in situations where there is sufficient knowledge to justify a multidimensional approach. The other alternative is for the psychotherapist to try to master as many modes of explanation as possible and to use clinical intuition and experience to apply a particular mode of explanation to a particular patient. This approach leaves the therapist open to new experience and, if his clinical hunches are right, could make him more effective. The disadvantage of this approach is that no therapist can possibly master and utilize all modes of explanation and that the therapist who remains ecumenical for too long is at risk of becoming nihilistic or cynical. Eventually such nihilism or cynicism may be communicated to patients. Perhaps the best approach to the problem of explanation is for the therapist to feel free to hold to many beliefs but to try and master one belief system thoroughly enough so that he can always rely on it as a firm explanatory base. New explanatory systems can then be integrated into the basic system as the therapist's perspectives change. It is also essential that the therapist believe in some type of explanation. Good therapists can be ecumenical, but they cannot be nihilistic.

SOME PERSONAL METHODS

It should be clear by now that there are many ways of doing psychotherapy and that each therapist must eventually develop his own style. I have already given many hints as to mine, but it might be useful, at this point, to expand a little on some of the ways I utilize the helpful elements in psychotherapy. One difficulty I have in doing this is that these days I rarely use individual psychotherapy as an exclusive intervention but will more frequently use family therapy or a combination of individual and family therapy. Much of what I will report here, though reported in the present tense, describes my therapeutic behavior in the recent past.

By virtue of being a physician, psychiatrist, and professor, I am a socially sanctioned healer. The reader might assume that this in itself gives me enough power to exert a therapeutic influence over my patients, but my experience is that it often does not. We live in an era in which it is difficult for people to respect, trust, and rely on authority of any kind. Physicians and psychiatrists in particular have not successfully weathered the current wave of antiauthoritarianism. Having spent a large part of my career treating convicted criminals and alienated students (two groups who are not exactly awed by the psychiatrist's authority), I have developed a number of techniques for gaining power in psychotherapeutic relationships which I may use with many different kinds of patients. These techniques consist primarily of demonstrating unanticipated honesty and openness and undercutting the patient's critiques of psychotherapy by partial agreement. I try to take a nondefensive posture which says to the patient, "I am optimistic that I can help you, but I will make no false promises." Some aspects of this approach can be illustrated by considering a number of statements which might be made by patients and how I might respond to them.

Patient: I know that psychotherapy doesn't work; I don't know why I'm here.

Therapist: Psychotherapy doesn't always work, but there is good evidence that it does help most people most of the time. Most of my patients seem to get better.

Patient: Psychotherapy demands so much change. I don't know if I can really change myself at all.

Therapist: One way of looking at change is that there is very little difference between the adaptive capacities of a happy person and those of a miserable person. You don't have to change very much in therapy and I don't expect massive changes. But even a tiny bit of change may make a substantial difference in your levels of comfort and effectiveness.

Individual Psychotherapy

Patient: Psychiatry is such a vague field. Do you really know what you're doing?
Therapist: Most of the time I think I do, but a lot of the time I'm not so sure. I just try my best.

Patient: I can't bring myself to trust you.
Therapist: You have no reason to trust me. You don't know me well enough. You'll just have to find out if I'm trustworthy or not.

Patient: You psychiatrists are detached and uninvolved. You're only in this for the money.
Therapist: This is hard work. I wouldn't be doing it if I didn't get adequate compensation. You'll have to learn to judge for yourself whether I really care.

Patient: You couldn't possibly understand or accept my values.
Therapist: Perhaps I won't. The most I will promise you is that I will try to honestly inform you of what I don't understand or accept.

Patient: You're just going to brainwash me in here.
Therapist: To a certain extent that's true. I probably will try to get you to adopt new perspectives on the ways you act and think.

Patient: I need a real friend, not a store-bought friend.
Therapist: Neither you nor I know yet whether we even want to be friends, but I can assure you that sometimes my patients and I do get quite fond of one another and this seems to make it easier for my patients to find other friends.

Patient: I need to know more about you. I can't relate to somebody who is so distant.
Therapist: What would you like to know? I'll tell you anything that I don't consider to be an infringement on my privacy. Later on in therapy, however, if you ask me about myself, I may want to look more deeply into the reasons for your asking.

Patient: If I let you know me, you'll hate me.
Therapist: That's certainly possible, but that's one of the risks you'll have to take. I can tell you that, as a rule, the better I know my patients the more I like them.

Patient: I have to do it alone. Accepting help makes me feel weak and degraded.
Therapist: That's a lot of bunk. Everybody needs help at some time or other. You're just courageous enough or lucky enough to have looked for it.

Patient: I'm afraid that if I get into therapy I'll become dependent on you.
Therapist: That certainly is a risk in psychotherapy. The most I can say to reassure you is that this dependency usually has a time limit.

Patient: You can't possibly understand me. We come from entirely different backgrounds and cultures.
Therapist: Perhaps you're right. The best we can both do is make some effort to communicate with each other.

Patient: I'm afraid I might fall in love with you.
Therapist: You might come to feel affectionate toward me, and that would be OK. I can promise you that I will not take advantage of your feelings.

Patient: Everything about you suggests to me that you are a male chauvinist.
Therapist: Sometimes I'm afraid that I am, but I try not to be and I try to keep my chauvinistic feelings out of therapy.

Patient: You're too straight to understand me.
Therapist: Maybe I am. Maybe Not. It's up to you to find out how straight or kinky I really am.

Patient: What school of psychotherapy do you belong to, doctor?
Therapist: I'm afraid I'm very wishy-washy. I'll use whatever works.

Patient: Have you ever had psychotherapy?
Therapist: Sure. I spent four years in psychoanalysis.
Patient: You may have had therapy, but you probably started it for training purposes.
Therapist: No. When I started therapy, I was really hurting.

As I write this, I am embarrassed by the seductiveness of my therapeutic behavior. The elements of seductiveness are hopefully secondary, however, to my efforts to establish my position as an authority and to create a therapeutic climate characterized by straightforwardness and empathy.

I have previously noted my willingness to have the patient identify with my approaches to problem solving and my willingness to clarify my own values. With regard to the issues of caring or lovingness, I try to be as empathic as I can. With highly disturbed patients who need emotional support I go out of my way to emphasize their positive characteristics. I provide reassurance and stroking to the greatest extent possible without being phony. My use of directiveness or nondirectiveness in shaping behavior is in large part determined by my assessment of the patient's need for autonomy. Patients who have been disabled by an emotional illness have already had their autonomy seriously compromised and are often relieved when they receive direct suggestions. With less disturbed patients I will try to be more subtly persuasive and allow the patient to make his own decisions as to when to experiment with new behaviors. There will still be many times, however, when it is apparent both to the patient and to me that some new behavior is called for, and I might say, "Why don't you just quit fooling around and do it." Whether being directive or nondirective, I use all of the techniques of reinforcement and extinction that were described earlier.

At times psychotherapists have made efforts to try to develop specific types of reinforcing and extinguishing responses to specific types of behavior patterns (Aichorn 1953, Kohut 1968). While efforts to match specific psychotherapeutic techniques to specific patient behaviors are obviously useful, we still do not have any data which show how this can be done. Every therapist tends to develop his own style of relating to patients with different personality traits. In my own psychotherapeutic work, I tend to offer little reinforcement for the intellectual ruminations of obsessive patients. I may interrupt them if they are talking in a circumstantial manner and are showing little affect. I will be very reinforcing if they are spontaneous. In dealing with schizoid patients, I am less concerned with content and make strenuous efforts to keep them talking. I feel that any kind of benign human interaction is helpful to those individuals. With impulsive patients I will reinforce talking about feelings and try to discourage inappropriate actions. With hysterical patients, I sometimes say that I will listen to complaints for only a given part of the hour, perhaps five minutes, and then expect them to talk about something else. Another technique I employ with these patients involves focusing on their use of language. Hysterical patients often use their language to exaggerate the extent of the suffering.

They will describe an ordinary headache as "the worst anyone has ever had" or mild anxiety as "absolutely unbearable." I try to tell them that such language elicits both internal and external reinforcement of the symptom and makes it worse. I also interrupt them when they are using hyperbolic language and ask them if they can use more accurate descriptive terms.

In dealing with information expansion, I am particularly interested in the patient's gaining information as to how he influences and is influenced by his social environment, and because this information is easy to obtain in family therapy, I find it useful to combine family therapy with individual work. With selected patients, I am also willing to undertake the difficult process of relating past experience to present behavior and will use psychoanalytic techniques which frustrate the patient in order to gain greater access to unconscious material. I will not use such a technique, however, with patients who are highly disturbed or who are not fully capable of appreciating its possible advantages or disadvantages. With regard to the issue of explanation, I must admit to being hopelessly ecumenical. As I review my practices over the last two decades, I realize that at various times I have been attracted to the postulates of Freudian, Adlerian, Hornevian, Sullivanian, Gestalt, existential, Rogerian, reality, and rational emotive therapy. I have experimented with modes of explanation derived from each of these schools with different patients and sometimes with the same patient depending on how I viewed the patient or depending on how I was being influenced at a particular time by my personal interests, my reading, or my involvement with charismatic teachers. I have always tried to obtain a follow-up on the status of patients I have treated for more than a few months and have been able to obtain subjective reports of outcomes from most of them. Using these very rough data, I have been unable to find any relationship between the theoretical commitment I held at the time I was treating a patient and the actual outcome of therapy.

TERMINATION

A discussion of psychotherapy would be incomplete without some consideration of the problem of termination. There are many methods of termination, and actual techniques are determined by the therapist's theoretical orientation (Freud 1937,

Saul 1972). Some therapists practice time-limited therapy. The majority of therapists, however, will encourage the patient to terminate only when he appears to have achieved certain types of learning. In practice, of course, many patients will terminate therapy long before they have achieved their initial goals or the goals of the therapist. Sometimes the patient wishes to stop therapy as soon as he experiences symptomatic relief. Other patients get bored with therapy or decide it is not worth the money. In a highly mobile society many therapeutic encounters are terminated when either the patient or the therapist moves to a new geographical area.

Most schools of therapy agree that termination is likely to be a difficult task for the patient. Patients are advised to begin discussing their feelings about treatment several sessions before termination actually occurs. Some therapists feel that termination goes best when the patient gradually decreases the frequency of sessions. A patient who has been seeing a therapist two times a week may cut down to once a week for several weeks and then to every other week for a few more weeks. Other therapists do not believe in such tapering or weaning and insist that the frequency of visits remain constant until the end. Most of the time the therapist waits for the patient to bring up the issue of termination. When patients have been in treatment a long time, however, and seem to be too dependent upon the therapeutic relationship, the therapist may initiate termination.

In my own work I have gradually become less authoritarian in determining when patients should terminate. For the most part my patients terminate whenever they feel like it. If a patient wishes to terminate and I feel that his disorder has not improved or has deteriorated, I may encourage him to continue therapy with me or with someone else. If the patient seems to be better, however, and is in no imminent danger of developing disabling symptoms, I will merely urge him to spend a session or two discussing termination before leaving. I have developed this approach because I do not feel I have sufficient capacity to predict how much therapy or change is good for a given individual. If the patient says he can get along without therapy and seems to be functioning well, I do not feel justified in urging him to stay in therapy to achieve goals which may reflect my values rather than his. The patient can always return to therapy if it turns out that termination was premature.

I make minor exceptions to this practice. Some patients contract with me for a long-term therapy experience in which they are seeking specific changes in personality or character traits. When these people ask to terminate before they have achieved their goals, I will remind them of their initial goals. I assume that if they contracted for long-term therapy, they were sufficiently aware of the repetitive nature, or chronicity, of their maladaptive behavior, and that even if they are feeling better, they might still do well to continue to seek personality change. I am also concerned about early termination by patients who have had major psychoses or depressive disorders. These patients are so prone to use denial mechanisms and are in such great need of sustained help in dealing with their disorders that I feel I have not done an adequate job unless I have worked with them for at least several months.

When nonpsychotic patients who have been in therapy for several months are relatively improved but seem to be making no further progress, I will frequently recommend termination. Some are relieved to hear this. Others view it as a rejection. It is important that the patient be allowed several hours to discuss termination instituted by the therapist. When patients have been insistent on remaining in therapy, I have either acquiesced to their wishes or have helped them find another therapist.

Although I have no set rules about tapering off the frequency of interviews, I do tend to behave ritualistically in the final hour. I ask patients to review the positive aspects of their therapy and to verbalize their disappointments in therapy. If the patient is talking only about the positive aspects, I will make sure he has ample opportunity to express negative feelings. If he talks only about negatives, I will ask him to consider positives. I do this because I believe that all patients are ambivalent about therapy, and their ambivalence may bother them later if it is not fully expressed. I also use the final hour to provide the patient with as much explanation of the causes of his disorder as I can. As a rule I give patients a clear and friendly message that they are always welcome back. Patients are reassured that they can return at any time and that they should never be ashamed to come back to therapy to work on old or new problems. I encourage patients I have seen in long-term therapy to keep in touch with me and let me know how they are doing. They have, after all, become friends and some form of continued communication may ease the pain of separation for both of us.

PSYCHOTHERAPY IN HOSPITAL SETTINGS

Individual psychotherapy is often recommended for patients who are hospitalized, and usually it is the younger, inexperienced clinician who is called upon to provide this treatment. The neophyte may assume that psychotherapy in the hospital setting will proceed in the same manner that it proceeds in an outpatient setting. This assumption is wrong. There are conditions related to hospitalization which require considerable modification of the usual psychotherapeutic approach.

Much of the work of psychotherapy begins with the patient's discussion of problems in his current environment, and since the hospitalized patient's current environment is an artificial one, the material he brings to the therapeutic hour will be significantly influenced by that reality. Unfortunately, the patient's experiences in the hospital environment are likely to be limited and stereotyped. They may not be similar to the kinds of experiences which have been influential in creating the patient's difficulty in his real environment. When the patient is seen in outpatient psychotherapy, discussion of his day-to-day life will usually clarify his problems and provide material which will define his need for new learning experiences. Discussion of the hospitalized patient's day-to-day experiences provides fewer clarifications or insights.

Hospitalization also facilitates the development of behavior which may be unrelated to the patient's initial problem. The hospitalized patient leads a life in which many areas of choice and responsibility are closed off. Most of his needs are taken care of by others, and many decisions as to what he will do from moment to moment are made by others. He is, in effect, living in a regressed condition reminiscent of childhood. Regression which is a by-product of hospitalization is quite different from that deliberately created in psychoanalytic psychotherapy. It is not induced through therapy but imposed upon the patient. It is not restricted to the therapeutic situation, but permeates every aspect of the patient's life. The hospitalized patient's regressed status will influence his interaction with the therapist. Much time will have to be spent dealing with behaviors, such as demandingness, rebelliousness, or passivity, that are created by the fact of hospitalization. The therapist will be preoccupied with sorting out which of the patient's behaviors are related to the initial disturbance and which are related to hospitalization. Sometimes the problems created by hospitalization are so urgent to the patient that the therapist will have to work very hard to get the patient to focus on the initial disturbance.

Another complicating factor in doing psychotherapy in the hospital setting is that the therapist is likely to have a highly ambiguous relationship to the patient with regard to issues of power and authority. If the psychotherapist is a psychiatrist who is also responsible for the patient's ward management, the therapist will usually assume varying degrees of control over the patient's daily activities. The hospital psychiatrist has the power to decide what the patient does from moment to moment, who will visit with the patient, what medications the patient will receive, and when the patient will leave the hospital. If the patient is involuntary committed or knows he will be committed if he tries to leave the hospital, the doctor's power is almost absolute. It is difficult to retain so much control over the patient's freedom and at the same time be the patient's therapist. Certainly the effectiveness of a nondirective approach will be limited. Nondirectiveness is based on a kind of permissiveness in which the therapist provides few suggestions to the patient and the patient enjoys complete freedom to do whatever he wishes outside the hour. If the inpatient psychotherapist is also responsible for the patient's total management, he cannot offer the patient such freedom. The therapist can try to relate to the patient within the psychotherapeutic hour as if the patient had the freedom to make his own choices outside the hour, but this is an inherently inconsistent and dishonest approach which is likely to confuse and irritate the patient.

It is possible to create a system of service delivery in the hospital in which the physician who is administratively responsible for the day-to-day needs of the patient is not the patient's psychotherapist. Someone else, either another physician, a psychologist, a social worker, or a nurse, may be designated as the psychotherapist, and an administrative structure can be created in which the designated psychotherapist has little or no input into decisions made about the patient. This kind of structure is often used in long-term hospitals where patients may stay from six months to years and allows the therapist to maintain a rather nondirective permissive role. It is also frequently used in rehabilitative programs in prisons and training schools. In hospital units where patients stay for only several days to a few weeks, however, it is usually inconvenient to separate therapeutic and administrative

Individual Psychotherapy

roles, and the psychiatrist is asked to assume both. Many psychiatrists begin their training in this kind of unit and do not receive adequate warning as to how the ambiguities of their assigned role may limit their effectiveness as therapists.

A final complicating factor in the hospital setting is that patients have many daily interpersonal encounters with individuals other than the designated therapist. In a good hospital setting patients regularly work with occupational therapists, recreational therapists, nurses, and social workers, and frequently develop close and therapeutic relationships with these professionals. If the designated psychotherapist is a physician, he may have the most power in deciding what is to happen to the patient, but he may not be the professional who has the opportunity to develop the most intimate relationship with the patient. His power to bring about change through use of a professional relationship may be significantly less than that of other professionals.

It may be useful to consider psychotherapy with inpatients in terms of the helpful elements which have been described as characteristic of all psychotherapies. The patient's faith and hope in the powers of the healer are likely to be strengthened in the hospital setting. Hospitals are often viewed as citadels of knowledge and they may be nationally recognized for their medical accomplishments. The patient quickly learns that within the hospital setting the physician-psychotherapist (even though he may be young and inexperienced) is perceived as a powerful person and a socially sanctioned healer. The power bestowed upon the physician-psychotherapist may increase the likelihood that the patient will follow his advice and perhaps wish to identify with him. It is also probable that the physician-psychotherapist's efforts to be empathic and positively reinforcing may have a more powerful impact in the inpatient than in the outpatient setting. When a person with great authority over the patient's life praises the patient or empathizes with him, the patient is likely to feel better.

At the same time the effectiveness of inpatient psychotherapy may be limited by the therapist's administrative power. If the patient reveals material which lets the hospital therapist know the depths of his despair, the patient may find himself deprived of freedom or may be required to take medicine he does not want. In the inpatient setting the patient may realistically fear that self-disclosure will lead to actions on the part of the hospital staff which he will perceive as punishments. Much of the tension-reducing value of psychotherapy will be lost, and the patient's capacity to form an honest, intimate relationship with the inpatient psychiatrist will be compromised. The patient's fear of self-disclosure plus the artificiality of the hospital setting will also limit the richness of the material brought into the therapeutic hour. There will therefore be less opportunity for the patient to learn new responses within the therapy situation or to acquire new information. The physician-psychotherapist does have the advantage of being able to orchestrate the hospital milieu to provide precise reinforcement and extinction of the patient's behavior once he can determine what behaviors are in the patient's best interests. But since the patient may not be disclosing his difficulties freely, it will be difficult to determine the specifics of the patient's needs.

Because of these considerations and because so many hospitalized patients are too incapacitated or too poorly motivated to integrate a great deal of new learning, it is generally wise for the physician-psychotherapist to attach modest importance to individual psychotherapy in the hospital setting. Many interventions other than individual psychotherapy can be more efficiently used. The focus of inpatient psychotherapy should be on defining the main problems which led to hospitalization, on explaining the use of other interventions, and on using the therapist's authority to provide direct guidance as to how the patient can resolve his problems (Tucker and Maxmen 1973). There will always be a few patients who will prove responsive to intensive inpatient psychotherapy. The goal of brief hospitalization for most patients, however, should be primarily that of providing the patient sufficient symptom relief to get back to his natural environment where he can benefit from individual psychotherapy as well as other interventions.

Beginning psychotherapists are likely to seek more ambitious goals. They note that their hospitalized patients often have powerful responses toward them and mistakenly assume that these responses represent a form of transference which can be worked with in a classical psychoanalytic fashion. This is a dangerous assumption. The regressed behavior which the inpatient shows in psychotherapy may have absolutely nothing to do with the therapeutic relationship. It may simply be related to the therapist's power or to the fact that the patient is living a life which reinforces regressed behavior. Incorrectly dealing with such behavior as a transference phenomenon results in frustration for both patient and therapist. The patient may try to accept the therapist's interpretations of transference phenomena but find it difficult to relate his feelings toward the therapist to past experiences since these feelings may have nothing to do with the past. The therapist will have difficulty in obtaining information that corroborates his hypothesis about the patient's transferences and will exaggerate his perception of the patient's resistance. If the therapist persists in his efforts to treat the patient with traditional techniques, there may eventually be a disastrous breakdown in communication.

There is still one other problem which arises in the psychotherapeutic treatment of hospitalized patients. In these days, when continuity of care is considered an essential aspect of a health delivery system, the physician-psychotherapist will often try to provide psychotherapy to the patient in both the outpatient and the inpatient setting. Sometimes the physician assumes total responsibility for the patient during the course of hospitalization and, in so doing, must adopt an authoritarian role. As soon as the patient gains outpatient status, however, the therapist may try to shift to a permissive role. It is difficult for the patient to deal with this shift. If a therapist who has just recently had total control over the patient's life suddenly takes the stance that he is no longer going to try to influence what happens to the patient outside the therapeutic hour, the patient may have a hard time believing him. Whenever I have attempted to continue psychotherapy with patients over whom I have previously exercised power in the hospital setting, I have found that it has taken several weeks or months for the patient to stop fearing my authority and to trust my permissiveness. The task of continuing outpatient psychotherapy with a person the therapist has treated in the hospital is not impossible, and sometimes it is even expedited by aspects of the relationship that were nurtured during hospital treatment. But the therapist will be wise to anticipate that trust and intimacy in the continuing relationship will develop slowly.

INDIVIDUAL PSYCHOTHERAPY AND OTHER INTERVENTIONS

From all that has been said up to now, it should be apparent that individual psychotherapy is a flexible intervention which can be paired with any other intervention. There is no evidence that combining individual psychotherapy with pharmacotherapy, behavioral therapy, group therapy, or family therapy diminishes the value of the individual work, and there is evidence that some combinations of individual with other therapies are advantageous.

The major problem the therapist has in combining individual psychotherapy with biological or behavioral treatments is that of having to shift between permissive and directive approaches. I have already considered some of the problems of shifting from authoritativeness to permissiveness. Shifts in the opposite direction may also be difficult. When a specific behavior therapy is instituted during the course of more traditional psychotherapy, the patient has to be urged to follow directions carefully. When drugs or other biological interventions are added during the course of psychotherapy, the patient must be willing to accept the clinician's recommendations. Therapists who are comfortable in giving their patients advice will have little difficulty in providing their patients such directions. Therapists who are more committed to a nondirective approach will have to be careful in explaining their shift in therapeutic behavior to patients. When I institute a behavior therapy with a patient I have been treating in a more nondirective psychotherapeutic mode, I will usually say something like the following: "Look, some of your behaviors seem to be making it impossible for you to function effectively outside of therapy and are also interfering with your capacity to work in psychotherapy. There are some techniques available for changing these behaviors rather rapidly, which require that I give you certain tasks to perform and that you follow my directions carefully. Are you willing to try to do this while we continue psychotherapy?" So far I have not seen this kind of approach lead to a diminution of the patient's willingness to disclose himself or a diminution in his capacity to develop transference reactions. Therapists who fear that combining behavioral techniques with nondirective psychotherapy will compromise the purity of the nondirective approach can, of course, ask another clinician to do the behavior therapy.

As a rule I do not use antianxiety drugs when treating patients with individual psychotherapy unless the patient is going through a bad experience or asks for medication. I will then either prescribe these drugs on a time-limited basis or will give the patient a prescription for a certain amount of the drug (for example, fifty 5 mg. Valium tablets) and tell him: "There will be little harm in your using this drug on those rare occasions when you are having a difficult time. I am giving you a prescription and am leaving it up to you to be responsible for how you use it. The medicine can be habituating, so I will have to warn you to use it sparingly and will have to trust you to let me know if you feel you are using it too frequently." When antidepressant or major neuroleptic drugs must be prescribed during the course of therapy, I will usually explain to the patient that I believe there is a part of his behavior which he can control only with inordinate difficulty, that I do not want him to feel responsible for that behavior, and that it should be treated biologically. I will try to make it as clear as possible, however, that he needs to continue to work on other aspects of his behavior in psychotherapy and that drug treatment will help him to do so.

When patients in individual psychotherapy focus primarily upon the unsatisfactory manner in which they are interacting with others and mention the possibility of a group experience, I have no hesitancy in recommending concurrent group psychotherapy. Since I do very little group therapy, it is necessary that I find a group therapist for the patient who feels comfortable with the patient's continuing to see me. I regularly do a certain amount of family therapy even with those patients I am treating primarily with individual psychotherapy. Usually at the beginning of therapy I will conduct a diagnostic family interview as part of the evaluation process. I will also make it clear that both the patient and I have the right to request that other family members be brought into the hour whenever either of us feels that it will facilitate the therapeutic process.

CO-THERAPISTS IN INDIVIDUAL PSYCHOTHERAPY

It has become customary for many group and family therapists to work with co-leaders. This practice is uncommon in individual psychotherapy. Yet there are times when asking a second therapist to help treat a single patient may be quite helpful. In the early years of my practice I often found myself so preoccupied by the suicide threats or the erotic or aggressive manipulativeness of certain patients that I could not treat them effectively. I worried too much about them, was inclined to be overcautious in dealing with them, and often could not bring myself to respond to them as firmly or as lovingly as I felt necessary. About ten years ago I learned that the simplest thing to do when I was in trouble with any patient was to bring in a colleague and have him sit in on one or more of our sessions. Sometimes the colleague functioned as a consultant and merely gave me advice about the patient or about the therapeutic relationship. At other times the colleague functioned as a co-therapist and we both treated the patient. I found that this relatively simple (albeit expensive) modification of the usual psychotherapy format helped both me and my patient. Having another person in the room took enough pressure off of me so that I could look at what was happening more objectively. It made me less fearful and freer to deal with my own feelings. Patients who were temporarily stalled in their therapeutic work because of erotic transferences or extreme demandingness or dependency were, in the presence of two therapists, able to view me more realistically and to get back to more constructive psychotherapeutic work. Most important, I found that potentially suicidal patients were less frightening. With a second therapist in the room I felt that if the patient actually did kill himself, I could share my grief, my guilt, and my sense of personal and professional loss with another person. This made it possible for me to relate to the patient more as a professional and less as a concerned but intimidated friend.

I now advise all of my students to feel free to call in a co-therapist or a consultant whenever a patient is not doing well or if they are unduly troubled by the therapeutic relationship. Psychotherapists need to retain a certain degree of comfort if they are to help patients. A therapist and patient who are stalemated in a dysfunctional relationship both need outside help. Therapists should never feel demeaned when they ask for such help. While in the short run co-therapy may appear expensive, it is ultimately much cheaper than therapy that is unsuccessful.

ETHICAL ISSUES

The ethical problems in individual psychotherapy are more subtle but no less powerful than those in biological or behavior therapy. Individual psychotherapy may influence the patient more slowly than other therapies, but it has a pervasive influence over all aspects of the patient's life. When the patient enters individual psychotherapy, his only goal may be symptom relief. He soon learns, however, that he is expected to achieve emotional growth and that such growth will not be achieved unless he changes many aspects of his life. Therapists try to help their patients learn to lead a good life. The values which underlie that good life, however, are in large part defined by the therapist. When the therapist takes on the responsibility of telling another how to live, he has assumed an awesome ethical burden. Psychotherapists have periodically shown a disturbing lack of humility and an unreflective arrogance in assuming that their own version of the good life is best for their patients.

There is nothing inherently wrong in trying to teach people to live the best possible life. Philosophers, politicians, and theologians have done this for centuries. The psychotherapist, however, in addition to being a philosopher and political and spiritual advisor is a scientist. Some of the directions of influence he tends to exert upon the patient are based on fact or testable hypotheses. Others are based on personal convictions or faith. Psychotherapists do not always clarify to patients when they act on the basis of faith. The potential damage that can be done when belief systems sustained primarily by faith are presented to the patient as scientific fact can be illustrated by reminding ourselves of the destructive messages so many psychotherapists have conveyed to women. For many years female patients were told that passivity, dependency, and even subservience toward their mates were desirable and healthy qualities. Too much assertiveness in females was viewed as pathological. Even the sexual needs of women were misinterpreted by male therapists. Women were viewed as incapable of experiencing multiple orgasms and were told that, if they could have only clitoral but not vaginal orgasms, they were immature. These belief systems, which had no basis in scientific fact, were conveyed to the patient with the aura of scientific truth. Such imposition of powerful male chauvinistic values upon female patients has undoubtedly contributed to the oppression of women in general and to a worsening of the condition of many female patients.

It is difficult to divorce ethical issues from practical issues in psychotherapy. Many people do not improve in psychotherapy, and some get worse. It is probably that some patients get worse because the values they learn in psychotherapy are not suitable for their own lives. A person who has been persuaded to diminish his abrasive responses to others may have difficulty if he continues to live in an oppressive environment. Or a patient who lives in an environment where others expect him to be passive and content may find that his new-found skills in assertiveness or self-actualization do not serve him well. In the course of psychotherapy, patients may be persuaded to examine and resolve problems in a manner that eventually diminishes the quality of their lives. The patient's decisions regarding marital problems are especially important. Nobody knows how many people who enter long-term individual psychotherapy eventually divorce their spouses, but most therapists feel the number is high. (In my own practice I cannot recall ever having treated a married patient in long-term psychotherapy who did not seriously contemplate divorce.) Therapists are likely to err when they exert too much influence over the patient's decision making regarding a troubled marriage. The changes the patient makes in his marriage during or following psychotherapy may seem quite desirable at the time, but they may not be in his long-term interests. If the patient is influenced to adjust to a stormy marriage and to make the best of it, his unhappiness may persist and even escalate. Patients who are subtly influenced to seek divorce may feel an initial sense of elation but may soon discover that their lives become even emptier. Before the advent of women's liberation I and many other therapists may have failed to help some female patients because we subtly encouraged them to remain in an oppressed marital situation. Today other patients may be hurt by being subtly persuaded to seek a kind of liberation or freedom which often turns out to mean nothing more than freedom to be miserable and lonely.

In the course of writing this chapter, I treated a forty-five-year-old woman who was massively depressed. Her depression developed six months after she separated from her husband. The patient's marriage, which had lasted for twenty years, had been an unhappy one in which she was severely oppressed by her husband. A year before she left her husband she had entered psychotherapy for mild depression and to seek help with marital problems. Her therapist tried to involve the husband in therapy, but he was uncooperative. As the therapist became more familiar with the patient's miserable home situation, he began to counsel the patient to seek divorce. Eventually the patient became convinced of the wisdom of her therapist's advice and separated from her husband.

She found a job, rented an apartment, hired a feminist lawyer, and for a few weeks felt liberated and happy. She then began to note that her oldest children, who had elected to stay with her husband, were reluctant to visit her. They felt she had rejected them. Most of her friends, who had

Individual Psychotherapy

been friends of both her and her husband, seemed less interested in continuing their relationship with her than with her husband. Even her brothers and sisters rarely came to see her. Eventually her feeling of liberation was replaced by feelings of intense loneliness. After many years of living in an oppressed state, she simply did not have the skills or the opportunities for building a new and independent life. Her feelings of sadness quickly escalated to somberness and suicidal preoccupation. She developed vegetative signs of depression and was hospitalized. In the hospital, the patient's condition deteriorated. She stopped eating and began to voice paranoid ideas. Her condition became so serious that she was eventually treated with ECT. As she came out of her depression, the hospital staff made many efforts to try to reinstitute some of the patient's supportive relationships with family and friends. We had only limited success. Although the patient was fearful of living alone once again, no one was willing to take her in. At the time of her discharge, we had no options but to send her to a halfway house and have her continue outpatient psychotherapy.

It would obviously be helpful if therapists would be more restrained in imposing their values upon patients. A value the therapist considers universally relevant may not be suitable for a particular patient. When the therapist exerts subtle or direct pressure to make the patient behave in a certain way, the patient is entitled to know what value systems underlie the therapist's efforts to influence him. If the therapist's directions of influence are determined by values rather than by facts and the patient knows this, the patient can at least have a dialogue with the therapist as to how he should respond to the therapist's influence.

In *The Politics of Therapy* (1971) I described other ethical problems of psychotherapy in some detail. One common by-product of psychotherapy is a tendency to explain one's disturbances in terms of intrapsychic factors and to be distracted from experiencing or dealing with an oppressive environment. Some symptoms can be created or influenced by conditions of social oppression. If these symptoms are treated by asking the patient to look inward and explain his behavior to himself in a manner that allows him to accommodate to oppression, psychotherapy becomes a force for continuing the status quo. Of course, psychotherapy can also, by providing explanations which relate the patient's disturbances to an oppressive environment, encourage patients to take steps to change the environment. Ultimately, much of the patient's response to the environment will be influenced by the manner in which the therapist is able to clarify the role the environment plays in creating his disturbance. The only practical way of dealing with this problem is for the psychotherapist to be rigorously evenhanded in helping the patient examine all of the possible causative factors in his disturbance. Systems of psychotherapy which focus too exclusively on intrapsychic forces can encourage the patient to accept situations which are not in his best interest. Systems which place too little emphasis on the individual's role in creating his disturbance can encourage the patient to take self-defeating actions and can distract the patient from the need to make changes in his own behavior.

Another possible risk of psychotherapy is that patients may be unable to free themselves of dependency ties to the therapist. Many who enter psychotherapy are lonely and unwilling to commit themselves to leading an autonomous and responsible life. The therapist who appears loving and strong may be viewed as the answer to their existential problems. These patients may feel safe only when they are in psychotherapy, and they are terrified at the prospect of being without a therapist. They can justify continued psychotherapy only by remaining symptomatic and they are usually able to generate just enough symptoms to stave off termination. Most patients will become quite dependent upon the therapist during the course of long-term psychotherapy. Usually these dependent feelings recede as the patient begins to feel better and obtains gratification outside the therapeutic situation. When the patient's dependency is not diminishing and his future pursuit of happiness seems directed more toward involvement with the therapist than with the outside world, the treatment program must be altered. Either the patient should see a new therapist or become involved in some new form of therapy, such as group or family therapy; or a co-therapist should be brought into the therapeutic relationship.

Therapists, unfortunately, may reinforce the patient's dependency for selfish reasons. There are obvious narcissistic gratifications for the therapist who treats patients who are attractive, intelligent, or gifted, or who relate to the therapist in a worshipful manner. If the therapist enjoys too much the status and adulation such patients bring him, it is relatively easy for him to foster a kind of dependency that keeps the patient in therapy for years instead of weeks or months. The therapist's financial needs may also interfere with his acting in the patient's best interests. Not uncommonly, wealthy and interesting patients are kept in therapy too long. It is easy to rationalize such practices as being in the patient's best interest. The therapist can always convince himself that the patient needs more work on some new problem or that a deeper and more profound reeducative effort will be more helpful to the patient than moderate symptom relief or behavioral change. And of course patients are easily persuaded to follow their therapist's suggestions. (I do not wish to be overcritical or sanctimonious in making these statements. As I look back over my own practice, I can think of a number of instances in which I kept patients in therapy too long. At the time I believed my decisions were in their best interests, but in retrospect I cannot be certain that I was not using theoretical arguments to rationalize economic motivations.)

Patients who do not fall into the wealthy or YAVIS category can be hurt by therapists in quite different ways. Not infrequently the lower or middle class patient is evaluated by a clinician and told that he needs intensive long-term psychotherapy. The patient then reports that he cannot afford the therapist's prices and is told that he can elect to be seen less frequently or can seek therapy in a clinic or mental health center. Even if the patient is fortunate enough to find somebody who will work with him at an inexpensive clinic or mental health center, it is not likely that he will be seen with the frequency which the initial evaluator recommended. Such patients are likely to begin therapy with a bitter and insecure attitude. They have been told (correctly or incorrectly) that they need a certain kind of intensive treatment. They discover that they must settle for something else. If the therapist does not emphasize the elective nature of intensive therapy and particularly if the therapist communicates that intensive therapy is a necessary condition for healing, the patient feels as though he has been told that he needs major surgery but has instead been offered only palliation. Poorer or less interesting people may also suffer the indignity of being referred from clinic to clinic and from therapist to therapist. After three or four evaluations, such a patient, who is told that he needs a certain kind of treatment but will have to wait for it or will have to accept a lesser treatment or an inexperienced therapist, will be rightfully discouraged. The tendency of therapists to reject poor or uninteresting patients who are often quite severely disturbed reflects negatively on the ethical standards of all the mental health professions.

I have previously noted the importance of confidentiality. While most therapists are scrupulous in this matter, occasionally therapists will gossip and reveal secrets that are embarrassing or harmful to patients. Some therapists write about patients in lay or professional journals and either fail to gain the patient's permission to do so or fail to disguise the material. At times therapists may be too cavalier in sharing patient material with investigative agencies without the patient's informed consent. Each of these practices is clearly unethical.

The issue of exploitation of the patient's erotic feelings toward the therapist has only recently begun to receive serious attention from patients and professionals. Nobody knows how many therapists have had sexual relationships with their patients, but the practice seems increasingly common, and I have sat in on enough ethics committees of state psychiatric societies to know that it is not infrequent. In dealing with cases that are brought to the attention of an ethics committee, it is usually easy to see the pernicious effect of sexual activity between therapist and patient. The patient feels exploited, used, and distrustful of therapists in general. I have seen a few such patients who might have been significantly helped by a nonsexual therapeutic relationship but who, following a sexual encounter with their therapist, developed more severe dysfunctions which were refractory to psychotherapeutic intervention. It can of course be argued that ethics committees learn only of the negative effects of sex between therapist and patient and that such interactions may be useful to some patients. Since there are no controlled studies of such practices, this argument cannot be refuted. It would seem unlikely, however, that an interaction which serves the therapist's needs, perhaps even more than the patient's, can really be therapeutic. The experience of being in a passive and helpless role, of seeking help from an authority who must be trusted, and of then being used by that authority for sexual gratification seems inherently dehumanizing.

The issue of love between patients and therapist is more complicated. In a general sense it is probably true that all therapists and patients love each other. Sometimes this love can become very intense and there is a mutually shared wish to continue an intimate relationship outside of therapy. If the patient is alone in such a wish, these feelings can usually be handled by reassurance, interpretation of possible transference reactions, and

Individual Psychotherapy

by the therapist's steadfast humility in accepting such feelings while not taking advantage of them. If the therapist also loves the patient, however, and wants to extend that intimacy beyond the therapeutic hour, the situation is more complicated. (As more women become therapists, I have seen a few instances in which they have fallen in love with their patients. So far I have not known of any women therapists seducing their patients.) In supervising psychiatric residents, I have encountered several situations where therapist and patient have fallen in love with each other. In such situations I have usually recommended that the patient find another therapist and that if the couple want to continue seeing each other, they should do so without having any kind of professional relationship whatsoever.

I am regularly amazed to discover how many of my male colleagues have married their own patients. In most cases, the therapist was married to someone else at the same time he began seeing his future wife as a patient. There are a number of possible explanations for this phenomenon. It is hard for the therapist to resist the adulation of a very attractive patient. If the therapist is having difficulty in his personal life, the patient's love and worshipfulness toward him will be especially welcome. Therapists, perhaps more than other people, also undergo major personality changes throughout their careers. They often make changes which are not complemented by changes in their spouses. They come to view themselves as different, more mature people than they were when they married. The attractive patient may be viewed as the person they would initially have sought as a spouse if only they had been healthier or more self-actualized. While I feel a certain cynicism and sadness about the tendency of so many of my colleagues to marry patients, this practice cannot be viewed as unethical. Many of these therapist-patient marriages seem, at least superficially, to be good ones. The patients enter into such relationships quite willingly, and perhaps the only victim is the therapist's initial spouse.

This brief review of ethical problems should make it clear that individual psychotherapy is hardly a harmless interaction. Some practitioners and patients assume that, if individual psychotherapy does not get people better, it at least does not make them worse. This is inaccurate. A certain number of people are damaged by individual psychotherapy. Some patients cannot tolerate the stress created by the therapist's frustrating behavior or by the demand that the patient be responsible for and change many aspects of his behavior. Other patients may become habituated to being in a helpless role and will escalate symptoms to stay in therapy. Still others will learn to behave in ways that please the therapist but do not serve their own interests. The patient starting psychotherapy should be fully informed about all of these risks. Such knowledged does not diminish their enthusiasm or their faith in psychotherapy but, rather, allows them to become more equal and more autonomous partners in the therapeutic relationship.

Chapter 8

Group Psychotherapy

During my psychiatric training and early years of practice, I did a great deal of group therapy. For a variety of reasons, however, I stopped doing group therapy about nine years ago. My more recent knowledge of groups is based primarily on observing other therapists at work, discussions with colleagues, reading, and some participation in workshops or encounter groups. The reader will therefore find less case material in this chapter than in others.

Group therapy is a treatment in which a therapist deliberately establishes a professional relationship with several emotionally disturbed people who meet with the therapist as a group for the purpose of helping each troubled person find a more comfortable and effective adaptation. The therapeutic process consists mainly of verbal interactions between group members and between group members and the therapist. All of the helpful factors that operate in individual psychotherapy operate also in group. The group, however, is an artificially created social system. Each of its members is influenced by the interpersonal transactions within that system as well as by the activities of the therapist, and some aspects of helpfulness appear in distinctive form in group therapy.

The group therapy field is blessed with a relative absence of the professional territoriality which pervades the fields of biological treatment, behavior therapy, and individual psychotherapy. There is much harmony between psychologists and psychiatrists in this field (they even write books together), and skilled people from each of the mental health disciplines have considerable opportunity to work with groups (Lieberman, Yalom, and Miles 1973).

Group therapy is less expensive than individual therapy. A therapist doing individual therapy who sees a single patient every half hour can see three patients in ninety minutes. If he sees a group of nine patients together for ninety minutes, he is multiplying his services threefold. If two therapists see a group as co-therapists, the dramatic economic advantage of group therapy is diminished, but group therapy will still be more economical than individual.

What is cheaper is often viewed as inferior, and many clinicians consider group therapy less valuable than individual therapy. I have previously noted that there are no convincing data to support this view. Not surprisingly, some therapists who are committed to the group approach believe that group therapy is equally or more effective than individual treatment for helping certain types of patient. Group therapists believe that it is usually an error to refer a patient for group therapy simply to help the patient save money or to conserve the resources of a clinic staff (Yalom 1975). It is probably essential that group therapists take this attitude. The element of faith or hope in the powers of the healer cannot be maximized unless both therapist and patient believe in the healer's methods. Patients who enter group therapy believing it second best may not profit from the experience, and therapists offering group therapy primarily because it is less expensive may not be effective.

At this moment we have few criteria supported by data to tell us whether a group or an individual approach is indicated in a given case. The choice in many instances rests with the patient's or the therapist's preferences. Given a choice, the majority of people who are experiencing emotional difficulty would probably elect individual over group therapy. If this preference were honored, a large number of patients would be excluded from groups. Therapists seem to make referrals for group therapy primarily on the basis of their familiarity with group techniques and their belief in the efficacy of the group therapy process. Some therapists refer most of their patients to a group; others refer none.

In actual practice there are a few clinical criteria for including certain types of patients in certain types of groups, and there are more criteria for excluding certain types of patients from certain types of groups. These criteria are usually based on the definition of the patient's most serious problem and on the purpose of the group. The criteria for selection or inclusion will become somewhat clearer after the goals of various types of group therapy have been described briefly.

GOALS

One common type of group therapy involves working with people who share the same problem. Individuals troubled by obesity, a chronic mental disorder, or an inability to be assertive may join groups which have the specific purpose of increasing their capacity to control appetitive behaviors or of teaching them such social skills as assertiveness or socialization. In this kind of group the patient is urged to take some responsibility for his behavior, but personality change or growth is not anticipated. Considerable emphasis is placed upon exhortation, directiveness, positive reinforcement, and inspiration.

Patients addicted to alcohol or other drugs may also be seen in groups which use an inspirational or exhortative approach. The goal here is, again, to help them develop greater control over appetitive behaviors. Some of these groups, however, require the patient to seek goals which go beyond simple control of addictive behaviors. Such groups as Alcoholics Anonymous and Synanon urge their members to make major changes in life style and to adopt new sets of values. These groups, which are run by nonprofessional leaders, use a variety of techniques such as abreaction and confrontation to facilitate personality change.

Criminal offenders are also likely to be treated in groups. When juvenile delinquents or adult offenders participate in group therapy, there may be several goals. The group might have the specific purpose of helping the offender survive conditions of legal restraint (usually imprisonment), or of helping the offender develop better control of antisocial impulses. Both types of group will emphasize educative and supportive techniques. Other group approaches to the offender, however, may be based on goals of maximizing more profound personality change. Here, the offender may be urged to adopt new value systems and to assume responsibility for his behavior. The techniques used in this approach may be identical to the techniques used in the more classical form of what I shall shortly describe as interactional group therapy.

Another major direction of group therapy is toward treating people with different problems. Patients who enter these groups usually suffer a variety of forms of anxiety and depression and can also be described as having a variety of maladaptive personality traits. The purpose of these mixed groups is to help each individual solve his own problem through his relationships to the therapist and other group members. Personality change or emotional growth is viewed as an essential concomitant of symptom removal or problem solving. These groups, which rely heavily upon interaction among all members and the therapist, are sometimes called interactional groups. They are commonly used in outpatient settings.

While participants in mixed or interactional groups may suffer from diverse symptoms, they are not likely to differ greatly from one another in terms of the severity of their disturbances. Efforts are usually made to ensure that there are no great disparities in the levels of personality strength or ego functioning of the various members. Some therapists will include psychotic patients in such groups, but most believe this unwise (Rosenbaum and Hartley 1962). Individuals treated in interactional groups are likely also to be more or less similar with regard to such qualities as age and socioeconomic class. Interactional groups, then, are usually heterogeneous in terms of the patient's presenting problems but homogeneous in terms of the personality strengths of their members and in terms of demographic variables.

Mixed or interactional groups have received the most attention in the group therapy literature. Leadership of such groups requires considerable technical skill, and these groups are alleged to facilitate powerful and enduring behavioral change. Most of my comments throughout this chapter will focus upon this type of group.

Another group approach, which has become popular in the last two decades, is designed not to treat disturbed people but rather to help any kind of person experience emotional growth. I am of course referring to the T-group or encounter group, in which people with dissimilar problems (including some who maintain they have no problems at all) meet for a time-limited period to learn more about themselves and to expand their potentials. Certain demographic qualities are common to encounter group participants. They are usually under fifty years of age and tend to be from upper or upper-middle class socioeconomic groups. Like many patients who actively seek a growth experience in other types of psychotherapy, they tend to have liberal rather than conservative values with regard to such issues as race, sex, and religion. While the encounter group movement originated in efforts to educate people to understand human behavior, encounter groups have gradually become directed toward helping participants change maladaptive patters of behavior. Many people who experience themselves as quite disturbed now enter such groups. Some schools of encounter group training no longer make distinctions between therapy and growth, and the boundary between traditional therapy groups and encounter groups has become less distinct.

GUIDES TO THE PRESCRIPTION OF GROUP THERAPY

The clinical indications for using group therapy with people with similar problems are relatively clear. People who abuse alcohol or who are obese respond well to the inspirational and supportive approach of such groups as Alcoholics Anonymous, Weight Watchers, or TOPS (Take Off Pounds Sensibly). Committed membership to AA is currently acknowledged to be the most effective intervention for controlling alcohol abuse (Riply and Jackson 1959). Groups which incorporate behavioral approaches are helpful in treating obesity (Levitz and Stunkard 1974). The efficacy of group therapy with people who abuse drugs other than alcohol is unproven, but group therapy of proven addicts, particularly with the assistance of former addicts, is likely to be helpful (Polatin 1966). The group format has obvious advantages in teaching assertiveness. It allows for the creation of situations in which assertive behaviors can be rehearsed and, when successfully performed, reinforced (Lazarus 1968). The usefulness of group therapy as an aid to resocializing chronically disturbed hospitalized patients is also apparent. These patients must interact with others if they are to develop the social skills required for functioning in society, and the group is a relatively benign environment in which to begin practicing such skills.

Group therapy is often the treatment of choice for delinquents. On the basis of my own experience in working with and supervising groups made up of adolescent or adult offenders, I am convinced that group therapy is highly effective in helping offenders survive the ordeal of imprisonment gracefully. It also seems to increase the impulse control of the offender, at least while he is still in prison. I have also seen quite good results in terms of outcome, such as personal growth or better impulse control after legal restraint is removed, following rather long-term group treatment of offenders. Offenders who work upon common problems in groups have a way of empathizing with one another and of cutting through one another's defensiveness, which is helpful and which may facilitate higher levels of self-disclosure and relatedness than are possible in individual therapy. For these reasons and for the sake of economy, group therapy may be the favored intervention for a clinician working in prison. It must be appreciated, however, that these statements are based on clinical experience and uncontrolled studies. Controlled research in the correctional area has produced discouraging results, and there is no firm evidence that any form of therapy with offenders produces personality changes (Martinson 1974).

The indications for the more classical interactional group treatment of people with dissimilar problems are difficult to define. One way of approaching the problem is to consider which individuals should be excluded from such groups. Most group therapists exclude individuals who are experiencing crisis reactions. They feel that the person who has experienced some recent loss or who must deal with recent changes in status may need more direct support than can be provided in an interactional therapy group and would be unable to function as a group member with the capacity to help others. Individuals in crisis are generally so involved with the threat of disruption of relationships in their real lives that they have great difficulty summoning the energy needed to form therapeutic relationships within the group. Patients who experience a crisis related either to accidental events or to an inability to cope with developmental tasks are probably better treated with individual or family therapy, or with a combination of the two.

My own bias (unsupported by data) is that psychotic patients do not do as well in interactional groups as in individual therapy. Participation in a group requires some ability to relate to a variety of people, to perceive and integrate a variety of difficult and often contradictory messages, and to have a realistic view of how one is influencing the nature and quality of communications with others. People who are having difficulty in thinking logically or in perceiving reality accurately may be overwhelmed by such a task. They are more likely, in my opinion, to learn about themselves in a sustained relation with one person whose methods of communication or style become increasingly familiar and understandable. If psychotic patients in a group find the level of sensory input confusing, they can, of course, withdraw from interaction more easily than they could in individual therapy. Such withdrawal, however, is not desirable in any form of treatment except as a temporary defensive measure. Furthermore, the individual therapist has an easy way of dealing with psychotic patients who seem overwhelmed by the demands of a dyadic relationship. The therapist can shift the topic to one which is more neutral and less threatening to the patient. The patient can then find a comfortable level of relationship with the therapist without having to withdraw. This simple accommodation could not take place in group therapy without compromising the needs of the other members. (For the sake of clarity it may be well to remind the reader that I am arguing that psychotic patients be excluded only from interactional groups. These patients can do well in resocialization groups where they work together with individuals at similar levels of dysfunction.)

As will be noted shortly, an important aspect of the therapeutic power of the group is its cohesiveness. To achieve maximum benefit from group therapy, patients must feel a certain attraction to the group and must develop a certain degree of pride in being a group member. It is also important that group patients not impede the function of the group by being unable to respond appropriately to the issues under current discussion or by focusing attention solely upon themselves. For these reasons many group therapists will exclude highly paranoid, narcissistic, hypochondriacal, hysterical, or antisocial patients from their groups. To the extent that therapists believe these people cannot identify with the group or cannot participate in group processes without monopolizing or disrupting them, they tend to refer them for individual psychotherapy. Here it must be noted that there is no clear consensus among group therapists as to exclusionary criteria (Fagen and Shepherd 1970). Each of the above categories of patients has been successfully treated in some groups. There is also some disagreement as to whether homosexual patients can be successfully treated in groups where other members are heterosexual. Some therapists may exclude homosexuals from interactional groups, but others feel that homosexuals respond well in such groups and do not impede group function.

The immediate needs of a particular group may also lead to exclusion of certain people. Generally, group therapists look for a certain balance in the age, sex, and intelligence of participants. A patient may ask for help at a time when no appropriate groups are available. Rather than have the patient wait, it may be more compassionate and practical to refer such a patient for individual psychotherapy.

Some patients reject group therapy on the grounds that it represents too much of a threat to their confidentiality. In my experience and that of others, violations of confidentiality are rarely a serious problem once the group is formed (Foulkes and Anthony 1965). But it is sometimes hard to convince patients that the group will provide the level of confidentiality they are seeking. If a patient cannot be convinced that his confidentiality will be protected, there is little point in continuing to recommend group therapy and individual therapy will be preferable. There are an increasing number of people in our society, such as government workers and industrial executives, who have secrets that cannot be shared with others without endangering their livelihood. These individuals may also be especially vulnerable if any unflattering information about them is leaked to their adversaries. It is interesting in this regard to speculate how successful the Nixon administration's Plumbers would have been in obtaining information about Daniel Ellsberg had he been treated with group rather than individul psychotherapy.

All of this suggests that individual and group psychotherapy should not be viewed as interchangeable interventions. Even the indications for interactional group therapy designed to bring about personality growth are slightly different from the indications for growth-oriented individual psychotherapy. My own practice is to recommend interactional group therapy primarily for patients who have chronic symptoms of anxiety or depression which are not circumscribed or easily delineated but which seem related to long-standing maladaptive personality traits. In making such decisions I try to exclude patients who may be disruptive to the group, who may not fit in because of problems of timing, or who feel they must be protected with an exceptionally high level of confidentiality. I am also more likely to recommend group therapy for patients able to define specific interpersonal problems, particularly interpersonal problems with peers rather than with family members. If the patient needs to learn better ways of relating to people with whom he must develop new bonds, the development of relationships with strangers in a group will be a useful and effective learning experience. If a patient's difficulties seem centered mostly upon relationships with family members, I will usually recommend individual or family therapy or a combination of the two.

Finally I do not push too hard in recommending group therapy for patients who insist on individual therapy. If they have their minds set on individual therapy and join the group only reluctantly, they are likely to become early dropouts, and their participation in the group will be a bad learning experience.

THE BASIC FORMAT

Patients are usually selected for group therapy after being interviewed individually by the therapist. During these interviews questions regarding the group are answered directly and there is considerable explanation of what kinds of patient behavior are most desirable in a group setting. Emphasis is placed on self-disclosure. Each member must be prepared to talk about actions, feelings, and thoughts which he may experience as shameful, unacceptable, or unforgivable. The group member is assured, however, that he will not be forced to reveal things he does not want to and that he will be allowed to choose the time at which he discloses himself. To facilitate the process of self-disclosure, members are cautioned that they should try to avoid discussing group matters outside the group, but that if they do, they must conceal the identity of the group participants.

The number of patients usually selected for a therapeutic group varies between four and nine, with most therapists preferring six to eight. This contrasts with the encounter group, in which fifteen to twenty members may participate. Traditional or interactional therapy groups tend to be open, in the sense that they allow new member to enter whenever older members leave. They are characterized also by having no time limit. As members drop out and are replaced, the group can take on a totally different character. Training or encounter groups differ insofar as they are closed groups which do not add new mmbers and which meet for a fixed period of time. In a therapy group each participant may terminate at a different time and has the opportunity to work through his particular problems of termination with both the therapist and the entire group. Termination in a time-limited group is a different matter, and all members must focus together on the issue of leaving one another.

Many groups are treated by co-therapists. There are various theories as to why this might be useful. Some therapists believe that having two therapists produces a wider variety of transference responses. Others emphasize the capacity of two therapists to support each other and to assist each other in understanding group processes. Still others view the co-therapist format as taking pressure off the individual therapist so that he can at times remove himself from the therapeutic field and focus upon the observational part of his participant-observer role. There is also disagreement as to the ideal pairing of co-therapists. Some emphasize the need to have co-therapists of relatively equal experience, while others believe that disparities here need not be a problem; they argue that the group can be used as a sort of on-the-job training for the less experienced co-therapist. All group therapists emphasize that the co-therapist must have enough mutual trust and respect to openly discuss their concerns about the group and their own interactions in it (Rabin 1967).

There are three general ways in which a therapist will relate to the group. Some, particularly of the transactional analysis or Gestalt schools, deal with one patient at a time. A patient who volunteers to "work" interacts with the therapist while the rest of the group for the most part look on passively. Each patient eventually has a turn to work on his own problems. While merely observing the interaction of one patient with the therapist may provide a great deal of learning, this kind of treatment has much in common with individual therapy (Berne, Steiner, and Dusay 1973, Corsini 1973).

A more common format is for the therapist to emphasize interactions between group members and briefer interactions between himself and group members. The therapist is seeking as many individual-to-individual interactions as possible and may view the interactions between two group members as being just as valuable as interactions between himself and a member. In this format the therapist is often quite open about his own feelings and values. While he retains leadership of the group, he is not likely to be viewed as a figure markedly different from other group members. He is in a more or less egalitarian position and is not likely to be experienced as mystical (Yalom 1974, Stoller 1968).

A third format is one in which the therapist, while encouraging some group interaction, has as his main focus his own interaction with the group as a whole. The group is assumed to have certain inherent qualities which influence the manner in which its members relate to the therapist and to each other. The therapist seeks to deal with these mass group phenomena by relating to the entire group as if they were a single patient. Here the therapist is clearly an individual apart from other group members. He retains a certain distance and mystery which provide him with power. This format has been developed largely by psychoanalytically oriented group psychotherapists (Rioch 1970, Ezriel 1950).

Any of these three formats may be adhered to in a relatively consistent manner by group therapists loyal to a particular theoretical school. But in practice most group therapists emphasize the second format, in which they focus upon interaction among all members, while remaining flexible in shifting to other formats whenever they feel such a shift is indicated.

HELPFUL FACTORS

The same factors which are helpful in individual therapy are helpful in group therapy. There are, however, important differences in the manner in which these factors exert influence in a group. Some are more and others less powerful in the group setting.

Faith and Belief in the Powers of the Healer

Patients who enter group therapy must of course have some belief that it will be helpful. The elements of faith and belief are especially important during the early phases of treatment. Groups cannot provide each members as much attention or support as might be available in individual therapy, and during the first few sessions group patients are likely to become discouraged. As many as one-third may drop out of the group in the first dozen meetings. Sometimes the experience of seeing an occasional member of the group profit from interactions during the initial sessions may help to sustain hope in the therapeutic process. Still, many patients will feel neglected, and the group therapist must work hard to sustain each patient's belief in a favorable outcome. He does this by virtue of his optimism and his capacity to communicate that optimism to the patient. If the therapist does not believe that the group experience is the best intervention for each patient in the group, fewer patients will remain in treatment and fewer will benefit.

In Western society the process of healing (outside of some religious settings) has traditionally been accomplished in a dyadic interaction. Individuals rather than groups are identified as healers, and when a person is in trouble, he tends to seek the counsel of a single healer rather than a group or a group led by a healer. This attitude may be changing as our society gradually accepts group therapy and the encounter movement, but it is still true that most people who are troubled will put more faith in a healing experience in which they have the exclusive attention of the healer. Because of these social attitudes, the elements of faith and hope are likely to be somewhat weaker in group therapy than in individual.

Identification

The way identification with the therapist's traits and values influences the patient in group therapy is significantly different from the way it influences the patient in individual therapy. In group therapy there is less opportunity for the individual patient to interact directly with the therapist, and there is less opportunity for the individual patient to see how the therapist might deal with problems similar to his own. Because the therapist may try to foster interaction among group members as well as between himself and the group, the amount of time the therapist exposes himself to interaction with any single patient may be less than in the individual setting. On the other hand, group therapies are more open to revealing their traits and values than are individual therapists. This lack of reticence provides group members a clearer picture of what the therapist is really like. Patients also have the opportunity to observe the therapist interacting with other people. They can, for at least a brief period, be relatively detached observers of the therapist's behavior and can identify with nuances of that behavior they might not have observed if they were preoccupied with their own interactions with the therapist. Finally, the therapist can exert a powerful influence by shaping group values or norms.

During the early phases of group therapy, the therapist, through demonstrating qualities of nonjudgmental acceptance, respect, patience, honesty, spontaneity, and self-disclosure, can model a set of values likely to influence all members of the group. Eventually, the group members will react to one another in a manner similar to the way they anticipate the therapist would react to them. Each patient can also anticipate that many of the responses of other patients to him and to others will be influenced by therapist's values. In effect, the group develops a new set of norms or values modeled after the therapist's behavior, and these values or norms will pervade subsequent group interaction. The therapist has actually created a social system characterized by adherence to the kinds of values he wishes to impress upon his patients. Functioning as a distinct entity or social system, the group will transmit the therapist's values to each member in a powerful manner, perhaps even more powerfully than the therapist could transmit them in a dyadic relationship.

Group Psychotherapy

There is another kind of learning by identification or modeling which occurs in groups and which is unrelated to the therapist. Group members can serve as desirable role models for one another. One group member may find some of the other members' attitudes, problem-solving behaviors and values useful. He may wish to incorporate these into his own behavioral repertoire.

Caring and Lovingness

While the patient in group psychotherapy will receive less nurturance and attention from the therapist than the patient in individual psychotherapy, he will certainly not be deprived of care and lovingness. Other group members will, in a properly functioning group, provide each member a considerable amount of empathy, positive reinforcement, and concern. The patient can be compassionately understood and "stroked" by several individuals rather than by one. He can also feel the concern and commitment of several individuals. In some ways the care and lovingness of other group members may be experienced as more meaningful than the care and lovingness of the therapist. Other patients, after all, are not being paid to care. Their involvement may be experienced as more genuine than that of the therapist.

The capacity of the group to be loving depends upon its cohesiveness. Group cohesiveness has been defined most simply as "the attractiveness of the group for its members" (Frank 1957). Those groups in which individual members value the group highly and which have a strong sense of solidarity or oneness can be thought of as cohesive. They are likely to meet the members' needs for empathy, positive reinforcement, and concern. A cohesive group can powerfully influence its members to experiment with new behaviors. Group cohesiveness is increased when the therapist behaves in a manner which fosters group norms of lovingness, acceptance, tolerance, and group loyalty. He does this not only by modeling these values but also by selectively reinforcing the behavior of any group member which reflects these values. Once the therapist and the group are successful in achieving cohesiveness, each individual can bask in the lovingness of the group climate. The group may then become the most prominent source of intimacy and concern in the patient's life.

The mutuality of caring and lovingness in the group setting provides an additional advantage to group therapy. Each patient is not only a recipient of care and lovingness but also a provider. Each group member is something more than a patient. He is also a helper. There is a certain amount of altruism in every person. The process of helping others satisfies altruistic needs and increases one's self-esteem. Helping another person may also provide a patient a temporary but often quite useful distraction from his own problems.

Tension Reduction

The tension-reducing aspects of revealing unpleasant thoughts or feelings are probably more powerful in the group than in the individual setting. There is greater risk taking involved in disclosing oneself to several people who may be relative strangers than to one person who is a socially sanctioned healer. The nonjudgmental acceptance of the patient's disclosure by the group is a greater reward than similar acceptance from a single professional. As more members disclose their thoughts, feelings, and actions, the patient in group therapy also comes to appreciate that he is not as unique or deviant as he might have thought. Most patients harbor feelings that their own inner thoughts and feelings may be uniquely unacceptable to anyone else. Listening to other patients express thoughts and feelings he has experienced himself reassures the patient that others are in the same boat. The patient may find that he can easily understand and accept thoughts and feelings that were considered unacceptable or deviant by another group member. This may make it easier for the patient to accept aspects of himself which he considers unacceptable or deviant.

Learning

Because he has fewer one-to-one transactions with each patient, the group therapist cannot use processes of extinction and reinforcement with the individual patient as frequently or as directly as he might in individual psychotherapy. Instead he must try to create a group climate (norms or values) in which all members of the group learn to respond to each participant's actions in a manner which will create new learning. This means that the group must learn to extinguish certain behaviors by refusing to respond to them the way others in the patient's life have responded, and must learn to provide high levels of reinforcement when desirable behaviors appear. It is sometimes difficult to teach these skills to a group. Group members are not professionals. They have their own problems and often misinterpret the communications of other members. Even when they accurately assess the behavior of others, they may not know how to respond to it therapeutically. In the beginning of treatment the group may respond to one member's anger with retaliation or withdrawal, or it may respond to a member's recitation of symptoms with too much attentiveness or alarm.

It is the therapist's responsibility to show the group how to diminish undesirable reinforcement and to increase desirable reinforcement. Sometimes he does this by direct intervention. He may, for example, request group members to curtail responses which reinforce symptomatic behavior. The therapist can also do a certain amount of explanation and point out how maladaptive behavior can be reinforced by the good intentions of others. The most powerful educative force in this situation, however, is the therapist's own behavior. As noted previously, group norms and, therefore, group patterns of reinforcement are developed largely through a process of identification with the therapist. One factor which facilitates the therapist's educative efforts is the freshness of the situation. Group members do not in the beginning know one another, and as strangers they have not developed fixed patterns of relating to one another. They are, as a rule, quite willing to accept the roles which the therapist models.

Much of the new learning in groups is facilitated by the manner in which unrealistic and maladaptive behaviors are repeated in the group setting. Past experience with significant figures in their lives lead group members to have unrealistic or distorted expectations of both other members and the therapist. These can be considered transference responses. Transference in groups (defined loosely as projecting onto people to whom one relates in the present feelings, thoughts, and wishes derived from experiences with significant figures in one's past) is ubiquitous. Other group members, as well as the therapist, become important people one must relate to and rely upon for help. The group which consists of a variety of individuals of different ages and sexes will elicit a large variety of transference responses related to each participant's previous experiences with siblings, parents, peers, or children.

Some group therapists believe that each patient will create relationships within the group that will, in effect, lead to a recapitulation of their behavior within their family units. They argue that the group, more than the individual setting, allows for a thorough reexperiencing of conflicts related to early learning within the family (Fagen and Shepherd 1970). Whether the group setting allows each patient to recapitulate his family setting is debatable. But there is little doubt that the group does allow for a rich variety of what have been called corrective emotional experiences. Patients may relate in certain ways to the clinician and to other patients and will anticipate certain responses from these individuals. When they receive an unexpected response, the maladaptive behavior will not be reinforced and the patient will be directed to examine the meaning of that behavior. Response patterns as well as attitudes and emotions are then likely to be altered. This is the same process which occurs in individual psychotherapy, but in group therapy corrective emotional experiences are more frequent and occur around a richer variety of issues. The group also provides the advantage of numbers or consensus in helping the patient see that some of his responses to others may be distorted. Several participants can point out to the patient that an angry, passive, or seductive response to another member or to the therapist was inappropriate to the situation. There may also be consensus in the sense that several members will provide a corrective response to the patient's behavior and several members may present the patient the message that his dysfunctional behavior must be related to some aspect of his previous learning.

The group is at a disadvantage in dealing with transference responses when other group members behave in a manner that may reinforce the patient's maladaptive responses. A patient who has experienced serious rivalry problems with a sibling may become competitive with another group member. If that member is in fact competitive with the patient, his responses to the patient are unlikely to be corrective and the transference aspects of the patient's behavior will be obscured. Here, the therapist must clarify the maladaptive aspects of each individual's behavior and must hope that other group members will be aware of that maladaptiveness and be willing to comment on it. Often the therapist may have to wait till one or another participant in the competitive process begins to improve and can relate more realistically to the other. There is also the possibility that with the passage of time one of the competitive group members will become inappropriately competitive with a different group member who will have different kinds of problems, who will not respond in a competitive manner, and who therefore will not reinforce competitive responses.

Once the group reaches an appropriate level of cohesiveness, it can become a powerful instrument for persuading each member to experiment with new behaviors—in or out of the group—and a powerful reinforcer of such behaviors. The patient in group therapy may desire the approval of the group even more than the patient in individual psychotherapy desires the approval of the therapist. If a number of people with whom the patient has become deeply involved urge the patient to try out a new behavior, they are likely to be successful. The patient in a cohesive group is also very much aware that his efforts to risk a new behavior will be amply rewarded.

The group has an additional advantage in shaping new behaviors by virtue of its being a small laboratory in which each patient can experiment with new behaviors. A male patient who has trouble talking with members of the opposite sex can risk new approaches toward female members of the group in a setting where the penalities for failure are few and the rewards for success are many. Assertive or intimate responses can be encouraged in the group, can be rehearsed there, and can eventually be generalized to situations outside the group.

Information

Group therapy may be the most effective intervention for helping the patient gain new information about how others view him and how the responses of others toward him are related to this view. In individual therapy the only sources of such information are the patient's reports and the therapist's observations. In the group, however, there can be an unlimited number of interactions between the patient and others which can be observed by the therapist. The therapist is in a position to gain relatively accurate information as to how the patient is influencing others, and he can communicate this information to the patient. Moreover, other group members can tell the patient how he is influencing them, and sometimes the entire group can provide feedback attesting to the accuracy of these observations. As is true in individual psychotherapy, such feedback enables the patient to identity his responses and sometimes his feelings toward others more accurately. Similar information can be generated in family therapy, but as a rule the patient may already know a great deal about how he is influencing those with whom he interacts on a regular basis. The experience of discovering that even relative strangers frequently perceive the patient in a manner that is different from the manner in which he perceives himself can have a powerful impact upon him.

As noted in an earlier chapter, it is always possible that the way the patient is coming across will be misread by those with whom he is interacting. People respond to others not only on the basis of the stimuli others emit but also on the basis of their own perceptions and needs. Presumably the therapist has some skill in determining to what degree his experience of the patient is related to his own needs. The therapist's reading of how the patient is coming across has a low probability of being distorted. Patients in a group, however, may be more prone to interpret their experience of another patient in terms of their own needs. Their perceptions of any particular patient may be inaccurate or distorted. The entire group may at times be in strong agreement as to the impact of one of its members and yet may be seeing that patient's behavior in a distorted manner.

It is important that the therapist, through modeling, teach all group members to have a certain humility in making comments as to how others are coming across. Language is important here. If the therapist says to a patient, "You are angry," or says, "You seem angry," he is making a comment which has the stamp of authority or cloture. It is usually better to say, "I am experiencing you as angry." This language tells the patient something about how he is coming across, but also allows discussion of the possibility that the influence the patient is having on others may be related to the therapist's unique way of experiencing him. The issue is not closed; further dialogue is possible. If the therapist provides a suitable model for the group and if the patient hears often and gently enough that others are experiencing him in a certain way, he will eventually gain some understanding of his own role in influencing others.

The group can provide quite accurate and unbiased feedback as to how the patient is coming across but do it in a manner that is hostile and destructive. Scapegoating, in which a particular member is attacked and rejected, is common in groups (Friedman 1978). It usually appears after the group has reached a certain degree of cohesiveness and has become deeply influenced by the therapist's values. Often it is precipitated when the therapist feels or acts negatively toward a particular group member. The therapist cannot prevent himself from emitting cues toward a particular patient that may seem to provide the group license to attack that member. But he must be assiduous in preventing any member from being attacked too frequently or too harshly. Information as to how one is coming across is unlikely to be heard or accepted unless it is provided in a climate of care or lovingness.

The group setting offers no advantages over the individual setting in helping the patient gain accurate information as to what others in the environment outside the group expect of him or are doing to him. It does, however, provide a rich opportunity for the patient to gain information as to how he is influenced by the behavior of others. Each patient in group therapy is confronted with a wide variety of interpersonal stimuli which bear considerable similarity to the interpersonal stimuli encountered in everyday life. In the group setting the patient may be exposed to feelings of tenderness, anger, rejection, or seductiveness. His emotional and motoric responses to such stimuli can be observed by the therapist and the group. The therapist, and at times other group members, can help the patient become more aware of these responses.

The major informational input of group therapy is determined by the manner in which group members relate to one another. Gaining information as to how one influences or is influenced by others requires that one interact with others. Such interactions in the group are maximized by urging the members to express feelings toward one another that exist in the present. Talking about the past is unlikely to elicit interaction. Each member may simply devote a great deal of time to his reminiscences. Focusing upon the present is more likely to elicit interaction. Most group therapists will allow patients to spend a certain amount of time talking about their past lives or their day-to-day experiences, but they will usually try to bring the discussion back to what is happening in the group.

The therapist focuses upon the here and now by relentlessly directing members to express their immediate feelings toward one another. If a member talks about feelings or experiences he has had outside of the group, the therapist may ask him to imagine what that feeling or experience might be like if it involved group members. Comments about activities outside the group are related, sometimes metaphorically, to experiences within it. I will not expand here upon the variety of techniques group therapists have developed for keeping the contents of treatment in the here and now but will reemphasize that here and now material is the most prized content in group therapy, since it allows for maximization of learning as to how one influences and is influenced by others (Fagen and Shepherd 1970).

While the group provides a superb setting for getting patients to interact with one another and learn from their interactions, it cannot be assumed that interaction in itself will provide each patient sufficient information. The therapist must also try to explain how group interactions influence each patient. This means that he must make frequent use of such comments as "I notice that whenever you try to get close to John and Mary you come across in a clinging, dependent manner that seems to turn them off" or "I notice that whenever the female members of the group try to talk with you about nonsexual matters you seem uninterested." Skill in this form of explanation requires considerable knowledge of people and is sharpened by experience. As a rule, the therapist must limit the extent to which he allows other group members to assume the role of commentator or explainer. Group members view this function as belonging to the therapist. If a group member tries to assume this role, it may be perceived by the group as an attempt by the individual to assume a special position of expertise or power within the group. The group is more comfortable and the therapist more effective if the leadership role is left primarily to the therapist.

Group therapy cannot be as effective an intervention as individual psychotherapy in helping the patient reconceptualize old information or gain new information regarding the past. Even if the focus of the group is directed more toward the past and less toward the here and now, there is no way in which each member could ever have sufficient time to examine and reconstruct the relationship of his past experiences in the group setting. Furthermore, group patients do not regress in the same way individual patients do. While they have transference responses toward the therapist and others, they do not develop a transference neurosis that is characterized by total involvement with or infantile expectations of the therapist.

A number of psychoanalytic schools of group therapy have argued that the group can be viewed as a single entity which develops properties of its own and which, by analogy, can be viewed as a single patient relating to the therapist (Whitaker and Lieberman 1964, Wolf et al. 1969). The analytic group therapist may assume that a comment from any individual member reflects the position of the entire group, and the therapist will respond to that comment as though the total group had spoken. By treating the entire group as one patient and by focusing on forces alleged to operate in all groups, the therapist can work with the group as though it had its own personality, defense mechanisms, and symptoms. A certain amount of group regression is believed to take place, and group transferences toward the therapist may be assumed to be part of that regression. It is hoped that as the group works on its problems as a group, information generated as a result of therapist-group interaction will be used by each member to deal with his own problems. This kind of work can be related to psychoanalytic theory, but it should be clear that even this format allows for relatively little reconstruction of past material by the individual patient.

Explanation

Patients in group therapy, like patients in individual therapy, seek and receive explanations of their behavior. As in individual therapy, the therapist offers direct explanations or indirect explanatory cues which help the patient understand his disorder as the therapist understands it. In a group setting, however, an additional factor operates. Each member will eventually incorporate some of the explanatory style of the therapist and this will be reflected in the way each member relates to other members. In a smoothly functioning group it is probably easier for the patient to accept the therapist's explanatory system because it is usually echoed by other group members.

As noted earlier, group therapists who work with one group member at a time usually hold to the theoretical models of transactional analysis or Gestalt therapy. Those who focus exclusively on the group as a single entity tend to support explanations based on psychoanalytic theory. The large group of therapists who focus on maximizing interaction among group members borrows heavily from psychoanalytic doctrine but also emphasizes socially oriented, interpersonal, or self-actualizing theories associated with Sullivan, Horney, and Rogers (Fromm-Reichman 1950, Rose 1969, Rogers 1965). In this kind of therapy the patient is likely to receive the message that, because of ungratifying experiences with significant figures throughout his pretherapy life, he has developed a poor sense of self-esteem and a number of defensive and unsatisfactory ways of relating to others.

The group tries to teach him that improvement will be related to his developing the capacities to see himself as an acceptable, likeable person and to find effective ways of relating to others. Implied in these messages is the additional communication that the patient may not be responsible for what has happened to him before treatment, but that as a result of the gains made in therapy he is now in a position to seek and achieve a responsible and self-actualizing future.

A BRIEF NOTE ON ENCOUNTER GROUPS

There seems little justification for discussing, in a book on emotional disorders, a technique for changing human behavior which was never intended as treatment for disordered behavior. Many encounter group leaders continue to insist that they are interested only in educating people or in helping them grow and that they have no wish to provide treatment (Goldberg 1970, Burton 1970). But since so many patients find their way into these groups and since the goals of these groups seem to be expanding to include therapy, some discussion is in order.

Encounter groups meet for a fixed time—usually several hours, for a weekend, or on a daily basis for one or two weeks. During the brief periods of encounter (or treatment), efforts are made to achieve maximum interaction between participants. The values of openness, honesty, and self-disclosure are emphasized, sometimes to the point of an almost religious intensity. To maximize interaction early in the course of the experience the therapist may use a number of techniques which involve asking members to perform some interpersonal exercise (for example, holding hands with another member or staring into another member's eyes for several minutes). As group members interact, the leader functions similarly to the group therapist in shaping group values, utilizing extinction and reinforcement, and expanding each patient's knowledge of his own behavior. The focus on here and now material is even more intense than in interactional group therapy. Discussion of past material is deliberately and sometimes emphatically discouraged. While encounter group leaders will try to create a group climate of care and lovingness, they are not as committed to providing emotional support as are interactional group therapists. Some encounter group leaders will deliberately foster a confronting and stressful environment. The emphasis in encounter groups is on bringing about rapid and sometimes spectacular change. It is assumed that since the participants are not emotionally disturbed people they can tolerate a high degree of stress without becoming emotionally disturbed.

Some recent and rather thorough studies of encounter groups suggest that certain therapist behaviors (irrespective of theoretical orientation) are more regularly associated with favorable outcome than are others (Lieberman, Yalom, and Miles 1973). Therapists who focus more on cognitive processes and help patients develop explanations of what they experience in the group have superior results. In general, better results are obtained by flexible therapists who do not view self-disclosure and expressiveness as ends in themselves, who are at times willing to allow members to deal with personal material outside the here and now, who do not make the group situation stressful, and who emphasize group cohesiveness.

ADDITIONAL DIFFERENCES BETWEEN GROUP AND INDIVIDUAL PSYCHOTHERAPY

Group therapists who try to create a climate of maximum interaction among members and between members and therapist are likely also to be highly self-disclosing and open in their relationships with the group. Although they adhere to the leadership role by paying close attention to the group process, by shaping group norms, and by making comments and interpretations, they have in many ways a relatively egalitarian stance toward the group and try to be free to be themselves. Group therapists do not feel guilty in accepting this freedom. Most believe that by being self-disclosing and open they are helping to shape a desirable group climate. My own experience and that of many therapists who have done both group and individual psychotherapy is that group therapy, while making many demands on the therapist, tends nevertheless to be more relaxing and enjoyable for the therapist than individual therapy. The interaction with patients is less stuffy, less restrained, and more playful. There are more participants available to correct the therapist's mistakes, and once the group is cohesive, the therapist need not be too concerned that an ill-timed or insensitive remark will result in a drastic curtailment of communication.

While the group therapist is free to be open during the therapy hour, he has less flexibility than the individual therapist when it comes to shifting roles in the therapeutic relationship. It is usually unwise for the group therapist to suddenly become more directive and authoritarian in a group setting. Such a change would have a negative impact upon the system of group norms he has previously worked so hard to develop. Group members who have seen the therapist in a more relaxed role and who have come to value his authenticity would consider inauthentic his assumption of a directive or authoritarian role. The group therapist must also try to relate to each member in a more or less similar manner. If one member should suddenly become quite disturbed, the group therapist would have to limit his use of a directive or authoritarian role in helping the patient, lest his role shift have an adverse influence on the group process. The individual therapist has less trouble in shifting roles. He can have a significant impact upon patients without being open, transparent, or even authentic. His mystery and distance may make it a little easier for him to shift from a permissive to a directive position without contradicting previous presentations of himself. If the patient should become more disturbed and if the therapist should have to become more directive, the therapeutic alliance might not be shaken. Even if the patient were troubled by the therapist's shifting roles, there would be ample opportunity to deal with the patient's concerns without having to worry about the effects of his shift on other patients.

Persuading people in a group to relate to one another and to the therapist can be difficult. The group therapist may often resort to a number of specialized techniques or gimmicks to facilitate interaction. A here and now orientation is emphasized by such exercises as asking beginning patients to take turns in discussing how they have experienced one another during their first meeting. Involvement with the therapist is fostered by his treating everything that group members report of their lives outside the hour as a metaphoric communication related to concerns about the therapist. If a patient talks about problems with authority figures, the group therapist may say, "You may be wondering if you are going to have similar problems with me." Some group therapists videotape their sessions and encourage the group to review the tapes in their absence (Berger 1970). Some groups may be asked to meet periodically without the therapist (Wolf 1949). Some therapists prepare a summary of each session and mail it to each patient so that it can be reviewed before the next meeting (Yalom, Brown, and Block, in press). Encounter group leaders have used a number of techniques to increase group trust, including asking a member to allow himself to fall and to rely upon other members to catch him. One of the most interesting techniques used in a group setting is having the patient hold an imaginary dialogue with himself or some significant figure in his life (Otto 1970). Some groups which rely heavily upon confrontation may ask each member to take a turn in the hot seat. This requires that the whole attention of the group be focused upon him, often in a critical manner (Schultz 1967). Finally, the group is an ideal setting for letting various participants dramatize the conflicts of a particular individual by deliberately taking on certain roles (Moreno 1945, 1953). In this technique, sometimes called psychodrama, the therapist may actually create scenarios relevant to some of the patient's major conflicts and have the patient and selected group members act the critical roles. As the patient reenacts his problem in the presence of the therapist and the group, he has the opportunity to gain new perspectives on his behavior and is in an ideal situation to practice new behaviors.

FURTHER TECHNICAL PROBLEMS

The group requires certain minimum standards of conduct from each member. Behavior that can be tolerated in individual therapy may be totally disruptive to the group. Disorganized behavior or paranoid behavior is usually always disruptive to an interactional group, but less spectacular behaviors, such as volubility, withdrawal, self-aggrandizement or self-righteousness, can also be disruptive. Some patients monopolize groups and never give others a chance to speak. Others never become involved enough to benefit from group participation, while still others take a holier than thou attitude toward group members and group issues and make it impossible for the group to develop a climate of acceptance.

During the process of group selection, the therapist of course tries to weed out individuals suspected of monopolistic, withdrawn, or self-righteous tendencies. His selection skills, however, are not always reliable. Some patients may behave like good group candidates in the evaluation interview and then turn out to be problems in the group. Faced with such a patient, whose behavior is clearly destructive to group interaction, the therapist must either exert strenuous efforts to control or change that patient's behavior or must help the patient leave. The latter alternative is often necessary and requires that the patient leave with as little damage to his self-esteem as possible. Patients who leave groups under duress, or even voluntarily, may find themselves feeling uncertain as to what they might do next to find help with their problems. It is essential that either the therapist or the referring clinician assume responsibility for finding another kind of treatment if it is still needed.

Another problem in group therapy is the formation of subgroups. Very often two or more patients within the group will be quite attracted to one another. They may begin meeting with one another outside of the therapy hour, and sometimes these liaisons will become overtly sexual. Formation of such subgroups is usually destructive of the group therapeutic process. The members of these subgroups tend to set themselves aside from other group members and do not interact freely with them. They may not even interact freely with each other during the session, sometimes reaching agreements among themselves as to the limits beyond which they will not disclose themselves in the hour. There is no way in which the therapist can legislate subgroups out of existence. He can warn group members at the beginning that the formation of such groups should be avoided. But he cannot control what happens outside the hour. Most therapists adopt the tactic of insisting that if subgroups or sexual liaisons form, their existence and the manner in which their existence influences the group must be discussed within the group meeting. If patients accept this suggestion, it is possible to keep the subgroup members from becoming too isolated from the rest of the group and from disrupting the group process.

SOME THEORETICAL CONCERNS ABOUT GROUP INTERVENTIONS

One of my own prejudices about group therapy is that it allows for too much fake self-disclosure. There is no way of knowing whether patients in individual psychotherapy are really more honest in disclosing themselves, but, having observed therapy groups and having both observed and experienced encounter groups, I believe that honesty is less prevalent in the group setting. Many patients develop a group "script" in which they regularly act in certain ways and make certain confessions. They may do this hour after hour in group therapy or encounter experiences without ever revealing other facets of themselves. Groups are usually too eager to accept at face value any form of self-disclosure. A patient in group therapy finds it somewhat easier than a patient in individual therapy to maintain distance by obfuscatory or irrelevant self-disclosure.

These considerations are perhaps inapplicable to highly cohesive therapy groups in which members have been working with one another for a period of time, but they are relevant to other kinds of group intervention. In my own experiences in two encounter groups, I found myself almost deliberately playing a game. I began by seeking a great deal of attention at the beginning and by revealing my narcissism and aggression. Other group members would then attack me, often quite angrily. I would respond defensively to these attacks for a time, and would then gradually begin to acknowledge my lack of insight as to how I was influencing and being influenced by others. At this point I would confess my insecurities and underlying lack of self-confidence. I revealed my more passive, more lovable side, and the group responded with praise and affection. Afterward I was welcomed as a contributing member, but I was never again challenged during the encounter experience. In effect I was allowed to withdraw. My behavior in these groups may in fact represent an accurate picture of one aspect of my behavioral repertoire, but it is hardly a very important part of my behavior. It is an aspect of myself about which I already have insight and it does not trouble me enough to want to change it. Since I do not believe that my skills in manipulation are any greater than those of most people of my educational level, I suspect that many other group participants were going through similar, more or less stereotyped maneuvers in order to enjoy the interactional process of the group without having their defenses threatened. Of course I am talking here about people who are not troubled when they enter the group and who do not see themselves as patients. Both of the groups in which I was involved were dedicated to the goal of growth rather than treatment. I suspect that most of the participants, including myself, were looking for distraction, fun, and excitement.

Another theoretical concern I have about groups is that it is often difficult to generalize the group experience to natural experiences in the community. Most interpersonal interactions in American life take place either within the family setting or in dyadic relationships. In ordinary social intercourse we are not involved with groups very often, except at work, at school, or at parties. At work or school the group's function is to complete some sort of task. At parties the major goal is having fun. The group therapy format, in which people are brought together and reveal themselves to one another in order to receive help and to grow, is not relevant to very many life situations. Of course the learning experiences within the group can to a large extent be generalized to dyadic and family relationships. But because the group setting lacks a certain naturalness, there is reason to doubt that this will happen. All of this makes me wonder if this highly individualistic society, which so esteems privacy, might not impose inherent limits on the group approach.

ETHICAL PROBLEMS

The ethical problems in group therapy are roughly similar to those in individual therapy, but there are some important differences. I have repeatedly noted that the helpful factors do not operate very effectively at the beginning of group therapy, but that they operate very powerfully once the group has developed a certain level of cohesiveness. The group does not have a great deal of influence on its members at the beginning of therapy, and this is reflected in a high dropout rate. Those who remain in the group, however, may be susceptible to an even more powerful source of influence than that imposed upon patients in individual psychotherapy.

It is extremely difficult for a patient to resist the persuasive powers of a group with which he is involved. The high potential for positive reinforcement is too seductive. A patient involved in a cohesive group will also be cautious about doing things that risk the group's displeasure. Here the fear of losing reinforcement will favor conformity. In such a climate there is always a danger that independent thinking, creativity, and a need for privacy can be labeled and quashed as antigroup behavior or resistance. We should remind ourselves that the group setting has been used for decades by various social groups to inculcate certain social or political attitudes into its members (London 1970). Groups are used to bolster conformity in both communistic and capitalistic nations. Therapy groups, of course, try to resist imposing a monolithic value system upon patients. But there is always the risk that a group will shape the patient's attitudes and values in a direction that may not be in his best ultimate interest.

The group can also be harmful to individual members. Those who are scapegoated and not sufficiently protected by the therapist can leave the group with markedly diminished self-esteem. Other participants may feel compelled to reveal themselves prematurely in a manner which they experience as demeaning or frightening. We know that the rate of casualties, or emotional disturbances, following involvement is high in encounter groups (Yalom and Lieberman 1971). While casualty rates may be equally high following interventions which have not been studied as extensively as encounter groups, the data on the potential harmfulness of these groups should not be ignored.

Sometimes the dangers of groups can be more eloquently expressed by those who have been serious participants and who have directly experienced the power of the group. The following excerpts are from a paper my daughter wrote during her junior year of college as an assignment for a course which consisted primarily of an encounter experience. She is directing her remarks primarily against the encounter movement, but some of her comments would be relevant also to many therapy groups.

POLLYANNA VERSUS THE GRINCH
by Judith Ann Halleck

This paper will be the battleground of a fight between Pollyanna and the Grinch. Pollyanna is that part of me that is seeking to find the redeeming good in my experience in Psychology 105; the Grinch is ferreting out all of the bad it can find. Within the actual experience, the Grinch won. I have walked away with bitter, sad feelings. If the Grinch wins this battle too, I don't believe that will be so bad. Time alters one's attitudes. The experience is still fresh to me. Later it will shift into a new perspective.

I have learned about group process from this experience, seeing how one group developed its norms and dealt with its problems. I've witnessed its effect on individuals, helping, curing, and disappointing. I have learned of its tremendous power and the power of the leader, seen them go to work on a scapegoat, felt the pressure of being the deviant, halfway succumbed to that pressure, and afterward felt my own strength in not having fallen total prey to the operation. I feel that I was wounded, but the cut was not too deep. Only one day has passed and already I feel my sense of autonomy growing.

So Pollyanna is cynical, but the "glads" she finds are genuine. I feel sadder but wiser, which qualifies as a "glad." I feel drained yet stronger. And I feel defeated but proud of myself. . . .

Groups are very powerful. Too powerful, I believe. Those people involved in the group movement have a grave ethical responsibility in their hands. The matter is complicated by the lack of really definitive data on group effects and how to control them. . . .

Rogers (1970) theorizes that the reason people fear that there will be traumatic effects in groups is that they really fear change. I cannot accept this explanation in terms of my own personal experience. He says that when people hear of a dramatic experience, they leap to the conclusion that groups are bad and psychologically destructive. I believe groups can be bad and destructive, and I do not fear change. I have worked very hard at changing myself for a long time. I have initiated change-oriented therapy and have actively altered my behavior. However, this is a very personal thing to me. If I make the mistake of joining an encounter group while working on self changes, I may risk psychological damage. Agendas may be pushed that I am not ready to tackle or that I have already resolved and need to reinforce not question.

There is a sort of change I do fear, and it is a very legitimate fear. That is coerced change. It may be quite covert and unintentional, but because the group is such a powerful influence on the individual, it can, and does, easily occur. This is what I was resisting so strongly. Yes, I can change. Yes, I can listen to feedback. Yes, I can be intimate and trusting and loving. Yes, I can break down and cry. Yes! Yes! Yes! I *can* do all of the things you want me to, but that's the barrier. You want me to—you the group, you the leaders—you want me to do these things to satisfy your needs, the need to help, psychological voyeurism, conforming to group norms. And I won't. It is not natural; it is forced.

I can, and do, do these things in the real world because it is real. An encounter group is an artificial community, or club, or clique—it's engineered. The people in the group are strangers not tried and true, trustworthy friends. Real, close friendships must develop through actual experiences with each other and be proven over time. A group is no place to be intimate. The importance of intimacy is denigrated if it can be achieved so readily and superficially. . . .

Self-disclosure itself as an issue. Are there really benefits to revealing one's inner depths to people who were strangers a short time ago and soon will be as distant as strangers again? Koch mentions the professor

Rogers describes, who was told to "come out from behind the lectern Doc" and subsequently revealed his innermost feelings to the group.

Koch (1971) asks: "Is it not possible that this 'perceptive' and contained man was pressured into relinquishing something gallant and proud in his make up? Is it not conceivable that even if disclosure had made him *feel* somewhat better, he had *become* somewhat less? Cracking masks, in Rogers's sense, could be therapy, but is could be brainwashing." I suspect the tone of this paper makes it obvious that I would answer *yes* to Koch's questions. I do think these are serious questions about a serious ethical dilemma in psychology.

When I entered the group I did not feel this strongly. I had instinctual fears that did not crystallize into anything easily grasped. Accused of wanting the experience to turn out badly, I'm not able to deny it. I thought I was trying to make things work out honestly and openly, but it may be that those uncrystallized feelings were more powerful than I thought. I may have hoped to fail to become an integrated member because, in retrospect, I am glad that I did not. I still like most of the individuals in the group very much but I do not like the group, and feel satisfied leaving it.

(Pollyanna got creamed.)

In the last decade there has been a disturbing trend toward coercing people to participate in encounter groups. Executives, government employees, students, and members of religious groups are sometimes urged to receive some type of training or encounter experience. Sometimes coercion is subtle. A person may be given a covert message that the group experience will make him a more efficient employee or that it may be a precondition for advancement. Students may be told that participation in a group is looked upon favorably by a professor or by an academic department. Sometimes coercion is direct. People may be told that they must participate in a group if they hope to hold on to their jobs, to advance in their work, to obtain course credit, or to graduate from a training program. Such coercive intervention can have a drastic outcome. I have treated several patients who were coerced into participating in encounter groups and whose disturbances were either precipitated or exacerbated by the experience.

Here we are dealing with a situation which exceeds the boundaries of ethical conduct. There is absolutely no justification for requiring a person who is not looking for help and who is not bothering anyone else to reveal himself in a group setting. There is no justification for imposing even subtle penalties upon people who resist the group experience because they do not enjoy it and wish to retain their privacy. Changes in current coercive practices could be facilitated if encounter group leaders would simply investigate the voluntariness of each participant's involvement and refuse to work with any person who has been coerced into joining. Malpractice litigation in this area would also help. Any person who is subtly or directly coerced into participating in a group and who feels damaged by the experience should have the opportunity to seek legal judgment against those who coerced him and perhaps against the group leader. I suspect that only this kind of litigation will decelerate the kind of evangelical commitment to the encounter experience which leads to coercive intervention.

Finally, the expansion of the group movement seems related to a general sense of alienation in American society (Packard 1972). I and others have written at length about the forces in American life that are contributing to alienation (Burrows and Lapides 1969, Marcuse 1964). One aspect of our current alienation is an enhanced experience of rootlessness. Even if we can identify with the values of a community, we may not stay in it long enough to feel part of it. Loneliness is a mounting problem in a society where so many are strangers. The group is an obvious antidote to loneliness. One of its purposes is to teach the participant how not to be lonely. But as long as the social environment remains alien, the new skills learned in the group setting may be inapplicable in the real world. If this situation remains constant, a point is reached at which group therapy becomes more than just a means of solving the problem of loneliness. It becomes the solution to the problem. Thousands of people in America have become "group addicts" who spend much of their spare time attending encounter groups and workshops. I suspect they are searching for something far more basic than symptom relief or emotional growth. I suspect they are searching for company.

It might be asked, What is wrong with people using the group setting as a means of finding the kinds of intimacy and honesty which may not be available in the family or community? Doesn't the group setting provide those essential ingredients of a humanistic existence which are now lacking in American life? Isn't an artificial intimacy better than none at all? I will acknowledge that group therapy and the encounter movement are probably fulfilling the humanistic needs of many Americans, but I am concerned about their popularity on two accounts. First, to the extent that the group compensates for deprivations of intimacy in American life, it distracts the participants from examining and dealing with the cause of this deprivation. When the group itself becomes the solution to a problem, we are tempted to diminish our efforts to find direct ways of resolving the problem. Accepting group therapy as a natural treatment for loneliness is tantamount to accepting the status quo. Second, I am concerned that the use of the group as a source for discovering intimacy leaves the individual too vulnerable to the dictates of others. The group, as I have noted repeatedly, is a powerful shaper of attitudes and values. Those who rely on the values of whatever group they are currently involved in for guidance in life must develop flexible life styles and are constantly susceptible to the influence of changing group values. Whether or not such rapid change really enhances their humanistic potential is debatable. People can also, of course, be influenced by the values of the family or community; but I believe that such influence, which is usually imposed upon an individual in early life, is clearly defined and consistent and does not create as great a need to compromise identity and autonomy as does reliance on groups.

Despite all of my negative criticisms of groups, I sometimes fear I am a latent "groupie." In the course of writing this chapter, I was asked to testify in a civil rights case in San Francisco and flew there one Sunday morning from the East Coast. I arrived in the early afternoon, very tired but unwilling to spend the few free hours I had in this lovely city resting in my hotel room. I had worked all through the plane trip and had not talked to anybody all day except for some stereotyped and meaningless interactions between myself and airline employees. I realized that I would be alone for several more hours and was intensely lonely. I began to wonder who I could call. I had some old acquaintances living in that area whom I had not seen in many years. It did not seem fair to intrude on their Sunday afternoon without warning. I had a few ex-patients and ex-students living in the Bay Area who would probably have felt honored or obligated to see me. But I felt that intruding upon them to ameliorate my loneliness would be an even greater discourtesy. Even if I possessed the skills to make casual friends at a bar, superficial conversation or even superficial sex would not have satisfied my hunger for intimacy. It was at this point that I began to yearn for a group. It occurred to me that it would be very nice if every American had the opportunity to join an organization which allowed him to drop in to a group meeting at a certain time, any day, no matter where he was. If a member knew that an instant group were available in any city he was visiting or to which he had moved, he could be constantly assured of a kind of intimacy that is simply not available in most aspects of American life. My fantasy went beyond the creation of a Kiwanis, Elks group, or church group. The group I was imagining would be structured around values of honesty, acceptance, and self-disclosure. It would demand nothing of me other than honest participation in the moment. It would provide me feedback and stroking in a climate largely created by a value system quite similar to my own.

When I returned home, I shared my fantasy with several colleagues. They surprised me by taking it seriously. One colleague thought it repugnant, but that it might be something that we would be seeing in the future. Another colleague, a prominent group therapist, suggested half jokingly that we develop the fantasy into a reality and create an organization (in which we would, of course, receive one percent of the membership dues) for providing this kind of group membership service throughout the country. For me, the fantasy and my discussion about it afterward served as a poignant reminder of the powers of the group to ameliorate loneliness. It will be interesting to see how these powers will be used in the future.

Chapter 9

Family Therapy

In contrast to all other interventions, family therapy is an intervention which consistently focuses upon a significant part of the individual's naturally occurring interpersonal environment. It is a treatment in which individuals who are a significant part of the patient's natural interpersonal environment are brought into the treatment and are seen together with the patient. The goal of family therapy is to increase the patient's comfort and effectiveness not only by changing the patient's behavior but also by changing the behavior of those who have been brought into therapy with him. (As I will note frequently throughout this discussion, techniques of behavior modification directed at manipulating interpersonal events are very helpful in facilitating the process of family therapy.)

There is no clear consensus among family therapists as to how much of the patient's natural environment should be brought directly into the treatment process. In the first part of this book I defined family therapy somewhat idiosyncratically as including conjoint work with any people who are involved in significant relationships with the patient, even if they are not members of the patient's nuclear or extended family. This definition is a generic one which incorporates many different kinds of efforts to influence patients by changing the natural interpersonal environment. The actual units treated may include married couples, members of the nuclear family, or members of the extended family. Sometimes a large group of individuals who have a significant relationship to the patient or to the nuclear family are included in treatment. This intervention is called social network therapy (Speck and Attneave 1972). Married couples may also be treated in groups and sometimes several nuclear families are treated as a group. The latter intervention is called multiple family therapy (Lacquer et al. 1964). My use of the term *family therapy* may be troubling to some readers since it includes therapy with people who are not really family members. I retain the term, however, because I do not want to coin a new and cumbersome phrase such as *natural interpersonal environmental therapy*.

WHO IS THE PATIENT IN FAMILY THERAPY?

In family therapy the therapist will become involved in transactions with the patient, with other family members, and with the family as a whole. The patient will have transactions with the therapist and with other members of the family. He will also have the opportunity to observe the therapist's interaction with other family members. All of this bears some resemblance to group therapy, but in a family setting the use of such multiple transactions creates a different set of theoretical, practical, and ethical issues. One of the most difficult issues is defining who is to be the patient. In the group everybody but the therapist and co-therapist are patients. In family therapy the question of who is being treated is more nebulous. There are three ways of dealing with this issue.

First, it is possible to keep the focus of treatment primarily upon the patient. Family members can be dealt with in terms of the manner in which they have helped to develop and sustain the patient's disturbance. They can be urged to behave in ways that might be more helpful to the patient on the basis of their concern for a loved one. They can be instructed as to how they might respond to the salutary changes the patient makes in therapy so that they are not overly stressed by these changes and do not interfere with them. Family members treated with this approach can be viewed either as helpers of the therapist who are participating in efforts to create the best possible environment for the patient or as participants in a therapeutic process in which they as well as the patient are expected to change. The latter view comes close to defining all participants in family therapy as patients.

In a second approach to the question of who the patient is, all participants in the family therapy process are unequivocally

Family Therapy

perceived as patients. Each family member is viewed as needing some form of treatment. Each is asked to change his behavior not only because it may be helpful to the original patient but also because it is assumed that it may be helpful to him. The family therapist's focus may often be on the original patient, but it can also shift, at times, to each member of the family. In effect, family therapy, like group therapy, can be used to treat several patients at the same time. A major justification of this approach is the common clinical observation that members of the patient's family are often as emotionally disturbed as the patient.

A third way of conceptualizing family therapy deals with the family as social system. Families have certain important functions such as providing an environment of intimacy and helping individual members deal with the community. In the course of fulfilling these functions, families develop rules and individual members must take on certain roles. These rules and roles govern much of the interaction of the family unit and, ultimately, the behavior of each of its members. Family transactions cannot be fully understood in terms of the interaction of individual personalities. They must be understood as events which are in large part determined by the rules and roles of a unique system. No individual who is a part of that system can be totally understood without understanding the total system. It is also impossible to bring about change in one element of that system without influencing all the other elements. Viewed in this light, family therapy can be considered an effort to treat the total family unit, or to treat the family as a system. The question of who the patient is becomes irrelevent. The entire family system is the patient.

Considerable clinical data support the systems approach. Anyone who has treated families has noted the tendency of family members to resist changes in one another, particularly change in the member who is viewed as the patient. Another common observation is that when the patient begins to behave in a more healthy, adaptive manner, other members of the family may become disturbed. It is extremely difficult to explain these events as simple transactions betweeen individuals who function autonomously. These events are best viewed as efforts upon the part of interdependent elements within a system to maintain homeostasis, or a steady state of equilibrium.

Some family therapists try to use all three approaches. They will insist that they are treating the person initially identified as the patient and the family system at the same time. Or they will insist that they are treating each family member and the family system at the same time. The longer family therapists practice, however, the more likely they are to become committed to exclusive reliance on the third treatment model, in which it is the family as a system rather than its individual components which must be treated. A commitment to treating a system rather than a patient or patients leads to modes of thinking and practice which will seem strange to the clinician who has not worked with families. Family therapists tend to deemphasize the pathology of the individual and to view pathology as residing within the family system. They view the person who seeks help, or who is defined as needing help, not as *the* patient but as the *identified* patient, the *designated* patient, or the *index* patient.

This kind of thinking is not easily accepted by the clinician, particularly by the clinician who is a physician trained to deal with individual variation and individual psychopathology. If family therapy is to be integrated into the medical model, the medical model must be expanded and made holistic. It is no longer possible to focus upon a dysfunctional aspect of one individual's existence and label it a disease. It becomes necessary to view human suffering and its alleviation in terms of a model that deals with a complex system of individual-environmental interaction. Although modern family therapy was developed largely by physicians, family therapists have had considerable difficulty in accommodating their conceptualizations to the realities of medical practice. One practical problem here is integrating the systems approach with the issue of health insurance. This problem is becoming more frequent in clinical practice. There have been times when I have hospitalized several members of a family in order to deal with the problems of a family system. On more than one occasion the insurors have refused to pay for any but the designated patient unless I would put a diagnostic label on the other family members. Sometimes these individuals were not experiencing any overt disabling symptoms, and I could not in good conscience label them. As family therapy and health insurance expands, our society will have to make decisions as to whether it wishes to insure the health of systems as well as the health of individuals. Insuring the health of all of the components of a social system makes sense to those who take a systems approach to the problems of mental health, but it is not easy to explain to nonpsychiatric physicians or to private or public insurance agencies.

ONE-DIMENSIONALITY

In my own family work I tend to begin by focusing on the individual identified patient and will not shift my focus to viewing all family members as patients or to viewing the family system as the patient unless certain conditions are met. I believe that systems-oriented family therapy is only one of many useful interventions and that it can be successfully combined with other interventions in treating emotionally disturbed patients. Unfortunately there has been a gradual retreat from eclecticism on the part of some of the more prominent family therapists. Some family therapists come close to insisting that it is futile and perhaps irrelevant to try to treat individuals. They view psychopathology or dysfunction as largely generated and sustained by family systems, and in their enthusiasm for the systems approach are prone to neglect the individual. I do not mean to imply that family therapists do not become deeply involved with individuals. As a group, family therapists are among the warmest and most sensitive clinicians I have known. In their more recent writings, however, a certain disdain toward other approaches has gradually emerged (Haley 1971). Systems theory is reified and invoked as a general explanation for all varieties of clinical phenomena. Such an approach is often more mystifying than enlightening. The explanations offered by systems theory are subtle, capable of multiple interpretations, and difficult to validate experimentally. The family therapy movement, like the psychoanalytic movement, is in danger of promulgating a rigid, one-dimensional approach to the treatment of emotional disorders. Several factors may be fueling this trend.

As family therapists have expanded their awareness of the impact of the environment upon the individual patient, they have become correctly preoccupied with the dangers of treatment that ignores the influence of the environment. If an emotional disorder is even partially based upon environmental or family determinants and if a clinician then views that disorder as residing totally within the individual, the environmental forces that created the disorder are strengthened. Labeling a suffering person as a patient and treating him outside the context of his environment can be a powerful factor in sustaining his illness. Family therapist are deeply sensitive to the issues involved in the politics of therapy. They see biological therapists, behaviorists, and other psychotherapists as unwittingly acting in collusion with the family to continue to support the scapegoating of the designated patient.

Family therapists are deeply concerned about iatrogenicity, or the capacity of socially sanctioned interventions directed at changing the individual to create and perpetuate illness. From everything I have said up to now, it should be apparent that I am quite sympathetic to their concerns. I do not believe, however, that the remedy for dealing with the deleterious effects of a one-dimensional approach which ignores the environment should be the adoption of a one-dimensional approach which ignores the individual.

Another reason why family therapists may be moving toward one-dimensionality is that they are caught up with the excitement of exploring the new vistas open to them once they have come to appreciate the influence of the environment. Family therapy is a relatively new intervention, having gained popularity only in the last two decades. It has not been dominated by the influence of any single individual but rather by a group of highly dedicated and innovative psychotherapists. The pioneers in this group began using family techniques quite independently of one another. When they began to share their findings, they did so with an air of exuberance and optimism that became contagious. Family therapists feel they have come upon a new way of conceptualizing emotional disorders and treating people which is intellectually exhilarating, emotionally gratifying, and likely to be helpful to most patients.

The more prominent family therapists are sensitive, charming, and charismatic. They have developed highly individualistic ways of operating. Some of them are delightfully playful and funloving. They proudly describe the family movement as being in a "healthy, unstructured state of chaos" (Ferber, Mendelsohn, and Napier 1972). Unlike many other practitioners they are open in their arguments and eager to expose their methods to one another. All of these qualities appeal to the *zeitgeist* of our times. Family therapy has a powerful appeal for practitioners, both young and old, who are looking for new and exciting ways to treat patients. Proponents of family theory have suddenly discovered that they can influence a large audience of mental health professionals. At the same time the field is too new to have accumulated much scientific data. Family therapy is dominated by fascinating theories and innovative techniques, but the validity of the theories and the efficacies of the techniques are unproven. In the field of mental health, there is an unfortunate tendency for the excitement and vibrancy of a new movement which has not yet begun to accumulate much data or to develop research methodologies to encourage a certain degree of mysticism and one-dimensionality.

TERRITORIALITY

Although most of the pioneers in family therapy have been psychiatrists, the field is remarkably open to input from all mental health professionals. The capacity to understand the impact of a complex system upon its individual components is not fostered by the training experience of any of the individual professions. Neither psychiatrists nor psychologists receive extensive training as to the impact of the environment upon individuals. Social workers have developed a keener sense of how family members influence the patient, since their role in mental health teams has traditionally been that of dealing with the patient's family. They have naturally been attracted to the family therapy movement and have been welcomed as respected practitioners. So far the field has enjoyed the benefits of a climate in which no single mental health profession has sought to own the right to practice family therapy. Family therapy is still a more or less revolutionary movement which fosters a high degree of egalitarianism. A psychiatrist who is committed to family therapy may have much more communication with, and respect for, a social worker who has similar commitments than he would have toward a fellow psychiatrist who does not do family therapy.

RESPONSIBILITY

In treating families the therapist must be concerned with the manner in which all participants deal with the issue of responsibility. Member's of the patient's family will vacillate between attributing responsibility for the patient's plight to the patient, to themselves, or to fate. When first interviewed, family members will frequently seem eager to blame the patient's condition upon events beyond anyone's control, such as bad genes or accidents. Early in treatment they may also express feelings that the patient has perversely brought his condition upon himself. Usually, however, if family members are allowed to talk about their feelings regarding the patient's disturbance to a noncondemning therapist, they will reveal that they have also been blaming themselves. Conjoint work with the patient and the family provides a unique opportunity to deal with the issue of responsibility in an equitable and more or less rational fashion.

Family therapists have developed some interesting ways of keeping people from hurting one another by irrational assignment of blame. These techniques help resolve unrealistic guilt feelings and maximize the sense of responsibility of all participants. The very act of bringing the family into the treatment gives the family a powerful message that the blame cannot be imposed solely upon the patient or upon the patient and fate. Bringing the family into the treatment gives them an implied message that they may have some responsibility for creating or sustaining the patient's disturbance. This message is quickly tempered, however, when family members realize that they need not sit by helplessly and watch the patient suffer. Once family members accept some responsibility for the patient's condition, they appreciate that they can help as well as hurt him. From the beginning of therapy, assignment of blame to family members is made in a very gentle manner. Family members may be told how they are hurting the patient, but they are not condemned for doing it. Rather, their oppressive behaviors may be labeled as misguided attempts to help the patient or as evidence that they too have serious problems.

The imposition of blame upon family members is also attenuated by efforts of family therapists to attribute responsibility to the patient. The patient may be told that he chose to behave in a certain maladaptive way in order to deal with family problems. One common technique family therapists use is to relabel the patient's symptoms and to define them as something the patient is doing for positive as well as for negative reasons. A young patient who becomes symptomatic may be told that he has created his disturbance in order to hold his parents' marriage together. Or a wife who has just had an affair may be told that she is just trying to "heat up" her marriage. The patient will then have difficulty in denying responsibility for behavior that has altruistic motivations. Labeling the patient as a responsible individual enables other family members to react to him with normal emotions of dependency, affection, and anger. They are free to treat the patient as an equal. At the same time each family member must assess his own role in creating conditions that encouraged the patient's symptomatic behavior. Blame is more or less equally distributed and no one is saddled with unrealistic guilt.

Family members are also told in therapy that many of their responses to one another are efforts to maintain the equilibrium of the family system. Gradually, family members begin to view that system as an impersonal force which has a power greater than any of its members. Family therapists do nothing to discourage this view. They try to give the message that each member may be accountable for his input into the family system, but that to the extent the system has an autonomous quality, no member need be too self-recriminatory with regard to the negative consequences of system malfunction. The system, in effect, becomes an element of fate for which no single individual is responsible. There is a rather subtle process involved here in which the intensity of self-blame of each of the participants is reduced.

GROWTH

Except when dealing with crisis situations, family therapists are concerned with the emotional growth of the patient and other family members. Generally, family therapists are even more vague than individual or group therapists in stating the values which determine growth. There is one aspect of growth, however, about which they are quite specific. They often define growth in terms of differentiation, or the capacity of each member to understand and accept his role in the family and to develop a role which allows for an identity outside the family. Sometimes a family member functions in an interdependent relationship to other family members, and sometimes he functions independently of the family. The clear demarcation of these activities and the acceptance of a proper blend of interdependence and independence are viewed as essential elements of emotional growth. In one popular school of family therapy, differentiation is defined in terms of the capacity of the individual to find an identity or sense of self which remains uninfluenced by the family relationship system (Bowen 1971). A differentiated individual, according to this view, has the capacity to approach tasks or functions in an intellectual or cognitive manner unencumbered by emotional attachments which would interfere with maximum performance.

However they define growth or differentiation, systems-oriented family therapists usually assume that growth in one family member will influence all other members. They believe that families may resist the growth or differentiation of a single member, but that if a single family member persists in his determination to grow or differentiate, other family members will eventually follow his example. Family therapists also believe that the process of family therapy will usually promote differentiation and diminish the tendency for participants to remain enmeshed in the family system. They will often insist that if the patient is to grow he must go back to the family and understand and confront the factors inhibiting his growth.

POWER IN FAMILY THERAPY

People who are signigicantly involved with one another will have many conflicts regarding power, and the issue is critical in family therapy. One important consideration is the power of the therapist. Once the family unit accepts the therapist as a person who will have some influence over family interactions, the family as a system has already changed. Introducing a new element into any system will modify the nature of transactions throughout the system. But the therapist must do more than just enter the family system. He must also find a way to direct it. Relationships in family therapy are often changed by the efforts of therapists to urge or persuade family participants to experiment with new modalities of interaction. The family therapist has sometimes been viewed as an individual who not only becomes an actor in the family play but may also become its director (Minuchin and Barcai 1969). Family therapists make no apologies as to their efforts to manipulate small social systems. They insist upon complete power to control the flow of interaction within their offices. During the therapeutic hour they often behave as benevolent despots. (My own observations of the more prominent family therapists lead me to believe that they are natural leaders who are rarely reluctant to take a benevolent form of control over chaotic situations.)

Therapists trained in the more unobtrusive and passive style characteristic of psychoanalytically oriented or nondirective individual psychotherapy may find the family therapist's unabashed and naked use of power somewhat shocking and even repugnant. In recent years I have presented many audiences the proposition that all interventions can be conceived of as political insofar as they endow the therapist with an enormous capacity to influence the distribution of power within social systems.

Individual psychotherapists, particularly psychoanalysts, have reacted to this message with anger, perplexity, or dismay. The response of family therapists has been, "So what else is new?"

In addition to being concerned with their own power, family therapists are also attentive to the distribution of power within the family system. Too much or too little power in one element of the system may result in system dysfunction, particularly when the system is under stress. In general, families function most effectively when there is a clear delineation and distribution of power based upon family rules and roles. Parents, for example, should have a certain degree of power to set family rules with regard to the children. Each family must negotiate rules which define the extent of influence each family member will have in decisions regarding finances, living arrangements, and family holidays or entertainment. The family therapist usually has personal views as to what are ideal or perfect distributions of power within the family. Many of his activities in therapy can be conceived of as efforts to have the family identify with these views and use them to develop their own rules for assigning power. In my own work I have developed a rather simple formula for determining distribution of power within family units. Greatest power should be assigned those with the greatest capacity or willingness to assume reponsibility (in the sense of obligation rather than accountability) for family functions and with the greatest knowledge to guide the family system in its tasks of providing a source of intimacy for one another and in relating to the community as a whole. This formula can be used by the therapist to provide a certain degree of rational input into the power struggles of family members.

Family therapists are also concerned with shifts in power which develop when the patient becomes symptomatic. They are interested not only in the manner in which labeling the patient sick may deprive him of power but also in the manner in which the patient can use his symptoms to control others. In carefully examining the patient's environment, family therapists note that symptomatic behavior often elicits new attitudes toward the patient and new interactions between other family members. These may be consciously or unconsciously wished for by the patient. Family therapists never view the identified patient as totally powerless. They may even consider him the person with the most influence upon the family system.

VARIETIES OF FAMILY STRESS

I have repeatedly emphasized the relationship of environmental stress, and particularly interpersonal stress, to emotional dysfunction. The clinician must have some idea as to how the behavior of those who interact with the patient can have an adverse influence. Environmental stress cannot always be described in stimulus-response language. It must be viewed also in terms of communication deficits and in terms of attitudes and of expectations significantly related individuals have of one another. Most of the theory in this area is derived from studies of married couples and nuclear and extended families. I will present some of the conventional theoretical material but will try also to describe the impact of stress upon other types of interpersonal systems.

Evaluation of the family environment requires that the clinician have some knowledge as to how people do things to one another in a way that makes one or more of them function maladaptively. A more succinct way of putting this is, How do people make one another miserable? There is ample evidence that the individual who experiences a large number of stressful events becomes more susceptible to physical and emotional dysfunction (Holmes and Rahe 1967, Engel 1960). Many of the more common stresses of life are generated in interpersonal systems. There is little disagreement among clinicians that high levels of interpersonal stress are, in a general way, correlated with emotional disorders. It is less clear, however, whether specific kinds of symptoms are generated by specific kinds of interpersonal stress patterns. Family theorists have at times claimed to have found patterns of family relatedness which are regularly associated with certain types of behavior disorders (Lidz 1969). These patterns of relatedness can be viewed either as a direct form of stress or as aspects of a dysfunctional system which make some individuals in that system highly susceptible to extrafamilial stress. Some family therapists who done extensive studies of families with schizophrenic children believe it possible to define certain maladaptive patterns of relationship within these families. They believe these relationship patterns are inherently stressful to the child who becomes schizophrenic and are a necessary but not sufficient condition for the appearance of schizophrenic behavior (Wynne et al. 1958). Other clinicians have tried to relate various kinds of family structure to delinquent behavior (Hallowitz 1963). All of this

Family Therapy

research is inconclusive. We have many interesting hypotheses, but at this time we are still speculating when we try to relate specific patterns of stressful interpersonal transactions to specific symptomatology. Most of the following material will describe how interpersonal stress creates symptoms, but little will be said about how it creates specific symptoms.

One of the most obvious ways in which people can make one another miserable is by being cruel. Rudeness, selfishness, and efforts to inflict physical and psychological pain upon others are unfortunate characteristics of human behavior. As a rule these behaviors are emitted by individuals with whom one does not have a close affectional relationship. But this is not always the case. People who live and work together in or out of a family relationship can also be cruel to one another. Cruelty is especially painful when it comes from individuals from whom one is seeking love or other varieties of positive reinforcement. Often the victim of cruelty has played some role in eliciting aversive responses from others. But some individuals may be victimized for reasons utterly beyond their control. A mother, for example, who is raising the child of a man who has abandoned her may express her angry feelings toward the rejecting spouse by treating the child cruelly.

Any naturally occurring group of peers may scapegoat a member whose behavior is slightly unusual or deviant. Groups of individuals working in a highly competitive setting such as a corporation or an academic department often create situations of intense rivalry in which some individuals are treated cruelly. People who are thrown together in a common living arrangement or who belong to an organization that is trying to accomplish a particular task may also hurt one another. Sometimes these groups create stress for certain members sufficient to make them become patients. This process and its treatment and prevention through a type of family therapy can be illustrated by the following examples.

A nineteen-year-old girl came into a student mental health clinic complaining of feelings of depression. Preoccupied with thoughts of suicide she related her difficulties to problems in living in a sorority where she felt ostracized and at times despised by other members. Her visit to the clinic had been precipitated by her overhearing a conversation in which several of her sorority sisters expressed the wish that she be asked to leave the sorority. The patient had joined her sorority because her mother had belonged to the same organization. From early adolescence her family had communicated their expectation that she would follow in her mother's footsteps. The patient's value system and orientation toward college, however, were quite different from those of most of her sorority sisters. She was a basically shy person who felt uncomfortable in large groups but who was highly devoted to her studies. She was not especially attractive and had little success in dating. During her early career in the sorority her fellow members tried to involve her in a variety of social experiences which the patient found discomforting and stressful. She perceived herself as a social failure and responded to this self-view by becoming more committed to her studies and more withdrawn from sorority activities. Her sorority sisters viewed her withdrawal as snobbishness. They began cutting her out of intimate conversations and ignoring her. During the year preceding her admission to the clinic, two different roommates with whom she lived briefly had asked for room reassignments. The patient made several good friends outside the sorority and made excellent grades, but as the academic year progressed, she found herself dreading going back to the sorority house at the end of the day. She wanted to feel more part of the sorority group but had no idea how she could do this. She suspected that many of her sorority sisters were saying malicious things about her behind her back, and when she overheard the conversation in which her sorority sisters expressed the hope she would leave, her worst suspicions were confirmed.

A major part of the therapeutic intervention with this girl involved asking her current roommate and the officers of the sorority to meet together with the patient and the therapist. During a two-hour session, the other sorority members were made more aware of the degree of the patient's pain and isolation. They expressed considerable guilt over their own behavior as well as concern for the patient. The patient became more aware that she had been behaving in a manner which others perceived as snobbish or arrogant. She also began to perceive the possibility that her sorority sisters could have positive as well as negative feelings toward her. The meeting ended with the patient resolving to try to participate more actively in sorority activities, with the other members feeling a commitment to become involved with the patient, and with some resolve on the part of all participants to try to sustain a more open pattern of communication. Following this group session the patient's symptoms were quickly alleviated. She remained in the sorority for another semester, sustained amicable but not close relationships with her sorority sisters, and then made a voluntary decision to resign. She did not experience further symptoms during her academic career.

Family Therapy

The choice of treatment in this case was crisis oriented. It can be argued that the patient might have benefited more extensively from some form of individual therapy or therapy with her nuclear family which would have helped her resolve certain self-defeating patterns of behavior or freed her from the oppressive influence of her parents. The decision for brief therapy with the group with whom she lived was made on the basis of my belief that the patient had considerable psychological strength and plenty of time to find ways of dealing with her maturational problems if she could sustain an appropriate degree of comfort. My hope was that modification of the oppressive factors in her immediate interpersonal environment would give her an opportunity to use her natural strengths to develop a more adaptive behavioral repertoire.

During the mid-1960s black athletes at many universities began complaining about discrimination against them by coaching staffs. At that time I was the director of student health psychiatry at a major university and was approached by black faculty members who asked if I could help with the problem on our campus. Together with a black colleague I arranged for a day-long meeting between the head coaches and representatives of both black and white athletes. In this session the black athletes expressed a variety of serious complaints cogently and powerfully. They were able to show how they were being oppressed both by the university system as a whole and by the various members of the coaching staffs. In the course of the meeting a great many things were learned about the university as a whole, but there was also considerable learning about the actions of various members of the athletic department. All participants gained greater awareness that the university system as a whole was not sufficiently concerned with the educational needs of the athletes. (At the time of the meeting no black athlete had ever managed to finish four years of school and graduate.) Some coaches were unaware that some of their actions toward black athletes were oppressive. The black athletes were unaware that some of the coaches' actions which they interpreted as racially oppressive were actually related to general coaching methods experienced as oppressive by white as well as by black athletes. The most surprising aspect of the meeting was the revelation of the great degree of affection all of the participants had for one another. As athletes they shared certain common bonds of respect and affection. These positive feelings had not previously been acknowledged. The meeting terminated with certain concrete recommendations for changes within the educational and athletic systems. Perhaps more important from the standpoint of therapy, it left the black athletes feeling more reassured that there would be some diminution of oppression within the educational and athletic systems (which turned out to be true) and it left all participants feeling closer to one another.

Those who are interested in the competitive aspects of university athletics might wish to know that there was no improvement in the athletic performance of any of the teams involved. The positive outcome of the intervention could only be described in terms of helping the participants learn to treat one another better, to feel better about themselves and others, and to function as a group in a manner which diminished the likelihood of some members being exploited.

While both of the above examples involved work with groups of people not related to one another by birth or marriage, the interventions were significantly different from those used in group therapy. The participants knew one another and did not share a common symptom. They were involved with one another on a day-to-day basis and quite capable of hurting one another. As naturally occurring groups, their dynamics were investigated and treated in the same manner as one would deal with a nuclear or extended family.

In nuclear and extended families interpersonal oppression is usually less blatant than in other naturally occurring groups. The most common way in which family members hurt one another directly is not through aversive behavior but through withdrawal of affection and support. The impact of withdrawal of reinforcement upon any individual will vary according to the nature and degree of that withdrawal, upon whether it is sudden or gradual, massive or slight. The person who experiences himself as losing affection and support he had previously become accustomed to enjoying is vulnerable to highly unpleasant affects such as anxiety or depression. If the person who is withdrawing has found new sources of reinforcement from other people or from other activities, the person who is being rejected also loses power in his relationship with the person who is withdrawing. If he wishes to regain power and to regain the support and affection of that person, he will have to make some changes in his own behavior. Sometimes the person who is feeling rejected may respond with anger, threats, or pleas. Quite frequently the anxiety and fear one

Family Therapy

experiences when reinforcement is diminished, or where there is a threat of its removal, is defined and elaborated as a symptom. Once the person who has experienced rejection is defined as a patient, the person who is withdrawing may become guilty and concerned. The patient often hopes that symptomatic behavior will allow him to recapture the affection of the loved one. Frequently this does happen, at least temporarily, and the existence of the symptom may alter the power equilibrium between the two individuals.

An endless variety of symptoms can be treated or sustained by this process. Many patients who develop symptoms labeled hysterical begin to do so as a response to withdrawal of reinforcement from their spouses. After several years of marriage one spouse, usually the husband, may begin to invest energy in his career or in other persons which was previously invested in his wife. If the wife cannot recapture his interests or develop alternative sources of reinforcement outside the marriage, she may develop symptoms such as sexual dysfunction, phobic behavior, or depression. This will bring her the attention she seeks from her husband, but such attention may also reinforce her symptoms. Eventually an equilibrium develops in which the marital relationship is sustained at the expense of one individual's becoming chronically symptomatic. (I am omitting the issue of the role the patient plays in allowing or sometimes even encouraging the initial withdrawal of the spouse. I do not mean to imply that the patient is a totally innocent victim of this process.) Hospitals in the United States are filled with patients who are disabled by this process. At the time I was writing this section, almost a third of the patients on my hospital service (some males as well as females) were suffering from symptoms directly related to this type of marital strife. Here are three representative cases:

A forty-year-old woman was hospitalized with a complaint of headaches over a period of two years which had been proved refractory to ordinary treatment. The patient had been treated by several doctors and received a number of thorough work-ups to rule out organic dysfunction. All of these evaluations failed to reveal the presence of structural or functional pathology. She claimed that only strong analgesics relieved her pain and had managed to obtain prescriptions for a number of drugs, including Demerol, which she used frequently. Doctors in her home community knew her well, felt defeated in their efforts to help her, and finally recommended she enter a psychiatric hospital. She did so reluctantly and for the first few days of hospitalization refused to admit to any emotional problems. She talked mostly about her pain and her need to receive large amounts of analgesics. After a few days, however, she became more comfortable in the hospital setting and was able to discuss some of her interpersonal difficulties. The headaches had appeared shortly after a local industry where she was employed closed down, and she was unable to find another job. There were other important stresses in her life. Her father had died two years prior to the onset of the headaches, and the patient had felt much more responsible for the care of her mother, with whom she had always had a conflictual relationship. She was also experiencing difficulty in raising her adolescent children. She resented their demandingness and rebelliousness but worried that they would soon be leaving home. The last problem which the patient discussed was her marital relationship. In the early years of the marriage she and her husband had been quite close. With the birth of the children he seemed to become much more involved in his job and spent more time with male friends and less time at home. She also suspected that he had begun having extramarital affairs. By the seventh year of her marriage she had lost interest in sex, and three years later her husband also seemed to lose interest. She and her husband lived together in a casual and cool manner, holding occasional conversations about family tasks or the children but rarely talking about their feelings toward each other and rarely having any kind of intimate moments, sexual or otherwise. During these years the patient saw herself as gratified by her children, her friends, her status in the community, and her job. With the death of her father and her need to deal with her mother and adolescent children, the patient tried to get closer to her husband but was unsuccessful. She continued to derive considerable satisfaction from work and friends. When she lost her job, however, and could not find another one, she felt helpless.

Once the patient's headaches began, she spent more time in bed and less time taking care of household chores. Tasks of housecleaning and meal preparation were often left to the husband and children. She noted that her husband became more solicitous and concerned about her whenever she was in great pain. As her headaches continued her husband began to spend more time at home; he took her to various doctors and became very preoccupied with her condition. He even began to show a new kind of tenderness in relating to her.

When the rest of the family was brought into the conjoint interview, they fully confirmed the patient's story. The husband admitted that his relationship with his wife had been quite distant during the years preceding her disturbance, but that they were getting closer now. The children noted that they had been more solicitous toward their mother since her headaches had developed.

A thirty-eight-year-old married woman was admitted to the hospital after deliberately taking 100 milligrams of Valium. This was her third apparent suicide attempt in the past two years. She complained of sadness, loneliness, and a feeling that life was not worth living. These symptoms had gradually developed during the preceding four years. The patient was frank in discussing her current living situation as unsatisfactory and ungratifying. Her main activities in life were taking care of her household and her three preadolescent children. Her husband was preoccupied with a highly successful career as a business executive and was gone from the home for long periods of time. The patient bitterly stated that his career came first, his children second, and she third. Prior to her marriage at twenty-four, she had seen herself as a career-oriented person, and had, during the early years of her marriage, worked as a physical education instructor. With the birth of the children, however, she and her husband began to have bitter struggles about the issue of her working. In the course of these struggles both partners became distant from each other. The patient fought hard for her liberation, but the husband was unrelenting and finally had his way. By the time the third child was born the patient was resigned to not working and to staying home and taking care of the children. As her bitterness over this situation grew and as her husband's distancing increased, the patient's dysphoric moods became more frequent and of longer duration. Her husband could not empathize with her sadness and was not very interested in hearing about it. After her first suicide attempt he became much more concerned about her. He began to spend more time at home, but his new attention toward her was focused upon viewing her as a patient. In the first conjoint family session he insisted upon viewing her depression as a disease which he expected to be quickly treated. He assumed that successful treatment would enable her to return to her functions as a housewife and would free him to pursue his previous activities.

A forty-eight-year-old professor of English was hospitalized for symptoms of alcohol abuse and depression. He had been symptomatic for approximately three years. Before his difficulties began, his career had been moderately successful and he had felt that his family life was gratifying. During the early years of his marriage his wife, an extremely bright and well-educated woman, had contented herself with staying home and taking care of the house and children. In her late thirties, however, she went back to work as a teaching assistant at the same university at which the patient was employed. She was highly successful in her work and began gaining job promotions at the same time that her husband's career was stagnating. Her work took her away from home on many evenings, and she also began to do a lot of traveling. At first the patient was pleased with his wife's success and proud of her, but he gradually began to feel neglected by her and overshadowed by her accomplishments. His serious drinking and depression began at a time when it became clear that she would soon be offered a high level position in the university administrative structure. His hospitalization was actually precipitated by her having received an offer to become a dean at the university. Shortly after he heard of the offer, he went on a three-day drinking spree and threatened to hang himself. The wife responded to his behavior by assuring him that she was willing to forgo her advancement at work if he was too sick to be able to tolerate the diversions of attention from him which would be required by her new job.

 In each of these cases there were of course factors other than withdrawal of intimacy in the marital relationship which contributed to the patient's disturbance. In each case, however, this withdrawal followed by a certain degree of intimacy once the patient became symptomatic was a factor that had to be dealt with if the patient's symptoms were to be alleviated. In cases of this type conjoint marital therapy can be helpful for a variety of reasons. It helps the patient develop a clear sense of the nature of the problem and to separate the role of his own behavior from the marital interaction as causative factors in his disturbance. Defining the problem also provides direction for using family therapy to initiate change. Sometimes the partners can renegotiate their marital situation in a manner satisfactory to both. In other instances the patient may learn to develop new ways of dealing with a marriage in which levels of intimacy will remain minimal. Sometimes it becomes clear that modifications cannot be made and that the best solution is divorce. Any of these changes may alleviate symptoms.

 Profound emotional reactions are also likely to develop when one partner in a relationship threatens a complete withdrawal of reinforcement by trying to end the relationship. When two people have been intimately involved with one another over a long period and one wishes to dissolve the relationship while the other does not, the person who wishes to continue the relationship is likely to be badly hurt. The pain is especially deep when the withdrawing partner has found a new love object. Threatened or actual dissolution of such intimate relationships between men and women are becoming quite common in America. With an increased acceptance of sex before marriage, many individuals now experience several prolonged and intimate relationships during their premarital years. Each termination of a relationship puts one of the partners at risk of becoming depressed. The marital contract is also providing less and less assurance of permanence. As divorce rates climb, emotional responses to separation which reach clinical proportions also seem to increase. Middle-aged women are especially vulnerable to being abandoned. They have often invested much of their lives in their husbands and families and are ill prepared to deal with the world on their own. Their emotional responses to threatening or impending divorce are, not unexpectedly, powerful. Among younger people, one sees emotional problems as a response to separation somewhat more frequently among women, but this situation is changing rapidly. As we approach greater equality between the sexes, young males are being rejected almost as often as young females, and their response to rejection is just as intense.

Some people seem to weather the stress of unwanted separation by experiencing a mild depression of several months' duration and then finding a new interest or a new partner to compensate for the loss of reinforcement. These people seem to view their discomfort as part of the natural trials and tribulations of life, and they do not become patients. But some individuals who are rejected become symptomatic. Symptoms are more likely to develop when the withdrawing partner is caring enough or guilty enough to respond to the rejected person's misery by promising to remain in the relationship at least temporarily. The rejected person observes that his misery forestalls separation and is likely to escalate his suffering and define it as an illness. This situation is especially pernicious when the withdrawing person provides ambivalent or mixed messages about his desire to remain in the relationship while he actually wishes to get out. The patient then has little chance of recapturing the positive qualities of the old relationship, has no opportunity to work through separation in a more or less adaptive manner, and is likely to remain seriously symptomatic in an effort to hold on to whatever remnants of the relationship are still available. This process also fills our hospitals with patients.

A twenty-four-year-old male graduate student was transferred to a psychiatric ward from an intensive care unit after recovering from the effects of an overdose of aspirin. He related his suicide attempt to despondency over his girl friend's wish to terminate their relationship. They had been living together for over a year and had been seriously contemplating marriage. Two months prior to the hospitalization, the girl friend had become interested in another man. She gradually began to hint to the patient that she was not ready to get tied down in a permanent relationship and wanted the option to see other men. He resisted this vehemently. Several weeks before the patient's suicide attempt, she suggested that they stop living together. He pleaded with her to change her mind, but she was persistent. His suicide attempt occurred the day she was to move out. During the first two days of his hospitalization on the psychiatric ward, the patient was morose, talked about the hopelessness of his future, and wished that he were dead. On the third day his girl friend visited him and during a very emotional and tearful interaction told him that she now realized how much he cared about her and how much she was hurting him and that she would rescind her decision to move out. At this point the patient's symptoms completely abated, and he asked to leave the hospital. At the same time the girl friend requested an interview with me and informed me that she really did not want to continue the relationship. She had told him that she would return to live with him because she couldn't bear to hurt him anymore. She admitted that she really wished to move in with her new lover and hoped that we would cure the patient's depression as soon as possible so that she would be free to do this. I told the girl friend that sooner or later she would have to be honest with the patient and that it would make sense for her to do this while he was still hospitalized. She reluctantly agreed. I saw both of them together for several sessions, during which it became apparent that she was quite ambivalent about leaving the patient. Some part of her promise to continue to stay with him had been determined by her guilt and concern about him, but another part was determined by real and longstanding affectional ties which were still present. At the same time she was able to say that while she was ambivalent, she was leaning toward terminating the relationship. As the girl friend moved back and forth in her resolution to leave or stay, the patient's symptoms escalated or diminished in accordance with her position. Eventually she made a clear statement that she was going to terminate the relationship, stop seeing the patient, and stop participating in couple therapy. The patient again became suicidal at this point and had to be kept in the hospital for three more weeks. Once the acute risk of suicide was diminished the patient entered individual psychotherapy as an outpatient. He gradually worked through his feelings about the separation, found new interests, and began to regain a sense of confidence and health.

A forty-eight-year-old woman was admitted to the hospital with symptoms of crying spells, insomnia, anorexia, and suicidal ruminations over the last two months. During this time she had lost ten pounds. Her symptoms were directly related to her husband's having asked for a divorce. Once the symptoms appeared, the husband agreed to delay divorce proceedings, but he continued to talk about his intention to eventually leave, and the relationship between the couple became strained and distant. The husband was a successful physician. The couple had married while he was still in medical school and she was working as a nurse. For the most part she had viewed her marriage as successful and happy. One of her children was still in college and two others were successfully pursuing careers. Both the patient and her husband had enjoyed his financial success, and both were active socially. Many people in the community considered them an ideal couple. During a conjoint marital interview it became apparent that the husband, who was in his early fifties, was experiencing a type of existential crisis. He had made all the money he needed, was somewhat bored with his work, missed his children, and felt that his wife was becoming prematurely old and unattractive. He had become sexually involved with a young woman who was a former patient, and while he was ambivalent about marrying her, he felt that his current marriage was strangling him and that he had to get out. The wife saw herself as betrayed. She had given up her nursing career to be a housewife and mother, and felt that she had no capacity to find a gratifying role in life without her husband's continued support. She could not conceive of the possibility of finding another man. The husband's decision to temporarily postpone divorce proceedings did not seem to relieve the patient's symptoms, and she was treated with antidepressant medication. This resulted in some relief. As conjoint marital interviews continued during her hospitalization, it also became apparent that both partners wanted to continue to work together on the issues of their aging, the departure of their children, and their inability to gratify one another at this stage of their marriage. Conjoint marital therapy was continued on an outpatient basis. On several occasions the children were brought into the therapy session. The patient's depression gradually improved and antidepressant medication was gradually withdrawn. In this case the couple decided to stay together.

These cases, in addition to illustrating one of the ways in which family stress creates symptoms, also illustrate some of the dangers of failure to explore and treat the environment. If a conjoint approach had not been used in the first case, it is quite likely that the patient would have been exposed to ambivalent and often dishonest messages, which may have eventually resulted in escalation of his symptoms and possible suicide. The patient was not able to find a new and nonsymptomatic adaptation until he had experienced the reality of his girl friend's departure. In the second case, treatment of the patient designed to change only her and not the natural environment might have alleviated her depression but would have deprived the husband of the opportunity to receive help he badly needed and might have pushed him toward a separation which was neither in his nor his wife's best interest.

FAMILY STRESS AND FAMILY THEORY

Up to this point I have dealt with interpersonal stress within family systems insofar as it can be directly related to the apparent needs and motivations of individuals. There are more subtle forms of interpersonal stress in family systems which can only be understood by examining complex transactional processes. Here it becomes necessary to examine both the manner in which family members communicate with one another and the unconscious needs or motivations of individuals within the family system. Much of the following material is based on theories proposed by various family therapists to explain the behavior of members of nuclear and extended families. It has less relevance for understanding the transactions of those who are not related by genetic origin or by marriage.

Family members may be stressed when communication processes within families are deficient. Many people are unskilled in communicating their needs and feelings to loved ones. If a husband is not told by his wife that she likes him to behave in certain ways during lovemaking, he will be unsuccessful in pleasing her; she is then likely to become less affectionate toward him. Her inability to communicate her needs and expectations puts both of them in a stressful situation. Children who do not have a clear idea of what their parents expect of them will also be stressed. They want to please their parents and receive affection for being "good," but they cannot be "good" unless parents let them know how they expect them to behave. Children are especially vulnerable when they receive different and conflicting messages as to what each parent expects of them. Sometimes such messages put the child in a position where he cannot please one parent without displeasing the other (Blos 1962). Since the child needs the love of both parents and wishes to please both, any actions he takes in response to their communication may bring him stress and pain.

In one form of communication which has been extensively studied and which is believed to be especially stressful to children, the child is given messages that provide two differing and usually contradictory injunctions (Bateson et al. 1956). A parent may say one thing, yet seem to mean another by his voice or gestures. The child, for example, might be encouraged to express a courageous opinion and then, when that opinion is expressed, it will be disparaged by the parent—who encouraged it—as unloving, disloyal, or disobedient. The paradoxical element of communication is even more evident when a parent gives the child a message that he wants the child to express anger toward him or to be more independent. There is no way the child can act in an angry or independent manner without satisfying the wish of the parent and therefore the child cannot truly be angry or independent. Children who frequently receive such communication from parents and who are conditioned from an early age not to inquire as to the exact meaning of the parent's communication can become dependent, angry, self-punitive, and lacking in trust in their own capacity to use language to communicate. The relationship of exposure to this kind of communication during early childhood to subsequent development of severe emotional disorders, such as schizophrenia, has been postulated but certainly not proved (Jackson and Weakland 1959). There is considerable clinical evidence, however, that this kind of communication is frequent in families of disturbed children and that it is usually stressful to children.

Family members may also communicate in ways that are not responsive to one another's needs. People do not always listen to one another attentively. They may be so preoccupied with their own needs that they fail to respond to either verbal or nonverbal cues in a manner which meets the needs of others. A request on the part of one family member for certain responses on the part of others may be ignored, misunderstood, or reinterpreted in terms of the requesting party's motivations. A husband who requests more intimacy from his wife may find her unresponsive. If he persists, she may tell him to stop bothering her and that he is only interested in sex. If the husband is simply seeking more intimacy, his wife's response will be highly stress inducing. An adolescent may ask his parents for permission to have later hours because he wants to feel more mature and responsible. His parents may respond to this request with a quick No, and if he is persistent, they may tell him that he is only looking for more time to run around and do things that are bad for him. Such a response is obviously stressful. Sometimes a request for cognitive communication may be responded to emotionally, or a request for emotional interaction may be responded to cognitively. An adolescent may ask how much of an allowance he will be receiving in the next month so that he can prepare to meet his expenses and find that his parents loudly criticize him for always wasting money. A wife who has prepared an excellent dinner and dressed seductively in the hope of having an exceptionally romantic evening with her husband may receive no response from him other than a compliment to the effect that she cooks well and looks nice. Here stress is created by the unwillingness or inability of one family member to respond at an appropriate emotional cognitive level to another.

It is obviously desirable that family members communicate with one another in as honest a manner as possible. This does not always happen. Spouses may lie to one another, parents may lie to children, and children may lie to parents. Any kind of dishonest communication is eventually stressful to one or another member of the family system, because it deprives family members of the accurate knowledge they need to deal with one another. The most common cause for lying is fear of losing affection. People will often distort the truth so that they can be seen in the best possible light by those whose affection they seek. Another motive for lying is to gain power. The person who distorts information presented to others retains more accurate information than others and can use this information to gain control of subsequent interactions. Occasionally lying between various family members can be conceived of as altruistic. It is sometimes unwise for married couples to discuss their premarital sexual experiences too extensively with each other or to be too open about their sexual fantasies toward others once they are married. In some marriages it may be unwise for the spouses to be too open in discussing extramarital affairs with one another. It is also usually unwise to burden children with too much information about difficulties parents are having in their own lives and particularly about difficulties they are having with one another. The keeping of secrets becomes less altruistic when involved family members begin to suspect a secret is being kept. In such a situation imagination tends to run rampant, and fantasies as to what is happening or has happened are likely to be more stressful than hearing the truth. Often the revealing of a secret within a family situation will drastically relieve the burden of unrealistic fears and fantasies which the symptomatic member has experienced.

Several years ago I treated a woman who became seriously depressed following an extramarital affair. Her husband knew about the affair but did not behave punitively toward her, and the patient responded well to individual psychotherapy. Two years after her affair, the patient began to suspect her husband of having an affair of his own. Her suspicions were based on a gradual cooling of his ardor for her and some deterioration of the intimacy of their relationship. She was absolutely convinced that if he did get involved with another woman, he would leave her forever. When she asked him about extramarital activities, he denied them. Gradually, the patient became preoccupied with alternating feelings of anger at her husband and fear of abandonment. Eventually she became depressed and reentered therapy. This time I interviewed the couple conjointly, and while the husband initially denied extramarital involvement, after several sessions he admitted that he had recently slept with several women. He insisted that he was not emotionally involved with any of them and had no wishes to leave his wife. The patient was markedly relieved to have this information. She learned that her suspicions were not based on faulty reality testing, she was reassured that her husband had no intentions of leaving her, and she felt much less guilty about her own indiscretions. The couple's marriage did not continue on a stable path, but the revelation of the secret did relieve the patient's depression.

Much of the therapeutic work in family therapy is focused upon communication. The family therapist must pay careful attention to the quality of communication between family members and must note the presence of defective, unresponsive, inconsistent, or dishonest communication. Family members must be taught to communicate clearly, directly, and honestly. They must also learn to become better listeners and to respond to the communications of others without discounting or negating what others are saying.

Another important source of stress in family systems is related to the tendency of family members to develop unrealistic and unfulfillable expectations of one another. The influence of such expectations may be powerful. A husband may hope that his wife will treat him as his mother did and expect her to develop his mother's qualities. Similarly, a wife may try to make her husband more like her father. In other marriages, people may try to extinguish in their spouses any traits that remind them of their parents. In most marriages each partner makes some effort to mold the other into an idealized image, and that image is heavily shaped by experiences with parents. In its most benign form, this process is resolved by communication, negotiation, and accommodation. In some marriages, however, the efforts of one spouse to put another into certain unrealistic roles are relentless. The battles over such role assignment may create considerable marital turmoil, an obvious source of stress.

Further stress is created when one of the partners is willing to behave unrealistically, according to the other's desire. Sometimes a spouse will accept an irrational role assignment because it fills some of his or her immature needs. It is not uncommon to see marriages in which one partner is highly dependent upon the other, almost to the extent that he or she is being fathered or mothered by the other. These marriages may have a certain stability, but they leave both members vulnerable to dysfunction when the family is forced to deal with such developmental tasks as raising children, or with crisis situations in which the spouse who has assumed the parental role is disabled or otherwise prevented from carrying on this function (Pittman et al. 1966).

Family therapists are especially impressed with the capacity of families to relentlessly cast certain children in certain roles (Framo 1965). A particular child may be labeled the bright one, the aggressive one, the slow one, the helpless one, or the bad one. Such role assignment, which may have little or no basis in reality, can begin very early in that child's life. While labels or roles may be assigned on the basis of minimal or nonexistent data, the expectations of parents and their efforts to see them realized lead to self-fulfilling prophesies. The child who resists an irrational role assignment may risk exclusion from the family system. Eventually he begins to act as his parents expect him to act and his behavior is then cited as evidence of the accuracy of their designation. Any kind of extreme and irrational role assignment can cause difficulty in the family system. The child who is viewed as the responsible one may be asked to take on responsibilities he is not ready to assume. The child who is designated the bad one may be scapegoated, and, as his defensive responses to such scapegoating are then cited as evidence of his badness, he risks being defined as a patient. In another form of unrealistic or irrational role assignment, children may be encouraged to gratify their parents vicariously by indulging in behavior the parents may have fantasied enjoying but never did. This type of mechanism is sometimes invoked as an explanation of juvenile delinquency (Johnson and Szurek 1952).

A particularly common and highly maladaptive form of irrational role assignment involves casting children in roles where they are asked to accept some of the responsibilities and powers which should belong to one of the parents (Framo 1970). One or another parent may relate to a particular child in a manner which requires the child to provide that parent emotional gratification not provided by the spouse. The child is not only forced to assume responsibility prematurely but also risks rejection by the parent whose functions he replaces. This kind of irrational role assignment is often referred to as *role blurring*. Children can also be stressed by putting them in the role of perpetual child (Satir 1964). Some families actively resist allowing the child to accomplish the developmental task of separating from the family. The child is loved if he remains childish, unloved if he seeks maturity. This pattern is often combined with role blurring. The child may be prevented from maturing because demands are made upon him to fulfill relationship needs with one of the parents, needs usually fulfilled in exclusive transactions between parents.

Family theorists place heavy emphasis upon irrational role assignments and role blurring in explaining a great deal of maladaptive individual behavior. Their emphasis is not supported by experimental data but rather is based on inferences made as the therapist observes family members interacting with one another. These inferences have led to elaborate theories of family system pathology which are often quite useful for providing direction for family intervention.

One explanation of irrational role assignment is borrowed from some of the more obscure and esoteric aspects of psychoanalytic theory (Fairbairn 1952). It is assumed that parents who have a great deal of influence upon their child will continue to exert that influence as the child matures to adulthood, even if they are not in direct contact with their offspring. The influence of one's parents can, in effect, be viewed as incorporated into every individual's psychic apparatus. Every person has mental images of parents and other significant figures, and these images exert a guiding influence over his behavior. The images may be even more influential when the incorporated object has been lost through death or other forms of separation. As a rule the internalized images represent both the positive and negative aspects of the relationship between the individual and his parental figures. Psychoanalysts believe that these positive and negative feelings toward introjected objects can then be projected onto spouses and children. In theory this process may help the individual symbolically recapture the old love objects now represented by members of the current family. The individual will relate to real family members as though they were significant figures in his past life and in so doing will protect himself from the pain of loss and mourning. Reality factors, of course, have some influence in such role assignment. A child who has some characteristics in common with a departed parent is likely to be related to in ways reminiscent of how the individual related to the parent.

This type of explanation may not appeal to those who are unfamiliar with psychoanalytic metapsychology, but it does provide one way of understanding how a parent or spouse can develop highly unrealistic expectations of other family members and can work in a relentless manner to see these expectations fulfilled. It also provides some directions for treatment. If each participant in the family system can know why he is projecting a role onto someone else, or why he is being asked to accept a projected role, the motivations to continue the process may be weakened and the motivations to resist it strengthened. In situations in which it is hypothesized that one or more parents are projecting aspects of their own parental introjects onto children, it also makes sense to have the parents talk about and try to reexperience problems with their own parents and perhaps to go through a process of mourning and accept the fact of separation from their parents.

A more common and less convoluted explanation of irrational role assignment, or role blurring, is derived from theories as to how families define and sustain the role functions of various members (Minuchin 1974). The family system can be divided into subsystems which have specific survival and developmental tasks. In a family with children the children alone or the parents alone can be viewed as a subsystem. Each subsystem has boundaries which can be considered the rules defining how the subsystems interact. Boundaries protect the differentiation of the family system. If they are too rigid and particularly if they are too ill-defined, the family is prone to dysfunction. Families lacking well-defined boundaries between subsystems may relate to one another quite intimately and may function adequately while not under stress. Their members, however, are not thought of as having differentiated or individuated in terms of role or function. They are often spoken of as intermeshed in the family system or trapped in the "undifferentiated family ego mass." When situations related to new developmental tasks or crises arise, some component or individual in the family system is unable to assume the differentiated role function that would enable him to cope.

Role blurring is most likely to occur when the parent subsystem is functioning in a manner which provides its members insufficient gratification. Communication problems between parents, their power struggles, their efforts to assign irrational roles to one another, or their tendency to withdraw from one another may lead to a situation in which one of the parents turns to a child for gratification of needs that should be filled by the spouse. If one accepts this kind of explanation, an important task of family therapy is the definition of boundaries between subsystems, in this case the parental subsystem and the child subsystem, and finding ways of strengthening the parental subsystem by helping the spouses develop more gratifying transactions.

A third type of explanation of irrational role assignment, or role blurring, which is in many ways similar to the second is based on the concept of three-person relationships or triangles (Bowen 1966). It is assumed that two-person relationships are inherently unstable and that some tension is created whenever such relationships are in danger of becoming more intimate or more distant. A state of equilibrium is then created by involving a third party in the transaction. The communications to and expectations of the third party reflect needs and functions which are more appropriate to transactions between the original dyad. In family systems a parent may attack a child when he is angry at a spouse. Or a child may be used to take sides in an argument between the parents. In each of these examples an interactional triangle is created. Some family theorists view the family as a series of such interlocking triangles in which various members are regularly put into roles which are not congruent with their actual needs or sense of selfness (Bowen 1965). If these explanations are accepted, one focus of family therapy must be on helping all participants become aware of the parts they play in the process of triangulation so they may avoid or control their continued participation in these roles.

Some family therapists believe that the dysfunctional system can be broken by inducing a shift in the triangle. This can be done by getting one of its participants to behave in ways congruent with his sense of selfness. These therapists will work with various dyads involved in the interactional triangle in an effort to help the triangulated parties achieve separateness. It is not uncommon for family therapists who adopt this explanatory system to work only with the parents of a disturbed child. The child, who is the identified patient, may be left out of therapy altogether. Therapists of this orientation sometimes work with a single individual in an effort to diminish triangular interaction and consider such work a form of family therapy.

One interesting corollary to the concept of triangulation is that the family therapist is also at risk of being used to resolve emotional conflicts within two-party systems by becoming triangulated or enmeshed in their conflicts. Family therapists committed to the concept of triangulation believe that if they can continue working with families without becoming enmeshed in the family system, they will have established a therapist-family relationship which may in itself be a sufficient condition for change.

It will be useful to remind the reader once again that this type of explanation is based not on experimental data but on clinical inference. It should be noted also that much of family stress theory is relatively new, and I have not, in the above synopsis, even begun to capture its richness or intricacies.

INDICATIONS FOR FAMILY THERAPY

Indications for the use of family therapy should be based on evaluation of the family system. In the course of evaluation some therapeutic work will be done, but the main function of the evaluation is to give the clinician some idea of how other family members or the family systems are influencing the patient. While family *therapy* may not be indicated for all patients, family *evaluation* is. It is common these days for some practitioners to claim that treating certain patients by using or not using certain interventions is poor clinical practice or even malpractice. As a rule, such statements are overdrawn and unnecessarily provocative. It should be abundantly clear from everything that has been said up to now, however, that I am convinced that treating a patient without attempting to evaluate his environment is poor clinical practice. The family is perhaps the most significant part of the patient's environment, and its evaluation should be routine.

Some clinicians would argue that the family can be evaluated without having them meet conjointly with the patient. Although the practice of interviewing and even counseling the patient's family in separate sessions has for many decades been common clinical practice, I consider it a distinctly inferior manner of obtaining data on how the family influences the patient. When parents, spouses, or children are interviewed independent of the patient, they may be able to provide useful historical information. But in this kind of family evaluation there is little opportunity to observe how family members interact with one another and how they stress or reinforce the patient. There is little opportunity to observe how the patient influences the family and none to accomplish even minimal therapeutic work. Finally, there is the risk that failure to interview all family members together may simply reinforce the patient's illness role or scapegoated position. When family members are seen separately, neither they nor the patient is likely to gain sufficient appreciation of the impact of the family system upon the patient, whose maladaptive behavior is likely to be defined as the total problem.

In evaluating the family conjointly, the therapist looks for all the kinds of stress I have described in the previous section. He tries to determine the extent to which people are hurting one another, either directly or through withdrawal of affection. He looks for defective or idiosyncratic patterns of communication and for irrational role assignment or blurring in family roles. He also tries to determine how the patient's symptoms influence the family system. Finally, he evaluates the manner in which family members may be reinforcing the patient's disorder. (I have not devoted much space here to the importance of reinforcement in family systems because the issue was discussed at length in the first part of the book and will be discussed further in a later part of this chapter.) If the clinician determines that family stresses and reinforcements are important factors in creating or sustaining the patient's illness, he should recommend family therapy.

It is, of course, easy to find something wrong with any family, and family therapists are prone to overdiagnose pathology in the family system. In fact family theorists who believe that symptoms are always related to family dysfunction will always find something wrong with the family system. My own position is that not all those who become patients are part of dysfunctional family systems. The patient is a part of many social systems other than the family, and these systems can create just as much stress for him. (The educational system is often given insufficient attention in evaluating the environment yet can play a role in creating transient or recurring symptoms in many young people.) Some symptoms may be determined primarily by biological factors, and the family's strained relationship with the patient may be a response to dysfunctional behavior rather than its cause. Sometimes the family system may have played a role in the development of the patient's symptoms but may subsequently have changed to the extent that its current influence on the still symptomatic patient is minimal. Even when there is some dysfunction in the family system, the small amount of therapeutic work which can be done in one or two evaluation interviews may be of significant help to the patient, and further family therapy will not be indicated. Family therapy, unlike family evaluation, is not required for every patient. Though I work primarily with highly disturbed patients who have a high probability of being members of dysfunctional family systems, I end up recommending family therapy for fewer than two-thirds of my patients.

Even when family therapy seems indicated, certain practical realities may limit its usefulness. In a highly mobile society, it is often difficult to bring family members together for a long enough period of time to do much therapy. Many people in our society over the age of eighteen do not live near their parents. Siblings may be scattered over all parts of the country, a geographical reality which puts obvious limits upon the use of family therapy. The unwillingness of various patients and family members to participate in an extended form of family therapy must also, at times, be honored. Some patients prefer to go it alone, and nothing

Family Therapy

will dissaude them. The patient's family members may be fearful of what might happen to them in family therapy, and while efforts can be made to reassure them, some will refuse to participate beyond the evaluation sessions.

Sometimes a patient will resist family therapy because of a wish to hold on to the reinforcements generated by the disturbance. In such situations, other family members may be so distressed by the extent to which the patient's symptoms are governing their lives that they push for family therapy with more vigor than the patient. Here it may be possible to persuade the patient to participate in family therapy, but unless the patient's motivations change there are limits to the amount of therapeutic progress possible. Sometimes the patient's disorder is clearly related to family system dysfunction, but no member of the family system wishes to change. The patient and family members may have reached a state of equilibrium which allows the system to tolerate the patient's symptomatology. In such situations it is sometimes wise to "leave bad enough alone" (Pittman and Flomenhaft 1970). Such families are certainly at risk of future dysfunction, but the therapist has little justification for imposing treatment upon a system in which each of its members does not want treatment.

A thirty-five-year-old man was incapacitated by an avoidance reaction characterized by a compulsive need to avoid touching anything that he felt might have been contaminated by other people's urine. His symptoms had escalated to the point that he was afraid to touch doors to doorknobs for fear that somebody, who had gone to the bathroom and not washed his hands, might have touched them. At times he was unwilling to open his mail. The symptoms had been present for over seven years, and had resulted in the patient's retirement as permanently disabled and in his leading a reclusive life with his wife and children. His retirement pension enabled the family to live comfortably but modestly. The patient had sought psychotherapy from a number of different therapists over the years, but none of these interventions was successful. Efforts were then made to treat him with a behavioral approach. With the use of sophisticated self-control methods, combined with techniques for encouraging exposure, his symptoms began to abate. There were limits, however, to the extent of his improvement. The patient's level of comfort increased as did his range of activities, but his symptoms still restricted him in his social and geographical mobility. At this point a family evaluation was requested. The patient and his wife were seen together, and she presented herself as a person who had become quite accustomed to catering to the patient's irrational fears. She had learned to treat him as a child and seemed to be comfortable in her mothering or nursing role. Although the patient professed to be seeking total symptom relief, it was apparent to the therapist that he had great fears of getting so well that his wife would not cater to him. He also feared loss of his pension. In the second session, the wife expressed some wistful thoughts that it would be nice if the marital relationship would change and her husband could assume more independence. The patient listened attentively and said nothing, but in the third session, both partners emphatically stated that they could see nothing being accomplished in family therapy, that it was a wast of their time, and that they wanted the sessions to end. We suspected that the patient had become frightened of the prospect of change and had played a major role in dissuading his wife from continuing therapy. She seemed quite willing to go along with him. Family therapy was terminated, and behavior therapy continued on an intermittent supportive basis to help the patient sustain the small amount of improvement he had made.

FAMILY THERAPY AND OTHER INTERVENTIONS

Some patients who experience anxiety or depression as a result of crisis reactions but who are not psychotic may respond to family therapy without any other intervention. Family therapy may also be a sufficient treatment for people who have personality disorders, and whose periodic experience of anxiety or depression seems clearly related to high levels of family dysfunction. For many patients, however, family therapy is insufficient. In much of my own work I tend to combine family therapy with other approaches and feel free to use drugs, individual psychotherapy, and behavior therapy (here I am not talking about the use of behavioral techniques as part of family treatment) as concurrent interventions. I am not impressed with the concern of some family therapists that efforts to treat the patient with techniques designed to change the behavior of individuals will compromise the patient's position within the family or will impede the process of family therapy. Combined therapies will not diminish the usefulness of family therapy as long as the patient and members of his family appreciate that symptoms have many causes. It is not too difficult to teach the patient and his family that one part of the difficulty is related to the family system and must be treated with family therapy and that another part is related to other causal factors and requires a different kind of treatment. As long as all parties understand the reasons for using other therapies concurrently, there is little danger that any other therapy will diminish the usefulness of family therapy.

A BASIC FORMAT OF FAMILY EVALUATION AND THERAPY

It is difficult to talk about a basic format for an intervention still in the throes of development and currently being implemented in a wide variety of ways. The basic format I present here is, in large part, my own. Though similar formats are used by other clinicians, the reader should be aware that there are many other ways of structuring family therapy.

The first issue the clinician has to deal with is assembling the family for an evaluation. It is rare for a nuclear family to present itself as a troubled family requesting help. Spouses are somewhat more likely to request marital evaluation or therapy, but many couples who might benefit from a family therapy approach never request it. In most cases the clinician beings with a patient who is troubled or who is troubling others, and the clinician must take the responsibility for recommending an evaluation and assembling the family. In arranging the evaluation interviews, a decision must be made as to how many family members will be asked to participate. If the patient is a young single person, should siblings as well as parents be invited? If he has children, should they be invited? My preference in the early phases of evaluation is to concentrate on the nuclear family. If the patient reveals, however, that there are other people in life with whom he has a significant relationship, I will invite these people as well. This may mean bringing in grandparents, aunts, uncles, and even neighbors, friends, and paramours. I try to be flexible in making these decisions and rely heavily on the patient's wishes and on what I perceive to be his needs.

A considerable amount of persuasion may be required to bring the various participants together in a family interview. The first person who has to be persuaded is the patient. Many patients will resist a family interview. They will insist that the problem is theirs alone and that they do not wish to hurt their families by exposing them to the scrutiny of a mental health professional. Many patients profess concern about the health problems of members of their family. They imagine that the family evaluation will lead to highly stressful confrontations and fear that these confrontations will irreparably damage some vulnerable member of the family system. Some patients view the proposed family session as one in which they will be embarrassed and humiliated. They may fear that the therapist will join the family in ganging up on them. Other patients, usually young people, are concerned that they may be infantilized in the therapy session and that their efforts to seek autonomy will be compromised. It is always difficult to know whether the efforts of patients to resist family evaluation are based on genuine and perhaps realistic fears, or on efforts to resist change in their own behavior or in the family system. This is an interesting theoretical question, but not one of great practical importance. The only critical issue here is convincing the patient that a family interview is necessary.

It is usually helpful to reassure the patient that efforts will be made during the family evaluation to preserve the dignity and status of each individual. The therapist should try to make clear that he will not take sides and is simply trying to find a better way to understand the patient and the family system. It is also helpful to reassure the patient that his autonomy will be protected and that family intervention might even help him find more independence. The key factor in persuading the patient, however, is the therapist's commitment to the belief that family evaluation is useful. Beginning therapists unfamiliar with the powerful therapeutic effects of family intervention tend to make timid or perfunctory efforts to request family meetings. Not surprisingly, the patient rejects these suggestions. More experienced therapists simply insist to their patients that family evaluation is an essential part of the patient's treatment. When the therapist communicates his determination and persistence, the patient will usually go along. When I first started doing family evaluation and therapy, I found many patients reluctant to participate. Now that I am more comfortable with the technique, it is extraordinarily rare that one of my patients refuses a family interview.

The clinician may encounter similar reluctance on the part of families to be interviewed together with the patient. Frequently they fear that they will be blamed for the patient's disturbance.

Family Therapy

They may worry that they cannot speak freely in front of the patient. Many family members are fearful of mental health professionals and worry that their own emotional difficulties, which they may have kept hidden, will be exposed once they begin to talk with the clinician. Other family members will initially refuse to bring in small children. They argue that children are innocent and unaware of the severity of the problems within the family and that it would be cruel to expose them to such harsh realities. A few family therapists are inflexible and insist that small children as well as all other members of the nuclear family be brought into the evaluation session. In my own practice I am not persistent in requesting the attendance of younger children, but this may be because I am not comfortable in working with children in a therapeutic setting. Sometimes family members will volunteer to talk to the therapist or one of the clinical staff but will not agree to a conjoint interview with the patient. Some clinicians will accept this compromise and use a separate meeting with family members as a way of persuading them to accept a conjoint interview. In my own practice I insist that the first family interview be conjoint unless the patient is severely disturbed and disorganized.

As is true for the patient, the best way to persuade family members to participate in family evaluation is for the therapist to be reassuring and to present a relatively nonnegotiable stance. Family members should be told that their involvement is a critical part of the patient's treatment. They should be assured that they will not be blamed, embarrassed, or humiliated during the sessions. It is important that the clinician take an attitude of matter-of-fact certainty that the patient's improvement is to a large extent dependent upon the family's cooperation. Such a stance, playing heavily upon the guilt of family members, is at times justifiable, I feel, in order to get them to a family interview. (Such manipulation should, of course, stop once the family agrees to come.) Ultimately, the experience and commitment of the therapist are crucial variables in involving the family in a conjoint evaluation. It has been several years since I have failed to persuade at least one or two of the patient's significantly related family members to participate in the evaluation process.

It is often difficult to decide when to begin family evaluation with a patient who is psychotic. There is usually no problem when the psychosis is abating or is chronic, but patients who are confused, in a state of panic, or combative should have their family evaluations postponed. I assume that these individuals are in no position to give informed consent for a family interview, and I prefer that they have some understanding of what the family interview is about and some capacity to agree to it before I am willing to arrange it. As soon as I feel that the patient can understand the purposes of the interview, can agree to participate in it, and can tolerate the stresses of an hour-and-a-half session without becoming too disturbed, I will initiate the family evaluation.

Once the family has been assembled, I will make a brief comment about the nature of the patient's disturbance, and if the patient has already been in treatment, I will review the progress or lack of progress to date. I will then launch into a speech which goes approximately as follows: "There are many reasons why people become emotionally disturbed. Sometimes it has a lot to do with traits that may have been inherited or with unfortunate experiences people may have encountered during various parts of their lives. Sometimes people learn ways of dealing with the problems of life which are never adequate and which always seem to get them into trouble. Any person who is experiencing emotional difficulties is usually having unsatisfactory relationships with other people. Often the patient creates these problems, but sometimes other people may be equally involved. To really understand the patient we must look at as much of his current world as we can, and you family members are a very important part of that world. So we are gathered here today to take as careful a look as we can at how all of you are influencing the patient and how the patient is influencing all of you. It is absolutely necessary that we try to conduct this investigation without worrying about who is to blame. The question of blame is almost impossible to figure out; it rarely helps to blame yourself or anyone else. If we get too concerned with blame, it will interfere with our efforts to understand what is going on."

Following this speech, I say, "Who would like to start helping all of us figure this out?" Usually it is the patient's spouse or parent who begins the discussion, and usually they begin by asking me questions about the patient. I try to answer these questions as succinctly and accurately as I can. Such questions as What is wrong with the patient? are answered primarily by describing what seems to be bothering the patient rather than by affixing labels. A common response is that we are not as yet sure what is wrong with the patient and that we are all participating in the evaluation that is designed to help us find out what is wrong. If there are very clear data that the patient is experiencing a psychotic process, particularly if it is a chronic disturbance, I will be more willing to label the disturbance and try to explain what we know about it. Another common question is What can we do to help? My response to this is usually "We really don't know yet. That's what we're here to find out."

After asking a few questions and receiving responses, family members will often begin talking about historical aspects of the patient's disturbance or about the patient's development. At this point all members usually begin to participate. The patient will frequently want to correct others' perception of the events leading up to his disturbance and other family members may wish to correct the patient's perceptions. I try to involve all family members at this point, and to elicit their view of what has happened. The history obtained in this process is in itself useful. It is likely to be more accurate than history obtained from interviewing either the patient or the family members separately. Through these different versions of history the therapist gains a more useful and accurate picture as to what has actually happened.

In the course of reviewing historical information, the family will eventually begin to focus upon problems between themselves and the patient. Sometimes these are presented as problems in the past, but I am always alert to evidence of their continued influence. During the course of the session I also try to shift the focus of problem discussion to the recent past or present. While doing this, I am constantly trying to find ways in which family members are stressing the patient. I look for patterns of reinforcement within the family and particularly for behaviors which reinforce the patient's symptoms. I am also concerned with the manner in which the patient may be using his symptoms to influence the family. I have no hesitation in pointing out or labeling any process of influence when I can observe it. Often such interpretation is of immediate benefit to the patient.

While I do not feel that major efforts should be made to change the family system during an evaluation interview, I do make some attempt to examine the family system and to comment on system processes. If, during the early part of the interview, family members direct all of their interactions to the patient or to myself, I will at some point begin to make inquiries as to the problems of other family members and the manner in which they relate to one another. I am looking for patterns of communication within the family and for family rules which seem to create boundaries and govern interaction. I also try to determine if the patient or others have been put into irrational roles or if generational boundaries have become blurred. All of these evaluations give me some idea as to what type of family relationship patterns need to be changed or restructured if the family agrees to continue in systems-oriented treatment. At this point in the evaluation process, the family as a unit is not yet in treatment and my primary obligation is to the patient. If I make any interpretations as to the dysfunctional quality of the family system, I do not expect that this will result in major system change. My purpose in making such comments is usually to support the patient and to motivate all participants to continue in family therapy by showing them how they have been adversely influencing one another.

It is my practice to spend an hour and a half to two hours in the evaluative session; if I do not then have a clear picture of what is going on, I will ask for a second session. After two such interviews I usually have a fair picture of how family stress or family system dysfunction may be related to the patient's disturbance and whether or not it is useful to continue family work.

I use the above evaluation format with hospitalized patients as well as with outpatients. There are some problems with using any kind of family intervention in an institutional setting. Family members must sometimes travel long distances to be interviewed and the patient is in the dependent position of having to rely on their good intentions to participate. If the family members do agree to come, it is relatively easy for them to avoid seeing themselves or the family system as contributing to the problem since the patient is so obviously incapacitated and has been temporarily removed from the system. Some family therapists have suggested that it may be impossible to treat a hospitalized patient with a family approach—unless all family members are hospitalized—because the loss of power the patient experiences by virtue of hospitalization strengthens the dysfunctional family equilibrium (Rosenbaum and Hartley 1962). In my own experience this is not true. Family evaluations and family therapy can be conducted while the patient is hospitalized and even when a great deal of emphasis is placed on the patient's disturbance. One technique I use to impress other family members with the need for their continued participation is to stress the seriousness of the patient's disturbance and confess my inability to help the patient without their assistance. I will never allow the patient simply to be dropped off at the hospital like a car in need of repair. I feel no guilt or loss of professional status when I tell the family that our hospital staff is not absolutely certain as to what is wrong with the

Family Therapy

patient and that we do not believe we are capable of "repairing" his disorder on our own. The key to this approach is getting the family to become responsible partners in the patient's treatment.

There are certain special problems regarding confidentiality in family therapy. Clinicians whose practices are devoted almost exclusively to family therapy often see families without first having contact with the identified patient. Here the clinician's therapeutic contract may be with the family as a system rather than with any individual. If during the course of evaluation or treatment the patient or family members request separate conferences, if these are granted, and if the therapist is told things that he is asked not to share with other family members, the clinician need not honor such requests. There has been no contract made to protect any individual's confidentiality in relation to another family member. The situation is somewhat different when the clinician has begun to evaluate the individual patient before the family conference takes place. Here the patient may have revealed things to the clinician that he does not want shared with family members, and it is usually wise to honor the patient's request. If family therapy continues, this material will usually be revealed to the family anyway, and if the clinician does not honor the patient's request he may be betraying a contract or trust that was implied in the initial one-to-one evaluation.

Often after an initial conjoint family evaluation, parents or spouses will ask to see the clinician alone. Sometimes they wish to tell things to the clinician which they want kept from the patient. If the clinician grants these interviews, and it is my practice to do so if the patient consents, it is prudent to begin the interview by telling the family member that the clinician reserves the right to reveal anything that is discussed during the session to the patient.

If it is decided to continue family work beyond one or two evaluation sessions, some kind of contract must be negotiated. At the beginning of therapy it is usually easiest to develop a contract in which family members and the patient agree to seek new ways of relating to one another for the purpose of alleviating the patient's symptoms. It should be made clear that the patient or other family members may become involved in other kinds of therapy concurrently. I have also found it useful to inform the family unit at the beginning of therapy that it is likely that the overall focus of therapy may quickly switch from the patient to other family members, and that ultimately the focus is likely to be on helping the family function as a better system. Some family therapists never explicitly tell family members about such probable shifts in emphasis. I believe this is an error. Family members should know exactly what they are getting into.

With most families I eventually shift my focus to trying to change the family system during the course of therapy. The shift is likely to be accompanied by certain changes in therapeutic goals and methods. If the focus is on the patient, much of the therapist's effort must be directed toward persuading various participants to change their behavior so as not to stress the patient and to modify the way they reinforce him. If the focus is on the family system, the therapist must be concerned with changing relationship patterns between all participants. In pursuing the latter goals, a number of manipulations or restructuring devices can be used. All of these techniques are designed to disrupt a dysfunctional equilibrium in the family system and to encourage more adaptive methods of interaction. Their actual use is determined by the therapist's diagnoses of dysfunctional processes and by the therapist's idea of what constitutes an adaptive equilibrium for a given family. Obviously, diagnoses of specific aspects of family system malfunction must often be based on inference and judgment. Only a few highly skilled therapists can quickly "read" a family system and decide how it should be changed. And we can never be sure that even the experts are making good inferences and judgments. In a later section I will list a number of techniques which family therapists frequently use to restructure family systems. Here, I would like to note that I tend to use these techniques only when I feel that my "reading" of the family system is fairly accurate.

I usually see the family once weekly for a session of an hour and a half. Family therapy need not, however, be so frequent. When the family is not dealing with an immediate crisis they can benefit from one or two visits a month. I also try to keep family therapy relatively brief, usually from five to thirty sessions. If the patient has improved and the family has accomplished some of the goals negotiated when the therapist shifted to a systems approach, the family group is usually eager to leave therapy. I make no effort to persuade them to continue. Some family therapists have what I would consider to be more utopian growth goals for the family system. They are committed either to helping each family member achieve his fullest individuation or to trying to make the family an almost perfectly functioning system. I consider these goals too ambitious. In the absence of any firm evidence that a smoothly

Family Therapy

functioning family system is possible or even desirable, there is little justification for the therapist's insistence upon prolonged treatment.

The process of termination of family therapy is usually not very difficult. If the therapist has done his work well, each member will have an increased sense of autonomy or individuation. Family members rarely develop the same kind of dependency upon the therapist that patients develop in individual or group psychotherapy. One major reason for this is that family members can derive a great deal of gratification from one another outside the therapeutic setting. If the therapist is able to teach them more gratifying methods of relating to one another their continuing needs for the therapist are minimal. Termination should be conducted in a manner which provides the family easy access to further therapy at a later date. Much of the future development of the family depends upon circumstances which are unpredictable and outside anyone's control. Even the most smoothly functioning family can be adversely influenced by stresses emanating from the society as a whole or by extrafamilial stresses which impinge heavily upon one member. It is always difficult to predict how families will respond to developmental tasks related to the growth of children, taking in new members through marriage, or to the geographic mobility of various members. The best that can be done is to bring the family to a point of relatively smooth functioning, hope that they will have good luck in the future, and remain available to them if they are not so fortunate. I believe that most of the families I have treated briefly will need no further care, but, admittedly, I have not done family therapy long enough to bolster this impression with data.

EXPERIENTIAL VERSUS STRUCTURAL APPROACHES

The theoretical orientations of family therapists of different schools play some role in determining their technical approaches to treatment. Efforts have been made to distinguish between family therapists whose interventions are based on theories used in individual and group therapy and those whose interventions are related to specific theories regarding family life (Beels and Ferber 1972). The first group is sometimes referred to as the experiential school. They encourage family members to express feelings toward the therapist and other family members and try to make family members more aware of the meaning of their behavior. Experientially oriented therapists use techniques that are highly influenced by those developed in group theory. Emphasis is placed on facilitating self-disclosure and emotional expression between family members and the therapist. Experiential family therapists are not greatly preoccupied with family theory or diagnosis and tend to be skilled clinicians who rely heavily on their subjective awareness and intuition (Haley and Hoffman 1963). At the other end of the scale are family therapists who rely upon well-developed theories of family function to determine the nature of their interventions. Their focus in therapy is upon communication between family members and upon the realtionship system through which communication is transmitted. They tend to be active and even aggressive in restructuring family interaction so as to change communication patterns and the roles various members play in the relationship system (Minuchin et al. 1967).

It is very difficult to know if these classifications have any meaning in actual practice. If one watches experienced family therapists of either the experiential or the structural school at work, their technical interventions are not very different. It is only when experienced therapists are asked to describe their reasons for using various interventions that they invoke different levels of explanation and seem to get into theoretical disputes. Most family therapists, including myself, fall somewhere in the middle of the experiential-structural continuum. We use many of the approaches discussed in the previous two chapters to help individual family members understand and change their behavior. At the same time, we frequently shift into a systems approach and use deliberate manipulations based on theories of restructuring family interaction.

CO-THERAPISTS IN FAMILY THERAPY

It is common for family therapists to use co-therapists. Therapists who come out of the group therapy school are perhaps a little more likely to prefer this format. As contrasted to group therapists, family therapists are somewhat less concerned with co-therapists having equal levels of sophistication and skill, and many will work together with any student whom they respect and with whom they feel relatively comfortable (Napier and Whitaker 1972). I am personally very enthusiastic about the co-therapy format. First of all, it provides an excellent training opportunity

Family Therapy

for the less experienced therapist. I started out doing family therapy as a novice co-therapist with Dr. Carl Whitaker and found this an extraordinarily useful training experience. I have subsequently continued to do family therapy using trainees in psychiatry, psychology, or social work as co-therapists, and have found that even inexperienced co-therapists pick up cues that I miss. They will often detect patterns of interaction of which I am totally unaware. They will sense the need to provide emotional support to a family member I may be ignoring or unduly stressing. The sharing of responsibility with a co-therapist enables me to be a little more courageous in expressing feelings or making suggestions I might have been too timid to make if I were alone with the family. Most important, the presence of a co-therapist enables me to detach myself from the field periodically and to think about what is going on. Family interactions are terribly complicated. In dealing with the dysfunctional family, the therapist often feels overwhelmed and unable to get any kind of intellectual or emotional grip on what is happening. When two therapists are available, one of them can actively deal with moment-to-moment transactions while allowing the other to quietly sit back and try to conceptualize what is happening.

HELPFUL FACTORS

The seven helpful factors considered in the chapters on individual and group psychotherapy operate also in family therapy, though the manner in which they exert influence and the techniques by which they are implemented are slightly different. At the risk of being repetitious, I will remind the reader once more that the factors are interrelated, that they function concurrently, and that they are considered separately only for convenience.

Faith and Belief in the Powers of the Healer

The family therapist starts out at a distinct disadvantage in exploiting the family's faith in his healing powers. Some participants in family therapy do not view themselves as being in need of healing. They may enter family therapy with reluctance, distrust, and skepticism. The family therapist cannot rely on a long history of tradition to enhance his image as a healer. Family therapy is a relatively new intervention. It has not been heavily publicized and its potential advantages are not easily grasped by the uninitiated. Furthermore the family therapist is unlikely to rely upon mysticism to impress his patients. In most approaches to family therapy, the therapist is quite open in allowing others to observe his work. Frequent use of co-therapists, one-way vision rooms, and videotaping emphasize the open and even public aspects of family intervention. Some patients may be favorably impressed with the therapist's willingness to go public and will view it as a manifestation of his high level of confidence. Other patients will view the therapist's openness as demeaning to his stature as a healer and will be unimpressed with a therapist who cares little for the trappings of mystical power.

The therapist must compensate for his initially minimal power base by grasping as much power as he can in the initial interactions. This he does in a variety of ways. Through his initial explanations and questions and through his quick assumption of an active rather than a passive role, he implies that he knows what he is doing. Family members usually have no idea what to anticipate during the first family session. They are likely to be confused and frightened. They may be willing to concede a great deal of power to the therapist who seems to be the one person in the room who has some idea of what might be happening. Participants in family therapy are often told that they are responsible for what goes on outside the therapy session, but that within the hour they are guests in the therapist's own territory or "home" and that the therapist will assume full control of the rules governing transactions (Minuchin 1974). Family therapists catch people off guard when they are explicit in clarifying that they will control what happens during the therapeutic hour. Most patients are impressed with therapists who have so few trepidations about defining their power base.

Family therapists also gain power by combining a gentle, empathic approach with a demonstration of their own wisdom. In most forms of individual or group psychotherapy, therapists tend to wait until they have a great deal of data before they interpret or comment on therapeutic transactions. In family therapy such hesitation is uncommon. Family therapists will very quickly try to decipher patterns of relatedness and communication and will point them out to the participants almost immediately. To the extent that these interpretations are correct, the family therapist quickly attains the status of a perceptive and powerful person. Some family therapists are especially skilled in making comments that would be considered outrageous if made in ordinary company.

Their interpretations are not only clever; they are startling and sometimes infuriating. By saying things that are not ordinarily said in polite company, or by mentioning the unmentionable, the family therapist establishes himself as an unusual person, powerful enough not to be intimidated by the conventional rules of interpersonal transactions.

Identification

The factor of identification operates differently in family therapy than in individual or group psychotherapy. The therapist cannot serve as a desirable model for every member of the family unit; there is simply no opportunity for the therapist to relate closely to any single member for a prolonged period of time. Nor can the family therapist have as much influence in modeling group norms as he might in group therapy. The family already has a set of norms or values. While the therapist may want to tamper with them or change them slightly, he cannot create them.

There are two ways in which the family therapist might attempt, through the factor of identification, to make slight changes in the relationship patterns or value systems of families. First, he can demonstrate the possibility of modes of interaction that have not been used by the family in the past. He does this by modeling them in his interactions with family members during the therapy session. Members of dysfunctional families often relate to one another in grim and desperate ways. Most family therapists are eager to show family members how they can be more playful with one another. The family therapist usually feels free to tease, joke, and even flirt with his patients. There is little danger that such actions will cut off communication from family members—it is more likely, in fact, to elicit imitative responses from them. If small children are brought into the session, some therapists will spend a considerable amount of time getting down on the floor and playing with them. Through such behavior the therapist is, of course, demonstrating a certain amount of care and lovingness. If asked why he does this sort of thing, he would say that he is trying to show family members they are missing out on the possibility of having fun with one another. There is, of course, a bonus in all this for the family therapist. Most clinicians have more fun doing family therapy than any other intervention (at least I do), and I suspect this is because the family therapy format provides a theoretical rationale for abandoning the mask of professionalism and enjoying one's playfulness.

A second way in which the family therapist can model more useful modes of family interaction is by revealing a great deal as to how he relates to his own family. During a session family members may demonstrate a particular kind of relationship pattern. The therapist will then note that something quite similar to what has been observed often happens in his own family. This self-disclosing response brings the therapist closer to the family and tells them that many of the transactions they have visualized as unique and intolerable are not too atypical and can be viewed as acceptable ways of dealing with everyday problems of family life. (This process contains elements of empathy and reinforcement as well as identification.) Therapists will also talk about their weaknesses in relating to their own family members. In so doing, they are modeling an accepting attitude toward behavior that might ordinarily be considered deviant or shameful. The family therapist is always trying to help family members adopt a lighter view of what they have in the past considered life and death situations. His own good humored disclosure of how he has dealt with similar problems helps facilitate this process.

Caring and Lovingness

Family therapists tend to be liberal in expressing empathy. Although therapists will at times take sides and help strengthen the position of a person under attack, they will try to identify also with other participants and to express compassion and interest in their plight. The practice of distributing blame among various family members on a more or less equal basis facilitates the expression of empathy. To the extent that each member feels that the therapist neither fully blames him for or fully exculpates him from creating family problems, each member is likely to feel correctly understood. The family therapist also has at least some influence in modifying group norms. As the family members observe the therapist responding to various members in empathic and caring ways, they may begin to model some of their own responses on those of the therapist and may become more empathic themselves.

The family therapist is liberal in providing noncontingent positive reinforcement for the family as whole. Family therapists often comment on the family's strength, its devotion, its lovingness, or its power. Sometimes a family can be indirectly complimented by being told how complicated, how resistive, or how crazy it is. These appellations are presented in a way that

Family Therapy

allows family members to feel that they are part of an unusual and unique group. It is easy for the therapist to reinforce the family as a unit without being phony. Each family really is unique. Even experienced family therapists are often awed by the various patterns of interaction families develop in order to maintain a functional or dysfunctional equilibrium. By communicating his awe and respect, the therapist reinforces the family as a unit, helps each member feel a kind of pride in the family, and at the same time gains a certain degree of power to influence family interaction.

Tension Reduction

In traditional group and individual psychotherapy tension reduction is achieved by self-disclosure and abreaction. The display of such emotions as fear, sadness, anger, or love is usually viewed as highly desirable. Family therapists are less certain as to the desirability of using the therapeutic session for this kind of expressivity. Family therapists on the experiential end of the family therapy continuum welcome a considerable degree of emotionally charged transaction in the therapy hour. Other family therapists, however, discourage displays of emotionality. They may even try to reduce expressivity during the hour by directing family members to take a more cognitive approach toward their problems. Their view is that families have probably been interacting with one another on a highly emotionally charged basis for many years and that bringing this same pattern of interaction into the therapy hour is not likely to be useful (Haley 1957). On this view, some family units may achieve maximum tension reduction by talking things over calmly.

My own view of this issue is that there are usually many feelings between people who have been living together for years which may never have been expressed. I try to use the family session as a vehicle for discharge of tension by encouraging catharsis or open expression of how family members feel about one another. At times I will even allow family arguments to reach a heated level and will do little to interfere with these battles. Like other family therapists, however, I am aware that such expressivity in family therapy is not always useful, and in many instances can be viewed as a defense mechanism or an effort to resist change. Often families will reenact battles in the therapy hour which have characterized their relationships outside of therapy for many years. In the permissive atmosphere of the therapy session negative feelings can escalate. When people who have been hurting one another for years continue the process of hurting one another in front of the therapist, there is a real risk that their discharge of emotions will not reduce tensions but will simply make each party angrier. In this regard it must be noted that family members, unlike group therapy members, bring their battles home with them once they leave the hour. Whatever has been said during therapy is not a secret restricted to the therapeutic hour but is something that each participant must continue to deal with on a day-to-day basis. For all of these reasons it is wise for the family therapist to put some limits on expression of negative emotionality during the therapy hour. There are many ways of doing this. The clinician can interpret angry emotionality as a sign of love and passion, and this message may be startling enough to stop a fight. Or the clinician can shift the interaction to a more cognitive level by asking questions which direct the family members to consider a less emotionally charged subject. Sometimes the clinician must be quite forceful in terminating an argument. This may require that he gain the contestant's attention by loudly demanding it or by doing something unexpected, such as picking up a book and reading it, or by simply leaving the room.

Learning

The process of bringing about behavioral change through use of extinction and reinforcement is, of necessity, somewhat slow in individual psychotherapy. The therapist must wait for undesirable behaviors to appear if he is to respond to them in ways that are not reinforcing. An even more difficult problem is how to get desirable behaviors emitted so that they can be reinforced. If the therapist is directive, he can try to use authority to encourage the patient to experiment with a new behavior within the therapeutic session, but even when there is a very good patient-therapist relationship, there are limits to the patient's willingness to do the therapist's bidding. It is even more difficult for the individual therapist to control the processes of extinction and reinforcement outside of the therapy hour. The group therapist has a different kind of problem. A wide variety of maladaptive behaviors are emitted in groups. New behaviors can be shaped within the structure of the therapy hour with less use of authority than is required in individual therapy. The problem with artificially created groups, however, is that they have few advantages over individual therapy in extinguishing or shaping behavior in real life situations outside of the therapy hour.

The family therapist works directly in a field in which all emitted behaviors represent a major part of each individual's real life repertoire. More important, this field is a system which is in a dynamic state of equilibrium. The behavior of individuals in that system is dependent upon intricate patterns of reinforcement which various members present to one another at any given time. If all members of the system are put into the same room at the same time and if efforts are made to change patterns of relationships in any part of the system, there will be changes in the manner in which various members reinforce each other throughout the total system. If one aspect of old behavior within a system is extinguished, the system must restore itself to equilibrium by creating new behaviors. If a new pattern of relationship is reinforced, older patterns are likely to be extinguished. There is no assurance that the new patterns of relationship will be sustained outside the therapeutic session. But since new patterns of interaction have already appeared with significant or real figures within the therapy setting, the problem of generalization to real situations outside the therapy setting is not nearly as great as it is in group or individual therapy. Often the family therapist can bring about impressive changes in the behavior of several family members by making only minor efforts to manipulate the family system. Such manipulations may not require a massive use of authority. Here are examples of how this process works:

A nineteen-year-old woman being seen in family therapy with her parents was having difficulty expressing either angry or positive feelings toward her father. The therapist noted that whenever she began to express any type of emotion toward him, the mother quickly intervened and either defended the father or started an argument with the daughter which would deflect the daughter's emotions toward her. The therapist pointed this out and asked the mother if she would remain silent the next time the daughter expressed some feelings toward her father. The mother cooperated and allowed father and daughter to have a long emotional interchange in which they expressed both positive and negative feelings toward each other. Both felt that this was the first time that they had talked seriously to one another. The mother, confronted with the observation that her husband was able to handle feelings involving the daughter quite adequately, began to see him in a new and more respectful way.

A middle-aged couple and their three children were being seen in conjoint family therapy primarily for treatment of the mother's moderate depression. During the hours she frequently complained to her children and to the therapist about the shortcomings of her husband. The thrust of her complaints was that he was selfish and was never aware of her needs. The therapist pointed out the pattern of her complaints and asked her to talk directly to her husband and tell him what she expected of him. She complied and to her surprise her husband responded by stating that he had never been quite sure what she wanted from him and felt that he could now make a more committed effort to gratify her. He had previously tried to ignore her complaints to the children or had become angry whenever he overheard them. As repeated efforts were made to have the wife talk directly to the husband and as he began to comply with some of her requests, her complaining about him to the children and others diminished and her depression improved.

In the first example the therapist temporarily extinguished a response of the mother which prevented communication between father and daughter. This led to the development of new patterns of communication which were mutually reinforcing. It also led, indirectly, to some changes in the relationship of husband and wife. In the second example the therapist temporarily extinguished the mother's tendency to communicate feelings about her husband to her daughters, and she was asked to experiment with the new behavior of talking directly to her husband. This pleased the husband and led to his delivering highly positive reinforcement to her. The children were freed of this burden of having to listen to complaints about their father, and one can surmise that they were then able to relate to him in a different way.

Both examples are rather typical of the kinds of minor manipulations family therapists use to bring about broad changes in family systems. In each case the therapist directed family interactions by requesting one family member to stop performing a given behavior or to start performing a new one. In effect he created new family scenarios or new conditions of interaction which expanded the learning opportunities of all participants.

It will be useful here to review briefly some of the many techniques family therapists have developed for restructuring the family system. One technique (previously discussed in the section on responsibility) involves redefining the patient's symptom as an effort to help the family. If the therapist is insistent on maintaining this new view of the patient, other family members

Family Therapy

can no longer treat the patient as a disturbed person, and the patient has less opportunity to act like one. This not only diminishes reinforcement of the patient's symptomatology but also creates a situation in which family members and the patient must find a new way of relating. These new patterns of relationship are sometimes mutually reinforcing and can sometimes be sustained outside the therapy hour.

Family therapists also use this relabeling technique in dealing with a number of family transactions other than those related to overt symptomatology. Behaviors of various members that would ordinarily be seen as aversive or noxious are sometimes relabeled as efforts to help the family or as efforts to gain greater intimacy. A wife's angry outburst toward her spouse, for example, may be interpreted as a manifestation of the great emotion and concern she feels toward him. If the wife accepts this interpretation, she may be willing to risk experimenting with less noxious ways of gaining intimacy. If the husband accepts the possibility that his wife's anger reflects passion, he may respond to it in a totally new fashion.

Another manipulative device involves focusing upon one member. One way to do this is to take sides. The family therapist may, for example, take an adolescent child's side in an argument over the need for privacy. This brings about a shift of the power equilibrium within the family. Since the child now has a powerful ally, the parents must find a new way of relating to him. As noted in the last two case examples, the therapist can also restrict the activities of a particular family member. This is an especially powerful technique when restrictions are put upon the member who seems to dominate the system. A mother who does most of the talking during the hours and who seems to be trying to speak on behalf of other family members can simply be asked to remain quiet (some therapists might even ask her to leave the room or to step behind a one-way mirror and observe rather than participate in the process). At this point the mother ceases to have control and other family members must find new ways of relating to each other and to the therapist. Sometimes the therapist will restrict the activities of a person who is not dominating the system with a very specific goal of trying to improve communications between members of a particular subsystem. A child who has been forced into an irrational role assignment related to his parents' inability to gratify one another can be asked to remain silent (or to turn his chair away from the family unit) while the therapist encourages the parents to discuss their problems. Being unable to use their child to solve problems between themselves the parents will have to work on new ways of relating. Still another technique is to focus upon the healthiest member of the family system and encourage that person in his effort to individuate. Such efforts may be resisted by the rest of the family system, but if one individual can free himself from enmeshment within the family system, other members who have been using him to gratify irrational needs will have to find new ways of relating to each other.

Sometimes the therapist can initiate change by asking two family members to try to relate to one another in a different manner. A husband and wife may be requested to spend more time doing things together without the children. Or a parent who is having difficulty relating to a particular child may be asked to find some activity he and that child can enjoy together. Often a parent who is putting too much responsibility on a particular child can be asked to put a certain amount of responsibility on a different child. If the family members follow these directives, they may find that their new behaviors lead to responses on the part of other family members which are positive reinforcers.

Family therapists can also change certain kinds of dysfunctional equilibria by teaching family members slightly different methods of communication. One common technique is to discourage any talk of past family history which is characterized by efforts on the part of one person to blame another. Family members can be encouraged to talk about the here and now and to express their feelings as they exist in the present. Emphasis can also be placed on teaching each person to speak for himself and to communicate his own wishes and feelings toward any other member by speaking to that member directly (Satir 1964). If family members are put under a slight amount of pressure to communicate in a more open and direct manner, subtle patterns of interaction related to the use of language can be changed. Finally, family members can be taught to make new and more adaptive responses to one another's communications. A child can be taught to ask for clarification when his parents' communications are ambiguous. A family member who regularly responds in an angry manner to the provocation of another can be persuaded to try responding in a more affable or even joking manner and to see what happens. His new response to a provocative communication may serve to extinguish it.

Family Therapy

This listing of techniques merely touches upon the rich variety of ways in which the therapist can create new learning experiences for members of the family system. They are based on efforts to change patterns of interpersonal reinforcement by temporarily disrupting the equilibrium of a social system. Their effectiveness can be understood in terms of how new patterns of learning develop when the equilibrium of a system changes.

Operant conditioning can also be used in family therapy in a more direct manner. Specific behaviors within the family system can be singled out for extinction or reinforcement (Liberman 1970). The effective use of direct behavior modification in family therapy requires that the therapist have a highly positive relationship with the family unit. The therapist must give specific advice, and the family members must have faith and trust in the therapist if they are to follow his advice. Once the family's cooperation is gained, the therapist and family begin to explore new ways in which various family members would like to see one another change. Careful inquiries can be made as to how one or more family members respond to the undesirable behavior of another. It may be noted that certain undesirable behaviors are reinforced by solicitousness and concern. Or they may turn out to be reinforced by fighting, nagging, or withdrawal. Once these reinforcers are identified, the family members delivering them can be given specific advice as to how they can respond differently. If they are willing to follow the therapist's directives, the undesirable behavior may be extinguished.

Family therapists who use behavioral techniques have also developed methods of shaping new behaviors between family members which are gratifying and mutually rewarding. These therapists believe that there is usually little to be gained by focusing upon family conflicts or arguments but that there is much to be gained by focusing upon ways in which family members can be nicer to each other. In a common technique known as contingency, contracting family members are asked to list ways in which they would like to see other family members behave (Stuart 1971). There is a tendency for family participants to begin by listing requests for decelerating negative behaviors. They must be discouraged from doing this since attempts to diminish the frequency of a behavior requires the use of aversive stimuli or extinction patterns which are unlikely to be effective and which may already have been used ineffectively within the family system. Family members should be asked to request changes in behaviors that can easily be measured, such as taking out the garbage, spending a certain amount of time with the children, or going out to dinner. It is best if each party to the contract lists an equal number of requested changes the initiation of which would involve a more or less equal amount of effort on each participant's part. A working husband and a homemaker wife, for example, might develop a contract in which the husband agrees to do the dishes, spend a certain amount of time talking with his wife and children each evening, and take his wife out once a week if the wife will prepare the evening meal, be attractively dressed at dinner time, and provide him a certain amount of physical attention. Such contracts can, of course, be much more elaborate and specific, and the more specific they are the more likely they are to be followed. Sometimes contracts can even be arranged in which the behaviors of one participant can be counted and can be rewarded with tokens which can then be used to "purchase" certain specified reinforcements from the other participants.

I have found contingency contracting useful with families who have developed long-standing patterns of trying to control one another through negative reinforcement (shouting, threatening) and who are inclined to spend most of their therapeutic sessions complaining about one another. There is a theoretical assumption implied in contingency contracting which once explained to family members becomes titillating (Stuart 1969). Ordinarily, family members, particularly spouses, see the behavior of their mates as determined by personality traits which are unmodifiable. Couples soon learn that it is difficult to change one another's personalities. As long as they believe that their spouses are insensitive, passive, or overaggressive they cannot find new ways of dealing with them. If, however, the spouse is viewed as *behaving* indifferently, *behaving* passively, or *behaving* too aggressively, and if they can learn that such behavior can be changed by altering the way in which the spouse is reinforced, there is no longer any need to feel helpless. They learn that they can change the behavior of the spouse by changing their own behavior. This is a powerful message. As a rule we tell patients in psychotherapy that they should never try to change others but should focus only upon changing themselves. Family therapy holds out the additional possibility that changes in self can be specifically designed to lead to changes in significant others.

Family Therapy

Information

Participants in family therapy have the opportunity to learn a great deal about how they influence one another. Each individual will learn how he comes across to other family members, how this influences their responses to him, and how he is influenced by the behavior of others. Family members, of course, already know quite a bit about how they have been influencing one another before they get to therapy, and new information generated about interpersonal transactions may not have as startling an impact as it would in group therapy. Nevertheless, there is much new information related to the process of interaction that can be gained. Quite often, even individuals who have lived together for years do not have accurate perceptions as to how they come across to one another or how they are influenced by one another. The family therapist can maximize the availability of such information by using techniques similar to those of group therapists. Specifically, he must try to keep the content of the material in the here and now and must encourage a high degree of interaction among family members and between family members and himself. If the therapist adheres to these goals, the family members will usually begin to reveal how they influence one another. Such information provides direction for the therapist in manipulating the family system and helps family members define the precise nature of behaviors they may wish to change.

The family therapy format would, in theory, seem ideal for helping the patient generate new information (or reconstruct old information) regarding the past. If the patient's parents are present in the session, they can probably provide more accurate information as to what happened in the patient's early childhood than the patient can, and the patient should be able to learn a great deal about the origins of his current behavior. While a certain amount of this material may be generated in family therapy, there are inherent limits to the usefulness of such an approach. In effect, focusing upon the past would have many of the qualities of trying to psychoanalyze a patient with his family present. It is unlikely that family members, who would be present primarily for the purpose of providing information, could sustain interest in the process for very long. It is difficult to speculate as to what kind of transference responses could be developed or what kind of corrective emotional experiences could occur in a situation where the figures who were originally involved in creating the maladaptive learning are still present. There would be so many variables involved in such a hypothetical situation that it would be mind-boggling. Perhaps this is why family therapists do not focus heavily upon the past in helping the patient gain awareness of unconscious motivation.

It should be noted here that some family therapists will encourage all participants, including the parents of the identified patient, to talk about their families or origin in some detail. The goal here, however, is somewhat different from the goal of reconstructing the past in individual psychoanalytically oriented psychotherapy. This technique is used to trace patterns of family interaction through several generations, and to try to determine if these patterns bear any similarity to patterns in the present. Efforts are made to help each participant become more aware of how his own past family experiences influence his current behavior in the family (Framo 1976).

The unique information-expanding aspect of family therapy relates to the manner in which it helps the patient discover what needs and expectations significant figures have of him. At the beginning of therapy, the patient may have to infer this information by observing the manner in which family members relate to each other and to the therapist. Later in therapy, family members will communicate their needs and expectations more explicitly. This information allows the patient to make rational and self-serving choices in dealing with the family system. No other form of therapy can provide this information so directly.

Explanation

Family therapists feel somewhat freer than do group or individual psychotherapists to indulge their pedantic impulses and explain their theories to patients. They are not preoccupied with developing transference responses, and they tend to eschew efforts at mystification. Experiential therapists tend to extol the virtues of self-expression, openness, and growth to their patients. Family therapists who hold to more structured approaches are also willing to explain such concepts as irrational role assignments, generational blurring, triangulation, and individuation. Strangely enough, many families who benefit from family therapy do not seem interested in seeking elaborate explanations of the causes of their problems, or how they were resolved. The new patterns of relatedness which develop in successful family therapy may be so inherently gratifying that some families seem able to maintain them without benefit of explanation.

BEYOND THE FAMILY

Family therapy is one of the most promising and exciting interventions for helping emotionally disturbed people. Some who practice family therapy feel that their work will eventually provide new insights into the nature of human behavior which can then be applied to a large number of social problems. The family can be viewed as a small social system which bears many resemblances to the system of the community or the greater society. Within the family system, it is possible to study the manner in which such human needs as intimacy, freedom, responsibility, power, mastery, and privacy are maintained. It is possible to gain insights into how such maladaptive social behaviors as violence, delinquency, and social withdrawal develop. Some family therapists have flirted with the idea that the principles of relationship which make for a healthy family can be translated into principles which might ultimately help create a better society. My own view is that treating families does help therapists become more aware of social problems and more insightful into the nature of transactions between social units, particularly around such issues as power and freedom (Halleck 1976). Whether this awareness will eventually prove useful in dealing with social problems involving larger systems is, however, uncertain. Some advocates of the family therapy movement have expressed optimism that treating families—which are, after all, important units in our society—will eventually improve the healthiness of the total society (Satir 1970). Here I must interject a more sobering opinion.

The family is only one of many social systems impinging upon the individual. While the family exerts influence upon its individual members, the family system itself is susceptible to the influence of economic, political, and religious systems. Social change constantly puts pressure on family members and family systems to redefine their roles. Families in a technological society must adjust to an ever-increasing rate of change. The problems of finding a useful and relevant role for the elderly, finding an equal role for woman, sustaining a certain amount of authority for parents, and finding productive and contributing roles for youth impinge upon all American families. Some families, by virtue of social stresses such as poverty or racism, have even greater difficulties in maintaining a gratifying and useful position within the society. One way of viewing the family is as an intervening variable between the individual and stress engendered by the society. The stresses which impinge on the family will be processed in the family structure so that they eventually will exert certain kinds of influence on the individual.

When family therapists label a family dysfunctional or disturbed, they may be repeating, on a larger scale, the same error they accuse other clinicians of making when they label an individual dysfunctional or disturbed. The disturbance of a family may well represent a symptom of the larger society's inability to fulfill its functions. A dysfunctional family can be taught to operate more smoothly and thereby eliminate the suffering of certain of its members. As long as the larger social system remains dysfunctional, however, and is failing to meet the needs of family units as well as of individuals, the family is likely to experience continued difficulty. In some instances, helping a family deal with a symptom such as the delinquency of one of its members may actually diminish its capacity as a unit to create change in the larger social system. Delinquency may be determined by individual variation or by family dysfunction, but social oppression is probably its most important determinant (Clark 1970). The delinquency seen in our urban ghettos, for example, is most easily explained as a response to a dysfunctional society. To the extent that the family system is taught to change its relationships in a manner that extinguishes the delinquent behavior of one of its members, the family as a unit may be less aware of the impact of social oppression upon its members and less willing to do anything about it. The short-run gain of improving a particular family's function may contribute to the enhancement of a long-run stabilization of a dysfunctional society. I am not suggesting that clinicians should stop treating families, I am merely pointing out that, viewed in terms of larger systems, the political consequences of family intervention are not too different from those of intervening with the individual. Any clinical intervention can strengthen the status quo, often, an oppressive status quo.

These seemingly esoteric considerations do have practical clinical implications. There are powerful limits to the extent to which the clinician can use his position to try to change oppressive aspects of the larger social system. But in working with families as well as with individuals there is no reason why the clinician cannot sustain or expand the awareness of families, as well as individuals, as to how the society influences them. There is nothing, for example, to stop the clinician from teaching disadvantaged

Family Therapy

families and individuals to interact more effectively with social agencies, and there are no rules which prevent him from at times intervening directly with agencies on behalf of the patient or family. In my own work with families, I always try to help them maintain some perspective as to how they are influenced by society. In dealing with oppressed families I make no effort to curb their realistic resentment of social conditions. Rather, I remind them how these conditions have contributed to family pathology.

FURTHER ETHICAL PROBLEMS

Family therapy is a relatively new intervention. It has been subjected to less scientific evaluation than any intervention thus far described. Given the lack of data as to the usefulness of its theory or techniques and given the enormous power the family therapist assumes in trying to change the lives of several individuals, one would hope that family therapists would undertake their interventions with great humility. Consider for a moment some of the risks involved. The family therapist often brings people into a treatment situation who are not troubled, who have never defined themselves as patients, and who may have little enthusiasm to participate. In the course of family therapy these individuals may be humiliated, shamed, attacked, provoked, and made to feel guilty. Often a family member who is not viewed as the identified patient may become so disturbed as to become a patient. Family therapists often note that a family member who is not the identified patient may become disturbed when the identified patient begins to improve. Presumably when family therapy works smoothly, all members, including those who were not initially symptomatic but who became symptomatic during the course of treatment, will eventually come out the better for the experience. But there is no conclusive evidence that this actually happens. It is conceivable that some people who become symptomatic as a result of family therapy may remain symptomatic. Even if such a change in the family system helps the identified patient, there are grave ethical implications to this kind of therapeutic outcome.

The majority of families enter family therapy with the motivation of helping the identified patient or of finding better ways of dealing with him. It is difficult to know the extent to which they initially wish to change the manner in which they relate to one another but they rarely enter therapy with the conscious wish of restructuring the family system. It is therefore reasonable to ask from where or from whom the family therapist derives the right to restructure a family. The only answer to this question must be that he derives the privilege to restructure the family by virtue of knowledge and experience that tell him what is best for the family. Given the limits of any clinician's knowledge of what is best for a family, the precarious ethical basis of such restructuring should be obvious.

During the course of writing this chapter I was talking to a group of residents about the power of the family therapist and was commenting on how the family therapist must sometimes play God. I then inadvertently blurted out, "It's OK to play God as long as you're humble about it." My students immediately recognized the contradictory nature of my statement and burst out laughing. I joined them in their laughter but in retrospect began to wonder if there might be a kernel of truth in my statement. The best family therapists I have known are willing to assume a great deal of power in dealing with the family, but they also seem to have a sense of awe in using that power. They are extraordinarily gentle and kind people. Even when they manipulate, provoke, or attack, they seem to have a profound appreciation of the limitations of various family members to tolerate stress, and they rarely push participants beyong their limits. I have seen brilliant family therapists such as Carl Whitaker say things to patients which would have been outrageous or insulting in almost any other context and noted that his remarks were experienced by family members as friendly and helpful.

My main concern about the power of family therapy relates to the activities of novices in this field who often try to mimic the actions of the masters without having the knowledge, skills, and empathic capacity of the masters. Family therapists often argue that it is difficult for even an inexperienced therapist to do much damage in dealing with the family. They insist that the family system has innate homeostatic mechanisms which will protect it from the aversive or insensitive intrusion of the therapist. In my own experience I have found little to contradict this assertion, but I am still not reassured that an arrogant or insensitive family therapist could not inflict psychological damage upon both the identified patient and other family members.

I am also concerned about the tendency of some family therapists to be so certain of the efficacy of the family therapy

Family Therapy

format that they fail to fully treat the problem of the individual initially identified as the patient. Family therapists who are systems purists sometimes forget that there are aspects to the patient's symptomatology that are autonomous on either a biological or a learned basis and which are refractory to systems intervention. When they insist on using family therapy as the sole mode of intervention, their ideological commitment deprives the patient of essential treatment.

Finally, I would be more comfortable with the field of family therapy if its practitioners would show a little more appreciation that the elements involved in their definitions of a healthy family are determined by value judgments. I especially wish that they could more fully appreciate the arbitrariness of their view of family growth. The value of individuation so often invoked by therapists is one that is most relevant in a capitalist society. It may not, however, be useful to certain oppressed family groups in our society who must remain firmly enmeshed if they are to survive. Taken to their extreme, commitments to such values as self-differentiation, self-realization, or self-actualization can lead to self-indulgence. I would strongly question whether we have enough knowledge at this time to impose these values upon all families in therapy. I have little knowledge of how family therapy is practiced in socialist as opposed to capitalist countries. It would be reasonable to surmise, however, that the values which would define emotional growth in a socialist country would be quite different from those which define personal growth in America. Urie Bronfenbrenner (1975) recently discussed some aspects of this concern:

> I was testifying at a congressional hearing on the results of a study I had conducted documenting the progressive deterioration, over the past twenty-five years, of the family and its position in American society, and the concomitant decline in measures reflecting the psychological and social development of children. After I had finished, a legislator posed a question. Every year, she said, congressional committees were being presented with more and more compelling evidence that the nation's families and children were in deep trouble. Yet, year after year, the nation refused to act. "Other countries are willing to make the commitment, why aren't we? As a psychologist, how do you explain that?"
>
> After the usual disclaimer about the lack of relevant research, I speculated that the explanation might lie in our strong ideological

commitment to individual freedom and responsibility. This ideology, I suggested, had historical roots: most of us were descendants of men and women who had come to our shores in rebellion against authority of one form or another. Witness the first flag of independent Massachusetts with its old inscription: "Don't tread on me!" In succeeding decades, the growth of the nation geographically by "going West" and economically by free enterprise had further strengthened the conviction that responsibility for success or failure lay, in the last analysis, within the individual himself and not in external circumstances.

But my questioners were not so easily satisfied. That's all very well for the past, they said, but what about the present? With the frontier gone and free enterprise much hobbled, what keeps these attitudes alive? Today, what forces or institutions focus on and foster individualism and reinforce the doctrine of "Do your own thing"?

I do not remember what exactly I said. I think I made some unkind remarks about big business, and quoted William James on the price America pays for "worshipping the bitch-goddess Success." But I remembered all too well my unspoken thoughts and feelings. As I sat there in the witness chair, I recalled the puzzlement of some of my colleagues abroad about how American psychologists define and deal with human problems: the amount of time we spend testing and treating the child; the parent; or the patient; rather than the situation in which he or she lives. Our tendency to seek and advocate the solution of personal problems through the direct intervention of the professional; our preoccupation, in psychological practice and research, with sex, aggression, and achievement, as against cooperation and concern for others; our anxiety about dependency and conformity; our emphasis on freedom from the bond of social roles, both within and outside the family; our search for existential experience; and, perhaps, the most revealing, our definition of the highest goals of psychological development in terms of "self-actualization."

Chapter 10

Back to Reality:
Training and Service Delivery

I have presented my version of an ideal system for evaluating and treating patients with emotional disorders. Obviously my version of what is ideal does not reflect current realities of clinical practice. Too few practitioners are willing or able to provide the kind of evaluation and treatment I have recommended, and the majority of Americans plagued with emotional disorders are unlikely to be treated with a multidimensional approach. This book would be incomplete if I failed to provide at least some recommendations for implementing the system of treatment I advocate.

One approach to improving mental health care would be to increase the number of skilled clinicians available. I have defined a clinician as a professional capable of diagnosing the patient with both classificatory and etiological approaches and of using his diagnoses to prescribe effective treatment. This task requires that the clinician at least be familiar with the pathology of emotional disorders, with the major theories of their causation, and with the major treatment modalities. None of the current programs for training mental health professionals adequately prepare trainees to meet these requirements. Training in psychiatry probably comes closest to being comprehensive. Psychiatric trainees have adequate opportunity to familiarize themselves with the various behaviors defined as emotional disorders, they learn some theories of causation quite well, and they have some opportunity to learn about all modalities of intervention. As physicians they have certain skills not available to other mental health professionals. They can prescribe biological interventions with considerable awareness of how these agents will influence the patient's physical state, and they can treat the physical side effects of these interventions.

Psychiatrists are also likely to be more aware than other mental health professionals of physical dysfunction as a causative factor in emotional disorders. Dysfunction of the nervous system as well as of other organ systems can be a significant etiological factor in many emotional disorders, and such dysfunction is often treatable. It can be argued that a nonpsychiatric mental health professional who is scrupulous in ascertaining that all of his cases are evaluated by an internist or family practitioner can do just as good a job as the psychiatrist. Most psychiatrists will, after all, use nonpsychiatric physician consultants in checking out suspected organic pathology, and once the presence of such pathology is ascertained, they will usually turn the patient over to the consultant anyway. This argument fails to consider that the psychiatrist's training in both medicine and psychology should provide him unusual skill in hypothesizing the existence of major physical disorders in emotionally disturbed people. The psychiatrist is probably more skillful in making such hypotheses than any other physician. After years of training in nonpsychiatric and psychiatric medicine, the psychiatrist develops an intuitive sense that certain symptoms which may appear emotional in nature are likely to be caused by serious physical dysfunction.

While the psychiatrist's medical training provides him certain advantages in dealing with emotionally disturbed patients, there are other clinical attitudes, expectations, and behaviors which the psychiatrist is likely to learn during medical training that may be disadvantageous. The most critical of these are:

1. The physician develops an attitudinal set which leads him to neglect the study of environmental variables. He learns to focus exclusively on the individual. There is little chance anywhere in medical school to learn about the role of the environment in creating and sustaining a disorder. In nonpsychiatric medicine this is unfortunate. In psychiatric practice it is tragic. Psychiatrists who never learn to study seriously the role of the environment or to use interventions which change the environment (and there are many who never do) can never be adequate clinicians.

2. In nonpsychiatric medical practice patients are almost always cooperative and motivated to get well. Often they are even grateful. The medically trained clinician learns to expect patients to behave that way. Many emotionally disordered patients,

however, are uncooperative and poorly motivated. They don't like to take prescribed medication and frequently request medication the doctor does not wish to prescribe. They are argumentative, resistant, and sometimes hostile. They are rarely grateful. The psychiatrist who expects his patients to behave like other patients is likely to be profoundly disappointed. If he cannot learn to adapt to the new set of responses he receives from patients, he is likely to become trapped in an adversarial approach to patients in which he is constantly exhorting them to behave in ways in which they do not want to behave.

3. Physicians are not trained to deal with the subtle ramifications of the issue of responsibility as it relates to clinical practice. They are used to imputing blame to nature or acts of God. When they must learn to use treatment modalities which require assigning responsibility to the patient, they have a great deal of difficulty in developing a consistent model for dealing with the issues of blame and responsibility.

4. Physicians are trained to act. They reflexively try to do something to the patient and to do it as soon as possible. In treating emotional disorders, however, there are few situations which call for immediate action. As a rule, action should be taken slowly and deliberately. In many instances "benign neglect" is preferable to hasty intervention. The psychiatrist must unlearn response tendencies directed toward immediate resolution of problems. Many psychiatrists never develop sufficient patience to be effective clinicians.

5. Physicians are used to considerable authority over other professionals as well as over patients. In some aspects of practice, however, the psychiatrist must learn to work with teams made up of other professionals. Other professional team members do not wish to be treated in an authoritarian manner, and team functioning is more efficient if there is a spirit of egalitarianism among team members. Some psychiatrists never learn to temper their authority and are ineffective in working with other professionals in team settings.

The psychiatrist's training is also seriously deficient in certain theoretical and clinical areas. Many physicians who begin psychiatric training have never had a course in psychology. The trainee is unfamiliar with learning theory or personality theory. He is unlikely to have studied general systems theory or sociology, knowledge of which would increase his awareness of the relationship of the environment to the patient. These deficiencies are never fully remedied in psychiatric training. Most training programs focus heavily upon classificatory diagnosis and the use of biological interventions. They also teach a great deal about the psychoanalytic theory of personality development and how to provide a form of individual psychotherapy which is usually based on psychoanalytic theory. There are a few training programs which emphasize behavior, group, or family therapy, but these are exceptions. In most programs these interventions and the theories which underlie them are taught perfunctorily. I do not know of any psychiatric training program in which the trainee receives enough experience with all modes of treatment to gain an adequate sense of how they can be efficiently prescribed.

Next to training in psychiatry, training in clinical psychology comes closest to providing the qualifications for becoming a clinician. Psychologists generally have adequate training in psychopathology and learn many different perspectives on etiology. They learn a great deal about personality theory, learning theory, and sociology. In some of the better programs, they learn also how to provide individual, group, and family therapy in addition to behavior modification. In contrast to psychiatrists, they have little difficulty in grasping the importance of the environment in creating emotional disorders. The research-oriented training of clinical psychologists should also, in theory, leave them relatively open to accept the relevance of a large variety of theories and interventions, clinical psychology programs focusing almost exclusively on behaviorism being possible exceptions.

There are some obvious factors which limit the probability that psychologists will become clinicians. They cannot prescribe biological interventions, and most never learn the indications for biological interventions. Psychologists either avoid treating severely disturbed patients or treat them inappropriately with a program that excludes biological intervention. Another problem is that psychologists do not receive extensive clinical experience during training and may spend more time studying the literature and conducting research than in actually dealing with patients. Part of the problem is that they have only limited access to clinical training opportunities. In most hospital and community clinic settings, the psychologist trainee is unlikely to receive the amount of attention given to the psychiatric trainee. The psychologist trainee is given only limited responsibility for evaluating and prescribing treatment programs for patients. The best training experience for psychologists, in terms of quality of supervision and opportunity to assume responsibility, is usually in university student health clinics or counseling centers. Here the trainee is likely to encounter patients who are financially well off, highly motivated, and not very disturbed. As a result of this kind of training, few clinical psychologists learn to deal with severe disorders, to work with lower socioeconomic groups, or to take full responsibility for their patients.

For the past five years I have invited postdoctoral fellows in clinical psychology to spend four months training on my inpatient unit. They work closely with the psychiatric resident, but also assume many of the functions of psychiatric residents. Each psychology trainee is assigned several patients. The psychiatric resident takes full responsibility for the nonpsychiatric medical needs of these patients and writes all orders for medication. The psychology trainee is given full responsibility for managing and providing all other aspects of treatment. He is expected to participate in decisions as to the use of biological interventions and is responsible for prescribing and orchestrating the patient's complete treatment program in the hospital. (This system creates a certain amount of extra and usually undesired work for the psychiatric resident, who functions almost as a medical consultant to the psychologist. To avoid morale problems, the psychology trainee provides a compensatory service to the psychiatry trainee by teaching him about behavior modification and psychological testing.) Most of the psychologists who have gone through this experience have performed superbly. Because they have had more training in treating emotional disorders, they outperform the residents after only a few weeks on the service. More important, they learn to take responsibility for diagnosis and treatment, and are able to function as clinicians. I believe that if these trainees could have a longer experience with this type of training and could continue to work in close collaboration with physicians, they could eventually practice as clinicians. Unfortunately, psychologists have few opportunities to receive even four months of the kind of training I have described, and four months of such training is definitely insufficient.

It is unlikely that training in social work could make one a clinician in the sense I have given the term. A major problem here is the length and intensity of training. Social workers have limited experience in working with patients and even less in assuming full responsibility for them. They may have some opportunity to develop skills in group, individual, and family psychotherapy, but they learn almost nothing about biological interventions. In most schools of social work they are also unlikely to learn behavior therapies. Much of social work training is directed toward helping the student gain greater awareness of the influence of the environment upon the patient. While social workers are usually quite sensitive to this issue, their training is not always relevant to work with patients. The social work trainee spends a good deal of time learning how to deal with social agencies that influence the patient and only a limited amount of time on the interpersonal aspects of environmental influence. If the social worker is to become a clinician, he must seek additional training which goes beyond that provided in the two-year social work curriculum.

Training in nursing also suffers from brevity of clinical experience and lack of opportunity for the trainee to assume full responsibility for treatment of emotionally disordered patients. Many of the skills learned in nursing school are related primarily to physical aspects of medicine and are not relevant to the treatment of emotional disorders. Unless the nurse takes graduate work and can work in settings where it is possible to gain a certain degree of extracurricular training in using all clinical interventions, he is unlikely to develop the skills required of a clinician.

At one time it was felt that the family practitioner would be an ideal person to treat many forms of emotional disorder. The family doctor already has a relationship with patients for whose physical care he is responsible. He is often the first person to hear complaints suggestive of psychological dysfunction. Delivery of mental health services would be simplified if the family practitioner could function as a clinician. Unfortunately, the early hopes that family practitioners would become deeply involved in the diagnosis and treatment of emotional disorders have not been realized. It has been my experience, with family medicine programs originally conceived to provide substantial training in psychiatry and the behavioral sciences, that as time passes both program leaders and students lose interest in such training. The major problem here is the demands of family practice on the physician's time. Family practitioners quickly realize they do not have the time to perform any but the most perfunctory kind of psychotherapy with patients. They also find that they have only limited time available to do diagnostic evaluations. Given these limits, family practitioners are prone to hasty diagnosis and heavy reliance on biological interventions, often making errors in diagnosis and using the wrong drug and the wrong dosages. Increasingly disillusioned, they lose interest in dealing with emotionally disturbed patients and routinely refer them to psychiatrists.

Given the realities of current training and practice in the mental health professions, there are only three ways to improve training and thereby increase the number of competent clinicians. The first and most obvious solution is to accept the current reality and designate the psychiatrist as the clinician who will assume primary responsibility for diagnosis and prescription. If we could train a greater number of psychiatrists in an integrated, multidimensional approach to treatment, patients would certainly receive better services.

Training psychiatrists to be competent clinicians should not, in theory, require a massive restructuring of psychiatric training programs. These programs could be adequate if they provided greater theoretical grounding in psychology and sociology and taught the specific skills required for behavior modification, group, and family therapy. It would also be necessary to teach psychiatric trainees to integrate these interventions with psychopharmacology and individual psychotherapy.

Unforunately, these changes would be difficult to implement. The trend in psychiatric training these days is toward greater one-dimensionality, with heavy emphasis upon biological intervention. While this trend is perhaps only temporary, it would be quite difficult at this time to expand the teaching of psychology or sociology in psychiatric training programs. It might also be difficult to convince the leaders of training programs of the need to teach an integrated approach to treatment and of the need to provide practical experience in all intervention modalities.

A second solution might be to resurrect the idea of creating a training program in which students learn just enough medicine to comprehend the biological aspects of diagnosis and treatment and spend the rest of their time on psychology, sociology, and the skills involved in psychotherapy and behavior modification. For decades now a number of clinicians have advocated creation of a new degree which combines the best training of medicine, psychiatry, and psychology. The holder of this degree would be able to prescribe medication and would have a far broader understanding of human behavior than is currently possessed by psychiatrists.

But the professions of psychiatry and psychology have resisted the creation of a new profession. Although there have been several serious attempts to create programs which would grant the degree of Doctor of Mental Health or Doctor of Psychotherapy, enthusiasm for such programs is currently at low ebb. One reason for this is that the major professional associations in psychology and psychiatry have opposed licensure of graduates of these programs. Those who have worked to develop new programs have learned, often bitterly, that the organized professional associations will oppose them in a powerful and decisive manner.

A third solution is to have well-trained clinical psychologists (and in some instances social workers and nurses) learn more about the use of biological interventions and pool their skills with internists and family physicians so that, in effect, "the clinician" becomes a team of two. This approach is being developed in some family practice clinics, but a major problem is that few psychologists (or other nonmedical professionals) have sufficient understanding of biological interventions to be competent diagnosticians. Often neither the psychologist nor the family physician is fully capable of performing diagnostic function, and, while their treatment skills may complement each other in many ways, the team often fails to properly evaluate the patient.

Perhaps because of my bias as a psychiatrist it seems to me that right now the easiest way to increase the number of trained clinicians is to define the psychiatrist as the person most likely to be a clinician and to focus our efforts on creating psychiatric training programs which teach an integrated multidimensional approach to the patient. I am also convinced that it would be possible to deliver good mental health care services to the American people without drastically increasing the number of psychiatrists currently being trained. It is more important to focus upon the quality of psychiatric training than upon the number of psychiatrists trained. It is critical to recall here that I am not defining the clinician as the person who necessarily carries out the prescribed treatment. He may provide treatment if he wishes, but his major role is diagnosis and prescription. There is no reason why other professionals, including family practitioners, psychologists, social workers, and nurses, could not work with the psychiatric clinician to deliver a full range of mental health services to all patients.

The psychiatrist's role as diagnostician and prescriber of treatment has already been noted. The family physician would be a second key member of the team, referring patients to the psychiatrist for evaluation and assuming responsibility for many of the biological treatments the psychiatrist prescribes. The family physician would also be available to treat the patient's physical complaints and, if he wishes, some of the psychological problems that can develop as a result of physical illness. In consultation with the psychiatrist he might also initiate preventive measures with regard to both physical and emotional disorders. Family practitioners who wish to invest the time and energy in developing diagnostic and psychotherapeutic skills might also be able to do a certain amount of clinical evaluation and psychotherapy.

The third key member of the team I would call simply the psychotherapist. This person would probably have a professional background in psychology, social work, or nursing. Ideally, he would be skilled in providing all modalities of psychotherapy, including individual, group, family and behavior therapy. If one psychotherapist possessing all these skills could not be found, more than one could be employed. A treatment team might, for example, have one psychotherapist who does most of the family work and another who does most of the behavior modification. I view the three key members of the team as functioning in a relatively egalitarian manner. The psychiatrist would not supervise the treatment provided by the family physician or the psychotherapist unless he had expertise in the specific modality beyond that of the others.

While the psychiatrist's main function would be diagnosis and prescription of treatment, this does not mean he would "never get his hands dirty." To keep up his diagnostic skills, he would have to stay involved in treatment activities and might elect to treat a certain number of patients with several or all intervention modalities. The psychiatrist might also wish to become especially skilled in one intervention, but his usefulness to the team would not be based on that skill.

This team approach would remedy many of the problems of mental health service delivery in the United States today. But if we are to implement effectively this approach, we must resolve five other critical problems in service delivery.

1. We need to develop a system of health care delivery which increases the likelihood that all patients will have access to multidimensional treatment. The mere existence of an increased number of clinicians with a multidimensional approach is not sufficient.

2. We need to diminish the disparity between the levels of care available to poor and affluent people. Poor people currently receive far less attention from skilled practitioners than do those who can afford to pay for private services. A democratic society should be unwilling to tolerate these inequities.

3. We need to diminish the rivalries and battles among the various mental health professionals for control of the psychotherapy market. It will be impossible to develop a team approach to treatment unless this "cold war" between the professions is stopped. When a patient needs some form of psychotherapy, he should be treated by a therapist who can offer the most effective services for the least expense. The task orientation of each professional should be based on his functional skills rather than on a "trade union" mentality or territorial needs.

4. We need to provide more effective outpatient or partial hospitalization care for a large percentage of patients currently being hospitalized. Too many patients are currently treated in hospitals when they could be more effectively and economically treated in other settings.

5. We need to provide better services for the severely disturbed. In both public and private sectors, with both inpatient and outpatient care, there is a disturbing tendency for professionals to select the more attractive relatively healthy patients for intensive treatment, particularly for psychotherapy. This perpetuates a system in which the sicker patient is likely to receive poorer care than the healthy patient.

All these needs can be met by modifying the behavior of those providing health care services. The principles of operant conditioning suggest this modification can best be achieved by changing the manner in which clinical practices are positively reinforced. Negative reinforcement or punishment is unnecessary and undesirable. Positive reinforcement can be either internal or external. Practitioners have learned to reward themselves when they behave in a manner consistent with certain internalized values and attitudes. But while it is possible for individual practitioners to change their internal perspectives and patterns of self-reinforcement, little can be done to modify the internal reinforcement systems of thousands of practitioners. It is necessary, therefore, to concentrate on external reinforcement, one major source of which is the professional peer group. Since the practitioner seeks the approval of colleagues and is reinforced when his practice meets professional standards, it should be possible to change his behavior by changing the values and ideologies of the profession. This would seem the most benign way of changing the clinician's behavior, but it is none too practical. We cannot legislate values and ideologies; the most we can do is exhort and persuade our colleagues to live up to certain standards, and there are obvious and important limits to the powers of exhortation and persuasion.

Another external and very powerful reinforcer of the clinician's behavior is money. In a capitalist society the behavior of all people is largely influenced by monetary reinforcement. Mental health professionals are not immune to this influence. In recent decades our society has shown an increasing willingness to manipulate monetary reinforcement so as to shape the behavior of consumers and providers of all types of services. For the purpose of our discussion, it is unimportant whether greater government control of monetary reinforcement is either desirable or necessary. Such control is a reality of our era. It is a reality that already exerts a powerful influence on clinical practice, and it will be even more powerful in the future.

Increasingly the costs of mental health care are not being directly paid by the patient but are being paid instead by private insurors or government agencies. Third-party payment will expand drastically if and when national health insurance is initiated. National health insurance can be viewed as a massive effort to restructure the behavior of consumers and providers of health services by changing the contingencies of monetary reinforcement for both groups. Financial savings or financial rewards can be structured so as to program the behavior of each actor in the treatment process.

The issues of third-party payment and national health insurance are, of course, much too complex to be fully understood simply in terms of operant conditioning. Many other systems-related variables are involved. Speculations about some of the possible systemic consequences of increasing or changing current systems of third-part payment are beyond the scope of this book. The most I will attempt here is to show how monetary reinforcements can be structured to change the behavior of practitioners in a way that will more effectively meet the needs of consumers.

If government agencies and private insurors are to function without going bankrupt, they must develop standards which define and limit appropriate services for each patient. Whatever type of national health insurance is implemented, it will have to include some standards for determining what treatments will be reimbursed with what patient and for what duration. Because of the obvious need for professionals to have considerable control over the manner in which they practice, all planners have thus far insisted that these guidelines be developed by professionals. The appropriateness of a given treatment should be determined by fellow practitioners through a process called peer review. The federal government has already formalized this process by creating Professional Standard Review Organizations (PSROs) mandated to develop treatment guidelines for determining reimbursements for Medicaid and Medicare services and eventually for national health insurance. Private insurors also are seeking stricter reimbursement guidelines.

It is my hope that some of the guidelines for multidimensional treatment presented in this book might be used by Professional Standard Review Organizations to develop reimbursement standards. If practitioners are more likely to be reimbursed for using a multidimensional approach, they will be more likely to use such an approach. Here it might be useful to reassure the reader that there are limits to my grandiosity. Most of my recommendations for treatment have not been validated as useful by scientific experimentation. I have presented only guidelines, not imperatives. Whatever reimbursement standards are eventually developed by PSROs will be the product of a continuing dialogue between representatives of different viewpoints. I am hoping merely that my viewpoint will be heard.

I am convinced, however, that there is sufficient justification for constructing a system of third-party payment which would discourage inappropriate one-dimensional treatment. If a patient has been receiving a given type of treatment for a certain period of time and has not responded to it, the third-part agency could intervene and demand that the treatment be evaluated. Such an evaluation could be conducted by peers who I hope would be open to considering a multidimensional approach. If the peer review committee concludes that the patient is receiving the wrong treatment or that some new combination of treatment should be added, the third-party agency could refuse to reimburse the patient's continued treatment unless the practitioner agrees to provide the recommended treatment. I am excruciatingly aware of the probability that such dictatorial monitoring can seriously limit the freedom of both the consumer and the practitioner. Eventually, however, we are going to have increased monitoring and control of the behavior of providers of health care in one direction or another. I am merely suggesting that such control be in the direction of favoring multidimensional treatment.

The issue of diminishing the gap between the quality of services currently received by poor and affluent people can begin to be resolved by providing some form of mental health insurance for all our citizens. Citizens who can pay for all types of treatment will have a greater opportunity to receive all types. Such a step will certainly not result in an immediate or massive change in the way poor people are treated. It is probable that they will continue to seek psychiatric services less frequently than affluent people and that practitioners will still invest most of their energy in treating patients whose socioeconomic class is similar to their own. But providing every citizen in our country the same potentiality for paying for health care services through insurance would be a great step forward in relieving the inequities in our current system.

Third-party payment can be used to help resolve the problems created by professional rivalries if we are willing to devise a system in which the various specialities are given the highest rewards for providing the services at which they are most skilled and in which various professionals are rewarded equally for providing equal services. A crucial issue here is getting the psychiatrist, the person most likely to be the clinician, to spend more time in evaluating patients and prescribing treatments and less time actually conducting the treatments. One way this goal could be achieved through monetary reinforcement would be to pay the psychiatrist a greater amount per hour for evaluation than for treatment. If the psychiatrist assumed the responsibility for the biological treatment of a patient, he would be reimbursed at the same rate as the family practitioner. The amount of reimbursement offered for providing an hour of psychotherapy could be made the same for all professional groups, whether psychiatrists, social workers, or nurses. The only issue here would be competence. Under this system, it would be necessary to license various practitioners as psychotherapists. Members of any professional group could be reimbursed by third-party agencies if they could demonstrate their mastery of the skills involved in the provision of psychotherapy and behavior modification. Under such a system, there would be nothing to prevent the psychiatrist from doing as much treatment as he wanted to do, but he could obviously earn more money by spending more time in his most appropriate role.

One of the reasons too many patients are hospitalized is that our current system of private and public health insurance rewards doctors more for hospitalizing patients than for treating them in nonhospital settings. It would be tragic if this system were to continue to be sanctioned. Most of the national health insurance plans thus far proposed provide liberal benefits for partial hospitalization, and their implementation would lead to considerable improvement in the existing system. But I am not convinced that coverage of partial care will in itself lead to more judicious use of hospitalization. My experience working in both hospitals and partial care units has been that the practitioner devotes more time to treating the same number of patients in partial care than in a hospital. If the financial rewards per patient were the same in either situation, there would be a temptation to hospitalize patients who might have done as well or better in a partial care clinic. This would not only be bad for patients but would unnecessarily penalize the taxpayer. On way of dealing with this problem might be to provide the doctor a higher fee for treating people in a partial care or outpatient unit than for treating them in the hospital.

The final problem, of getting practitioners to treat sicker people, particularly sicker people with lengthy and costly interventions such as psychotherapy, may be insurmountable even manipulating the contingencies of third-party payment. We could legislate that treatment of patients with severe disorders be reimbursed at a level higher than the treatment of less disturbed patients. This, however, migh stigmatize the severly disturbed and might also encourage practitioners to diagnose more severe disturbances and to encourage patients to act more disturbed. One step we might take would be to recommend that any emotionally disturbed person who has been in a mental hospital or correctional setting for over a certain period of time (perhaps two months) be defined as in need of special treatment. Subsequent treatment could be reimbursed at a level higher than for other patients. If this were implemented, there would be little danger of stigmatizing such a patient, since he would already have been hospitalized. The danger of overdiagnosis would be attenuated since the patient would not be eager to seek lengthy hospitalization, and the practitioner would gain no immediate advantage by affixing upon the patient the label of a serious disorder. The extra costs involved in treating these individuals in outpatient settings might well be compensated by the money saved in preventing their subsequent incapacitation and hospitalization.

My suggestions are presented in a terse, incomplete manner, not to serve as mandates for change, but to illustrate how service delivery problems could be solved by manipulating monetary reinforcement. The reader who is annoyed by my depiction of the practitioner as a person who can be manipulated by economic rewards should be assured that I believe that nonmaterialistic reinforcements also shape clinical behavior. Sometimes it is difficult to separate the influence of monetary reinforcement from the influence of professional and personal standards in ascertaining what actually determines the practitioners's behavior. It is possible to develop clinical standards which will rationalize or justify high earnings for the clinician. But standards can also be held to for idealistic reasons, and these standards might just happen to encourage practices that are remunerative. A practitioner who firmly believes that only psychoanalysis will cure patients will naturally gravitate toward treating a few relatively affluent people for long periods of time. A practitioner who firmly believes that only biological treatment is effective will treat many patients of varying classes for short periods of time. Each practitioner might make a large amount of money, and each might correctly argue that financial rewards have little influence on his style of practice. I emphasize this point because I have no wish to impugn the behavior of any of my professional colleagues. In my view they have been far more idealistic and far less mercenary than most other groups in our society.

The task of writing this book has made me more optimistic as to the possibility of providing better treatment for the emotionally disturbed. We cannot, of course, alleviate all forms of mental suffering, but technologies are available which can help the majority of those plagued with emotional disorders. These technologies will get better and better. Our problem is that we have not learned to use existing technologies efficiently and humanely. We are too restricted by the parochial teachings of our own past to have learned to use effectively all dimensions of treatment. It is my hope that professionals dedicated to bringing about helpful changes in their patient's behavior will seek and welcome similar changes in their own behavior. We will achieve the goal of multi-dimensional treatment more quickly to the extent that we approach our patients with open minds and a relentless commitment to study and confront the complexities of human behavior.

References

Adler A. (1924). *The Practice and Theory of Individual Psychology.* New York: Harcourt Brace.
Adler, A. (1931). *What Life Should Mean to You.* Boston: Little, Brown.
Aichorn, A. (1953). *Wayward Youth.* New York: Viking.
Akiskal, H.S., and McKinney, W.T. (1973). Psychiatry and pseudopsychiatry. *Archives of General Psychiatry* 28:367–373.
Akiskal, H.S., and McKinney, W.T. (1975). Overview of recent research in depression. *Archives of General Psychiatry* 32:285–308.
Alexander, F. (1956). *Psychoanalysis and Psychotherapy.* New York: Norton.
Alexander, F., and Ross, H. (1952). *Dynamic Psychiatry.* Chicago: University of Chicago Press.
Alexander, J.F., and Parsons, B.V. (1975). Short term behavioral intervention with delinquent families. *Journal of Abnormal Psychology* 81:219–225.
Appleton, W.S., (1976). Third psychoactive drug usage guide. *Diseases of the Nervous System* (January):39–51.
Avery, D., and Winokur, G. (1976). Mortality in depressed patients with electroconvulsive therapy and antidepressants. *Archives of General Psychiatry* 33: 1029–1037.
Ayd, F.J. (1975). Treatment resistant patients: a moral, legal and therapeutic challenge. In *Rational Psychopharmacotherapy and the Right to Treatment,* ed. F.J. Ayd. Baltimore: Ayd Medical Communications.
Ayd, FJ. (ed.) (1974). *Medical, Moral and Legal Issues in Mental Health Care.* Baltimore: Williams and Wilkins.

References

Azrin, N.H., and Nunn, R.G. (1973). Habit reversal: a method of eliminating nervous habits and tics. *Behavioral Research and Therapy* 11:619-628.

Baehr, G. (1954). The comparative effectiveness of individual psychotherapy, group psychotherapy and a combination of these methods. *Journal of Consulting Psychology* 18:179-183.

Barber, T.X., et al. (1974). Cardiovascular control. *Aldine Annual of Biofeedback and Self Control:* 297-421.

Bateson, G., Jackson, D., Haley, J., and Weakland, J. (1956). Toward a therapy of schizophrenia. *Behavioral Sciences* 1:251-264.

Beck, D.F. (1975). Research findings on the outcomes of marital counseling. *Social Casework* 56:153-181.

Beels, C., and Ferber, A. (1972). What family therapists do. In *The Book of Family Therapy*, ed. A. Ferber, M. Mendelsohn, and A. Napier. New York: Jason Aronson.

Benson, R. (1975). The forgotten treatment modality in bipolar illness: psychotherapy. *Diseases of the Nervous System* 36:634-638.

Benson, H., Beary, J.F., and Carol, M.T. (1974). The relaxation response. *Psychiatry* 37:37-46.

Berger, M. (1970). *Videotape Techniques in Psychiatric Training and Treatment.* New York: Brunner-Mazel.

Berne, E. (1964). *Games People Play.* New York: Grove Press.

Berne, E. (1966). *Principles of Group Treatment.* New York: Oxford University Press.

Berne, E., Steiner, C.M., and Dusay, J.M. (1973). Transactional analysis. In *Direct Psychotherapy*, vol. 1, ed. R. Jurjevich. Coral Gables, Fla.: University of Miami Press.

Berzins, J.I. (In press). Therapist patient matching.

Betz, B., and Whitehorn, J.C. (1956). The relationship of the therapist to the outcome of therapy in schizophrenia. *Psychiatric Research Reports* 5:89-105.

Blackwell, B. (1973). Drug therapy, patient compliance. *New England Journal of Medicine* 289:249-252.

Blanchard, E.B., and Young, L.D. (1974). Clinical applications of biofeedback training: a review of evidence. *Archives of General Psychiatry* 30:573-589.

Blos, P. (1962). *On Adolescence: A Psychoanalytic Interpretation.* Glencoe, Ill.: Free Press.

Boss, M. (1963). *Daseinsanalyse and Psychoanalysis.* New York: Basic Books.

Bowen, M. (1965). Family psychotherapy with schizophrenia in the hospital and in private practice. In *Intensive Family Therapy*, ed. I. Boszormenyi-Nagy and J.L. Framo. New York: Hoeber.

Bowen, M. (1966). The use of family theory in clinical practice. *Comprehensive Psychiatry* 7:345–374.

Bowen, M. (1971). Toward the differentiation of a self in one's own family. In *Family Interaction*, ed. J.L. Framo. New York: Springer.

Brady, J.P. (1972). Systematic desensitization. In *Behavior Modification, Principles and Clinical Applications*, ed. S. W. Agras. Boston: Little, Brown.

Bronfenbrenner, U. (1975). Letter. *American Psychological Association Monitor* 6:2.

Brooks, A. (1974). *Law, Psychiatry and the Mental Health System*. Boston: Little, Brown.

Burrows, D., and Lapides, F.R., ed. (1969). *Alienation: A Casebook*. New York: Crowell.

Burton, A., ed. (1970). *Encounter*. San Francisco: Jossey-Bass.

Busse, E. W. (1972). The presidential address: there are decisions to be made. *American Journal of Psychiatry* 129:1–9.

Caplan, G. (1964). *Principles of Preventive Psychiatry*. New York: Basic Books.

Carpenter, W.T., McGlashan, T.H., and Strauss, J.S. (1977). The treatment of acute schizophrenia without drugs: an investigation of some current assumptions. *American Journal of Psychiatry* 134:14–20.

Cartwright, R.D., and Vogel, J.L. (1958). A comparison of changes in psychoneurotic patients during matched periods of therapy and no therapy. *Journal of Consulting Psychology* 23:411–413.

Chartier, G.M. (1971). The A-B therapist variable: real or imagined? *Psychological Bulletin* 75:22–23.

Clark, R. (1970). *Crime in America*. New York: Simon and Schuster.

Coppen, A., Peet, M., and Bailey, J. (1973). The effect of long term lithium treatment on the morbidity of affective disorders. Internal Report, Medical Research Council Neuropsychiatry Unit. Epson, Surrey, England.

Corsini, R., ed. (1973). *Current Psychotherapies*. Itasca, Ill.: F.E. Peacock.

Crane, G.E. (1973). Persistent dyskinesia. *British Journal of Psychiatry* 122:395.

Davis, J.M. (1975). Which patients need ECT? *Medical World News* October, 1975.

Davison, G.C. (1976). Homosexuality: the ethical challenge. *Journal of Consulting and Clinical Psychology* 44:157–162.

Detre, T.P., and Jarecki, H.G. (1971). *Modern Psychiatric Treatment*. Philadelphia: Lippincott.

Dollard, J., and Miller, N.E. (1950). *Personality and Psychotherapy*. New York: McGraw-Hill.

Eitlinger, L., Laane, C.V., and Langfeldt, G. (1958). The prognostic value of the clinical picture and the therapeutic value of physical treatment in

References

schizophrenia and the schizophreniform states. *Acta Psychiatry and Neurology Scandinavia* 33:33-53.

Elkes, J. (1966). Introduction to Psychopharmacology. In *Biological Treatment of Mental Illness*, ed. M. Rinkel, pp. 437-449. New York: L.C. Page.

Ellis, A. (1962). *Reason and Emotion in Psychotherapy*. New York: Lyle Stuart.

Ellis, A. (1973). Rational-emotive therapy. In *Current Psychotherapies*, ed. R. Corsini. Itasca, Ill.: F.E. Peabody.

Engel, G. (1960). A unified concept of health and disease. *Perspectives in Biology and Medicine* 3:459-470.

Eysenck, H.J. (1952). The effects of psychotherapy: an evaluation. *Journal of Consulting Psychology* 16:319-324.

Eysenck, H.J. (1959). Learning theory and behavior therapy. *Journal of Mental Science* 105:61-75.

Ezriel, H.(1950). A psychoanalytic approach to group treatment. *British Journal of Medical Psychology* 23:59-74.

Fagen, J., and Shepherd, I.L. (1970). *Gestalt Therapy Now*. Palo Alto, Calif.: Science and Behavior Books.

Fairbairn, W.R.D. (1952). *An Object-Relations Theory of the Personality*. New York: Basic Books.

Ferber, A., Mendelsohn, and Napier, A., ed. (1972). *The Book of Family Therapy*. New York: Jason Aronson.

Fieve, R.R. (1970). Lithium in psychiatry. *International Journal of Psychiatry* 9:375-412. New York: Jason Aronson.

Fieve, R.R., et al. (1975). Lithium carbonate in affective disorders: IV. A double blind study of prophylaxis in unipolar recurrent depression. *Archives of General Psychiatry* 32:1541-1544.

Fish, J.M. (1973). *Placebo Therapy*. San Francisco: Jossey-Bass.

Ford, D.N., and Urban, H.B. (1965). *Systems of Psychotherapy*. New York: Wiley.

Foulkes, S.H., and Anthony, E.J. (1965). *Group Psychotherapy: the Psychoanalytic Approach*, 2nd ed. Baltimore: Penguin Books.

Framo, J.L. (1965). Rationale and techniques of intensive therapy. In *Intensive Family Therapy*, ed. I. Boszormenyi-Nagy and J.L. Framo. New York: Hoeber.

Framo, J.L. (1970). Symptoms from a family transactional viewpoint. *International Psychiatry Clinics* 7:125-171. Boston: Little, Brown.

Framo, J.L. (1976). Family of origin as a therapeutic resource for adults in marital and family therapy: you can and should go home again. *Family Process* 15:193-211.

Frank, J.D. (1957). Some determinants, manifestations and effects of cohesion in therapy groups. *International Journal of Group Psychotherapy* 7:53-62.

Frank, J. D. (1961). *Persuasion and Healing.* Baltimore: Johns Hopkins Press.
Frank, J. D. (1971). Therapeutic factors in psychotherapy. *American Journal of Psychotherapy* 25:350-361.
Frankl, V. E. (1960). Paradoxical intention: a logotherapeutic technique. *American Journal of Psychotherapy* 14:520-526.
Franks, C. M. (1969). Behavior therapy and its Pavlovian origins: review and perspectives. In *Behavior Therapy: Appraisal and Status,* ed. C. M. Franks. New York: McGraw-Hill.
Franks, C. M., and Wilson, T. S. (1975). *Annual Review of Behavior Therapy, Theory and Practice,* p. 589. New York: Brunner-Mazel.
Freud, S. (1937). Analysis terminable and interminable. *International Journal of Psycho-Analysis* 18:373-405.
Freud, S. (1952). *Collected Papers, 1924-1950.* New York: International Psychoanalytic Press.
Freud, S. (1955). *The Standard Edition of the Complete Psychological Works of Sigmund Freud,* ed. J. Strachey. London: Hogarth Press.
Freud, S. (1961). Moral responsibility for the content of dreams. In *Nineteen Complete Psychological Works of Sigmund Freud,* vol. 19, p. 131. Stanford Edition.
Friedman, A. S. (1975). Interaction of drug therapy and marital therapy in depressive patients. *Archives of General Psychiatry* 32:619-637.
Friedman, W. (1978). *How to Do Groups.* New York: Jason Aronson.
Fromm-Reichman, F. (1950). *Principles of Intensive Psychotherapy.* Chicago: University of Chicago Press.
Gardos, G., and Cole, J. O. (1976). Maintenance of antipsychotic therapy: is the cure worse than the disease? *American Journal of Psychiatry* 133:32-36.
Gelder, M. G., Marks, I. M., and Wolff, H. H. (1967). Desensitization and psychotherapy in the treatment of phobic states: a controlled inquiry. *British Journal of Psychiatry* 113:53-73.
Glasser, W. (1965). *Reality Therapy: A New Approach to Psychiatry.* New York: Harper and Row.
Glueck, B. C., and Stroebel, C. F. (1975). Biofeedback and meditation in the treatment of psychiatric illness. *Comprehensive Psychiatry* 16:303-321.
Goldberg, C. (1970). *Encounter: Group Sensitivity Training Experience.* New York: Jason Aronson.
Goodwin, D., et al. (1973). Alcohol problems in adopters raised apart from biological parents. *Archives of General Psychiatry* 28:238-243.
Grinker, R. R., ed. (1956). *Toward a Unified Theory of Human Behavior.* New York: Basic Books.
Grinspoon, L., and Shader, R. I. (1975). Psychotherapy and drugs in schizophrenia. In *Drugs in Combination with Other Therapies,* ed. M. Greenblatt. New York: Grune and Stratton.

Group for the Advancement of Psychiatry (1975). *Pharmacotherapy and Psychotherapy: Paradoxes, Problems and Progress.* New York:
Haley, J. (1957). Marriage therapy. In *Active Psychotherapy*, ed. H. Greenwald. New York: Atherton Press.
Haley, J. (1963). *Strategies of Psychotherapy.* New York: Grune and Stratton.
Haley, J. (1971). Family therapy. *International Journal of Psychiatry* 9:233-242.
Haley, J., and Hoffman, L. (1963). An interview with Carl Whitaker. In *Techniques of Family Therapy*, pp. 265-360. New York: Basic Books.
Halleck, J. A. Pollyanna vs. the Grinch. Unpublished manuscript.
Halleck, S. L. (1967). Hysterical personality traits, psychological, social and introgenic determinants. *Archives of General Psychiatry* 16:750-757.
Halleck, S. L. (1971). *The Politics of Therapy.* New York: Jason Aronson.
Halleck, S. L. (1976a). Another response to homosexuality: the ethical challenge. *Journal of Consulting and Clinical Psychology* 44:167-170.
Halleck, S. L. (1976b). Family therapy and social change. *Social Casework* 57:483-493.
Hallowitz, D. (1963). *Family Unit Treatment of Character Disordered Youngsters, Social Work Practice.* New York: Columbia University Press.
Harper, R. A. (1961). *Psychoanalysis and Psychotherapy: 36 Systems.* Englewood Cliffs, N.J.: Prentice-Hall.
Harper, R. A. (1975). *The New Psychotherapies.* Englewood Cliffs, N.J.: Prentice-Hall.
Harris, M. B., and Bruner, C. G. (1973). A comparison of self control and contract procedures for weight control. *Behavior Research and Therapy* 11:523-529.
Havens, L. (1972). *Approaches to the Mind.* Boston: Little, Brown.
Hirsch, S. R., et al. (1973). Outpatient maintenance of chronic schizophrenic patients with long active flupnenazine: double blind placebo trial. *British Medical Journal* 1:633-637.
Hogarty, G. E., Goldberg, S. C., and Schooler, N. R. (1975). Drug and sociotherapy in the aftercare of schizophrenia: a review. In *Drugs in Combination with Other Therapies*, ed. M. Greenblatt. New York: Grune and Stratton.
Hogarty, G. E. and Goldberg, S. C. (1973). Drug and sociotherapy in the post hospital maintenance of schizophrenic patients: one year relapse rates. *Archives of General Psychiatry* 28:54-64.
Hollister, L. E. (1975). Polypharmacy in psychiatry: is it necessary, good or bad? In *Rational Psychopharmacotherapy and the Right to Treatment*, ed. F. J. Ayd. Baltimore: Ayd Medical Communications.
Holmes, T. H., and Rahe, R. H. (1967). The social readjustment rating scale. *Journal of Psychosomatic Research* 11:213-218.
Horney, K. (1937). *The Neurotic Personality of Our Time.* New York: Norton.
Jackson, D., and Weakland, J. (1959). Schizophrenic symptoms and family

interaction. *Archives of General Psychiatry* 1:618-621.
Janov, A. (1970). *The Primal Scream: A Revolutionary Cure for Neurosis.* New York: Putnam.
Johnson, A., and Szurer, S. A. (1952). The genesis of antisocial acting out in children and adults. *Psychoanalytic Quarterly* 21:313-323.
Jones, M. C. (1924). Elimination of children's fears. *Journal of Experimental Psychology* 7:382.
Jung, C. G. (1929). *Contributions to Analytic Psychology.* New York: Harcourt, Brace.
Jung, C. G. (1953). *Collected Works.* Ed. H. Read, M. Fordham, and G. Adler. Princeton, New Jersey: Princeton University Press.
Kanfer, F. H. (1971). The maintenance of behavior by self-generated stimuli and reinforcement. In *The Psychology of Private Events: Perspectives on Covert Response Systems*, ed. A. Jacobs and L. B. Sachs. New York: Academic Press.
Kant, O. (1940). Types and analyses of the clinical pictures of recovered schizophrenics. *Psychiatric Quarterly* 4:676-700.
Kaplan, N. S. (1974). *The New Sex Therapy.* New York: Brunner-Mazel.
Kazdin, A. E. (1975). *Behavior Modification in Applied Settings.* Homewood, Ill.: Dorsey Press.
Kelly, D. (1973). Sterotactic limbic leucotomy: a preliminary report in forty patients. *British Journal of Psychiatry* 123:133-140.
Kety, S. S. (1974). From rationalization to reason. *American Journal of Psychiatry* 131:957-963.
Kimmel, H. D. (1974). Instrumental conditioning of autonomically mediated responses in human beings. *American Psychologist* 29:325-333.
Klein, D. F., and Davis, J. M. (1969). *Diagnosis and Treatment of Psychiatric Disorders.* Baltimore: Williams and Wilkins.
Klerman, G. L. (1975a). Combining drugs and psychotherapy in the treatment of depression. In *Drugs in Combination with Other Therapies.* New York: Grune and Stratton.
Klerman, G. L. (1975b). Neuroleptics: Too many or too few? In *Rational Psychophamacotherapy and the Right to Treatment*, ed. F. J. Ayd. Baltimore: Ayd Medical Communications.
Klerman, G. L., et al. (1974). Treatment of depression by drugs and psychotherapy. *American Journal of Psychiatry* 131:186-191.
Koch, R. (1971). The image of man implicit in encounter group therapy. *Journal of Human Psychology* 11:107-128.
Kohlenburg, R. J. (1974). Treatment of a homosexual pedophiliac using in vivo desensitization: a case study. *Journal of Abnormal Psychology* 83:192-195.
Kohut, H. (1968). The psychoanalytic treatment of narcissistic personality disorders. In *Psychoanalytic Study of the Child* 23:86-113.

Kubie, L.S. (1950). *Practical and Theoretical Aspects of Psychoanalysis*. New York: International Universities Press.
Lacquer, H.C., et al. (1964). Multiple family therapy. In *Current Psychiatric Therapies*, vol. 4, ed. J. Masserman. New York: Grune and Stratton.
Laing, R.D. (1967). *The Politics of Experience*. London: Penguin.
Langfeldt, G. (1956). The prognosis of schizophrenia. *Acta Psychiatry et Neurology Scandinavia* supplement 110.
Landfield, A.W. (1971). *Personal Construct Systems in Psychotherapy*. Chicago: Rand-McNally.
Langsley, D., and Kaplan, D.M. (1968). *The Treatment of Families in Crisis*. New York: Grune and Stratton.
Langsley, D., Stephenson, W., and McDonald, J. (1964). Why not insure partial hospitalization? *Mental Hospital* 15:16-17.
Lazare, A. (1973). Hidden conceptual models in clinical psychiatry. *New England Journal of Medicine* 288, 7:345-350.
Lazarus, A. (1968). Behavior therapy in groups. In *Basic Approaches to Group Therapy and Group Counseling*, ed. G.M. Gazda. Springfield, Ill.: Charles C Thomas.
Lazarus, A. (1971). *Behavior Therapy and Beyond*. New York: McGraw-Hill.
Lazarus, A. (1973). Multimodel therapy: treating the basic I.D. *Journal of Nervous and Mental Disorders* 156:404-411.
Lazarus, A. (1974). Multimodal therapy: basic ID. *Psychology Today* 7:59-63.
Lemert, E.M. (1972). *Human Deviance: Social Problems and Social Control*, 2nd ed. Englewood Cliffs, N.J.: Prentice-Hall.
Levitz, L.S., and Stunkard, A.J. (1974). A therapeutic coalition for obesity: behavior modification and patient self-help. *American Journal of Psychiatry* 131:423-427.
Liberman, R.P. (1970). Behavioral approaches to family and couple therapy. *American Journal of Orthopsychiatry* 40:106-118.
Lieberman, M.A., Yalom, I., and Miles, M. (1973). *Encounter Groups: First Facts*. New York: Basic Books.
Lidz, T. (1969). The influence of family studies on the treatment of schizophrenia. *Psychiatry* 32:237-251.
Lipkin, M.K., Dyrud, J., and Meyer, G.G. (1970). The many faces of mania. *Archives of General Psychiatry* 22:262-267.
Livingston, K. (1969). The frontal lobes revisited: the case for a second look. *Archives of Neurology* 20:90-95.
London, P. (1964). *The Modes and Morals of Psychotherapy*. New York: Holt, Rinehart and Winston.
London, P. (1970). *Behavior Control*. New York: Harper and Row.
Luborsky, R., Singer, B., and Luborsky, L. (1975). Comparative studies of psychotherapy. *Archives of General Psychiatry* 32:995-1208.

Luthe, W., ed. (1969). *Autogenic Therapy*, vols. 1-5. New York: Grune and Stratton.
Mahoney, M.J. (1974). Self reward and self monitoring techniques for weight control. *Behavior Therapy* 5:48-57.
Mahoney, M.S., and Thoresen, C.E. (1974). *Self Control: Power to the Person.* Monterrey: Brooks-Cole.
Malan, D.N. (1973). The outcome problem in psychotherapy research. *Archives of General Psychiatry* 29:719-729.
Mann, J. (1974). *Time Limited Psychotherapy.* Cambridge, Mass.: Harvard University Press.
Marcuse, H. (1964). *One Dimensional Man.* Boston: Beacon Press.
Mark, V.H., and Ervin, F.R. (1970). *Violence and the Brain.* New York: Harper and Row.
Marks, I.M. (1972). Flooding (implosion) and allied treatments. In *Behavior Modification, Principles and Clinical Applications*, ed. W.S. Agras. Boston: Little, Brown.
Marks, I.M. (1976). The current status of behavior psychotherapy. *American Journal of Psychiatry* 133:253-261.
Marks, I.M., Boulougouris, S.C., and Marset, P. (1971). Flooding versus desensitization in the treatment of phobic patients: a cross-over study. *British Journal of Psychiatry* 119:353.
Marmor, J. (1975). Report in *Psychiatric News*, November 5.
Martinson, R. (1974). What works?—questions and answers about prison reform. *The Public Interest* 35:22-54.
Maslow, A. (1968). *Toward a Psychology of Being.* Philadelphia: Van Nostrand.
Masserman, J.N., ed. (1965). *Science and Psychoanalysis*, vol. 1, *Integrative Studies.* New York: Grune and Stratton.
Masters, W.H., and Johnson, V.E. (1970). *Human Sexual Inadequacy.* Boston: Little, Brown.
Masters, W.H., and Johnson, V.E. (1972). The rapid treatment of human sexual dysfunctions. In *Progress in Group and Family Therapy*, ed. C.J. Sager, and H.S. Kaplan. New York: Brunner-Mazel.
Matza, D. (1969). *Becoming Deviant.* Englewood Cliffs, N.J.: Prentice-Hall.
May, P. (1968). *Treatment of Schizophrenia: A Comparative Study of Five Treatment Methods.* New York: Jason Aronson.
May, R. (1969). *Love and Will.* New York: Norton.
May, R., Angel, E., and Ellenberger, H.F., eds. (1958). *Existence: A New Dimension in Psychiatry and Psychology.* New York: Basic Books.
Mechanic, D. (1969). *Mental Health and Social Policy.* Englewood Cliffs, N.J.: Prentice-Hall.
Meltzoff, J., and Kornreich, M. (1970). *Research in Psychotherapy.* New York: Atherton Press.

References

Menninger, K.A. (1958). *Theory of Psychoanalytic Technique.* New York: Harper and Row.
Menninger, K.A. (1963). *The Vital Balance.* New York: Viking.
Miller, N.E. (1974). Biofeedback: evaluation of a new technique. *New England Journal of Medicine* 290:684-685.
Minuchin, S. (1974). *Families and Family Therapy.* Cambridge, Mass.: Harvard University Press.
Minuchin, S., and Barcai, A. (1969). Therapeutically induced family crisis. In *Science and Psychoanalysis*, vol. 14, *Childhood and Adolescence*, ed. J. Masserman. New York: Grune and Stratton.
Minuchin, J., et al. (1967). *Families of the Slums: An Exploration of Their Structure and Treatment.* New York: Basic Books.
Mitchell, K.R., and Mitchell, D.M. (1971). Migraine: an exploratory treatment application of programmed behavior therapy techniques.. *Journal of Psychosomatic Research* 15:137-157.
Moreno, J.L. (1945). Psychodrama and the psychopathology of interpersonal relations. *Psychodrama Monographs* 16:3-68.
Moreno, J.L. (1953). *Who Shall Survive?* New York: Beacon House.
Muncie, W. (1959). The psychobiological approach. In *American Handbook of Psychiatry*, vol. 2, ed. S. Arieti, 1st ed., pp. 1317-1332. New York: Basic Books.
Napier, A., and Whitaker, C. (1972). A conversation about co-therapy. In *The Book of Family Therapy*, ed. A. Ferber, M. Mendelsohn, and A. Napier. New York: Jason Aronson.
O'Connell (1976). *The Clinical Use of Lithium.* New York: Biomedia.
Offenkrantz, W., and Tobin, A. (1974). Psychoanalytic psychotherapy. *Archives of General Psychiatry* 30:593-607.
Otto, N. (1970). *Group Methods to Actualize Human Potential.* Berverly Hills, Calif.: Holistic Press.
Packard, V.A. (1972). *A Nation of Strangers.* New York: David McKay.
Pelletier, K.R., and Garfield, C. (1976). *Consciousness East and West.* New York: Harper.
Perls, F. (1969). *Gestalt Therapy Verbatim.* Berkeley, Calif.: Real People Press.
Pincus, J.J., and Tucker, G.J. (1974). *Behavioral Neurology.* New York: Oxford University Press.
Pittman, F.S., and Flomenhaft, K. (1970). Treating the doll's house marriage. *Family Process* 9.
Pittman, F.S., et al. (1966). Techniques of crisis family therapy. In *Current Psychiatric Therapies*, vol. 6, ed. J. Masserman. New York: Grune and Stratton.
Polatin, P. (1966). *A Guide to Treatment in Psychiatry.* Philadelphia: Lippincott.

Prien, R.R., Caffey, E.M., and Klett, C.J. (1972). A comparison of lithium carbonate and chlorpromazine in the treatment of excited schizoaffectives. *Archives of General Psychiatry* 27:182-188.

Rabin, H. (1967). How does co-therapy compare with regular group therapy? *American Journal of Psychotherapy* 21:244-255.

Rackman, S. (1971). *The Effects of Psychotherapy.* Oxford: Pergamon.

Razin, A.M. (1971). "A-B" variable in psychotherapy: a critical review. *Psychological Bulletin* 75:1-21.

Rennie, T.A.C. (1939). Follow-up study of 500 patients with schizophrenia admitted to hospital from 1913 to 1923. *Archives of Neurology and Psychiatry* 42:877-881.

Rifkin, A., et al. (1972). Lithium carbonate in emotionally unstable character disorder. *Archives of General Psychiatry* 27:519-523.

Rioch, M.J. (1970). The work of Wilfred Bion on groups. *Psychiatry* 33:56-66.

Ripley, H.S., and Jackson, J.K. (1959). Therapeutic factors in alcoholics anonymous. *American Journal of Psychiatry* 166:44.

Rogers, C.R. (1954). *Client Centered Therapy.* Boston: Houghton Mifflin.

Rogers, C.R. (1961). *On Becoming a Person: A Therapist's View of Psychotherapy.* Boston: Houghton Mifflin.

Rogers, C.R. (1965). The therapeutic relationship: recent theory and research. *Australian Journal of Psychology* 17:95-108.

Rogers, C.R. (1970). *Carl Rogers on Encounter Groups.* New York: Harper and Row.

Rose, S. (1969). Horney concepts in group psychotherapy. In *Group Therapy Today*, ed. H.N. Ruitenbeek. New York: Atherton.

Rosenbaum, M., and Hartley, E. (1962). A summary review of current practices of ninety-two group therapists. *International Journal of Group Psychotherapy* 12:194-198.

Rosenhan, D.L. (1973). On being sane in insane places. *Science* 179:250-258.

Satir, V.W. (1964). *Conjoint Family Therapy.* Palo Alto, Calif.: Science and Behavior Books.

Satir, V. (1970). *Peoplemaking.* Palo Alto, Calif.: Science and Behavioral Books.

Saul, L.J. (1972). *Psychodynamically Based Psychotherapy.* New York: Jason Aronson.

Scheff, T.J. (1966). *Being Mentally Ill.* Chicago: Aldine.

Schofield, W. (1964). *Psychotherapy: The Purchase of Friendship.* Englewood Cliffs, N.J.: Prentice-Hall.

Schofield, W., Hathaway, S.R., Hastings, D.W., and Bell, D.M. (1954). Prognostic factors in schizophrenia. *Journal of Consulting Psychology* 18:155-166.

References

Schukit, M., Robins, E., and Feighner, J. (1971). Tricyclic antidepressants and monoamine oxidase inhibitors. *Archives of General Psychiatry* 24:509–514.

Schultz, W. (1967). *Joy: Expanding Human Awareness.* New York: Grove Press.

Schwartz, A. (1974). Psychiatry's drift away from medicine. *American Journal of Psychiatry* 131:129–134.

Shader, R. (1975a). Fear of side effects and denial of treatment. In *Rational Psychopharmacotherapy and the Right to Treatment*, ed. F.J. Ayd. Baltimore: Ayd Medical Communications.

Shader, R., ed. (1975b). *Manual of Psychiatric Therapeutics.* Boston: Little, Brown.

Shevitz, S.A. (1976). Psychosurgery: some current observations. *American Journal of Psychiatry* 133:266–270.

Sifneds, P.E. (1974). *Short Term Psychotherapy and Emotional Crises.* Cambridge, Mass.: Harvard University Press.

Skinner, B.F. (1953). *Science and Human Behavior.* New York: Free Press.

Skinner, B.F. (1971). *Beyond Freedom and Dignity.* New York: Knopf.

Skinner, B.F. (1974). *About Behaviorism.* New York: Knopf.

Sloan, B.R., et al. (1975). *Psychotherapy versus Behavior Therapy.* Cambridge: Harvard University Press.

Smith, M.B. (1969). *Social Psychology and Human Values.* Chicago: Aldine.

Snyder, S.H. (1976). The dopamine hypothesis of schizophrenia. *American Journal of Psychiatry* 133:197–201.

Speck, R., and Attneave, C. (1972). Network therapy. In *The Book of Family Therapy*, ed. A. Ferber, M. Mendelsohn, and A. Napier. New York: Jason Aronson.

Stoller, F.H. (1968) Accelerated interaction: a time limited approach based on the brief, intensive group. *Interactional Journal of Group Psychotherapy* 18:220–235.

Stoller, F.H. (1969). Videotape feedback in the group setting. *Journal of Nervous and Mental Diseases* 148:437–466.

Storrow, A.H. (1967). *Introduction to Scientific Psychiatry.* New York: Appleton-Century-Crofts.

Stuart, R.B. (1969). Operant-interpersonal treatment for marital discord. *Journal of Behavior Therapy and Clinical Psychology* 33:675–682.

Stuart, R.B. (1971). Behavioral contracting with the families of delinquents. *Journal of Behavior Therapy and Experimental Psychiatry* 2:1–11.

Stürup, G.K. (1968). *Treating the Untreatable.* Baltimore: Johns Hopkins Press.

Sugerman, A.A. (1975). Non-CNS side effects of neuroleptics. *Psychiatric Annals* 5:61–70.

Sullivan, H.S. (1953). *The Interpersonal Theory of Psychiatry.* New York: Norton.
Szasz, T. S. (1965). *Psychiatric Justice.* New York: Macmillan.
Szasz, T.S. (1970). *The Manufacture of Madness.* New York: Harper and Row.
Thoresen, T.E., and Mahoney, M.J. (1974). *Behavioral Self Control.* New York: Holt, Rinehart and Winston.
Troshinsky, C.N., Aaronson, H.G., and Stone, R.K. (1962). Maintenance phenothiazines in aftercare of schizophrenic patients. *Penn Psychiatric Quarterly* 2:11–45.
Truax, C.B., and Carkhuff, R.R. (1967). *Toward Effective Counseling and Psychotherapy.* Chicago: Aldine.
Tucker, G.J., and Maxmen, J.S. (1973). The practice of hospital psychiatry: a formulation. *American Journal of Psychiatry* 130:887–891.
Tyrer, P., Candy, J., and Kelly, D. (1973). Phenelzine in phobic anxiety: a controlled trial. *Psychological Medicine* 3:120–124.
Uhlenhuth, E.H., et al. (1966). Drug, doctor's verbal attitude and clinical setting in the symptomatic response to pharmacotherapy. *Psychopharmacologia* 32.
Valins, S., and Nisbett, R.E. (1971). *Attribution Processes in the Development and Treatment of Emotional Disorders.* Morristown, N.J.: General Learning Press.
Vaillant, G.E. (1962). The prediction of recovery in schizophrenia. *Journal of Nervous and Mental Diseases* 135:534–543.
Waelder, R. (1952). Psychiatry and the problem of criminal responsibility. *University of Pennsylvania Law Review* 101:383–390.
Watson, J.B., and Rayner, P. (1960). Conditioned emotional reactions. *Journal of Experimental Psychology* 3:1.
Weissman, M.M., et al. (1974). Treatment effects on the social adjustment of depressed patients. *Archives of General Psychiatry* 30:771–778.
Wexler, D.B. (1973). Token and taboo: behavioral modification, token economics and the law. *California Law Review* 61:81–109.
Whitaker, D.S., and Lieberman, M. (1964). *Psychotherapy Through the Group Process.* New York: Atherton Press.
Wilder, J.F., Levin, G., and Zwerling, I. (1966). A two-year follow-up evaluation of acute psychiatric patients treated in a day hospital. *American Journal of Psychiatry* 122:1095–1101.
Wilson, G.D. (1967). Efficacy of "flooding" procedures in desensitization of fear: a theoretical note. *Behavior Research and Therapy* 5:138.
Winstead, D.K., et al. (1974). Diazepam on demand. *Archives of General Psychiatry* 30:349–359.

References

Wolberg, L. R. (1967). *The Technique of Psychotherapy*. New York: Grune and Stratton.

Wolf, A. (1949). The psychoanalysis of groups. *American Journal of Psychotherapy* 3:529–557.

Wolf, A., et al. (1969). *Beyond the Couch*. New York: Jason Aronson.

Wolpe, J. (1961). The systematic desensitization treatment of neuroses. *Journal of Nervous and Mental Diseases* 132:189.

Wolpe, J. (1964). Objective psychotherapy of the neuroses. *South African Medical Journal* 26:825–835.

Wolpe, J. (1969). *The Practice of Behavior Therapy*. New York: Pergamon.

Woodruff, R. A., Goodwin, D. W., and Guze, S. B. (1974). *Psychiatric Diagnosis*. New York: Oxford Press.

Wynne, L. C., et al. (1958). Pseudo-mutuality in the family relations of schizophrenics. *Psychiatry* 21:205–220.

Yalom, I. (1974). Existential factors in group therapy. Strecker Monograph Series, XI, The Institute of the Pennsylvania Hospital.

Yalom, I. (1975). *The Theory and Practice of Group Psychotherapy*. 2nd ed. New York: Basic Books.

Yalom, I., Brown, S., and Bloch, S. (In press). The written summary as a group psychotherapy technique. *Archives of General Psychiatry*.

Yalom, I. and Lieberman, M. (1971). A study of encounter group casualties. *Archives of General Psychiatry* 25.

Index

A

Aaronson, H. G., 208
Adler, A., 361
Aichorn, A., 367
Akiskal, H. S., 43, 305
alcoholism, behavioral treatment of, 276-77
Alexander, F., 107, 343, 361
Alexander, J. F., 17
Angel, E., 38
Anthony, E. J., 394
antianxiety drugs, 221-24
antidepressant drugs, 210-17
antipsychotic drugs, 193-210
appetitive disorders, treatment of, with behavior therapy, 267-79
   alcoholism, 276-77
   eating disorders, 277-79
   sexual inadequacy, 271-76
   sexual variations, 267-71
Appelton, W. S., 194
attitude, clinician's, in practical issues in concurrent use of interventions, 133-35
Attneave, C., 422
autonomy, and motivation in ethical issues, 144-56
Avery, D., 225
Ayd, F. J., 154, 208
Azrin, N. H., 282

B

Baehr, G., 13
Bailey, J., 219
Barber, T. X., 284
Barcai, A., 430
Bateson, G., 445
Beary, J. F., 73, 232
Beck, D. F., 17
Beels, C., 465
behavior modification
   "soft," as behavior therapy, 284-96
   techniques of, and general clinical problems, 279-83
behavior therapies, 241-301
   basic learning concepts, 241-51
   behavior modification techniques and general clinical problems, 279-83
   biofeedback, 283-84

Index

ethical considerations, 296-301
general issues, 241-45
principles of, 251-58
   diminishing behavior, 255-58
   increasing behavior, 252-55
"soft" behavior modification, 284-96
treatment of appetitive disorders, 267-79
   alcoholism, 276-77
   eating disorders, 277-79
   sexual inadequacy, 271-76
   sexual variations, 267-71
treatment of fear responses, 261-67
uses of, 245-48
belief, and faith in powers of healer
   in family therapy, 467-69
   in group therapy, 397-98
   in individual therapy, 327-28
Benson, H., 73-232
Benson, R., 221
Berger, M., 410
Berne, E., 305, 362, 396
Berzins, J. I., 19
Betz, B., 18
biofeedback, as behavioral therapy, 283-84
biological hypotheses, in relating diagnosis to treatment, 42-44
biological interventions, 165-239
   antianxiety drugs, 221-24
   antidepressant drugs, 210-17
   antipsychotic drugs, 193-210
   electroconvulsive therapy, 224-28
   ethical use of, 232-39
   evaluating indications for, in clinical evaluation of patient and environment, 70-75
   general diagnostic issues, 171-80
   lithium treatment, 217-21
   psychosurgery, 221-29
   relaxation training, 229-32
   specific diagnostic issues, 180-93
   territorial issues, 169-71
   See also interventions; treatment
Blackwell, B., 207
Blanchard, E. B., 284
Bloch, S., 410
Blos, P., 445
Boss, M., 305
Boulougouris, S. C., 265
Bowen, M., 429, 451, 452
Brady, J. P., 230-32, 264
Bronfenbrenner, U., 485-86
Brooks, A., 234
Brown, S., 410
Bruner, C. G., 277
Burrows, D., 418
Burton, A., 408
Busse, E. W., 305

C

Caffey, E. M., 15
Candy, J., 212
Caplan, G., 106
caring and lovingness
   in family therapy, 470-71
   in group psychotherapy, 399-400
   in individual psychotherapy, 334-39
Carkhuff, R. R., 19, 362
Carol, M. T., 73, 232
Carpenter, W. T., 14, 209
Cartwright, R. D., 19
Chartier, G. M., 19
Clark, R., 482
clinical problems, general, and behavior modification techniques, 279-83

clinician, attitude of, in practical issues in concurrent use of interventions, 133-35
See also psychotherapist
Cole, J. O., 15, 207, 209
conditioning, as basic learning concept
  classical, 249
  operant, 250-51
Coppen, A., 219
Corsini, R., 396
co-therapists
  in family therapy, 466-67
  in individual psychotherapy, 377-78
Crane, G. E., 205

D
Davis, J. M., 15, 16, 74
Davison, G. C., 268
Detre, T. P., 16
diagnosis
  general, issues of, in biological interventions, 171-80
  related to treatment, 29-68
    biological hypotheses, 42-44
    diagnosis, 32-39
    environmental hypotheses, 50-53
    and how current therapies work, 61-63
    and hypotheses to modes of intervention, 53-61
    individual-environment interaction, 39-42
    informational hypotheses, 47-50
    learning hypotheses, 45-47
    values and choice of, 63-68
  specific, issues of, in biological issues, 180-93

and use of individual psychotherapy, 314-21
Dollard, J., 45
drugs, as biological intervention
  antianxiety, 221-24
  antidepressant, 210-17
  antipsychotic, 193-210
    extrapyramidal side effects, 203-10
    side effects of neuroleptics, 200-203
Dusay, J. M., 396
Dyrud, J., 72, 183

E
Eagleton, Sen. Thomas, 25
eating disorders, behavioral treatment of, 277-79
Eitlinger, L., 74
electroconvulsive therapy, as biological intervention, 224-28
Elkes, J., 11
Ellenberger, H. F., 38
Ellis, A., 260, 306, 362
Ellsberg, Daniel, 394
encounter groups, and group psychotherapy, 408-409
Engel, G., 432
environment
  accidental versus patient-created, 91-100
  and patient, clinical evaluation of, 69-117
    evaluating indications for biological interventions, 70-75
    evaluating indications for information-expanding interventions, 77-85
    summary of, 114-17
  postsymptomatic, 106-14
  presymptomatic, 87-91

Index

in relating diagnosis to treatment, 50-53
response to, and developmental change, 100-106
Ervin, F. R., 229
ethical issues
  in behavior therapies, 296-301
  and considerations, 136-59
    conclusion, 159
    motivation and autonomy, 144-56
    politics of therapy, 136-44
    treatment choice and degree of severity, 156-59
  in family therapy, 483-86
  in group psychotherapy, 414-20
  in individual psychotherapy, 378-86
  and practical issues, 119-20
  in use of biological treatments, 232-39
evaluation, family, basic format of, and family therapy, 457-65
experiential approach, versus structural approach to family therapy, 465-66
explanation
  in family therapy, 480
  in group psychotherapy, 407-408
  in individual psychotherapy, 359-63
extrapyramidal side effects, to use of antipsychotic drugs, 203-10
Eysenck, H. J., 13, 107
Ezriel, H., 396

F

Fagen, J., 305, 393, 402, 406
Fairbairn, W. R. D., 450
faith, and belief in powers of healer
  in family therapy, 467-69
  in group psychotherapy, 397-98
  (hope) in individual psychotherapy, 327-28
family therapy, 421-86
  basic format of family evaluation and, 457-65
  beyond family, 481-83
  co-therapists in, 466-67
  ethical problems, 483-86
  experiential versus structural approaches, 465-66
  family stress
    and family theory, 444-52
    varieties of, 432-44
  growth, 429-30
  helpful factors in, 467-80
    care and lovingness, 470-71
    explanation, 480
    faith and belief in powers of healer, 467-69
    identification, 469-70
    information, 479-80
    learning, 472-78
    tension reduction, 471-72
  indications for, 452-56
  one-dimensionality, 425-27
  and other interventions, 456-57
  patient in, 422-24
  power in, 430-31
  responsibility in, 427-29
  territoriality in, 427
fear responses, treatment of, as behavior therapy, 261-67
Feighner, J., 215
Ferber, A., 426, 465
Fieve, R. R., 15, 217
Fish, J. M., 327
Flomenhaft, K., 455
Ford, D. N., 126
Foulkes, S. A., 394
Framo, J.,L., 448, 449, 480
Frank, J. D., 31, 56, 326, 327, 399

Frankl, V., 266
Franks, C. M., 11, 276
Freud, S., 57, 125, 306, 312, 328, 368
Friedman, A. S., 15, 404
Fromm-Reichman, F., 407

G
Gardos, G., 15, 207, 209
Gelder, M. G., 16
Glasser, W., 306, 362
Glueck, B. C., 232
Goldberg, C., 408
Goldberg, S. C., 14, 64
Goodwin, D., 276
Grinker, R. R., 30
Grinspoon, L., 64
group psychotherapy, 387-420
  basic format, 395-97
  encounter groups, 408-409
  ethical problems, 414-20
  goals, 389-91
  guides to prescription of, 391-94
  helpful factors, 397-408
    caring and lovingness, 399-400
    explanation, 407-408
    faith and belief in powers of healer, 397-98
    identification, 398-99
    information, 403-407
    learning, 400-403
    tension reduction, 400
  and individual psychotherapy, 409-11
  technical problems, 411-12
  theoretical concerns about group interventions, 412-14
growth, in family therapy, 429-30

H
Haley, J., 31, 266, 425, 466, 471

Halleck, J.A., 415-17
Hallowitz, D., 432
Harper, R. A., 6, 125, 327
Harris, M. B., 277
Hartley, E., 390, 462
Havens, L., 31
Hirsch, S. R., 209
Hoffman, L., 466
Hogarty, G. E., 14, 64
Hollister, L. E., 196, 199
Holmes, T. H., 432
hope, and belief in power of socially sanctioned healer in individual psychotherapy, 327-28
  See also faith
Horney, K., 331, 361-62, 407
hospital, as setting for individual psychotherapy, 371-75

identification, with therapist
  in family therapy, 469-70
  in group psychotherapy, 398-99
  in individual psychotherapy, 328-34
indications, for family therapy, 452-56
  See also diagnosis
individual psychotherapy, 303-86
  co-therapists in, 377-78
  diagnostic issue as to who should receive psychotherapy, 314-21
  ethical issues in, 378-86
  general structure, 322-25
  and group psychotherapy, 409-11
  Halleck's personal methods, 363-68
  helpful factors in, 326-63
    caring and lovingness, 334-39

hope and belief in power of socially sanctioned healer, 327-28
identification with therapist, 328-34
information, 346-59
learning in, 340-46
tension reduction, 339-40
in hospital settings, 371-75
and other interventions, 375-77
and responsibility, 306-11
termination, 368-70
territoriality, 311-13
theory and technique, 321-22
information
in family therapy, 479-80
in group psychotherapy, 403-407
in individual psychotherapy, 346-59
information-expanding interventions, evaluation of indications for, in clinical evaluation of patient and environment, 77-85
informational hypotheses, in relating diagnosis to treatment, 47-50
instructional learning, or observational learning, as behavior therapy, 251
interaction, individual-environment, in relating diagnosis to treatment, 39-42
interventions
biological see biological interventions
clinical evaluations increasing efficiency of, 114-17
group, theoretical concerns about, in group psychotherapy, 412-14

information-expanding, evaluation of indications for, 77-85
other than and with individual psychotherapy, 375-77
other than family therapy within family therapy, 456-57
practical issues in concurrent use of, 120-36
clinician's attitude, 133-35
with moderately disturbed patients, 125-28
with severely disturbed patients, 120-25
synergistic, 128-33
timing of multiple interventions, 135-36

J

Jackson, D., 41, 445
Jackson, J. K., 391, 464
Jacobson, E., 264
Janov, A., 339
Jarecki, H. G., 16
Johnson, A., 449
Johnson, V., 272, 275
Jones, M.C., 249
Jung, C., 361

K

Kanfer, F. H., 258
Kant, O., 182
Kaplan, D. M., 106
Kaplan, N. S., 272
Kazdin, A. E., 258
Kelly, D., 212, 229
Kety, S. S., 41
Kimmel, H. D., 283
Klein, D. F., 15, 74
Klerman, G. L., 16, 64, 74, 194, 212
Klett, C. J., 15
Koch, R., 416, 417

Kohlenburg, R. J., 269
Kohut, H., 367
Kubie, L. S., 121

L

Laane, C. v., 74
Lacquer, H. C., 422
Laing, R. D., 41
Landfield, A. W., 18
Langfeldt, G., 74, 88
Langsley, D., 17, 106
Lapides, F. R., 418
Lazare, A., 31
Lazarus, A., 32, 247, 248, 391
learning; basic concepts in, as behavior therapy, 248-51
  classical conditioning, 249
  observational or instructional learning, 251
  operant conditioning, 250-51
  in family therapy, 472-78
  in individual psychotherapy, 340-46
  in relating diagnosis to treatment, 45-47
Lemert, E. M., 137
Levin, G., 17
Levitz, L. S., 391, 452
Liberman, R. P., 477
Lidz, T., 432
Lieberman, M. A., 387, 406, 409, 415
Lipkin, M. K., 72, 183
lithium treatment, as biological intervention, 217-21
Livingston, K., 229
London, P., 126, 414
lovingness, and caring
  in family therapy, 470-71
  in group psychotherapy, 399-400
  in individual psychotherapy, 334-39
Luborsky, I., 16, 317

Luborsky, R., 16, 317
Luthe, W., 232

M

McDonald, J., 17
McGlashan, T. H., 14, 209
McKinney, W. T., 305
Mahoney, M. J., 258, 277
Malan, D. N., 23
Mann, J., 316
Marcuse, H., 418
Mark, V. H., 229
Marks, I. M., 16, 246, 263, 265, 339
Marmor, J., 326
Marset, P., 265
Martinson, R., 392
Maslow, A., 362
Masserman, J. N., 30
Masters, W. H., 272, 275
Matza, D., 286
Maxmen, J. S., 374
May, P., 38
Mechanic, D., 345
Meltzoff, J., 13
Menninger, K. A., 30-31, 361
Meyer, A., 29-30
Meyer, G. G., 72, 183
Miles, M., 387, 409
Miller, N. E., 45, 283
Minuchin, J., 430, 451, 466, 568
Mitchell, D. M., 284
Mitchell, K. R., 284
modification, behavior, self-control techniques in, 258-61
Moreno, J. L., 411
motivation, and autonomy in ethical issues, 144-56
Muncie, W., 29

N

Napier, A., 426, 466

neuroleptics, side effects of, 200-203
Nisbett, R. E., 20
Nixon, Richard M., 394
Nunn, R. G., 282

O
observational or instructional learning, as behavior therapy, 251
Offenkrantz, W., 359
one-dimensionality, in family therapy, 425-27
Otto, N., 411

P
Packard, V. A., 418
Parsons, B. V., 17
patients
  and environment, clinical evaluation of, 69-117
  environment, 85-114
  indications for biological interventions, 70-75
  indications for information-expanding interventions, 77-85
  summary of, 114-17
  in family therapy, 422-24
  moderately disturbed, concurrent use of interventions with, 125-28
  severely disturbed, practical issues in concurrent use of interventions with, 120-25
Pavlov, I., 249
Peet, M., 219
Pelletier, K. R., 45
Perls, F., 340
Pincus, J. J., 107
Pittman, F. S., 448, 455
Polatin, P., 391

power, in family therapy, 430-31
practical issues
  in concurrent use of interventions, 120-36
  and ethical issues, 119-20
Prien, R. R., 15
psychosurgery, as biological intervention, 228-29
psychotherapist
  faith and belief in healing powers of
    in family therapy, 467-69
    in group psychotherapy, 397-98
    in individual therapy, 327-28
  identification with, as factor in individual psychotherapy, 328-34
  See also clinician
psychotherapy. See family therapy, group psychotherapy, individual psychotherapy

R
Rabin, H., 396
Rachman, S., 13
Rahe, R. H., 432
Rayner, P., 249
Razin, A. M., 19
Rennie, T. A. C., 15
relaxation training, as biological intervention, 229-32
research evidence, on treatment model, 7-22
  results, 20-22
responsibility
  in family therapy, 427-29
  and individual psychotherapy, 306-11
Rifkin, A., 217
Rioch, M. J., 396
Ripley, H. S., 391, 464

Robins, E., 215
Rogers, C., 10-11, 29, 304, 306, 338, 362, 407, 417
Rose, S., 407
Rosenbaum, M., 390, 462
Rosenhan, D. L., 174, 286
Ross, H., 107, 343

S
Satir, V. M., 449, 476, 481
Saul, L. J., 369
Scheff, T. J., 107
Schofield, W., 19, 182
Schooler, N. R., 64
Schukit, M., 215
Schultz, W., 411
Schwartz, A., 158
self-control, techniques of, in behavior modification, 258-61
service delivery, and training, 487-501
severity, degree of, and choice of treatment, as ethical issue, 156-59
sexual inadequacy, treatment of, by behavior therapy, 271-76
sexual variations, treatment of, by behavior therapy, 267-71
Shader, R. I., 16, 64, 74, 188, 197, 206, 212
Shepherd, I. L., 305, 393, 402, 406
Shevitz, S. A., 229
side effects
  extrapyramidal, to use of antipsychotic drugs, 203-10
  of neuroleptics, 200-203
Sifneos, P. E., 316
Singer, B., 16, 317
Skinner, B. F., 37, 250, 283
Sloan, B. R., 11, 13, 306
Smith, M. B., 33

Snyder, S. H., 193
Speck, R., 422
Steiner, C. M., 396
Stephenson, W., 17
Stone, R. K., 209
Stoller, F. H., 281, 396
Storrow, A. H., 107
Strauss, J. S., 14, 209
stress, family
  and family theory in family therapy, 444-52
  varieties of, in family therapy, 432-44
Stroebel, C. F., 232
structural approach, versus experiential approach to family therapy, 465-66
Stunkard, A. J., 391, 452
Stuart, R. B., 477, 478
Sturup, G. K., 345
Sugarman, A. A., 198
Sullivan, H. S., 362, 407
Szasz, T., 137, 220
Szurer, S. A., 449

T
technique, of individual psychotherapy, 321-22
tension reduction
  in family therapy, 471-72
  in group psychotherapy, 400
  in individual psychotherapy, 339-40
termination, of individual psychotherapy, 368-70
territoriality
  in biological interventions, 169-71
  in family therapy, 427
  in individual psychotherapy, 311-13

theory
  family, and family stress in family therapy, 444-52
  of individual psychotherapy, 321-22
  therapeutic intervention, relating hypotheses to modes of, 53-61
  See also intervention; therapies; treatment
therapies
  behavior, 241-301
  current, working of, and relating diagnosis to treatment, 61-63
  electroconvulsive, as biological intervention, 224-28
  politics of, ethical issues in, 136-44
  See also behavior therapy
Thoresen, C. E., 258
timing, of multiple interventions, as practical issue in concurrent use of interventions, 135-36
Tobin, A., 359
training, and service delivery, 487-501
treatment
  of appetitive disorders, with behavior therapy, 267-79
    alcoholism, 276-77
    eating disorders, 277-79
    sexual inadequacy, 271-76
    sexual variations, 267-71
  biological, ethical use of, 232-39
  choice of, and degree of severity, as ethical issue, 156-59
  of fear responses, as behavior therapy, 261-67
  with lithium, as biological intervention, 217-21
  relating diagnosis to, 29-68
    biological hypotheses, 42-44
    diagnosis, 32-39
    environmental hypotheses, 50-53
    and how current therapies work, 61-63
    and hypotheses to modes of interventions, 53-61
    informational hypotheses, 47-50
    learning hypotheses, 45-47
    values and choice of, 63-68
    See also biological interventions; interventions
treatment model, need for, 3-28
  research evidence, 7-20
  resistance to integrative models, 22-28
  results of research, 20-22
Troshinsky, C. N., 208
Truax, C. B., 19, 362
Tucker, G. J., 374
Tryer, P., 212

U
Uhlenhuth, E. H., 18
Urban, H. B., 126

V
Vaillant, G. E., 182
Valins, S., 20
values, and choice of treatment, 63-68
Vogel, J. L., 19

W
Waelder, R., 308
Watson, J. B., 249
Weakland, J., 445
Weissman, M. M., 64, 216
Wexler, D. B., 281

Whitaker, C., 406, 466, 467, 484
Whitehorn, J. C., 18
Wilder, J. F., 17
Wilson, G. D., 265
Wilson, T. S., 276
Winokur, G., 225
Winstead, D. K., 224
Wolberg, L. R., 361
Wolf, A., 406, 410
Wolff, H. H., 16
Wolpe, J., 16, 30, 57, 263-64
Woodruff, R. A., 36
Wynne, L. C., 432

Y

Yalom, I., 326, 387, 388, 396, 409, 410, 415
Young, L. D., 284

Z

Zwerling, I., 17